COGNITIVE FOUNDATIONS OF NATURAL HISTORY

COGNITIVE FOUNDATIONS
OF
NATURAL HISTORY

Towards an anthropology of science

SCOTT ATRAN

CHARGÉ DE RECHERCHE
CREA-CNRS
Groupe de Recherche sur la Cognition
Ecole Polytechnique

and

RESEARCH SCIENTIST
Department of Anthropology
University of Michigan

CAMBRIDGE
UNIVERSITY PRESS

Published by the Press Syndicate of the University of Cambridge
The Pitt Building, Trumpington Street, Cambridge CB2 IRP
40 West 20th Street, New York, NY 10011–4211, USA
10 Stamford Road, Oakleigh, Victoria 3166, Australia
and Editions de la Maison des Sciences de l'Homme
54 Boulevard Raspail, 75270 Paris Cedex 06

First published 1990
First paperback edition 1993

Printed in Canada

Library of Congress cataloguing in publication data
Atran, Scott 1952–
Cognitive foundations of natural history: towards an anthropology
of science / Scott Atran.
p.   cm.
Bibliography.
Includes index.
ISBN 0-521-37293-3
1. Folk classification.   2. Cognition and culture.   3. Natural
history – Classification.   I. Title.
GN 468.4.A87   1990
303.4.'5 – dc20   89-36129   CIP

A catalog record for this book is available from the British Library

ISBN 0-521-37293-3 hardback
ISBN 2-7351-0296-3 (France only) hardback
ISBN 0-521-43871-3 paperback
ISBN 2-7351-0510-5 (France only) paperback

For my brother Dean,
and my teacher, Margaret Mead

CONTENTS

PREFACE

The following pages are intended to resolve a paradox, which a puzzle turned up. The puzzle, I encountered at the start of graduate study in anthropology: most introductory courses and texts began by proclaiming the psychic unity of humankind, only to proceed straight to the study of cultural variations. Having so long combated the ethnocentric view of Western thought as innate or inevitable, anthropologists had largely come to renounce all appeal to nativism as scientifically absurd and ideologically pernicious. But in philosophy, psychology and linguistics the argument over universals of human cognition was being vigorously pursued. A new nativism arose free of those simple-minded presuppositions that most anthropologists had rightly disowned.

For the profit of people – like myself – who were perplexed by the issue of universals, I conceived a debate between Noam Chomsky and Jean Piaget: then (in 1975), as now, their respective outlooks on universals had the most far-reaching implications for the study of cognition (including its biological aspects). The meeting was organized by the Royaumont Center for a Science of Man (see Royaumont Center 1980). As the discussion unfolded I came to think that Chomsky was, in the main, right and Piaget wrong: no logical or empirical grounds supported the claim that the innate and universal foundations of human thinking reduce to an undifferentiated intelligence, which is responsible in the same way for all cognitive operations.

Why, indeed, make the *a priori* assumption that all, or even some, of the interesting (i.e. species-specific) domains of human knowledge and experience are structured alike? It is hardly plausible that the rich and diverse sorts of adult mental competence are induced, learned or constructed by general procedures from the poor and fragmentary experiences of childhood. More likely, there are a variety of fairly well-articulated modes of human thinking – inherently differentiated components of human nature acquired over millions of years of biological and cognitive evolution.

Now for the paradox, which Piaget suggested such reasoning leads to. Suppose, in Chomsky's fashion, that each fundamental type of human knowledge arises from a specialized cognitive aptitude; then science, which is patently different from other forms of human knowledge, should also be innately grounded in some special "science-forming faculty." But suppose also that science integrates the various domains of human knowledge, and in ways contingent upon unforeseen insights into the relations between domains. From this latter supposition, it follows that science cannot exist apart from (alongside or prior to) its constituent domains; hence, it cannot constitute a distinct faculty. Intuition underscores the paradox: it is clear that the growth of scientific knowledge, whether in a culture or individual mind, lacks the quasi-automatic character evident in the acquisition of such ordinary forms of knowledge as linguistic competence, spatial appreciation, facial recognition, color perception or the apprehension of living kinds.

But the paradox goes deeper, undermining the distinctiveness of ordinary forms of knowledge as well. If science does truly integrate the various ordinary domains, it therefore obliterates their boundaries and disintegrates their supposedly fixed and special characters. Supposing that the cognitively maturing adult thinks as a would-be scientist, then talk of the mature individual retaining any specialized cognitive faculties no longer seems to make much sense.

The paradox disappears, I believe, when one drops the related presuppositions that science tends to thoroughly integrate the domains of ordinary human knowledge and that cognitive maturation necessarily proceeds in the direction of scientific reasoning. In fact, science scarcely affects ordinary thinking about customary matters, and most adults become highly competent cultural performers without any scientific knowledge. Children, tribal peoples, modern layfolk – even scientists in their nonworking hours – readily partition the ordinary range of human experience according to cognitive domains that are pretty much the same across cultures. By and large, these domains remain structurally stable and are adequate for dealing with the phenomenal world of ordinary human experience.

To illustrate this rather spontaneous and steadfast acquisition of "common sense," I analyze folk knowledge of living kinds. The development of science evinces no such spontaneity and stability. There appears to be no specially constituted "science-forming-faculty," although there may be more general "regulative" principles on rational explanation and intelligibility. Rather, certain sciences seem fitted to specific common-sense domains. This book takes the example of systematics – the science of biological classification – which emerged as an elaboration of universal cognitive schema common to all and only folkbiological taxonomies.

Natural history, like natural philosophy, transcended the bounds of common sense by calling upon various representational techniques that increased the depth and extent of its coverage of the facts. Although by no means restricted to this or that domain of common sense, such techniques still had to operate with the materials of this or that domain in mind. The moral: theories and analogies that allow us to speculate beyond common-sense domains must originally be formulated in terms of them, that is, with pointed reference to the cognitive "givens" of our species.

Perhaps the psychological condition that science initially be compatible with common-sense universals imposes insurmountable barriers to some lines of scientific advance. Even so, there would be little cause to lament the role of common sense in the growth and understanding of science. For it is owing to the constraints of common sense that science develops at all and can be made accessible to the children of contemporary Stone Age peoples just as readily as to our own sons and daughters. The present book endeavors to make this obvious.

A good deal of the subject matter integrated into this book was originally scattered in earlier presentations. Part I draws on these sources: "Covert fragmenta and the origins of the botanical family" (*Man*, 18:51–71, 1983), "The nature of folkbotanical life-forms" (*American Anthropologist*, 87:298–315, 1985), "Ordinary constraints on the semantics of living kinds: a commonsense alternative to recent treatments of natural-object terms" (*Mind and Language*, 2:27–63, 1987), "Do natural kind concepts form a natural kind?" (Paper delivered to the second session of the Franco-British Project on "Language, Communication and Cognition", London, May 1988; "Basic conceptual domains" (*Mind and Language*, 4: 7–16, 1989).) Many of the arguments for Part II initially appeared in "Pre-theoretical aspects of Aristotelian definition and classification of animals: the case for common sense" (*Studies in History and Philosophy of Science*, 16:113–163, 1985).

Part III contains ideas from an article, "Origins of the species and genus concepts: an anthropological perspective" (*Journal of the History of Biology*, 20:195–279, 1987), and from a paper, "The commonsense basis of Buffon's *Méthode naturelle*" (delivered to the "Colloque International Buffon 88," Paris – Montbard – Dijon, June 1988). Much of the material in Part IV derives from the following: a series of lectures given to the Department of Social Anthropology, Cambridge University (at the invitation of Jack Goody, winter term, 1984), my course "Culture and Communication" (taught jointly with Dan Sperber at the Ecole des Hautes Etudes en Sciences Sociales in Paris, 1985–1986), and the paper "Whither the new ethnography?" (delivered to the King's College Research Centre Conference on "Complex Culture Categories," Cambridge University, March 1988).

I am particularly grateful to Clemens Heller, President of the Maison des Sciences de l'Homme, for the institutional support that carried me through the lean years, when much was in question. Other institutions helped along the way: Columbia University, the Fondation Fyssen, the Fritz Thyssen Stiftung and, especially, the Centre National de la Recherche Scientifique and the National Science Foundation Scholar's Award Program in the History and Philosophy of Science (Grant No. SES-8507896). Professor Jacques Barrau, of the Museum

National d'Histoire Naturelle de Paris, kindly offered what proved to be a rewarding and lasting association with the Laboratoire d'Ethnobotanique et d'Ethnozoologie (now the Laboratoire d'Ethnobiologie-Biogéographie). The newly formed Groupe de Recherche sur la Cognition (CREA – CNRS) at the Ecole Polytechnique provided the forum of ideas and technical means for the final realization of this work.

A deep intellectual debt is owed Dan Sperber, whose knowledge and science encouraged my awareness of certain fundamental issues treated here and served to harness some of the wilder hypotheses. I have also profited greatly from critical discussions and correspondences with Alexander Alland, Brent Berlin, Claudine Friedberg, David Hull, Jonathan Hodge, Pierre Jacob, Ernst Mayr, Georges Métailié, Phillip Sloan and Peter Stevens. Generous years of advice from Lawrence Hirschfeld and the affection bestowed by my family were indispensable to the doggedness and completion of my enterprise. A very special thanks goes to my daughters, Tatiana and Laura, and to my son Emiliano, for much of the joy that animates my life and work.

1

COMMON SENSE: ITS SCOPE AND LIMITS

> *Philonous:* I am content, Hylas, to appeal to the common sense of the
> world for the truth of my notion. Ask the gardener, why he
> thinks yonder cherry-tree exists in the garden, and he shall tell
> you, because he sees and feels it; in a word, because he perceives
> it by his senses.
>
> (Bishop George Berkeley, *Third Dialogue Between*
> *Hylas and Philonous*, 1713)

INTRODUCTION

Ever since Plato, many philosophers have held common sense in poor esteem.
This is particularly notable in scientific circles, which tend to dismiss the popular
assumption that people do know most of what they ordinarily think they know
as a vestige of "Stone Age metaphysics". Science, it appears, is the only
trustworthy claimant to a true comprehension of the world, whereas common
sense is but faithworthy for savages, children and the uneducated rabble. It is
unfortunate that philosophers and historians of science have sold common sense
so short. For once its proper scope and limits are understood, much that seems
obscure in the development of science becomes plain.

True, there is much in quantum mechanics and relativity theory, as in
evolutionary theory and molecular biology, that is counter-intuitive, or at least
has no precedent in everyday thought. But a comprehension of the basic
conceptual frameworks of, say, classical mechanics and classical systematics was
instrumental in the critical formulation of the corresponding modern scientific
theories. Manipulation of these frameworks, in turn, pivoted on awareness of
the scope and limits of common sense.

Common sense is used here with systematic ambiguity to refer both to the
results and processes of certain special kinds of ordinary thinking: to what in all
societies is considered, and is cognitively responsible for the consideration of,
manifestly perceivable empirical fact – like the fact that grass is green (when it
really is perceived to be green). Interpreted in this way, common sense also
includes statements pertaining to what is plausibly an innately grounded, and
species-specific, apprehension of the spatio-temporal, geometrical, chromatic,

chemical and organic world in which we, and all other human beings, live our usual lives.

G. E. Moore puts the matter in this light:[1]

> The "Common Sense view of the world" ... is "in certain fundamental features" wholly true. What is meant by saying that so-and-so is a feature or item in "the Common Sense view of the world"? Something like this: That it is a thing which every or very nearly every sane adult, who has the use of all his senses (e.g. was not born blind or deaf), believes or knows (where "believes" and "knows" are used dispositionally). Does one need to add: And of which, for many centuries, it would have been true to say this?   (1962:280)

Common-sense beliefs are beyond dispute not because they happen to accurately describe the facts, but because that is just the way humans are constitutionally disposed to think of things. Of course, this does not define the term "common sense" precisely nor expressly say what are the common-sense beliefs. "Common sense" itself is not likely a natural-kind predicate of the science of cognitive psychology – a piece of cerebral architecture that functions in behavior with lawful regularity. But, as we shall see, cognitive psychology and anthropology can illustrate common sense, for instance plain thinking about the world in terms of universal color schemata, rigid bodies, biological taxa and so forth.

The actual realization of these cognitive universals depends upon the fragmented and limited experience available to us. But such experience does not so much shape our beliefs as activate our native dispositions to extend particular encounters to generalized sets of complexly related cases: to be able to divide the world into cats and dogs, one must experience cats and dogs; but it is our prior cognitive disposition to categorize animals with animals and species members with species members that allows us to distinguish such experiences *qua* cats and dogs.

As such, common sense is not to be confounded with "good sense" (or the *sensus communis* of the Roman orators). That is the mental capacity for exemplifying proper judgment, as when we say of a wise or handy man that he shows good common sense in his choices.[2] The willful (or pragmatic) kind of judgment implied is unequally shared within a culture and its criteria may vary across cultures. But what concerns us here is equally accessible to the sage and the ignoramus, the skillful and the clumsy, no matter what the culture. It is very plausibly a part of our evolutionary heritage, like the human disposition to categorically distinguish an artifact from a living kind. No speculation can possibly confute the grounds for this common-sense view of things because all speculation must start from it. There just is no other place to begin to think about the world.

Speculative reason (Cartesian *bon sens*) is thus unable to cut the umbilical cord that binds it to common sense, and so undermine it. Still, one can go beyond our ordinary ways of thinking about things. Speculation can reveal the bounds of such thinking and thereby prevent common sense from exceeding its proper authority – for common sense remains valid only so long as it is restricted to the manifestly visible dimensions of the everyday world, that is, to *phenomenal* reality. Studied reflection and measured experimentation, however, can lead to knowledge of another world – a nonphenomenal world of astronomical, microscopic and evolutionary dimensions – that can only be vaguely perceived, if at all, with the apparatus of self-evident intuitions that belongs to common sense.

Common sense, then, is an indubitable source of truth for knowledge of the readily experienced local world, but fallible as a means of insight into the scientific universe. This, opines Peirce (1935), is what the eighteenth-century Scottish common-sense philosophers did not fully appreciate:[3]

> The Scotch failed to recognize ... that the original beliefs only remain indubitable in their application to affairs that resemble the primitive mode of life ... Modern science, with its microscopes and telescopes, with its chemistry and electricity, and with its entirely new appliances of life, has put us in quite another world; almost as much so as if it had transported our race to another planet. Some of the old beliefs have no application excepted in extended senses, and in such extended senses they are some-times dubitable and subject to criticism. (5.445, 5.513)

Thus, while the Scots may have overrated the validity of common sense, others have certainly underrated it. This book is an effort to restore the balance of knowledge between common sense and science by reinterpreting their relationship in light of new evidence and recent research in anthropology and psychology. It approaches its subject, not from the more traditional philosophi-cal, historical or sociological perspectives, but from a vantage that I think is more basic and necessary to all of these: that of cognition. By "cognition," I mean quite simply the internal structure of ideas by which the world is conceptualized.

Everyone who has ever done or thought about science has entertained cognitive claims about how the world can or should be thought of. But curiously little attention has been paid to the conceptual origin and structure of those claims – to what it is about the human mind that makes our species capable of thinking scientifically. I should like to apply this "cognitive" perspective with a view toward explaining the successive scientific incarnations, transformations and mutations of what Hume called "that original stock of ideas," which human imagination may indeed exceed but never be altogether free of.

In this scenario, common sense does not preclude, but neither does it include, any magical, mythico-religious, metaphorical or other "symbolic" elaboration of the empirical world. Any symbolic utterance is nonpropositional, however one chooses to look at it: logically, no fixed meaning (not even a context-relative one) can be assigned that would permit a coherent evaluation of entailments;

empirically, no determinate factual content can be attributed whose consequences experience might definitely confirm or disconfirm; and psychologically, no specific mnemonic structure can be accorded for consistent storage and recall of information. In multiplying senses and metaphors, symbolism leaves the interpretation of any utterance significantly "open-ended."

To go beyond the "bare" facts of common sense and into the world of science, then, one must first of all recognize that symbolic reconstruals of the world do not constitute explanations of the facts. Because symbolism cannot systematically pattern old facts, *a fortiori* it cannot consistently project patterns to new facts. It is this insight, suggests G. E. R. Lloyd, that distinguishes the Greek *physiologoi* from the *magoi*, and the Hippocratic doctors from the purifiers (*kathartai*):

> Mythological "aetiologies" are explanations only in a quite restricted sense. To attribute earthquakes to Poseidon is, from the point of view of an understanding of the nature of earthquakes, not to reduce the unknown to the known, but to exchange one unknown for another. While Poseidon's motives can be imagined in human terms ... *how* an earthquake occurs is not thereby explained nor indeed at issue. If there is no question of assigning a historical origin to an interest in causal explanations of *some* kind, the deliberate investigation of how particular kinds of natural phenomena occur only begins with the philosophers: it was they who first attempted to explain what thunder, lightning, eclipses and the like are in terms of more familiar phenomena and processes.   (1979: 52–53)

But in order to explain new or unfamiliar phenomena, the familiar phenomena of common sense would have to be codified and theoretically construed. Without such standardized referents there could be no judgment of progress achieved. That is why, as Kirk (1960) cogently points out, "gross departures from common sense were carefully avoided by the Presocratics."

For example, the resolution of problems connected with the spatio-temporal position of the heavenly bodies depends upon a correct appreciation of the scope and limits of common sense. The shape of the earth, the position of the sun and the like are determined by calculation; however, such calculations (which were partly developed as aids to navigation) are based on the assumption that various other objects *are* how and where they commonsensically appear to be. It is only because we start by equating the physical positions of the things around us with the observed positions of standardized referents that our more sophisticated methods of locating objects like the sun and projecting the curvature of the earth can lead to confirmable results. Such standardized referents, taken together with their apparant spatio-temporal position, are precisely those things around us with which we are most intuitively familiar.

In this respect, what happened in natural history is not unlike what occurred in natural philosophy. A series of biological types emerged to provide a taxonomic system of reference for the comparative study of organisms.[4] It is by

4

developing notions of species, genera, families and classes that natural historians managed to progressively standardize what was already – at least to some extent – common to the viewpoints of ordinary folk everywhere. Ultimately, this framework would provide a practical basis for the comprehensive survey of beings the world over, and a conceptual foundation for the theoretical elaboration of their interrelations. How this transition in our apprehension of the living world from setting to subject came about, all herein aspires to show.

This inquiry has four parts, which are broadly as follows:

Part I, "Folkbiology," looks at some of the principal features of the common-sense background to natural history, focusing on how people the world over ordinarily classify locally perceived living kinds. The perspective is that of ethnobiology, a branch of cognitive anthropology concerned with studying the ways members of a culture apprehend and utilize the local flora and fauna. A significant contrast comes to light both in regard to the ordinary categorization of artifacts and the extraordinary scientific classification of living kinds.

Two decades of intensive empirical and theoretical cross-cultural work seem to reveal that folkbiological classification is taxonomic, being composed of a rigid hierarchy of inclusive classes of organisms, or taxa. At each level of the hierarchy the taxa, which are mutually exclusive, exhaustively partition the locally perceived biota. Lay taxonomy, it appears, is universally and primarily composed of three absolutely distinct hierarchichal levels, or ranks: the levels of *unique beginner, generic-specieme* and *life-form* (cf. Berlin et al. 1973).[5]

A unique beginner refers to the ontological category of plants or that of animals excluding humans. Some cultures have single words to denote the botanical or zoological realm, like "beast" for nonhuman animals. Other cultures employ descriptive phrases, like "hairs of the earth" (*muk gubul nor*) for the plant kingdom of the Bunaq of Timor (cf. Friedberg 1984). Some societies use a special marker for the unique beginner, like the numerical classifier *tehk* for plants, as with the Tzeltal Maya (Berlin *et al.* 1974). Still others forego the use of any specific words, phrases or markers, although it seems that from an early age all humans conceptually distinguish the class of plants and the class of animals, as indicated by studies of young Mayan (Stross 1973) and American children (Dougherty 1979; Macnamara 1982), New Guinea highlanders (Hays 1983), Indonesian natives (Taylor 1984): thus, although some English speakers ordinarily contrast "tree" with "plant", both are covered by an unamed category of THINGS WHICH GROW OUT OF THE GROUND (Wierzbicka 1985).

The basic level is logically subordinate, but psychologically prior, to the life-form level. Ideally it is constituted as a *fundamentum relationis*, that is, an exhaustive and mutually exclusive partitioning of the local flora and fauna into well-bounded morpho-behavioral gestalts (which visual aspect is readily perceptible at a glance). For the most part, taxa at this level correspond, within predictable limits, to those species of the field biologist that are spatially sympatric (i.e. coexisting in the same locality) and temporally nondimensional (i.e. perceived over at most a few generations). At least this is the case for those organisms that are readily apparent, including most vertebrates and flowering plants. Because the frontiers of a cultural group do not always coincide with the boundaries of a set of sympatric species, partitioning can fall short of the ideal: for instance, migrating birds may be only intermittently or vaguely perceived. But this basic folk kind also largely conforms to the modern genus, being immediately recognizable both ecologically and morphologically. As we shall see, the species-genus distinction is largely irrelevant to the common-sense vision of the world. In the local world of most folk, species usually lack congeners so that species and genus are habitually coextensive. That is why I have designated the basic folkbiological kind "generic-specieme."

The life-form level further assembles generic-speciemes into larger exclusive groups (tree, grass, moss, quadruped, bird, fish, insect, etc.). A salient character-istic of folkbiological life-forms is that they partition the plant and animal categories into contrastive lexical fields. The system of lexical markings thus constitutes a pretheoretical *fundamentum divisionis* of features that are positive and opposed. The opposition may be along a single perceptible dimension (size, stem habit, mode of locomotion, skin covering, etc.) or simultaneously along several dimensions. By and large, plant life-forms do not correspond to scientific taxa, whereas animal life-forms more or less conform to modern classes, save the phenomenally "residual" categories of "bug," "worm," "insect" and the like. These popular invertebrate groupings are exceptions because human perception of them is not as evident.

Such uniform taxonomic knowledge, under socio-cultural learning con-ditions so diverse, likely results from certain regular and domain-specific processes of human cognition, although local circumstances undoubtedly trigger and condition the stable forms of knowledge attained. Meaning for living-kind terms can thus be analyzed in a fundamentally distinct way from the semantics of other object domains, such as the domain of artifacts and perhaps that of chemical and physical substances as well. All and only living kinds are conceived as physical sorts whose intrinsic "natures" are presumed, even if unknown. Consequently, the semantically typical properties that the definition of a living-kind term describes may be considered necessary – not merely likely – in virtue of the presumed underlying nature of that kind. For instance, we can say that a dog born legless is missing "its" legs because we presume that all dogs are quadrupeds "by nature"; but we cannot justifiably say that a legless beanbag chair is missing "its" legs simply because chairs normally have legs. It is this presumption of underlying nature that underpins the taxonomic stability of organic phenomenal types despite obvious variation among individual exemplars.

The scientific conception of living kinds differs from the folk conception by allowing that any of the typical properties of a kind may prove to be incidental to its real nature. Bats, for example, have many of the typical properties of birds and ostriches have many of the typical properties of mammals; nevertheless, bats are mammals and ostriches are birds. But even today common-sense meaning is not directly tied to scientific reference. If laypeople accept modification of a folk taxon, it is because the scientific taxon proves compatible with everyday common-sense realism; if not, the scientific concept can usually be set aside, and the lay notion persists as a "natural kind" regardless. Thus, owing to their singular morphologies and ecological roles, bats and ostriches are fairly easy to conceptually isolate and taxonomically realign. By contrast, tree and sparrow remain American folk kinds with presumed natures, although they do not conform to scientific (phyletic) lines.

Despite the relative autonomy of common sense implied in the fact that folkbiological taxa are not demarcated like scientific taxa, folk and scientific classifications have tended to share a basic presumption. The idea is that living kinds naturally fall into "groups within groups" by virtue of a systematic embedding of their existence-determining physical properties. Only, while folk suppose that patternings in morphological aspect and ecological proclivity are determined, science has come to focus on the determination of genetic affiliations. Throughout history, people have assumed that the primary locus of underlying properties responsible for the regularities of living kinds occurs at roughly the level of the nondimensional species.

Part II, "Aristotelian Essentials," is concerned with rethinking Aristotle's much maligned essentialist doctrine by highlighting its folkbiological foundations. From this vantage, his biological works seem largely geared to providing a principled understanding of the differences and similarities between folk taxa according to the distribution of vital functions through the ranks. It turns out that Aristotle did not apparently entertain many of the notions traditionally attributed to essentialism, such as the idea of eternally fixed species and the belief that variation within species does not constitute a legitimate object of study.

For Aristotle, individuals belong to a species as a joint function of parentage and environment. Thus, the examination of deviation from type can factor out the various contributions of heritage and milieu that are responsible for how organisms "come to be" essentially like others, that is, for their *genesis*. Moreover, because species are integrally bound to their respective environments, and because environments may change, species are neither necessarily constant nor everlasting.

To the query "What is nature?" the philosophically inclined might respond: "what there is" or "the totality of things." But there is a prephilosophical sense in which "nature" differs from the artificial, on the one hand, and the supernatural, on the other. From a pretheoretical standpoint, natural things, like a robin or Robert, differ from robots and the Redeemer by reason of immanent causality: that is, in virtue of those causal factors that are peculiar to the type of thing and make it whatever it is – a bird or a man. What separates Aristotle's idea of "nature" (*physis*) from, say, the notion of "nature" (*unuq*) entertained by the Bunaq of Timor (Friedberg 1984:1350) is simply this: whereas humans the world over ordinarily presume each distinct living kind has its proper nature, Aristotle further assumes that all the distinct natures of folktaxonomic living kinds (as well as those nonliving sorts modeled on the living) are causally connected. That is why Aristotle's *physis* has the dual meaning of "a given kind" and of "Nature" in general.

Aristotle's primary task was to find a principle of unity underlying the diversity of ordinary phenomenal types. In practice, this meant systematically deriving each basic-level generic-specieme (*atomon eidos*) from a life-form (*megiston genos*). It further implied combining the various life-forms by "analogy" (*analogian*) into an integrated conception of life.

Aristotelian life-forms are distinguished and related through possession of analogous organs of the same essential functions (locomotion, digestion, repro-duction, respiration); for example, bird wings, quadruped feet and fish fins constitute analogous organs of locomotion. The generic-speciemes of each life-form are then differentiated by degrees of "more or less" with respect to essential organs. Because these organs are essential, and naturally "for the better," they are necessarily adapted to the special requirements of each species' habitual environment (*bios*). Thus, all birds have wings for moving about and beaks for obtaining nutriments. But, whereas the predatory eagle is partially diagnosed by long and narrow wings and a sharply hooked beak, the goose – owing to its different mode of life – is partially diagnosed by a lesser and broader wing span and a flatter bill. The principled classification of folkbiological taxa "by division and assembly" (*diaresis* and *synagoge*) ends when all taxa are defined, that is, when each generic-specieme is completely diagnosed with respect to every essential organ. Such definition, however, does not pertain to a species in the abstract, but to a community of organisms-in-their-environment.

This first sustained scientific research program differed from modern science in its preoccupation with explaining the familiar and known, rather than with exploring the unknown for its own sake. The program failed owing to a fundamental antagonism between what were effectively nonphenomenal means and the phenomenal end sought. To explain the visible order of things Aristotle had recourse to internal functions. But such functions cannot be properly understood if, as with Aristotle, they are referred primarily to their morphologi-cal manifestations. Moreover, as any folk naturalist, he recognized no more than five or six hundred species. He knew that there were kinds not present in his own familiar environment, but he had no idea that there were orders of magnitude of difference between what was locally apparent and what existed world-wide. Given the (wrong) assumption that a phenomenal survey of naturally occurring kinds was practically complete, Aristotle hoped to find a true and consistent system of character selection by the trial and error method. Nevertheless, by inquiring into how the apparently diverse natures of com-monly apprehended species may be causally related to the Nature of life, Aristotle established the theoretical program of natural history.

Part III, "Herbals to Systems," examines the developments that led from herbalism to systematic botany and analyzes the attempt of science to overcome the limits of common sense with the aid of rational intuition. Two stages in this advance of natural history are especially noteworthy: the elaboration of the taxonomic species as a perpetually self-reproducing unit from a common seed, and the codification of the genus as a perceptually and mnemonically privileged rank immediately superordinate to the species.

After Aristotle, the practice of copying descriptions and illustrations of living kinds from previous sources superseded actual field experience in the schools of late antiquity. Well into the Renaissance, scholastic "naturalists" took it for granted that the local flora and fauna of northern and central Europe could be fully categorized under the Mediterranean plant and animal types found in ancient works. Herbals and bestiaries of the time were far removed from any empirical base.

Only when German, Dutch and Italian herbalists of the sixteenth and seventeenth centuries returned to customary intuitions of nature did progress become possible. But they persisted in using a Latin (or latinized Greek) nomenclatural type whenever a similar local species could be attached to it. This fostered the comparison of ancient and foreign types to local forms. In addition, a series of technological innovations allowed a permanent record of the knowledge gained: the preservation of dried specimens in herbaria, the establishment of botanical and zoological gardens, advances in the art of woodcut and the invention of movable type.

Folk knowledge was thus recovered, set against standards for comparison and fixed for communication across local boundaries of time and place. Information was exchanged among different communities without loss of specificity and accumulated, and a worldwide catalogue of species could be envisaged. The problem, then, would be to systematize the welter of new forms into an overarching taxonomy that would be as psychologically convenient as folk-taxonomy in providing an intellectual map of the readily visible organic world.

The first step towards a systematic global classification involved fixing the species as an eternally self-perpetuating entity. Although ecological and reproductive criteria are usually covariant indicators of local species status, only the latter would provide cross-community status to morphological groupings: the most commonly perceived features of local species would also be those that usually happened to breed ever true. The permanent filiation of locally visible types would yield sempiternal forms, and thus sanction the principle of systematic comparison and placement within higher groups extending in scope to the world at large. Species now fixed reproductively and eternally, rather than ecologically and locally, could be abstracted from context and fit into a universal morphological scheme.

Together with the introduction of specific breeding criteria, the emergence of the genus concept was initially motivated by historical difficulties that exploration had posed for common sense. The genus was originally designed to allow the reduction of species by an order of magnitude to equivalence classes whose number and quality the mind could easily manage again (from over 6,000 known species to some 600 genera). The place of a new species in the natural order of genera would be initially determined in either of two ways: (i) By empirical intuition, that is, readily visible morphological agreement with a European representative or some other preferred type-species of the genus, or (ii) by intellectual intuition, that is, analytic agreement with the generic fructification according to the number, topological disposition, geometrical configuration and magnitude of its constituent elements. But the one would ultimately be commensurate with the other, thus allowing a mathematical reduction of the new species to its associated type by reason of their common fructification. As a result, the customary surety of the folk naturalist might be rationally extended to a world-wide scale. This was the gist of the "natural system."

Part IV, "The Scientific Breakaway," explores the intellectual dissociation of natural history from folkbiology during the late eighteenth and early nineteenth centuries, which paved the way for the birth of modern systematics. Motivating the theoretical break were both practical and more speculative agendas. Practical concerns led from a rational system of genera to an empirical method centering on families and classes. The genus lost its role as the chief taxonomic rank and there was a dynamic reassessment of the relation between species and higher-order taxa in terms of biological functions, anatomical structures and historical processes. At the same time, the speculative program that sought to unify the visible forms of life in a "great chain of being" (*scala naturae*) reached its culmination through the theory-forming "Analogy of Nature." With the realization of this program, a global patterning of visible plant and animal forms was found inadequate for understanding the underlying order of life. As a result, natural history's common-sense preoccupation with comprehending phenomenal reality gave way to biology's quest to explain the unforeseen.

The genus's defining character – the fructification – was crucially a rational notion, although metaphysically sanctioned as the seat of life. It required conceptual isolation of those analytically prized characters of the visible fruit and flower that could be apodictically arranged into a preset combinatory system. The detachability and reducibility of visible parts to computable characters was, however, *prima facie* less warranted in the case of animals; the parts of animals immediately lend themselves to consideration as functionally interjoined organs rather than as visibly juxtaposed features.

Moreover, conservation of animal life-forms blocked attempts to dissolve animal (and therefore ultimately plant) kinds into a single table of rational characters. A set of generic characters proposed for one animal life-form would fail to apply to the others. Even if functionally analogous, the essential organs of each great class of animals hardly manifest similarity in their external features: no logical expression of the means for acquiring nutriment would link, say, the conformation of a mammal's teeth to the structure of a bird's beak.

The system was able to dispense with plant life-forms. They are fundamentally provincial indicators of ecological status tied up with our understanding of the way local kinds interrelate and appear to us. Devoid of local context, however, plant life-forms represent only what Linnaeus would qualify as "lubricious" morphological groupings. In contrast, our appreciation of vertebrate life-forms (perhaps because we ourselves are vertebrates) is not so far removed from an objective appreciation of morphological affinities between vertebrates themselves. From the Renaissance onwards, the analysis of zoological forms proceeded mostly within the framework of separate monographs treating distinct animal life-forms. Special concern for these life-forms effectively ruled out a wholesale approach to animal organization from the start. But because there were initially many fewer animals to worry about than plants (wild animals especially being harder to spot in nature, to relocate for study and to examine without destroying), the problem did not seem at first compelling in face of the myriad plant forms that occupied the attention of those naturalists seeking a global system.

Also lessening the importance of the genus was the geometrical rate of exploration and discovery. Recall that the genus was introduced in an effort to cope with a number of plant species approximately one order of magnitude above that which ancient and Renaissance herbalists ordinarily faced. But once awareness of new forms had increased by yet another order of magnitude, the family became the new basis for taxonomy.

The family was itself rooted in local groupings that folk implicitly recognize but seldom name, such as felines, equids, legumes and grasses. These "covert" groupings generally do not violate the boundaries of modern families, but they may cross life-forms: for example, among the family of legumes may be found herbs, vines, trees and bushes. Furthermore, unlike taxonomically arrayed generic-speciemes and life-forms, the local series of covert groupings does not cover the local environment with a morpho-ecologic quilt but is riddled with gaps. A strategy emerged for closing the gaps: by looking to other environments for similar as well as different family "fragments," and by using such partial series drawn from many different environments, European naturalists sought to fill the lacunae in any and all environments with a single worldwide series of families. This strategy became the "natural method."

Only by giving the correlation of visible characters at the family level a physiological dimension, however, could one affirm the family's biological integrity. This alone would justify the family category's claim to ontological status and still uphold the quest for a visible order spanning the entire living world. The analysis of zoological classes provided the grounds for an abstract notion of anatomical integrity that could support the visible arrangement of families. The family thereby became the prime locus of speculation as to those material causes linking species together into the larger apparent unity. But soon after, the family itself lost its status as the favored taxonomic rank. That dealt a fatal blow to the idea that taxonomy should aim principally at a visible order. By then, a clear epistemic break had emerged between science and common sense, although this did not mean that the one would ignore the other.

The speculation that guided the natural method of arranging life's visible forms centered on the idea of a "great chain of being" organized according to Newton's "Analogy of Nature" or Locke's "Rule of Analogy." The Rule says that all of nature's kinds must be compounded of the same properties found to constitute the readily perceptible "mid-level" phenomena of everyday experience. In natural history, man was the mid-level ideal·in relation to which all other forms of life were to be organized according to visibly apparent species, genus, family and class. Introduced from natural philosophy, the theory-constitutive "Analogy of Nature" combined and carried through three older research-orienting analogies of natural history: man as the perfect animal, the plant as an upturned animal, and the organism as a microcosm.

Granted that the analogies of mythico-religious thought, like the formative analogies of science, are free creations of the human mind that are not bound to sense experience. In fact, the three principal analogies of natural history were also part of European symbolic lore. But the fount of such ideas has scant bearing on the course of science. What matters is how they are used. Contrary to mystical analogy, the goal of scientific analogy is ultimately to reduce itself to "dead metaphor," not to produce eternally open-ended "truth." It aims to ultimately terminate any metaphorical imprecision by (ideally) accommodating one subject to another in a wholly determinate manner. Because such accommodation often does not (and usually cannot) occur at the phenomenal level of sensible intuition, a nonphenomenal accommodation is sought. In this way, formative analogies become prime constituents of scientific abstraction and law-making. They are used to show that familiar things belong to more extensive classes of objects and processes, which depend for their occurrence on more pervasive relational or structural properties that are not immediately obvious.

People may be particularly susceptible to comprehend and elaborate certain original formative ideas of science because these have privileged connections with basic cognitions. Such, it seems, is the idea of the "great chain of being." Assuredly, the thesis of a continuous progression of living forms is neither obviously part nor parcel of folktaxonomy in which diversity is manifest. Still, the putative nature of the chain intuitively maintained much in relation to more fundamental folk conceptions: the exploration of continuity instituted a research program for seeking out a graduated system of relationships among *commonly apprehended living kinds*; and it did this by centering comparisons on man, that is, on *basic knowledge of humans and human activities*.

In other words, the terms of the analogy were essentially common sense "givens." That is a reason why the analogy was initially compelling and also readily sustained. For once unleashed in the scientific community's cognitive environment, such a speculative "virus" would spread contagiously among minds, owing to its affinity with universal cognitive dispositions. But it could also be elaborated and transformed in ways that more rigidly structured basic cognitions might not be.

The resultant knowledge of organic variation and underlying connection was originally intended to facilitate the ordering of phenomenal kinds. Eventually, it became a primary object of interest in itself, with knowledge of phenomenal kinds serving merely to facilitate its study. This "gestalt" shift between object and ground was a hallmark of the passage from natural history to biology. Yet, to get from the familiar to the unfamiliar involved not so much a radical rupture with common sense, as maintaining a continuing access through its reevaluation.

In all, my aim is to show how our universally held conception of the living world is both historically prior to, and psychologically necessary for, any scientific – or symbolic – elaboration of that world. As we shall see, ordinary notions of species (generic-specieme), family (covert fragment) and class (life-form) not only continue to provide epistemic access to our usual environment, but also cognitive access to the biological universe at large. At least this aspect of common sense, then, constitutes everyday knowledge of nature, while also serving as a natural heuristic for regulating our scientific dealings with the cosmos. Science, in turn, not only produces novel understanding of the universe, but also marks the true bounds of our common vision of the world. Between science and common sense, there need not be any contradiction or conflict.

PART I

FOLKBIOLOGY

And God called dry land Earth; and the gathering together of the waters he called the seas: and God saw that it was good.

And God said, Let the earth bring forth grass, the herb yielding seed, and the tree yielding fruit after its kind, whose seed is in itself, upon the earth: and it was so.

And God said, Let the waters bring forth abundantly the moving creature that hath life, and bird that may fly above the earth in the open firmament of heaven.

And God created great whales, and every living thing that moveth, which the waters brought forth abundantly, after their kind, and every winged bird after his kind: and God saw that it was good.

And God blessed them, saying, Be fruitful, and multiply, and fill the waters in the seas, and let birds multiply throughout the earth.

And God said, Let the earth bring forth the living creature after his kind, large beast (*bihaimah*), and creeping thing, and brute of the earth after its kind: and it was so.

And God said, Let us make man in our image, after our likeness: and let him have dominion over the fish of the sea, and over the bird of the air, and over the large beast, and over all the earth, and over every creeping thing that creepeth upon the earth.

(Genesis I)

2

FOLKTAXONOMY

2.1 IN THE BEGINNING....

There are unmistakable cross-cultural regularities in the structure of folkbiological classifications. But these regularities go much deeper than purported historical parallels between, say, the Renaissance herbals of Western Europe and Chinese pharmacopoeia. The only significant systematic resemblances between European orderings of flora and fauna and those of other great civilizations apparently owe to a biological conception of the world common to folk everywhere. In particular, all known cultures appear to entertain notions of: (i) biological species, at least those "nondimensional" species (i.e. coexisting in the same locality over a few observed generations) of vertebrates and flowering plants that are manifest and phenomenally salient for human beings, (ii) sequential patterns of naming (e.g. "oak," "shingle oak," "spotted shingle oak"), (iii) taxa construction by means of an appreciation of overall patterns of morphological regularity (variously termed "habitus," "facies," or "aspect"), (iv) overarching animal "life-form" groupings that more or less correspond to modern zoological classes (e.g. bird, fish), and (v) overarching plant "life-form" groupings that have no place in modern botanical taxonomy but are nonetheless of obvious ecological significance (e.g. tree, grass).

To say the systems of encyclopedic thought that pertain to the natural world in other civilizations exhibit "precursors" or "parallels" to what was to emerge as Western science actually tells little about the truly significant similarities, at least in natural history. Concentration on historical parallels also tends to obscure the fact that the course of natural history in Europe after the Renaissance was determined by novel empirical problems whose solution required a singular kind of mechanical rationality. For instance, the conceptual apparatus that emerged in Europe to deal with the unceasing discovery and exploration of new sources of information did not arise in China. Thus, no Chinese herbal or encyclopedia organizes more than a thousand or so basic kinds of plants – roughly the same number found in all known folkbiologies and also in the works of Ancient and Medieval Europe, the Middle East and Meso-america.[1] The Chinese empire, it is true, encompassed many different sub-cultures whose respective folktaxonomies collectively sum to thousands of species. Yet, there is no evidence of any systematic attempt at a taxonomic organization of morphological information beyond that already present in any folktaxonomy.[2]

In contrast to pre-literate societies, however, cultures with writing do have an additional point in common: whether in Ancient Greece, Egypt, India, Meso-america or China, there is an effort to report the presumed medicinal properties and social virtues of popular groupings of plants and animals, and to organize those attributes in summary fashion. Yet, profitable as it may be to compare the diverse organizational schemata civilizations use, there seems to be no principled cross-cultural correspondence between them. For any such schema, which orders the presumed relationships between plants and animals according to socially utilitarian or symbolic criteria, is necessarily idiosyncratic and culture specific. This is so because utility is contingent upon historical and environmen-tal context, and because symbolism has no constraint of logical consequence or empirical verifiability (or falsifiability) that would allow consistent interpre-tation across cultures. Again, the only systematic cross-cultural correspondence involves a universal, common-sense appreciation of morphological patterns of similarity and difference among groups (of species) within groups (of life-forms).[3]

In his dedicatory epistle to the founding work of systematic botany, Andrea Cesalpino (1583) disclaims the practices of earlier natural historians who, like Dioscorides,

> assembled [plants] by medicinal properties . . . . Others have classified alphabetically, so that one can more easily store content in memory . . . . But the classification that unites plants by their natural affinities may be considered the easiest, the surest and the most efficacious, be it for the memory or for the study of [a plant's secondary] properties.

In a natural system, then,

> Genera and species are constituted neither from medicinal properties, nor by reason of some use, nor from the place in which they occur. These are all accidents. (26)

By attempting to proceed straightaway to an account of the various virtues of natural kinds, without first carefully describing those kinds in regard to morphological similarities and differences, ancient and medieval herbalists succeeded only in confounding our spontaneous appreciation of natural relationships: "It seems," notes Tournefort (1694:7), "that the more they enriched medicine, the more they threw botany into confusion."

Likewise, for Buffon (1749,I:49–50), an originator of the empirical method in zoology, natural history must, first of all, furnish the "exact description of each thing." The ancients failed to fulfill the necessary condition of an adequate natural history because:

> they did not believe that things which were of no use were worthy of study . . . . One could cite the twenty-seventh book of Pliny, *Reliqua herbarium genera*, wherein he places together all the herbs which he does not greatly value, so that he contents himself with naming them alphabetically, indicating only certain of their general characteristics and uses for medicine.

Buffon opposes the efforts of those, such as Cesalpino, Tournefort and Linnaeus, who would arbitrarily impose a rational system on nature; nonetheless, he is in accord with the systematists on this necessary prerequisite to a correct natural history. He also agrees that "exact description" should be limited to readily perceptible characters of external morphology so as to do justice to an intuitive feeling for natural affinity – a feeling of the kind that someone unaffected by tradition or prejudice might experience in an unpeopled earth. Detailed examination of internal anatomy and the use of the microscope, no less than medicinal virtues, would therefore be effectively excluded from a determination of generic pedigree no matter how admittedly useful they might be for understanding physiological function or generation.

What is curious here is the suggestion that ancient natural history angled away from something so obvious: odd because neither Cesalpino, Tournefort nor Buffon presumed that people before them had ever classified plants or animals in accordance with such supposedly apparent intuitions – what Linnaeus (1751 sec. 168) would also intend by *primo intuitu ex facie externa*. If the learned scholars of Greece, Rome and the Renaissance failed on this score, surely it would be folly to suppose that more primitive ancestors or contemporary pre-literate peoples could do better – the unspoiled savage of Montaigne and Rousseau notwithstanding.

There are, to be sure, striking resemblances to be found between the ancient herbals of Greece and Rome, their Medieval and Renaissance derivatives, and those of Mesoamerica, the Middle East, China and India. Frequently there appear to be "unnatural" groupings of plants, that is, groupings based not on any readily perceived morphological similarity, but on the basis of some acknowledged virtue. In European herbals since Pliny, for instance, various species of Euphorbiaceae are often grouped with plants of other families because of a similarity in the texture and color of the sap which was valued as a medicinal purgative. Similarly, in the sixteenth-century Aztec herbal known as the Badianus Manuscript (Emmart 1940), two illustrated plants appear: the *tohmioxihuitl* ("hairy plant"), belonging to the tribe Chichorieae of the Compositae, and *memeyaxiuhtontli* ("little milk plant"), a species of *Euphorbia*. These are also linked together on the basis of their milky juice – a juice thought to increase lactation in women.

It would be a mistake, however, to conclude as so many have from such observations, that knowledge of living kinds was exclusively, or even primarily, a practical knowledge dependent on cultural virtues.[4] Admittedly, the initial task of natural historians, or *rhizomotists*, was to provide a written record of features of plants (and animals) deemed beneficial or harmful to man's well-being, especially the "hidden" aspects of roots, sap and entrails. But such performative knowledge was itself dependent on a rich and prior competence with respect to the visible patterns of the living world. It does indeed appear that herbals tend to make their appearance at a rather advanced stage of city-state development; yet this hardly indicates "the late advent of interest in plants" (Singer 1927:2) as such.

A common-sense appreciation of phenomenal reality is, it seems, largely independent of culturally parochial concerns; however, this knowledge of the visible patterns of the organic world does function provincially, that is, within the local bounds of everyday experience. Such basic competence appears to be fundamentally the same in all times and places since humankind first acquired rights to the Linnaean title, *Homo sapiens*. It would be so easily accessible to all, and the visible patterns it reveals so immediately obvious, that there would be no need for members of a given culture to instruct one another in such knowledge. In a classic study of Aztec folk botany, for instance, Paso y Trancoso (1886) presents a much more detailed appreciation of plant life "for its own sake" than the Badianus herbal would lead one to suspect.

Similarly, with respect to the folk classifications of the Tzeltal Maya of Mexico and the Aguaruna Jivaro of Peru, Berlin (1978:10–11) notes that more than a third of the named plants in both societies have no known social use, nor are they poisonous or pestiferous. Like the overwhelming majority of named plants, however, those apparently lacking in cultural utility are also grouped according to "overall perceptual similarities": "This finding would seem to controvert the view that preliterate man names and classifies only those organisms in the environment that have some immediate functional significance for survival."

A closer examination of Theophrastus's *Historia plantarum*, which provides the touchstone for many later European herbals, shows that a discussion of cultural virtues is predicated on the following premises: that shared virtues are necessary consequences of similarity in underlying essential nature (*physis*), and that there is often no better sign of similarity in nature than a popular intuition of overall resemblance in readily visible morphological aspect (*eidos, idea, schema, morphe*). In other words, learned communication *presupposes* the principled acceptance of morphological types, as Aquinas so aptly noted: "figura est signum speciei in rebus naturalibus" (*Summa theologiae* III,74,iii).

Yet, even in late Antiquity the common-sense foundations of natural history were often ignored. Subsequent developments only aggravated this neglect. Following the Renaissance, proponents of a rational system and empirical method for the worldwide ordering of plants and animals emphasized the problem of finding universal standards of agreement about morphological affinity. But the solutions offered were primarily considered to be philosophical novelties; only incidentally, if at all, were they thought of as labored reorganizations of basic common-sense dispositions to classify organisms.[5]

As the requirements of a worldwide taxonomy were increasingly drawn from nonintuitive modes of reasoning and observation, explicit recourse to customary knowledge diminished. The hierarchy of common-sense categories that systematist and methodist alike initially accepted began to break down under the burden of incorporating a prodigious number of intractable, exotic organisms. In their everyday lives natural historians, like everybody else, could scarcely do without these categories; yet, intermittent awareness of this circumstance emerged only in the reluctant acknowledgment that people are ordinarily susceptible to the conveniences of intellectually outworn traditions. Unhappily for those who desire to know more than just the chronological sequence of scientific discovery, appreciation of the matter has barely improved since Darwin. The cognitive factors that have historically compelled and enabled the mind to resolve a vast array of scientific puzzles have thus been left mostly in the dark. Consider the following:

In the seminal work on the history of botany to Darwin, Julius Sachs (1875/ 1890)[6] provides the framework for innumerable subsequent interpretations of the course of natural history. Sachs's rather simple-minded premise is that science has its origins in the "unprejudiced" and "involuntary" inductive associations of perceptions and ideas. In the beginning, these associations were concerned with practical matters: "In the effort to promote the knowledge of plants for practical purposes by careful description of individual forms, the impression forced itself on the mind of the observer that there are various natural groups of plants which have a distinct resemblance to one another in form and other characteristics" (4). Once the mind was freed from the grip of traditional schools, natural groups could be intuited through the simple enumeration of observations: "The perception of a natural affinity among plants could only be obtained from exact description a thousand times repeated, never from the abstractions of the Aristotelian school, which rested essentially on superficial observation" (17).

Whether in regard to the human individual or species, the inductivist view of the growth of knowledge denies that there are innate or culturally untainted ideas. One eminent anthropologist sees the physical and social environment of a young child as a continuum, which contains no inherently separated "things": "The child, in due course, is taught to impose upon this environment, a kind of discriminating grid which serves to distinguish the world as being composed of a large number of separate things, each labeled with a name" (Leach 1964:212).

From this standpoint, it follows that there are not *any* intrinsic differences in our cognitive dispositions to classify natural or artificial objects or qualities.

According to philosopher and biologist J. S. L. Gilmour (1940:365), for instance, the classifier simply experiences a vast number of sense-data which are then grouped together for this or that "purpose":

> the important point to emphasize is that the construction of these classes is an act of reason, and hence provided they are based on experienced data, such classes can be manipulated at will to serve the purpose of the classifier . . . . The classification of animals and plants . . . is essentially similar in principle to the classification of inanimate objects.

This approach joins two ideas. It holds with the English empirical philosopher John Stuart Mill (1889:467) that of all logically possible classifications there is only one that is simultaneously "the most important" and of the greatest "general interest." It also adheres to the Vienna School's "phenomenalist" version of logical positivism that denies to the brain any cognitively meaningful *a priorisms*" (cf. Carnap 1928). In this respect, the belief that: "there are such 'natural kinds', differing in some 'fundamental' way from other, 'artificial' methods of classifying the same objects, is very difficult to sustain; a more useful way of looking at the situation is that these so-called 'kinds' are classes showing a high degree of correlation of attributes, differing only in degree from other classes with a less high correlation" (Gilmour and Walters 1964:5).

The only significant difference between classifications, then, is the degree to which some culturally parochial "special purpose" is allowed to favor certain attributes over others. Initially, all classification was presumably subject to the purposeful dictates of symbolic passions and economic needs and, in the last analysis, to reason itself: "many of the taxa concerned, including families, genera, and species, were recognized more than two thousand years ago, and 'created' by man, not on account of any bioligical, far less phylogenetic, interest in them, but in response to man's need to use living things for food, clothing ornament, and other purposes" (11).

Admittedly, post-Renaissance systems were less culturally parochial than folk classifications. But they were still artificially biased to an arbitrary *human* concern, namely, *deducing* a natural series of plant and animal types. From this standpoint, the Renaissance herbals came closer than the classical systems of Linnaeus and others to a "natural classification" in "the modern, logical sense" (cf. Gilmour 1937). Nevertheless, even initial classifications of living kinds, which supposedly differed little intellectually from groupings of artifacts, had a "natural," that is, "inductive" element. Taxonomy today, however, clearly "has a much wider scope"; that is to say, modern systematics tends to an unbiased appreciation of covariation in attributes.

Earlier ethnobiological inquires tended to reinforce (because they presupposed) this empiricist view of abstract science emanating from, and culminating in, a concrete and parochial folk knowledge:

Primitive tribes, such as our Indians, depended immediately upon their floral environment first of all for food . . . . Under such conditions of intimate dependence upon the vegetation of their habitat a people would naturally be induced to become acquainted with all the plants which grew about them, and which held so large a practical interest.

(Gilmore 1932:320)

The living-kind categories of folk would assumedly not be the abstract categories of genus and species; rather, "plants fall under a number of classes, according to their uses for food, architecture, dress and adornment, domestic life, domestic arts, agriculture, medicine as folk medicine, religion and folk-lore" (Hough 1897:37). And when it is recognized that "Indians of the lowest Brazilian tribes can differentiate all the species and even all the varieties of palms," they can only be "guided by a kind of special sense, or by tact . . . having [nothing] in common with intellectual processes so-called" (Lévy-Bruhl 1923/1966:445).

A respected naturalist summarizes well the standard view of the course of natural history (Croizat 1945:52–53; cf. Greene 1983,I:100–101). Initially, "of necessity," humans classify plants into "the most useful and the noxious." Then, with writing, progress is made: "*describing* these plants under chapters such as 'Plants with roots that can be eaten', 'Herbs which are good in love potions and magic brews', and the like [w]e may, of course, take into account the fact that some of these plants are tree-like and perennial, and others fugacious weeds." Over time, as awareness becomes "more self-conscious and firmer," we are able to grasp "the fact that certain groups, like the leguminosae, characterized by common kinship, may well happen to include trees, shrubs and herbs, and may be useful or not for immediate material needs."

Upon closer examination, however, each stage of the story collapses. It is, first of all, inconceivable that modern systematics had its origin in the work of the herbalists, as Sachs contends, rather than the systematists. Granted, there is an "unmistakable difference" between herbalist and systematist in regard to the origin of studied efforts to distinguish natural affinities at various levels. But the difference is not between unbiased "induction," on the one hand, and *a priori* deductions, on the other. Rather, the difference is between no plan at all and a theoretically elaborated, if ultimately skewed, blueprint for *predicting* or project-ing antecedently held intuitions of natural affinity to exotic and intuitively unaccessed sorts (thus also facilitating discovery of hitherto unknown properties of known sorts). The systematists, in other words, presupposed *all* that the herbalists intuitively knew with respect to local patterns of natural affinity. Such prior knowledge was necessary, but not sufficient, for an attempt at systematic generalization on a world-wide scale.

There is, moreover, no such thing as a "sense datum" language of the kind presumed by Gilmour to underlie categorization of artifacts, colors, chemical substances, living kinds, etc. The phenomenal data of experience are organized into qualities, bodily objects, gestalt forms, and so forth, often quite independently of human will (though not of the structure of the human brain) and in ways distinctly appropriate to differently organized cognitive domains. For example, a perceptual analysis for the domain of living kinds has little bearing on a perceptual analysis for the domain of artifacts; consideration of whether a surface constitutes, say, a "table-top" or a "seat" depends upon function and context in ways that judgments over what constitutes a "head" or "wings" do not.

Of course some aspects of visual processing may be the same for different domains of natural categories, but this tells us nothing about the structure of the specific domains in question. Lay classifications of colors, inorganic substances, diseases, kinsfolk and artifacts are all *prima facie* very different in structure from one another and from living-kind taxonomies. Any deeper organization principles (such as taxonomic ranking) that may cross cognitive domains must be shown, rather than assumed. To date, no such demonstration exists.

What of Croizat's presumed sequence from particularly functional groupings of plants, to generally useful categories of trees, shrubs and herbs, and on to natural taxa that cross-cut these categories? It suffices here to signal what the rest of the chapter aims to show, namely, that tribal peoples *simultaneously* recognize all of these divisions of the plant world for what they are, and do not confuse their respective merits. There is one significant difference between folk appreciation of the value of such divisions and the standard view of their respective worth: groupings such as tree, herb and shrub are generally named and considered natural groupings that may be useful or not, whereas such cross-cutting taxa as the legumes, orchids, and other plant forms, though also considered natural, usually are not named. As will hopefully become evident, however, the reasons for this difference in appreciation apparently have nothing to do with the "special" concerns of pre-scientific folk, or with a less refined capacity for induction.

The more "general" the classification – so the story goes – the wider its "inductive validity" (Gilmour 1940). Based on "overall similarities" of "many" features rather than "few" features, it is also supposedly "multi-purpose" and not especially restricted in its range of uses. Logically speaking, however, the distinction thus drawn between general and special classification is untenable.

There is no possibility of assessing "overall similarity" without an antecedent determination of point of view. Otherwise, there can be no criteria of identity for deciding just what a feature *is*, much less what it resembles (e.g. molecular features, or atomic features, do not play a role in the assessment of similarities between bodily organs). Moreover, there may be indefinitely many purposes which any given classification *serves*, but which need not have figured into the original *design*. Because there is no logical limit to the discovery of new uses, there is no definite way to determine, *a priori*, to what extent one classification is more multi-purpose than another. Of course, classification may be ceremonially prescribed for some end, such as herbals for medicinal or ritual use. But, as we shall presently see, *this* sort of special-purpose classification is not directly pertinent to an understanding of folkbiological taxonomy.[7]

These truisms are largely ignored by the pheneticist (or neo-Adansonian) movement in systematics, which maintains that there exists, free from "mental anticipations," a notion of "overall similarity" that yields "natural" groupings.[8] Long ago, however, Locke rightly came to the skeptical conclusion that neither a science of natural history, nor natural philosophy, could arise upon such grounds: "This way of getting and improving our knowledge in substances only by experience and history, which is all that the weakness of our faculties in this state of mediocrity, which we are in this world, can attain to, makes me suspect that natural philosophy is not capable of being made a science (1689/1848 IV,xii,10)."[9] Only to the extent that systematics *is* theory-laden can it pretend to represent lawful knowledge about the world.

Finally, it is worth mentioning the oddity of the inductivist reconstruction of science for the cognitive procedures it entails. There is an *a priori* assumption that the development of taxonomic notions proceeded via principles of sensory association, habit formation, enumeration and so forth. No questions are posed concerning how such rich and complex notions of biological groupings could possibly be acquired on the basis of the inductivist's simple – indeed trivial – principles. A more reasonable investigation of the development of biological classification should rather begin by looking at the groupings that *have* been acquired, *then* asking what possible cognitive operations might enable one to come up with these various biological sorts.

From this perspective, one just may discover that it is "simpler" for human beings in ordinary circumstances to think of trees and grasses, rather than medicinal roots or herbs that require the additional cognitive operations associated with special interests. One might also find out that, in fact, the elaborate cognitive assessments of modern taxa differ appreciably from somewhat more spontaneous notions of tree and grass, but not so very much from spontaneous notions of oak and clover. One could then plausibly conjecture that modern taxa did not emerge by simple "refinements" of those cognitive procedures affiliated with the acquisition of ordinary groupings, but by a mix of procedures, some customary and some not, fit to the extraordinarily different circumstances of science.

2.2 A BASIC LEVEL

The primary operation in the classification of living kinds, whether for the field naturalist or the museum taxonomist, is the aggregation of organisms into basic-level taxa. This means partitioning a set of individual organisms into classes, or taxa, that are in some sense homogeneous with respect to specified attributes: "Such a problem faces us when we attempt to sort individual organisms into 'species'" (Jardine 1969:37). This basic partitioning of the living world into homogeneous groupings involves the construction of well-bounded configurations, or "morphotypes." Such visual types can then be sorted among higher taxa by "comparing mental images of whole specimens as wholes . . . what have been called *Gestalten*" (Cullen 1968:176).

Though comparing whole images of specimens, "observational homologies" are established between them (Inglis 1966), that is, a judgment of *absolute resemblance* is made between the corresponding structures of different exemplars of the *same* type. The corresponding homologous structures of the various exemplars of the type are deemed wholly equivalent for classificatory purposes, and logically identical with respect to the ideal-typical pattern, or "species" structure (Regan 1926). The various exemplars thus become token "namesakes" of the species type (Owen 1866). This, in essence, is the Aristotelian notion of the basic-level organic grouping, or *atomon eidos*:

> With regard to animals, there are those which have all their parts mutually identical . . . . Some parts are specifically identical in form, for example, one man's nose and eye are identical with another's nose and eye; one's flesh is identical with another's flesh, one's bone with another's; and the same applies to the parts of a horse, and of such other animals as we consider identical to one another by species (*eidei*); for as the whole is to the whole, so every part is to every part. (*Historia animalium* 486a14f.)

Yet, as Simpson (1961:23) notes, in the practice of classification the abstraction of the biological species "is not always the *first* operation, and in identification it never is." In many cases, it seems that generic, rather than specific, groupings are easiest to sort. This is because the exact delimitation of biological species as breeding isolates is often difficult in practice owing to the complication of perceptually aberrant mutants, incomplete fossil records for historical or paleontological species, and phenotypically similar "sibling" species that can usually be identified only by careful observation and experiment over time.

In Cain's (1956:108) view, the genus is "the smallest 'kind' or 'sort' recognisable without expert study." For plants, observes Cronquist (1968:30), "if the circumstances permit we try to define genera in such a way that one can recognize a genus from its *aspect*, without recourse to technical characters not readily visible to the naked eye." Sprague (1940:449) describes the taxonomist's basic sorting process in terms of a "bird's eye view":

> the faculty of appreciating what is called the 'facies' of the plant is invaluable . . . . It is a general effect produced on the eye by the sum total of all the visible external characters, many of which are not actually employed in technical descriptions owing to the difficulty of expressing them in precise terms . . . . The better sixteenth-century descriptions of plants, such as those of Valerius Cordus, can be best understood by treating them as word-pictures designed to supply mental images.

Similarly, in zoology "the basic or one might say primitive step in classification" involves "nontechnical recognition," which "is normally not by separate characters but by a mental image of the whole animal" (Simpson 1961:12). Thus, "we can visualize that primitive man, in the process of domestication, picked plants [and presumably animals] on the basis of their generic features without discrimination as to species" (Li 1974:723).

This historically and conceptually primary stage of scientific classification, then, would appear to correspond to the basic operation in folkbiological classification the world over. According to Bartlett (1940:351), the concept of the genus is the most natural and useful level of classification, inasmuch as it is "the smallest group that everyone might be expected to have the name for in his vocabulary." Berlin (1972:55) notes that basic-level folk taxa fit this requirement because they are, in fact, "the first to be encoded in the ethnobotanical lexicons of all languages." The same appears to be true of folkzoological taxonomies (Berlin *et al.* 1973).

The principal characteristic of the basic "folkgeneric," as Berlin (1978) calls it, is its readily perceived "aspect." Hunn (1975a) reports that the "gestalt" character of the folkgeneric lends itself to "instantaneous recognition"; but he further argues for an intuitive justification of folkgenerics on empirical grounds of "inductive recognition" of a "multiplicity of [visible] distinctions." Within any given local environment it is usually the case that no two coexisting folkgenerics occupy the same habitat so that "it is inevitable that differences [between basic folk taxa] . . . will be reflected morphologically and/or behaviorally" (Hunn 1975b:320; 1976:523n).

In a study of seals and their allies (Pinnipedia), Scheffer (1958) indicates some further properties of such "genera" usually distinguished by the natives: (a) at least one variate does not overlap with other genera when comparing individuals of same age and sex; (b) the way of life is distinctive; (c) the breeding range is confined to one or two broad niches; and (d) different genera do not interbreed in the wild. Although some taxonomists tend to view modern genera similarly (cf. Inger 1958:383), Simpson (1961:189) objects that these features "are all characteristic of . . . the evolutionary species, not genus"; as for the native, such an account "has some validity for the species, as field workers know," but not for the genus. Indeed, for Bulmer and Tyler (1968:350), basic folk taxa, or "speciemes," are "logically comparable to modern species."[10]

Now, if Scheffer's point is that the natives first tend to class the Pinnipedia into groups possessing the features listed above, how can such properties attach to species, since, according to Simpson, the species is supposedly rarely the first step in "nontechnical," or "primitive" classification? And if, as Berlin (1973:267–68) concedes, basic folk taxa closely correspond to scientific species "in Bulmer's sense," that is, in regard to "multiple distinctions of appearance, habitat and behavior," how can they also resemble modern genera? The apparent dilemma is resolved once it is realized that the distinction between species and genus is largely irrelevant to a basic appreciation of the flora and fauna of a local environment.

Historically, the distinction only assumes a modern character in connection with Europe's Age of Exploration. A taxonomic notion of species as a perpetually self-reproducing unity from a common seed was introduced by Cesalpino (1583:1,28) in the first treatise on systematic botany (see section 6.3

below). A conception of the genus as a perceptually and mnemonically privileged rank immediately superordinate to the species was originally codified by Tournefort (1694:13–14) (see section 7.3 below). But these historical occurrences pertain to the necessity of constructing a worldwide classificatory order – an order transcending local concerns.

Within any local community the layman readily perceives "gaps" between groups of organisms. For the most part, these apparent discontinuities in the local flora and fauna correspond to species differences. Among the Tzeltal Maya, for example, Hunn (1976) reports that nearly all (95%) animal generics correspond to recognized scientific taxa, three-fourths (75%) to scientific species and more than half (57%) to "isolated species" having no congeners in the local area. So, in the majority of cases species and genus are extensionally equivalent and hence cannot be distinguished perceptually.

When congeneric species are perceived as each having generic status it is usually because they are ecological isolates. As Dwyer (1976a:430) notes in regard to the Rofaifo of New Guinea: "when closely related species co–occur, they will diverge significantly in the ecological strategies they adopt and often in the morphological correlates of those strategies" (cf. Diamond 1972). This is especially so if the species fall within families that are locally monogeneric or minimally polytypic. That such cases are not infrequent may be expected given the general disposition of a local flora and fauna. In the case of the local flora of the Bunaq of Timor: "one may note that ... certain botanical genera are represented by few species, certain families by few genera and that the Bunaq therefore have but a partial vision of the botanical world wherein certain plants seem to them completely isolated and hence determinable without confusion" (Friedberg 1970:1128). Thus it happens that folk nomenclature contains numerous basic terms that denote only isolated species.

For those instances where generics seem to be underdifferentiated, that is, where a folkgeneric subsumes two or more species, it is often legitimate to ask, along with Bulmer (1970:1088): "How many of these cases include species which the professional botanist can only distinguish by very fine points so that the layman could justifiably regard them as natural units sharing a wide range of attributes? How many of them include only plants [or animals] which are relatively unfamiliar?" Indeed, because the genera of a local family usually occupy a single adaptive zone in a particular community, identifying the congeneric species of a polygeneric family can pose problems of recognition even for the trained taxonomist because of overlap in aspect and ecological proclivity (cf. Diver 1940).

In sum, within any given local community a principled distinction between genus and species is usually impossible perceptually because most genera are monospecific. The distinction is frequently also irrelevant conceptually inasmuch as the species of locally monogeneric or minimally polytypic families may have the same sorts of morphological, geographical and behavioral correlates as the genera of locally polygeneric families. In such cases, the perceptible morpho-ecological distance between species of the monogeneric or minimally polytypic family more or less corresponds to that between genera of the polygeneric family (cf. Berlin 1982a). Finally, the distinction is often inconsequential to anyone but a geneticist or micro-evolutionary theorist (e.g. sibling species that occupy the same niche and manifest virtually identical phenotypes). For the most part, then, local species are marked by "generic gaps" in the local economy of nature, and have no rivals to compete with for generic status.[11] That is why I label the basic level of folktaxonomy "generic-specieme."

Most of the time, then, the generic gap is filled by what Mayr (1969:37) has called "the nondimensional species" because it lacks the geographical and evolutionary dimensions of space and time:

> At a given locality a species of animal is usually separated from other
> sympatric species by a complete gap. This is the species of the local
> naturalist, the species of Ray and Linnaeus .... Combining properties of a
> single local population, the nondimensional species can usually be delimited
> unequivocally.

Being akin to the folk concept, Mayr notes accordingly that the nondimensional species has its primary significance with respect to sympatric and synchronic populations.

It is somewhat misleading to argue, however, that the manner of delimiting basic local kinds is the same for the folk naturalist as it was for Ray and Linnaeus, namely, as a breeding unit: "The word species in biology is a relational term: A is a species in relation to B because it is reproductively isolated from them" (26). For folk, as for Aristotle and later European herbalists, reproductive criteria, though *usually sufficient*, are not always necessary. The necessary condition is an ecological distinction that marks a morpho-geographical gap in the readily perceptible local economy of nature.[12]

Necessary breeding criteria were initially introduced into classical natural history in order to fix species status *within* a particular community, so that a systematic comparison and grouping of species could be made *across* communities. The idea was to provide a universal (or "natural") physical means (or "mechanism") for species production, that is, for the appearance and mainten-ance of morphological regularity in any given location. It was to be wholly internal to the species – part of its "essence" – and independent of external factors connected with environmental regulation. A permanent fixation of the limits of morphological variation (the degree of permissible morphological difference) for the species would justify abstracting a morphotype by omitting all but its most usual features as irrelevant. With the morphotype thus extracted from context, the comparison and grouping of species could be made entirely on the basis of cross-specific regularities in morphotypical characters. Because universal "natural" taxonomy was worked out by botanists who, following Aristotle, first thought that most, if not all plants, propagate asexually, criteria of genealogical linkage rather than cross-fertility were initially chosen to ensure conspecificity.

2.3 LIFE-FORMS

The first two of Adanson's (1763:cciv–ccvj) sixty-five so-called "artificial" systems of botanical classification pertain to plants grouped by the *ensemble* of their external morphological features, but particularly by stem structure and height: vines, trees, shrubs, undershrubs and herbs. Most modern commentators on the history of biology have followed Adanson in assuming that these groupings were "unnatural." Supposedly Aristotelian, their first confirmable trace in botany presumably originated with Aristotle's student, Theophrastus: "So far as classification is concerned, the influence of the Aristotelian School showed itself chiefly in the long survival of the division into trees, shrubs, and herbs" (Arber 1953: 331). What the commentators do not agree on is the precise sense in which such divisions were "artificial" or "unnatural" (cf. Benson 1962). This disagreement owes, in part, to conflicting interpretations of "natural" classification given by rival schools of modern systematics. The other, more serious, source of the disagreement rests on a vague and misguided appreciation of the popular conceptual foundations of biological taxonomy.

According to Cain (1959b:234–35):

Cesalpino [the first systematist] using [the Aristotelian] principle, said that the most important thing a plant could do was feed (in order to exist at all) and consequently the first division must be into woody (with a more perfect system of distributing food internally) and non-woody. The principal difference, therefore was between herbs on the one hand, and trees and shrubs on the other ... By the time of Linnaeus, the first division was seen to be so unnatural that it was dropped.

On this account, the primary life-form division into "tree" and "shrub" was the *a priori* product of "deductive" reasoning.

Yet, one finds these groupings in Greece well before Plato and Aristotle proposed logical division (e.g. in the works of Empedocles). Moreover, Cain misleads in asserting that Linnaeus rejected such divisions simply because they represent *a priori* holdovers from philosophical tradition. Linnaeus argues that they are as "lubricious" as they are "seemingly natural" (1751 sec. 209): although like animal life-forms they are the product of the common man's classificatory "natural instinct" (1751 sec. 153), unlike animal life-forms they are too fuzzy in their boundaries *when devoid of ecological context* to possess philosophical verity. Granted, then, that such divisions were not Aristotelian in origin, but more primitive and popular, then they must be "special-purpose" in the sense of utilitarian; for, "prior to the sixteenth century virtually all attempts at 'classification' were of this utilitarian type" (Mayr 1982:148).

The ethnobiological evidence, however, indicates the case is otherwise. Such divisions, it appears, are universal, spontaneous and orderly in ways that do not accord with accepted senses of "artificial" or "special-purpose." The first botanical life-form to appear in any language seems to be "tree," that is, a plant usually taller than a human adult and usually ligneous. For Brown (1977), though, the existence of one life-form, so conceived, necessarily implies at least covert recognition of another life-form, "herb," or a plant usually smaller than a human adult and usually herbaceous. Thus, the ancient Chinese proto-encyclopedia, *ERH YA*, devotes two of fourteen chapters to plants: one is called "explanation of trees" (*shi mu*) and the other, "explanation of herbs" (*shi tshao*) (cf. Bretschneider 1893).

According to Brown, it is "size" rather than "woodiness" that constitutes "the universally critical, underlying distinction" between tree and herb (or "non-tree"). The Delaware Indians, for instance, seem "to regard any plant over human height as a tree" (*hitukw*), whereas the attributes of herb (*skikw*), "are ambiguity and being shorter than a human adult" (Miller 1975:438–39). American children learning ordinary botanical life-forms also initially partition the familiar flora into "large plants" versus "small plants" (Dougherty 1979). Adult Americans include such non-woody plants as the palm and banana in their tree category, whereas the Tzoltzil of Mexico include in their herb category (*c'i lel*) ligneous plants which are stunted or gathered in their early stages of growth (Laughlin 1975). The Brou of Cambodia also incorporate in their herb category (*bat*) such ligneous shrubs; and trees (*loong*), though of variable height, are "generally superior to [adult] human size" (Matras & Martin 1972:6).

For Brown (1977:332–3), this initial dichotomization of the botanical world owes primarily to a basic cognitive tendency to linguistically partition perceptual dimensions that are salient for human beings: "The oppositional characteristics of dimensional concepts, such as height, width, depth, etc. are usually encoded by two terms, and only rarely are finer dimensional distinctions lexically carved out." The fact that "tree" rather than "herb" is the first labeled may owe to a universal cognitive disposition to emphasize the positive aspect of the dimension (cf. Greenberg 1966:53).

For the Rangi of Tanzania the distinction "above/below" is also a necessary criterion for initial life-form status, but not sufficient. "Woodiness" alone seems to decide if a shrubby plant is a tree or an herb; for, plants are "distinguished from each other, *miti* being large and/or woody and *masambi* being small and non-woody" (Kesby 1979). Likewise for the ancient Hebrews, the generally herbaceous life-form, *esev*, could include undershrubs with hard stems whereas *etz* would include woody shrubs, or bushes, and trees (Genesis I, 2).

The combination of the criteria of size and woodiness may lead to a further partitioning of the plant world into four life-forms, as among the ancient Greeks and Romans or later European herbalists. According to Theophrastus (*Historia Plantarum* I,iii-lv) plants are subdivided into: (1) tall and woody trees (*dendron*); (2) woody bushes or ligneous shrubs of small or medium height (*thamnos*); (3) small or medium suffrutescent undershrubs (*phrygia*) with ligneous stems, low and wide-spreading branching patterns and herbaceous foliage that usually withers after fruiting; and (4) small, herbaceous herbs and grasses (*poa*).

Two other life-forms are encountered nearly as frequently as shrub and undershrub for which the dimensions size and/or woodiness are insufficient, viz., vines and grasses. The Brou, for example, consider vines, *jomuu*, to be either herbaceous (e.g. *Pericampylus glaucus*) or ligneous (e.g. *Willugbeia cochinchinensis*). Here spatial orientation of the stem, rather than size, seems to be critical. For the Tzeltal life-form, grass (*ak*), the blade-like stem distinguishes these plants from other herbs and herbaceous shrubs (Berlin *et al*. 1974).

Occasionally mushrooms, as for the Brou, and possibly mosses, as in the case of the Batak of Sumatra (Bartlett 1926), also assume life-form status. This may owe more to the distinctive role they are perceived to play in the local economy of nature than (just) to their readily visible external morphology (i.e. habitus). For the non-flowering plants (exclusive of the ferns perhaps) may generally be construed as "residual" categories with no clearly defined morphological aspect. In this sense, Ray's *Musci* – which includes confervae, lichens, liverworts, mosses and clubmosses – is not so much the artificial product of some *a priori* system, as Sachs (1875/1890:73) implies, but the perceptual remainder of those small and often hidden plants that lack phenomenal resolution for human beings.

Similarly, whereas the vertebrates are distinguished into major life-form groupings (e.g. quadruped, bird, fish), the invertebrates usually are not. Rather, they are thrown together under the single "residual" life-form, "bug," or into a pair of residual life-forms, the many-limbed "insects" and the virtually limbless "worms." When set against the morphological and behavioral standards of man and his vertebrate cousins, invertebrate forms lack phenomenal resolution with regard to size and ecological proclivity.

For example, among the Hill Pandaram of South India, *puchi* is a "residual category ... which includes insects, crustaceans and several other categories" (Morris 1976). Like considerations apply to the categories *agbiro* in Zandeland (Evans-Pritchard 1963), *makoki* for the Rangi and *remes* (or *sheretz*) for the ancient Hebrews (Genesis I,1; Leviticus XI). Generally speaking, while the vertebrate life-forms often constitute distinct biological classes within a single phylum, the invertebrate life-form "is distinctly heterogeneous, demonstrating little criteria clustering" (Brown 1979a:806), often including representatives of many different classes and even phyla.[13] The Linnaean invertebrate classes, *Vermes* (worms) and *Insecta* (bugs), are plainly residual in this way.

For most folk, man is the standard for a comparative appreciation of the animals, but is not himself an object of comparison. The Rangi viewpoint is typical – to be human is not to be CREATURE OR BEAST:

> To Rangi, the resemblance between "*vanyama*" [mammals] and people is most strikingly seen in their having blood, in their genitals and in their manner of giving birth. However, to say that they are more like people than are, say, *ndee* [birds] ... is not to say that people are "*vanyama*." That would be insulting to Rangi, as such comparisons usually are in other societies. The category *vantu* [people] is separate [from other life-forms]. Implicitly, *vantu* are the subjects who do the classifying, not the objects which are classified. (Kesby 1979:44)

As we shall see, Aristotle did manage to introduce man among the life-forms (see section 5.1 below); however, it was not until Linnaeus (1735) defied charges of heresy by including man *within* the class (life-form) of mammals that man became a veritable object of classification.[14]

Admittedly, there often exist broad categories that include most ordinary kinds of local flora or fauna and whose scope is functionally delimited, like "domestic" versus "wild." But on closer examination it appears that life-forms are also present. For example, previous study indicates (Colloquium 1986) that the Inuit of East Hudson Bay, like those of Baker Lake to the West (cf. Paillet 1973), have (at least) two overlapping systems of functional categories. The game animals (*umajuq*), which exclude insects, shellfish, mollusks and domestic animals (*umajuquti*) like the dog and horse, can be subdivided in either of two ways. On the one hand, they may be segregated into animals too small to feed a family (*umajurait*), sufficient for a family (*umajuit*) or big enough for a whole community (*umajumarit*). On the other hand, they may be distinguished as sea animals (*imarmiutait*), including the polar bear, land animals (*nunamiutait*), like the ptarmigan and fox, or lake animals (*tasiqmiutait*), including trout and some seals. Now, fish may be small, medium or large, and lake or sea animals, whereas birds may be small or medium and sea or land animals. But my questioning of Inuit hunters also lends evidence for life-forms: all and only birds (*tiqmiut*), fish (*iqaliut*), bugs (*hupaquit*) and "bottom-lying sea creatures" (*iqamiut*) like mollusks and shellfish. Mammals, by far the most perceptually evident creatures in the austere economy of nature of the Arctic, are here (as elsewhere, cf. Kesby 1979:43) not put into a single life-form. This is not because they are residual, but because like other salient and pervasive phenomena in any conceptual field they simply comprise the linguistically unmarked case.

The relative phenomenal salience of life-forms in human appreciation of the local economy of nature has rather obvious repercussions for people's consequent ability to variously use this appreciation in their day-to-day lives. But to attribute the conception of life-forms to the social functions they come to assume is to put the cart before the horse. Thus bugs are not, in the first instance, functionally residual. Bugs simply lack phenomenal resolution for humans because size and ecological proclivities are of a different order of magnitude (they are phenomenally lumped together much as light is at the end of the color spectrum). General lack of awareness, of course, may be a factor in subsequent lack of concern with function and use.

Still, a number of specialists in the field would trace the origins of life-forms – especially plant life-forms – to their assumed social functions. For example, Witkowski, Brown and Chase (1981), maintain that life-forms such as tree and herb develop originally, not from perceptions of differences in size or gross morphology of plants, but from extensions of such functional concepts as "wood" and "weed." Brown (1979b) calls the process whereby a life-form emerges from a more directly functional concept, "referential expansion": "Mayan languages, for example, have developed ['herb'] life forms through expansion of words designating 'weeds,' 'medicinal plants,' 'underbrush,' and 'greens' [i.e. designations related to gardening and/or curing] to small herbaceous plants in general." The primary evidence for referential expansion is linguistic: e.g. the words for "wood" and "tree" are often the same; however, if there is a separate word for "tree" in the language, then there is also a word for "wood" (or "timber," etc.) whereas if there is a word for "wood" there needn't be a word for "tree."

Bulmer (1970), who considers life-forms "artificial," intimates a similar understanding of the matter with regard to Karam (New Guinea) folkbotanical life-forms:

> There are two large taxa, *mon*, ("tree" though this does not include the Panadanus palms, black-palms, bamboos, hollow-stemmed forms such as Piperaceae, or tree-ferns) and *mn* "vines" ("climbing or creeping plants with strong stems"). Both *mon* and *mn* are polysemous, *mon* referring to "timber", "firewood" and "fire" as well as "tree", and *mn* to "rope", "string" and "fibre" as well as "vine" . . . terms for tree also being used for "timber" and "firewood" suggests that these taxa may be defined as much by cultural evaluation (technological utilization, dietary and culinary status, economic and ritual significance) as by their objective biological characteristics.
>
> (1974)

"Referential expansion" thus implies a conceptual shift from the functional to the morphological wherein the empirical domain of the concept extends to nonfunctional (or only potentially functional) objects. The argument rests on the observation that a substance marked by its functional value (e.g. "wood," "rope"), or lack of value (e.g. "weed") eventually becomes polysemous with the plant type that is the source of that substance (e.g. "tree," "vine," "grass").

Now, even if the original life-form term is polysemous with a derived substance of functional value, this does not imply that apprehension of life-forms is invariably based upon an evaluation of functional factors. For, if the emergence of "tree" necessarily implies at least an implicit awareness of "herb," and since there is apparently no *a priori* or necessary functional underpinning to this dichotomization of the plant world, then the origin of these life-form concepts would seem to be independent of concerns with social function and use.[15] Furthermore, it will not do to argue that referential expansion simply consists in relaxing the functional component of the definition and stressing only the perceptual component (Brown 1982:220–21). The perceptual features attaching to the artifact "timber" and the living kind "tree" are quite different in nature: those which attach to "tree" are virtual properties that include phenomenally typical attributes of trees, whereas the only perceptual attributes logically characteristic of "timber" relate to being wooden and cut.

There remains the possibility that the functional concept was historically bound to the nonfunctional term. This possibility, however, has nothing to do with *concept* learning or formation, though it may have something to do with social structure: "Speakers of languages uniting "wood" and "tree" usually live in small-scale societies while speakers separating them usually live in large, state societies" (Witkowski *et al.* 1981:8). But counter-examples are readily at hand. In both modern and ancient Hebrew, for example, the word *etz* is polysemous for "wood" and "tree," yet both ancient and modern Israel represent large state societies (by the standards Witkowski *et al.* go by).[16]

It won't do to argue that correlations in the social sciences are not perfect. Principles must be offered to account for *deviant* cases, and no such principles appear. The rather blithe conclusion that such correlations in the lexicon permit one to gain access to conceptual history is not well-founded and *prime facie* refutable. To say that the lexicon "broadly reflects cultural concerns and relationships with the natural environment" (Witkowski *et al.* 1981:11), or that language "broadly reflects" how we think about the world, is to say little of substance. At present, linguists have only the barest indication of the enormous complexity of lexical structures; and one has even less idea of the composition of the extremely diverse conceptual domains to which those linguistic systems are attached.

In another variant of the functional argument, Hunn (1987) argues that TREE is not biologically natural; however, neither is it quite artificial (much as the color green has no particular interest for the physicist, yet does mark a real, if somewhat arbitrary, interval in the color spectrum). Functional considerations of wood use supposedly raise this admittedly "perceptually compelling" group to the level of a well-defined higher order folkbiological taxon. In fact, the intrusion of functional considerations is entirely superfluous. The natural discontinuities apparent in the conception of TREE pertain to processes of evolutionary convergence bound to ecological considerations in the competition for sunlight. People naturally tend to find trees phenomenally compelling because of their evident ecological role in determining local distributions of flora and fauna – just go into a forest and *look*. Certainly children – be they American (Dougherty 1979) or Maya (Stross 1973) – don't learn WOOD-USE when they learn TREE.

2.4 EXCEPTIONS THAT PROVE THE RULE

The logical difference in taxonomic status between folk life-forms and generic-specieme is twofold. First, there is the obvious fact that the latter's extension is a subset of the former's. Second, there is a difference in the nature of their respective intensions. Life-forms appear to partition the domains of animal and plant into a contrastive lexical field. The system of lexical markings at the life-form level constitutes a logical *division* of the category into positive attributes that are opposed along one or more perceptible attribute-dimensions (spanning size, orientation, mode of life, etc.). If only one attribute-dimension is used to span the life-forms then a single feature is diagnostic for each life-form, if more than one dimension is involved then each life-form is diagnosed by some conjunction of features.[17]

By contrast, the partitioning of the local flora and fauna into generic-specieme groupings represents a relational, rather than divisional, segregation of organisms into well-formed configurations. The features of a given generic-specieme are bound to one another as integral parts of the singular configuration in which all those features participate. So what characterizes, e.g., "raccoon-ness" is the whole image-pattern typically associated with the raccoon (Hunn 1976). Features of one generic-specieme configuration thus have no necessary link to features of any other generic-specieme configuration.[18] With life-forms, though, the diagnostic features of any two life-forms are often linked along the dimension(s) spanning all the life-forms in a field. As Hunn has convincingly argued, life-forms do not appear to have the same sort of configurational integrity. Moreover, unlike the conceptual boundaries of generic-speciemes, those of life-forms are seemingly subject to conventional manipulation.

It is by no means "evident" (Ellen 1986:87), however, that life-forms are any less "inductive" (in the rigorous sense of being confirmed by favorable instances) or further removed from experience than generic-speciemes. The fact that generic-speciemes more closely accord with scientific taxa than life-forms is not a matter of experiential efficacy *per se* (predicting habitual covariations in perceptible patterns) but of the different experiential ends they serve. Unfortunately, the issue is only confused by widespread recourse to inductivist terminology, which ethnobiologists have borrowed from anthropologically ill-informed philosophers and practitioners of systematics. Extrapolating from Berlin *et al.* (1966), Hunn (1982) thus assimilates "inductive," "polythetic" folkgenerics to "general" classification and "deductive," "monothetic" life-forms to "special" classification (see section 2.1 above). This appreciation owes much to biologists Sokal and Sneath (1963) who, in turn, were elaborating on Gilmour (1937). Although compatible with Gilmour's avowed adherence to logical empiricism and Sokal and Sneath's vociferous "operationalism," it proves inconsistent when applied to empirical domains not built by simple inductive enumeration or to thoughts not forged operationally (including thoughts related to folkbiology as well as modern systematics).

It may well be that generics, more than life-forms, are identified by many features and that a mnemonic stock of family resemblances usually serves to recognize instances of generic-speciemes. Yet, either category of taxa has logically necessary features as well. In this respect, it is by "logical fiat" that generic-speciemes are perfectly well-bounded. Moreover, taxa at both levels support inductions. Thus, not only can it be inferred that distinct taxa of any given life-form share visible aspects of overall morphology and behavior with respect to the local economy of nature; it may also be presumed they share unseen or unknown properties as well (cf. Rips 1975).

In the case of generic-speciemes, the covariance of readily perceptible features in a singular configuration serves to support inductions with respect to habitus, or that aspect of overall external morphology that can be apprehended at a glance. The configuration need not be a static display, but may well include behavioral action schemata, such as the way a tree bends in the wind (cf.

Friedberg 1972) or a tiger stalks. Delimitation of life-forms, though to some degree dependent on external morphology, primarily serves to mark the boundaries that living kinds have in relation to one another and in relation to ourselves.

It is not a logical necessity that our intuitive appreciation of generic-speciemes supports a wide range of inductions related to morphology and behavior. But it may well be a fact of our evolution. Our brains might be wired to spontaneously apprehend groupings in a local environment that roughly correspond to nondimensional kinds, much as we might be wired to apprehend other "natural" substances (e.g. bodily objects), qualities (e.g. focal colors) and relations (e.g. temporal causality and geometrical extension). For each of these domains modern science provides a somewhat different story, but one that our intuitions closely approximate – at least for the restricted dimensions of perceptibly evident everyday life. There is likely less direct wiring and more choice involved in our diagnoses of life-form boundaries than in our construction of generic boundaries; but the choice of boundaries is made in support of induction (with respect to habitus and habits of life in a local environment).

Size alone may not be as important as place in human ecology; that is, the life-form divisions seem to be made on the basis of those habits of life that determine the place of each being in that local environment pertaining to man's everyday life. The ecological importance of life-forms is attested to by the fact that modern botany retains them only in ecological contexts. Concerning their particular salience from a human point of view, however, subjective appreciation of what plants are *relative to us* has little bearing on an objective appreciation of what plants are *relative to one another* once the bounds of the local environment have been transcended: trees are bigger than people, and grasses smaller; trees are where birds most often perch and grasses where most quadrupeds forage; trees determine exposure to sun and moisture – and hence the density of other vegetation, and the possible habitats of many of the animals familiar to local folk. Yet such totalizing ecological frameworks are scarcely of value in organizing knowledge of the world of nature outside the orbit of man's everyday life.

For this reason they were ultimately banned from taxonomy; once devoid of local context they become "scabrous" and "lubricious" when utilized as frameworks for organizing flora world-wide (Linnaeus 1751 sec. 209). Nevertheless, plant life-forms did continue to serve Linnaeus as "natural" frameworks for organizing an understanding of *local* flora, and still do so for the ethnobiologist and professional naturalist. As for folkzoological life-forms, for the most part the non-residual vertebrate divisions correspond to scientific classes: mammals, birds, fish, etc. Perhaps since we ourselves are vertebrates, the subjective (life-form) appreciation of vertebrates *as they appear to us* turns out to be not so very far removed from a morphologically objective appreciation of vertebrate classes. But the folk naturalist and scientist interpret these groups quite differently. For folk, such groupings represent locally distinct modes of life, ecological roles and morphological frames, not genealogical lines.

So far, the argument has been that life-forms generally represent an exhaustive partitioning of the local flora whose boundaries are determined by convention. These conventions do not seem to owe to any evident cultural purpose; and they are logically structured into a contrastive field marked by abstract diagnostics that are positive and opposed. Berlin *et al.* (1973:219; cf. Hays 1979), however, note two situations that ostensibly violate these general conditions on life-form structure: the "unaffiliated" generic-specieme, which is apparently included under no life-form, and the "ambiguously" affiliated generic-specieme, which is seemingly attached to more than one life-form. Unaffiliated generic-speciemes might be of two sorts: they are "almost without exception cultivated and/or morphologically peculiar in some fashion."

An example of the morphologically distinctive unaffiliated generic-specieme is the Aguaruna taxon, *ikamas* (Berlin 1976). This is the only form of cactus present in the locale. As such, it is likely perceived by the Aguaruna to play a distinctive role in the economy of nature; however, it is also likely that should a new species of cactus be introduced into the area it would be included with *ikamas*. The Aguaruna may thus judge the cactus to be conceptually equivalent to other life-forms in view of its distinct morphology relative to the overall habits of the surrounding floral (and faunal) life. In that case, the cactus would not be so much an unaffiliated generic-specieme as a monogeneric life-form.[19]

The failure of ethnobiologists to consider the possibility of monogeneric life-forms stems from certain unsatisfactory formalist assumptions. In line with Kay (1971), Berlin *et al.* (1966) characterize taxonomic levels as extensionally inclusive "sets of organisms," thus ruling out monotypy *a priori*. Kay's "taxonomy," however, does not even meet the minimum condition of observational adequacy for either folk or Linnaean taxonomies. Each taxon represents a class of objects partitioned into two or more mutually exclusive subordinate taxa that are extensionally defined as proper subsets of the superordinate class of objects. By definition, a monotypic taxon would contain only one subordinate taxon whose extension is an *improper* subset of its superordinate taxon. The subordinate taxon would thus be extensionally equivalent to its superordinate and, hence, conceptually indistinguishable from it since, by assumption, taxa are nothing more than their simple extensions. Instead of representing disjoint sets of taxa, the taxonomic hierarchy would merely reflect levels of set inclusions. In such a formalism ranks are precluded on the purely dogmatic grounds that all synthetic (empirical) concepts should be exclusively definable in terms of the logic of set theory.

Leaving aside this dubious (and, alas, again inductivist) bias,[20] the peculiar characteristic of monogeneric-specieme life-forms is that they appear to have intuited aspects of both generic-speciemes and life-forms. Like generic-speciemes their facies are readily perceptible at a glance – as an immediately recognizable "gestalt." Like life-forms they occupy a distinctive role in the economy of nature. Because they are so distinctive, they may be easily marked *intensionally* by diagnostic characters chosen from dimensions spanning the other life-forms. For instance, in Aguaruna, the twining vine-like palm (*cayú duká*) can be segregated from the other large palms (that comprise the Aguaruna life-form, *sínki*), the other twining plants (*dáek*), the other erect woody plants (*númi*) and the small herbaceous plants (*dúpa*) by a rather simple set of diagnostic oppositions.

If one considers taxonomy to operate as a logically convenient system for accessing intuitional structure of the living world, then the most obvious way to access a grouping that has the intuitional characteristics of both the life-form and the generic-specieme would be to index it twice, once as a life-form and once as a generic-specieme. In this way, the logical system remains complete. It covers all our intuitions and organizes them into easily accessible domains that can be readily compared and contrasted (in part, automatically, that is, by logical inference) with respect to habitus and habits of life. Double indexing with respect to rank – by divisional and relational contrast – thus marks the truly weird and isolated groupings, highlighting their abnormality (for easy access and scrutiny) while perfectly integrating them into our overall picture of living nature.

Perhaps like reasoning could be applied to the more important cultigens in regard to folksystematics and nomenclature. As an example of a cultivated unaffiliated generic-specieme for the Aguaruna Jivaro of Peru, Berlin (1976) cites the manioc plant (*máma*). Boster's (1980) study of Aguaruna practices of manioc naming and patterns of reference, however, indicate that in the process of cultivation manioc has attained a distinct and isolated status in the economy of nature owing to man's constant and direct intervention. Similar considerations lead Rogers (1963) to argue that some cultivated species cannot be considered in the same way as other plants in regard to matters of naming and affiliation:

among plants at the species [i.e. folkgeneric-specieme] and subspecies levels there are apparent and wide differences between natural and cultivated plants. These discrepancies indicate that modern systematics and nomen-clature, aimed primarily at natural populations, cannot be appropriately applied to cultigens.

In this case cultural significance *would* affect taxonomic status, but only to the extent cultural meddling has actually altered perception of relative distinctive-ness in the economy of nature (cf. Geoghegan 1976).

What, then, are to we make of Bulmer's (1970) claim that questions of "cultural cosmology" must be considered in reference to the special status of isolated speciemes? In the case of the Karam (New Guinea) taxon *kobt* (cassowary), for instance, Bulmer (1967) notes that its referents are indeed "aberrant" creatures by perceptible-ecological standards: it is an exclusively terrestrial bird that has no wings and doesn't fly; it also has heavy, strong and very human-like leg bones, and a large bony casque on the top of its skull; and its behavior is correspondingly odd. Still, such factors allegedly do not suffice to explain its distinct status in Karam taxonomy. Why not? The reasons given are two: the cassowary is clearly a "specieme," yet it is isolated linguistically from the other speciemes and often contrasted with the larger (life-form) groupings such as the flying vertebrates (bats and birds); and it has a privileged place in Karam ritual and mythology.

Now, should the Karam be presented an emu or ostrich they would, I imagine, be as likely to group them with the cassowary as would Australian aborigines (who value the emu) and African tribesmen (who put a symbolic premium on the ostrich). In this vein, Sperber notes that although the Dorzé of Ethiopia accord a singular status to their one snake taxon, *shosh*, when a Dorzé travels to the nearby Rift Valley where many other snake species are found, the traveler invariably applies *shosh* to them as well: "This demonstrates that snakes are not a species [i.e. generic-specieme] without a genus [i.e. life-form], but a genus that contains, *de facto*, a single well-known species, *de jure*, an indefinite number of species" (Sperber 1975a:15).

Logically, then, there is no anomaly. The cassowary is simply a monogeneric life-form with but one known representative specieme, much as the aardvark is the only known species of the monospecific scientific order Tubulidentata. Monogeneric life-forms are exceptions that prove the rule.[21] Nor must the undeniable socio-symbolic import of a taxon be considered in ascertaining a taxonomy's logical or substantive nature.[22] Perceptual aberrance often serves to focus symbolic evocation, although it also frequently happens that perceptually aberrant monogeneric life-forms have no special symbolic status. Thus, Hunn (1975b:310) cites the Tzeltal folk taxon *mayil ti bal* (armadillo) as an "unaffiliated generic," but he emphasizes that "no extraordinary ritual significance is attributed to these 'anomalous' animals."

Finally, consider those "ambiguously affiliated generic-speciemes" that appear to attach to more than one life-form (Berlin 1976:388–89):

> *cincák* is a good example. The taxon covers a major portion of . . . the Melastomataceae, a common family of tropical plants . . . unambiguously recognized by a unique leaf venation pattern . . . . Species of this family have variant botanical life form characteristics at maturity, and they include trees, shrubs, herbs, and rarely herbaceous vines.

The description of *cincák*, however, resembles more that of the (usually covert) family fragment than a folkgeneric-specieme. Family fragments, as opposed to generic-speciemes, often do constitute groupings whose constituent species are variously associated with different life-forms. As we shall see in the following section, one reason fragments are seldom named is that they comprise an "extrataxonomic" scheme based on association of habitus only and whose members may cross-cut the named groupings of the taxonomic system. Nevertheless, such fragments do seem to be occasionally named by the Aguaruna. This may be the case, for example, with respect to family fragments in Aguaruna bird classification (Berlin *et al.* 1981; cf. Taylor 1978–1979).

Accordingly, those unaffiliated and ambiguous generic-speciemes that ostensibly violate conditions of life-form structure may, in fact, represent situations which are either extrataxonomic (family fragments) or actually consistent with such conditions (monogeneric-specieme life-forms).

To review, then, what seems to be the nature of folkbiological life-forms: They appear to represent a holistic appreciation of the local biota that is compatible with humankind's usual existence. They seem to reflect gross morphological patterns that subsume any number of generic-speciemes that play similar roles in the economy of nature seen from a phenomenal perspective, that is, within the (nondimensional) local ecology we are normally compelled to deal with. They do not, and are not meant to, deal with the large stretches of geographical space and evolutionary time that the higher taxa of modern systematics must comprehend. They are not phylogenetically "natural" (at least folkbotanical life-forms are not), but neither are they more "artificial" or "special purpose" than higher-order scientific taxa. They are anthropocentrically biased, though not usually in any culturally purposeful way.

In short, folkbiological life-forms partition the everyday world of human experience with local flora in ways that are "natural" to the human mind as it partakes of the activities of ordinary life. Even scientists employ them, as do we all, when there is no longer direct concern with the extraordinary, nonphenomenal problems of minute and vastly extended stretches of space and time.

2.5 FAMILY FRAGMENTS

There is considerable cross-cultural evidence of other non-utilitarian morphological groupings that are less well-defined than the standard taxonomic groupings of generic-speciemes and life-forms. Although their morphological aspect is usually more far-ranging than generic-speciemes but less so than life-forms, they may also cut across life-forms. Unlike the standard taxonomic groupings, however, they do not constitute an exhaustive partitioning of a local flora or fauna, nor even a well-connected partial sequence. Frequently, they just are not named. But they are important to an ordinary understanding of local nature, and more crucial still to historical attempts to transcend the limits of that understanding. As we shall see, it is to such groups that Cesalpino adverts when he speaks of botanical *genera innominata*, and which in the zoological realm Aristotle refers to as *eide anonyma*.

Perhaps the first modern author to notice the relationship between covert folk fragmenta and the family concept in biological taxonomy was Bartlett. Reflecting on the folkbotanical classification of the Batak of Sumatra, he notes:

As to plants in general, there is a partial classification, going to genera or species in hundreds of instances, but leaving many plants unclassified, regarding which all the native botanist will say is that there are trees, herbs, vines, ferns, or mosses. Any very slender sedge is *si marithe-tihe*, "the one who passes for *tihe*" or "the *tihe*-like one" (*tihe* being a particular kind of sedge) and many other designations of this are very broadly but discriminatingly classificatory. Here we have an inkling of the family concept and a name which is linguistically a reflection of the same kind of thinking that gave us the botanical family names in current scientific use.   (1940:354)

Often, however, "it is recognized that there are very similar kinds, but nobody bothers to give them names."

The covert nature of many implicitly recognized plant groupings was again later stressed by Conklin for the Hanunóo of the Philippines: "midgroupings were made, of course, but not according to a structured terminologically-identifiable system" (1954:97). This observation motivated ethnobiologists to seek out evidence for such unnamed mid-level groupings since it seemed implausible that native classifiers, who Conklin showed were able to discriminate hundreds of biologically valid genera, species and varieties, would content themselves with simply collecting these numerous named groupings under a few marked life-forms. It appeared unlikely that the keen eye of the folk naturalist would miss the more obvious suprageneric groupings entirely.

Berlin and his associates were the first to develop a method explicitly aimed at "searching for possible subgroupings within contrast sets of large numbers," that is, within life-forms. The names of the immediately included taxa of each major life-form name, written on slips of paper, were presented to informants with instructions to scan the lists and place in separate piles those names that applied to plants judged to be similar to one another (Berlin *et al.* 1968:292). In this way, they were able to show that the Tzeltal of Mexico implicitly recognize numerous unnamed groupings which appear to be intermediate between generic-speciemes and life-forms.[23]

Later, Berlin argued that mid-level groupings occasionally might be named, especially if they were initially formed to accommodate rare plants or newly introduced plants of foreign origin. These names would presumably disappear once the unfamiliar plant had become familiar enough to have its own distinctive facies. Thus, in the case of introduced grains, it was suggested that the Tzeltal conceive of the new forms as "a single unsegmented pattern" recognizable at a glance without reference to the more familiar generic with which it had been initially associated: "The final result will be the ultimate loss of the intermediate taxa as *named* categories, although conceptually they will continue to remain" (1972:78).

After considering Shoshoni bird classification, though, Hage and Miller (1976) concluded that covert categories may be far from unstable when they assume names. Not only may these names be retained in the subsequent historical development of folk taxonomy, but such named categories may even be a source of new life-forms. For Numic speakers such as the Shoshoni, a typically small bird (*huittsuu*) or typically large bird (*kwinna*) may come to be associated with other birds of similar dimensions. The term for the typical bird may, at first, simply bring to mind the associated generic-speciemes; but over time the name of the typical bird itself becomes a suprageneric label for all birds of that kind. The birds are henceforth assembled into two named groupings, the large birds (*kwinna*) and the small birds (*huittsuu*). In due course, one or the other grouping may come to represent all the birds (Hage and Miller cite examples of Numic languages where *huittsuu* predominates, others where it is *kwinna*). The name *not* chosen to represent all the birds may, in fact, disappear from the folkbiological lexicon; however, those intermediate categories that eventually do supply the life-form names, and that "are simply covert categories . . . which have become labelled," endure to become arguably the most stable super-ordinate groups of all.

How, then, do we reconcile Berlin's claims with the findings of Hage and Miller? The answer, it appears, turns on the fact that the situation described by Berlin has actually little, if anything, to do with that described by Hage and Miller. The conflict dissolves once it is realized that the "intermediate categor-ies" discussed by Berlin really cover three distinct sorts of conceptual problem: (i) the incorporation of unfamiliar groupings into the taxonomic system, (ii) the emergence of life-forms, and (iii) the formation of covert fragmenta properly so-called.

In the first case, a foreign species is initially assimilated to the taxonomic framework by associating it with the name of a more familiar generic specieme. Once the foreign species acquires its own distinctive aspect it becomes a generic-specieme in its own right and is designated as such by a distinctive label. The name of the more familiar generic-specieme no longer attaches to it. The conceptual affiliation between old and new may yet persist "covertly," but it is not the case that this process necessarily constitutes *the* source of the covert family-level morphological complexes discussed by Berlin and others. Such occasional covert attachments may or may not be integrated into pre-existing family-level complexes. But there is no evidence that such complexes develop by first being named and then having the name disappear. Covert family-level complexes seem to arise without ever having been named, and in ways which are not bound to the process of assimilating unfamiliar species into the taxonomic system. The incorporation of foreign species into the taxonomic system could conceivably affect the development of a family-level complex; however, such a process of incorporation seems to be neither a necessary nor sufficient condition for the emergence of a complex.

The second situation described by Hage and Miller appears to bear little relation either to the incorporation of unfamiliar species or to the emergence of family-level complexes. What they describe is the development of life-form taxa from their typical generic-speciemes, such that the typical generic-specieme label may eventually come to mark the whole life-form, which includes other generic-speciemes more or less related to the typical generic-specieme by aspects of habitus and habits of life. In this respect, Berlin (1972) describes a process noted earlier by Trager (1939) whereby the name of a typical, salient generic-specieme becomes polysemous with the life-form; among certain tribes of the American Southwest, for example, the term for 'cottonwood' is the same as that for 'tree'. Hage and Miller suggest that the "typical" generic-specieme may be only the typical representative of one pole of the size dimension which structures the life-form space.[24] But, again, this process seems not to be necessarily related to the assimilation of only rare or foreign forms into the taxonomic system, nor to the emergence of family-level morphological complexes as such.

The confusion between the three processes owes partly to the techniques employed by Berlin and company in their elicitation of covert categories. They presented informants only with the names of generic-speciemes and specifics *included under* a given life-form. Thus, the method of elicitation may have unduly restricted recognition of covert complexes only to those which happen to fall entirely within the range of a given life-form. Given this undue restriction, there would be no reason to suspect that the development of such a complex involves processes that do *not* exclusively operate upon generic-speciemes *within* a life-form. It would then seem only natural that the development of the life-form itself should be related to processes which operate exclusively upon its constituent generic-speciemes, including processes related to the formation of covert complexes within a life-form. But if, as appears to be the case, covert complexes need not be constrained by the internal structure of animal life-forms, and if, as also seems to be the case, such complexes may cut across botanical life-forms, then the putative connection between the development of life-forms and the emergence of covert complexes becomes quite tenuous.

One indication that covert complexes may cut across botanical life-forms is found in Hays's (1976) study of the Ndumba (Highland New Guinea) folkbotany. To elicit covert complexes from nonliterate informants he asked them to verbally enumerate those plants which came to mind when the name of a given generic-specieme was invoked. The names thus enumerated were, in turn, invoked and informants were again asked to specify the plants' names that readily came to mind. For each target generic-specieme invoked, a set of associated generic-speciemes was elicited. Comparing these sets, Hays was able to confirm fairly consistent overlappings; that is, each generic-specieme found in the overlap tended to coincide with other generic-speciemes in the overlap regardless of which generic-specieme in the co-occurring group served as target.

Informants assembled covert complexes akin to modern botanical families in their overall morphological aspect. Since botanical families cut across life-forms, folkbotanical complexes might reasonably be expected to do so as well should it be the case that such complexes actually provide the common-sense ground for the family concept in natural history. Consistent with this supposition, Hays notes that: "while some plant name co-occurrences are understandable with reference to the folk taxonomic system ... others seem problematic" because they appear to cross-cut life-forms.

Although Hays surmises that the problematic cases may owe to "informant error," there are indications that unnamed morphological complexes do transverse the life-forms of other folk (cf. Friedberg 1970). In any event, what ethnobotanical evidence there is suggests that recognized complexes generally do not violate botanical families, and those that do "tend to be rather tightly focused in a single family" (Berlin 1982b). As for zoological complexes, these do not so much cross-cut animal life-forms as operate independently of the internal structure of the life-form space. So if, as seems plausible, vertebrate life-forms are structured as to size and perceived degree of remoteness from humans, then one should not expect, say, the common cat and the lion, or the boar and the pig, to be closely associated within the life-form space of mammals or quadrupeds.[25] Nevertheless, they are usually related covertly.

Another significant factor in the formation of covert complexes noted by Hays concerns the "chaining effect" first analyzed by Hunn (1975a) in reference to American folk ornithological classification. Thus, a chain of three taxa, x, y and z occurs if x is perceived to be directly linked to y but not to z, and z is perceived to be directly linked to y but not to x. The links in the chain, however, need not be symmetrical since one may consider x and y more related than y and z. This may help to explain why it is that the longer the chain, the less likelihood there will be a common name; for, long and especially asymmetric chains may contain few features common to all, or even most, of the generic-specieme links in the chain:

> The Kalam [New Guinea] are well aware of certain groupings higher than species, in which a number of species (which are in fact zoological "genera" or "families") share a complex of morphological and behavioural characters. Notable examples, where the Kalam appreciate the association of four or more related species are: Hawks and falcons; parrots . . . . I must stress that they do not have standard names for these "natural" groups . . . but their reality in Kalam thinking is unquestionable . . . . On the other hand, where a "natural" group of only 2 or 3 species exist in Kalam territory . . . Kalam do tend to have names for them. (Bulmer 1979:62)

Similarly, for the Aguaruna (Peru) whose "complexes are remarkably similar to well recognized ornithological taxa at the family and sub-family levels," it seems that "at least some of these mid-level complexes are named" (Berlin *et al.* 1981).

Suprageneric folk complexes thus appear to be built on habitus relations similar to those aspects of the facies which mark generic-speciemes. The difference being that the aspectual ties at the level of family-fragment may be considerably weaker than the well-bounded configural relations of generic-specieme morphology. Additionally, unlike the local series of generic-speciemes, the series of local fragments does not span the whole of the recognized flora or fauna. Only some of the generic-speciemes link up in chains of varying lengths, without these segments all joining together. Consequently, this intermittent awareness of overarching morphological pattern would be relegated to a fuzzier secondary echelon and remain largely unacknowledged.

The folk categories of generic-specieme and life-form, which rank "groups within groups," thus constitute the fundamental setting for humankind's ordinary apprehension of the local flora and fauna. But they prove to be inadequate for comprehending the living world at large. After the Renaissance, the ordinary bounds of sense were transcended. The complete embedding of the whole array of generic-speciemes within life-forms, which so thoroughly construed the local ecology morphologically, lost much of its relevance. It is not that this first echelon of common sense falsely apprehended the world; it simply did not have the wherewithal to deal with nonphenomenal problems bound to horizons of an altogether different order.

All the same, it was common sense itself which, having reached the limits of its first line of understanding, thereby evinced recognition that a problem existed for science to treat. Crucial, perhaps, to that recognition was an awareness that science could draw its initial means of tackling the problem by appealing to the secondary echelon. In fact, it was the attempt to constitute a determinate series of local fragments that inaugurated the "natural method" (in botany first, then zoology) that lasted from Linnaeus to de Jussieu and beyond.

Once the family level became the principal focus of systematics, a few salient features could be used to mark and name the most readily apparent fragmenta: legumes, palms, umbellifers, labiates and so forth.[26] Naming the morphologically more "diffuse" local chains of species would depend on the method's global progress; that is, the proper delimitation of all families would mean comparing the fragments of other foreign environments in order to fill out the partial series of every local environment. This world-wide morphological series, in turn, would provide the observational foundations of modern taxonomy. At least partial empirical continuity between folk and evolutionary taxonomy would be assured by the fact that the more phylogenetically related groups are generally those with the greatest aspectual affinity.

Yet, how does common sense go about logically securing a stable notion of aspect in the first place? And how resistant is this notion to variation and diversity – and to scientific discovery itself? Here the special logic, or semantics, of ordinary living-kind terms plays a critical role. The nature of that special logic, its differences from the semantics of other object domains (e.g. artifacts) and its relative independence from the nomological constraints of science occupy the next chapter.

3

THE SEMANTICS OF LIVING KINDS

3.1 DOMAIN SPECIFICITY

This chapter focuses on two basic issues concerning the scope and limits of our common-sense understanding of the living world. The first is whether the scope is restricted or wide: whether there are domain-specific cognitive universals that account for the peculiar kinds of regularities apparent in folksystems of knowledge and belief world-over; or whether those regularities are the product of general processing mechanisms that cross such domains as living kinds, artifacts and substances. To claim, as I do, that living kinds are everywhere ranked into transitively structured taxonomies, with no other natural-object domain so structured, favors restricted scope. Wide scope is implied in an opposing contention: that categorization of all natural objects centers on prototypes, and that the perceptual nature of prototypes as well as the somewhat indefinite extension of their range is partly determined by functional considerations of use and context.

The second issue concerns the following: whether, in ordinary use of substance terms, humans naturally aspire or cede to indications of (nomological) omniscience regarding the structure of the universe at large, including its astronomical, microscopic and evolutionary dimensions; or whether, under normal constraints of everyday life, humans principally seek to know better their more limited phenomenal world by rightly denoting just *its* natural kinds, that is, those kinds – including living kinds – we most readily apprehend owing to the natural selection of our cognitive make-up. The "causal theory" of "historico-scientific determinism" implies that all human knowledge-seeking aims beyond the ordinary bounds of sense; for when interpreted as a theory of cognition it makes common-sense meaning necessarily dependent on scientific

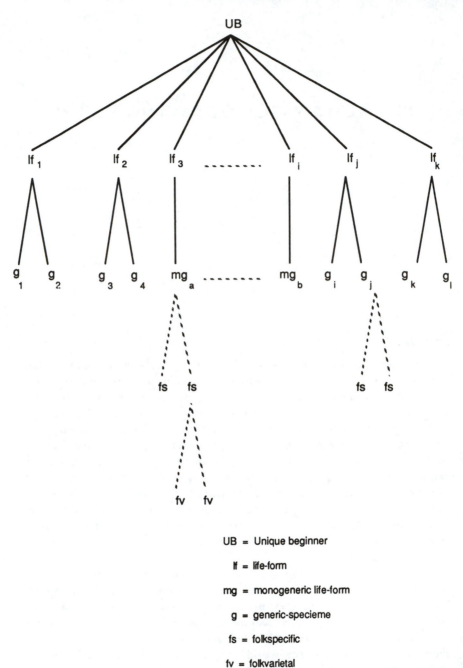

Figure 1
Schematic relationship of universal ethnobiological taxonomic categories
(modified from Berlin, Breedlove and Raven *American Anthropologist* 75, 1973)

reference. By contrast, here it is argued that no such necessary condition exists in day-to-day life. Natural science, in other words, does not canonically establish conditions of meaning or truth on everyday discourse about the world.

These considerations, then, signal problems both with current views of conceptual structure in cognitive psychology, especially prototype theory, and with the psychological and anthropological implications of causal theories of meaning and reference in recent philosophy of language.

Not all concepts are equal. Different conceptual domains may require or tolerate different kinds of supporting environments. Some domains, particularly those where more or less spontaneous learning takes place, may need supporting environments with only a minimum of previous, culturally imposed structure. The environment's role would be merely to provide the physical targets that trigger the learner's attention. To say, in such cases, that we actually learn from the exemplars that occasion learning obviously begs the question of what may count as a legitimate datum. It is the conceptual structure of the domain that tells us what the entities are and how they are to be organized and interpreted.

In brief, it is logically impossible that humans are able to conceptually generalize from limited experience without pre-existing structures that govern the projection of finite instances to their infinitely extendable classes. It is an entirely empirical question whether or not these principles cross domains, and, if they do, which domains they cross. No *a priori* assumption in the matter is justified. The implication for research strategies is clear: in the absence of sufficient further evidence, results from a potentially autonomous cognitive domain should not be extended to other domains. We should be prepared to discover that, after all, the structure of human concepts is varied and sundry. But how are specific domains to be identified?

The existence of universal domain-specific cognitions is not tied exclusively, or even necessarily, to cross-cultural pervasiveness. The social subordination of women, for example, appears to characterize all known cultures (e.g. cultural "universals" in the sense of Lévi-Strauss 1949/1969a). It could even be argued that there is some biological grounding for this condition. There is no reason, however, to attribute the varied ways people psychologically process this pervasive social phenomenon to some universal cognitive mechanism. Conversely, the ability to develop and understand mathematics may be rooted in some fairly specific cognitive mechanisms, which human beings are innately endowed with (cf. Chomsky 1988). But if so, many cultures do not require that people use this ability. Nor is it occasioned by every environment. Mathematics does not spontaneously arise irrespective of social context, but seems to require a richer and more sustained sequence of experience and instruction in order to flourish than, say, basic grammatical knowledge, color perception or appreciation of living kinds (cf. Rosskopf *et al.* 1971).

A more revealing indication of basic, domain-specific knowledge comes from a source that has barely been tapped: the study of cultural transmission. Some bodies of knowledge have a life of their own, only marginally affected by social change (e.g. color classification, ordinary living-kind categories) while other bodies of cultural knowledge (e.g. totemism, molecular biology) depend for their transmission, and hence for their very existence, on specific institutions. This suggests that culture should not be viewed as an integrated whole, relying for its transmission on undifferentiated human cognitive abilities. Rather, it seems that human cognitive resources are involved in different ways in the many more or less autonomous psychological subsystems that go into the making of culture.

Admittedly, the acquisition of all cultural knowledge depends upon its mode of transmission. But the acquisition of certain basic forms of knowledge does not seem much influenced by the sequence in which it is communicated; that is, *what* is learned does not much depend on *how* it is passed along. For example, Boster (1987) finds that cultures tend to make finer discriminations of passerines than nonpasserines, regardless of the social practices relating to these birds; rather, what matters are phenomenal characteristics (passerines comprise a relatively large order with graded differentiation in morphological features and ecological proclivities). More generally, the structure, scope and depth of taxonomic knowledge of living kinds is roughly comparable across similar physical environments regardless of whether it is "ideologically formless" in one society or has a "high rhetorical profile" in another. Thus, the Hanunóo of the Philippines possess detailed basic botanical knowledge that they take every occasion to demonstrate and pontificate upon (Conklin 1954); but the Zafimaniry of Madagascar, whose tropical environment and swidden technology are rather similar to that of the Hanunóo, appear to pass on their equally detailed basic botanical knowledge quite informally and with scarce commentary (Bloch 1988).[1]

An additional source of evidence for domain-specificity stems from developmental psychology. For it is logical to suppose that the basic structures of human cognition are those which severely constrain, and therefore greatly facilitate, the rapid acquisition of cultural knowledge. Increasingly, cognitive psychologists are coming to seriously entertain "the proposition that domains are functioning, self-regulating [cognitive] systems (in contrast with global structure or an indeterminate number of components)" (Turiel and Davidson 1986:115).

Experiments in the field indicate accordingly that young children – be they American (Keil 1986) or Yoruba (Jeyifous 1985) – categorically distinguish ARTIFACTS from LIVING THINGS, and come to presume that only the latter constitute "natural kinds" with underlying essences. An ongoing project of Keil (1988) and his colleagues further indicates that even preschoolers have some presumptions of the underlying nature of species, however rudimentary. In other words, the youngsters clearly "have some beliefs about what are not likely to be biologically relevant properties, regardless of salient characteristics." Most of the kindergartners tested did not allow temporary and intermittent alterations (e.g. paint that wears off a tigerized lion) to signal changes in kindhood, and even 3-year-olds tended not to admit costume change (e.g. putting a horse in a zebra outfit) as a change of identity.[2]

Thus, the youngest children tested to date appear to evince some knowledge that animals of a kind share properties that are not readily apparent. Moreover, earlier studies by Keil (1979) in two cultures also suggest that preschoolers are apt to categorically restrict certain predicates, such as "grow," to plants and animals only (the children thought it did not make sense to say, e.g., that rocks grow). This intimates that at least some concepts are constrained to the category LIVING KIND, however underdifferentiated the underlying biological "theory" that unifies conceptions of animals with those of plants. Unfortunately, for reasons that should become clear in the final section of this chapter, cognitive psychologists have overgeneralized or ignored some of the more compelling domain-specific aspects of LIVING KINDS.

Appreciation of artifacts, too, might be governed by innate expectations: "even preschoolers clearly believe that artifacts tend to be human made and that natural kinds are not" (Gelman 1988:88; cf. Keil 1986). Although, for lack of systematic analysis, the character of these expectations is still somewhat open to speculation, it seems that in this domain as well humans are able to categorize fragmented experiences and, with little or no "trial and error," extend the resulting categories to an indefinitely large set of complexly related experiences. As in any other area of cognitive endeavor, it is difficult to imagine how such spontaneous learning could succeed without a powerful set of *a priori* organizing principles.

A bit more evidence is at hand regarding initial expectations about three-dimensional rigid bodies, and the spatio-temporally contiguous relations of physical causality between them (Spelke 1987) and for intentional causality in animate beings (Gelman *et al.* 1983). In important respects, then, it appears that in addition to innate expectations governing the spontaneous learning of language (Chomsky 1968) and such basic perceptual categories as colors (Kay and McDaniel 1978), humans are also endowed with the means to spontaneously develop concepts and views in accordance with "naive" notions of biology, psychology and physics. It seems likely that the list of distinct, innately determined cognitive domains will turn out to be longer. For example, there is mounting evidence for the domain-specificity of certain aspects of preschoolers' knowledge of social relations (Hirschfeld 1988; cf. Turiel and Davidson 1986) and for preverbal numerical skills (Starkey *et al.* 1983; cf. Gelman 1980).

Selective cerebral impairment and selective preservation of certain cognitive categories can provide further clues for domain-specificity (Warrington and McCarthy 1983; Hart *et al.* 1985). There is an increasing body of literature in neuropsychology that refers to "category-specific" deficits in brain-damaged patients. In particular, there is considerable evidence not only for a distinct "gnostic field" of living kinds (Konorski 1967), but also for "modality specific semantic systems" that involve both visual and verbal understanding of artifacts versus living kinds (Warrington and Shallice 1984).

More specifically, Sartori and Job (1988) describe impairments that differentially affect the basic and superordinate levels of living kind taxonomy.[3] McCarthy and Warrington (1988) provide similar hints at a specialized information processing system for plants and animals. They describe a patient with a trauma to a small region of the left temporal lobe who, when asked to describe a species, could only associate it with a life-form. For example, when the patient was asked to define the word "pig" or "rhinocerous," he replied, "Animal" (taken in the polysemous sense of MAMMAL). Asked to define a dolphin, he could only guess, "A fish or a bird." But when asked to describe "lighthouse," he said, "Round the coast, built up, tall building, lights revolve to warn ships." These findings, surmise McCarthy and Warrington, "call into question the widely accepted view that the brain has a single all-purpose meaning store."

Perhaps the most significant support for domain-specificity, however, comes from conceptual analysis. The object is to show that a given domain is ordinarily structured in a specific way that differs radically from the ways other domains are ordinarily structured. In particular, anthropological and psychological findings clearly suggest that the mind organizes the domain of living kinds in a very different way from that of artifacts, and perhaps also naturally occurring chemical and physical substances, no matter what the culture. The rest of this chapter provides a conceptual analysis of the LIVING-KIND domain.

3.2 MEANING AS A MOTLEY

The studies of Eleanor Rosch and her associates on "natural categorization" represent that work in cognitive psychology that most informs, and is most informed by, current work in ethnobiology. Widely recognized is the historical significance of their devastating attack on the hitherto generally held view that every substance concept is signified by a boolean conjunction of simple attributes and that each referent is characterized exclusively in terms of them.[4] But the collaboration between psychology and anthropology has yielded dubious results.

For example, one crucial support in the assumption that folkbiological taxa are functional in a utilitarian sense, or "special purpose," rests on a faulty notion of "taxonomy" that ethnoscientists used throughout the 1960s (Frake 1961; Conklin 1962; Lévi-Strauss 1962/1966; Berlin et al. 1966; Kay 1971):

> Categories are generally designated by names (e.g., *dog, animal*). A *taxonomy* is a system by which categories are related to one another by means of class inclusion. The greater the inclusiveness of a category within a taxonomy, the higher the level of abstraction. Each category within a taxonomy is entirely included within one other category (unless it is the highest level category) . . . . The term *level of abstraction* within a taxonomy refers to a particular level of inclusiveness. A familiar taxonomy is the Linnaean system. (Rosch 1978:30)

Now, the notion of "category" above has little to do with the categories of biological classification.[5] More important, neither folkbiological systems nor the Linnaean system fit the usual definition of "taxonomy" given in the psychological and anthropological literature. In fact, it is difficult to imagine *any* naturally non-arbitrary order of groups of things that fit.

In biological classification, "category" denotes a hierarchical *rank* and not the taxonomic grouping, or taxon, itself. Taxa are the elements of categories. Organisms are the elements of taxa. Species, genus, family and class are Linnaean categories. Generic-specieme and life-form are folkbiological categories. Disjoint taxa are termed higher and lower with respect to one another not because they stand in any inclusion relations, but because they are members of different categories: "robin", "pike" and "gnat" are taxonomically related to "cat" by reason of common generic-specieme rank (the same class of classes), and not by reason of inclusion of reference within some shared superordinate taxon (class). If one tried to analyze the Linnaean system in terms of levels of abstraction and terminal contrast one would wind up with a biologically confused collection of taxa (e.g. with monospecific families and orders placed at the same level of inclusion as species and monospecific genera).

Applied to folkbiology such faulty notions produce an equally odd collection of groupings. Thus the bottom line, or basic level, of folktaxonomy is here determined exclusively by the linguistic artifice of "terminal contrast." Terminal contrast occurs between those named groupings that include no additional named groupings. The terminal level not only indiscriminately mixes in monogeneric life-forms with generic-speciemes, but also those taxa found below the rank of generic-specieme, that is, at the level of what ethnobiologists call the "folk-specific" (e.g. red oak, white oak) and "folk-varietal" (e.g. spotted white oak). Unlike the distinctions between life-forms and generic-speciemes, this further differentiation of (some, but rarely all) generic-speciemes into folk-specifics and varietals is usually made on the basis of one (or a very few) culturally significant features (cf. Berlin 1978).[6] Little wonder then that their inclusion into the "basic level" appears to make for a biologically confused and culturally idiosyncratic system of classification:

> Although an initial claim that folk plant classifications mirrored the Linnaean system and were thus universal [Diamond 1966] this has been shown [in ethnobiological studies of terminal contrast] to be largely a product of casual observation and failure to distinguish loan words from indigenous classifications.   (Rosch 1975:198)

Such "casual observations," though, consisted of findings extrapolated from a detailed study of New Guinea birds (including reference to folk ornithology) by one of zoology's foremost taxonomists (Mayr 1941).

When this faulty notion of taxonomy is fused with prototype theory the error is only compounded. Much experimentation and discussion by advocates of prototype theory favors the notion that "good" instances or average examples of any given concept are crucial to determining the concept's proper extension, that is, the set of objects that fall under the concept and to which the term(s) associated with the concept truly applies. Moreover, it is assumed that the actual extension of such prototypically based concepts is indeterminate and that membership in the set is in truth a matter of "more or less."

Take the concept FRUIT. Most mature English speakers would likely contrast FRUIT and VEGETABLE. They would also probably agree that some examples of FRUIT, like apples and oranges, are more representative of FRUIT than are, say, tomatoes and avocados. In fact, in some contexts, such as being served as entrees rather than as dessert, tomatoes and avocados might be considered instances of VEGETABLE (Bright & Bright 1965:258 n.6). Thus, whether or not a given item instantiates the concept depends on the extent to which that item perceptually resembles focal types and on the degree to which it fulfils their usual sort of function.

Now, as with Rosch and company, and like many studies in "semantic memory," VEGETABLE and FRUIT, which actually fall within the conceptual realm of artifacts, are equated with living kinds *per se* (see also Smith *et al.* 1974; McCloskey and Glucksberg 1978; Loftus 1977). In general, when living kinds enter the space of concern with human function and use, such as eating, gardening (weeds and flowers), farming (beasts of burden), entertainment (pets, circus and fair animals), they cease to be of taxonomic importance. For items that pertain to the conceptual space of human function and use, then, there may well be "unclear cases" of category affiliation, but this has no direct relevance to folkbiological classification.

Prototype views of meaning also generally carry the complementary assumption that a single semantic theory of family resemblances pertains to the intension of (at least) all ordinary kind terms. In other words, the class of defining attributes that constitutes the intension of the term is not a class of attributes that are severally necessary and jointly sufficient, but a "polythetic group" or "imperfect community" (cf. Needham 1975). Consider "game":

> you will not see something that is common to them *all* . . . . Look for example at board-games, with their multifarious relationships. Now pass to card-games; here you may find many correspondences with the first group, but many common features drop out, and others appear. When we pass next to ball-games, much that is common is retained, but much is lost . . . . I can think of no better expression to characterize these similarities than "family resemblances."   (Wittgenstein 1958:31e–32e)

Thus, whereas prototypes allegedly affect the extension of living-kind terms, "family resemblance" is somehow supposed to delimit intension. Implicit in this supposition is the "working assumption . . . that in the domains of both man-made and biological objects, there occur information rich bundles of attributes that form natural discontinuities [and] these bundles are both perceptual and functional" (Rosch & Mervis 1975:586; also Anglin 1977:262). In a study of family resemblances, Rosch and Mervis claim for both domains "empirical confirmation of Wittgenstein's argument that formal criteria are neither a logical nor psychological necessity." Yet *no* experiment in this study dealt with living kinds as such. And apart from obvious conditions, like "is an artifact" and "is a living kind", it seems all artifacts tested here and in Rosch's other studies have necessary functional, if not perceptual,[7] properties,[8] whereas none of the basic or superordinate living kinds in the other studies have necessary functions.[9]

From the standpoint of understanding common-sense conceptual organization of the living world, the chief problem with prototype theory considered as (part or all of) a general theory of meaning is that it fails to distinguish the semantic structure of living kinds from that of artifacts (e.g. Smith & Medin 1981:5). Of course, implicit rejection of inherent differences between logical and conceptual processes that determine the taxonomic ordering of living kinds and those governing conceptualization of artifacts is not exclusive to advocates of prototype theory. Unwarranted extension of findings across these domains is part of a more general assumption that all "natural-object" domains are semantically of a sort.[10] But prototype theory constitutes a particularly enticing entrapment because it does highlight a seemingly powerful cross-domain mode of information processing.

The mind, it appears, is endowed with at least two general sorts of information-processing strategies: those that are strictly rule-bound and those that are not. Perhaps these general strategies were naturally selected to allow humans to handle both apparently law-governed phenomena and less regular patterns of nature. But whatever their evolutionary history, domain-specific rules define the entities that can be organized in a given domain. Once these entities are defined they can be put to use. The way they are put to use may depend on the particular contexts and tasks at hand. Prototypes facilitate the patterning of input for use in memory and for one's actual dealings with the day-to-day world by describing similarities among particularly useful, salient or familiar clusters of exemplars. Prototypical patterning is thus contingent on memory and use. Because memory and use are influenced by context, prototypical patterning transforms in accordance with changes in history and society, with the extent and nature of such transformations varying as much as individuals and cultures vary. By contrast, concepts that are delimited by domain-specific rules are bound to hold fast whatever the contexts of their use, while remaining largely ahistorical and transcultural in their broad outlines.

It may well be that prototypicality judgments serve as mnemonic and recognitory heuristics in all domains. But this does not pertain to the *meaning* of terms in those domains. For example, although the numbers one, two and three are conceivably prototypical prime numbers they are no more nor less perfectly "prime" than any other unfactorable numbers (cf. Armstrong *et al.* 1983). Likewise, Rosch's prototype indicator, "perches on trees," no more defines "bird," than, say, "wears a white smock" indicates the meaning of "nurse." But prototypicality judgments are likely as crucial to mnemonic processing strategies and perceptual verification procedures for living-kind concepts and terms as they are for others.

Concepts for both artifacts and living kinds are rule-bound. But the apparent hierarchichal structure between artifact concepts and terms is not: "furniture" is not part of the definition of "chair", although "animal" is part of the definition of "cat".[11] Perhaps artifact concepts evolved to deal with human contingencies whereas living kind concepts were naturally selected to treat more or less omniprevalent products of nature. In any event, the internal structure of the artifact domain is clearly less strictly rule-governed and more susceptible to prototypical patterning than the internal structure of the living-kind domain.

Thus, when the prototypical structure of artifact groupings is set against the rigid notion of transitive hierarchy it is plain that artifacts are not organized taxonomically. It is not just that an "atypical" subordinate category (e.g. "piano") may cross-cut contrasting superordinate categories ("furniture", "musical instrument"). Even a prototypical representative (e.g. "chair") of a superordinate category ("furniture") can itself have atypical subordinates (e.g. "car-seat") that are not thought to belong to the superordinate category (i.e. not "furniture"). Suppose the organization of living kinds is also conceived in terms of varying degrees of typicality. It too, then, must fail to exhibit the transitivity implied by hierarchical levels of inclusion and contrast, much less that of rigid ranking (D'Andrade 1970, Kay 1975, Randall 1976, Hampton 1982).[12]

As indicated in the last chapter, however, it appears that lay taxonomy is rigidly structured in terms of three transitively tiered levels, and may be characterized thus (see Figure 1):

1. Every natural object is either a living kind or not.
2. Every living kind is either a plant or an animal.
3. Each plant or animal belongs to one and only one basic taxon, GS.
4. No two basic taxa share all of their characteristic phenomenal properties; that is, for all GS_i and for any GS_j, GS_j lacks at least one readily perceptible feature characteristic of GS_i.
5. Every basic taxon, GS, belongs to only one life-form taxon, LF.
6. For every LF_i there is at least one phenomenal property, D_i, which is characteristic and diagnostic in the sense that for all LF_j, D_i is not characteristic.

The claim for universal principles of folkbiological taxonomy is not for the universal status of particular *taxa*, only for taxonomic *categories*. Taxa are particular groups of organisms, whereas categories are ranked classes of taxa. In other words, taxa and categories comprise different logical types. The categories of generic-specieme and life-form are universal. The delimitation and placement of particular taxa are not. Applied to a local biota, universal taxonomic principles (including presumptions of underlying natures) tend to yield basic-level groupings that correspond to biological species, at least for the phenomenally salient vertebrates and flowering plants.

Formal taxonomic constraints are deductive and inductive. The deductive constraint requires transitive inference as to group adherence: if one discovers a new kind of oak, then one knows it to be a tree. The inductive constraint allows for inferences as to the general distribution of taxonomic (and ancillary morpho-ecological) features throughout the local flora and fauna: if one discovers two organisms to possess a feature, then one may infer that the feature belongs to all organisms in the lowest ranked taxon containing the two. The inductive character of life-forms pertains primarily to the ecological and morphological relationships between species. Some cultures classify bats with birds, others place bats with quadrupeds, still others accord bats their own (monogeneric) life-form status, depending upon the bat's perceived relationships with the totality of the local fauna (and flora). As the distribution of ecological boundaries and morphological characters varies from one locale to another, so may life-form boundaries. All the same, universal taxonomic principles operate.

Hierarchical ranking of living kinds is apparently unique to that domain. The field structure for artifacts, while often confounded with that of living kinds, is in fact quite different. For one thing, that taxa of the same category are disjoint precludes artifact groupings entering into ranked taxonomies. Not only can artifactual items belong to more than one "taxon" within an inclusion series (a wheel-chair as both "furniture" and "vehicle") but a given item may belong to different series (the same item as a crate used for packing furniture or as a table used as a piece of furniture).

Also, artifacts fail to meet the deductive and inductive requirements of ranked taxonomies. They are not ordered into transitive hierarchies, and it is hardly plausible that we *induce*, say, that chairs are naturally four-legged or that vehicles have wheels from the fact that chairs are normally observed to have four legs and vehicles are usually seen with wheels. Talk of artifact "natures" is idle as well. For example, one and the same item can literally *be* an instance of "waste paper basket" in one context and "taboret" in another if oriented differently. It is the fact that artifacts are defined by the functions they serve, rather than by any inherent perceptual properties, that allows a given (morphologically self-same) item to belong to different categories of artifacts in different circumstances. But, e.g., a dog is always a dog.

Still, according to Rosch (1973:111), just as: "some colors to which English speakers apply the word 'red' are 'redder' than others[,] some breeds of 'dog' (such as the retriever) are more representative of the 'meaning' of dog [than a Pekinese]." But the analogy with color is untenable. If a Pekinese is not properly, or only peripherally, a dog, what other kind could it be confused with? It may be difficult to decide where "red" ends and "orange" starts, or whether a given item is a "cup" or "bowl" (cf. Labov 1973, Kempton 1978); however, this is certainly not so for "dog", "oak" or any other such living kind. Perhaps there is a lesser degree of confidence in the judgment (especially the child's judgment) that a Pekinese or Boston terrier is a dog and not another basic kind such as a cat, than in the judgment that a retriever or German shepherd is a dog rather than a cat. But Pekinese and Boston terriers cannot *be* anything but dogs. Here, as elsewhere, interesting findings for one domain, inconsiderately applied to another, risk being trivialized. Until independently assessed semantic domains can be *shown* to be similar, meaning should be assumed a motley, not a monolith.

In what follows, meaning for living-kind terms is analyzed as being fundamentally different from other object terms. Ordinarily, people conceive of the typical properties a living-kind's definition describes as necessary – not merely possible or usual – in virtue of the kind's presumed underlying nature. So, e.g., legless tigers are still classed with animals considered quadrupeds "by nature." Cross-culturally, people presume that living kinds have (possibly unknown) natures with propensities responsible for perceived regularities of those kinds. This presumption that a nature and its propensities produce characteristics typical of a kind – whenever normal conditions obtain – underlies the taxonomic stability of all (and likely only) living-kind terms despite obvious token variation among individuals of a type. Such a presumption together with absolute ranking of taxa into "generic-speciemes" (e.g. chicken) and "life-forms" (e.g. bird) has no parallel in the notoriously "open textured" realm of artifacts.

3.3 NATURE AND NECESSITY

One objection to characterizing ordinary living kinds in terms of necessary features is the fact that biologists "now recognize that membership in a biological species cannot be predicated on possession of necessary and sufficient conditions" (Hunn 1982:832). This is supposedly because in science it is occasionally unclear to which taxon a given organism belongs, and there is no assurance that defining nomological features of structural homology or genetic constitution can be ascribed to all and only members of a taxon:[13]

> These developments in biological classification are relevant to a psychology of concepts . . . . The most likely place to look for classical definitions of flora and fauna is the language of biology, and to the extent that the classical view fails here, it will likely fail as a psychological theory as well.
> (Smith and Medin 1981:31–32)

Moreover, argues Rey (1983:239n): "So far as the Classical View is concerned, the situation in biology seems to be even worse than [Smith & Medin] describe, given the on-going competition between [theoretically rival] taxonomies." Yet, this ongoing competition among theories in biological systematics may be no more pertinent to our understanding of everyday living-kind terms than the ongoing controversy over the nature of various subatomic particles and forces is to our ordinary concept of BILLIARD BALL. This is not to deny that science and common sense may interact. It is only to deny that our customary ontological commitment is necessarily bound to that of the scientist. Thus, the fact that *scientific* data do not wholly conform to *common-sense* classification is hardly a compelling criticism of the classical view as it applies to ordinary language.

Admitting ordinary kinds on their own terms, rather than as stand-ins for the ideas of science, there still seems to be an obvious objection to positing *logically* necessary features that uniquely characterize a living kind: a given exemplar may always lack one or more of these typical features. In line with this objection, Ziff (1960:184) claims that any attempt to define, say, "tiger" in terms of such characteristic features as "being striped" or "quadrupedal" would lead to the absurd conclusion that a three-legged tiger which had lost its stripes is a *contradictio in adjecto*. As Fodor (1977:148) remarks, cows differ from other animals in:

> familiar ways, but it is no part of the MEANING of *cow* that cows say 'moo', and give milk, and look thus-and-so. These are not NECESSARY truths . . . a cow that did not say 'moo' would still be a cow, and so would one that did not give milk or was purple.

If these objections hold, it would appear that only a "family resemblance" of perceptible features can cover the full extension of many living-kind terms, and that for such terms all perceptible features are merely contingent (Mervis & Rosch 1981). The "ness" (or linguistic equivalent in other languages) that seems to attach to ordinary living kinds would then appear to denote only the prototypical "configuration by which members of the category . . . are recognized" (Hunn 1976:514). Instead of definitions there could only be "default values" (Miller & Johnson-Laird 1976). But consider this anthropological observation as to why, for instance, a bean-bag chair hasn't "its" legs though a legless tiger has "its":

> If an animal does not actually possess a feature ascribed to it by its definition, then it possesses it virtually: not in its appearance but in its nature. In such conditions it would be hard for empirical evidence to contradict the definitions of folk taxonomies. (Sperber 1975a:22)

This is more than just a grammatical point: we can say of a tiger born without legs that it didn't ever get *its* legs, but not of a bean bag chair that it didn't ever get *its*. Sperber further implies that, say, a plucked bird is still thought to have *its* feathers "virtually" just as a coneless pine "virtually" has *its* cones.

This is why it is appropriate to hold, for example, that tigers are always "quadrupedal by nature" while tables aren't.[14] Thus, although for American folk being taller than a person and having a perennial stem seems to be criterial for being a tree (since non-woody palms and banana plants are classed as trees), insofar as bonsai are trees they are still "by nature larger than a person". If predicting entailments in the lexical field of living kinds requires the abstract property "by nature larger than a person" for marking a "tree", then if a given referential token (exemplar) of the semantic type (the concept TREE) lacks the property's perceptual correlate it is a contingent fact of the world and extrinsic to the semantic logic of living kinds.

Yet, how is it that there is no anomaly? How can "quadrupedal" ever be truthfully predicated of tigers that never have four legs? Knowing the meaning of a living-kind term must at least put us on the right track in search of an answer. For, if not, then what in the world can meaning conceivably be about? Since an object may fail to manifest all aspects of the meaning of the term under which it falls, to consider such aspects as conditions that must hold for the object *to be* seems counter-intuitive. The problem is not simply one of a three-legged tiger losing or growing back a defining property, but of perhaps never having it in fact. The knowledge problem for ordinary living-kind terms thus appears to require at least this for its resolution: grasping the meaning of the term involves knowing that, in principle (if not how, in fact) instances which fall within the true extension of the term necessarily *would* manifest the attributes. This requires explication:

In line with Aristotle, let us first make the following rough distinctions. Of the whole set of attributes of a given living kind, there is a subset that is intrinsic to that kind and a subset that is incidental to it. For example, if it were true that tigers are large, striped felines seen only on Tuesdays, then being a feline and being large and striped would be among the intrinsic attributes of tigers and being seen on Tuesdays would be incidental to tigers. Thus, the counterfactual (7) is true:

7. "It would not be a tiger, unless it were feline"

And (8) is false:

8. ★"It would not be a tiger, unless it were seen on Tuesdays"

But what of (9)?

9. (?)"It would not be a tiger, unless it were striped"

To answer, we are first obliged to note that the intrinsic attributes of a living kind appear to come in two grades, one more essential, but less well known, than the other. The essential trait, or nature, (e.g. the peculiar felinity of tigers) "underlies" the better known perceptible features (e.g. being large and striped); that is, the perceptible features of a kind are *presumed* to be natural consequences of, or to be *naturally caused* by, the essential nature of that kind, even if the essential nature is largely unknown and perhaps effectively unknowable.

Now, being a natural consequence is dependent on a "normality" clause. When an exemplar possesses an essential underlying trait – for example, when Tio the tiger has its peculiar felinity essentially – then *whenever normal conditions obtain* it will necessarily manifest the perceptible features of its kind. So, we believe (10):

10. "It is *natural* for tigers to be four-legged, that is what we *expect* to happen unless something physically *hinders* their normal maturation" (cf. Aristotle *Physica* 199b15 and section 4.2 below).

In other words, it is presumed by most folk that every individual of a given living kind has each an inner causal nature that normally leads the individual to mature in accordance with the morphological type of its kind. But it is possible to envisage situations where normal conditions do not obtain, where some external or internal event has broken the putative natural chain which physically links Tio's having a particular essential nature and Tio's being large and having stripes. Unusual environmental perturbation or natural malfunction, such as shaving Tio or Tio being a naturally deformed dwarf would be examples of such interference.

We ordinarily cope with such situations by distinguishing semantic properties of the kind from the naturally manifest perceptible features of particulars. We say of the shaven Tio that it has no stripes, but that it is "striped by nature". Hence, (9) now suitably modified as (11) by an implicit normality clause is true:

11. "It would not be a tiger, unless it were striped by nature"

In other words, in virtue of its essential nature, the tiger is endowed with the *propensity to manifest* four legs, and will so manifest them in fact whenever normal conditions obtain.[15] In effect, it is to propensities (e.g. inherently quadrupedal) that semantic properties advert and not to manifest features *per se* (e.g. actually four-legged).

When fully analyzed, the common-sense locution "by nature" yields the ontological relation *because of* in the following sense: let p be a naturally manifest feature, and P the corresponding propensity; then:

12. Nec $(P(x)$ & normal conditions obtain $---->p(x))$

A manifest feature p, as such, is not essential to members of a kind; rather if and when it does occur, then we say it "necessarily occurs by nature" because of P (and of the underlying nature of which P is an integral part).[16] This common-sense notion of natural necessity is a conditional necessity: it will be necessary that if p is manifested, then if the organism has the propensity P to manifest p as a constituent of its essential nature, and normal conditions obtain, then indeed p is manifested. To discover the physical nature of individuals of a kind is thus to find out *what it is* for them to have the necessary features they would have were normal conditions to obtain. Because two generic-speciemes cannot share all their natural features, they cannot have (or be discovered to have) natures of a kind.

But what happens when appearances do not cooperate with our typical (meaning-induced) expectations? How do we know to classify "deviant" cases with "normal" ones? The strategies for coping with these situations are basically two, one pertaining to environmental circumstance, the other to origin. Because local generic-speciemes are in the main well-bounded geographically and ecologically, organisms that occupy the same niche and interact with members of one kind, and are clearly not identified with any other kind, are presumed to be of a kind with the organisms with which they interact. If genealogical linkage is also observed, all the better. But for folk in pre-scientific societies, an awareness of genealogical linkage may not suffice in itself, especially if distinct morphological varieties (or even males versus females, juveniles versus adults) of the same species occupy separate niches. For the sophisticated layperson who is influenced by the scientific assumption of historical continuity between organisms of a kind, a plausible genealogical linkage appears sufficient to establish a transtemporal identity in kind between morphologically dissimilar individuals.

But this genealogical linkage need not be exclusively phylogenetic as science would have it. For example, hawks and sparrows are American folk kinds, but they are morpho-ecologic kinds that are not phyletically unitary; nonetheless, it suffices to know that some bird is the progeny or progenitor of a hawk or sparrow in order to be able to class that bird as a hawk or sparrow.[17]

What of deviance in respect of life-forms? One must realize that to class an organism under a life-form is not simply to presume it has the nature of that life-form; rather, it is to predicate of the organism membership of one or the other of the generic-speciemes that has as part of its nature the nature of its life-form. So, as Theophrastus (1968:25) stresses, when mallow, which is normally not like a tree, grows tall like a tree it departs from its "essential nature" (*physis*). In this case mallow is said to be merely "tree-like" (*apodendroumeni*), and not a tree "by nature" (*physei*)'. Similarly for American folk, although pussy willows may not always look like trees (especially in parts of the western United States), the fact that they are considered willows, and that willows are considered trees, implies that pussy willows are nonetheless trees.

The theoretical significance of a cross-cultural presumption of essential natures that underlie the stability of folkbiological taxonomy is threefold. First, such a presumption saves the facts, namely, the rigidly ranked structure of folkbotanical and folkzoological taxonomies observed the world over. Despite obvious variation among exemplars of a given folk kind, there is little doubt that perceptually prototypical and atypical individuals veridically instantiate the kind. To presume an underlying nature makes sense of this.

Second, in addition to being observationally adequate, a presumption of essence is a descriptively adequate rendition of native intuitions. For it renders such ethnographic observations as these immediately comprehensible: among the Tobelo of Indonesia (Taylor 1978/79:224):

> one often hears of a particular small sapling ... 'this weed (*o rurubu*) is a tree (*o gota*)' (non-contrastive sense of *o rurubu*); or of the same sapling ... 'this is not a (member of the) herbaceous weed class, it is a tree' (*o rurubu* here contrasts with *o gota*).

And it does so by appealing directly to informants' views about the organization of the biological world: "Thus, for Rofaifo [of New Guinea] species share an essence which ... immediately renders the idea, species, intelligible in a natural (biological) sense" (Dwyer 1976a:433).

Finally, more than a glimmer of explanatory adequacy appears with the postulation of such a presumption of physical essence. A universal belief in underlying nature constrains the character of semantic and conceptual knowledge for living kinds generally. It does so in a way that helps to explain the relatively uniform acquisition of such knowledge across cultures and the relative ease with which it is acquired by the children of any given culture (cf. Stross 1973; Macnamara 1982). A presumption of essence plausibly enables the young child to rapidly fix a morphotype in mind, despite very limited perceptual encounter with exemplars. This, in turn, allows the child to immediately classify and relationally segregate an example from instances of all other taxa.

Clearly beliefs about essences cannot be *post hoc*. They must constitute conceptually *a priori* impositions on the taxonomic ordering of perceptual stimuli into morphotypes. Otherwise, how would it be logically possible for the child to take an instance of experience and "instantaneously" predict its extension to an indefinitely large set of complexly related instances? The child, it seems, just perceptually "fills in" abstract taxonomic schema that are naturally at the mind's disposal. Even in the absence of any confirming instance, it suffices to presume that, e.g., elms have a distinct nature for people with an incomplete concept of ELM to communicate effortlessly.

Presumption of underlying nature is also a necessary condition for any appreciation of the temporal development (maturation) or spatial distribution (ecological proclivity) of individuals of a species. It is .thus prior to any knowledge of the cultural utilizations of a species *qua* species. For example, the Inuit of East Hudson Bay have a dozen or so terms for various developmental stages of the reindeer linked to socially important uses (Roué 1986). But only the presumption that reindeers all have the natures of their kind allows this.

The cross-cultural disposition (and possibly innate predisposition) to think this way about the organic world is perhaps partly accounted for in evolutionary terms by the empirical adequacy that presumptions of essence afford to human beings in dealing with a local biota. Knowledge of species *qua* biological species, and knowledge that organic individuals naturally fall into groups within groups, is a knowledge humankind shares, whether bushman, layman or scientist. Such knowledge determines the way we see the world and regulates our inductions about what we do not see.

In brief, living-kind terms are conceived as "natural kinds" whose intrinsic nature, or (to use Locke's notion) "real essence," is presumed, even if unknown. The essential role of possibly unknown underlying structure is to permit variation, and even change, in reference without a change in the corresponding phenomenal type classed in the dictionary. By incorporating auxiliary empirical knowledge (e.g. on metamorphosis, courtship behavior, genetic structure, niche sharing, and so forth) into encyclopedic theories of underlying traits, one may thus come to include, for example, the caterpillar under the concept of BUTTERFLY and the tadpole under that of FROG, despite the fact that caterpillars and tadpoles share few, if any, perceptible features with normal frogs and butterflies. Theories of underlying traits may also facilitate acceptance of mutants, ecological variants and so on. As a result, we are able to accommodate unusual and novel aspects of the physical world to our conceptual system without compromising our basic stock of ordinary knowledge.

Variation within type is understood by mere presumption of an underlying nature and knowledge of local ecology. But when exotic species are reported, or actually introduced, into the local scene on a large scale (as among sections of post-Renaissance Western society) a more elaborate notion of underlying natures and their origins is required to accommodate the new to the old without destroying the local taxonomic scheme. This elaboration may be partially deferred to science, but not wholly inasmuch as science often rides rough shod over the local order. This overriding concern with maintaining the integrity of our ordinary knowledge about the living world distinguishes terms used by both sophisticated and uninformed folk from those employed in fields of science.

3.4 PHENOMENAL REALITY AND NOMIC THEORY

Inter alia, the causal theory of "historico-scientific determinism" denies that a principled distinction exists between ordinary and scientific ascriptions of meaning to living-kind terms (cf. Schwartz 1979, Macnamara 1982, Rey 1983, Devitt and Sterelny 1987). According to Kripke's (1972) account, a causal relationship is established via an initial baptism ceremony between a natural substance term, a (first, typical or otherwise privileged) sampling of objects and an underlying physical trait. This link is preserved by a descendent linguistic community committed to the term's "rigid designation" – whatever the experts may determine *that* to be. The extension of the term simply becomes the set of objects having that physical trait which is nomically responsible for the existence of those objects (with all their dispositional features). That trait, however, is not determined by features of any concept that language users may attach to the term, no matter how appropriate those features might at first seem.

A problem with this scenario is that it fails to account for actual historical changes in reference. Thus, English colonists first used the term "indian corn", that is, maize (indigenous to America), to denote a variety of "corn", that is, wheat; just as *kašlan ʔišim* (the Mayan term for "Castillian maize"), that is, wheat, was used by Indians to signify a foreign variety of *ʔišim*, that is, maize (Berlin 1972).[18] Over time, the unfamiliar kind proved to be of such significance in the local ecology that the generic-specieme term, "corn", was eventually applied to maize only. In a similar development, the Mayan term for deer (*čih*) was ultimately transferred to sheep introduced by the Spaniards (with deer now referred to as a variety of "forest sheep", or *teʔ tikil čih*). Such transference of reference is obviously not a mere conventional twist, but turns upon a complex appreciation of the local relations between species which folk taxonomy expresses. This precludes there being some originally privileged or otherwise isolated sample that historically somehow (and Kripke never does tell us just how) fixes reference.

It would, however, be consistent with rigid designation to parry the objection by arguing that, in calling maize "corn", the colonists performed a new baptism which simply ousted the old. How and why this new baptism came about, although psychologically and anthropologically important issues, would not be philosophically pertinent. It suffices to note that terms designate rigidly only after baptism occurs. As in the case of proper names, it may not be essential that Kripke be called "Kripke," but once he is called that the name picks him out rigidly.

All this is logically possible; however, it ignores history and hardly accounts for matters of psychological or anthropological fact, matters that concern the ways human beings actually think and behave. Historically, the rigid designation story gives not the slightest clue as to the reason for a term's shift in reference, because it fails to acknowledge that there must be continuity in the reference of folk-biological kinds with respect to the whole local biota and the taxonomic structure which describes it. Psychologically, "baptism" is just too impoverished a notion to imply much at all about mental processing.

A psychologically plausible correlate of baptism for ordinary-kind terms might be deemed *expected ostension*, that is, the act of making apparent (one's intention to make apparent) what every human being would naturally expect to be manifest to anybody. Linked to the cross-cultural stability of the living-kind conceptual domain, we find that the learning of ordinary living-kind terms is remarkably easy and needs virtually no teaching. At a limit, one need only once point to a plant or animal (in a garden or zoo, or even in a book) to have a child immediately classify it and relationally segregate it from all other taxa. Of course, the naming might be (and in a garden or zoo is likely to be) done with pedagogic intent: "this, children, is a sheep." But it may just as well occur in an utterance not at all aimed at teaching: "let's kill the sheep in the picture." Here the verb "kill" is sufficient to indicate that what is pointed to in the picture is a living thing, and innate expectations about the organization of the biological world ensure that that thing is basically of a kind with its species but not basically a kind with all other living things.

Humans, let us suppose, are endowed with highly articulated cognitive faculties for "fast-mapping" the world they evolved in, and for which their minds were selected. The "automatic" taxonomic ordering of phenomenal species, like the spontaneous relational ordering of colors (Kay and McDaniel 1978), would then be a likely product of one such faculty.[19] Intuitively, ostension of living kinds works extremely well for humans in any culture, and at any age, because it calls our attention to what it is about the (biological) world that comes most naturally to everyone's mind, that is (all and only) readily perceptible species. For living things, then, expected ostension invokes a semantic primitive, namely, "species", in a sense of a readily perceptible kind of plant or animal that necessarily differs typically, and by nature, from all other species.

In Putnam's (1975:141–2) version of the causal theory, "natural kind" terms,[20] such as "tiger", can be given by an "ostensive definition" with the following empirical presupposition: that the creature pointed to bears a certain sameness relation (say, *x is the same creature as y*) to most of the things which speakers in the linguistic community have on other occasions labeled "tiger". Leaving aside the historical fiction of baptism, the interesting claim is that this nomological relation of sameness may be "operationally" determined by a conceptual stereotype.

Although Putnam offers no explicit account of how stereotypes actually operate, one which does ample justice to his proposal is as follows: first, select a sampling of exemplars as distinct from one another as is compatible with the taxon's stereotype. For maximum generality, foils chosen from other taxa could serve to demarcate limits of compatability. One would then seek the most specific nomic relation that holds between every pair of exemplars and which cannot be extended to pairs containing a foil. Failing that, one would look for the nomic relation covering the widest variety of pairs in the sampling. Thus, assuming that whales were at one time ordinarily included under "fish" and bats under "bird", no nomic relation would have been available for all and only those pairs of exemplars falling under "fish" or "bird". For example, if one of the exemplars of a fish-pair were a whale then the most specific nomic relation applicable to all fish-pairs would extend to the mammals. So, rather than obliterate the distinction in "meaning" between "mammal" and "fish", here the preferred strategy would be to accept the nomic relation with the greatest partial scope, viz., that which characterizes fish exclusive of whales.

There are problems, however. Consider "sparrow". If scientific taxonomy is indicative of nomic relationship, then "sparrow" as commonly perceived does not have a nomic extension: it is ordinarily taken to denote only species of plain-colored birds in the finch family and birds of the genus *Passer* in the weaver family. To accord with science, ordinary users of "sparrow" would probably not restrict the term to plain-colored finches, since the most specific sameness relation applicable to plain-colored finches also applies to goldfinches and canaries (which are normally perceived as foils to "sparrow"). Moreover, the restriction excludes birds usually accepted as sparrows by Americans (e.g. the house sparrow), and typically viewed as such by the English. The alternative is to limit the term to the widest (i.e. highest ranked) grouping wholly included within the common extension of "sparrow", such as the genus of weavers (as opposed to any one of the heterogeneous collection of plain-colored finch species). But this would mean that our most typically American sparrows (e.g. the chirping sparrow) are not really sparrows at all, and that is plainly counter-intuitive.

Kripke argues that such considerations "may make some people think right away that there are really two concepts . . . operating here, a phenomenological one and a scientific one which then replaces it. This I reject" (1972:315). His point is that common-sense terms must ultimately either prove co-extensive with some nomic kinds, or simply cease to be natural-kind terms. Kripke fails to appreciate that the "phenomenological concept" may persist *as an underlying trait term* regardless of science's opinion on the matter. "Hawk" and "sparrow" persist as underlying trait terms because their usual denotations are readily perceived to be components of local nature; the Tzeltal Maya, for instance, recognize similar taxa (Hunn 1977:143,190). The traits underlying common-sense kinds need not be (or need not even include) nomic traits, though sometimes they may.

With pre-scientific folk there is usually, and with sophisticated laypeople seemingly always, a presumption of historical continuity between common-sense traits, or natures, to the effect that "like begets like." But this presumption of historical continuity does not, as with science, necessarily imply descent from a common ancestor: sparrows do beget sparrows but not in a phyletic line. Also, with sophisticated laypeople there is usually, and with pre-scientific folk seemingly always, a presumption that it is in the nature of a kind to bind its members together into an interactive ecological community (cf. Bulmer 1974:12). So, genealogical and ecological criteria largely figure into a determination of the nature of a common-sense kind. Socially functional criteria, though, do not. Indeed, if ordinary living kinds were to depend upon social functions, Kripke could justify his claim that they then cease to be natural-kind terms; but nothing of the sort happens.

"Tree" and "grass" are cases in point. Once perfectly respectable taxonomic terms, they have now disappeared from systematics; however, unlike countless ill-fated terms for microscopic and extinct organisms which have since gone the way of phlogiston and the ether, they have not also vanished from common parlance. This is because trees and grasses are phenomenally, though not nomically, natural kinds. In other words, they plainly *look* as if they must be natural kinds, even though *scientifically* they are not. Supposing evolutionary taxonomy to be the best available representation of the true structural history of plants and animals, then trees and grasses are not central historical subjects. This is not to deny the ecologist's legitimate interest in the "objective" correlates of their phenomenal properties, any more than it would be to deny the physicist's circumstantial concern with color phenomena. But to extrapolate from Quine (1969:127), cosmologically, trees and grasses would no more qualify as kinds than would colors.

That there is a definite anthropocentric bias in these pretheoretical divisions cannot be gainsaid. But such (possibly even innate) bias can in no way be construed as a variant of some utilitarian or cultural viewpoint. "Tree" is no more derived from a functional preoccupation with wood than "green" is derived from a cultural preoccupation with plants in general (see section 2.3 above).

The layperson's stubborn adherence to the (phenomenal) validity of everyday-kind terms thus markedly contrasts lack of prior commitment to the (nonphenomenal) terms of science.[21] Take "animalcule", which first arose in the scientific and popular literature of the late seventeenth century as a natural-kind term for all microscopic organisms (including spermatozoa). By the end of the following century this term had ceased to denote a natural kind. Although today the term barely lingers as a qualifier to a heterogeneous collection of microorganisms (barrel animalcule, wheel animalcule, etc.), "animalcule" is no more considered a natural-kind term by scientist *or* layperson than is "caloric".

It is not that scientific developments cannot affect common-sense appreciation of the perceptible world. Only, the theory of ordinary meaning is not directly related to scientific reference in a way that levels the distinction between the terms of common sense and science. Evidence of scientific incompatibility between sortals is neither necessary nor sufficient to indicate lack of an underlying trait compatible with common-sense realism. Under what circumstances does one decide when two sortal terms are connected to the same natural-kind term in virtue of some common underlying trait (e.g. "maple" as applied to the red maple and the sugar maple) and when not ("wolf" applied to placental mammals of the dog family versus the marsupial wolf, Thylacine)? One such condition of "compatible common-sense realism" may pertain to the fact that the largest grouping with an immediately recognizable morphological configuration, or facies, is usually restricted to the biological family or order. Thus, many a heterogeneous collection of species falling within a given family or order, if previously considered a phenomenal kind, is likely to remain so whatever the state of scientific knowledge. Beyond the level of family or order, the aspectual tie between members of a previous kind is generally too vague to preserve the kind intact without the aid of other apparent factors such as a shared role in the local ecology: thus, allowing dissociation of whales from fish, salamanders from lizards, marsupial from placental mice, lampreys from eels, hedgehogs from porcupines, etc.

Dissociations of this kind usually happen in either of two ways: at the life-form level, or at a level intermediate between generic-specieme and life-form. As already indicated (see section 2.5 above), such intermediate groupings are recognized by folk whether or not (in fact, mostly not) explicitly named. Mostly they correspond to fragments of a scientific family or order. But they do not constitute an exhaustive partition of the local flora or fauna. This is not surprising given the fact that associations of family and order are pocketed with gaps in any locality, unlike associations of species (generic-speciemes) and life-forms which form a morpho-ecologic quilt across a local area. In contrast to taxonomically arrayed generic-speciemes and life-forms, the boundaries of these usually covert groupings are fuzzy, while the core is generally the recognizable facies of a modern family or order. Accordingly, generic-speciemes only peripherally associated with such fragments are susceptible to dissociation. Thus, early English settlers in Australia probably combined an implicit grouping of marsupial and placental mice by weak association of morphological aspect. But today few Australians would think marsupial and placental mice are of a kind.[22]

Dissociation at the life-form level occurs most readily for generic-speciemes whose phenomenal affiliations with their respective life-forms are only marginal (although from a strictly logical standpoint there is no *taxonomic* anomaly). Most often, folk views on the extension of these life-forms differ from scientifically construed extensions of the corresponding classes in regard to what, from the folk viewpoint, are rather marginal cases (and for natural history traditionally the most problematic): bat, ostrich, whale, etc. Indeed, as often as not these marginal groupings assume a separate life-form status of their own; hence they are treated as monogeneric life-forms. As such, they differ from the other life-forms in being minimally polytypic and in having a role which is restricted, rather than wideranging, in the overall local economy of nature. Given the tenuous phenomenal associations such groups thus bear to other groups in respect of life-form, modern folk are amenable to a shift in their life-form status which would be in conformity with scientific opinion.

These (tentative) conditions on "compatible common sense realism" argue against any straightforward reduction of common-sense terms: phenomenal conditions appreciably constrain the intricate relationship between common sense and science. In this respect Dupré (1981:69) aptly stresses that: "the general picture is of science as a largely autonomous activity, in spite of subtle and pervasive interactions with the main body of language." But when assessing the relationship between the classifications of organisms in ordinary language (OLC) and in scientific taxonomy, Dupré errs in imposing a "functionalist viewpoint" on OLC:

> A group of organisms may be distinguished in ordinary language for any number of reasons: because it is economically or sociologically important (Colorado beetles, silkworms or Tsetse flies); because its members are intellectually intriguing (trap-door spiders or porpoises); furry and empathetic (hamsters and koala bears); or just very noticeable (tigers and giant redwoods). (1981:69; also Wierzbicka 1985:242)

Porpoises do intrigue folk. They are evocative because, along with whales, they are phenomenally aberrant at the life-form level; however, their evocative or symbolic power is not the *source* of their taxonomic status. Hamsters may be empathetic, but their taxonomic status is no different from that of the rat, raccoon, house cat or tiger. And when, as with silkworms, there is a finer appreciation than is usually the case with invertebrates, it is not because of their functional importance as such. Rather, it is because constant and direct intervention by man actually creates an isolated role for them in the local environment, which makes them phenomenally salient. The anthropocentric bias, it seems, is fundamentally cognitive and phenomenal, not functional in a socially parochial and pragmatic sense.[23]

At the generic-specieme level of classification (to which Dupré's examples above belong) ethnobiologists largely agree that considerations other than morpho-ecologic affinity are rather peripheral. Apart from invertebrates and cryptogams, when disagreement between science and common sense occurs at the generic-specieme level it is usually because the reproductive criteria of the scientist conflict with the morpho-ecological criteria of the layperson. Most often these two sets of criteria overlap at the generic-specieme level; but when they do not, ordinary folk generally refrain from acceding to scientific opinion. In regard to most bugs and non-flowering plants, as these are not salient species-wise, they are often lumped into residual taxa. But the residual character is phenomenally compelling enough to resist scientific pressure to restrict, say, "moss" to the bryophytes or "worm" to the annelids.

So far as I can see, then, there is no scientific advance which would *necessarily* lead to a restructuring of lay taxonomy. Moreover, people need not, and normally do not, seek to reconcile the fact that such American folk kinds as "tree", "bug", "thistle", "butterfly" and "hawk" have no biologically valid extensions, or that French folk taxa like *abre, fauvette, milan* and *roseau* do not conform to scientific (phyletic) lines. When it does happen that some common-sense taxon falls within the extension of a scientific taxon, then folk *may* come to accept a modification of the common-sense taxon so that it corresponds more closely to the scientific taxon (e.g. including whales with the mammals and excluding bats from the birds). But this is only possible if the scientific notion can be given a phenomenal expression, and if expert opinion is not incompatible with everyday common-sense realism.

Yet, even if such an accord proves feasible, the lay concept still diverges from the scientist's, that is, the folk taxon differs in structure from the evolutionary taxon. For example, the layperson may regard "mammal" as an "air-breathing, warm-blooded, milk-giving" creature. The evolutionary taxonomist, however, may well view "Mammalia" as a portion of the genealogical nexus of evolution. As such, it would be a term for a logical *individual* localized in space and time and not, as with the layman, a term for an eternal class (Ghiselin 1981; cf. Hull 1978). Axiomatizations of evolutionary theory (or at least the formalized subset known as "selection theory") that are compatible with Mayr's (1982:273) widely accepted definition of the species as a "reproductive community of populations . . . that occupies a specific niche in nature," use species terms as primitives for denoting populations conceived as individualized "Darwinian subclans" (Williams 1985). Thus, although there may be considerable systematic correspondence between the actual extensions of biological and folkbiological taxa, no such correspondence occurs with regard to intension. For scientific taxonomies – at least modern evolutionary ones – do not assume the necessity of fixed sets of manifest attributes nor do they presume the existence of fixed essences or natures.

Most accounts by causal theorists exhibit an indiscriminate switching of evidence and argument between different scientific fields and domains of common sense. By and large, they have failed to notice that while consideration of the underlying scientific nature of kinds may be pertinent to chemistry and physics, it holds little relevance for evolutionary biology (cf. Dupré 1986). Conversely, talk of popular conceptions of the underlying natures of kinds may have different implications for common-sense appreciations of inorganic substances and living things. Ignoring this, causal theorists may be misled into assuming the unity of science, the homogeneity of common sense and the singularity of the relationship between science and common sense. It seems more plausible to view ordinary conceptions of the natural world as involving fundamentally different common-sense conceptual domains, and to see the disunity of science as the product of a varied elaboration of these distinct domains. Consider:

Humans appear to be inherently disposed to classify living kinds according to presumptions about their underlying physical natures. Cross-cultural evidence indicates that people everywhere spontaneously organize living kinds into rigidly ranked taxonomic types despite wide morphological variation among those exemplars presumed to have the nature of their type. But people may be less spontaneously disposed to so organize their diverse apprehensions of substances. If so, the relatively weak internal structure of the ordinary substance domain may be susceptible to the borrowed influence of strong common-sense presumptions about underlying nature. This (still very speculative) hypothesis might account for the historical fact that scientific essentialism was initially and primarily geared to the organic realm and then, derivatively, to the inorganic realm. It would also seem to accord with ontogenetic findings (reported in the next section) that children acquire appreciation of the inductive limits and allowable metamorphoses of biological kinds before becoming correspondingly competent judges of the underlying natures of substances.

Thus, it may be that weak or tentative popular intuition about the structure of a rather heterogeneous domain (if a domain it is) of physical and chemical substances succumbs to deep scientific knowledge about their underlying natures and theoretical unity. But if so, the argument hardly goes through for the biological domain. In that domain, strong popular intuitions about the underlying natures of living kinds may endure whatever science says, and biology itself may dispense with fixing natural kinds – or at least their presumed underlying natures – altogether. In other words, a strong common-sense intuition of biological kinds works against any general pattern of deference to the scientist on the matter of natural kinds. Indeed, continued reference in scientific discourse to species *as if* they were law-abiding natural kinds indicates just how strong may be *the scientist's deference* to common sense in the matter of biological kinds.

3.5 KINDS OF NATURAL KINDS

Interpretations of recent experiments in developmental psychology tend to deny that young children spontaneously attribute underlying natures to all and only living things (Carey 1985a, Keil 1986, Gelman 1988). Rather, the claim is that youngsters gradually come to make attributions of underlying natures to all (but not necessarily only) living things as they become exposed to increasingly sophisticated notions of empirical theory formation, that is, as a result of (formal or informal) instruction in matters that draw upon scientific theories (through schooling, nature programs on television, etc.). Before children learn to embed empirical concepts in theories, they supposedly treat living kinds in much the same way as they treat artifacts. This view generally accords with the cognitive claims of causal theory in suggesting childrens' progressive awareness and deference to science in their ordinary use of empirical terms and concepts.

More specifically, Keil concludes that preschoolers do not treat the terms for biological kinds – or those for nonartifactual substances – as natural-kind terms. This is presumably why, for example, younger kids believe a skunk made to look like a raccoon really is a raccoon. Thus, "while we may initially become acquainted with various natural domains through the most characteristic [i.e. prototypical] properties of their instances, we move beyond such representations to an increasingly rich causal structure that tells us how and why a thing came into being" (Keil 1986:151). Carey suggests that because the natural laws connecting different appearances to the same underlying reality are not immediately obvious, and must be learned through exposure to some sort of scientific instruction, young children cannot appreciate the deeper causal unity underlying the existence of plant and animal kinds. For example, "6-year-old children taught that dogs and flowers have golgi [an invented property] widely attributed golgi to inanimate objects"; that is, *living thing did not constrain induction*" (Carey 1985a:155). In a similar vein, Gelman argues that preschoolers fail to realize that natural kinds afford richer causal explanations than artifacts to account for differences between appearance and underlying reality. For both artifacts and natural kinds, then, the youngsters "draw inferences concerning internal parts and function equally often": "To 4-year-olds, two apples are no more likely to have the same internal parts than a golfball and a football" (Gelman 1988:91).

These studies, I believe, are vitiated by two general problems (although these problems are not both equally represented in the authors cited). The first concerns the (by now familiar) confusion between plant kinds *per se* and those "artifacts" of plant origin that are categorized by the social functions they serve, such as vegetables, fruits and flowers. This confusion tends to obscure the differences between how young children treat artifacts and how they treat living kinds; although the investigators do acknowledge that even the youngest children categorically distinguish artifacts – as being consequences of human intentions – from things which are not.

The second problem involves the unanalyzed assumption that there is a general class of "natural-kind" terms and concepts that ordinarily includes animals and plants as well as chemical and physical substances. The notion of "natural kind" used in the cognitive literature is ambiguous. Sometimes it is used to refer to any concept that supports lawful empirical generalizations of the sort scientists are concerned with. Sometimes "natural kind" is taken to denote all natural things commonly judged to possess underlying essences. Conflating these two uses, however, forces a convergence between science and common sense, between ordinary understanding of living things and ordinary understanding of inorganic substances, and between scientific elaborations of these ordinary appreciations.

The term "natural kind" is most frequently used in the cognitive literature to refer to those "basic-level categories of naturally occurring objects" (Gelman 1988:69) which "scientific disciplines evolve to study" (Carey 1985a:171). Flowers and fruits, then, would not be natural kinds. Certainly ordinary ideas – especially children's ideas – of FRUIT are not made in conjunction with FLOWER, as in the botanical concept of FRUCTIFICATION. Rather, FLOWER, FRUIT and VEGETABLE are ordinarily assimilated to social functions (see section 3.2 above). Apples are not, as Gelman suggests, kinds of fruit, and flowers are not, as Carey implies, kinds of plants – at least in the way, say, that pines are kinds of trees and kinds of plants (cf. Wierzbicka 1984, 1985 – although she nevertheless believes flowers are kinds of plants but trees are not).

Thus, although preschoolers may experience the same sorts of difficulties in imposing consistent hierarchical relations on fruits and flowers as they do on artifacts (cf. Rosch *et al.* 1976), they appear to be much better at biological taxonomies. Accordingly, even 3-year-olds are significantly better at both forming and labeling animal taxonomies than food hierarchies that include fruits (Waxman 1985). Indeed, by the age of 4 or 5 young Maya children consistently classify over 100 botanical kinds by taxonomic rank, excluding "pseudo-generic" flowers (Stross 1973).

Considered in this light, Gelman's finding that preschoolers are no more inclined to concern themselves with the internal structure of apples than they are with that of golfballs skews the evidence in favor of the claim that children initially lack presumptions about the underlying natures of living kinds. There is a similar problem with Carey's evidence against there being a distinct ontological category of LIVING KIND before the age of nine or ten. What her experiments seem to show is the following: (i) given new knowledge of an unknown property of flowers, young children "were not inclined to consider either animals or inanimate objects relevantly similar to flowers" (1985a:152); (ii) given knowledge that an animal and flower had the property, there was no more likelihood of young children attributing that property to only living kinds than to inanimate objects as well (155); and (iii) young children have "a great difficulty in rationalizing the inclusion of an animal and a plant into a single category" (158). Concerning (i) and (ii), note that flower was the only representative of the category PLANT.[24] As for (iii), it may well be that young children are unable to *rationalize* the grouping of plants and animals in a single category, but this does not imply that they cannot include them in one.

Carey's findings do suggest that the "naive biology" of the animal domain is initially a prototypically based extension of the child's "naive psychology" about why people organically function the way they do (e.g. an animal eats because food "makes him strong" and "he likes it"). But how comes it that children ever acquire a sensibility to instruction that eventually limits the biological extension of naive psychology to *just* plants and animals? Suppose the plausible candidates for (innate) *a priori* constraints on conceptual acquisition in the biological domain are restricted to a "naive psychology" and perhaps the induction-limiting category ANIMAL, but not LIVING KIND: how, then, is a biology – naive or otherwise – that further extends to all and only plants even conceivable? It seems more plausible that people's knowledge of the biological domain becomes "theory-driven" because they entertain prior presumptions about underlying organic natures rather than the other way around. This would accord with anthropological data that tend to show the universal presence of similarly structured plant and animal taxonomies even in the absence of any evidence for a totalizing organic theory.

Still, the findings that indicate the progressive transfer of biological properties from HUMANS to ANIMALS to PLANTS have to be accounted for. Suppose, as Gelman *et al.* (1983) suggest, children initially distinguish HUMANS and ANIMALS within the superordinate ontological category ANIMATE OBJECTS. Suppose also, in line with Keil (1979), that children possess an overriding ontological category LIVING THINGS that includes the subordinate categories ANIMALS and PLANTS.

Suppose further, with Carey, that theories are geared to integrating domains of knowledge. Now, these suppositions (and the empirical findings that underscore them) might also support the following scenario:

Because HUMANS and ANIMALS are adjacent ontological domains, as it were, then one might expect children to initially borrow from their knowledge of HUMANS to begin to organize and merge their knowledge of ANIMALS and PLANTS. So, although children may initially entertain only presumptions, rather than knowledge, of the underlying natures of animals and plants, they could use their knowledge of human biology (cum psychology) to begin the process of organizing and merging their knowledge of animal and plant natures. Conversely, children might initially borrow from their presumptions of the underlying natures of living things in order to better organize their knowledge of HUMANS and merge this knowledge with that of other LIVING THINGS. This scenario would accord with the apparent fact that whereas 3-year-olds do not seem to categorize humans along racial lines, by the age of 5, children presume that the morphological differences signaled by their society correspond to essential underlying differences between human groups (Hirschfeld 1988); Hirschfeld and Denhiére unpublished data). More will be said shortly about this – admittedly quite conjectural – process of domain integration. For the moment, let us return to the implicit claim that people ordinarily attribute an underlying nature to a species only when it is conceived as a biological essence embedded in a general theory of living things.

According to Keil, people come to attribute underlying natures to empirical kinds to the extent that such kinds become embedded in causal theories. But in non-Western societies, we are told, "the causal structure underlying natural kinds" may be very different from that of modern science (1986:146). Thus, following Keil's experimental protocols, Jeyifous (1985) found that, among the Yoruba of Nigeria, people come (at different times depending on expertise) to judge that a sheep which has acquired all the prototypical features of a goat is still a sheep. A Yoruba subject may justify this judgment not by notions of descent or reproduction but by a sort of "metaphysical logic," by which the subject "might discuss how the two animals were created by different gods in certain ways and how such origins override simple changes in characteristic features" (Keil 1986:146). By appealing to such "elaborate causal theories," then, the Yoruba are able "to override what Horton [1967] calls 'common sense', which closely resembles knowledge based on characteristic features."

Now, this domain-general notion of "common sense," which is based exclusively on characteristic associations among phenomenal features, is as implausible as the cross-cultural notion of scientific "theory" proffered by Keil (and Horton). Creation myths, magical incantations and other forms of symbolism, or "metaphysical logic" are no more necessary to Yoruba comprehension of species *qua* species than they are to our own. To call such symbolic speculations "theory" or "science" and to make them the fount of original conceptions about "natural kinds" is to deprive notions of scientific theory and natural kind of virtually all significance (see sections 9.1 and 9.2 below).

What the experimental evidence does indicate is that young Yoruba, like young Americans, do not initially elaborate a conception of underlying nature that is invariant under morphological transformation, or a causal theory that integrates all specific natures into an overall view of biological Nature. But this does not mean they do not believe all living kinds have underlying natures, or that all living kinds are ranked into taxonomies. Even adults may be disinclined to allow knowledge of underlying biological nature to completely override morphological concerns because of the strong common-sense presumption that underlying natures normally produce recognizable organic types. The Rofaifo of New Guinea, for example, clearly conceive of species as essential kinds (Dwyer 1976a) but may refrain from grouping together morphologically dissimilar organisms with divergent ecological proclivities, even when reproductive ties are known (Dwyer 1976b).

Like symbolic speculation in other societies, Yoruba "theory" consists of open-textured evocations that neither consistently nor exclusively apply to all and only living kinds. It can thus hardly account for the essential kindhood and taxonomic unity of organic species in Yoruba thought. Yoruba symbolism may indeed be invoked to elaborate upon living kinds and to extend the notion of essential kindhood beyond the biological domain, but this constitutes no evidence that Yoruba come to conceive of species as essences only by embedding them in causal theories – much less in symbolic speculations.

With this in mind, consider another anthropological claim concerning the allegedly indissociable relationship between conceptions of "material essence" and "theories" of "causality" in traditional West Futunan (Vanuatu, Polynesia). Keller and Lehman (1988) argue that the semantic representations associated with the theory-embedded concepts of material essence, or *hkano*, presuppose "culture-specific cosmological assumptions." *Hkano*, it seems, can only be defined with respect to an "elaborate" and "formal theory" wherein it functions with other "causally related" concepts like *ata*, or "efficacious image," as "theorems" in a "larger encyclopedic theory of the world":

EFFICACIOUS IMAGE is something that shares recognized perceptible attributes with the typical representation of a culturally significant thing having a MATERIAL ESSENCE. The shared perceptible attributes creating a link between a *hkano* and its *ata* indicate an intrinsic sympathetic connection between the MATERIAL ESSENCE and its EFFICACIOUS IMAGE. By virtue of this connection, magical performances involving the EFFICACIOUS IMAGE can produce effects in the thing itself. Significantly, but not exclusively, EFFICACIOUS IMAGES are recognized in rock formations.

Because the West Futunan "theory" of MATERIAL ESSENCE employs culturally parochial elements, as any symbolic speculation does, the empirical "domain" to which it applies is neither "basic" nor "universal" in the sense, say, that the domain of focal colors is. It is "constructed" rather than given "*a priori*":

the case exemplified may be the principles of life or resemblance and its significance . . . . A domain need not be universally defined in any obvious way; the one in question is unlike "animal", "plant" or color in this sense.

Note, however, that the "typical" or "default" sense of *hkano* refers to living things: "MATERIAL ESSENCE is the obvious, basic component of culturally significant, perceptible, typically (in a 'default' sense) living kinds of things such as pigs, coconuts and people but also including speech, song, canoes and playing cards."

In this respect, the "theory" in which *hkano* is embedded closely resembles the Medieval Doctrine of Signatures with its hermeneutical notion of "essence." But, as we shall see in a later chapter, the Doctrine of Signatures hardly comes to a theory that is consistent in reasoning or application, and the hermeneutical connections between "essence" and "appearance" are no more causally related than are *hkano* and *ata* (see section 9.3 below). Indeed, Keller and Lehman concede that "the features themselves of the two categories bear no necessary or predictable relation to one another save for the fact that they must not be the same." In brief, the theory of causality purported to underlie notions of MATERIAL ESSENCE is neither consequent in its "logic" nor in its empirical uses. Neither is such "theory" necessary to these Polynesian islanders' taxonomic conceptions of all and only plant and animal species as *ne mauri* or LIVING THINGS (cf. Dougherty 1983).

It may well be true that science does develop, in the first instance, by embedding and connecting concepts of material essences in empirical theories to support lawful inductions across a domain. But the notion of "natural kind" as often understood by cognitive psychologists – namely, as a theory-embedded essence – masks the fact that empirical theories and material essences do not always go together: physical chemistry may have both theories and essences, but evolutionary biology appears to have only theories, and folkbiology seems able to get by with just essences.

Upon closer examination, the increasingly popular claim among cognitive psychologists, that natural-kind concepts only emerge as theory-embedded concepts, turns out to be trivially true or likely false. On the one hand, if natural-kinds terms are conceived as terms that state lawful inductive gene-rations, then it is trivially true that understanding such terms depends on our ability to form theories that support such generalizations. But contrary to the ordinary language domain of taxonomically arrayed folkbiological kinds, there is no theoretically unified biological domain to which this generalized notion of "natural kind" applies. In science, lawful generalizations may be stated with reference to such diverse "natural kinds" as the species category (e.g. "phyletic lines are composed of successive species"), a particular species taxon (e.g. "*Homo sapiens* has 48 chromosomes"), taxa that are not strictly (mono)phyletic ("fish have three-chambered hearts"), ecological kinds that cut across evolutionary taxa completely (e.g. "trees have adaptations to compete for sunlight"), and so forth. Exposure to such rather diverse theoretical notions, then, could hardly be expected to account for the taxonomic unity of popularly conceived animal and plant kinds. Too strong a pull by biological theory on everyday thought would only undermine the basic conceptual framework for establishing empirical relationships among folkbiological kinds.

On the other hand, if natural kinds are considered in terms of underlying natures or essences, then it is false to claim that the more we know theory the more we come to consider (folk)biological kinds essentially. In fact, the more we come to know science, the *less* we are likely to consider species and other biological kinds as having underlying natures: evolutionary theory teaches us that no taxon has a specifiable genetic composition that is unique to the taxon and that functions with lawful regularity in phylogenesis. Presumptive notions of biological species as essential kinds are pretheoretical, and while perhaps compatible with certain stages of theory development, they may cease to be conceived essentially at later stages. Again, popular conceptions of biological kinds do not, and could not, so strictly depend upon the sort of theory-driven conceptions found in modern science.

By contrast, consideration of physical and chemical substances as essential kinds may well depend on these empirical concepts becoming theory-embedded. Findings by Keil (1986:146), Gelman (1988:93) and Carey (Smith, Carey and Wiser 1985) indicate that a rich causal understanding of the underlying similarities and differences between kinds of substances develops later and at a slower pace than causal knowledge of living kinds. Perhaps this is related to the apparent fact that children initially distinguish ways of inferring the semantic features and physical properties of non–solid substances from ways of inferring the categorical attributes of solid substances (cf. Soja 1987). Possibly, people have to come to *learn how* to attribute essential kindhood to substances that span distinct ontological categories (e.g. ice and water) before they know what may count as a substantial essence, whereas people simply *presume* which are the essential living kinds.

The unexplored implication is that the idea of "underlying nature" undergoes theoretical elaboration by children first and foremost in regard to living kinds. Humans may have to be taught much more and longer about substances in order to comprehend them as "natural kinds" (either in the sense of essential kinds or kinds that simply imply lawful generalizations of some sort or other). Indeed, while there is ample cross–cultural evidence pointing to universal presumptions of "underlying nature" for living kinds, there is presently little evidence to show that people everywhere consistently treat physical and chemical substances as material essences with underlying physical natures. Although people everywhere do seem to categorically distinguish naturally occurring substances from artifacts and living kinds, the basic stock of substances (e.g. air, earth, fire, water) ranges widely across history (e.g. brimstone, lime, caloric) and across cultures in a way that basic notions of species or life-forms do not.

Let us return now to conjectures about domain integration. The anthropological evidence to date points to reasonably well-delimited domains of ANIMALS and PLANTS, which are both taxonomically structured into ranks (generic-specieme, life-form) according to universal presumptions of underlying nature. Other evidence already cited indicates the presence of such additional empirical domains as HUMANS, ARTIFACTS and, perhaps, SUBSTANCES. The internal structure of these other domains has been barely explored, and in the absence of detailed anthropological and psychological study into the cognitive structure of empirical domains any hypothesis about domain integration is hazardous. Moreover, since no interesting information-processing model for any domain has ever been proposed, no *psychological theory* of the ways cognitive domains are structured or integrated is presently in the offing. The following speculation, however, seems plausible given what little is known.[25] If anywhere near correct, it illustrates in an intriguing way some themes that are further elaborated in later chapters.

Human cognition, it appears, is handily eclectic. People tend to make use of whatever cognitive means they readily have at their disposal in order to make further sense of the world. The idea of underlying essence, which seems to be universally and spontaneously available to people for hierarchically classifying and understanding living kinds according to type, might be variously extended to other domains. For instance, apparent morphological distinctions between human groups are readily (but not necessarily) conceived as apparent morphological distinctions between animal species – that is, in accordance with presumptions about underlying physical natures. These presumptions underscore the establishment of social hierarchies and the tenacity of racism. Arguably, such presumptions have harmed humans in their dealings with one another. As Darwin remarks in his *Notebooks*: "Animals – whom we have made our slaves we do not like to consider our equals. – Do not slave holders wish to make the black man other kind? . . . to consider him as other animal – ."

But presumptions of underlying nature also seem to have benefited humans in their dealings with the world by helping to make the initially heterogeneous domain of physical and chemical sorts more manageable. Today, the concept of essential kind continues to play an active part in physics and chemistry (most notably through the periodic table and crystallography), whereas evolutionary biology no longer presumes that species (and *a fortiori* taxa of any other rank) have underlying natures of a definite sort or that the terms for species function as natural kind predicates in biological laws (cf. Hull 1987).

Plausibly, the more children are required – and people try – to come to grips with the world, the more they will attempt to integrate their knowledge of it. Yet, no necessary or inevitable pattern of domain-crossing appears when the basic cognitive disposition, to conceive of living kinds as material essences with underlying natures, is further elaborated and transfered to such "nearby" empirical domains as HUMANS and SUBSTANCES. To be sure, essences can be further extended to artifacts and even events (e.g. songs and storms), although most probably only in the sort of intermittent fashion prevalent in symbolism (myth, magic, religion, etc.).

Later, we will have occasion to distinguish such "first-order" cognitive dispositions to conceive of species essentially from "second-order" cognitive susceptibilities to further elaborate, transfer and integrate such conceptions (see especially section 9.2). For the present, simply note in line with Sperber (1985a:83) that first-order dispositions are "treated by the mind as true descriptions of the world just because they are so stored ... they are automatically tested for mutual consistency and in particular consistency with perceptual inputs." They tend not to be taught or learned, but spontaneously formed by the mind with a minimum of triggering experience from the environment.

Conceptions formed by such basic dispositions, such as the folktaxonomic idea of species, thus develop under strong logical and perceptual constraints. They convey highly specific, manifest knowledge about the everyday world, which is as rigidly circumscribed as it is empirically adequate and consistent. By contrast, second-order susceptibilities elaborate upon first-order representations of the world to produce concepts requiring "greater flexibility and weaker filtering mechanisms" (84). These second-order concepts tend to be less intuitively obvious, less domain-specific, less logically and perceptually constrained, more open to cultural variation and more dependent on instruction than first-order concepts. Their continued use in symbolic speculation, and in such pseudo-sciences as raciology, requires that they be – to some degree – vaguely applied, logically inscrutable and empirically opaque. By contrast, their creative use and ultimate adequacy in science depends upon eventually limiting their application in ways that are empirically and logically consequent. This will hopefully become more evident as we proceed to trace the cognitive history of the notion of species and other biological concepts in subsequent chapters.

The epistemological aim of lay taxonomy differs from that of scientific taxonomy. Both provide a classification that is a key to nature, but they have different presumptions about what that nature is. For folk, nature can never be completely "hidden," the presumption being that at least some of the typical features of a kind are necessary, rather than incidental, to its real nature.

It is debatable whether rival scientific theories are logically comparable (Popper 1963) or incommensurable (Kuhn 1962). But, whatever scientific epistemology is adopted, there is a methodological presupposition to the effect that science seeks to decompose and explain the known in terms of the unknown. Common sense distinguishes itself from science by aiming principally to maintain the familiar composition of the world and, if necessary, to assimilate the unknown to the known.

Science and common sense thus do not presuppose the same ontologies,[26] and their respective semantic frameworks deal, as it were, with "different" worlds. That science does not recognize sparrows or trees as evolutionary entities does not eliminate them from the ontology of everyday life, which layperson and scientist alike ordinarily adhere to. In this respect, science's failure to displace or influence folkbiological taxonomies does not result from the layperson's conceptual ignorance, obstinacy, lethargy or naivety. It owes rather to the fact that folk "automatically" come to systematic grips with the everyday world in ways that are substantially different from the scientist's relentless endeavor to understand the cosmos.

Folk, on the one hand, expect experts to scientifically deal with trees (and ecologists do), even though trees do not constitute a valid botanical taxon. On the other hand, scientists talk of species as natural kinds when they wish to educate other scientists or laymen about aspects of the species. Such behavior on the part of layfolk and scientists hardly substantiates the story of a unilineal causal connection between science and common sense. Rather, it reflects the varied and distinctive characters of common sense and science, and the intricate relations between them.[27]

Indeed, if it is true that biological species do not have underlying natures, and that the predicates denoting them do not enter into general laws, then any scientific treatment of biological species as "natural kinds" with determinate (genetic) natures would show that science is as much a hostage to the dictates of common sense as the other way around. The stubborn fiction that species are natural kinds allows layfolk to tie into science and scientists to log in to lay discourse; while persistence in treating trees as a natural kind allows us all to tap in to science so as to further our understanding of an obvious and compelling part of our natural ecology.

Although the relative autonomy of common-sense notions of living kinds is underscored by the fact that folk treat them essentially while biology does not, historically the difference wasn't always so clear cut. Until Darwin – and arguably still among some taxonomists today – scientific classifications shared a presumption with lay classifications that the constituent taxa are natural kinds with underlying natures.

But whereas for folk the primary interest has always been in determining and grouping species according to morphological aspect and ecological proclivity, natural history after Cesalpino and Linnaeus gradually came to focus on determining species' genealogically-related affinities. It was Aristotle, however, who first set the stage for the scientific breakaway by attempting to connect all species natures into one unified conception of Nature. Henceforth, natural history became the science of *theory*-embedded essences. By contrast, common-sense appreciation of species and their underlying natures has never been strictly governed by this epistemological principle of "all for one, and one for all."

Part I aimed to establish the cognitive autonomy of folkbiology, both with respect to other common-sense domains and with respect to modern systematics. The remaining parts are intended to show how and why a science of biological classification developed at all. Understanding the why and wherefore of science requires a comprehension of the nature of common sense and the steps required to transcend it – if only to throw away the ladder after having climbed it. The first step turns out to be a matter of Aristotelian essentials.

PART II

ARISTOTELIAN ESSENTIALS

Socrates: If I asked you what a bee really is, and you answered that there are many kinds of bees, what would you answer me if I asked you then: "Do you say there are many kinds of bees, differing from each other in being bees more or less? Or do they differ in some other respect, for example in size, beauty and so forth?" Tell me, how would you answer that question?

Menon: I should say that they are not different at all from one another in beehood.

Socrates: Suppose I went on to ask: "Tell me this, then – what do you say exactly is that in which they are all the same, and not different?" Could you answer anything to that?

Menon: Oh, yes.

(Plato, *Meno*)

4

ESSENCE AND ENVIRONMENT

Historians and philosophers of biology are, for the most part, in accord with the view that "essentialism" has been the principal source of sin in systematics, and the cause of centuries of stagnation. Many agree with Bertrand Russell's (1945:165) judgment of Aristotle, which seems to echo the warning against the pernicious Naphta of *Magic Mountain*: "His form is logic, but his essence is confusion" (Mann 1940:404). In contrast to the "scientific revolution" that began in the natural philosophy of the sixteenth century, natural history supposedly continued to wallow in what Popper has described as "the empty verbiage and barren scholasticism" of "the Aristotelian method of definition" (1950:206). Following Popper, for whom essentialism reflects a confusion of word meanings with an explanation of how their denotata actually came to be, Hull argues that: "The conflict between reality and theory was largely ignored by early taxonomists both because they did not understand the logic of Aristotelian definition very clearly and because even scientists have a way of not noticing what conflicts with their philosophical presuppositions" (1965:316; cf. Popper 1963:20).

It is not so much that later taxonomists did not understand what Aristotle had to *say* about definition, they just were not aware of the fact that Aristotle himself confounds words with things (i.e. the statement of the truth-conditions for the proper application of a term with a principled account of the existence of its referents). It is this intellectual myopia that is taken as "responsible for taxonomists retaining what is loosely called a static species concept, which in turn is responsible for species being divested of reality" (Hull 1965:316; cf. Hull 1985). This is supposedly so even though "the names of taxa cannot be defined in terms of essential characters without falsification on a scale which should have been evident even to the most critical investigator with only a limited knowledge of the organisms being classified." Indeed, Simpson (1961:36n.), in his brief history of systematics, goes so far as to warn the reader of Aristotle's pernicious effect on the mind: "I tend to agree with Roger Bacon that the study of Aristotle increases ignorance. Nevertheless, the founders of taxonomy were themselves students of Aristotle and Aquinas (among many others of that lineage) so that the subject is to some extent necessary for my purpose."[1]

Also citing Popper, Mayr contends that Aristotle, like Plato and "all essentialists," betrayed both common sense and the true course of science, by ignoring the obvious variations in nature for the sake of discovering "the hidden nature or Form or essences of things": "All these methodological essentialists also agreed with Plato in holding that those essences may be discovered and discerned with the help of intellectual intuition [i.e. analysis, logic]; that every essence has a name proper to it, the name after which the sensible thing is called" (Mayr 1969:66–67; cf. Popper 1950:34; Cain 1958:146).

Essentialism, then, is a philosophy of marked discontinuity. It is thus resistant to change both as a means of representation:

> Presented with the welter of diverse forms to be classified, a taxonomist can greatly simplify his task if he pretends that certain properties are "essential" for definition. (Hull 1965:316)

and in regard to what is represented:

> This philosophy, when applied to the classification of organic diversity, attempts to assign the variability of nature to a fixed number of basic types at various levels. It postulates that all members of a taxon reflect the same essential nature, or in other words that they conform to the same type. This is why the essentialist ideology is also referred to as typology. Variation, consequently, is considered by the typologist as trivial and irrelevant. The constancy of taxa and the sharpness of the gaps separating them tend to be exaggerated. (Mayr 1969:67)

For my part, I have so far failed to find any natural historian of significance who ever adhered to the strict version of essentialism so often attributed to Aristotle. Nor is any weaker version of the doctrine that has indiscriminately been imputed to Cesalpino, Ray, Tournefort, Linnaeus, A.-L. Jussieu and Cuvier likely to bear up under closer analysis. Most often, it is invoked against one's own rival school: the back pages of the technical journals are filled with pheneticists and phylogeneticists accusing one another of being reactionary throwbacks to an outworn tradition – their theoretical baggage filled with vestiges of statically contrived types and artificially fixed orders. In general, I think one should be wary of extending any of the familiar doctrines ending in

-ism over more than a limited number of generations; and even then the conventional suffix may reflect little else than stability in the grammatical function of a fluid and volatile composition of ill-tuned ideas.

Notwithstanding such tendentious use of history, contemporary arguments are frequently decided on strict scientific grounds, not by doctrinal allegiance. The case is otherwise for historical figures who may be remembered, or forgotten, only as "precursors" with regard to problems that currently agitate systematics; for the historical past often appears merely as an imperfect prelude to the modern present. The problems were there all the time, only they were viewed cockeyed through filters of traditional ignorance, prejudice and superstition.

Forgotten in this anachronistic and Procrustean view of history are the facts: the elaboration of the distinction between the biological species and genus, the advent of the family concept and, ultimately, the ascendancy of the notion of phylum. All of these developments, though, are embedded in the gradual and profound shift from common-sense understanding of local, everyday experience, to ever more reflective attempts to cope with worldwide novelty: from the layman's spontaneous treatment of what is rare and strange in the world in terms of the readily visible and familiar patterns of the phenomenal order of things, to the naturalist's progressive effort to deal with unceasing discovery by means of the hidden causes and nonphenomenal processes of biology.

To reduce all this to "two thousand years of stasis" is to nullify a monumental movement in human thought – a movement which, by the eighteenth century, was at least able to offer up the whole of the living world, including man, as an object of study and insight. For all intents and purposes, it was Aristotle who began this movement; although it was for others to carry it through in ways that he could scarcely have imagined. Such a movement was possible at all, however, only because access was assured by a common-sense appreciation of the living world shared not only by Aristotle and Linnaeus, but by ordinary folk everywhere.[2]

The principal task of Aristotelian philosophy and science, or metaphysics, is to determine the essential nature of common sense ontology so as to reveal these different pieces of the world as instances of, or more justly as teleological tendencies *to*, order and beauty. As a result, Aristotelian speculation goes beyond simple common sense; that is to say, those intuitively obvious aspects of common sense that are visibly manifest and iterated in ordinary language constitute necessary, but not sufficient, conditions for a determination of how the world is structured. Speculation aims to connect intuitively separate and dissimilar features of the everyday world (distinct relations, qualities and substances) into a harmoniously integrated universe. In it, each thing will be shown to have its proper place relative to every other in the economy of nature. Accordingly, the determination of essences involves a mixture of commonsensical and aesthetic criteria. Because such a determination is not strictly manifest, true natures are partially hidden from immediate, sensible intuition. The discovery of these partially invisible, essential truths is the goal of a properly "scientific" knowledge (*episteme*) of nature (*physis*).

Aristotle uses the term *physis* with systematic ambiguity. In its popular sense, the term refers to an inherent program for development that accounts for the morphotypic regularities of ordinary living kinds.[3] Being the philosopher he is, however, Aristotle also provides *physis* with a technical sense, namely, the principle of movement and rest in Nature. But the two senses are intimately connected: the philosophical conception of Nature writ large consists in the principled integration of those various particular natures presumed to underlie the everyday kinds of common sense.

In this respect, Aristotle's attempts to analyze world-structure differ significantly from the Presocratic physical philosophers (*physiologoi*). In their efforts to find a reality-principle that would unify the diverse phenomena of mind and body, and the various kinds of inanimate and animate objects, the Presocratic physiologers opted for a materialistic aetiology that effectively denied to each living kind (and to living kinds in general) their specific natures. Empedocles (*On Nature* fr.8), for example, held the common-sense presumption of such natures to reflect an unwarranted projection of ordinary language onto the ontological plane.

It seems justified, then, to insist that Aristotle's robust sense of experiential reality led him "to react against the excesses of idealism and restore the phenomenal world to something like its proper place in man's schematism of his experience . . . at last Aristotle redirected knowledge towards the common-sense world of our experience" (Kirk 1961 13–15). Still the problem remained for Aristotle, as for his predecessors, of unifying the apparent variety that common sense presents. This is the problem that articulates Aristotle's biological investigations – a problem that common sense alone cannot resolve.

The revelation of nature's underlying order proceeds by showing how, and why, the sundry common-sense kinds of phenomenal substance lawfully connect as true "natural kinds." As Gaukroger (1978:95) notes: "Natural kinds are self-differentiating, but this does not mean that our everyday speech automatically exhibits these kinds: this is part of the reason why demonstration is needed." A taxonomy, or hierarchically ordered division (*diaeresis*), is the instrument (*organon*) that makes apparent the rationale (*logos*) inherent in the process to order and beauty. It displays the process as a *system* of definitions *per genus et differentiam* (*sive differentias*) beginning with the highest category (*genus summum*), and ending with the last species (*infimae species*).

If this procedure is to count as demonstrative proof, it is necessary to know all the species that fall under the genus (*APr.* 68b27).[4] But this is not enough. The study of instances merely provides one with knowledge "that a thing is so" (the fact) but not yet "why a thing is so" (the understood fact) (*APo.* 99b–100b). To know why a thing is so, is not only to know that it is, but also from whence it came, how it came, and because-of-what it came to be. Aristotle soon realized, however, that, at best, division can only *point to* these essential aspects of beings, but cannot *prove* they are essential (*APr.* 46a31–46b11; *APo* 91b14f.). In addition, he also tacitly acknowledged that there was no sure-fire method of "induction" (*epagoge*) for determining essential relations. For each field, or "genus," of science discovery of the right means of differentiation would be a matter of trial and error, although guided by an intuition (*nous*) of the general principles by which division of the field might be carried out (*de An.* I,1).

Moreover, by Book Z of the *Metaphysica* the purpose of definition by genus and species is to exhibit and determine the nature of material substances whose species and essence are quite clearly distinguished from one another. Essence *per se* is thus no longer a proper object of definition, at least for living kinds and all natural substances, because in such cases essences cannot be extracted from the matter upon which the generation of species depends: "for the objects of natural science, while distinguishable ideally from the matter in which they reside, are not actually separable; in Nature man generates man, but the process presupposes and takes place in natural material already organized by solar heat and so forth" (*Ph.* 194b10 f.; *Metaph.* 1036a24–9).

A major source of error in the interpretation of natural history is thus owing to a misleading analysis of Aristotle's theory of Logical Division that has been unduly influenced by the idealism of some of the Oxford scholars, most notably H. W. B. Joseph (1916). Such analyses tend to maintain that Aristotle accepts the parallelism between the division of geometrical forms and that of biological kinds *as a matter of observed fact* (cf. Ross 1949). But everything in Aristotle's biological works indicates this is not so.

Indeed, species are not necessarily either eternal or constant, insofar as they are subject to shifting material conditions that may enter into a determination of the optimal (i.e. species-typical) course of generation and growth. Thus, "certain animals became (*egeneto*) quadrupeds because their soul could not support their weight" (*PA* 686b1); for it was "inevitable" that "nature gave" to quadrupeds forelimbs, instead of hands and arms, so that they could be placed under the body for support. This does not mean that Aristotle holds a doctrine of "natural selection," but he does believe that those kinds which exist do so in virtue of their *materially* adapted nature. Since material conditions may change, so may the nature of adaptations.[5]

4.2 "INDUCTION"

Aristotelian speculation about the hierarchical nature of our diversely connected world begins with an inquiry into the general aspects of the ordinary Greek's everyday knowledge of the worldly things around him: of those self-evident sorts manifest in common parlance, and spontaneously accepted by most everyone. Thus, for any particular state of affairs, one might ask: What is it? What-like is it? What size is it? Where is it? How does it look? How does it lie? In what is it? etc. (cf. Ryle 1938). The set of terms that would provide sensible (not necessarily true) answers to these and other similar fundamental questions are said to belong to the same "category": "for example, animal and knowledge:

footed, winged, aquatic, two-footed, are differentia of animal, but none of these is a differentia of knowledge; one sort of knowledge does not differ from another by being two-footed" (*Cat.* 1b16). What can be sensibly said of animals cannot be sensibly said of knowledge, and vice versa, because animals and knowledge belong to different categories.

Thus, whatever can be truthfully said of one kind of animal can be sensibly predicated of all other kinds of animals, even if the predication is false (e.g. it makes sense to ask whether or not fish, quadrupeds, insects are winged even though most are not). But not everything that can be sensibly predicated of animals can be sensibly predicated of plants (e.g. it is literal – though perhaps not metaphorical – nonsense to ask whether animals have roots and leaves, or whether plants sleep and have babies). Still, there are predicates which can be sensibly applied to plants as well as animals, such as "live" and "die." This means that plants and animals, although they have different ontological status, nevertheless must belong to the same ontological category (one that can be described, in part, by the predicates that can sensibly be applied to both plants and animals). The categories, then, represent those ontological domains that sensibly share no predicates, and no manner of existence, with one another, such as substance, quality, quantity, place, time, etc.

The most important category in the Aristotelian scheme is that of substance (*ousia*), and "the actual Aristotelian substances are preeminently the biological objects, living things – which means, in practice, the higher animals, metazoans, the ones he could see" but also "higher plants, metaphytans" (Furth 1987:23). The contents of this category are not produced by *a priori* reasoning, but by an extractive use of common-sense intuitions. Here, one begins with the sensible *phainomena* of everyday experience, especially visible phenomena:

All men desire by nature to know. An indication of this is the delight we take in our senses; for even apart from their usefulness they are loved for themselves; and above all others the sense of sight .... The reason is that this, most of all the senses, makes us know and brings to light many differences between things. (*Metaph.* 980a21–27)

The primary objects of knowledge are those sensible things that *can* be named in ordinary speech. Although different languages might have different sounds for denoting things, the things denoted, as well as the thoughts that represent those things, are pretty much common to humankind: "now spoken sounds are symbols of affection in the soul, and written marks symbols of spoken sounds. But what these are in the first place signs of – affections of the soul – are the same for all; and what these affections are likenesses of – actual things – are also the same" (*Int.* 16a3).

Owing to our innate mental make-up, these things are represented to us first as sense impressions, then as memories (*APo.* 99b–100a). If the experience is sustained, a thing is named and represented in our minds as a nonmaterial form; that is, the sense organ receives the form of the object perceived without its matter. The sense organ, which always has the potential for actually assuming the forms of objects, thereby becomes the object. Thus, "knowledge that exists in actuality is identical with its object" (de An. III,5). In the limiting case (where there is no cause of change inherent in the object, as with artifacts) and at first sight the form (morphe) is simply the exterior morphological aspect (schema) of the object (Metaph. 999b16). This is the usual, Presocratic sense of the term eidos.[6]

The constituents of this initial level of analysis appear to correspond to what psychologists call "basic object" terms (cf. Rosch et al. 1976). Such terms apparently represent the initial referential groupings of very young children, the named groupings to which adults primarily assign objects and the first groupings to be assigned a lexical label in a given semantic (categorical) domain in the evolution of a language. The objects that fall under the extension of these terms seem to share gross perceptual and/or functional features. These terms presumably divide the world of objects into maximally distinguishable sets of entities, and constitute the most inclusive groupings for which a concrete image of a class of objects can be formed. In this sense dogs and chairs, for example, are more basic to the domains of living kinds and artifacts respectively, than, say, mammals (quadrupeds) or dalmations and furniture or high-chairs. In other words, basic-object terms represent the most intuitively accessible level of object categorization.[7]

From this basis one continues the analysis of substance upwards by "induction":

> there is a primitive universal in the mind (for though one perceives the particular, perception is of the universal – e.g. of man but not of Callias the man); again a stand is made in these, until what has no parts and is universal stands – e.g. such and such an animal stands, until animal does .... Thus it is clear that it is necessary for us to become familiar with the primitives by induction (epagoge), for perception too instills the universal in this way.
> (APo. 100a–b)

This process of induction, however, is not to be confused with enumerative induction or abstraction by omission of irrelevant content. It is, rather, "an intuition that will apprehend the [general] principles." In Aristotelian terms, it is that which makes predication possible (Granger 1976:161).

Peirce has dubbed this freely speculative inference by which one is led to intuit the general principle, "abduction." Abduction has a dual role of hypothesis and concept formation. With regard to hypothesis formation, it is meant to account for the plausibility of that mainstay of Aristotelian science, the syllogism (Apr. 68b15–37). It is an intuitive inference from a given result of a possible deduction and a proposed general premise to the contingent (minor) premise of the syllogism:

> The form of inference, therefore, is this: The surprising fact, C, is observed; But if A were true, C would be a matter of course. Hence, there

is reason to suspect that A is true. Thus, A cannot be abductively inferred, or if you prefer the expression, cannot be abductively conjectured until its entire content is already present in the premiss, "If A were true, C would follow as a matter of course."   (Peirce 1935,VI:522–528)

But *epagoge* must simultaneously furnish the conceptual universals that figure as possible constituents of hypotheses; that is, it must ultimately yield *definitions* that can then be used in syllogistic demonstrations. Of course, a definition of something, in terms of those properties that inhere essentially, necessarily and universally in that something, potentially involves a syllogism; however, such a definition is not in itself a demonstration. For example, a definition of "man" as a "rational being" supplies the terms of the universally quantified hypothetical: "for any x, whenever x is a man, then x is a rational being." This proposition can then be taken as the major premise of the syllogism whose middle term consists of the actual knowledge that "Socrates is a man," from whence the conclusion that "Socrates is, therefore, a rational being."

At first glance, Aristotelian abduction of conceptual universals seems to be no more than a means of tapping the layman's intuitions about his usual linguistic ontology. In this respect, psychologists have been able to show that even very young children recognize well-bounded ontological divisions of various levels of generality. These may be delimited in terms of predicate spanning (cf. Keil 1979, 1983) or by means of inductive projections; for example, if one is told that two unrelated animals possess some unknown property then one is likely to predict that all and only animals possess that property, and that, for example, even a worm is more likely to possess a "natural" property of humans than is a mechanical monkey (cf. Gelman *et al.* 1983; Carey 1985a). By way of such methods of testing ordinary intuitions one may eventually arrive at various ontologically distinct levels, or domains (e.g. animals versus plants, chemical substances versus artifacts, living kinds versus inorganic substances). Ultimately one may end up with the all-inclusive category of "things that may be thought about." This category, and each distinct sub-level, represent criteria of identity; for, without them, there is no way on earth to limit the otherwise limitless inductive possibilities for assessing similarities. They are fundamental regions of object-giving intuitions that are psychologically prior to, and necessary for, learning which objects go together in the world (see section 3.5 above,[8] especially note 25).

But for Aristotle common-sense awareness is not quite the world; criteria of cognitive identity are not actual modes of being. Only materially realizable substances are proper subjects of (ontological) predication; only the category of SUBSTANCE is existentially primary: "it is only of a concrete thing, as such, that one can speak of its 'coming to be' in the full sense of coming into existence" (*Ph.* 190a31 f.). Still, there is a close relationship between cognitive (psychological) and metaphysical (scientific) notions of what something is. The world as it really is proves to be intimately bound up with our ordinary ways of knowing things. For Aristotle, something cannot be identified as *being the same thing* simply by pointing to a certain spatio–temporal relation between two states of the same object, such as spatio–temporal continuity as with Kant. For two things to be states of the same object a necessary relation must hold among the phenomenally typical, or naturally realized, properties associated with the states of the object being referred to. There is no such thing as *being the same* without essentially being *the same such-and-such*. To know which object is being referred to is to know that it is such a thing; and to know that it is such a thing is to presume to know *why* – in virtue of what kind of thing – it is that the object in question has the recognizable states it does have.

Thus, to know what, for example, individual men are, is to know the species and genera into which these primary substances fall:

> It is by stating the species or the genus that we appropriately define any
> individual man; and we shall make our definition more exact by stating
> the former than by stating the latter. All other things that we state such as
> that he is white, that he runs, and so on, are irrelevant to the definition.
>
> (*Cat.* 2b31–36)

Unlike purely "accidental" non-substance attributes such as color, secondary substances are "in" no other individuals, species and genera. The secondary specific and generic substances can also be subjects of predication insofar as they represent aspects of existence; the genus ANIMAL, for instance, may be predicated of the species MAN (though not vice versa). But when species and genus are taken together *quâ* definition of mankind, then this definition of men is predicable only of individual men; only individuals are primary and ultimate subjects of predication.

There are also naturally realized, but nondefining, properties common to animals. These do not directly pertain to substance, and yet are not purely accidental. Among them are the readily visible parts (*moria*) of the morphotype (*eidos*) (e.g. feet, feathers, scales, tails, hair, etc.) (*PA* 645b5). Even though living kinds are initially distinguished by similarity of overall morphology, including similarity of these "essential accidents" (*PA* 644b7), such features cannot enter into the definition inasmuch they do not point to the causes of their presence in the organism (*PA* 645b14).[9]

Nonetheless, essential accidents play a crucial role in the process of forming scientific definitions, for two reasons.[10] First, they provide the principal means of access to the problem of underlying causes; for the common-sense awareness of pattern (*paradeigma*) – an awareness that makes no distinction between essential diagnostic and essential accident – is the most reliable indication that nature is being systematically organized. Such commonly perceived regularities of type are thus deemed "causal necessities." Second, explanation of essential accidents, once their causes have been discerned, is indispensable to a principled understanding of why the common-sense realism of ordinary humankind is valid.

Such understanding certifies that we need not hold to common sense merely on trust, nor need we fear that we mistake appearance for reality. The world we readily apprehend is, for good reason, the world that is: "an acquaintance with a thing's incidental properties greatly promotes an understanding of its essential nature; as we are best qualified to speak of a thing's essential nature when we are able to give an account of all or most of its properties as they are directly experienced" (de An. I,1).[11] Nevertheless, a grasp of the essential accidents of a being, although necessary, is not sufficient for an understanding of what, exactly, that being is (or is not); for, "the things that stand out as plain and obvious at first glance are confused mixtures, whose elements and initiating principles become known only on subsequent analysis" (Ph. 184a21–3).[12]

Such a causal analysis is at once material and logical. It is logical to the extent that the determination of form from the highest genus to the lowest species implies what Balme (1980:6) describes as a "progressive quantification of matter": "the movement from general to particular should not proceed by adding new differentiae but by determining more and more precisely the forms with which the division began" (e.g. motile, footed, bipedal). It is important to stress, however, that "quantification" refers only to an increasing specification of functional proportions rather than to a numeration of distinctions. Quantification ends when further differences (e.g. color and sex in the case of living kinds) split intuitively familiar natural kinds.

This determination is empirical to the extent that each quantification must correspond to a sensibly apparent, and constant, qualification of the last species. As A. C. Lloyd (1962:87) notes: "a differentia which is an essential property is to be distinguished from an accident by observation and experiment."[13] But constancy is not enough: the constant features must be logically, because causally, related. The fact that appendages of most animals come in symmetrical pairs is less significant than the fact that they are motile; for the former fact is true only in virtue of the latter fact (and not vice versa), which is essentially bound up with the search for food.

The essential diagnostic of a species of animal is a part of its typical, morphologically complete, and normally functioning adult state (acme), as that end state is the complete being (PA 641b31). It is the part that points to the cause of that, rather than some other, species' coming-into-being (genesis). It is the functional aspect of form to which the flow of movement and matter leading to a mature member of the species is directed by nature. All animal species must eat and defend themselves in order to develop, but it is owing to their distinct natures that species actualize the same animal matter, following the same animal "cause" (i.e. the need to eat and survive), in fundamentally different ways.

Epagoge, then, is required to do much more than simply yield de facto universals. It must not only factor out the natural properties from the purely accidental aspects of a being (e.g. getting wet or wilted), but also the truly essential from the natural incidents of the common-sense type. For example, it is because of its canines that the dog is able to hunt, eat, grow and mature to look and behave as a dog is expected to; and it is because it has canines, as essential parts of its nature, to tear its food and defend itself that it does not require the defensive horns of other animals nor the extra stomachs needed to complete mastication (*PA* II,2). All such induction-insight assumes (a) the self-evidence of common-sense intuitions from which diagnostics are to be extracted, and (b) the rational acceptance of diagnostics as necessary premises of syllogisms.

Ontological definition is thus not to be achieved through an analysis of the linguistic meaning of species terms, as Hull (1965:318) implies, that is "by properties connected conjunctively which are severally necessary and jointly sufficient." Aristotle is explicit on the point: "Definition is a unitary discourse, not by simple conjunction (*syndesmos*) . . . but by the essential unity of its object" (*Metaph.* H,6). Definition is thus meant to reveal those existence-determining principles (*archai*) responsible for the unitary career of an object, that is, for its identity through changes in space and time. Because any definition must reveal the generative principles responsible for the existence, or coming-into-being (*genesis*), of a thing it cannot be purely descriptive, but must carry existential import. In addition to the individuals and properties with which modern logic deals, there are also natural kinds whose relations to individuals are not the same as the relations between individuals and properties.

As Moravcsik (1975:635–6) aptly notes, there are two reasons why natural kinds cannot be defined in terms of necessary and sufficient nominal features: "on account of the Aristotelian instantiation requirements, but also on account of the naturalness conditions assumed by statements describing the nature and potentialities of species." For instance, a dog (normal, healthy, etc.) is an animal that has canines "by nature" (*physei*). It is the latter condition that also precludes defining natural kinds in terms of their token extensions. Thus, it could turn out that exemplars of dogs lack canines, although all dogs are "potentially" canine:[14] for "each inner principle makes always for the same goal of its own, if nothing interferes . . . if nothing hinders" (*Ph.* 199b15 f.). For Aristotle, this is fundamentally a principled rendition of the common-sense view of living kinds.

4.3 FORM AND MATTER

The Presocratic physiologers thought to resolve the problem of deviance between token and type (i.e. between experience and concept) by dissolving all underlying natures into a general Nature. Nature was ultimately to consist only of one or more of the material "elements" (earth, fire, air and water) together with their qualitative "potential" or "powers" (hot, cold, wet, dry) as *archai*. The atomist ideal was a structural explanation of wholes in terms of a small number of parts and properties. These simples would be common to all things but mixed differently in different things as "temporary modifications" (*pathos*) of elemental substance. Although in the *Phaedo* the young Socrates tells us that he was first seduced by this maneuver, he came to view it as an affront to reason and common sense.

To resolve the problem of the ontological relation between token and type, Socrates argues that material explanation will not do. Material happenstance cannot explain why it is that exemplars should conform to specific types, nor how and to what degree exemplars actually do so conform. To understand how and why exemplars are actually generated in accordance with their underlying natures is to grasp the teleological *aitia*, argues Socrates. For the Platonic Socrates, as for Aristotle, the presentation of *aitia* corresponds to those "because" clauses that answer *dia ti* questions of "how" and "why" things come to be as they are. Socrates says that although he has not found the teleological *aitia* responsible for genesis (including material development), he has found "formal" *aitia* that account for the fact that there is a type at all.

These formal *aitia*, or "Forms," are but projections of conceptual types onto the timeless and spatially unextended ontological plane. A Form is an immutable, incorporeal and eternal *eidos* that cannot be known by sense experience, but only by "recollection" (*anamnesis*). We do not recollect that we actually possess such forms in us; rather, we discover "in us" an innate appreciation of them. What we discover within ourselves is thus the characterization of the Form as a "namesake." Although these Forms are not themselves responsible for genesis (material existence), it is nevertheless the case that: "each of the Forms exists and it is in virtue of participating in them that other things are named after [these Forms]" (*Phaedo* 102A10–B2; cf. *Republic* VII, 507A). More precisely: For any true phenomenal characterization, P, of an exemplar, x, there exists a (homonymous) Form, P-ness, such that $P(x)$ is true if, and only if, x participates in P-ness.[15]

Although Plato thus reinstates the common sense notion of "natural kind" as an ontological entity with an underlying nature, his doctrine does not account for the mechanics of participation, that is, for natural causality.[16] There is no account of how tokens come to resemble one another "for the most part" and yet remain undeniably different. Moreover, Plato's belief that token exemplars are somehow less real than their corresponding Forms is plainly contrary to common-sense realism, because we really do experience them. Accordingly, in an effort to preserve common-sense realism and the Greek conception of ultimate unity, Aristotle is led to an explanation of the common-sense notion of natural causality for natural kinds that not only aspires to save the phenomena, but also to systematically account for the fact that in this world it is *for the sake of the best possible material advantage* that phenomena conform by nature to specific types under given circumstances.

Aristotle notices that the usual accounts, of why the regularities commonly perceived in the world are as they are, come in four modes of explanation: formal (*morphe*), material (*hyle*), efficient (*aition*) and final (*telos*). These four modes together are taken to be ontologically grounded in nature itself. The nature of the physical world, in general, and the natures of living kinds, in particular, are constituted of these four "causes" of things being the way they are. Perceived regularities thus become "causal necessities" that exist "by nature"; that is, the nature of a thing shapes the outcomes of actions on and by it in lawful, patterned ways. A nature is the initiating (*archai*) and determining (*aitia*) principle of change, of becoming.

In effect, the constituents of a nature can be reduced to two – the form-of something and the matter-for something – because a nature considered as a composite of form and matter implies also a means of forming matter and a result. In the sublunary realm, including the world of living kinds, there can be no absolute distinction between matter (without any of the intelligibility of form) and (disembodied) form. In the living world, therefore, the form constituent of a nature has a material aspect expressed only as a potentiality for form that requires an appropriate material susceptible to being formed. Only the individual organism has a nature properly speaking, as it alone actually achieves a form by and according to nature.

The form an individual does achieve is a form which, in the end, comes to be for the sake of "an irreducible potential for form" transmitted via the male parent's semen (cf. Gotthelf 1976).[17] But the realization of that potential for form also depends upon the menses supplied by the female parent. The active motion imparted by the semen agitates the passive female matter in order to produce an organism, one in form with the male parent. However, insofar as the female matter itself has a (secondary) formal aspect that enters into the direction of the course of development, the offspring is never an exact replica of the sire, hence it can never be the result of fully actualized (primary) form. It can, however, be formed, not perfectly, but in accordance with its nature considered as an internalized pair of active male and passive female potentials. In other words, the male semen acts on the female menses in such a manner as to produce an organism, one in form with both parents. But what does it mean to be one in form with both parents? This can only be understood by adverting to the species-specific nature of individuals, considered as the grounds of those causal regularities of a type that implicates a whole *domain* of male form-potentials together with the materially *compatible range* of female potentials. To have the structure, nature or essence of, say, man is to have an internalized potential-pair that falls within the plane of humanly compatible male–female potentials.[18]

Whether or not an individual of the species will, or even can, manifest its species-typical properties, however, does not depend on active male and passive female potentials alone. It also depends upon the intrusive element-potentials of the environment. The condition of having a certain causal nature does not bring about the realization of the potential without some action somewhere in the circumstances: not just any action in the circumstances, but one that has the realization of the potential as a result. Only when the "right" circumstances exist that are conducive to the attainment of species-typical form can the individual be said to realize its species-typical form "by nature."

Specific regularities emerge via a characteristic process of *genesis* – of coming-into-being – that implicates an appropriate set of element-potentials in addition to the compatible sets of male and female potentials. As for the species itself, it is not an essence or a form *per se* but a universal mix of matter and form that has no actual existence besides, apart from, or prior to, the individuals of which it is composed. The defining properties of the species (and therefore of individuals of the species), as well as the merely species-typical but natural properties, are realized "according to nature" only "for the most part."

Although the characteristic attributes of both eternal and sublunary kinds are necessary, they are necessary in different ways. In both cases, the full complement of characteristic attributes include the essential attributes as well as those derivative attributes that naturally accompany the essential attributes as "proper" consequences that follow from the intrinsic nature of a thing.[19] But for mathematical eternals, necessity is absolute and cannot be otherwise (*Metaph.* 1015b7,1026b7), while for natural kinds necessity is merely hypothetical and follows only "for the most part" (*Metaph.* 1027a f.).[20] In other words, necessity is conditional upon the end state actually coming about. Thus, on the hypothesis that the mature organism (*acme*) will fully develop, then what is anatomically and morphologically typical of, and proper to, that species of organism will fully come about only because the "best possible" end state has come about. There is no guarantee that the best possible end state will be achieved in fact, but under normal circumstances it generally does tend to come about according to the organism's own "potential" (*dynamis*) and "in accordance with nature" (*kata physin*) (*GA* 731b20 f.; *Ph.* 199b15 f.).[21]

Aristotle's essentialism effectively boils down to an acceptance of common-sense animal universals as "natural" and "for the better." Given the pre-theoretical array of basically distinct kinds in the local environment, Aristotle seeks to understand what is good in their continuance over time, their diversity and ultimate connectedness in nature's overall plan. Since all life is perishable, continuance can only be renewal – a constant coming-into-being. The renewal of any particular kind is conditional upon three factors: the availability of the right sort of matter, the reliability of material forces, and the presence of a form-potential for combining matter in kind with the aid of material forces. The female menses (*katamenia*) is responsible for the first, the sun, wind, climate and available nutriments for the second, and the male seed for the third. The third factor is determinant (*aitia kai archai*) inasmuch as it conveys the life-giving soul.

The form-potential is invariably in the father's image; however, the actual form that is realized is always a "falling short" (*steresis*) of the father's likeness. Material happenstance (from insufficiency of coction in maternal matter to the heat of the South Wind) unavoidably deflects the unfolding of the causal process from its ideal course. By default, the offspring tends to resemble the more weakly determined form of one of its ancestors. If no individual form is dominant, "there remains only that which is common," namely, the species (*GA* 768b10). Because the determination of what, if any, individual form will dominate is partly a matter of material contingency or chance (*automaton*), only a species determination can be considered a naturally or normally occurring necessity.

At best, then, offspring can only be said to bear a species-likeness:

Creatures produce others of their kind, animals producing animals and plants producing plants, in order that they may share, so far as their several natures allow, in the eternal and divine. That is the ideal for which all creatures strive, and which determines their behavior, so far as their behavior is natural. But since mortal things cannot share continuously in the eternal and divine (because nothing that perishes can preserve its identity nor remain numerically one), they partake of eternity and divinity in the one way that is open to them, and with unequal success; achieving immortality not in themselves, but vicariously through their offspring, which, though distinct individuals, are one with them specifically (*eidei*).

(*de An.* 415a26–b1)

That is why there is always a kind (*genos*) – of men and of animals and of plants. (*GA* 731b25–732a2)

Because individuals cannot survive in number (as the same material entities), they strive to perpetuate themselves through sequences of ancestor-generating descendant. They persist by passing on their form, which is only more or less materially realized by their successors. The species arises as the product of this imperfect but causally sustained attempt at serial immortality. But there is no indication whatsoever that such a self-generating lineage is ever eternal or immutable in fact, only that organisms well-suited to stable environments naturally tend to breed true to form (cf. Lennox 1985).

The only "species" (*eide*) that Aristotle mentions as even approaching eternity are such subcategorical "genera" (*gene*) of substance as man, animal and plant. For Aristotle, species are not characterized by the genealogical progression of invariable forms from individual to individual. It is *not* the case that species exist "fixed and unchanging" (Lloyd 1968:88) "from all eternity . . . by the process of like generating like" (Sloan 1972:2). What seems to be eternal is the existence of (some) rational, sensate and vegetative souls. Also, natural genera are not defined by kinship *per se*. Rather, natural groups represent "best" adaptations given the joint constraints of inheritance and environment, but they are neither inevitable nor inexorable in God's eyes. Still, their diversity represents an optimal division of labor for the economy of nature, given the circumstances that do exist; and their connectedness, which enhances the beauty and intelligibility of nature, is for the everlasting good of God.

Even when viewed as a typical or normal pattern in nature, the Aristotelian species hardly entails accepting all variation as trivial or irrelevant. On the contrary, for Aristotle, the investigation of variation, or rather deviation, affords a means of ascertaining the extent and efficacy of nature's various causes. In fact, without such standardized referents the very idea of lawful variation would be inconceivable. Events are scientifically interesting only if they fall under laws; and they fall under laws of science by virtue of belonging to one natural kind or another. Monsters (*terata*), for instance, are notable inasmuch as they lack specific form. They are "amorphous" in the sense that they appear to combine two forms that should not ordinarily combine; however, they are comprehensible only to the extent that they fall under *some* kind or other, that is, only to the degree that they are recognized to belong to one of the higher genera (*GA* 769b11f.). To avow, as Aristotle does, that all creatures belong to some taxonomic *genos* is simply to maintain that any living nature has its place in Nature.

To locate the taxonomic position of an animal, then, is to be able to locate and study, systematically and factually, its material relationships with all other animals. True, taxonomy only exhibits material and formal cause; however, it presupposes the operation of efficient and final cause. Within a natural-kind taxonomy each generic level represents a kind of matter relative to the next, more specifically formed, level. Each more specific level, in turn, represents a transformation of generic matter, which is effected in accordance with nature's plan. In such a taxonomy actual substance pertains only to the last species (*atomon eidos*), since it alone divides into existing individuals. The process by which this transformation of amorphous matter into formed substance is effected is not exclusively the result of action upon the intrinsic properties of the generic matter, but of the interaction of these with other kinds of matter, such as the sun and the earth. Nature, being structured as it is, will always tend to transform a certain kind of matter in a specific way under given material circumstances. Taxonomy records the steps in this process by which particular natures are formed and materially joined in Nature. It implies, but neither demonstrates nor describes, the process itself.

The first order of business in the study of Nature involves an unambiguous theoretical determination of the material natures of intuitive species. In this way, Aristotelian science renders ontological primacy to what is psychologically basic. This construal of folk species, though, scarcely reflects an idealist strain in Aristotle's thought. Not only does he not allow idealization to encompass that which was not, or could not plausibly be expected to be, readily perceived (e.g. objects moving in the void, eternal species); but he limits all idealizations in the sublunary realm to probability only. The species is natural not because it is an eternally existing type. It is natural because it is the optimal morpho-behavioral career naturally available to an individual generated in the normal way, and raised in normal surroundings. Common-sense types are thus not to be mythically preserved at all costs despite the observation of individual variation. On the contrary, they may be accepted as real only to the extent that they make factual sense of such observations.

In this sense, teleology is not some intentional design brought in by analogy from elsewhere (e.g. purposeful human action). For Aristotle, it amounts to the best *material* hypothesis to account for the apparent regularity of the living world given the obtainable experience: "what he is saying is that there is a cybernetic control in biological processes over and above the simple actions of air earth fire and water, but still consisting only of their interactions within the complex" (Balme 1987c:285). Had others been able to demonstrate that the development of even the simplest part could be produced from a chance encounter of material elements (or even an externally forced experimental encounter), then Aristotle might well have embraced a materialistic aetiology without compromising his fundamental interest in locating the principles underlying the unity of nature. But to this day, no such demonstration exists.

Once one has listed the essential, teleological properties of species there is really nothing more for natural history to do. Since these universal aspects of individuals are the causes of everything else typical and knowable, to know them is thus to know all that science needs to know. Of course, knowledge does not lie in the mere listing of essential properties "without qualification, but relatively to the 'whole substantial nature' (*ousia*) of the thing in question" (*Ph.* 198b).

Such knowledge requires interlocking the properties of different natures within a hierarchical scheme of genus and differences: not only in order to furnish the terms for a syllogistic demonstration of the necessity of particular properties in specific individuals, but also to reveal the principles of unity underlying the diversity of ordinary phenomenal types. In other words, one must show how Nature produces natures: how it is that material forces and contingencies cause differences to appear in the divine wholeness of being.

This program represents the first try at a scientific taxonomy. But its importance is more than simply that of being a milestone in the history of science. For when divested of its outdated cosmic pretensions, this program contains much of enduring psychological – even epistemological – value about how reason and the world conspire to produce the common-sense vision of things.

In practice, Aristotelian systematics would involve a principled derivation of each basic-level generic-specieme, or *atomon eidos*, from a folk life-form, or *megiston genos*; and it would imply a method of combining by "analogy" (*analogian*) the various life-forms. This principled organization of "groups within groups" (*gene hup allela*) would thus represent the collection of folk kinds into an integrated notion of life. The next chapter looks into the mechanics and achievements of this program.

5

MATERIALS OF LOGICAL DIVISION

5.1 GENOS AND EIDOS

Given the pre-theoretical character of folkbiological taxonomy, Aristotle's problem of the reduction of habitual structures to their essential parts translates as the problem of reconciling the pre-theoretical divisional character of life-forms with the pre-theoretical relational character of basic kinds. Aristotle's solution was to superimpose one logical system – the contrastive hierarchy – upon another – the ranked taxonomy.

In pre-theoretical taxonomy each level, or rank, corresponds to a fixed level of reality. The *megista gene* apply to all and only life-forms, the *atomon eidos* to each and every basic kind: robin, cat, pike and gnat are all of the same rank (that of the *atomon eidos*), not because they stand in inclusion relations to the same *genos*, but because they partition reality in commensurable ways. In the logical division that applies to organ-systems (e.g. reproduction, digestion, locomotion) and their respective functional parts (e.g. testes, mouth, feet), however, *genos* and *eidos* do not represent fixed ranks corresponding to distinct levels of reality. Rather, any *genos* may be an *eidos* to some higher level *genos*. In such a scheme there are no fixed ranks, only relative levels of inclusion and contrast. Each *eidos* of a given *genos* must stand in "positive opposition" to every other *eidos* of that *genos*. Every functional part, then, is a "contrary" of another functional part at the same level of inclusion: e.g. fins, wings and feet are contrary functional parts of the organ-system of locomotion; split-winged and whole-winged are contraries of winged, etc. In order to determine the logical relationship between groups in a ranked taxonomy, though, no reference to inclusion or contrast is required, and the taxa compared may be disjoint: e.g. robin, gnat and bird stand in a definite relationship by virtue of their respective ranks, not by virtue of inclusion or contrariety.[1]

Although these two organizational schema are logically distinct,[2] their joint product yields an integral classification of the animal world. When the ranked taxonomy of life-forms and basic kinds is overlain by the grid of organ-systems and their functional parts, the result is simultaneously a ranking of all functional parts (by analogy, degree and identity) and a division of all phenomenal kinds (by means of a componential analysis of their vital parts). The disjoint kinds of common sense are thereby systematically "assembled" into life's functional manifold; and life's vital systems, in turn, are "differentiated" into viable kinds specifically adapted to the various exigencies of actual, material existence.[3] This, I believe, is not only the key to Aristotle's biology, but to much in his logical and metaphysical works as well.

In Part I we analyzed what appears to be a universal tendency of folkbiological classification to exhaustively partition the local flora and fauna into mutually exclusive basic types. Each type is readily distinguished from every other type at a glance according to its gestalt-like overall morphological aspect. Aristotle uses the term *atomon eidos* to refer to such basic-level folkbiological kinds, that is, to generic-speciemes.[4] It is the pretheoretical fact of a complete, relational series of well-bounded natural sorts that makes the common-sense living world the paradigm for Aristotelian science, and the prime candidate for a real division.

First, it fulfills the logical pre-condition on scientific explanation, namely, that *all* the species of a natural domain must be known for proper induction of the general principle (*APo.* 68b27). Second, it holds speculation to the epistemic constraint that one must "first take the appearances (*phainomena*) in respect to each kind, and only then go on to speak of their causes (*aitia*)" (*PA* 640a14). Third, it provides the prima facie evidence that the substantive requirement of natural science can be met: that it can be shown how and why "the *for-something's-sake* is present in the works of nature most of all, and the end for which they have been composed or have come to be occupies the place of the beautiful" (*PA* 645a24–26).

In the *Politica* (1266b16), Aristotle says that plants are for the sake of animals, and animals are for the sake of men. Consistent with scholastic and biblical tradition, the usual interpretation of the statement is that plants exist *for the purpose* of providing animals sustenance, and that animals, in turn, exist so as to provide food and service to men. Against this Balme (1972:96) argues:

Aristotle's comments on natural economy in fact refer ... not to a general economy of nature .... Aristotle means only that *A* is for the sake of *B* in the sense that *B* cannot happen without *A*. Man depends upon animals for food, and animals upon plants; if the latter were not present, the former could not be.

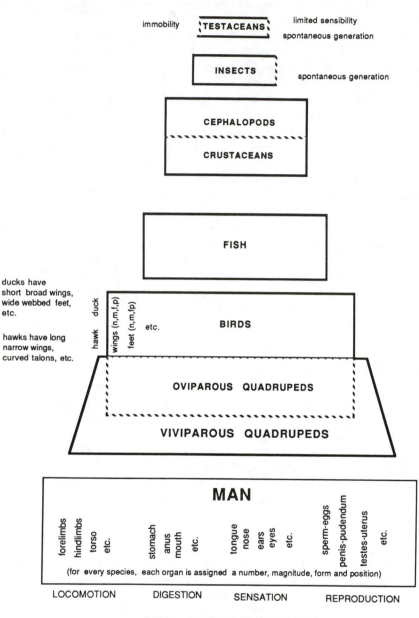

Figure 2
Schematic version of Aristotle's classification of animals

In other words, Aristotle's teleology implies no hypostasization of nature. Nonetheless, it is precisely the *pretheoretical* conception of a "general economy of nature" that provides the plausible grounds for such a teleology:

> In effect, the good of the army is in its ordered arrangement . . . . All things are ordered together somehow; but not in the same manner – fishes, birds, plants; and the world is not such that one thing has nothing to do with another, but they are connected: because everything is ordered with respect to a single end . . . all things must dissolve into their elements . . . by which all conspire to a harmony of the ensemble. (*Metaph.* 1075a)

In this conception, the living world appears as an integrated whole of interacting parts. Here no one kind exists solely for the sake of another, nor do all kinds come to be for the sake of man. This is the ordinary folk standpoint.

Take the rather typical case of the Pinatubo Negritos of the Philippines. Not only do they recognize hundreds of kinds of plants and animals, but they also have a detailed knowledge of the habits and behavior of each. The natives, it seems, classify animals and insects of no apparent benefit or danger because of their intimate connection with plant life. Conversely, there is also interest in plants that are of no direct use because of their significant links with the animal and insect world (Fox 1953:187–88).

Plants and animals thus seem to be classified in preliterate societies within a totalizing framework wherein the reciprocal roles of all readily perceptible plant and animal groupings in the economy of nature are appreciated. Bulmer (1974:12) refers this totalizing aspect of folkbiological classification to an "ecological" perspective:

> These continuities are particularly obvious where they occur in plants and animals which operate at an ecological scale approximately equivalent to that of man . . . a vast amount of apparently accurate knowledge is possessed about aspects of the integration of plant and animal communities – of the topographic, soil and climate conditions required by wild as well as cultivated plants, of the kinds of plants and their parts which provide food or refuge for different kinds of animals, of which animals prey upon other animals, and the role of birds and mammals in the propagation and dispersal of plants.

As a rule, the basic folk kind is an ecological species in that it is restricted to a particular niche. Its morphological constitution, as well as its courtship behavior, is usually well correlated with ecological strategies. But for folk generally, and Aristotle in particular, ecological strategy is the limiting material factor in the determination of kinds, and *not* reproduction of like from like. It is this circumstance that may well lie behind Aristotle's acceptance of the following account, and not any inclination to pay heed to fabulous stories: "One says that the proverb pertaining to Lybia, according to which Lybia always produces something new, owes to the animals of different families (*phyla*) uniting: as water is scarce, they meet in the small number of places that have sources, and they couple, even if they are not of the same species (*eidos*)" (*GA* 746b6–11; *HA* 606b19). Thus, unusual environmental circumstances may favor the creation of new kinds of animals, although once these kinds emerge they may then go on to reproduce themselves "naturally," that is, by "like being generated from like."

Consider, now, the "largest kinds" (*megista gene*): man and the viviparous quadrupeds, the oviparous quadrupeds and footless animals, birds, fish, cetacea (the sanguineous animals); cephalopods, crustacea, testacea, insects (the bloodless animals) (*HA* 490b7 f.). Elsewhere Aristotle implies that the listing of bloodless animals is complete (*PA* 523b1; *GA* 720b2). As for the sanguineous animals, although the groups mentioned include most vertebrate forms, there are those that are "intermediate" between these groups, such as the monkey and the bat. According to G. E. R. Lloyd (1961:73), these groupings are the product of a complex and novel way of distinguishing natural groups by multiple criteria of function and form. For anthropologists familiar with folk zoology, however, except for man and the bloodless groups, the *megista gene* are fundamentally no different from those major "life-forms" found in folkzoological classifications everywhere (cf. Brown 1979a). Aristotle himself emphasizes that "one should try to take the animals by kinds in the way already shown by popular distinction between *bird* and *fish* kind" (*PA* 643b11), inasmuch as they are "natural" (i.e. should not be split) and "rightly distinguished" (*PA* 642b10).[5]

It appears, then, that Leblond (1945:176n.116) is borne out in his claim that Aristotle "is inspired by common sense in choosing the largest genera." Leblond goes on to argue, however, that Aristotle's use of life-forms owes, in part, to his appreciation of "the complexity of reality" and, in part, to his "habitually conformist attitude." It is this latter factor that supposedly encouraged Aristotle's theoretical timidity and prevented him from offering a bold new approach to classification once he had rightly criticized the Platonist tendency to lose touch with reality (cf. Leblond 1939:295,298). Yet, there is hardly a trace of "conformism" in Aristotle's attitude towards common sense. Aristotle explicitly argues that common sense should be used only where manifestly correct (*PA* 644a16), and even then it is not, by itself, adequate to the task of the scientist (*Ph.* 184a21–3). Moreover, his introduction of man among the life-forms, and his elaboration of the invertebrate life-forms, represent profound alterations in traditional ways of apprehending living nature – changes whose effects continued to be vigorously debated (and with specific reference to Aristotle) by the likes of Linnaeus, Buffon, Lamarck and Cuvier. Solidly rooted in common sense but wholly novel in design, Aristotle's classificatory program appears a true successor to no other and a predecessor for all to come.[6]

Although Aristotle never completely abandons an anthropocentric telescoping of the animal kingdom, he does enhance the focus by analysis.[7] First, he includes man as an object along with the other animals.[8] In Aristotle's scheme, man is to serve as the standard of reference for a comparative functional morphology of the animal kingdom. The choice of man is justified, not only because man is "the best known" of the animals (*HA* 491a19), but because his functional morphology is the most "complex" (HA 539a4), "natural" (PA 656a10; IA 706a19, 706b9) and "perfected" overall (HA 608b4); however, not every acting limb or sensory organ need be, or is, most perfect.

In the main, then, the functions and parts of the other animals are less finished and apparent – this lack of perfectedness being marked by "small differences" in the progression of being that commences with man and ends with the bloodless testaceans (HA 588a19–b21). But it is a hierarchy that is far from being a regularly graduated ladder that can be consistently calibrated according to the number, diversity or power of the functional parts. For no part is uniquely bound to a function throughout the animal kingdom. For instance, the mouth of one kind of animal may be used for defense, but it need not be so used in another kind; and what one part lacks in function may be compensated for in another part, though not in any measurable way.

It would also be a mistake to view Aristotle as the precursor of Cuvier and the initiator of a general functional anatomy that compares animals to one another. For Aristotle, the animal is not fundamentally an agglomeration of functional systems per se (digestion, reproduction, respiration, circulation, etc.) as with Cuvier. Rather, it is a functioning morphological complex consisting of eyes, feet, stomachs, lungs, etc.: "The active and functional faculties reside in the non-uniform parts [i.e. not in the tissues but in the organs]: e.g. the mastication of food occurs in the mouth, and the faculty of locomotion in the feet, or wings, or parts analogous to these" (HA 489a27–30).

True, underlying functions are the ultimate causes, or ends, of life, in particular, and material nature, in general; however, it is the (mostly visible) organ and limbs (i.e. the non–uniform parts) that are primary units of analysis and classification. These organs and limbs are the immediate loci and direct instruments of the functions. The functions require the organs and limbs for their realization; just as the organs require (i.e. are the proximate ends of) the tissues (i.e. the uniform parts) while the tissues, in turn, proximately necessitate material elements (PA 646a12–b9). Morphological disposition is thus the highest positive sign of the underlying organization of a living kind and of the various functional relationships that link together all specific forms of life.

Nevertheless, Aristotle does provide at least the first comparative morphology that allows one to systematically compare other animals to man. Indeed, it is this systematic effort to exhaustively compare the structures and functions of other animals to man that led Aristotle to introduce the concept of analogy to unify all of life. Henceforth it would be possible not only to scrutinize the hitherto inscrutable invertebrates; even plants might be ultimately assimilable to the same systematic framework (PA 686b35, GA 717a21, 741b35; de An. II,1). The importance of this procedure for the development of natural history can hardly be overestimated, although its effects were intermittent for the better part of two thousand years. As late as the middle of the eighteenth century, Buffon felt compelled to defend Aristotle and insist that: "the first truth that comes out of a serious examination of nature, is a truth perhaps humiliating for man; it is that he must order himself with the class of animals" (1749,I:12).

It was Lamarck and Cuvier, however, who first grasped the systematic import of Aristotle's concluding remarks to the theoretical discussion of systematic zoology in *De partibus animalium* (645a16): "we must avoid a childish distaste for examining the less valued animals; for in all natural things there is something wonderful."[9] Although Swammerdam (1685) Réaumur (1734–1742) and other anatomists and morphologists had taken up the study of invertebrates,[10] there was to be no significant improvement in understanding their systematic diversity relative to the vertebrates before Lamarck and Cuvier. In the spirit of Aristotle, Lamarck (1809) believed that the study of invertebrates might yield "still more enlightenments" that could eventually lead to that "knowledge most important for arriving at the discovery of nature's laws and for determining its process (*marche*)."

The animal order would no longer simply be comprehended as a graduated attenuation of man's life functions to that murky near-vanishing point where insects and barely functioning crawling things lurk. To some extent, it would also be understood as a progressive ramification of the vitality of lowly creatures whose lives take on form and value in their own right. Eventually, working the animal order from both ends would unveil intervening biological organizations of different sorts, hence breaks in the one great scale of being. But it is only because the bugs were subjected to the same systematic scrutiny as man himself, that such advances were possible at all. In this, Aristotle is clearly the chief historical inspiration.

5.2 DIVISION AND ASSEMBLY

If commentators on the development of natural history tend to downplay the differences between Plato and Aristotle (cf. Lehman 1971), some classical scholars incline perhaps too greatly to Werner Jaeger's (1923/1948) thesis that Aristotle's biological works represent the maturation of his declining Platonism (Lloyd 1961), if not increasing empiricism (Bourgey 1955:124n). On G. E. R. Lloyd's account, for instance, Aristotle gradually proceeds in the *Organon* from an uncritical acceptance of Platonic division (*diaeresis*) to the more discretionary appreciation elaborated in the *Metaphysics*. The biological works then continue the process: beginning with a half-hearted attempt to use division in the *Historia animalium*, Aristotle goes on to criticize and abandon it in *De partibus animalium*, and eventually perfect his own method of classification by degrees of perfection of the offspring in *De generatione animalium*. To my mind, the claim that Aristotle *ever* rejected division is either ambiguous or false; nor is there compelling evidence to suggest that Aristotle ever held that classification by reproductive criteria alone was *sufficient*.

In Plato's *Phaedrus*, Socrates warns against those rhetoricians who would "make the same things appear to his hearers like and unlike." Instead, one ought to inquire into the "real nature of everything" by a "regular division." The proper execution of such a division involves two complementary processes: "first, the comprehension of scattered particulars in one idea"; second, "division into species according to their natural formation, where the joint is, not breaking any part as a bad carver might." Socrates then offers a very rudimentary sketch of dichotomous division, which is more fully elaborated in the *Sophistes* and *Politicus*. In the *Analytica priora* (46a–b), Aristotle argues contra the Platonists that division, as against syllogism, is powerless to demonstrate; nevertheless, syllogism combines those terms established by division. In the *Analytica posteriora* (91b), he further contends that division, which itself employs terms established by *epagoge*, while never apodictic is still the only method for exhibiting essence by definition that is known to be valid.

Taxonomic division, then, is the indispensable midwife for converting the universals extracted from common sense by *epagoge* into terms appropriate for syllogistic demonstration. For example, according to Aristotle we find:

> No animal that is polydactyl has horns. The reason is that the horn is only one means of defense and polydactyl animals have different means of defending themselves. To some [nature] has given claws, to others sharp teeth . . . .   (*PA* III,2)

Thus, if we are told of the discovery of a polydactyl animal, we can infer that it is hornless on the premise that all polydactyls are essentially hornless. We also infer, by inspecting the collateral terms of the taxonomic division, that members of the intermediate genus POLYDACTYL must have something in place of horns. Aristotle never had the least cause to alter this appreciation of division. Although he would come to reject the dichotomous division of Plato's later works, throughout his career he would continue to hold with his teacher in being "a great lover of these processes of division (*diaeresis*) and assembly (*synagoge*)" (*Phaedrus* 265C9 f.).[11]

The more usual view of Aristotle's forays into biological classification is that progressive concern with hard facts prohibited a unified division of the animal world that would necessarily dislocate natural (especially popular) groupings (cf. Daudin 1926a; Louis 1975). According to Larson (1971:24n.), for instance: "The result is not one system, but several, each with a set of 'essential' considerations, which, even when taken together, lack logical coherence." Much of the evidence for this position is gleaned from *Historia animalium I*. At first, Aristotle seems to follow some shallow dichotomies in the manner of Plato (e.g. animals may be aquatic or not; of the aquatic animals there are those that live by absorbing water and those that do not); but he goes on to show that such divisions are both incomplete (shellfish absorb neither air nor water) and cross-cutting (crabs walk like terrestrial animals).

The possibility of alternate dichotomies is apparent from Plato's own works. Thus, in the *Sophistes* (220A–B) Plato divides animals into those that "walk" and those that "swim," and the latter group are then subdivided into "winged" and "water-animals." In the *Politicus* (264D f.), though, animals are initially divided into those living on "land" and those living in "water," with the former subdivided into "winged" and "walking" animals. Plato's divisions, then, involve neither progressive nor exclusive differentiation. As Balme (1987b:71) notes: "Each form is added arbitrarily by intuition, and there is no order of priority nor hierarchy among them." By contrast, Aristotle insists that success- ive differentiation must ensure a final division that entails its predecessors and renders them "redundant" (*Metaph.* 1038a19; *APo.* 97a28).

Because the substantial unity of a living being is complex rather than simple, there can be no adequate dichotomous or polytomous division by one differentia at a time. Division by a single differentia, such as wild versus tame, often does not mark an essential aspect of natural kinds, that is, a part of the soul (*PA* 643a35). But even when essential aspects are involved, a single line of differentiation invariably splits natural kinds and leads to cross division (*PA* 642b10). For example, a division according to footed versus footless cannot be further subdivided without overlap in essential properties related to blood: some polypods are bloodless (centipedes) while some apods are red-blooded (e.g. snakes). Conversely, a division according to blood versus bloodless would leave some of the essential nature of animals related to locomotion on one side of the divide and some on the other.

If, however, one takes the popular divisions for granted, as between birds and fish, then it becomes evident that "each of these has been marked off by many differentiae, not dichotomously" (*PA* 643b12–13). It is clear from Aristotle's criticism of dichotomy, therefore, that one is compelled to offer alternate divisions *only if one assumes that division must proceed along a single dimension* (i.e. a single – dichotomous or polytomous – *fundamentum divisionis*). If, instead, one opts for a division along many dimensions simultaneously, by all differentia exhibited by the *definiendum*, then a *unique* classification may be both logically possible and empirically plausible.

What, then, of Aristotle's apparent suggestion in his logical and metaphysical works that division along a single *fundamentum* is the ideal means for achieving a proper definition?[12] A plausible explanation for the apparent "contradiction" in Aristotle's proposals for Logical Division is that he meant examples of division by one differentia at a time to be no more than merely illustrative of a novel logical technique, namely, division by *genos* and contrasting *eide*. This is not to say that Aristotle denied logical division to be the best, or only, means to achieve a proper understanding of natural kinds. It is only to suggest that division along a single *fundamentum*, rather than along multiple *fundamenta*, did not represent an important distinction for the purposes of illustrating a logical technique. In the biological works, though, the distinction would prove crucial.

Yet, even in the *Organon*, Aristotle clearly outlines the processes of division and assembly that will characterize classification in his biological works (*APo.* II,14):

> It is important to choose partitions and divisions. The method of selection consists of positing the genus that is common to all of the subjects studied: for example, if they are animals, then those which are the properties of all animals. Once this is achieved, next in turn is the first class [of subgenera]

remaining. One asks what are the necessary attributes that belong entirely to this class: for example, if it is the bird, then those which are the properties belonging to every bird; and so on down the line.

But Aristotle goes on to insist that analysis must not be restricted to "those things that have received a common name." Investigation should also take into consideration unlabelled groupings intermediate between life-forms and generic-speciemes, that is, covert fragmenta or *eide anonyma*:[13]

> For example, in the animals that have horns, we reveal as shared properties [of all horned animals] the fact of possessing a third stomach and only one row of teeth. The question which then poses itself is: of which species is the possession of horns an attribute? For one sees that it is by virtue of the fact of having horns that the properties in question belong to these animals.

Finally, there is another "method" of analysis, namely, by analogy:

> it is not possible, in effect, to find one and the same word to designate cuttle-bone, fish-bone and bone properly speaking; nevertheless, all these things possess properties that belong to them as if such things were of one and the same nature.

The object of a division, then, is to rigorously cut nature at its joints by carving the material *genos* into more precisely formed component *eide*. This is already implicit in the *Categoriae* (14b24). Thus, the animals may be divided into:

> beast and bird and fish – and none of them is prior or posterior; and things of this kind are thought to be simultaneous by nature. Each of these might itself be further divided into species (I mean beast and bird and fish); so there, too, those resulting from the same division of the same genus will be simultaneous by nature.

The *Metaphysica* (1054b27) further clarifies the matter: "Everything that differs, differs either according to the *genos* or according to the *eidos*: according to the *genos* when there is no common matter or generation from one to the other." Still, there are groupings that do seem to share something of nature, yet are not the same by *genos*; for example, birds, fish and sea mollusks all seem to have bone-like structures, even though these groupings correspond to different *gene*.[14]

Thus, although common sense is disposed to supply clear-cut groupings of animals (only some of which are named) that may be systematically analyzed in terms of the resemblances and differences of their readily visible parts, common sense does not obviously provide the means to systematically compare and contrast the largest groupings (*megista gene*), such as the quadrupeds, birds, fish, and the several invertebrate groups. That is why there is no *genos* including, say, birds and fish in "popular consciousness" (*hoi anthropoi*) (*PA*644a12–14). Even so, such groups evidently share a material nature, namely, animality. Aristotle's solution to the dilemma is implicit in the passage from the *Organon*: there must thus be "another way" to divide and assemble the natural realm than by *genos* and *eidos*, and that other way is *analogos*. This is not to say that division by analogy is a procedure that is logically distinct from division according to *genos* and *eidos*. Rather, analogy is the only way to *complete* a division by the analysis of structures not readily apparent. From a logical standpoint, groupings that differ as *megista gene* are but *eide* of ANIMAL, which is the same by analogy.

The *Historia animalium* (486a–b) makes even more explicit the notion of a complete division (3) that is to be established in accordance with common-sense classification at the basic (1) and life-form (2) levels:

1. With regard to animals, there are those which have all their parts mutually identical . . . specifically identical in form (*edei*) . . . .
2. When other parts are the same, but differ from one another by more or less, they belong to animals of the same *genos*. By *genos*, I mean, for example, bird or fish; because each is separated from the other by a difference according to *genos*, and there are many *eide* of fish and bird . . . .
3. There also exist animals whose parts are neither the same by *eide* nor by more or less, but by *analogian*.

Again, in *De partibus animalium* (644a19–22): "bird differs from bird by more or less or by degree (one is long-feathered, another is short-feathered), but fishes differ from bird by analogy (what is feather in one is scale in another)."

Analogy thus refers to functional equivalence in anatomically dissimilar parts; that is, morphologically dissimilar organs or limbs (and even blood, flesh or bone tissue) are judged analogous if they contribute, each in their own way, to maintain the same overall function in the life of the different animals to which those organs or limbs attach. Granted that certain organs or limbs may be less "perfect" than their analogs in realizing the life-sustaining functions: for example, the blood of the vertebrates is more perfected than the analogous liquid of the invertebrates; the reproductive apparatus of the viviparous quadrupeds is more perfected than the corresponding reproductive devices of all other creatures, and so forth. Still, nearly all animals possess all the basic life-sustaining functions, and are therefore morphologically and anatomically analogous.

The fact that certain groupings in *GA* seem to split ordinary kinds (e.g. fish and snakes are split into those that are oviparous and those that are ovoviviparous) does not imply the abandonment of common-sense kinds. All that is implied is that no single functional system, whether it be reproduction or locomotion, is enough to determine the underlying nature of ordinary kinds. Reproduction is only one factor in determining the actual existence of kinds; it is necessary but not sufficient.[15]

Accordingly, Aristotelian division would not only define each kind of organism that common sense makes apparent, but in so doing would systematically unify all kinds by defining (animal) *life* itself; for the soul just *is* the integrated product of its essential functions. This is the import of the oft ignored or misunderstood passage in the *Politica* (1290b25 f.):

> We should first have to answer the question "what is essential for every animal to have in order to live?" And among those essentials we should have to include some of the sense organs, the organs for digesting food, and for taking it into the body, e.g. mouth and stomach, and in addition to these, the organs of locomotion. If these were all that we had to consider, there would be variations in them (I mean several sorts of mouth, of stomach, of sense organs, and of locomotion), and the number of ways of combining these will necessarily make a number of different kinds of animals. For it is biologically impossible for one and the same species of animal to have different kinds of mouth or ears. So that when all possible combinations of these parts have been arrived at, they will comprise the species (*eide*) of animals, and the number of forms of animal life will be equal to the number of collocations of essential parts.

The first division of ANIMAL would thus include all and only those functional systems upon which animal life depends: nutrition, locomotion and sensation (*PA* 647a24). To this list could be added reproduction, although nutrition and reproduction really form one functional system (*de An.* II,4; *HA* 58913).

Each of these functional systems would then be analyzed in terms of its constituent organs, and the analogous character of each of these organs would be ascertained for each of the vertebrate and invertebrate *megista gene*. This is the task begun in *Historia animalium*. Within each of the *megista gene*, proportional differences of "more or less" in each vital organ would be analyzed for every one of the subordinate groupings of organisms. This is the process initiated in *De partibus animalium*.[16] If one considers that to each of the essential functional systems of animals corresponds a character-dimension, or *fundamentum*, then a logical division of animals is preserved by multiple differentiation. The organs (e.g. fins, wings, feet) comprising each system (e.g. locomotion) would thus correspond to essential divisions of the *fundamentum* that characterizes that system. Each species would then be delineated as the complex product of simultaneous, parallel divisions (i.e. with a specific kind of nutritional apparatus, and way of sensing, and manner of locomotion); that is, each species would be defined by multiple differentiae.

Take the *fundamentum* "organs of nutrition and digestion." According to Aristotle, there are nutritional-digestive organs that all animals share (*PA* 655b29) either by identity (*eidos*), degree or analogy (*HA* 589a13): the mouth (by which nutriments are introduced), the anus (by which residues are discharged) and the stomach (from which nutriments are absorbed into the body). The character of these organs are described for each of the *megista gene*. Thus, the quadrupeds, like man, have mouths with many teeth and a tongue, but "birds have for a mouth what one calls their beak" (*PA* III,1), while the cephalopods "have two teeth around that part which is called their mouth; and in this mouth there is a fleshy appendage in place of a tongue" (*PA* IV,5). Similar considerations apply to the other *fundamenta*.[17]

All other functional organs of animals are ultimately to be explained as being "for the sake of" these primary organs (*PA* 645b22). Once each of the *megista gene* is marked off by an analogous complex of vital organs, each organ of the complex can then be differentiated in parallel, and by degrees of "more or less," as one descends the hierarchy of subordinate kinds. For example, since all birds are winged, beaked and footed for locomotion and for obtaining nutriments, the hawk may be diagnosed as that kind of bird which has long and narrow wings, curved talons and a sharply hooked beak. By contrast, the duck – owing to its different mode of life in the water (*PA* 649b6–8) – can be diagnosed by a proportionately lesser and broader wing span, wide webbed feet and a flat bill. Division ends when all of the *infimae species* have been completely defined in this way (see Figure 2).

The essential telelogical differences that distinguish the functional parts of each generic-specieme within a life-form appear to be quantitative variations along a continuum of "more or less"; for example, beaks differ in being sharp and curved, straight, broad or long "according to the lives lived" (*PA* 693a11–23). But when the sum of these differences is taken for each species as a whole, the life-forms' several and necessary qualitatively distinct adaptations to the environment are expressed – for "nature makes organs relative to their function, not the function relative to the organ" (*PA* 694b12–15). In this way, division explains every difference of species and parts:

> The material used for lengthening legs in one species produces webbing between the toes in another. Taken individually and out of context, the organs of one species differ from another only in whether they have more or less length or breadth, hardness or softness, curvature or coarseness. Yet it is *also* true that each species possesses an organized set of adaptations, the best possible material for its specific *bios*.　　　　　　(Lennox 1980:342)

Such a division works because "nature does nothing in vain, but it acts always by seeking the best that is possible, so safeguarding the essence of each being and its particular end" (*IA* 708a9). Consequently, "we must recognize that if a small source is disturbed, many of the things after the source usually change with it" (*GA* 716b4–5). In this way "nature seeks out that which is adapted" (*HA* 615a25). It is, therefore, biologically impossible for one and the same species to have different kinds of mouth or ears. It is also biologically impossible for different species, living under different material conditions, to have the same kinds of mouth or ears; for nature always aims to realize that which is the best possible under given conditions. This is why each distinct kind of animal just *is* the uniquely integrated complex of its functional parts: birds of chase and prey, for instance, have keen sight, strong and large wings, thick legs, curved claws and a curved beak (*PA* III,1; IV,12).

Aristotle repeatedly emphasizes that such a division is *not* deductive, at least in the sense of yielding demonstrations. Furthermore, despite the aspect of implication that is at once formal (i.e. logical) and material (i.e. causal), it would be a mistake to view division as an inferential exercise meant to enable the number and kinds of last species to be *predicted*. Rather, division can succeed only if preceded, or accompanied, by a survey of each and every basic sort "like sparrow or crane and all" (*PA* 644a33–35). Division thus aims to reveal the essential natures of natural kinds that have been *independently* apprehended on the basis of overall morphological aspect and habits of life (*PA* I,4). It does this by reducing the habitual structures of pretheoretical kinds to essential parts, that is, by mentioning only those minimal aspects of overall morphology that serve to functionally distinguish each kind from every other kind.

Accordingly, Aristotle does not endeavor to deduce the basic kinds of the living world, only to order what was antecedently held by ordinary common sense. In this regard, he sharply differs from Linnaeus and the other classical systematists who would seek to tabulate the existence of unknown kinds (see section 7.4 below). True, there are important similarities between the method outlined in the *Politica* and *De partibus animalium* and Linnaeus' *Systema naturae*. In fact, Linnaeus would tacitly accept the method of multiple differentiation, at least for zoological classification; he would also insist, in keeping with Aristotle, that division ought not to violate common sense. But by shifting attention from, say, kinds of mouth to numbers of teeth, and effectively excluding consideration of stomachs and all internal organs, Linnaeus would show himself primarily interested in computing the natural order rather than in defining its cause.[18]

It is not that Aristotle rejects such an approach. He simply has no need of it. With only thirty or so exotic species to worry about, and less than 600 indigenous species to survey, his situation is fundamentally no different from that of local folk the world over (cf. Raven *et al.* 1971). In such a circumstance, there is no concern with reconciling the partial orders of many different local environments scattered over the various corners of the earth. There is, therefore, no warrant to systematically fill in the lacunae. Accordingly, Aristotle does not endeavor to predict a single, worldwide order in which all organisms, known and as yet unknown, would naturally fall into place.

Aristotle's reliance on folktaxonomy excused him from the dual necessity that would characterize post-Renaissance systematics: that of having to *build* a classificatory framework for species and *create* a taxonomic terminology for families and classes. He neither proposes a "top-down" system for deriving novel taxa as Linnaeus implies he does, nor a method for inductively constructing groupings of organisms from "the bottom up" as Buffon suggests he does. But this hardly substantiates the view that "there is no room at all for any animal taxonomy in the Aristotelian biological project" (Pellegrin 1987:313). Unfortunately, this view, which was first proposed and defended in Pellegrin's (1982) groundbreaking study of Aristotle's biology, seems well on its way to becoming the "standard view" among specialists in the field.

On this account, Aristotle's aim throughout is supposedly never a classification of all the groupings of animals. Rather, he seeks a definition of animal *nature*. Thus it is possible, even likely, that among the different kinds distinguished by common sense at any given level, there are overlappings of an essential nature. For example, among the viviparous quadrupeds the organs of defense are causally interrelated with those of digestion, yet these causal relations criss-cross species in various ways: fissipeds have no horns, but they have claws or teeth for defense; by contrast, animals with horns have no upper incisors and so need more stomachs to complete matiscation (*PA* 674a30); the camel, however, possesses neither horns nor upper incisors, but has a number of stomachs for digestion and a large size for defense (*PA* 663a1). In such cases, classification according to essential nature allows for no fixed series of taxonomic groupings between the generic-specieme and life-form levels. Spotty references to covert groupings that go unnamed in popular discourse allegedly only further demonstrate the "non-taxonomic nature" of Aristotle's enterprise (Lennox 1987:109).

Worse, neither does classification by essential functions and organs seem to preserve a constant level of taxonomic generality to which life-forms could refer. For example, among the *genos* "organs of defense" are such *eide* as hoofs, beaks, claws and horns (*PA* 655b2). The analogy *between* birds beaks and the horns of viviparous quadrupeds would thus correspond to the analogy of horns to hoofs *within* the viviparous quadrupeds. Similarly, the spines, bones and cartilage are said to indicate analogous relations *among* the fish (*PA* 653b35). Given the general lack of correspondence between taxonomic groupings and groupings by the functional nature of essential organs, it would thus seem useless to dwell on the definition and classification of kinds distinguished by common sense.

The fallacy in all of this lies with the presupposition that the common-sense kinds Aristotle's occasionally refers to were not organized to begin with, and that Aristotle forsook the attempt to organize them. It is a fallacy that owes to a general lack of awareness of folkbiology generally, and the pre-theoretical foundations of Aristotle's biology in particular. In fact, Aristotle believes a complete division of the kinds of common sense to be a necessary, if not sufficient, condition for a demonstrative understanding of the biological world.[19] The problem which he never solves, and whose resolution is a prerequisite to a complete division, involves a reduction of habitual structures to their essential parts. But before such a reduction could be systematically engaged, a *complete* knowledge of habitual structure would be needed. Aristotle does not belabor the point, though; not because pre-scientific groupings are "non-aetiological" and therefore devoid of scientific interest, as Pellegrin (1982:180) claims, but because such groupings are simply too obvious to warrant elaboration. Such groupings would be self-evident not only to Aristotle and the ordinary Greek layman of the time, but to common folk across cultures the world over, and likely in all times. This is so not only for life-forms and basic kinds, but for the covert groups (*eide anonyma*) as well.

It seems entirely convincing to argue, as Balme (1987b) does, that Aristotle's biology was "after the correct identification and grouping of differentia" according to their causal interrelationships, not the "making" of an animal classification. But the arguments in favor of Aristotle's supposed disinterest in taxonomy actually lend credence to the idea that he was primarily engaged in a causal resolution of the whole array of prefabricated folkbiological groupings. This is not just with respect to "regular" generic-speciemes and life-forms, but also "irregular" covert fragmenta and "isolated" monogeneric life-forms, such as the snake.

5.3 ANALOGY

For Aristotle, the similes likening God to an artisan, nature to art and the organism to the artifact are never intended as anything other than similes. They neither aim specifically to instigate an additional host of sundry symbolic associations, nor do they act as a summons to empirically investigate the possibility of a deeper and more precise basis for comparison. In other words, they are pedagogical, and *wholly* replaceable by nonmetaphorical explication. The comparison of man to animal, however, is assuredly more than pedagogical. It is theory-constitutive: it is meant to lead, and in fact did lead, to a comparative zoology; just as the analogy between plant and animal would lay the foundation for a unified biology (see section 9.4 below).

For ordinary Greeks, as for ordinary folk most everywhere, man's ontological status clearly places him in a category apart from brute beasts (see section 2.3 above). By suspending this categorical distinction, Aristotle is able to connect the popular, higher order categories of animal (bird, fish, viviparous quadruped, oviparous quadruped and the four main divisions of invertebrates) to one another through the notion of *analogous function*: organs having the same potential (*dynamis*) by analogy (*analogos*) are similar in nature (*physikon*). As in man, these often morphologically dissimilar, but functionally analogous, vital parts allow the organism to feed, propagate, feel and (in most cases) move; that is, the analogous organs enable something to *be* an animal.

Man provides the standard functions. Of all the animals man is most familiar and is most perfectly structured; that is, he functions in the most harmonious fashion vis-a-vis his environment. Thus, we discover that human hair is of the same nature as the fur of viviparous quadrupeds and the scales of fish and oviparous quadrupeds. Additionally, the gills of oviparous quadrupeds, crustacea and fish are of the same nature as the lungs of man and the viviparous quadrupeds. Even the lowliest insects have a liquid that performs functions analogous to blood. This implies that the bloodless animals (*anaima*), i.e. the invertebrates, must also have organs analogous to the brain and heart, as these organs are intimately connected with the circulation of blood and the maintenance of life as a whole. Moreover, as it is obvious that plants, too, eat and propagate in order to live and reproduce, there is license to extend analogies to plants as well: "From one seed is begotten one body, as for example, of one grain of wheat, one plant, of one egg, one animal" (*GA* 728b35; cf. *GA* 758b2–5, *HA*

539a15–25); and "if we differentiate and identify organs according to their [vital] functions, then the roots of plants will correspond to the heads of animals" (*de An.* 416a4).[20]

Although Aristotle's biology is unquestionably anthropocentric, this does not imply that he sought to reduce biology to what was already explicitly known about man. Thus, whereas man is known best with regard to external morphology, his internal parts "are, on the contrary, for the most part unknown, and so we must refer to the parts of other animals which those of man resemble and examine them" (*HA* 494b21 f.). In sum, Aristotle uses analogy as a vehicle of *reciprocal illumination* between terms to explore the structure of life in general and to create a science dealing with the subject.

In this respect, then, Aristotle's use of analogy is doubtlessly more than merely heuristic, as G. E. R. Lloyd acknowledges:

> To represent the animal world as forming a systematic whole requires a formidable effort of synthesis . . . the key concept used by Aristotle in establishing links *across* the main groupings of animals is that of similarity by 'analogy' . . . . The search for and reflection on points of comparison between different species provides Aristotle with one of the means of organising the vast body of data he had collected in his inquiry concerning animals   (1983:42)

Lloyd plausibly argues that Aristotle's use of man as the first term of the analogy was not a borrowing or an extension from previous popular beliefs or folklore. Less plausible is the claim that: "the anthropocentricity of his zoology may be said to correspond to the deep-seated preoccupation with the question of where man stands in relation to animals that runs through so many Greek (like so many non-Greek) myths" (42).

Nowhere, in fact, is there the slightest inclination in Aristotle to animism, although Aristotle's teleology is often attributed to the "anthropomorphising inclination of the Greek mind" (Kirk 1961:116; cf. Joly 1968:249).[21] There is only the occasional simile linking the process of physical maturation and the realization of thoughtful purpose: "Nature, like the mind, acts with reference to purpose (*heneka tou*), and this purpose is its end (*telos*)" (*de An.* 415b16–18); however, even such metaphorical allusions are rare in the biological works. Moreover, metaphor is hardly a commitment to anything at all. Symbolic speculation, as Aristotle well understood, differs from metaphor in that the former lays a claim to truth while the latter does not (see sections 9.3 and 9.4 below).

Still, according to Lloyd there is a closer tie to the symbolic analogies of tribal folk than first meets the eye. Indeed, Aristotle seems to be merely making explicit a traditional, and presumably culturally parochial, folk position by "providing such a position with an elaborate and detailed would-be rational justification" (1983:211).[22] From this standpoint, Aristotelian zoology can supposedly be linked to folkbiology from three standpoints: (i) the infiltration of "human, especially social, terms" in taxonomic analysis, (ii) the "anthrocentri-city" of taxonomy, and (iii) the appreciation of taxonomic "anomalies," "boundary-crossers" and "dualisers," which demonstrates that "the symbolic load poses obvious and fundamental problems for any system that purports to give a single comprehensive and consistent account of natural kinds" (1983:3). In each case, though, Lloyd simply assumes what he has set out to prove. Consider the following:

Alongside the principal characters that Aristotle considers in the *Historia animalium* in his search for the essential differences of a zoological taxonomy, he includes certain features of the animal's "social" behavior. He ponders over the differences between tame and wild animals, between the wicked and affection-ate, the aggressive and the timid, the noble and the scheming, the jealous and the generous, the sociable and the shy, and so forth. The use of such characters may seem "at first sight surprising," argues Lloyd; however, upon closer analysis they reflect the "assumption of the parallelism between the human and animal series, which is . . . a feature of Greek popular belief." In this way, the ideas of folklore become part of the science of natural history. All the same, "in practice, Aristotle pays far less attention to such matters as the jealousy of the peacock and the meanness of the snake, than to their anatomy, physiology and methods of reproduction or mode of locomotion" (1983:26).

In fact, though, such characters play no role at all in the attempt to set up a taxonomic system on the basis of the causes of the animal's coming-into-being. Aristotle emphasizes that because science is concerned only with causes, such differences as those between the wild and the tame are not really essential or proper after all (*HA* 488a27 ff.; *PA* 643b4–5).[23] Moreover, although ordinary folk often do impute human social characteristics to animals, such characteristics do not appear to figure into the exhaustive partitioning of local flora and fauna into basic (or even higher-order) kinds. This is so for Aristotle as well.

Concerning Aristotle's anthropocentrism, Lloyd argues that: "Aristotle iden-tifies proportionately far fewer of the species of lower kinds of animals than he does those of the higher, and while some of the brevity of his accounts of the former may be put down to the difficulties of observing very small creatures without optical aids, we may believe . . . that value-judgments have also played their part" (1983:36). Value-judgments are presumably evident in Aristotle's emphasis on "essential" parts, such as the external organs of locomotion, over less essential parts, like the internal muscles. Furthermore, while his belief in the heart as the seat of the soul may have prompted the search for an analogous controlling-center in the invertebrates, it also seems to have led to hasty conclusions (e.g. the misidentification of the cephalopod liver as its heart) and might have blinded him to the character of the nervous system.

Now, it is incontrovertible that Aristotle did value certain hypotheses and research strategies over others, as *all* scientific investigators after him have done. It is also incontestable that his theoretical inclinations led up blind alleys and caused him to misjudge certain findings, as has happened with all subsequent scientists. But there is nothing here that indicates the pervasive influence of folklore symbolism, popular uses of myth, religion or anything of the sort. Human beings the world over simply are not endowed with the perceptual apparatus to *see*, and thus to initially appreciate, the internal systems and external articulations of very small animals and plants, and are not disposed to spontaneously apprehend the internal complexity of living kinds in general. That is why (cross-culturally and historically through the mid-eighteenth century) the nonflowering plants and the invertebrates are usually lumped together in one or two "residual" phenomenal categories, and why speculations about internal anatomy often remain just speculations.

What, then, of such "anomalies" as the bat, which "dualises" bird and quadruped, and the seal, which cross-cuts the normal categories of fish and quadruped? Surely folklore is replete with the antics and mysterious powers of these morphologically abnormal creatures; and just as surely, avers Lloyd, Aristotle allows "intermediaries treated as anomalies, and in doing so he may be said to have the tacit support of a powerful, if unformalised, set of popular assumptions" (52). But what assumptions might these be? They are noticeably not assumptions of a mythical nature, because "these grounds never, in Aristotle's case, include an appeal to any supposed magical, mystical or sacred properties the animals were popularly held to possess" (48). In fact, even in such cases it is often evident that Aristotle is "proceeding along the usual lines of his discussion and keeps rigorously to his usual biological differentiae." Still, the fact that he refers to these anomalies as "deformed" supposedly reveals the influence of folklore.

Again, there is scant evidence in Aristotle's conception of dualizing, or equivocation (*epamphoterizein*), that suggests the intrusion of symbolic traditions in general, and Greek folklore, in particular. For the most part, those of Aristotle's dualizers that also have prominent roles in folklore just *are* phenomenally abnormal in regard to their overall morphological aspect. The taxonomic position of bats, seals, whales, ostriches and the like, though logically speaking never anomalous, is nonetheless often psychologically peculiar. In some societies the bat is classified with the bird, in others with the quadruped; in yet others it is given a separate taxonomic status equal to that of the bird and the quadruped (see section 2.4 above). But whatever taxonomic solution one opts for, the result is abnormality: if classified with the birds or quadrupeds, still it is morphologically and behaviorally distinct from the other birds or quadrupeds; and if given a position equal in status to that of the birds, quadrupeds and fish, still it lacks the numerical and ecological diversity of these other higher order taxa and constitutes a much more perceptually and behaviorally homogeneous taxon.[24] This peculiarity is attention-getting. Hence it renders such kinds choice subjects for symbolic speculation. But this need not have anything to do with folkbiological taxonomy *per se* (cf. Sperber 1975a).

Occasionally, dualizing owes to the cross-cutting of categories that are evidently of Aristotle's own construction. In these cases, Aristotle's analysis cannot be related to folktaxonomy, much less folklore. From this, Lloyd concludes that: "Dualising thus provides a remarkable case of interaction –

within Aristotle's zoology – of traditional beliefs and his own independent theorising" (1983:50). Of course, there is nothing remarkable about the fact that Aristotle often accepts common-sense judgments into his system and occasionally does not. But Lloyd sees this as quite something else: vestiges of folklore lingering in the advanced stage of a gradual effort to break loose from the myths and traditional symbolism of folk. Yet whatever vestigial folklore may be found in Aristotle's biological speculations, it does not constitute any *part* of his zoological classifications. This is scarcely surprising in view of the fact that myths and traditional symbolism also have so little to do with with making of folktaxonomy.

5.4 FAILURE'S TRIUMPH

Aristotle shared a commitment with pre-scientific folk in regard to common-sense epistemology and the phenomenal realism that goes along with it, namely, that we do know most, if not all, of the things that ordinary prople think they know as self-evident. But this commitment to common-sense realism hardly reflects a simple confusion of conventional meanings with reality. True, the ontology of the common-sense world includes intuitional entities to which discursively definite meanings are attached in ordinary language; however, the (conditional) necessity that informs the typical features of corresponding referents does *not* derive purely from verbal convention, but from the way the mind spontaneously organizes environmental information, that is, by presuming the perceived regularities of living kinds to be caused by underlying physical natures – when all things are equal.

Yet, it is only by extending common sense in ways that render it fallible and susceptible to falsification that knowledge of the world can possibly advance beyond self-evident experience. What is obvious and familiar is thereby reinterpreted so as to incorporate coherently the unfamiliar and unusual. Such extensions, however, require profound empirical insight coupled with bold theoretical speculation, as common sense alone provides no intuitions to confirm or deny. One of Aristotle's most significant contributions to the advance of science was to preserve common-sense intuitions while banishing all mystical, magical, mythico-religious and other "symbolic" endeavors to cope with those rare, deviant, or otherwise uncommon phenomena that were inscrutable, or partially inscrutable, to common sense.

For example, in order to account for deviance from the type, Aristotle supposed that either the normal environmental circumstances conducive to the organism's proper development were lacking, or some "accident" had occurred in the normal process of generation, or both. As a result, both normal variation and radical deviance could be assimilated to the same explanatory framework. In other words, Aristotle undertook the task of analyzing exactly in what respects things are, or are not, in fact equal. By relativizing the operation of underlying natures to specific surroundings, he sought to understand how natures may also shape the outcomes of actions in abnormal circumstances (e.g.

in the production of monsters). The various functional propensities, or potentials, of a nature would be realized, that is, fully developed morphologically,
only under appropriate conditions (which it is the task of the naturalist to
describe). Henceforth, the mechanics of reproduction and the interplay of
environmental circumstance would serve, along with comparative functional
morphology, as the principal means for empirically investigating possible – but
not immediately obvious – connections between "natural kinds."

This is not to say that Aristotle understood *episteme* the way we understand
science today, as the attempt to explain the known by the unknown or to
explore the unknown for its own sake. For Aristotle, the task was rather to
extend the familiar to the unfamiliar. As his student Theophrastus observed
when applying the Master's method to botany: "it is by the help of the better
known that we must pursue the unknown, and better known are the things
which are larger and plainer to our senses . . . for then in dealing with the less
known things we shall be making these better known things our standard, and
shall ask how far and in what manner comparison is possible in each case"
(*Historian Plantarum* I,ii,3–4). Although it is no longer simply a question of
reducing the unknown to the known in the manner of tribal folk, the kinds of
common sense remain not only psychologically primary, but ontologically
primary as well.

The problem that most agitated Aristotle, and which he was never able to
satisfactorily resolve, was how to select from among the well-known attributes
of a type the truly essential attributes that would hierarchically interconnect
with those of other types. There are two reasons for this failure. First, in
requiring that morphological features be directly tied to anatomical functions in
order to qualify as candidates for essential parts, he introduced an equivocation
into the notion of "natural affinity" that was not really treated until Lamarck
and Cuvier. The fact that similar morphologies might have quite different
functions, or that distinct morphologies might have similar functions, was not
properly understood.

Actually, Aristotle had little factual knowledge of internal anatomy. He knew
nothing of the muscles, for instance, nor of the differences between arteries and
veins. He even believed the brain to be an organ whose primary function was to
cool the blood. When he did use analogies from internal anatomy (e.g. gills and
lungs) it was only to determine the *existence* of function. Once the functions
were discovered they could presumably be used as a sufficient means for
reducing morphological features to essential characters; but without morphological agreement, essential agreement was not possible. Classification, then,
would be based on obvious morphological differences that could be functionally
interpreted, and not on functions as such.

Second, Aristotle never seemed to doubt that a *complete* survey of basic living
kinds was possible. Like any folk naturalist he dealt with no more than five or
six hundred species. Because Aristotle geared local division to an analysis of
antecedently known kinds, he did not foresee that the introduction of exotic
forms would undermine his quest for a taxonomy of analyzed entities.[25]

As long as analysis could be restricted to the kinds of a single *fundamentum relationis* of the ordinary folk sort the enterprise would seem plausible. But, in admitting exotic kinds to equal status with local types as the quest for the unity of nature demanded, Aristotle undermined the common-sense basis for supposing that a complete inventory was readily at hand, although it was not until the end of the sixteenth century, after the Age of Exploration, that the problem was recognized. Actually, it was only after this recognition that the procedure of Logical Division became a largely *a priori* affair. According to Aristotle, division could only be posterior to a complete survey of kinds. For Linnaeus and the other classical systematists, however, division would represent a rational means of accessing hitherto unknown types. Such preoccupation with the rational prediction of hitherto unknown possibilities has more to do with concerns shared by Galileo, Descartes, Spinoza and Leibniz, than by Aristotle.

Aristotle did not adopt the "principle of plenitude" intimated in Plato's *Timaeus* (cf. Lovejoy 1936/1964). Nor, therefore, did he deduce corollaries to the effect that "nature makes no leaps" (Linnaeus 1751 sec. 77) or that "everything which can be, is" (Buffon 1749,I,11). This is "because what is potentially possible need not be actualized" (*Metaph.* 1071b13). Aristotle did not imply, as Linnaeus would, that the number of basic kinds is predetermined logically, and therefore accessible by rational inference. Nor did Aristotle suggest, as a foreshadowing of Buffon, that there is a sensibly continuous progression of beings into which exotic forms could be readily interpolated upon visual examination. For Linnaeus and Buffon, the doctrine of fullness or continuity in the world would aim to give coherence to the cosmic order, because in their world common sense could not account for nearly so much as it could in Aristotle's. Moreover, the enormous variety of an ever increasing number of discovered organisms would tend to confirm eighteenth-century notions of a continuous grading of characters and a shading of forms one into the other. Although Aristotle also relied to a significant extent on external characters, his basic folk understanding of the living world offered much more *prima facie* support for the existence of perceptual gaps in nature.

In sum, Aristotle's initial ontological commitment was to common-sense appearances, that is, self-evident phenomenal reality. He went beyond common sense in trying to systematically engender such appearances by means of their underlying existence-determining principles. This was to be revealed in a taxonomy interlocking the essential attributes of different natures. In so doing, he sought to relate disparate phenomenal kinds to one another, thereby converting them into natural kinds that could be subsumed under unifying laws. In this, he was little different from other creative scientists who proceed by conceptual generalization, that is, by showing that phenomena initially perceived to be different, follow from the same principles (e.g. planetary motion and earth-bound projectiles).

Unlike the modern scientist, though, he did not seek to explain away the known world of everyday experience as the epiphenomenal manifestation of some deeper, unseen reality; for Aristotle, all natural kinds were phenomenal. Rather, he aimed to improve our understanding of the world as we ordinarily see it, and know it to be: not by refuting "naive realism," but by simplifying it. Practically, this meant knowing how and why properties of one intuitive kind could be generalized to another by identity, by degree or by analogy: it meant knowing which individuals were identical in their species nature (*physis*), to what extent each generic-specieme (*atomon eidos*) developed the essential characteristics of its life-form (*megiston genos*), and the functional principles whereby each life-form might partake of life in general.

Aristotle's scheme foundered because his conception of induction of general, connecting principles from the phenomenal data proved untenable. By restricting the domain of evidence to common sense, explanation as he meant it could not be achieved. On the one hand, even if function (as opposed to kinship) were the source of connection in the living world, the limitation of functions to the visible limbs and readily known organs would preclude an adequate understanding of functional anatomy (on the order, say, of Cuvier). On the other hand, as these principles were supposed to extend to organic nature at large, and not simply to segments of local fauna (and flora), the extended domain of evidence could no longer be certifiably complete. Without completeness, however, division would not be possible. Still, the idea of conceptual generalization – that is, lawful unification of disparate phenomena – did considerably benefit the advance of science.

To better understand the common-sense world, Aristotle introduced a science of organizing principles to go beyond it. But what began as a quest to simplify common sense, eventually turned to an anticipation of unknown and invisible evidence. In the end, that nonphenomenal realm would become the principal domain of scientific inquiry. Yet, this does not mean that philosophers and historians of science today can afford to ignore common sense as the outworn vestige of some "Stone Age Metaphysics." The epistemologist must contend with the fact that common sense remains our psychologically primary means of access to an initially unintuitive world of science; while the historian need consider that science progresses in no small measure in response to the insufficiency of our ordinary ways of dealing with extraordinary facts. To understand the scientific enterprise, then, is, first of all, to understand the scope and limits of common sense: "We must trust in perception (*aisthesis*) rather than theories (*logoi*) and theories, too, so long as what they show agree with the *phainomena*" (*GA* 760b31–33).

PART III

FROM HERBALS TO SYSTEMS

ANDREAE CAESALPINI
ARETINI

DE PLANTIS LIBER PRIMVS
CAP. PRIMVM.

VM natura plantarum illud folum genus animæ fortita fit, quo alantur, crefcant, & gignant fibi fimilia ; careant autem vi fentiendi, mouendiq; in quibus animalium natura confiftit : iure optimo plantæ longe minori inftrumentorum apparatu indiguerunt quàm animalia. Multæ enim funt partes in animalibus ad fenfum facientes, quæ multiplici forma & numero funt conftitutæ : plures adhuc in eifdem reperiuntur ad motus præftandos : nam huius gratia vniuerfa ferè offium fubftantia articulis diftincta eft, & caro in mufculos eft digefta neruis in omnes partes difcurrentibus ; fi præterea vifcera contemplemur, quæ altricis animæ funt inftrumenta, ob fimilem animæ facultatem, modicam quidem fimilitudinem cum plantarum partibus intuebimur ; fed in plerifq; maximam diffimilitudinem. Natura enim venarum, quæ alimentum ex ventre hauriunt, vt illud in vniuerfum corpus diftribuant ; aliqua ex parte refpondere videtur cum plantarum radicibus ; nam fimiliter hæ ex terra tanquam ex ventre cui implantantur, trahunt alimentum. Cum autem animalia exquifitiori ciborum genere indigerent, & multa eorumdem præparatione coctioneq; eorū radicibus ventres funt appofiti, aliiq; multi ductus ad alimenti excrementa feparanda. Quæ omnia plantis negata funt. Quo fit, vt corpora plantarum valde fimplici fubftantia conftare videantur, & maxime accedere ad naturam fimilarium, difcedere autem ab operofa organicarum compofitione. Quoniam autem altricis animæ opus eft gignere quale ipfum, fiue id ex alimento fiat ad conferuationem fingulorum, fiue ex femine ad fpecierum æternitatem : duæ ad fummum partes perfectioribus datæ funt, maxime neceffariæ : Vna, per quam fumant alimentum, quæ radix appellatur. Altera qua fructum tanquam fœtum ad fpeciem propagandam ferant, qui caulis vocatur in humili materia, caudex autem in genere arboreo. illa quidem fuperior, quia principalior licet intra terram condita fit ; viuunt enim multæ plan

A   tæ

The nature of plants determines only the following: nutrition, growth and reproduction. But plants lack the faculties of sensation and movement, which characterize animal nature. Plants thus have a much less complex working apparatus than animals.

In fact, there are numerous parts, with multiple and quite varied forms, that affect the senses in animals. Other parts, even more numerous, serve to assure movement: it is for this reason that almost all the bony material is separated by articulations, and the flesh is distributed in the muscles via the nerves, which run through all the parts of the body.

If, moreover, we examine the viscera, which are the instruments of the principle of nutrition, we assuredly note a slight similarity with the constitutive parts of plants because of a similar faculty of life; however, in most cases the differences between them are extreme. In effect, the veins, which draw food from the stomach for distribution throughout the body, appear to be in a certain respect the equivalent of the roots of plants; for plants likewise draw nutriment from the ground in which they are implanted – as from a stomach – through their roots.

But as for animals, they have need of more elaborate nutriment, involving long preparation and slow digestion; their stomach adjoins that which serves as their roots, and there are many other pathways for rejecting food waste. All this is absent in plants. So much so that plants seem constituted of a very simple substance, and while seeming to have many points in common with nature's beings, lack the laborious organization of organs.

Furthermore, because there must be a nutritive principle to produce the plant as it is, either there must be recourse to nutriment for the conservation of the individual, or to the seed for the perpetuation of the species. Two parts are thus attributed to perfect plants, necessary to the highest degree: a part that permits the absorption of nutriments, which is called the root; another part that carries the fruit – as a gestation – in order to perpetuate the species, which is called the stalk in small vegetation, and the trunk when talking of trees. The first part is superior to the other, although it is buried in the ground, because it is fundamental; in fact, numerous plants [have only a root and live by that alone . . . .]

(Andrea Cesalpino, *De plantis*, 1583)

(Author's translation of the first page of chapter 1, book 1, which discusses the positive and negative analogies between plants and animals as well as the idea that plant species perpetuate themselves by seed.)

6

ORIGIN OF THE SPECIES CONCEPT

6.1 BACK TO NATURE

After Aristotle and Theophrastus, a general disregard for careful morphological description and the degenerate practice of relying on authority rather than on first-hand experience increased in classical antiquity. In *Historiarum mundi*, Pliny defends experience as "the best teacher" in contrast to the degenerate practices of the schools, where: "it is more agreeable to sit on benches . . . than to go out into deserted places and look for different herbs at each season of the year" (XXVI,6). Still, Pliny's own descriptions are plagued by the very tendencies he condemns, and are on the whole inferior to the descriptions of Theophrastus. Unlike Theophrastus, or even Pliny, Dioscorides' verbal descriptions are tightly restricted to *Materia Medica*; while after Krateuas, figures tend to be ever more schematic and bare of detail (see Singer 1927).

Through the Renaissance, many scholastic "naturalists" merely assumed that the local flora and fauna of the temperate regions of Europe could be exhaustively apportioned among the Mediterranean plant and animal types depicted in ancient sources. The experiential foundations of those ancient works, though, had since ceased to be pertinent. This is because common-sense classifications are merely relevant to a local environment.

Judging by the number of extant copies, two of the most important early botanical treatises were Pseudo-Apuleius fourth-century *Herbarius* and Pseudo-Dioscorides' fifth- or sixth-century *Ex herbis femininis*. Both works draw on Dioscorides but are much more restricted in scope. The *Herbarius* portrays some 130 plants, while the *Ex herbis* depicts seventy one herbs. The *Herbarius* and *Ex herbis* often simply rely on arguments from authority, with later copies especially containing figures of generally poor quality and frequent mismatches between ancient and vernacular names (cf. Kästner 1896; Singer 1927).[1].

The chief reference for "Aristotelian" botany in the late Middle Ages was not Theophrastus, but a bogus version of Aristotle's lost *De Plantis* composed by Nicolaus of Damascus. This work, which continued to be attributed to Aristotle into the twentieth century, comprised the core of Roger Bacon's and Albert Magnus' thirteenth-century botanical works and did much to vitiate their occasional empirically well-grounded observations. Even the dominant botanical treatise of the sixteenth century, *Le grand herbier* (or *The Grete Herball*) was largely a third-hand mutilation of classical sources, fancifully illustrated and generally mediated by the second-hand descriptions of Avicenna, Albertus and others.

Only after the process was reversed by the great German, Dutch and Italian herbalists of the sixteenth and seventeenth centuries was classification again grounded in intuitions of natural affinity. These later herbalists persisted in using the Latin (or latinized Greek) name and description as a nomenclatural type to which local species could be attached; however, they no longer simply *assumed* an ancient type to be locally represented in the same fashion (or even at all). Thus Fuchs, one of the German "fathers of botany," remarks that *Centaurio minore* (i.e. *Centaurium umbellatum*) "grows in wet and damp places, notes Dioscorides . . . but I have often observed in our Germany that it grows in hard, dry, grassy fields and meadows" (1542:386).

Accordingly, the search for dubious ancient sources of common-sense truths about organisms in the local environment – with the consequent distortion of those truths – was transformed into a concerted effort to assimilate ancient and foreign material to local knowledge as far as possible. Although this renewed effort at local description proceeded in a somewhat refractory manner in order to correspond as closely as possible to the nomenclature of the ancients, it is precisely the search for such correspondence that prodded the herbalists to fix a medium of communication and to establish a shared repository of data about the living world. In so doing, the herbalists managed to go beyond common sense by transcribing folk understanding in a manner that could be transmitted across local boundaries of time and place. The idea of a worldwide system became conceivable; but only because customary intuitions of natural affinity, which are ordinarily restricted to a local environment, were recovered and fixed in such a way that they could be provided standards of expression for comparison and contrast.

Early European classifiers more or less followed the habit of local folk in reducing unfamiliar fauna and flora to locally familiar sorts of plants and animals. Friedberg describes the process for the Bunaq of Timor:

> Each time we asked them to name and classify a rare plant . . . they would try to attach it to . . . a series [i.e. a basic-level grouping], always on the basis of the plant's appearance – an appearance that is as much its morpho-

logy, anatomy as its odor or the texture of its fibers. One thus has the impression that if the informant does not know the name of a plant he can always find one in conformity to the logic of the classificatory system, by giving it the base name of the series which it most closely resembles.

(1970:1122-23)

Similarly, Dughi notes that the nomenclature of the ancient Greeks, and later that of the Latins, does not fundamentally differ from popular botanical terminology, such as that used by Provençal speakers in southern France: "Here drawn around certain paragon plants is a whole tribe of plants which are sometimes related, sometimes not, but which share traits of external resemblance with the paragon" (1957:136).

Theophrastus appears to treat many of the exotic plants sent back to Greece from Alexander's expeditions in just this way (Bretzl 1903). The banyan (*Ficus benghalensis*), for instance, is simply labeled an Indian "variety" (*syka indika*) of the common Mediterranean fig (*syka*, i.e. *Ficus carica*): "the whole tree is round and exceedingly large . . . the fruit is very small, only as large as a chickpea, and it resembles a fig. And that is why the Greeks named this a 'fig tree'" (*Historia plantarum* IV,iv,7). Similarly, Chinese authors of the sixteenth century compare wheat that "comes from western lands" to their own sorghum (*Sorghum bicolor*) and refer to it as "sorghum of jade" (*yushushu*) (Li Shizhen 1975-78/1590-96; see Haudricourt and Métailié 1985:17).

Now, this strategy, which is based on likeness of the whole or a part of the habitus, occasionally leads to an appreciation of natural affinity. For example, the English colonists were thus able to assimilate the widely divergent species of North American oaks to the rather narrow range of English trees denoted by "oak": for instance, "shingle oak" (*Quercus imbricaria*), "scarlet oak" (*Q. coccinea*), "dyer's oak" (*Q. tinctoria*) and so forth. If, however, the foreign species is truly exotic, such a strategy inevitably fails. Thus, it seems that when wheat and sorghum were first introduced to the Tzeltal Maya they were referred to as "Castillian maize" (*kašlan ʔišim*) and "Moor's maize" (*móro ʔišim*), respectively. Initially, then, these exotic forms appear to have been considered folkspecific variations of the indigenous generic-specieme *ʔišim*, that is, maize (Berlin 1972). Conversely, the English colonists likely thought of maize as an indigenous variety of wheat when they first called it "Indian corn."

Once an unfamiliar plant or animal is labeled and identified by perceptual analogy with the closest indigenous facies, though, it may itself assume a marked role in the local economy of nature. Accordingly, increased familiarity with the once unfamiliar plant or animal may eventually lead to the structuring of a distinct facies. When this happens the once unfamiliar species usually drops the base name of the indigenous generic-specieme to which it was originally attached and assumes its own unique label. Thus, for the folk of France today, the *Zea* plant is more commonly referred to as *maïs* than as the *blé de turquie* of former times.[2]

The same cognitive process that governs the incorporation of exotic species into the local scheme can also regulate the upgrading of native species in conformity with the ever changing relationships of local species to one another and to local folk. Again for the Tzeltal, the "armadillo-eared oak" (*čiknib hihte²*) may once have been viewed as but one of a number of specific variations of the generic-specieme "oak" (*hihte²*) along with such other folkspecifics as "white-footed oak" (*sakyok hihte²*) and "custard-apple oak" (*k'ewes hihte²*). At present, the "armadillo-eared oak" is separated from these other oaks. The latter group of broad-leafed oaks are now included under the optional rubric "true oak" (*bac'il hihte²*), or merely "oak" (*hihte²*), whereas the "armadillo-eared oak" is referred to these days as simply "armadillo-eared" (*čiknib*), with the appellation "oak" (*hihte²*) being entirely optional. *Čiknib* has thus attained the grade of a generic-specieme that encompasses the various native small-leafed oaks, while *hihte²* is left with only the broad-leafed oaks as specifics.

On occasion, though, the binomial qualification may linger: for example, while "Castillian maize" and "Moor's maize" currently rank as generic-speciemes, they maintain binomial form. What distinguishes today's situation from the past is that the indigenous generic-specieme is nowadays optionally marked by the attributive "true" (*bac'il*); hence, it too is nominally binomial in structure (*bac'il ²išim*): "Time and usage, however, will tend to neutralize the marking properties of the attributive forms *kašlan* and *móro* and the expressions will come to be conceived of as single, semantic units" (Berlin 1972:75).[3]

My own attempt to confirm this speculation with two other Mayan language communities, Itzá and Cakchikuel, tends to indicate that Tzeltal appreciation of wheat falls somewhere between them. The Itzá of San José region of Guatemala's Peten jungle were one of the last Mesoamerican groups conquered by the Spanish. To this day, the few remaining Itzá speakers apply the same binomial to wheat as they do to their "white" variety of maize (*iši'im saq*). In fact, until recently wheat was little used by the Itzá. By contrast, for some time wheat has been an important element of the environment for the numerous Cakchikuel groups of the more densely populated highland plains. The monomial representation of wheat (*siq*) is clearly distinguished from the binomial representation of white maize (*išin siq* or *išin saqhel*). Unlike the case for Itzá where the attributive form *saq* is never conceived as a single semantic unit to denote wheat, in Cakchikuel only when the attributive form *siq* stands alone does it denote wheat.[4]

Similar processes are evidently at work in the herbals of the three "German fathers of botany": Otto Brunfels, Jerome Bock (or Hieronymus Tragus) and Leonhart Fuchs.[5] The main difference between these Renaissance herbalists and ordinary folk concerns the original referential type. For the German herbalists, the type is frequently an ancient rather than local generic-specieme. Consequently, the process for incorporating new species seems to function in reverse. Instead of attempting to match foreign species to local types, it is more often a matter of matching local species to foreign types, although the principle is basically the same.

Take the Latin edition of Brunfel's *Herbarum vivae eicones* (1530-36). Here the author refers to the mallow of the ancients as simply *Malva*, but labels a second species found in Germany *Malva equina*, or "horse mallow." Yet, in the German edition it appears that *Malva equina* is no longer simply a variety of *Malva* because both species are now labeled with binomials: "horse mallow" is called *Rossbappelen*, and the original *Malva* is termed *Gaensbappelen*, or "goose mallow." The local generic-specieme has apparently achieved conceptual equality with the ancient type (cf. Bartlett 1940).

Consider, now, a slightly different example. In the *Kreütter Buch* (1539), illustrated and published in Latin as *De Stirpium* (1552), Bock distinguishes domestic and wild varieties of the ancient *Melissa* (*Mütterkraut*) from the common *Melissa vulgaris* (*Gemein Mütterkraut*). In *De Historia Stirpium* (1542), Fuchs proceeds to give the ancient type the optional marking "true" (*Mellissophylon verum*), while the common specieme is accorded the optional epithet "false" or "bastard" (*Mellissophylon vulgaris vel adulterinus*) – for, "according to the opinion of popular herborists there are two sorts of Melissa."

Still, it would be a mistake to conclude that either the binomial nomenclature of folk or that of the German herbalists evinces "the modern idea of the genus" (Bartlett 1940:355). For folk, binomial sorts generally occur at a taxonomic level below that of the generic-specieme. They are, more often than not, culturally idiosyncratic varieties that do not exhaust the local flora or fauna. Such folkspecific or folksvarietal taxa, as ethnobiologists call them, usually occur in sets of two or three members that contrast with one another on the basis of very few (and frequently only one culturally important) morphological characters (cf. Berlin 1978). Similarly, according to Greene (1983, I:106), the first Virginia colonists likely took the "White Walnut" (*Juglans alba*) and "Black Walnut" (*Juglans nigra*) of the New World to be strikingly different variants of the one known European type (*Juglans regia*).

True, for folk, as for the German herbalists, morphologically similar generic-speciemes are *occasionally* related binomially. But this does not mean that binomially labeled generic-speciemes that share a common base name are consistently deemed to group together at a distinct level of reality, or *rank*, superordinate to the basic level of folktaxonomy (as Greene and Bartlett suggest; also Dughi 1957:138). In other words, no definite relationship of genus to species can be established between *Bappelen* and all the *other* (disjoint) basic-level groupings noted by Brunfels, any more than between *'isim* and all other Tzeltal generic-speciemes. This is not to deny that linguistically related generic-speciemes may share recognized morphological characteristics. Only, such overarching groupings of affinities occupy neither a uniform perceptual stratum nor a fixed conceptual position in the classificatory scheme.

What is rightly intimated by Greene and Bartlett is that the work of German herbalists insinuates a shift towards local realism and away from the antiquated and bookish practices of the scholastic herbalists, who were mostly concerned with attaching local plants to the pre-existing names and descriptions of ancient types (cf. Meyer 1854–57; Sachs 1875/1890). Because plants of the more temperate regions of Europe were often quite distinct from the plants described by ancient authors of the Mediterranean world, such a literary exercise could only succeed in confounding the true affinities of plants. The German herbalists of the sixteenth and seventeenth centuries, like their French, Dutch and Italian contemporaries,[6] often persisted in using the Latin (or Latinized Greek) name and description as a nomenclatural type to which local species could be attached; however, unlike their scholastic predecessors, they did not simply *assume* the ancient type to be locally represented.

Concern with local conditions is particularly notable in Fuchs. Thus, under the section *tempus* in the chapter on *Cucurbita Sativa* (i.e. *C. lagenaria* L.), he notes:[7] "In Germany the fruit comes later owing to the chilliness of the country, and yet before autumn is done there is none left to find." Fuchs considerably advanced the art of naturalistic illustration and description, and did not hesitate to challenge the ancients. Lacking a notion of comparative morphology, though, he is disposed to emphasize only those aspects most characteristic of the plant in question. For example, considerations of the form and figure of the fruit lead him to posit three "genera" of *C. lagenaria*, where Pliny had mentioned only two: "Pliny, in the fifteenth chapter of the nineteenth book, makes two cultivated species ... we, have more regard for the form and figure of the fruit, have separated three."

Here Fuchs employs binomial nomenclature both for the superordinate specieme, *Cucurbita Sativa*, as well as for the subordinate specifics: *Cucurbita Oblonga* (*Lang Kürbſs*), *Cucurbita Maior* (*Gros Kürbſs*), *Cucurbita Minor* (*Klein Kürbſs*). Elsewhere he identifies binomial, trinomial and even quadrinomial variants of a type, some of which appear to be speciemes in their own right; as with Bock, for example, Fuchs has *Elleborus Niger Sylvestris* sharing a chapter with *Elleborus Niger Adulterinus Hortensis*, while *Elleborus Albus* occupies its owns chapter. This indicates that, at least in some cases, there is a recognition of affinities that overarch generic-speciemes. This is all the more apparent when affinities are noted between speciemes that are allotted separate chapters but do not exhibit nomenclatural ties:

> The Anethium grows in height up to a cubit and a half. It has several stems and branches. It has leaves as thin as thread, a yellow flower. The root, in the form of wood, is not very long. *The pompoms and umbels are like the fennel, with which it shares an almost total resemblance* [my italics].

But such broader notions of affinity still do not reflect an overriding order of relationships or represent absolute standards of awareness.

In the abbreviated German edition of his work, *Neu Kreüterbuch* (1543), Fuchs admits only 289 of the 600 or so species known to the ancients. The others, he argues, are not pertinent to the everyday knowledge of the common man. The remaining 200 plants that Fuchs depicts are not found in the works of the ancients. When he is able to locate a species that resembles one of the ancient types in overall morphology, he is careful to provide an illustration of the local representative and to note any apparent disagreement as to habitus, habit or habitat.

The naturalistic approach to plant knowledge progresses even further in Bock. A contributor to Brunfels's *Eicones* and a keen collector and observer of plants, Bock is more attentive than his predecessor to describing the particularities of plants "in our Germany."[8] For instance, he provides the first description of the pasque-flower, or *Herba venti* (i.e. *Anemone Pulsatilla* L.), that "unknown herb" which local folk call "dinner bell" (*Kücheschell*). Brunfels had earlier noted the existence of *Kücheschell* but chose not to describe it because it was unknown to the ancients.[9] As does Fuchs, Bock intermittently refers to more general relations of affinity between linguistically unrelated kinds, such as the similarity between the "acrid and fermented taste" of the pasque-flower and that of *Ranunculus*.[10] Furthermore, the sequencing of chapters manifests an awareness of the intuitive importance of "family" fragments of gramineous, umbelliferous, leguminous and labiate herbs. Bock also seems to be well aware that such family-level chains may cut across recognized life-forms. Consider rosemary and lavender, which are genera of labiates: "they are shrubs . . . therefore the proper place for them is away in Tragus's [i.e. Bock's] Third Book, among the woody growths . . . but he has both of these here in the First Book, at the end of the labiates, all the rest of which are herbs" (Greene 1983,I:333).

The naturalistic technique of the herbalists reaches its highest expression with Valerius Cordus. Cordus, who died while on a botanical excursion to southern Italy in 1544, published nothing during his short lifetime. His highly accurate descriptions of some 500 plants appeared only posthumously in *Historia plantarum* (1561).[11] This milestone in descriptive botany was edited and partially illustrated by the encyclopedic Zurich philologist, physician and naturalist, Konrad Gesner, who had previously prefaced the Latin edition of Bock.[12] In each description one usually finds accurate accounts of the movement, measurement and arrangement of leaves; the mode of origin and characteristic features of the stem, branches and flower; the numbers of loculi in the fruit and rows of seed; the habit of the root; as well as the taste and smell of the parts and the sap. The habitat of the plant also figures prominently, as do notions of qualitative relationships with other plants; and the mode by which ferns (trichomanes) propagate is intimated for the first time (cf. Sprague and Sprague 1939).

There is also some (intermittent) suggestion of a principled "generic" listing based upon a privileged notion of floral character. Each list is headed by a traditional or familiar type. For example, a list of twelve *Ranunculi* includes three northern European anemones and the pulsatilla; it begins with *Ranunculus palustris* (*Ranunculus sceleratus*), followed by *R. sardous, R. tertia* (*Anemone ranunculoides*), *R. quartus* (*A. nemorosa*), etc. Concern with floral structures also allowed Cordus to extend the scope of family chains; for example, by thus attaching bryonies to the squashes and melons. Accurate description allowed a conceptualization of some of the looser connections among family "chains," which an illustration could not as readily bring to mind.

Thus did the Renaissance herbalists conscientiously invert the focus of scholastic and medieval herborizing, which had tended to stray from common sense – that is, from the sort of folkbiological knowledge that customarily (and cross-culturally) passes for empirical fact. Local knowledge was recovered and precisely transcribed. Only then could it be transcended. A series of interrelated technological innovations helped to make this possible. In Germany, the invention of movable type and advances in the art of the woodcut facilitated the dissemination of information about specimens, and these developments were first advantageously exploited by Brunfels and Weiditz. Thus, regarding Weiditz's illustration of *Weissz Seeblum* in Brunfels's herbal, Jacobs aptly notes:

> The plant was taken out of the water, and the roots were cleansed. What therefore we see depicted is a water lily without water – isn't this a bit paradoxical? All relations between the plant and its habitat have been broken and concealed. And yet this is regarded as the first herbal with illustrations 'true to nature'; Weiditz was a pupil of Dürer's, and no doubt had learnt from the master the motto about nature: "*Wer sie heraus kan reissen, der hat sie*" – to tear out nature is to possess her.   (1980:162–63)

In addition, botanical gardens were opened, thus permitting observation of plants outside of their original environments. The simultaneous introduction of new techniques promoted in northern Italy by Luca Ghini for the preservation of dried speciments in herbaria allowed free exchange and reference back to actual specimens at all times of the year. Such was the novel heuristic value of these techniques that Gesner was led to boast that he could appropriately designate any exotic specimen if presented with the dried flower and leaf.[13] These innovations, together with the choice of Latin as a common tongue, allowed the herbalists to unambiguously communicate the details of their respective folk stocks and their exploratory inventories of the flora of neighboring lands. Henceforth plants could be physically isolated and their observable structure desiccated for all time.

To be sure, the Chinese, centuries before, had perfected a highly naturalistic art of coloured ink on silk scrolls that compares favorably with the paintings of Botticelli or Dürer: for instance, the twelfth-century "*Gardenia jasminoides* with *Litchi chinensis* and birds" on permanent exhibit at the British Museum. Furthermore, Chinese texts of the time already show a developed technique of wood-cut and use of block printing. For example, the illustrations of the thirteenth-century herbal, *Zhenghe Bencao*, offer clear morphological details that are fairly true to nature. But the associated morphological descriptions are rather poor (Shenwei 1957). More generally, nowhere in China, before the middle of the nineteenth century, does there appear to have been an attempt to analytically match morphological description to illustration. Thus, the late sixteenth-century herbal, *Bencao Gangmu*, provides somewhat richer descriptions (mostly in analogical terms; see chapter 2 note 2 above), but the illustrative engravings are very poor, especially when compared to those of Fuchs or Bock:

The encounter between plant practitioners and philologists seems rarely to have taken place, and in the thirteenth century a polygraphic author, Zheng Qiao writes: "most Confucian writings ignore things of the field and of nature; the peasants and market gardeners know nothing of literature. If there is no fusion of the two, the study of birds, quadrupeds, trees and flowers cannot be carried out successfully."

(Haudricourt and Métailié 1985:20)

Among the Chinese there was no qualitatively reduced structure such as could be "objectified" in the fixed spatial perspective of Renaissance art, with its "true nature" eternally set in the neutral tones of scholarly discourse.

6.2 CHARTING NEW TERRITORY

As a result of the naturalistic movement in herbalism, a worldwide catalog of readily visible forms could be envisaged with ancient Mediterranean types serving as paragons to which both temperate and exotic species might be attached. If no ancient type were available, a more familiar local sort could be substituted. In this way, speciemes would be more easily compared and contrasted. Local understanding, no matter how provincial initially, could then be related to a broader view of the world. To this end, Johann Bauhin[14] and his younger brother Caspar surveyed some 6,000 forms of plants, thus bringing the herbalist period in Western Europe to a culmination. The systematic worth of their surveys, however, is still a matter of some misvaluation.

Some commentators regard the group headings under each section of Caspar Bauhin's *Pinax theatri botanici* (1623), for example, as reflecting an unmistakable notion of the morphological genus, and the numbered forms under each heading as indicating a solid understanding of the biological species (Sachs 1875/1890:33; Singer 1959:79; Morton 1981:145). Some even regard Bauhin's way of naming plants as a foreshadowing of Linnaean binomial nomenclature and his arrangement of groups into sections, together with the sequencing of sections into books, as constituting the intuitive foundation for a system of natural families (Bartlett 1940; Guyénot 1941:14; Mayr 1982:157). But Caspar Bauhin's role as "precursor" in regard to species, genus and family is actually much less clear than might initially appear to the historian of biology unfamiliar with folkbiology.

Throughout the *Pinax*, group headings within a section are often mononomial, though just as often they are not, and the first numbered form listed in each group usually corresponds to the earliest known or most easily recognized type of the group. Consider the fourth section of book VIII, which treats only (some of the then-known) cucurbits, that is, members of the family of cucumbers, melons and squashes. The groups, with their "types," are as follows: Cucumis (*Cucumis sativus vulgaris*), Melo (*Mel vulgaris*), Pepo (*Pepo oblungus*), Melopepo (*Melopepo clypeiformis*), Anguria (*Anguria Citrullus dicta*), Cucurbita (*Cucburbita major sessilis*), Colocynthis (*Colocynthis fructu rotundo major*) and Cucumis Asininus (*Cucumis sylvestris asininus dictus*). All groups have several representatives save the last, Cucumis Asininus, which has only its type as representative.

At first glance, there is a striking concordance between this listing and Tournefort's listing of genera under the unnamed sixth section of his class of Campaniformes in *Elémens de botanique* (1694). All but one of Bauhin's group headings lends its name to a Tournefortian genus, with Bauhin's first type listed as first species.[15] Unlike Tournefort, though, Bauhin gives no special generic descriptions; unlike Linnaeus, he offers no familial designations; unlike Ray, he mentions no characters that might distinguish species as such. In fact, the resemblance between the fourth section of book VIII and the first eight sections in book XX of Pliny's *Historiarum mundi* is just as marked. Yet, Pliny could scarcely be taken for a precursor of Ray, Tournefort or Linnaeus. Indeed, all but two of Bauhin's group headings correspond to section headings in Pliny.[16] Furthermore, while Pliny generally treats but one generic-specieme in a section, it is that which Bauhin takes as his first type.[17]

Although Pliny seldom discusses more than one or two forms per section, whereas Bauhin sometimes names as many as twenty distinct forms for each group, no *principled* differences in the use of nomenclature are apparent. Moreover, Pliny explicitly notes the (family) similarity that squashes have with cucumbers and melons (*similes et cucurbitis natura*). In fact, there are no principled differences between folk nomenclature or understanding of family relationships and Pliny's or Bauhin's. Tzeltal knowledge of cucurbits is a case in point. The Tzeltal recognize, but do not label, a "covert" category of cucurbits that encompasses eight generic-speciemes (Berlin *et al.* 1974:421-24); six of these are native squashes and gourds (*c'um, mayil, c'ol, bohc, cu, c'ahko?*), and two are Old World imports (*melones, santiya*).[18] Except for the gourds *bohc* and *cu* which are cultivated subspecies of *Lagenaria siceraria*, each generic-specieme corresponds to a distinct scientific species. The majority of generic-speciemes each subsume two or more binomially labeled folkspecifics, with "pumpkin" (*c'um*), for example, having perhaps as many as ten: "soft pumpkin" (*sk'un c'um*), "hooked-neck pumpkin" (*luk' nuk' c'um*), "tree pumpkin" (*ste? c'um*) and so forth. Longer polynomial forms are absent from this covert Tzeltal category, but trinomial and even quadrinomial forms, though much less frequent than binomials, do appear in other categories.

The tendency, for the sake of convenience, to regard only such Bauhinian groups as appear to presage the genera and families of future taxonomists has thus led commentators astray; for these ostensibly "standard" groups exhibit no principled distinctions from ancient or folk groupings. In addition, examining some of Bauhin's more "problematic" groups, one finds far less regularity in nomenclature or appreciation of morphological affinity. These groups, which actually compose the majority of cases, differ appreciably from ancient (and folk) as well as future taxa. Often, the groups of a section exhibit no regular pattern of nomenclatural association or dissociation with one another; and the listed species of a group may bear no linguistic tie at all with the group heading. For example, the second section of book VIII lists the following groups:

Clematitis, Clematitis Indica, Clematis Daphnoides, Pericymenum, Apocynum, Asclepias, Polygonatum, Lilium Convalium, Monophylum and Laurus Alexandrina. Under the group Clematitis Indica, seven forms appear. The first three forms have polynomial structures that begin with the binomial indicating the group heading, namely, *Clematis indica . . .* ; the fourth and fifth forms begin with the binomial *Clematis malabarensis*; and the last two forms have names that in no way link them with the other forms of this or related groups of Clematitis: *Colubrini lignitertium genus in eadem provincia* and *Radex quaedam in Malaca*.

To make matters worse, many groups are notoriously heterogeneous. Take the very first section of Book I concerning "grasses" (*De Graminibus*). Nearly all of the twenty-four groups in the section have binomial, rather than mononomial, headings. Three groups include subgroups whose headings are usually trinomial in structure. The large majority of groups as well as subgroups of the section cross-cut two or more Linnaean genera. For example, the subgroup "Gramen paniculatum arvense" has four numbered forms, each of which corresponds to a Linnaean species of a different genus: *Gramen arvense panicula crispa* (*Poa bulbosa* L.), *Gramen panicula pendula aurea* (*Cynosurus aureus* L.), *Gramen segetum altissimum panicula sparsa* (*Agrostis spica-venti* L.) and *Gramen segetum panicula arundinacea* (*Aira cespitosa* L.).[19]

Yet it would be a mistake to see this lack of regular nomenclatural or morphological pattern as a return to the debased practices of late antiquity and medieval scholasticism, or as a deviation from the orderliness of folk classification and earlier Renaissance herbalism. In those cases where many more forms are known to Bauhin than to ordinary folk or to ancient and Renaissance herbalists, his comprehensive attempt to index all known plants leads to heterogeneity in nomenclatural and morphological affiliation. This is not because he abandons common sense, but because common sense alone is not intrinsically able to relationally segregate basic forms from one another when most of those forms originate in entirely different environments, and when the number of forms exceeds that of a normal locale by an order of magnitude.

In fact, the various nomenclatural combinations of the *Pinax* express rather consistent extensions of common-sense naming and segregating practices to problems that ordinary folk are not normally compelled to deal with. Only occasionally are folk required to attach an unfamiliar type to the basic stock of familiar types. For Bauhin, however, both locally familiar and ancient types were few and far between, and the whole of the then-known living world could not be commonsensically accommodated to these except in a fragmentary and piecemeal fashion. If, to a modern eye, family-level and generic-level chains of species can be discerned in Bauhin – the most accomplished of the herbalists – for him there is as yet no clear distinction between, nor conception of, species, genus or family.

Bauhin's *Pinax*, or "Chart," was little more than a catalog of forms and synonyms for the plants then known, which included not only plants of southern and northern Europe, but also many from the better explored coastal areas of Africa, Asia and North and South America. The *Pinax* did not provide a key to understanding the living world at large, although its practical value for cross-referencing was unrivaled for the better part of two hundred years. There was nothing in it to allow a systematic placement of kinds not originally surveyed in a fixed relation to known kinds. The systematists would seek to remedy this by logically codifying readily visible patterns of morphological affinity and dissimilarity. Because exploration was constantly yielding new kinds, a sure code would have to be automatically extendable so as to permit one to tabulate the place of any given local form of plant with respect to every other (possible) form in advance of all future discoveries.

6.3 SPECIES FOREVER

It was Andrea Cesalpino, professor at Pisa and papal physician, who first suggested a way whereby the intellect might detach itself from the overwhelming confusion of so many new sensible forms.[20] Yet, even Cesalpino's most novel contributions to the development of systematics have been severely misconstrued for lack of appreciation of the singular character of his "Aristotelianism." To be sure, Cesalpino's *Questionibus Peripateticis* (1571) constitutes a landmark in Aristotelian exegesis of the late Renaissance. But the botanical applications of the conclusions of this exegesis in *De plantis libri XVI* (1583) are designed to resolve empirical problems quite different from those envisaged by Aristotle, and wholly alien to the nonempirical concerns of the scholastics.

There are two principal and interrelated features of "Aristotelian essentialism," as the creed has come to be known among historians and philosophers: the dogma of the *eternal* fixity of species (Hull 1965), and the doctrine that any individual *necessarily* comes to be what it is in virtue of its species-specific properties, that is, those properties which define the essence of the kind of being that individual is and which therefore *make* the individual the particular individual it is (Quine 1966:173-4). It is important to note that while these features do characterize Cesalpino's essentialism, they do not appropriately apply to Aristotle. Moreover, the method of Logical Division employed by Cesalpino differs significantly from Aristotle's own method. This is not because Cesalpino "equivocated" in his use of the Stagirite's principles in order to reconcile *a priori* ideas with reality (Sachs 1875/1890), or because he was forced to make "concessions" in the analysis of material conditions (Bremekamp 1953a), but because he was faced with an organizing task markedly distinct from anything encountered by Aristotle.

For Aristotle, as we have seen (section 4.3 above), natural species represent temporally and spatially localized populations, the individuals of which bear a resemblance in the process of *genesis* – a process characterized by a range of active (male) form-potentials, passive (female) material-potentials and intrusive (environmental) element-potentials. The species is a naturally occurring empirical "necessity" – part of nature's ontological fold – that is nevertheless conditional upon an ideal constellation of material circumstances that may never, in fact, obtain. Such necessity is not eternal, because normal conditions for generation and growth may shift by chance (*automaton*), and nature's optimal course move along with them. Necessity is conditional, consequential and after the fact. It is not absolute, *a priori* or causative in the sense of being directed by a purposive force like God.

For Aristotle, as for Cesalpino, the form (*eidos*), or soul (*psyche*), of the individual organism is responsible for its physical organization and vitality (*de An.* 415b9-30). But in Aristotle's case, the life-giving principle (*archai*) and immanent form (*dynamis*) are shared *only* by a sire and its immediate progeny. Material happenstance (from insufficiency in the coction of vegetative female matter to the heat of the South Wind) unavoidably deflects the unfolding of the causal process from its ideal course, which is the actualization of the sire's form. By default, the progeny tends to resemble the more weakly determined form of one of its ancestors. If no individual form predominates "there remains what is common," namely, the morpho-geographic species (generic-specieme) as a limit at which a given range of female matter and male form are compatible (*GA* 768b10f.). Because the form-as-soul that the progeny in turn passes on to its offspring is determined by the former's actual form − not the original sire's − there is little, if any, chance for a perpetuation of any given form across generations. The immanent forms that are passed along to individuals of a species are similar, but not identical.

So, for Aristotle, only when certain environmental conditions obtain can the typical *morphe* emerge in a given individual whose underlying nature falls within a given range. Although Aristotle applies the term "nature" to (i) the underlying potential for development in the individual, (ii) the actual process of development, and (iii) the final result obtained, each occurrence of the term denotes a different ontological event (*Ph* II,i). These different events are closely related, but the relationship is in part governed by material contingency. This is not the case for Cesalpino, who collapses all three events into a single expression of Divine contemplation.

For Cesalpino, species are not unrealized optimal *tendencies* for individual development in the material conditions of nature *sub specie universalitatis*. They are everlasting, immanent forms for the material realization of God on earth *sub specie aeternitatis*:

> Eternity can only arise from the eternal: since the proper work of the vegetative soul is to engender its like, which makes for the eternity of the species, it is necessary that its substance not be corruptible. The reason for the eternal lies neither in corruptible existences taken individually, nor in their totality (1571 II,viii).

The environment really has no formative role to play. It can but facilitate or hinder the only natural, preordained sort of development possible, namely, that of an underlying nature of a specific kind into the mature form of a specific kind. The underlying natures that are housed in the seeds of the various individuals of a species are not merely members of a range of underlying natures that are similar in potential; they are identical *"ex semine ad specierum aeternitatem"* (1583:1).

Cesalpino adopts much of Aristotle's realist epistemology (cf. Dorolle 1929:22-23) and embraces Aristotle's instantiation requirement: contrary to the Platonist position, no form can exist without being materially individuated. But Cesalpino adds a heavy dose of Christian theology, which results in an unavoidably neo-Platonic slant. For both Cesalpino and Aristotle, human intelligence apprehends its objects rather than constructs them. Moreover, the world that appears to us – that is, which is visibly manifest – is fundamentally the only world that is. Intelligence extracts the universal aspects of reality apparent in individual bodies by a sort of "induction" (*epagoge*). Just as the vegetative soul of the organism is embodied in its whole morphology, so the intellectual soul of the human being is enmattered in its various sensory images of the world. But these images are themselves the disembodied presentations of the individual forms of particular organisms to the human mind. The mind, which is endowed with light-sensing capacity (when considered potentially), and light-giving quality (when actually operating), illuminates the clear, distinct and common idea in its several images. In the mind, then, "actual knowledge is identical with its object" (*de An.* 430a10-25) and through the mind objects become, as it were, conscious of themselves (Cesalpino 1571 II,viii).

In this way, the mind grasps what is universal in the individual (*universalia in rebus*). Whatever is thus universally intelligible, constitutes an immortal part of the cosmos. But for Aristotle, everything that occurs in the sublunary realm occurs as a persistent tendency that always falls short of perfection; whereas for Cesalpino, this unremitting tendency is itself an immanent perfection. In the one case, the continuous historical cycle of ancestor generating descendant is but analogous to the fixed rounds of the heavens; while in the other, abiding sublunary cycles are, ultimately, identical with the everlasting celestial circuit.

In Cesalpino's Christian cosmos, all movement must be considered an immanent striving, and ultimate attainment, of eternity and oneness with a perfectly whole, contemplative, unmoved God. Accordingly, Cesalpino holds with Albertus that the form-potential of the species is perfectly perpetuated over its individuals: *generatio naturalis terminatur ad perfectum* (Albertus Magnus *Quaestiones super de animalibus* XVI,20). It survives death and decay that it may achieve eventual redemption. With Albert's student Thomas, Cesalpino also maintains that the individual form-potentials of a natural lineage of organisms are exactly the same "in species," although actual forms do manifest "acciden-tal" differences owing to material deficiency or to the progenitor's weak generative virtue (*generans generat sibi simile in specie: fit tamen aliquando aliqua dissimilitudo generantis ad genitum quantum ad accidentia, vel propter materiam, vel propter debilitatem vitutis generativae*) (Aquinas *Summa Theologiae* III,74,iii). A species is thus a nature in continuous action.

As with the object of knowledge, so with knowledge itself: knowledge of universals is perfect, true, eternal and universal knowledge. On Aristotle's account, though, to the extent that a species (i.e. a natural lineage) exists in the world, it does so *only* as an aggregation of individuals similar, but not identical, in both actual form and form-potential. Moreover, insofar as the species exists in the mind, it offers no guarantee of certitude, but only of the likelihood and verisimilitude.

In the Aristotelian cosmos, physical forces operate only among the four elements in the sublunary realm, while the characteristic motion of celestial bodies is governed exclusively by the demands of geometrical perfection. Cesalpino breaks down this dualism not, as Galileo would, by postulating that physical causality permeates the entire cosmos, but by maintaining that the sublunary realm also attains a manner of perfection. This position allows Cesalpino to elaborate a novel conception of natural history and taxonomy. He goes even further than the herbalists in wrenching the object of inquiry from its actually perceived state of nature. Sensory assessment, other than the austere black and white representation of vision, is virtually banished from all description, as are considerations of ecological situation. From now on, the various interactions between humans, animals and plants could be effectively ignored at all general levels of statement.

Thus, all organisms have underlying natures that cause growth and development, just as they have mature and developed shapes that are caused by those natures. These mature shapes are direct manifestations of God on earth, which it is the privilege and duty of man to contemplate. There are different kinds of natures, systematically related to each other, as there are distinct kinds of shapes between which the geometrician can perceive the formal relations. Because natures are the causes of shapes, the formal relations that hold between natures – or their perceptible representatives and repositories (i.e. seed structures) – should themselves represent (as *simulacra*) the eternal relations that hold between shapes (i.e. perceived species) in the mind of the Divine Geometrician. The result would be a formal analysis of internal causal relations (*substantia*) (Cesalpino 1583:26). This would enable one to understand "the number and nature of principles" (1571 I,i) underlying the phenomena revealed by sense perception (*cognita*). By resorting to a formal analysis of causes (i.e. of natures), one could consistently maintain an attachment to the Aristotelian *episteme* without subscribing to the Aristotelian method of functional analysis, that is, without having to treat the development of natures under specified material conditions.

As for the task of constructing a universal taxonomy, this, it would appear, could best proceed by ignoring local circumstance. Only in that way might one hope to reduce the chaotic multiplicity of sensible forms to equivalence classes whose proportions the mind could once again manage. Recall that for Aristotle, classification aims to provide a complete division (*diaeresis*) and assembly (*synagoge*) of all *antecedently* known basic-level kinds (see section 5.2 above). The differentiae of such a classificatory structure must yield a progressive reduction of habitual, basic-level structures to their essential, functional parts. But before such a reduction could be systematically engaged, a *complete* knowledge of the habitual structures of all basic kinds would be needed. Given the fact that Aristotle acknowledges about the same number of basic kinds as any folk naturalist, it would seem to him plausible that such a precondition for classification could be met. But Cesalpino faces a very different task. For Aristotle, it is first necessary "to know all the species that fall under the genus" (*APr.* 68b27), "like sparrow or crane and all" (*PA* 644a25-30). Whereas for Cesalpino, one needs to know the genera before all of the indefinitely many species; for, "if there is unclarity in genera, species will necessarily be confused in many ways" (1583:25): "One must unite everything within homogeneous genera ... [which is] very efficacious for the memory, because an enormous number of plants are thus enclosed in a resumé, ordered by genera; hence, although a plant may have never before been seen, anyone can place it in its appropriate category; and if a plant has no name, anyone can call it by its generic name" (1583 dedicatory epistle).[21]

But before the right genera could be sought for reducing the multiplicity of new forms to tractable equivalence classes, it would be necessary to fix a criterion for the species even in advance of future discoveries. Without such a criterion there could be no principled justification for uniting basic-level sorts originating in different climes within the same genus. Such a criterion must, therefore, establish that morphological characters *usually* perceived to be constant are, in fact, those that *ought to be* constant according to God's eternal plan. This allows one to accept that (variations in) material conditions are irrelevant to the existence of species-types. Consequently, one is justified in extracting folk species from the environments in which they were first located, and converting them into abstract types that may be placed in a universal taxonomy.

Accordingly, the species criterion, though often attributed to Ray (Stearn 1957:156; Mayr 1982:256), or known as the "Linnaean species," is actually first introduced in *De plantis*:

> Plants that resemble one another in the totality of their parts generally
> belong to the same species. In effect, a small difference between plants is
> not always a sign of species difference; often the leaves, flowers and other
> parts are modified by diversity of location and conditions of cultivation ...
> if one sows the seed of a domestic species, wild plants will readily arise
> that are as indifferent in species as those which by cultivation or other
> means have been modified: for, like everywhere engenders like, according
> to nature and of the same species.   (Cesalpino 1583:26)

The local problem of accounting for token variation from the morphological type, which had so agitated Aristotle, could thus be reduced to the test of seeing whether a plant comes true to seed.

6.4 OMNIA EX OVO

As with many other late Renaissance thinkers who came out of the North Italian tradition of Aristotelian exegesis, Cesalpino owes his methodology and metaphysics more to Aristotle's *Organon* than to the biological works. This allows a large degree of freedom from the encumbrance of many of the subtle epistemological complications that Aristotle's biology would appear to introduce into an understanding of the sublunary realm, which includes organic life. As a result, the analysis of organic species can more readily proceed along a path that emulates the analysis of perfect celestial forms. In particular, it permits of various attempted solutions to certain problems of empirical generalization over organic species that Aristotle himself was not compelled to deal with. In addition to Cesalpino's essay, for instance, another such attempt seems to underlie the somewhat different treatment of the manner and order of acquiring knowledge from Aristotelian principles that is found in the works of the English anatomist, William Harvey, who studied in Padua at the beginning of the seventeenth century. The point should become clearer after consideration of an apparent shortcoming in Aristotle's theory of universals.

For Aristotle, a species is a universal that represents a mere possibility for the future course of optimal individual development. Strictly speaking, there are no universals in the world. Only individuals exist. Nevertheless, individuals can never be known *qua* individuals, but only *sub specie universalitatis*. In other words, the nature of individual existence can be grasped only as a particular realization of a global rule, or principle of nature, that causes matter to develop, that is, to change and yet persist for a time in identifiable form. Each actual embodiment of a principle, however, is always, to a greater or lesser degree, a "falling short" (*steresis*) of what the being ideally is by definition. The definition of a being does not exhibit the being's "complete actuality" (*entelecheia*), that is, all that it happens to be by way of realizing what the definition actually implies under given circumstances; rather, the definition of a natural substance denotes its "general form" (*eidos*). Logically speaking, the form of a thing indicates the species under which it immediately falls. From a physical perspective (*physikos*), however, it signals the end (*telos*) toward which individuals of the species are naturally disposed to advance as they mature. Since the goal, or optimal species form, is never perfectly actualized, it exists only as a partially unrealized material possibility.

But universals as they exist in the mind abstractly are different from the unfulfilled promise that universals represent in the material world. True, a universal in awareness, as in the world, is the potential (*dynamis*) in its every instantiation: whereas the potential of a universal in the world is in each individual that tends naturally to develop towards the common goal, that of a universal in awareness is in every exemplifying sensation, and in every summary or typical image left behind by such sensations. All the same, thought cannot function as a future eventuality; it must be a present reality. Accordingly, Aristotle furnishes human awareness not only with mere instances of a form (sensations and images), but with the form or idea as such. The form is there undeniably *alongside* the images from which it somehow derives: "the one beside the many which is a single identity with them all" (*APo.* 100a3-9; cf. *de An.* 432a12 ff.).

Aristotle leaves "intuition" (*nous*) the task of extracting the thought from sensory images; however, it is none too clear how this is supposed to work. In *De anima* (413b24-25, 429a10-11) "intuition" appears to be synonymous with "mind," or the independently active "theoretical intellect," while in the *Analytica posteriora* it seems to be merely a particular state of perceptual awareness or "insight" that requires no cognitive operation over and above simple abstraction (omission of irrelevant perceptual content). But scholastic debate over this problem of Aristotelian "induction" (*epagoge*) did not inevitably lead science to a dead end as is often claimed.[22] Thus, Cesalpino relies on "intellectual intuition" to justify the construction of a novel classificatory system according to *a priori* principles, while Harvey counts on "perceptual intuition" to produce self-confirming patterns of physiological processes after a sufficient number of repeated observations.[23]

Cesalpino begins his *Questionum peripateticorum* (1571), as does Harvey his *Disputations touching the generation of animals* (1653/1981), with a meditation on passages of Aristotle's *Physica* that are confronted with passages from the *Posteriora analytica*. According to the *Physica* (184a16-21):

> The natural path of investigation starts from what is more readily knowable and more evident *to us* although intrinsically more obscure, and proceeds towards what is more *self*-evident and intrinsically more intelligible .... The things that stand out as plain and obvious are confused mixtures, whose elements and initiating principles become known only on subsequent analysis. So we must proceed from the general character of a thing to its constituent factors; for what the senses discern most readily are concrete wholes .... A name, such as 'circle', gives a general indication of what is meant, while its definition (*horismos*) makes an explicit analysis of this meaning. Similarly, children begin by calling every man father and every woman mother, but as they grow older they learn to make suitable distinctions.

As universals are whole and wholes are easier to apprehend, one must proceed from the universal to the particular. The two examples given refer to intellection, but the lesson can also be taken to hold for the other aspects of concept formation, namely, sensation and imagination.[24] Thus, "in sensation the face of a man presents itself indistinctly to us, in its totality, before the eye, the nostrils, or the other parts of the face" (Cesalpino 1571,I,i); and:

> this same particular is abstracted in the imagination or laid up in the memory and appears obscure and confused, nor is it any longer apprehended as a particular but as some general and universal thing .... So any painter being about to draw a man's face, though he make a thousand draughts of it, yet does he each time draw a different face.
>
> (Harvey 1653/1981:11)

Each higher stage of thinking about the world, then, begins with an apprehension of universals that is a rash induction or a vague one. A further knowledge of particulars is required to rein in the induction to cover its proper extension (all and only those instances to which it truly applies) and intension (all and only those other objects of thought that it truly entails). A proper appreciation of intension requires an analysis of the genus into its component elements, that is, a division into species; and comprehension of the proper extent of each species, in turn, depends upon an intimate experience with repeated instances of the species.

Nevertheless, it is only by an induction (*epagoge*) from particulars that the universal can be grasped at all. This is the sense that Cesalpino and Harvey make of such a passage in the *Analytica posteriora* as this (81a37-81b9): "it is impossible to acquire knowledge of universals other than by induction . . . . But induction is impossible without sensation; and sensation applies to particular cases." It is also the case that knowledge of the principles of art and science proceeds by induction from those of lesser scope (*habitus*) to those of greater scope (100a10ff.). Moreover, the definition of what is generic in a given species comes only after definitional knowledge of the species is acquired (97b26ff.). Although one cannot, of course, know the species without *implicitly* knowing the genus under which it falls, one cannot be sure to what extent particular aspects of one's intimate knowledge of the species are truly generalizable to other species of the genus until after the comparison with other species is made.

Because of their very different methodological priorities, however, Cesalpino and Harvey tend to orient and implement these Aristotelian insights in seemingly opposed ways. Cesalpino's main concern is the classification of natural kinds according to principles that specify the essential similarities and differences between them (1583 dedicatory epistle; cf. Dorolle 1929:7-8). The constitution of Nature just is the interlocking of all its original, irreducible yet causally connected, specific natures. To discover the principles of nature is, therefore, to understand the principles of classification whereby genera are divided into species:

> But why, insofar as the discovery of the principles of nature is concerned, does Aristotle give the rule of proceeding from the universal to the particular, and not the inverse order? . . . one cannot obtain the number and nature of principles either by induction or by definition. Definition presupposes knowledge of its object: but one does not yet know at this moment what are the principles [to be used in constructing the definition]; now, induction shows neither the number nor the difference, but concludes with a [confused] unity among a multiplicity. This leaves the division of universal concepts into particulars whereby we may realize what we seek. (Cesalpino 1571,I,i)

For Harvey, however, the problem of finding principles by which to reduce genera and classify species is not primary. Rather, the chief aim of scientific inquiry is to gain knowledge of the primordial properties of nature. Unlike Cesalpino, Harvey was already involved with the revival of atomistic doctrines that would come to dominate English natural philosophy in the latter half of the seventeenth century, culminating with Newton and Locke. Contrary to Newton and Locke, though, Harvey still held fast to the neo-Aristotelian view of Nature as a community of specific and primary natures. There could thus be no question of finding a single common and universal nature from which all specific natures could be generated one after, or from, the other. Biological species and other natural kinds were not the special, or temporary, effects of general causes – that is, ubiquitous, cosmological forces. Rather, all such natural kinds represented the original and eternal constituents of a complete *scala naturae* without which the cosmos would not exist.

Nevertheless, one could reasonably hope to discover universal principles that operate and administer the career of each specific, pre-existent primordium by frequent observation and diligent experimentation with entities most familiar to us and most "perfect" in the scale of being. Only by much repeated experience with the properties we think we perceive in those things familiar to us can we be sure that those properties are truly properties of the entities we perceive: "Aristotle clearly shows that no man can be truly called prudent or learned who does not by his own experience, attained by repeated remembrances, frequent perception and diligent observation, comprehend that the thing is so" (Harvey 1653/1981:16).

Thus, one may observe by countless day to day "ocular inspections" and "dissections" the manner in which, say, a full grown chicken is generated from an egg. The task, then, is to further generalize this account of the manner of generation to "other different creatures," gradually stripping away all but those efficient and material principles common to every kind of animal (and, ultimately, to every kind of plant):

> Now this indeed I could not do in all kinds of animals, both because a sufficient number of them could not be had, as because others are so exceedingly small that they elude our eyes. Hence, it must suffice that I have done these things in those kinds of animals which are more familiar to us, and to their pattern the first beginnings of all other animals may be related.
> (Harvey 1653/1981:18)

Among the more familiar animals are especially the largest and most perfect ones, that is, the viviparous creatures. Their size renders observations and experiments "very easy" and their resemblance to man makes their development more or less "distinct" and well articulated. But evidence from less perfect, if familiar, animals must also be taken into account in order that we may know the true proportions of those material and efficient agents involved in the generation of organisms and the fabrication of their parts.

In other words, experience with a wide variety of species is required in order to know the extent to which findings relating to one species may be generalized to another. Only then is it possible to understand the general mode of generation observed by Nature in each specific nature. Thus, the right course of scientific inquiry proceeds from knowledge of particulars to knowledge of universals. Without the former, the latter "represents nothing but waking men's dreams and sick men's fantasies." Universals remain less surely known than particulars until such time as innumerable repeated observations of the latter give sufficient cause for attributing certitude to the former.[25]

Yet, ultimate understanding of "the hidden nature of the vegetative soul" and "the manner and order of generation in all creatures and its causes" is not derived from observation or experience, but is adduced from analogy:

> all the other animals agree with those I have enumerated, or at least with some of them, either generically or specifically, and they are procreated after the same manner of generation, or at least in a manner which may be compared with it by analogy. For Nature being divine and perfect is always consistent with herself in the same things. And just as her works either agree or differ, that is in a genus or species or some proportion, so her working, namely generation and fabrication, is in all of them either the same or different. (Harvey 1653/1981:19)

The procreative similarity of all living kinds, like the causal unity of the entire world, owes to cosmic circuits – circuits that ensure that patterns of finite observations would repeat ad infinitum.

But to implement the Aristotelian analogy of the causal unity of the world, Harvey requires a still broader metaphysical principle. The principle, which in later natural philosophy came to be called the "Analogy of Nature," rests on a complete ontological doctrine of the cosmic order. This involves the application of the Christian dogma of the perfection of God, or Divine Nature, to two older themes that are related to each other: the "great chain of being" and the unity of pattern in the macrocosm and microcosm. Neither theme constitutes a full-blown metaphysical principle or methodological rule for Aristotle.

The mechanist and atomist Analogy of Nature, which achieves its first complete expression in natural history in the works of Buffon, allows one to posit as real imperceptible material bodies while doing away with original special natures (see section 9.5 below). Later anatomists and mechanists thus use the Analogy of Nature in ways that directly counter Harvey's view of the world in important respects. For Locke, the natural kinds in the "chain of being" are compound bodies that differ only in the arrangement of their minute and insensible parts. The "chain of being" is constituted of natural kinds considered as compound bodies. In fact, there are no rigidly defined arrangements that set off all biological species from one another. Similarly, for Newton, all natural kinds are compounded transmutations of an original aethereal substance that functioned as a primitive *archai* (cf. McGuire 1967). For Harvey, though, natural kinds are constant and immutable.[26]

The end product of analogy is an understanding of the *ovum* as the uniform primordial pattern of everything living (*quodlibet primordium potential vivens*): "Therefore the primordia of all kinds of animals are called seeds and fruit, and so likewise all the seeds of plants may in a manner be called conceptions and eggs" (334). The fertilized ovum is the organized essence of material life, underlying nature of the individual and species, repository of the innate virtues of motion, change, rest and preservation (*principeo nempe motus, transmutationis, quietis, et conservationis*). It is the "soul" as "the form and species". (153).

The ovoid shape emulates the circular movement of the heavenly bodies that holds together the Aristotelian cosmos. By analogy, this also conforms to Harvey's earlier discovery of the circular movement of blood that preserves and regenerates the body. So too, then, are ova able to perpetuate the life-giving forms they embody across generations in a continuous historical cycle of ancestor generating descendant; for, ova are structurally the same in all individuals of a species, animated but untouched by any male semen, housed in the womb but nourished by their own blood and uncontaminated with any female's matter. All these circuits belong to the same cosmic movement first described by Aristotle in *De generatione et corruptione*. But Harvey's cosmos, like Cesalpino's, is a Christian one in which each circuit unrelentingly strives in its own way to attain eternity and perfect oneness with God:[27]

> This circuit makes the *genus* of the chicken eternal (*sempiternum*), while now the chicken and now the egg in a perceptually continuing series (*continuata perpetuo serie*) produce an immortal *speciem* from individuals that are transitory and fade away. And in this same way we behold many inferior [i.e. sublunary] things emulate the perpetuity of superior [i.e. celestial] things. (Harvey 1653/1981:150-151)

It appears, then, that the metaphysical positions of Cesalpino and Harvey regarding the organization of the cosmos and the eternity of the species are in accord with one another, though not entirely with Aristotle. Both require the existence of the eternal species for scientific ends, but for different, non-Aristotelian, ends. Unlike Cesalpino, Harvey did not set out to construct a rationally extendable taxonomy. But he did require the principle of a stable and unimpeachable taxonomy of genera and species. For this alone would permit inductions to go through based on observations that concerned only a limited number of organisms representing but a limited number of species.

Given similar findings in organisms of different species, Harvey could thus justify the likelihood of similar results in any of the higher-order groups, or "general," common to those species. Taxonomy would also guide selection of specimens to confirm results for the species or the genus, or to locate the dividing lines over which findings could be generalized only with restrictions or not at all. Only such rigorous constraints on Harvey's scientific program could warrant the hope of realizing his quest for a single primordial structure common to all living things.

Implicitly guided in this way by taxonomic constraints on allowable generalization, Harvey could claim discovery of the outlines of life's basic primordial structure. Its intimate architecture had yet to come to light, however, especially in regard to insects and plants. The quest for a general primordial structure was not yet the Cartesian or Newtonian quest for a universal set of laws that operate uniformly over *all* natural kinds; for Harvey, each species primordium remained an irreducibly distinct nature. Still, by following Harvey's axiom that plant seed and animal egg are conceptually and ontologically of a sort – *omnia ex ovo* – Ray (1686:40) would be able to contemplate an extension of Cesalpino's insights into the zoological realm: *Sicut enim in animalibus*. For the whole of the living world, then, as "every kind hath its seed" (Ray 1691:181), so might each kind ultimately be connected to every other by taxonomic principles. In a clearer and more concrete manner, Linnaeus – who chose the egg as his coat-of-arms when he was ennobled as von Linné – would take Harvey's premise "that living beings are generated from eggs" to the conclusion that all kinds could be perfectly arranged into one great *Systema naturae* (Linnaeus 1744:1).

To recapitulate: Basic-level folkbiological groupings have always provided an intuitive underpinning and empirical approximation for the scientific species. No more theoretical "justification" need be given for this spontaneous operation of common-sense realism than for color perception or apprehension of three-dimensional rigid bodies. Nor was any given by the likes of Cesalpino, Harvey, Ray or Linnaeus whenever there was express appeal to common sense. The difference between folk and science here is that on gives primacy to the ecological gap between populations, the other to the reproductive gap. Most often, though, the one is covariant with the other. With the introduction of reproductive criteria, any new species could be readily given cross-community status: the most commonly perceived features of local species would also be those that usually happened to breed ever true.

As the next chapter will illustrate, the status that underscored the permanence of these basically visible forms over time also sanctioned the principle of their systematic comparison and the possibility of their grouping within higher groups that transcend the bounds of local knowledge. Only if species could be confined to their eternally fixed circuits might a true system be constructed:

> There are as many species as there were created different forms in the beginning . . . . There are as many genera as differently constructed organs of fructification will bring forth natural species of plants.
>
> (Linnaeus 1736:15)

In its most complete form, the *Systema naturae*, which grew in Linnaeus' lifetime from a pamphlet of a few pages to a multi-volume work, was governed by two simple but powerful ideas. First, each species has a seed or egg different in nature, once and for always, from every other. Second, all specific natures should, and could, be fitted into a rigid and homogeneous hierarchy of pyramidally arrayed classes, orders (families) and genera.

In Part IV we will look at how folk life-forms and family-level fragments were systematically elaborated into classes and orders. But it is the genus that occupies us in the next chapter. For a short but crucial period in history, the genus would come to represent the primary rank of nature.

7

THE NATURE OF THE GENUS

All things, which for us can be truly distinguished, depend upon a clear Method that sets apart the similar from the dissimilar.
The more natural the Method for grasping discontinuities, the clearer our ideas of things.
The more objects we face, the more difficult it is to elaborate a method, but all the more necessary to do so.
Nowhere has the Supreme Creator exposed as many objects to the senses of man as in the Plant Realm, which covers and fills the globe we inhabit.
Thus, if there be anywhere a proper method, it is that whereby we may hope to obtain a clear idea of Plants.

(Caroli Linnaeus, *General Plantarum* Ratio Operis I, 1737a)

7.1 FRUITS OF REASON

For many a modern historian, philosopher and practitioner of biology, taxonomy today is still not wholly disabused of the folly of bookish systems, such as those of Aristotle, Cesalpino or Linnaeus. There is the opinion, for instance, that Cesalpino's bold initiatives to solve what must have seemed to the herbalists an intractable problem were doomed by his Procrustean effort to fit a new world into an Aristotelian framework inadequate even for the old. It is for his allegedly outworn attachment to the value of seeds and fruits in classification that Cesalpino owes his fame:

> This principle, and that of the prime importance of the division into trees and herbs, to which he also adhered, were direct deductions from the views of the Aristotelian school .... The empirical development of taxonomics at the hands of the Renaissance herbalists gave surer guidance than Cesalpino's *a priori* views. (Arber 1950:31–32; cf. Cain 1959b:234)

This view of Cesalpino's contribution to systematics is gravely flawed in at least three respects,

First, the Renaissance herbalists gave little, if any, guidance to the development of taxonomies. Their listings were either alphabetical or unconnected sequences of implicit folk groupings. Cesalpino not only captures most, if not all, of the intuitive regularities of folk and Renaissance herbalists, but seeks to analyze them morphologically and logically. Renaissance herbalists scarcely attempted anything of the sort.

Second, the partition of flora into tree and herb, though it may be justified *post hoc* by Aristotelian or (as in the case of Ray and Tournefort) non-Aristotelian reasoning, most certainly did not originate as "a direct deduction" from any set of *a priori* principles. This fundamental partition into what ethnobiologists call "life-forms" is common to tribal societies the world over. It characterizes ancient Hebrew, Chinese and Mesoamerican classification, as it does the lay classification of modern Israelis, Americans and Tanzanian tribesmen who could hardly be taken for devout Aristotelians.

Third, Cesalpino's appreciation of the value of fruits and seeds differs radically from Aristotle's. For Aristotle (and Theophrastus), as for Cesalpino, the seed and fruit are potential bodies of a certain type: vital loci wherein actual material forms are generated by heat (coction) from their underlying natures. In Aristotle, however, the species-type of the mature, realized organism is not determined exclusively by the seed, but only in conjunction with environmental conditions normally compatible with the functional adaptation of organisms whose underlying natures fall within a specific range. Although Aristotle, like Cesalpino, believes most plants to reproduce asexually, he still allows the environment to have a formative influence on the *optimal* morphology of the individual and hence on the composition of the species; Cesalpino does not. Nor does Aristotle (or Theophrastus) express the teleological thesis of the vital unity of the organism in terms of its *reduction* to an essential part. Other parts of the plant may come into play "for the sake of" the fructification – which is the plant's end – but a true classification must mention and make explicit this teleological character of the *other* parts.

Cesalpino's rationale for his reductive thesis derives from the dual role that he accords the characters of the fructification in the natural scheme of things. The natural scheme represents a contact point between God's eternal, rational order and the actual, imperfect, material conditions obtaining on earth. The fructification constitutes a natural intersection of these orders. It provides God substantive access to the material world – for the plant just *is* the material actualization of the fructification; and it permits humankind epistemic access from the material world to God. The taxonomic order is thus identical neither with the eternal order (conceptually whole and materially undifferentiated) nor with the sensible order (how things commonsensically appear to us under their various material guises). It is for this reason that the fructification elements chosen as the *differentiae* of classification need have no direct functional value, only rational value. Direct functional value pertains to the sensible realm exclusively. This is not Cesalpino's fundamental preoccupation; rather, he is concerned with the *rationality* imposed by God on the material being. That is why only the number (*numerus*), position (*situs*) and figure (*figura*) of the seeds and other selected floral organs are truly essential to taxonomy.

Having set the criterion for fixing species,[1] Cesalpino could go on to establish genera that would bring the chaos of an ever-expanding world of sensible forms back to some kind of intellectual order. He argues that the characters (*differentiae*) required for classification must pertain to the (morphological) nature of the plant only. Variable characters that alter with climate, soil or habitat, or through man's intervention, must be taken as "accidental" and unfit for demarcating the essential similarities and differences between plants. Qualities of texture, odor, taste and color are particularly subject to variation and can be used only as adjuncts to the austere visual cues of number, position and figure.

The first division of the plant kingdom – into those with a lignaceous habit and those with a herbaceous one – derives from popular classification; however, it can also be justified on the Aristotelian assumption that the first function of the "vegetative soul" is nutrition, and that the basic difference in habit reflects a fundamental difference in the mode of acquiring nutriment. For Cesalpino, roots and shoots were the parts primarily responsible for fulfilling the nutritive function. The root would absorb the food from the soil, while the leafy shoot would assimilate the absorbed food and distribute it to the other parts of the plant. Accordingly, the group of woody plants is characterized by the fact that the root and shoot are stronger and harder (*habitiori substantia, & duriori constant*) than in herbaceous plants (1583:27).[2]

In the second place:

> there must be a "vegetative" substance allowing plants to reproduce. This is the most important aspect wherever it is perfected. To this end were created the fruits and parts assuring the fructification. This particularity does not exist among all plants, only in the most elaborated. And as a function of the similarities and differences in the fructification, one must establish secondary genera for the trees as well as for the most humble plants. It matters little whether these genera be named or not; for they have not all been named. Only those of evident utility for man have been named, such as the legumes and grains.
>
> And if there were need of a third "vegetative substance," it would be necessary to institute a third partition – and to study in the same way this element as well as the parts destined for it – a partition that would divide the preceding genera. But insofar as the functioning of plants is summed up in the two elements previously discussed, the classification and division of genera will only take into account those elements. Numerous genera rightly appear to follow the mode of fructification; *for in no other part has nature produced such a multitude and distinction of organs as are observed in the fruit.*   (Cesalpino 1583:27, my italics)

Thus, Cesalpino's further divisions of the two main groups are based on those parts in which the next most important function of the plant is located, namely the fruits and seeds.[3] The characters derived from these parts are primarily meant to demarcate taxa at what is roughly the level of the modern family on up to the folk life-form.[4] Presumably, the fructification characters are enough to delineate these taxa *because the information content of the fructification is sufficiently detailed to make reference to other parts merely redundant*. So, when the fructification is constant, differences in parts of the stem, leaves or roots are "in a sense accidental" (1583:29). But this does not mean that other parts of the plant can be ignored. True, "all the organs over and above the root and pith (or 'heart') are for the purpose of fruit bearing" (1583:6), however, "to the extent that they are for the sake of the fructification" (*quatenus fructus gratia datae sunt*), a close attention to differences in these other parts may reveal hitherto unexpected differences in the fructification (1583:9). Moreover, divisions below the family level may be provisionally made on the basis of parts other than the fructification; the herbaceous Leguminosae, for example, are subdivided according to possession or lack of tendrils. In the end, though, all secondary divisions down to the level of species should proceed according to differences in the fructification.

Reliance on the information value of the fructification is not a direct deduction from *a priori* principles. It derives from a painstaking attempt to delimit unequivocally an exhaustive series of family-level "genera" in place of the intuitive and vaguely bounded family-level fragments of common sense. Because an exhaustive series of species could no longer be expected to serve as a complete basis for apprehending the order of the living world, another basis would have to be found in accordance with readily perceptible (commonsensical) notions of morphological affinity. The local series of family-level fragments seemed to provide the intuitive groundwork for just such a basis:[5]

> The plants are almost innumerable. So one must note intermediate genera, hardly mentioned, and containing the most distant species; but hitherto only a few have been revealed. For if one accepts the grains and legumes, which are commonly called cereals and vegetables, others can hardly be distinguished so clearly. And it is especially use that in fact justifies this selection rather than similarity in form – which is what we are looking for.
>
> (1583:25)

Although Cesalpino rightly notes that ordinary folk rarely name covert fragments, he errs in suggesting that they recognize only those having some special utility. In fact, popular groupings, that depend largely on affinity in overall morphological aspect and that tend to center about a single biological family, are recognized in folk societies, though seldom named (Berlin 1982b; cf. Berlin *et al.* 1981; Bulmer 1979:62). The same is generally true of Cesalpino's botanical *genera innominata*, as it is of Aristotle's animal *eide anonyma*.

Such groups are not usually named because, unlike the named folkbiological groupings of generic-speciemes and life-forms, family-level fragments do not appear to comprise a proper taxonomic series. That is to say, they do not constitute a mutually exclusive, exhaustive and relational partitioning of the local flora and fauna. For the herbalists as well, such groups represent more or less isolated sections of weakly-linked chains of generic-speciemes. The longer the section – that is, the greater the number of links – the fuzzier the section's composition. This is because any local environment is unevenly riddled with morphological gaps at the "family" level. Nevertheless, whether the family fragment is named (cf. Taylor 1978-79:227-228) or not (cf. Hays 1976:500), its morphological composition is occasionally such that its members cut across plant life-forms that do form a proper taxonomic series. Because overt inclusion of such fragmenta would destroy any (transitive) taxonomic order in which plant life-forms also appear, they tend to remain "covert" (see section 2.5 above).

This is likely the foremost factor in Cesalpino's decision to sustain the separation, for example, between ligneous and herbaceous Leguminosae. For, on Cesalpino's own account, except for the difference in stem habit, the two main classes of Leguminosae (i.e. woody and herbaceous) have the same differentiae. His insistence on maintaining the distinction, despite an obvious awareness of their morphological relationship, clearly derives from his commitment to the intuitively elegant structure of popular taxonomy, and not from blind adherence to metaphysical doctrine.

Cesalpino's dilemma is that of having to cross a conceptual threshold beyond which common sense is no longer pertinent in order to recapture the intuitive surety of common sense. The full complement of nondimensional species could no longer be grasped in its entirety; yet the nondimensional species is intuitively the most secure contact that human beings have with the diversity of the living world. Family-level fragments can provide only intermittent intuitive contact with the local flora and fauna; but if a way could be found, without violating life-forms, to complete an unequivocal series of such fragments by evening out the local gaps with knowledge obtained from the partial series of other environments, this would resecure the equivalent of local contact while vastly extending it.

Determining such a series would require a calculated blend of empirical and rational intuition. Like the herbalists, Cesalpino must first secure all the intuitive knowledge thus far accumulated relating ancient to local types: "as far as possible, I have felt it incumbent upon me to match each separate plant to its ancient names ... but without neglecting popular appellations" (1583, dedicatory epistle). By taking known European types and fragments as standard referents, more remote environments could then be scanned for species to fill out the fragmentary European chains; but once completed, a full complement of European-based family-level "genera" would presumably suffice as a summary framework in which any exotic species might find its "natural genus." If a foreign species were to occasionally show itself to be misplaced, this would be owing to some insufficiency in the initial description of the plant, and not to an insufficiency in the stock of available genera:

> In truth it is obligatory that in such a summary of plants, one amongst the rest may accidentally escape us; as with a soldier who sometimes sees himself placed in a division that is not his own, so it may happen that a

plant is classed in a genus that is foreign to it. This especially concerns the medicinal plants of far off countries, of which only the root or sap or wood or another part is transported, without us having the opportunity to have ever seen the entire plant.   (Cesalpino 1583, dedicatory epistle)

Empirical intuition alone, however, could never ensure an *exhaustive* and *unequivocal* delimitation of family-level "genera." The European core of fragments would itself be grounded in an intuitive appreciation of greater or lesser degrees of overall morphological affinity; foreign species would be attached as complements to that core on the basis of still weaker intuitions of affinity. Thus, for indefinitely many exotic species, and even for morphologically isolated European species, no clear and unambiguous decision on generic (i.e. familial) affiliation could be justified intuitively. Consequently, the closure and well-boundedness of individual genera, as well as the completeness of the whole sequence of genera, would have to depend upon rational principles. Accordingly, all empirically intuited genera must, in some way, be rigidly bound to a logical structure of fructification characters. This is the task to which books II through IV of *De plantis* are devoted. These books aspire to offer rational principles of discovery, but they generally succeed only as easy-to-follow keys to the identification of what was already intuitively known.

The way Cesalpino worked out his classification is speculatively reconstructed by Bremekamp (1953a; cf. Vines 1913), who suggests that he may have begun with a single intuitively well-grounded group of plants or with several such groups. Cesalpino likely chose the first track, argues Bremekamp, for that would have led to the "discovery of a large number of natural groups, and this ... would have encouraged him to proceed." But the families and sections of natural families that Cesalpino did produce were, to a significant extent, already known to local folk and the herbalists of the time: *Gramineae, Leguminosae, Liliaceae, Labiatae, Verbenaceae, Umbelliferae, Cruciferae, Ranunculaceae, Cucurbitaceae, Euphorbiaceae, Compositae, Rosaceae, Caryophyllaceae* and *Primulaceae*.

It seems more plausible, then, that Cesalpino attempted by trial and error to find logically elegant combinations of fructification characters that would *preserve* these intuitive groupings. Occasionally, the logical play of such characters could indeed lead to the discovery of natural groupings that intuition of habitus alone would not likely reveal: for example, factoring out the Boraginaceae from the Labiatae by the ovule's orientation. But the keying process could also yield morphologically mixed results: for example, herbaceous plants with bilocular fruits divide into those with a double caryopsis (umbellifers), those with a single freed seed in each fruit cell (*Mercurialis, Agrimonia, Poterium, Rubia, Galium*), those having several seeds in each fruit cell with the dissepiment perpendicular to the plane of symmetry (crucifers), and those having several seeds in each fruit cell with the dissepiment in the plane of symmetry (Scrophulariaceae, part of Solanaceae, *Plantago, Pyrola, Potamogeton*). All in all, though, Cesalpino managed to produce a logical key whose consecutive divisions include plants that usually belong to only one or two natural families –

not nearly so "deplorable" (Guyénot 1941:19) an affront to intuitions of natural affinity as might be inferred from cursory examination.

Cesalpino clearly favors certain aspects of the fructification, such as number of seeds per fruit, relative position of the petals and stamens with respect to the fruit, and figure of the seed, seed-receptacle and flower. But he provides no formal principle of priority by which to automatically demarcate plant groups. Nor does he fall back on functional priority. This lack of a definite principle of priority no doubt owes to his realization that, even if the more obvious intuitive groupings may be tagged with fructification characters, the tagging sequence can apparently follow no single logical line, or *fundamentum fructificationis*, if such groups are to be preserved. Yet without a single principled line of reasoning, the boundaries of the *less*-intuitive groupings would remain a subject of indefinite controversy, with arbitrary claims being made for the priority of different characters in different cases.

Cesalpino's logical key, then, is thus not quite a deduction. It takes the general form of a dichotomous division, although some stages of the division have more than two alternatives. At each step, a particular part (or complex of parts) of the fructification presents at least two features that oppose one another in number, position or figure. But these opposing features by no means exhaust the *logically possible* alternatives. Moreover, sometimes number is chosen as the criterion of opposition, other times form or position; and occasionally an opposing feature simply marks the absence of a certain number, position or figure. In brief, no attempt is made to exhaust all possible positive combinations of essential characters according to some universal rule. No logical derivation of plant groups is really offered: there is only a practical guide that unequivocally factors out subordinate genera that are otherwise too difficult to recognize immediately, either because they are too numerous or because their respective (overall morphological) aspects tend to shade into one another.

Later systematists sought to rectify the situation by removing the problem of classification even further from neo-Aristotelian concerns. The rational order would no longer be considered the logical nexus where corruptible matter meets eternal godly form. Rather, logical hylomorphism would cede to mathematical mechanism; that is, the rational order would be viewed as a mathematical trajectory tracing the workings of the Universal Artificer through the living world. The goal would no longer be a formally elegant indexing of plant forms, but a computational system whose basic rationalization need only be evidence of a mathematically efficacious sequence of morphological combinations. Such a system, Cesalpino could not envisage – for he lacked the technical vocabulary that would allow (Jung and Ray) a mathematical description of plant parts, and he failed to fix the genus (in the manner of Tournefort and Linnaeus) as a privileged level of reality to which *a* principle of computation might be applied.

To know the logical place of any one form would be simultaneously to know the possible morphological similarities and differences between it and all other forms. For classification to become this preset combinatory system of indefinitely many morphological possibilities, the character of number would have to shift from the ordinal to the cardinal; position would have to translate into topological disposition in respect of structural morphology; and figure would have to transform into geometrical configuration. In this way, a quantitative expression and reduction might be given to multidimensional similarities and differences in overall morphological structure.[6] Only then could one hope to traverse, automatically and simply, the whole complex of morphological arrangements in the living world without having to perform the superhuman feat of accumulating and committing to memory all the morphological facts. The system would still have to be made compatible with common-sense intuitions, though; otherwise it could lay no claim to a vital link with the sensible world.

7.2 TRIAL AND ERROR

For the better part of a century following the publication of *De plantis* there was little sustained effort at systematic classification. For the most part, Cesalpino's arrangement was ignored, although his plant denominations were often cited, as herbalists gave priority to describing the new species that exploration was revealing at an ever-increasing rate. Caspar Bauhin, for instance, knew of Cesalpino's work, but he did not understand it and thought that it would only confuse students of botany. The one major exception in this period was Joachim Jung (Jungius), professor of mathematics at Giessen and later of natural sciences at the Akademisches Gymnasium in Hamburg. Educated at Padua, Jung was undoubtedly influenced by both Cesalpino and Galileo.[7] He sought to develop Cesalpino's natural system by creatively applying the maxim of Galileo's *Il Saggiatore* (1623) that the book of nature "is written in mathematical language and the characters are triangles, circles and other geometrical figures."

Jung's approach to scientific methodology, however, differs from both Cesalpino and Galileo in that it does *not* use deductive analysis – whether logical division or geometrical demonstration – either as a technique for the solution of specific empirical problems or as a means to the apprehension of self-evident metaphysical principles. Like Harvey, who was also educated at Padua, Jung rejects the central tenet of logical *methodus* expressed in the works of the great Paduan Aristotelian, Giacomo Zabarella. According to Zabarella (1608, cols. 133-134) logic is the instrument "by which we are helped in acquiring knowledge of things"; however, "acquisition" is meant in two ways, only the first of which would prove acceptable to Jung and Harvey: as a set of teaching procedures (*ordines*), logic aims to communicate existing knowledge without ambiguity; but as a method of discovery (*methodus proprie dicta*), it aspires to provide new knowledge (cols. 138-139), being an instrument for yielding "knowledge of what is unknown from knowledge of what is known" (cols. 226-231).[8] For Jung and Harvey, though, the resolution of particular scientific puzzles, as well as the discovery of the premises of any scientific (or metaphysical) demonstration, are obtained by induction from experience.

Although Jung and Harvey were well acquainted with Bacon's work, their view of induction remained decidely Aristotelian: either by increasingly refined observation (Jung) or by repeated experience (Harvey), empirical simples would presumably manifest themselves, as would their combination into *necessary* truths. From this standpoint, a noble task of scientific investigation would be to prove previous theories – including one's own – false by rendering observation more exact. But while Harvey (1653/1981:443-453) relies on analogy for extrapolation and argumentation from immediate sense data, Jung (1982) looks to geometry.

Jung conceives of the scientific method as a critique, or *doxoscopus*, that inextricably combines logic and experience. It is geometry that provides everyday observations with the precision needed to make the scientific connections between them manifest:

> Just as the doctor must first purge the body of those substances that make it sick, so the task of *doxoscopus* must be to prepare a *tabula rasa* of the intellect in which the things of nature may be allowed to project themselves .... Already Galen had furnished the only sure method: start out from the most evident and general givens of everyday experience in order to progress little by little towards more difficult observations .... It is only after having found and defined the lowest levels of being that one could then constitute an axiomatic science of nature, in the manner of geometry that starts from the point, the line, the circle or the parallels.
>
> (Meinel 1985; 1984a)

The only explicit methodological principle that Jung accepts is Occam's razor; for this justifies the geometrical analysis of experience whose goal is to achieve a complete synthesis and resolution (*resolutio*) of complex experience by a finite combination of elementary principles. These principles are not, as with Galileo, mathematical principles of *discovery* that allow the natural scientist to abstract from the secondary qualities of sensible things so as to apprehend "real" underlying physical forms. Rather, they are strictly principles of sense experience, whose mathematical expression must be constructed after the fact.

Whereas for Galileo, Euclid's geometry provides a (partial) model of reality, for Jung the structure of the "geometrical" model in chemistry, as in natural history, is something that cannot be prejudged in advance of empirical scrutiny. There could be no mental anticipations of empirical generalization. Nor could one allow contrived experiments to confirm or deny such *a priori* considerations. So, there could be no conception of "law of nature" or "scientific method" in Galileo's modern sense. But if mathematical inference and law do not constitute the syntax and semantics of Jung's book of nature, at least geometry provides its alphabet.

In all of this, Jung's approach was destined to be a minor, if valiant, side effort in the theoretical development of natural philosophy. But in natural history there was a more sustained and fruitful wedding of enlightened Aristotelian and modern scientific ideas; and this is understandable given that the Aristotelian cosmos was built on a biological model, not on a model of inert substances. It is at this historical juncture that Jung's ideas of analysis found a special niche, but one that was methodological rather than epistemological. Both empirically and rationally inclined natural historians could profitably make use of his mathematized descriptions of plants without committing themselves to Jung's Aristotelian conception of science as classification and definition.

Unpublished in his lifetime, Jung's botanical lectures were edited shortly after his death by two former students, Martin Fogel and Johannes Vagetius. Through the five fragments of the *De plantis doxoscopiae physicae minores* (1662/1747), Jung proposes that all plants can be "accurately reduced to true genera by specific differences, according to the rules of logic" (69). In the first fragment, he questions whether the traditional life-form divisions of tree and herb are valid. Citing Theophrastus' description of the otherwise herbaceous mallow occasionally becoming "tree-like" (74), he argues that this is but one example where the popular distinction appears to break down.[9] Such a division cannot, therefore, be admitted as "philosophically" proper. He emphasizes the importance of the geometrical configuration and the topological interrelations of the floral parts and fruit for delimiting genera, but he also stresses the significance of leaf structure. Like Cesalpino, Jung acknowledges that variations in spiny texture, color, odor, taste, medicinal properties, location and time of germination are nonessential (77); but unlike Cesalpino, he argues that the number of flowers and fruits are accidental as well.

The *Doxoscopiae* had little direct impact on the course of systematics, but the short *Isagoge Phytoscopica* (1679/1747) established the foundations of analytic plant morphology. A handwritten manuscript was given to John Ray in the late 1650s, and its influence owes chiefly to Ray's use of its morphological principles in his own later systematic work. In the *Isagoge* the root, stem, leaf, flower and fruit are decomposed into analytically significant elements. The leaf, for example, is characterized as that which is laterally extended with respect to its point of attachment, such that there is a difference between its external (adaxial) and internal (abaxial) surfaces. The form of the leaf may be simple (e.g. lily), concave (e.g. onion) or compound. Compound leaves can be digitate (e.g. clover), paripinnate (e.g. pea), imparipinnate (e.g. rose) or triangulate (e.g. celery). The leaf margin is either whole or segmented, and if dissected, then laciniate, serrate, crenate or dentate.

Even more important for the development of systematics is Jung's distinction of the parts of the flower: calyx, corolla, stamens, style and ovary (fruit). Some flowers have no calyx (e.g. tulips and lilies), but when there is one it is either undivided (*perianthium simplex*) or divided (*perianthium compositium*). He sees that the number of lobes of the corolla marks off different species, and that flowers with five or six occur more often than those with three or four. Although, like Cesalpino, he ignores the reproductive role of the stamens, he associates differences in their number, disposition and configuration with different species; his description of the fruit, however, does not improve on Cesalpino's.

The restoration of interest in Cesalpino's system owes its chief impetus to a curious debate between the leading English naturalists of the second half of the seventeenth century. In his *Praeludia botanica* (1669:469) the king's physician and botanist, Robert Morison, attacked the unnamed author of the tabular classification of plants presented in John Wilkins' *Essay Towards a Real Character and Artificial Language* (1668). At the request of Wilkins, John Ray – the first eminent naturalist who was *not* a physician – had drawn up these tables in conformity to Wilkins' ideal grammar, proposing various alternative ways for dividing the same groups and including such "accidental" features as taste, color, odor, texture and location. In a letter dated May 7, 1669, Ray acknowledged that he knew the tables to be "manifestly imperfect and ridiculous," for they basically represented a linguistic rather than a natural demonstration (1848:41–42). But he was compelled by Morison's clear implication that the author of the tables was botanically incompetent to produce a more coherent system (cf. Raven 1942).

Morison proposed his own system against the "hallucinations" of the brothers Bauhin and claimed it to be drawn solely from nature; however, his assertion that the *nota generica* are to be sought exclusively in the fructification evidently derives from Cesalpino.[10] Ray had earlier proposed an alphabetical catalog of the local Cambridge flora as a prelude to a complete British flora; but at the conclusion to the catalog's *Index* he imagines, plausibly with Jung's recently communicated manuscript in mind, that "it would be possible to classify plants in many other ways, for example in respect of their roots or stems or flowers or seeds, though it is not my intention to pursue the subject further" (Ray 1660:103). Following Morison's attack, Ray set out to apply Jung's analytic morphology to Cesalpino's system, thus absorbing all that was worthwhile in Morison's method while endowing it with a precision that would ensure much greater success.

In the preface to his *Methodus plantarum nova* (1682), Ray argues that classification should not follow utilitarian or ecological criteria; rather, in line with Cesalpino, it should be based on "the similitude and likeness of the principal parts." Like Cesalpino, he implicitly allows consideration of all the elements of the fructification, although he emphasizes "principally" the seeds and seed-receptacles. On occasion he also accepts as "characteristic" marks drawn from the form of the roots or the locations of the leaves on the stem (e.g. Asperifoliae [i.e. the labiates]). Like Jung, Ray concedes that the division of plants into life-forms is "popular" rather than "philosophical," yet he chooses to retain the traditional distinction anyway (24-25). His most significant departure from Cesalpino, however, concerns the division immediately following that of life-forms: the division of herbs into those with either two seed-leaves (dicotyledons) or only one (monocotyledons) would eventually become a standard item in the classification of flowering plants.[11]

In the *Historia plantarum* (1686), Ray further elaborates his system in accordance with Jung's morphology, and fixes the criterion of conspecificity in the manner of Cesalpino:

> differences that issue from the same seed, be it in an isolated plant or in an entire species, are accidental and not the signs of a specific character . . . . The same is true of the animal world . . . the number of species in nature is certain and determined: *God rested on the sixth day, interrupting his great work* – that is, the creation of new species. Now the number of plants varying by the color of their flowers or their multiplicity is infinite: each year new variations are spawned that we reject and to which we refuse the title and the dignity of true species . . . these variations are due to changes in the sky, the earth or the alimentation. (Ray 1686:40)

As for ostensible cases of hybridization or "transmutation": "Observe, however, that such transmutation exists only between related species of the same genus; and it is likely that certain of these are not characterized by specific differences" (Ray 1686:43).[12]

These works mark a steady improvement in the delimitation of natural groups, especially those subdivisions that correspond to modern families of phanerogams. Yet, like Cesalpino, Ray fails to apply a single consistent basis for division throughout his classification, in order not to violate the more readily perceived intuitive groups. His "synoptic" tables resemble Cesalpino's logical key much more than they do a strictly principled division. In contrast, the Leipzig botanist, physician and chemist Rivinus (Bachmann) would shortly propose an elegant system whose major divisions depend solely on structural variations in the corolla of the flower. The definitive form of Ray's reply to Rivinus' *Introductio generalis in rem herbarium* (1690) appears in an exchange of letters reprinted in the appendix to the second edition of Ray's *Synopsis methodica stirpium Britanicarum* (1696a). Here Rivinus argues against the time-honored division of plants into life-forms, because it could not be fitted into a system employing "but one (sort of) natural character" (in Ray 1696a:4). As for Ray's own classification, Rivinus remarks:

> You concede the utility of characters chosen from the flower and fruit in order to distinguish subalternate genera. I feel the same, but while I consistently use them you waver, abandoning these essential marks whenever it seems appropriate. (in Ray 1696a:21)

To this, Ray replies that a classification that conforms to nature must occasionally use many characters drawn from the whole habitus. Indeed, no single part is truly essential:

> The correct and philosophical division of any genus is by essential differences. But the essences of things are unknown to us. Thus, in place of these

essential characters, characteristic accidents should be used . . . [that] join together plants that are similar, and agree in primary parts, or in total external aspect, and which separate those that differ in these respects.

(Ray 1696a:30-33)

At this juncture Ray's argument already has a definite Lockean flavor. But as Sloan (1972) notes, it is only in formulating a reply to the much more formidable system presented in Tournefort's *Elémens de botanique* (1694) that Ray clearly embraces some of the main ideas of Locke's *Essay* (1689/1848):

The essences of things are wholly unknown to us. Since all our knowledge derives from sensation, we know nothing of things that are outside us except through the power that they have to affect our senses in some particular way, and by the mediation of these impressions to cause a particular image to arise in the intellect. If the essences of things are immaterial forms, it is admitted by everyone that these are not encountered in any sensible means. If they are really nothing other than certain fixed proportions and mixtures of elements or natural minima, then these minima cannot be perceived by our senses, except with several instruments or aids.

(Ray 1696b:5)

Tournefort's classification displays even more logical elegance than Rivinus', while doing less violence to naturally perceived affinities. Nevertheless, argues Ray, the fungi have neither fruit nor flower, and most deciduous plants lack these organs for much of their lives. How, then, can such nonexistent or transient characters be "essential" to the life of plants? Moreover, since the roots and stem are always present, these organs would have a better claim to being essential, although hardly anyone would consider using only such parts as a basis for classification.

In his last important work, *Methodus plantarum emendata et aucta* (1703), Ray concedes that the fructification is usually preferable to other parts; however, it is by no means an infallible guide to the natural order of genera. In the (unpaginated) section *De methodo plantarum in genere* he writes:

For the memory and the right method one must, by way of a sign of recognition, adopt either one property with a generic character or a mark which is common to all the species already known . . . . This mark is very readily taken from the flower or the fruit of those plants that exhibit these marks, because these parts vary less often in the same genus than do the others; and they are, by their color, figure and other accidents, conspicuous and easily observable. Nevertheless, if in the future one encounters a plant which agrees in other parts and accidents with the rest of the species of the genus, but does not have the mark which we have taken for characteristic, then such a plant must be included in the genus with which it has several attributes in common.

The fructification is the most "natural" character for classification only in the sense that, of all the parts, it has the highest information content. All things being equal, it is usually redundant with the whole habitus. The natural priority of the fructification thus owes not to its functional essentiality, but to its practicality. In other words, it best fulfils the tenets of Occam's razor: "The characteristic marks of the genera must not be multiplied beyond necessity, nor accumulated to an extent more than necessary to determine the genus with certainty."

The fructification, though usually sufficient, is not always necessary. A proper characterization of any given genus must thus include a description of the entire habitus as a necessary preliminary. Only then can a characteristic mark be chosen that is redundant with the whole habitus, be it a mark selected from the fructification or from some other part:

> A complete definition is made up out of a *genus proximum* and an essential difference: but the essences of things are unknown to us, hence the essential differences of them also. However, since from the essences flow the same qualities, operations and other things which are accidents, there can be no surer mark of essential, and so of generic, agreement than to have many parts and accidents similar, or to have the whole facies (*faciem*), habitus (*habitum*), and contexture (*texturam*) the same.   (Ray 1703)

Although Ray follows Locke in claiming the real essences of beings to be unknowable, and the complex perceptions arising in our minds to be only nominal essences, he differs from Locke on two crucial points. First, Ray never abandons his belief in the absolute reality of species:

> I would not deny that universals have a foundation in things truly agreeing or similar in special parts or properties. This agreement is so great, especially in living things, that individuals of the same species are seen as having been made according to the same exemplar or idea in the Divine Mind . . . . From this it follows that species are distinguished essentially from one another and are not transmutable, and the forms and essences of these are either certain specific principles, that is, certain very small particles of matter, distinct from all others, and naturally indivisible, or certain specific seminal reasons enclosed by means of an appropriate vehicle.
> (Ray 1696b:vi)

For Ray, then, the nominal essence at the level of the species unequivocally signals the presence of a real essence, even though the underlying principles of the real essence may remain forever obscure. Locke, however, sees matters quite differently:

> I demand, what are the alterations that may, or may not, be in a horse or lead, without making either of them to be another species? In determining the species of things by our abstract ideas, this is easy to resolve; but if any

one will regulate himself herein, by supposed real essences, he will I suppose be at a loss; and he will never be able to know when any thing precisely ceases to be of the species of horse or lead.

(1689/1848 III,iii,13)

Second, Ray never seems to have accepted Locke's skeptical conclusion that a true science of nominal essences is impossible. For Ray, not only species, but higher genera as well, can be known to be real. For Locke, however, claims as to the reality of abstract types, whether species or genera, are "wholly unintelligible, and whereof we have scarce so much as any obscure or confused conception in general" (1689/1848 III,vi,10). Such claims, argues Locke, are the culture-bound illusions of ordinary language.[13] Ray, by contrast, considers phenomenal intuitions to be strong indications of true genera: so much so, in fact, that he appears to abandon earlier hesitations concerning the "philosophical verity" of life-forms. Indeed, on Ray's own accounting, morphological intuitions are surer signs of natural agreement than any philosophical principles.

7.3 ART AND INTUITION

Descartes insinuates in *Discours de la méthode* that to transcend the bounds of sense one must substitute analytic certainty for sensible intuition: "The analysis of the Ancients ... is so constrained by a consideration of figures that it cannot exercise the understanding without greatly tiring the imagination" (1637/1907, pt.2). Similarly, for Tournefort, part of the rationale for a botanical system is that "the study of plants does not greatly tire the imagination when undertaken with method" (1694:13).

To ensure the system a firm grounding in reality, Tournefort is obliged to establish a basis where the conflict between reason and customary modes of apprehension is minimal. This privileged point of contact between nature and art is the *genus*. Before Tournefort, "genus" referred to any group expressly including two or more species. With Tournefort, "genus" comes to denote only that conceptually fixed and perceptually unitary level of reality that *logically* ranks immediately above that of the species, but which is otherwise *perceptually* confluent with the species, that is, with a *bouquet* of morphologically similar individuals (1694:13).

Now, intuitively given genera are *usually* associated with distinct fructifications. Thus, on the basis of the rationalist principle of sufficient reason, there *must* be a naturally unique indexing of known and as yet unknown genera by fructification features. If gaps should appear in the sequence of characters, one must not forget that God has a horror of vacuums. This ensures, *a priori*, that genera still to be discovered by expedition will already have a fixed place within a preestablished series, whether or not we are in fact able to reason out what the series is. Implicit in this approach is the Cartesian credo of *veracitas dei*: if God has undeceivingly allowed us to *see* a part of nature's plan, then he has given us reason by which to *anticipate* the whole.

According to Tournefort:

> *the author of nature has fixed the appropriate marks of plants* .... Now if the genera are confounded, how do we represent species to ourselves? Nature, so it is said, seems wholly alien to any method. But even if this be conceded, experience convinces us that without a method in things so numerous and diverse as in botany one could but comprehend nature obscurely. Those who imagine that the correct distribution and naming of species depend upon men's fancy are not less mistaken. The Creator of all things, who gave us the faculty for giving names to plants, places in the plants themselves signifying marks from which should be sought that similarity required of species of the same genus. We can neither change these marks nor renounce examining and using them, if we would elimi-
> nate error. (Tournefort 1719:54)

If we fail to uncover the whole of nature's plan by such clear and distinct characters, it is because we, and not God or nature, are imperfect. As Descartes himself notes:

> our ideas and notions, being real things that come from God insofar as they are clear and distinct, cannot to that extent fail to be true. Accordingly, if we often have ideas that contain falsity, they can only be ideas that contain some confusion and obscurity ... that is to say, they are confused in us
> only because we are not wholly perfect. (1637/1907, pt.4)

At first glance, Tournefort's idea of the "naturalness" of genera seems to refer only to what is convenient for the mind: "It is much more convenient to reduce most of the known plants to 600 genera than to reduce them merely to two or three hundred, because most of these two or three hundred will be overloaded (*chargé*) with so many species that one will not be able to express their differences except by highly composed names" (1694:38). But it is clear from his insistence that genera must be "true" that Tournefort means by "naturalness" more than mere ease of memory. He advises that species judged to be "heteroclites or bastards or degenerates, if such terms be permitted," should not be allowed to encumber well-defined genera "because they do not have the essential marks of those genera to which they are attached"; in such cases, the heteroclites should be allowed to form distinct genera of their own, even if the genus contains only *one* species: "What is the necessity, for example, of following Morison in calling hops, *Convolvulus heteroclitus perenni, Floribus foliaceis, strobili instar*? Wouldn't it be better to make of it a particular genus, and to leave to it the name, *Lupulus vulgaris*, which is known the world over?" (1694:38).

Tournefort argues that the ostensibly mixed generic character of a heteroclite is an indication of a truly distinctive generic discontinuity in nature, which further exploration and more careful observation may confirm with new species. Nonetheless, the possibility exists that a genus will remain mono-specific (e.g. the *Belladonna*); and it is this possibility that underscores the fact that the genus represents a fixed level of reality, no matter what its specific content.

The crucial question arises, though, why six hundred genera?

Certainly the names of plants can be reduced to a mediocre number, if one wishes to fix on those which are necessary. One will have, so to speak, the key of this science in retaining the names of about 600 genera, under which can be brought the greatest part of known plants. It would be useless to burden the memory with all the synonyms that one has given them .... If after this cutting back (*retranchement*) one still thinks of complaining that the names of plants are too numerous, it would be to accuse nature of being too fecund in its productions. (Tournefort 1694:3)

The key to understanding the naturalness of genera, then, is the notion of "cutting back", or retrenchment, of the 6,000 to 10,000 known species of plants by one order of magnitude *to the same number of basic-level groups entertained by the ancients, by the German, Italian and Dutch herbalists, and by other folk* (cf. Raven *et al.* 1971). In short, the genus emerged as the "natural" accommodation of the rational mind to a perceptual reality that could no longer be contained within the ordinary bounds of common sense.

The unequivocal nature of the fructification would leave no doubt as to generic character. If the habitus, rather than the fructification, were chosen as the basis for the genus, however, then the genus would be bound to a morphological type. The choice of generic habitus would thus depend upon which species was chosen as the type. Such a choice would invariably be the subject of disagreement among authors who, because of their familiarity with their own environments, might prefer one species over another. The extension of the generic grouping would vary with the type chosen, and there would be potentially as many genera as species. In that case, the endeavor to replace limited common-sense surety with an equally certain global order would be doomed to failure, and the quest for a natural system would have to be abandoned.

Still, the need to reduce habitual structure to a characteristic part does not suffice to explain why the fructification was chosen, rather than the stem, leaf, root, or some combination of these parts. The traditional account has it that, by identifying the genus with its fructification – that is, with its reproductive parts – the genus could also assume the metaphysical status of a natural, generative force in the world. To classify by fructification would then be tantamount to explaining how the natural order necessarily came to be (cf. Sachs 1875/1890; Sloan 1972).

Tournefort, however, explicitly denies that functional importance has any bearing on the choice of the fructification or certain of its elements as essential generic characters:

Let one not say that nature, having no goal other than the production of fruits, requires us to consider these as the most noble parts of plants. There is no question here of nature's intentions, nor of the nobility of parts; rather, it is a question of finding expedients for the sake of distinguishing plants with all possible clarity; and if the least of their parts were more appropriate than those which are called the most noble, they should be preferred. (1694:26)

Actually, he goes on to argue, the roots appear to be the parts most essential to the life of plants, but they are scarcely indicative of the natural order of plants. So it would seem that Ray's criticism of Tournefort's reliance on "essential" parts that are, in fact, not immediately crucial to the life of plants is beside the point.[14]

Tournefort's "definition" of the plant in terms of root, seed, leaves, stem and flower is a direct appeal to lay knowledge: "All men have more or less the same idea, and [these parts] would be rendered more obscure, if one were to define them" (1694:21).[15] In this respect, he is simply rendering explicit what herbalists and systematists before him had implicitly assumed to be the "natural parts" of plants. The true nature of these parts, which any real definition would have to describe, could not be specified so long as the real nature of things were unknown to use. It suffices that we know what is, and what is not, a natural part.

Thus, starting with what is presumably both a natural and a customary decomposition of plants into their constituent parts, Tournefort proceeds to examine those elements that might be taken from the fructification as against those elements that might be taken from the other parts. He concludes that elements taken from other parts are too numerous if treated together; that is, "it is dangerous to descend into too great a detail, for fear that plants discovered in the future may lack a few of the essential parts thought to belong to the character of their genus" (1694:24). Or, they are too few if taken separately; for example, "differences of roots and stems are too small in number" (25). In the one case, there could be an unsystematic influx of new genera; and in the other, there might not be enough genera recognized for discerning an ordered connection between them.

The fructification would never have been adopted as the basis for botanical classification were it not for the fact that it usually accords with intuitions about which bouquets of plants seem naturally to go together. That is to say, the fructification is largely redundant with the whole habitus – not because it is the most vital part, but because it is the most complex morphologically. Still, the fructification does not always correspond to intuition, as acknowledged implicitly by Cesalpino and explicitly by Ray. A successful development of the system, then, would turn on the quest for a definitive resolution of the inevitable conflict between systematic art and intuitive nature.

Tournefort concedes Ray's point that many plants, including algae, mosses, and mushrooms, have no visible fructification pattern at all; hence, they must be diagnosed by some other part, until such time as a "true character" (*véritable caractère*) can be found in them that would be analogous to the visible fructification. Even when such characters are manifest, however, they are not always sufficient; for "if one only had regard for the flowers and fruits, it would be necessary to change several things which custom has, with some reason, authorized: for example, wheat, rye, oats, barley and all the species of couch-grass would have to belong to the same genus, since their flowers and fruits have much the same conformation (1694:28–29)".[16] But it would be wrong to think these grasses belong to the same genus: "One can establish as a general maxim in botany, that the flower and the fruit are necessary parts for establishing all genera whose species manifest flowers and fruits, but these parts do not always suffice to distinguish genera from one another" (30). Where the fructification alone does not suffice, "second order" genera may be established "in relation to other parts."

Moreover, Tournefort concedes that his, or any, natural system can only be considered partial and tentative. For him, a "natural" system of the rational mind only more or less follows the doubtlessly perfect logical thread by which God weaves together the world:

> It is necessary to note that whatever method one uses, however exact it may be, one will always believe it to be defective . . . . I know, moreover, that all new rules are subject to many contradictions, and I do not doubt that something first will be found to be said against the system that I propose. (1694:42)

According to Dughi (1957:181), it is precisely through such considerations that Tournefort manages to free himself from the scholastic metaphysics of his predecessors and successors: "The conception of the importance of organs of reproduction taken from Cesalpino led most notably Linnaeus to an all too scholastic principle that 'natural' genera must be defined uniquely with the aid of characters drawn from the five parts of the flower."

Dughi goes much too far, though, in attempting to distinguish Tournefort's concern with rational diagnosis from the "scholastic" concerns of Cesalpino and Linnaeus for whom: "The choice of these floral characters is no longer essentially inspired, as with Tournefort, by considering their diagnostic value, nor corrected by the eventual admission of vegetative [i.e. habitual] characters, nor, most importantly, completed by figures; conceived *a priori* it is restrictive by design." Concern with rational diagnosis is equally apparent in Cesalpino and, as we shall presently see, in Linnaeus as well. So, too, is there a willingness to admit a vegetative characters, at least provisionally. As with Tournefort, Linnaeus also rarely, if ever, diagnoses a plant (or animal) without first analyzing its entire figure (cf. Stearn 1959). What distinguishes Tournefort from Cesalpino and Linnaeus, then, is not adherence to rationalist principles, or admittance of other than fructification characters in the construction of the system. Rather, it is the fact that Tournefort considers the fructification characters to be epistemically, but not ontologically, essential to the natural order of plants. In other

words, Tournefort does not believe, as Linnaeus does, that possible variations on
the patterns of fructification represent the potentially viable modifications on
the theme of life itself – for reason cannot discover nature's real intentions, only
its resultant contours.

Still, it would be an error to conclude, as Linnaeus' French contemporaries
and rivals did, that Tournefort thus regards his classification as an *artificial* key
devoid of a natural basis: "Tournefort, not regarding his method as natural, but
as artificial, placed his genera in the same rank; Linnaeus took his pretentions
further" (Buffon 1749, I:18-19; cf. Adanson 1763:cv). Only with respect to
higher-order classes can the mnemonic simplicity of a single, visually agreeable
floral diagnostic be consistently preferred to more apparently natural, but vague,
intuitions of overall affinity – and even this preference may be justified only to
the extent that it leads to an effective keying out of natural genera. That is why
higher-order groups should be based on characters drawn from the same part of
the plant that is used to establish true genera.

In fact, Tournefort judges the fructification to be the only conceivable natural
basis for a system. He doubts only that his basis is *complete*. This doubt has a
twofold character. First, there is awareness of the fact that everything that has to
be marked is not yet fully available for analysis: "whatever part one takes, it is
sure that one will never find a method that is absolutely general, because . . . one
does not know the flowers and the fruits of all the plants" (1694:43).[17] Second,
even if the flowers and fruits of all plants were readily discernible, current
notions about which characters are sufficient would invariably change with
exploration and discovery (43).

7.4 PARADISE REGAINED

Linnaeus thought to resolve the doubts inherent in Tournefort's system by
decomposing the fructification into a precise combination of analytic elements;
for only a demonstrative science of botany based on rational principles could be
proved a true science (1751 sec. 19): "what I like are distinctions that are definite
and capable of demonstration" (1737b sec. 267). Faith in the epistemological
(computational) rationale for the system would once again be linked to the
acceptance of a metaphysical (essential) rationale (1751 sec. 88). Each genus
would thus be associated with a characteristic formula; and mathematically
regular patterns would be sought among these formulae to compute all
fundamentally possibly basic (i.e. generic) states of plant life: "These marks are
to us as so many plant letters, which, if we can read, teach us the character of
plants; they are written in God's hand; it should be our task to read them"
(1737a, *Ratio operis*).

As a result, discovery of new generic forms could be anticipated that would
accommodate as yet unknown species into the eternal order of things:

> The system is for botany the thread of Ariadna, without which there is
> chaos. Let one take, for example, an unknown plant of the Indies, and let a

botanophile leaf through descriptions, figures, every index; he will not find it unless by chance. But a systematist will determine it straightaway, be it old or new .... The system indicates the plants, even those it does not mention; this, the enumeration of a catalog can never do.

(1751 sec. 156)

To this end, he divided the flower into four parts (calyx, corolla, stamen, pistil) and the fruit into three (pericarp, seed, receptacle) (secs. 86,92). Each of the seven parts of the fructification is further subdivided into as many elements as readily strike the eye at first glance (seven for the calyx, two for the corolla, three each for the stamens and pistils, eight for the pericarp, and four each for the seed and receptacle). Linnaeus then calculates that these thirty-one elements, each comprising the four analytic variables of number, configuration, disposition and proportion (magnitude), would "suffice for 3,884 generic structures, or more than will ever exist" (sec. 167).[18] These generic structures would represent the unequivocal modes of possible existence, only some of which are ever actually realized. Having thus calculated all possible basic existential modalities, he is therefore reasonably assured that the fructification would provide for any new discovery, inasmuch as he had already succeeded in reducing nearly 7,000 of the 10,000 or so species of plants then estimated to exist, into a few hundred genera.

For Linnaeus, as opposed to Tournefort, each genus must correspond to a unique fructification (1736 sec. 159). There could be no place for "second-order" genera in Tournefort's sense: that is, genera that have the same fructification but are distinguished by other (second-order) characters of habitus (and so at first Linnaeus did not choose to recognize many of them). The reason there can be no exception is that genera represent nature's basic rationality. This rationality is determined by (and for) God. Botany, therefore, should be both testamentary and testimonial: as God's ideas are beautifully clear and distinct, so must nature's genera be.

Yet, there is no explicit account given in Linnaeus' many philosophical aphorisms of the metaphysical principles that justify his assertions that all genera are natural, that each genus is determined by a unique fructification, and that the fructification characters of genera constitute the foundations of a true science of botany. This lack of a sustained metaphysical argument is unfortunate, because it encourages the view that Linnaeus simply did not need to elaborate on his attachment to an all too obvious Aristotelian metaphysics (see Cain 1958).[19] For Linnaeus, however, natural essences are more like Platonic *universalia ante rem*, that is, eternal forms of being that subsist prior to their full material realizations. Indeed, individual existence itself loses its essential cast.[20] In this, Linnaeus is rather more in keeping with Spinoza who writes in the *Tractatus de intellectus emendatione*:

I do not understand here by the series of causes and real entities a series of individual mutable things ... for the existence of particular things has no connection with their essence . . . . That essence is only to be found in fixed and eternal things, and from the laws inscribed in those things as their true codes, according to which all individual things are made and ordered; nay, individual and mutable things depend so intimately and essentially on these fixed ones that without them they can neither exist nor be conceived. And these fixed and eternal things . . . will be universal kinds for us by grace of their presence everywhere and by their very great potency, that is, genera for the definitions of individual mutable things and proximate causes of all things.   (1972 secs. 100-101)

Linnaeus was the first to make consistent use of the recently discovered sexual aspect of the fructification in classification.[21] Because the genus is the first level at which the fructification pattern is apparently stable, there would seem to be nothing more natural than for the Creator of all things to bring his ideas of creation for the living world to fruition through these basic sexual sorts. If so, then the genus would have a rightful claim to being the primary ontological, as well as epistemological, unit of theoretical botany: "Botany rests on the fixity of genera" (1751 sec. 209; cf. 1737b sec. 284).

Genera thus conceived represent eternal modes for the realization of God's work in the living world. They are fundamentally rational modalities of existence; hence, their determination need make no reference to any spatio-temporal framework. Species, although eternal (1736 sec. 157), are nevertheless material realizations of, and for, the rational generic order. Even if no reference need be made to any *particular* time or place, species do have actual roles to play in the economy of nature. It is through the concrete interactions of species with one another and with their respective environments that the balance of material forces in the living world is held in equilibrium:[22]

All things contained within this universe loudly celebrate the infinite wisdom of the Creator . . . . All things are ordered successively and linked to attain the same ultimate end . . . all natural beings by turns tend a helping hand for the conservation of any species . . . the death and destruc-tion of the one serving always to re-establish the other.
                                                    (Linnaeus [Biberg] 1749 sec. 1)

By playing its proper material role, every species lives towards a rational end. Armed with its proper type of morphological structure, suited to its proper type of environment, each species materially preserves the fructification in its own best way: "That is why the Creator suspended each plant from its stem and peduncle, so that the mature fruit could be diffused by wind and storm" (1744/ 1972 sec. 64).

In granting ontological priority to the genus, as well as priority in the formal mode, Linnaeus in effect reverses the Aristotelian order. For Aristotle, the species represents a formal realization of some unformed generic matter (a relatively amorphous material substrate). In Linnaeus, the genus clearly has a prior and independent claim to formal existence. It is for this reason that the "theoretical disposition" of genera (*dispositio theoretica*) has a higher scientific value than the "practical disposition" (*dispositio practica*) of species within the system (1751 secs. 152,165); although it is still necessary to know species well in order to verify that the theoretical disposition is the right one.

Linnaeus declares that in a universal and orthodox system that theoretically disposes all naturally observed genera, the fructification is the only true foundation (*fructificationis vero fundamento*) (1751 sec. 26). By this he means that there is a single logical means of dividing the plant world, or *fundamentum divisionis*, that proceeds at every stage, and through all stages, upon one principle, namely, the *fundamentum fructificationis*. By canonically re-presenting the existential process whereby substance progressively unfolds itself into viable forms, one thereby "explains" their existence.[23]

Beginning with the notion of class, which corresponds to the "highest genus" (*genus summum*), a division is effected *per genus et differentiam* (*sive differentias*). It descends by "intermediate genera" (*genera subalterna*), including family-level groupings (*ordines*), until it attains all of the naturally observed genera (*genera proxima*) with their species (*species infimae*) (1751 sec. 155). In this manner, as groups become embedded within groups, the plant world takes on the aspect of a geographical map: its realm is fully partitioned into contiguous provinces; each province, in turn, is exhaustively divided into abutting territories; and each territory is entirely apportioned into districts that border on one another (1751 sec. 77).[24]

Rejecting Ray's synoptic tables and the other logical keys of the sixteenth and seventeen centuries as rationally unprincipled (1751 secs. 153,154), Linnaeus accepts the classifications of Rivinus and especially Tournefort as the first really systematic arrangements (1751 secs. 153,155). Nevertheless, argues Linnaeus, when assembling genera into higher groups, Tournefort adopts a convenient but "artificial" method. By contrast, in Linnaeus' view a true system can only be one that is both logically consistent and "natural" in a metaphysically well-founded sense.

Linnaeus' initial and most comprehensive attempt at a logical calibration of the natural system stresses the number of the stamens and the pistils. Because fertilization is the primary act in reproduction, the organs of fertilization are likely more essential to the plant than the floral elements that contain them. Moreover, the sexual organs, that is the stamens and pistils, are ever present, readily observed and compared, and characteristically formed in intermediate (family-level) groups in ways apparent even to the untrained eye (e.g. the two long and two short stamens of many labiates). In this scheme, classes represent different numbers and positions of stamens in the flower, and the orders within each class are derived from the number of pistils. The structure of this "sexual system" is to a significant degree arithmetic; however, the configuration, positioning and proportion of the sexual organs are also crucial to the determination of over half the classes and orders of flowering plants in the *Systema naturae* (1735; cf. Larson 1971).

In the *Classes plantarum* (1738), Linnaeus concedes that neither his, nor any other, system is truly natural. But he implies that his system preserves as many or more intuitively perceived natural groupings because it seeks to bring to light the essence of the flower, the plant and the group in an easily determinable manner. Still, the sexual system is the closest Linnaeus, or anyone else, ever came to a computation of the natural order. For instance, the different levels of the divisional hierarchy are characterized, in part, by integer sequences of stamens and pistils; however, even these partial sequences have (empirically motivated) gaps – it just so happens that there are no flowers with eleven stamens, so there can be no class of flowers with that number of stamens (1751 sec. 68).

Later, Linnaeus would come to regard positioning followed by configuration as the most reliable of the four analytic variables with magnitude and number as the least sure (1751 secs. 178,179). But there is nothing in the offing that remotely resembles anything like an analytic geometry, or even an arithmetic formulation, of natural plant forms. The problem is that no one part or dimension of the fructification can be assumed constant in all genera. Hence, any hierarchical ordering or derivation of characters must be presumed "artificial" until the essential characters of all genera have been located. Worse, there can be no *a priori* guarantee that the constant character chosen for any one genus is, in fact, truly invariant for that genus unless all of the species of the genus have been examined beforehand. In brief, all so-called "essential" characters must be presumed "factitious" until every species has been thoroughly described.

Still, Linnaeus continues to insist on Cesalpino's point that all is confused if genera are not first well-formed (1737b sec. 225, 1751 sec. 159), the sense of the point being that the genera must prefigure species. Genera need (more or less) anticipate species for reasons of common sense. Well before Linneaus, exploration had already yielded species too numerous to be remembered, and therefore too mentally unstable in the aggregate to serve as a sure basis for a complete ordering of living things (1737b sec. 213, 1751 sec. 256).

The task, then, would be to propose a *program* for the progressive construction of a natural system, such that the intercalation of new species tends to confirm the progress already made and to contribute to its further elaboration. In other words, the broad scheme of the generic order should, at any given moment, *more or less* anticipate the place of exotic species; and it should do so without being so rigidly formed that it cannot accommodate truly novel finds that might otherwise put the whole logically elaborated scheme at risk. Thus, between the artificial and the truly essential a compromise nevertheless seemed possible. It would be based on what Linnaeus calls "the natural character" of the genus in conjunction with a cautious use of habitual intuitions.

The natural character contains, at least initially, the analytic dimensions (numerical, proportional, geometrical, topological) of the seven basic parts of the fructification (calyx, corolla, stamen, pistil, pericarp, seed, receptacle). It thus includes both the essential and factitious characters.[25] To locate the natural character one first notes the basic parts of the fructification under the aspect of the four analytic variables in some familiar or ancient species. Then, "all of the other species of the genus are compared to the first and all discordant marks deleted; in the end the [true] character will thus be produced" (sec. 193).

Because nature is constrained by law, one should expect to find only limited variation in the combination of elements and variables that make up natural characters generally. Accordingly, Linnaeus seeks out "normal" or archetypical conformations that appear in natural characters, much as the physicist looks for "normal" conformations of atomic particles and variables that occur regularly throughout the periodic table. The most "natural" numerical condition, for example, is when the calyx has the same number of segments as the corolla, and this equals the number of stamens. Also, the pistils normally correspond to the fruit in the number of chambers, or the number of rows of seeds. In addition to "normal" structures, Linnaeus also attempts to systematically describe "exceptional" generic characters; for instance, the normal disposition of a pistil is its placement within the anthers, but in this respect *Arum* is a singular anomaly.

Once the natural characters of all genera were known, the basis of the system would be secure:

> If the essential characters of all the genera were discovered, this would greatly facilitate the study of plants . . . . But he, who having neglected the natural character, credits himself with knowledge of botany only misleads himself and others; because the [putative] essential character cannot but often induce one into error when it comes to new genera. The natural character is the foundation of genera, without it none can be rightly judged; it is, and will always be, the absolute foundation of a knowledge of plants.
>
> (1751 sec. 191)

Only after all the natural characters of all genera have been described could one go out in search of the true characters of orders and classes. In the meantime, "artificial classes take the place of natural ones until all the latter be known" (sec. 160); although one should always keep in mind that "the more the classes are natural, the more they are worth, all things being equal" (sec. 206).

Linnaeus concedes that botany cannot aspire to a rational system until the natural characters of all genera have been discovered. Because the exact delimitation of a natural character of a genus depends upon a complete survey of all species that fall under the genus, then a rational system cannot be judged complete before all species are known. It would seem, therefore, that the step of substituting the natural for the essential character, as the first goal of systematic botany, hardly solves the problem of constructing a generic system that prefigures the place of each and every species. But suppose the approximate scope of the genus could be determined by some relatively independent and reliable criterion, such as the habitus. This would yield an intuitive bouquet of species that could then be analyzed with a view to finding their natural character.

Admittedly, there is nothing sure about common-sense intuitions above the level of species. Nevertheless, folk-sense is quite capable of appreciating degrees of morphological affinity, and of recognizing whether one grouping of species is more or less aspectually homogeneous than another. Nobody was more aware of this fact than Linnaeus: "The habitus was the touchstone of the ancients; it is a stone that should be sharpened by modern [botanists]; it merits the greatest consideration, though it has its limits" (1751 sec. 209). Linnaeus' appreciation of the crucial role of customary notions of overall aspectual affinity thus concerns not only species, but also genera.

The significance of the habitus may seem obscured by the decisive importance of the fructification:

> the recommended disposition [i.e. classification] of plants must be drawn solely from the fructification . . . . All plants having relations in the parts of the fructification must not be distinguished in the theoretical disposition, all things being equal. (secs. 164,165)

To rely exclusively on the habitus would lead to interminable disputes about generic boundaries, and so condemn botany to chaos: "To be so attached to the habitus of plants that one renounces the principles of fructification . . . is to put foolishness in the place of wisdom" (sec. 209).

Nevertheless, appreciation of habitus is a *necessary* pre-condition for properly delineating genera: "One must consult the habitus for fear that one has too lightly formed a misleading genus." It is simply *not sufficient*: "Although habitual characters are not sufficient, nevertheless they most often make known the plant at first glance" (sec. 168). Practically, habitus and fructification are effectively on equal footing in the Linnaean system. This explains why generic names that bring to mind the characteristic fructification or (*vel*) the habitus are best (sec. 240).

When all things are equal, that is, in the normal circumstance, the habitus gives knowledge of the empirical scope of the genus at first glance (*primo intuitu ex facie externa*), and the fructification defines its limits (*definitio generis*). But in those infrequent cases when the boundaries set by the fructification appear to cut through habitual associations, problems arise:

> The Bidens (A) . . . has exactly the fructification of the genus *Bidentis*; but the Bidens (B) . . . absolutely manifests the fructification of the *Cereopfidis* . . . but if B is a variety of A, as appears likely, then it is not permissible to separate them; and I would not hesitate to reunite in one the genera *Bidentis* and *Cereopfidis*, for fear that the limits of genera are not destroyed. Thus posed, the habitus and nature militate against the principle and art. (sec. 209)

In some cases, then, it may be better in the short term to transgress art than nature. But if this happens too often, as it does in Morison and Ray, the thread of Ariadna becomes tangled and mayhem threatens. In any event, transgression of art can only be temporary; for in God, nature and art are invariably in accord.

Deeper analysis, then, must ultimately reveal that the natural character and habitus coincide: by adding or substracting features, natural character and habitus may be suitably expanded or reduced so as to agree in the species they extend to.

In assessing the natural character, stresses Linnaeus: "One must examine all the parts of the fructification, even those that escape sight, even with the aid of a microscope (to which one must nevertheless rarely have recourse); for without knowledge of the fructification, one can have no certitude of genus" (1751 sec. 192). This conditional appeal to the microscope actually represents a significant departure from previous systematic practice. Ray, for instance, warns: "one must not propose marks that require the attention and contention of minds, by obliging recourse to the microscope" (1703, *De methodo plantarum in genere*). Likewise, Tournefort refuses all characters that are not "readily perceptible (*sensibles*) and easy to note, without one being obliged to employ a microscope in order to discover them" (1694:14).

After all, a primary motivation for systematic inquiry lay in a heart-felt need to resecure the intuitive sureness of local knowledge by rationally re-establishing, and thereby extending, it to the world at large: the phenomenal order of things must be comprehended in terms familiar to it, by tracing obvious characters – at once logical and visible – through myriad sensible forms. Even Linnaeus concedes the overriding importance of easily visible characters that are immediately recognizable to the layman: "let no comparison that is not better known than one's own right hand be admitted in a character" (1751 sec. 198; cf. secs. 151,299). What, then, could justify the exceptional allowance of the microscope in the case of the fructification?

Ever since the pioneering work of Malpighi and Grew, naturalists had acknowledged the pertinence of the microscope to studies of the mechanics of generation in individuals. It was also universally presumed that the generative natures of (same sex) individuals of a species are identical. Since, on the principles of the system, the reproduction of species is intimately bound up with the propagation of (generic) fructifications, why should the generative natures of individuals and species be denied all expression at the level representing the integrated generative structure of the whole natural order? If it is allowed that the normally invisible natures responsible for the genesis of individuals and species may be partially revealed by the microscope, then why not also the natures of genera, which are the global products of, and reasons for, the genesis of individuals and species?

True, all inquiry into the unknown is still conditioned by, and for, the need to reconcile rational with empirical intuition. In this sense, Linnaeus seems very far from modern science, which seeks to explore the unknown for its own sake while using the known merely as a convenient stepping stone for such exploration.[26] But limited as it was to generation and fructification, Linnaeus' interest in reconciling the visible order with the hidden springs of life served as a powerful spur to the empirical study of angiosperm reproductive structure, including its microanatomical aspects.[27] It also provided the first important break with preformationism, that is, the theory that the embryonic individual is simply a minute replica of its species' mature adult type (see Ray 1691).[28]

Linnaeus' refusal to accept the widely held view that the process of generation can be reduced to the simple accretion of a miniature "germ" of the species plausibly stems from his denial of ontological primacy to the visually primary entity (i.e. the whole morphology of the species). The whole visible morphology of the species no longer serves in its capacity as an eternally fixed, impenetrable, two-dimensional surface of contact between the microscopic order of underlying natures and the order of sensible forms. Before Linnaeus, generative structure looked and acted like a miniature replay of the mechanics of whole, or part, of visible morphology. Underlying generative organization had only a maintenance function: to sustain the whole, visibly typical, species-pattern from generation to generation. With Linnaeus, whole species-types derive from the operations of a privileged organ-complex. Because species-type and organ-complex are not identical with one another, generation cannot be mere replication. As a result, speciation can be contemplated and generation explored to mutual benefit.

But the idea of speciation that Linnaeus actually advances is very much at odds with ideas of speciation as later understood by Buffon, Lamarck or Darwin. The same may be said for the generative processes held to be responsible for speciation. This is because the locus of generative forces in Linnaeus' world resides not in the individual, but in the genus. Because the genus is not considered to be primarily a materially functioning entity, the generative "mechanisms" associated with it appear as principles rather than processes. Although Linnaeus does refer the essential "composition" of the plant to a physical model that allows for a separation of its physical constituents, the distinctions between components are not made primarily on the basis of plant physiology. Rather, components are metaphysically distinguished as ontologically and conceptually irreducible posits. This metaphysical factoring involves a curious blend of the Aristotelian form/matter and Cartesian mind/body distinctions.

As with Cesalpino, the Linnaean principle of life is located in the soft inner part of the plant. This is the female "medulla" from which the pistils emanate. The female matrix contains the underlying nature of the plant. It is the essential bearer of life and producer of seeds. By contrast, the stamens derive from the corticle mantle, which conveys nourishment, rather than life *per se*, and is largely responsible for outward appearance. Species arise when the medullary substance of the generic prototype is covered with cortical "principles" (*principiis*) originating in *other* genera.

Linnaeus thus not only breaks from Aristotle's equation of the male principle with the essence of life; he also explicitly rejects, for the first time, the common-sense view that the typical characters of outward appearance (today we might say the "phenotype") are necessary indicators of underlying nature (or "genotype"). In particular, congeneric species may typically differ in habitus owing to the varying influence of the "vagabond" fathers, inasmuch as it is the cortex –

not the medulla – that controls the general aspect of the plant (Linnaeus [Ramström] 1759).

Species do not arise, then, as a result of crossings between congeneric species. On the contrary, "hybridization" occurs principally (and perhaps exclusively) between species of different genera.[29] "Speciation," in other words, refers to an operation wherein a limited stock of genera "mix" to produce a much larger number of species.[30] At first, Linnaeus may have viewed this operation as supernatural, having occurred only at the time of Creation. But once clearly in mind, the hybridization theory enabled him to renounce the numerical constancy of species in favor of eternal genera: "the [original] genera were mixed with each other by nature [not by God], and in this way in every genus so many were formed [over time] as at present exist" (Linnaeus 1764; cf. Linnaeus [Graberg] 1762). Still, once having arisen by crossing, species continue to be delimited in terms of a stable morphological arrangement – as ideal forms that perpetuate themselves by heredity: "Linnaeus renounced neither his idea of creation nor even his faith in the constancy of what was created, but only his views on the unchanged number of species" (Hofsten 1959:17; Leikola 1987). Concordance with common sense now appears complete. The genus occupies the place in Paradise that the basic-level folk grouping has in the local environment. Paradise, in fact, is the *ideal* local environment:

In the Oration, *De telluris habitabilis incremento*, Linnaeus (1744/1972) reveals Paradise to have been an ideal local environment in which all basic kinds were harmoniously concentrated. Linnaeus' Paradise is conceived to have been an island in the midst of waters that covered the rest of the earth. In fact it is modeled on Tournefort's (1717, II:xix) first-hand description of Mt. Ararat made during his journey to the Levant. Here are to be found all the world's climatic zones together with the distinctive flora and fauna representative of each zone:

> It is worth remembering what Tournefort relates in the tale of his voyage to the Orient. Assuredly, he rediscovered by the base of Mt. Ararat plants he had previously seen in Italy. Climbing a bit higher, he will have encountered plants that grow near Paris. The plants characteristic of Sweden are in a place more elevated; but those which are proper to the mountains of Switzerland and Lapland occupy the most elevated place of the mountain very near the snow covered summit.
>
> (Linnaeus 1744/1972:37)

As the earth's landmass, which originally consisted of Paradise alone, spread upon the waters, it did so in such a way that the climatic zones of the primordial island-center simply expanded in proportion to their initial dimensions. Hence, the present world may be divided into rather homogeneous areas: tropical, alpine, temperate and so forth.

Earlier on, it is true, Linnaeus had followed Ray (1691) in attributing the basic role in the ideal economy of nature to the founding couples (or hermaphrodites) of each of the world's various species, all of which were originally present in Paradise: "In this very pleasant garden, all the species of plants saw themselves assigned a station. In effect, each plant nourishes the insect appropriate to it" (1744/1972 sec. 19).[31] But it is later apparent that the generic prototype, rather than the species as such, plays the primary and original role of maintaining the balance of material forces in the living world: "This mode of multiplying plants does not interfere with the system or general scheme of nature; as I daily observe that insects, which live upon one species of a particular genus, are contented with another of the same genus" (1760/1790). As a result, generic-speciemes are not only extracted from their contingent material conditions and assimilated to morphologically constant taxonomic species; henceforth folk generic-speciemes may be considered virtually *identical* with their nonlocal congeners in regard to the place they occupy in the overall order of nature. The taxonomic order of genera thus becomes an ideal representation of the actual visible order of generic-speciemes that every layman is familiar with.

Indeed, the "practical disposition" of species within the system is only that – a pragmatic, binary denomination of each species.[32] The important element of the denomination is the upper-case generic name, which calls to mind the natural character. The lower-case "trivial" name is attached only to distinguish the species from its congeners until such time as all species have been carefully examined so that the essential character of the genus may then be educed. Once the essential character is educed, and the theoretical disposition of genera fixed, then the eternally essential themes of life, which species only instantiate, will be manifest.

In acknowledging the universal validity of habitual, unskilled intuitions but only the practicality of fructification characters, Ray had no ready means by which to complete Cesalpino's program and settle definitively the phenomenal boundaries of common-sense groupings within a well-formed natural order. An optimistic empiricist might see no problem here, but for a skeptic or a rationalist this would never do. Either the quest for a natural system would breed only temporary illusions of agreement, or *a priori* constraints on allowable possibilities would have to be rigorously adhered to. In effect Tournefort's rationalist alternative simply inverted Ray's priorities, admitting common-sense intuitions as useful but making the fructification characters universally decisive, at least in principle (see Tournefort 1697).

The argument between Ray and Tournefort was not between progressive Lockean empiricism, on the one hand, and regressive Aristotelian essentialism on the other – for Tournefort was no more an Aristotelian essentialist than Ray. Rather, the debate pitted Ray's mildly optimistic form of empiricism against Tournefort's mildly skeptical form of rationalism: if Ray followed Locke in believing real essences to be unknowable, he did not follow Locke in believing that nominal essences could never directly reflect reality; and if Tournefort followed Descartes in thinking that the true order of things might be indicated by *a priori* principles, he did not follow Descartes in thinking that such true indications necessarily reveal anything of real essences.[33]

Ultimately, Linnaeus also came to believe with Locke that real essences are effectively unknowable. Yet, he never doubted that reason gives a true indication of where they are. In line with Tournefort, he argued that the character determines only the possibility of knowing the genus, and does not itself constitute the essence of the genus: "know that it is not the character that makes the genus, but the genus that makes the character" (1751 sec. 169). But contrary to Tournefort, he considered the character to be a true mark of the underlying essence of the plant (sec. 88). By appealing to reason and the fructification, Linnaeus also differed from Ray, who sought to mark the location of real essences exclusively by aspects of the whole habitus that are primarily grounded in phenomenal intuitions, rather than in rational principles.

To allay any metaphysical doubts about the appropriateness or effectiveness of a true method in natural history, Linnaeus sought to mark the real essence of species through a rational determination of their generic characters. He would show the thread of life by which God weaves the natural order without necessarily revealing the hidden springs and forces that make such an order viable. Such was the aim of the "natural system."

Thus did Linnaeus see himself as a "second Adam" able to enumerate all the world's basic kinds, just as the first man had done in Paradise. The present world could be approached as the ideal local environment writ large: genera would occupy the role in the overall natural economy of the earth that each of the prototypical species had occupied in Paradise. The totalizing aspect of folkbiological knowledge that had been lost since the Renaissance now seemed on the verge of recovery for the world at large, and Paradise regained.

Unfortunately, as the next chapter shows, this first systematic attempt to recover the intuitive certainty of that common-sense paradise lost in the age following the Renaissance was short-lived: the disparity between fructification and habitus eventually proved much greater than anticipated; the computation underestimated the task of reduction by at least an order of magnitude; and no obvious generic standard could be found for animals. Attention to the families of plants and the classes of animals would then offer the last glimmer of hope for a phenomenal order of life.

PART IV

THE SCIENTIFIC BREAKAWAY

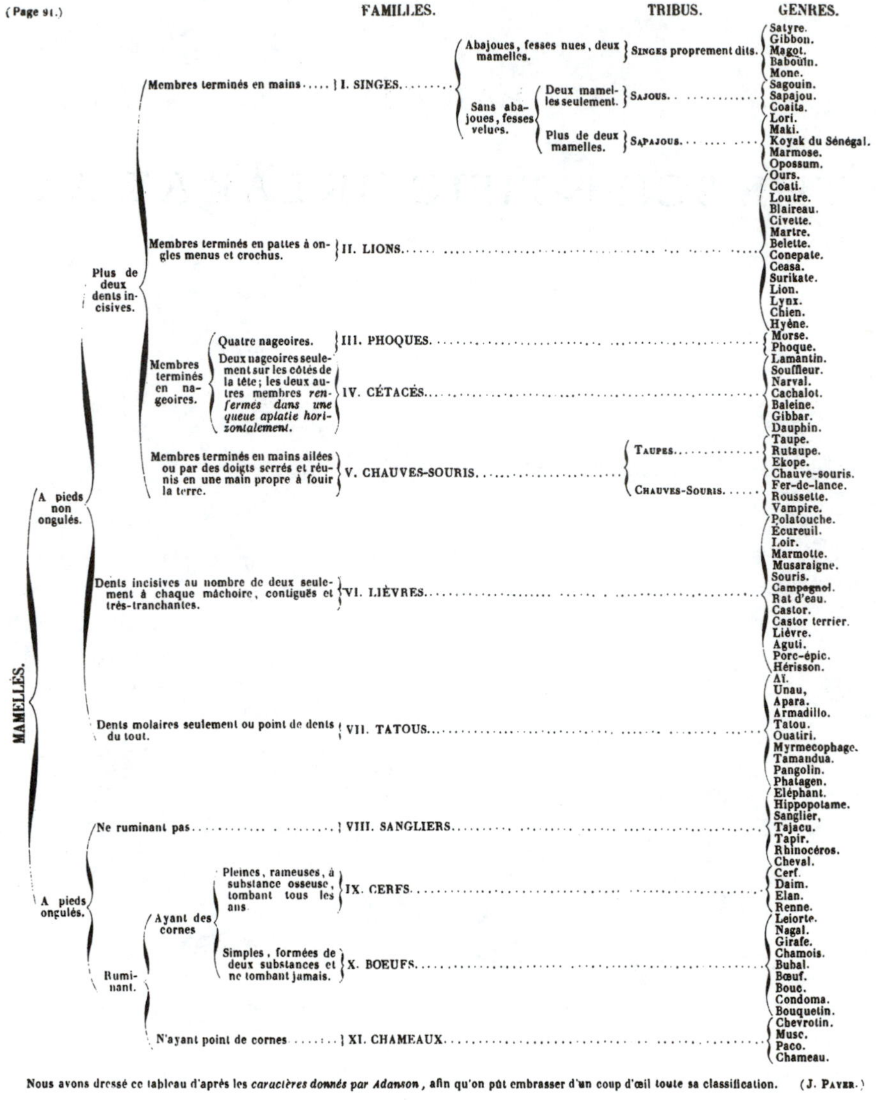

(Page 91.)   FAMILLES.   TRIBUS.   GENRES.

MAMELLES.

- **A pieds non ongulés.**
  - **Plus de deux dents incisives.**
    - Membres terminés en mains ..... } I. SINGES ....
      - Abajoues, fesses nues, deux mamelles. } SINGES proprement dits. — Satyre. Gibbon. Magot. Babouin. Mone.
      - Sans abajoues, fesses velues.
        - Deux mamelles seulement. } SAJOUS .... — Sagouin. Sapajou. Coaita. Lori. Maki.
        - Plus de deux mamelles. } SAPAJOUS .... — Koyak du Sénégal. Marmose. Opossum.
    - Membres terminés en pattes à ongles menus et crochus. } II. LIONS .... — Ours. Coati. Loutre. Blaireau. Civette. Marte. Belette. Conepate. Ceasa. Surikate. Lion. Lynx. Chien. Hyène.
    - **Membres terminés en nageoires.**
      - Quatre nageoires. } III. PHOQUES .... — Morse. Phoque.
      - Deux nageoires seulement sur les côtés de la tête; les deux autres membres renfermés dans une queue aplatie horizontalement. } IV. CÉTACÉS .... — Lamantin. Souffleur. Narval. Cachalot. Baleine. Gibbar. Dauphin.
    - Membres terminés en mains ailées ou par des doigts serrés et réunis en une main propre à fouir la terre. } V. CHAUVES-SOURIS ....
      - TAUPES .... — Taupe. Rutaupe. Ekope.
      - CHAUVES-SOURIS ..... — Chauve-souris. Fer-de-lance. Rousselle. Vampire.
    - Dents incisives au nombre de deux seulement à chaque mâchoire, contiguës et très-tranchantes. } VI. LIÈVRES .... — Polatouche. Écureuil. Loir. Marmotte. Musaraigne. Souris. Campagnol. Rat d'eau. Castor. Castor terrier. Lièvre. Aguti. Porc-épic. Hérisson.
    - Dents molaires seulement ou point de dents du tout. } VII. TATOUS .... — Aï. Unau. Apara. Armadillo. Tatou. Ouatiri. Myrmecophage. Tamandua. Pangolin. Phatagen.
- **A pieds ongulés.**
  - **Ne ruminant pas.** } VIII. SANGLIERS .... — Éléphant. Hippopotame. Sanglier. Tajacu. Tapir. Rhinocéros. Cheval.
  - **Ruminant.**
    - **Ayant des cornes**
      - Pleines, rameuses, à substance osseuse, tombant tous les ans. } IX. CERFS .... — Cerf. Daim. Élan. Renne. Leiorte. Nagal. Girafe.
      - Simples, formées de deux substances et ne tombant jamais. } X. BOEUFS .... — Chamois. Buhal. Bœuf. Bouc. Condoma. Bouquetin.
    - N'ayant point de cornes .... } XI. CHAMEAUX .... — Chevrotin. Musc. Paco. Chameau.

Nous avons dressé ce tableau d'après les *caractères donnés par Adanson*, afin qu'on pût embrasser d'un coup d'œil toute sa classification.   (J. PAYER.)

Figure 4
Michel Adanson's mammal classification (from *Cours d'histoire naturelle*, 1772)

8

THE METHOD OF FAMILIES
AND CLASSES

8.1 STRESS AND STRAIN

From the Linnaean standpoint, the success of any system would depend upon their being a rationally determined and perceptually evident set of true genera. Even an artificial system would have real value if capable of keying out these fundamental natural units. Only a rational determination could ensure an absolute reduction of species by an order of magnitude to cognitively manageable proportions. The truth of such a reduction, however, would require that the groupings so formed by reason and the fructification do in fact accord with habitually preceived associations. This is the import of the concluding remarks to Linnaeus' pedagogic philosophical summary, *Philosophia botanica* (1751): "In natural science, principles of truth must be confirmed by observation."

In the *Familles des plantes* (1763), Adanson attacks Linnaean genera as being misconceived in two senses. First, the Linnaean genera are artificially defined. There can be no *a priori* guarantee that genera formed by an inspection of habitus (*port*, i.e. the *caractère habituel* or *caractère de l'ensemble*), can be defined in terms of some part. This is so even if that part be the most notable, distinct and morphologically complex of parts – as the fructification admittedly is – and the part with the highest information content and frequency of covariance (redundancy) with respect to the whole habitus. Adanson rejects any justification of the principle of sufficient reason, whether (as with Tournefort) on purely rational grounds or (as with Linnaeus) on more deeply motivated metaphysical grounds (1763:cv). Rather, he calls for the use of any character that is distinctly perceived, taken from any and "all the parts" of the plants (1763:cv).

Second, Adanson deems the empirical basis for Linnaean genera to be insufficient. Many of Linnaeus' exotic genera are substantiated entirely by questionable herbarium material from foreign countries (e.g. the incomplete anatomy of dried flowers or badly pressed facies) or by figures supplied by uninstructed travelers (1763:cxcvi). Shoddy vertification thus seemingly goes hand in hand with rationalist prejudice.

The second of these objections posed no serious problem for Linnaeus. He could, and did, constantly upgrade his groupings with more reliable specimens and reports. These were often furnished by his own large, highly trained and motivated company of well-traveled students and disciples (cf. Stafleu 1971a). As for the first objection, Linnaeus did recognize apparent cases where "facies and nature militate against principle and art" (1751 sec. 209), but thought he could ultimately reconcile these ostensible conflicts: either by emphasizing certain features of the fructification (including its microscopic aspects) in order to form a singular fructification compatible with a habitual grouping, or by selectively ignoring certain readily perceived differences or affinities in habitus so as to juxtapose, or narrow down, habitual patterns in accordance with some fructification. After all, Malpighi and Grew were able to show by their microscopic examinations that some apparently atypical patterns of the fructification (especially concerning the flower) are actually not irregular; and nobody could reasonably argue with the idea that parts of the habitus might vary in significance as indicators of different groupings.

In fact, as *ad hoc* as this maneuvering may seem, it did accommodate relatively stable groupings that have stood the test of time. One reason for this stability owes to the fact that such groupings tended to do minimal violence to habitual intuitions. Another reason is the longstanding reverence that has been accorded this most convincing (if ultimately failed) attempt of the mind at a complete rational mastery of the manifest living world. The principal challenge to the Linnaean system – at least in botany – thus did not come from a frontal assault on its genera. It came from work on the family.

From Cesalpino to Ray, the family-level covert fragments of European folkbiology substantially underlay the series of *genera proxima* (or *genera majora*) – centerpost of systematic classification. During that period, systematics was very largely geared to completing the arrangement of European species into larger intuitive groupings. To the European naturalist's eye, the sequence of these larger groupings is pocketed with lacunae; that is, European family-level fragments just do not cover the whole of the European flora and fauna (cf. Lamarck 1785:442,451). But implicit in the early systematic work was the notion that one could round out the series of European fragments by attaching foreign species to them, thereby simultaneously creating a framework for systematically incorporating new forms without reducing them to the old: "Until they can be arranged in some order, like a great army in camp ... distributed in companies" (Cesalpino 1583, dedicatory epistle).

As long as this assumption remained unchallenged, the strategy would endure. But the realization gradually dawned that the handful of better-known European fragments were too fuzzy at their boundaries and too poor in content to readily or rigorously accommodate the ever increasing variety of exotic species. The completion of a worldwide system of family-level taxa would thus have to await a knowledge of *all* basic exotic groupings. This left the fundamental problem of reducing the world's species to manageable proportions unresolved; for it was precisely the prior, or "automatic," incorporation of basic foreign groupings that the system sought to ensure. Such is the difficulty Tournefort's genus was designed to overcome. Henceforth, the quest for a complete series of natural families (corresponding to Cesalpino's "genera") would presumably have to await a knowledge of the basic (Tournefortian) genera. These genera would be the most empirically and rationally tractable of groupings, and necessarily prior to the formation of the true higher classes: "to establish classes of plants, is precisely to discover that which several genera of plants have in common" (Tournefort 1694:40).

In the meantime, as a matter of convenience both for memory and for reason, Tournefort proposed a set of artificial *classes* and *sections* based on the structure of the flower and fruit. In trying to preserve, as best as possible, intuitions of higher groupings within the framework of a systematic derivation of genera, Tournefort succeeded in producing a didactic compromise between logic and experience. Although in the *Philosophia botanica* Linnaeus accepts the principle of compromise as a temporary expedient, his earlier and later works belie such half measures.

At first, Linnaeus was confident that by manipulating the number, relative size and position of the stamens and carpels he could produce a "sexual" system of classes and orders. The system was to be logically consistent, metaphysically well-motivated, intuitively confirmed and eminently practical as an entrée to established but numerous genera. Soon, however, he realized that the sexual system could never aspire to being other than a particularly useful contrivance – more opportune perhaps than Tournefort's, but no less factitious – and a mere "succedaneum" for the natural method (1751 sec. 160). Increasingly Linnaeus's work on higher-order groupings turned to the old project of completing the series of intuitively apprehended fragments. This project became for him the "primary and ultimate" aim of botany (1751 sec. 77):

> Botanists of our epoch have first of all preoccupied themselves with discovering the *Natural Classes of plants*, which is certainly of very great importance and requires much research. But as the plants hitherto dis-covered were not sufficient, this science has not yet been able to be completed. That is why it is incumbent upon botanists to know exotic plants with exactitude, in order to achieve the desired end . . . .
> Once the natural classes were established, we found plants so close [in habitus] that they could hardly be distinguished from one another, as happens with the umbellifers, siliques, legumes, composites, etc. For the majority of these plants grow in Europe, where they are easily recognized and discovered. But he who knows not several [kinds of] plants determines characters that are as facile as they are insufficient, which do not perfect

our science but rather entangle it; for the natural Method is the best acquisition of Systematic Science, without which all seems to us almost chaotic.   (Linnaeus [Gedner] 1752 sec. XII).

What prompted this reversal in priorities? Several factors came into play. Not the least of these concerns the abandonment of the folkbotanical life-forms (especially tree and herb, but also shrub, undershrub and vine) that continued to dominate the systems of Cesalpino, Ray and Tournefort – for such life-forms often violate natural families and hence block a coherent sequencing of genera within and between families. This step, though already intimated by Jung, Rivinus and Tournefort's mentor, Pierre Magnol, was only first properly appreciated by Linnaeus.

Another force in the reorientation of botanical systematics was the study of genera, which are wider in scope than species. Their examination could thus be expected to lead to a more sweeping appreciation of the morphological similarities and differences between plants than detailed scrutiny of every species ever could. By comparing genera to one another one could grasp more handily the proper range of fragments built around a core of European genera. It would also become evident that new fragments with a foreign core would have to be sought not only to accommodate exotic genera (e.g. Palmae), but also to claim those recalcitrant or "unaffiliated" European genera which eluded the more familiar fragments (e.g. Tiliaceae).

The emerging "natural method" for forming an exhaustive series of families worldwide would accordingly focus on perusal of genera – at least in the first instance – rather than species: "future botanists will be inundated with species and obliged in the end to abandon the species in order to restrict themselves to the genera" (Adanson 1763:cxiv).[1] It would not be necessary, however, to know them all: "The natural Method is not a chimera, as some authors pretend, who no doubt confound it with the perfect Method; and if it requires knowledge of a greater number of beings than we [now] possess, it does not require, as some believe, knowledge of all" (clxvj-clxvij).[2]

Perhaps the primary impulse for the ascendancy of the family concept over the botanical genus derives from an increasingly heightened awareness of quality and quantity of variation in the living world. Valmont-Bomare's *Dictionnaire d'histoire naturelle* (1791, II:397) notes that Adanson recognized some 25,000 species of plants and projected at least four times that number. This represents an order of magnitude above the number of species which originally figured in the estimations of Tournefort and Linnaeus.[3] It is not so surprising, therefore, that A.-L. Jussieu's *Genera plantarum* (1789), which became the standard for all future elaborations of the family-based pre-Darwinian "natural order," fixed the number of families at exactly one hundred. Clearly at work again is the same need to reconcile the demands of common sense with those of science that had originally compelled Tournefort to posit a layer of genera one order of magnitude above the basic folk level.[4]

In the sixth edition of the *Genera plantarum* (1764), Linnaeus propounds a view of organic creation that is obviously meant to justify the family as the primary rank in nature, and to account for the possibility of there being a much greater number of species than previously thought. In line with the Spinozistic doctrine of emanationism, the Creator is thought to proceed from the simple to the complex, from few to many, producing first the progenitor of the natural families (*ordines naturales*). These are then "mixed" (*miscuit*) among themselves by Him in order to create the progenitors of all genera.

Having stabilized the number of families at between fifty and sixty,[5] Linnaeus sought to accommodate the existence of 2,500–3,000 genera as follows: in the Beginning, the staid female element of any given family was mixed with the fifty to sixty "vagabond fathers" of the other families to produce fifty to sixty genera belonging to the family of the mother. This pattern of mixing was repeated for each family at God's instigation, thus yielding as many genera in each family as there are families altogether. In the course of time, the progenitors of the modern genera crossed with one another to produce modern species. In other words, the staid female element of the generic prototype *could* be mixed with the 2,500–3,000 "vagabond fathers" of all the genera to eventually assemble 2,500–3,000 additional species belonging to the genus of each mother (cf. Bremekamp 1953b). This pattern of "hybridization," which might ultimately supply several hundred thousand species, would be repeated as often as nature required (or as much as the discoveries revealed by exploration might demand).

Here Linnaeus renounces his earlier reservations over whether higher-order groupings are *intrinsically* as much a part of "art" as of nature (1751 sec. 162). They now have an equal or greater claim than genera to consideration as truly natural units. Indeed, in the posthumous *Praelectiones* (1792), Linnaeus surmises that only the families have proved constant since the world was first created. We might not ever be able to perceptually circumscribe, or rationally delimit, these most stable units; but that is because our appreciation of habitus is simply too vague, and our knowledge of the patterns and elements of the fructification too weak (1792:xvii). Moreover, conflict between the habitus and the supposedly normal patterns of fructification is just too blatant at the family level to countenance their mutual adjustment (or fudging).[6]

Not that Linnaeus ever admitted to there being no reproductive characters that accurately mark the families. Indeed, our eyes show us that the families are real, and our minds tell us that if reproductive characters provide true marks anywhere in organic nature (as they apparently do among the genera), then, by the principle of sufficient reason, they must do so everywhere. It is only that our eyes and minds will never be up to the task of "philosophically" delineating families by effecting a true rapprochement between perception and reason.

The same factors that led to a steady appreciation of the family in the Linnaean scheme resulted in a concomitant depreciation of the genus in nearly everyone eles's. Only the Linnaeans pertinaciously continued to esteem the genus as a true product of nature on a par with the species and the family. But for those unencumbered by this vestige of a lifelong devotion to the cause of the "natural system," the genus had lost its luster. It was unceremoniously demoted to an adjunct, stripped of its privileged rank and definition. Considered "all but arbitrary," its role as taxonomical midwife would be to merely ready summary patterns of species for the elicitation of natural families (Jussieu 1789:xxxvii).

8.2 AND THE WALLS CAME TUMBLING DOWN

Some of the really decisive arguments responsible for loss of faith in the integrity of the genus concept, and also for a profound reassessment of the nature of the species, came not from botany but from zoology finally come of age. Despite an auspicious start with Aristotle and renewed interest during the Renaissance, zoological classification soon thereafter began to lag far behind systematic botany. Menageries were already in vogue in the domains of fifteenth-century Italian princes, with Naples and Florence among the foremost. By the middle of the following century, the naming practices associated with zoological forms paralleled those introduced by the herbalists into botany. In the *Historiae animalium* (1551-1558), for example, Gesner's denomination of the various kinds of the fish, *Anthias*, is reminiscent of Cordus's description of *Renonculus* (see section 6.1 above): *De Anthiae prima species, De Anthiae secunda specie, De Anthiae tertia specie*, etc. (Gesner 1558). There are also occasional direct references to a "genus" of animals, such as the *Mustelae* (Gesner 1553). But for a host of reasons, there was to be little further advance in zoological systematics for the better part of two centuries.

For one thing, there was nothing in zoology like the bewildering admixture of plant forms to be sorted out. The accumulation of novel kinds was far less rapid in the case of animals. Animals – especially wild animals – were harder to observe, capture, transport, relocate, use and breed than plants. That is why the menageries were less plentifully stocked than the botanical gardens, and less representative of the world's fauna than gardens were of its flora. Hence, the search for missing structural affinities to complete the natural order of animals would be that much more difficult. Additionally, whereas by the end of the sixteenth century herbaria allowed year-round observations of dried plant speciments, the use of alcohol as a preservative for animals (first suggested by Boyle in 1663) came into general use only at the beginning of the eighteenth century. Because alcohol does not preserve skin covering and plumage well, the conservation of these important vertebrate diagnostics had to wait yet another half-century for Becoeur's arsenic soap (cf. Farber 1977).

The same factors that fostered the acquisition of new plant forms, and so encouraged professional efforts at convenient identification keys as well as wide-ranging "natural" systems, also promoted amateur collecting and herborizing. Although not directly engaged in systematic work, amateurs did facilitate professional exchanges. Only in entomology did collecting rival botany. For the professional, however, entomology remained a rather specialized endeavor with little direct influence on vertebrate zoology – the assumed basis of animal classification until Lamarck and Cuvier.

Besides, from the start it was obvious that dead specimens could be of no more than secondary importance in the appreciation of animals. This is because the relation of an animal's external anatomy to its internal functioning is much more apparent to us. Owing to a lack of movement, plants reveal a visually less striking articulation of functions. External characters can therefore be isolated more easily and arbitrarily. Animal parts, however, are perceived to be synergetic and so cannot be readily factored out for separate treatment.

To the common eye, plants are also internally much less differentiated. The important differences between them – even the functional ones – are largely manifest in the exterior parts: reproduction in the flower and fruit, nutrition in the roots, stem and leaves. Flowering plants, especially, seem to "wear" their characteristic organs on the outside for all to see, while animals appear to "hide" much more within. Accordingly, botanists could virtually ignore plant anatomy in the search for structural affinities: "It is this resemblance between plants that poses the difficulty of recognizing and arranging them; that is what has given birth to the methods of Botany, which have been worked out much more than those of zoology" (Buffon 1749, II:10; cf. Jussieu 1774:196; Candolle 1813:59).

Zoologists, for their part, could not justifiably free themselves of concern for internal structure. They even had a hard time abstracting away from the environment in respect to which characteristic organs seem to be adapted. In sum, ever since ancient times, the internal structure and functional anatomy of animals, as opposed to plants, revealed itself richer in detail, more complex and more indicative of natural affinities; but the absence of live specimens and techniques of dissection hindered understanding of overall animal structures and the relations between them.

The separation between external morphology and internal anatomy, which eased conception of a vast tableau spanning the plant world, would thus prove much more problematic in the case of animals. So, too, would the notion of a single logical grid that could overlay the visible expanse and provide the mind ready access to it. Accordingly, vertebrate life-forms (e.g. quadruped, fish, bird) were to remain the principal higher-order rank of zoological taxonomy throughout the eighteenth century, or until the anatomical and microstructural study of the phenomenally residual invertebrate life-forms (e.g. insects and worms) revealed that the vertebrates, taken as a whole, are no more inherently diversified than any of the major subgroupings of "bugs."[7]

One consequence of the continued primacy of folkzoological life-forms was the tendency to specialization that characterized post-Renaissance zoology. From Gesner to Ray, the great encyclopedic works in the field were usually composed of several monographs, each devoted to a single vertebrate life-form. More often, zoological investigators restricted their attention to one vertebrate life-form or another, such as Rondelet (1554) and Belon (1555) on the fishes or birds; or they focused exclusively on the invertebrates. As each life-form required its own particular arrangement, this effectively precluded development of an overarching system of animal classification.

When Linnaeus finally did try to formulate a global classification of animals through various editions of the *Systema naturae*, he felt obliged to preserve the life-forms in all their salient aspects: life-forms, or classes, must be distinguished from one another by similar external diagnostics, such as manner of skin covering and mode of locomotion (1767, I:20); they need have approximately the same diversity (number and kind) of subordinate groupings; and they should be conceived as occupying equal roles in policing the overall economy of nature so as to conserve its "proper proportions" (Linnaeus [Wilcke] 1760). The "essential" differentiae for animal classification, however, turn out to be characteristically different for each class, or life-form.[8]

Linnaeus, it is true, did attempt to justify both the unity of the animal kingdom and the integrity of each life-form in accordance with Aristotelian notions of analogous, but distinct, internal functioning (e.g. heart, blood respiratory apparatus). This would assumedly underscore the more obvious external resemblances and differences: *Divisio naturalis animalium ab interna indicatur* (1758). Moreover, the characters chosen for divisions within any life-form should, in principle, be drawn from those organs essential to the search for food, obtaining it, and converting it into digestible form: feet and teeth in Mammalia, fins in Pisces, beak and feet in Aves, feet in Amphibia, wings in Insecta, shell in Vermes.

Thus, whereas reproduction would serve as the *fundamentum* for botanical divisions, nutrition would serve as *fundamentum* in zoology. The choice of either one *fundamentum* or the other could be laid to convenience without any real compromise of metaphysical principle. All things being equal, either reproductive or nutritive indicators would do on the Aristotelian premise that nutrition and reproduction are not only functionally cooperative, but actually coextensive parts of the soul: "the same faculty of the soul is both nutritive and generative" (Aristotle *de An.* II,4).

Such nutritive characters would also be the mathematically most efficacious diagnostics, involving primarily the countable and figurable parts of the mouth and the body's appendages. But the essential organs, though perhaps functionally similar in each of the great classes of animals, manifest little resemblance in their external features. Hence, a system of readily visible divisions could at best take place within a class, never between classes. What logical expression, for instance, could link the conformation of a mammal's teeth to the structure of a bird's beak, or the structure of a fish's fins to the conformation of a reptile's feet? Furthermore, as not all of the essential characters are spatially contiguous (e.g. teeth and toes), it would be hard to find a single mathematically satisfying conformation to mark any subgroup. In short, the idea of a logically unitary system for the delineation and derivation of lower-order groupings was effectively ruled out by continued adherence to life-forms.

Even within a class there would be no uniform set of characters. Some of the supposedly defining features of Linnaean classes are wholly absent in some of the orders: within the Insecta, there is the wingless order of Aptera, while the shell-less order of Mollusca is found among the Vermes; and the initially monogeneric order of Serpentia (later increased to six genera) is negatively characterized as a footless order of Amphibia. For each order of Mammalia, the number and kinds of generic diagnostics may differ: the genera of the order Anthropomorpha are characterized by differences with respect to the number of forelimbs and hindlimbs, whereas genera of the order Pecora are diagnosed on the basis of digits and horns; and genera of the order Ferae are marked by the number of digits and mamma and by the conformation of the tongue.

Of still more significance for the fate of the genus in zoology, is the fact that there are no stable characters for defining genera within an order. Thus, most of the genera of the mammalian order Glires are distinguished by digits and the conformation of the tail (e.g. hare, beaver, squirrel), but the porcupine (*Hystrix*) is diagnosed by its spiny body (*corpus spinosum*) and human-like ears (*aures humanae*) (Linnaeus 1735). A rather typical example of inconsistency within the Aves concerns the genus *Fulica* of the order Grallae. While *Fulica* is characterized as having a convex beak (*rostrum convexum*), like birds of the order Gallinae, the Grallae are supposed to have only cylindrical beaks (*rostrum subcylindricum*) (Linnaeus 1758:139,156). Moreover, none of the listed species of *Fulica* possess all of the generic characters, although each of the species possesses some (cf. Stearn 1959).

As a result of such diagnostic inconstancy, there could be no unequivocal means of discursively identifying any privileged subordinate rank above that of the species. Although Linnaeus repeatedly emphasizes that the genus must operate as the certain natural basis of animal as well as plant classification, he admits that zoology has lagged behind botany in this respect (1744:206). In fact, only species and life-forms appear to furnish relatively stable and uncontroversial elements of animal taxonomy.

Even Buffon, the most persistent and influential opponent of the idea of system, accepts the reality of life-forms "for us" ("par rapport à nous").[9] Nevertheless, he disagrees with Linnaeus that life-forms *as we think of them* are real in themselves:

> Man has only thought (*imaginé*) general names in order to aid his memory ... then he abuses the [practice] by considering them as something real .... I can give example and proof of this without departing from the order of quadrupeds, which of all the animals man knows best, and to which he is consequently in a position to give the most precise designations. The name *quadruped* supposes that the animal has *four feet*. If it lacks two of these feet, like the sea-cow ... if it has arms and hands like the monkey ... if it has wings like the bat, it is no longer a quadruped; and one abuses this general designation when one applies it to these animals. For there to be precision in words, there must be truth in the ideas they represent.
>
> (1766,XIV:17-18)

On Buffon's account, this disaccord between life-form boundaries and rigorous notions of definition amply exemplifies why there will never be a truly consistent hierarchical division of animals. For even when intuition most directly reflects nature, as in the case of life-forms, the "nomenclaturer's" art conspires to falsify both.

For him, intuition of a phenomenal kind does not warrant belief in the corresponding existence of a natural kind. Only in the case of species, can our intuitions be well-delimited in accordance with nature. The proof is that we can ultimately provide a material causal description of the concrete existence of species that does not depend upon our perceptions alone (1749,II:3; 1765,XIII:i). In other words, general terms, such as those which refer to species, may be considered to denote parts of the real world, if that reality can be given a concrete physical expression. As we shall see in the next chapter, Buffon's notion of a concrete general term, such as a species term, differs from that of an abstract universal term, such as a genus term, when the objects denoted by the term are successively linked together in an uninterrupted causal chain. Such a chain comprises the continuous serial manifestation of a single historical event, namely, a genealogical lineage.

At first blush, Buffon's initial rejection of Linnaean genera proves to be somewhat misleading: "One finds that the lynx is but a species of cat, the fox and wolf only species of dog, the civet-cat a species of badger . . . the rhinocerus a species of elephant, the donkey a species of horse, etc., and all this because a few meager relations between the number of mamma and teeth of these animals, or some slight resemblance in the form of their horns" (1749,I:40). He later points out that this manner of forming "abstract" genera is still employed by contemporary explorers who would simply assimiliate the exotic fauna of America to the better-known animals of the old world (e.g. the puma to the lion, the jaguar to the tiger, the alpaca to the sheep, the lama to the camel). Such a "method" as this, therefore, amounts to no more than the popular custom of reducing the unknown to the known.[10]

But the real argument against the Linnaean genus, as Buffon was ultimately to stress, turns on the idea of its "essence." It certainly appears that the *lives* of the members of these distinct species do not depend on one another in the way that the life of an individual depends on the lives of other individuals of the same species, that is, as part to whole. In other words, Linnaean genera have no "concrete" spatial reality as reproductive communities, nor temporal existence as self-perpetuating lineages. Like mathematical objects and other "mental abstractions," the taxa of the Linnaean hierarchy are only "platonic ideas" (1749,I:37-40). Admittedly, if one could demonstrate that congeners are literally generated one from the other, or from a common ancestor, then one could argue for a "genus" or "family" that would include, say, the donkey, horse and zebra, or the fox, wolf and dog (1753,IV:378), But, as Kant (1790/1951 sec. 80) argues after Buffon, there is no evidence that such *generatio heteronyma* is anywhere to be found.[11] If essence conveys life, then genera do not seem to be essentially alive.

Yet, through his investigation of wild and domestic animals, Buffon gradually recognized that it is not always possible to verify, in fact, whether two varieties comprise really one species or two: perhaps the sheep is but a "perfected" form of goat, and the chamois merely a "wild goat" (1755,V:60). Soon after, Buffon acknowledged that one must judge species "as much by the climate and the natural [setting] as by figure and structure" (1761,IX:119). Not until Buffon had nearly completed a study of the mammals of the old and new worlds, however, did he realize that racial varieties that had migrated far from their source might come to assume the status of distinct local species.

In the end, Buffon (1766,XIV:311 ff.) would allow the possibility that a genealogical relationship could establish a real generic tie between species. But that tie would have to be grounded in more than simple intuitions of overall morphological, or even anatomical, affinities. Careful attention to detail in habitat, courtship behavior and other habits of life would prove just as important. Thus, it may turn out that while some of our "generic" intuitions coincide with reality (e.g. the natural kind that includes the horse, zebra and ass) some do not (e.g. the lion and tiger are judged not causally related by descent).

The practical consequences of Buffon's acceptance of genera were soon obvious. The more numerous and lesser-known birds could be conveniently surveyed by describing their genera, rather than species: "Instead of treating birds one by one, that is to say, by distinct and separate species, I shall unite several together under the same genus . . . being more or less of the same nature and of the same family" (1770,I:20). This tactic could presumably be applied to the other classes of animals and plants, the justification being that species were, after all, only relatively constant varieties that had devolved under the influence of the environment from the original prototypical species (*premier souche*) of the genus. Buffon, however, did not offer a doctrine of evolution; for the new species of a genus could only be the "degenerate" forms of an older prototype whose essence (or *moule intérieur*)[12] is eternally fixed.

Buffon's genus differs from the Linnaean genus in still one other critical respect; namely, that no principled distinction exists between the genus and the family. In the absence of a uniform set of logical diagnostics, no privileged rank above the species could be discursively isolated. For Buffon, "genus" and "family" are practically synonymous terms that denote networks of historically connected lineages.

True, Buffon sometimes uses both terms to denote groups that roughly correspond to modern genera: "Following the apes, another family (*famille*) presents itself, which we will indicate by using the generic name (*nom générique*) of baboon" (1766,XIV:4–5). He also occasionally refers to a "still smaller number of families" that approximate modern families or orders: for instance, the *quadrumanes*, which include old world apes, monkeys and lemurs (1766, XIV:358–363, 373–374), But no principled and consistent distinction is made between genera and families, nor could there be – for the only real group is the one whose species have descended from a first, spontaneously created, prototype: "as all these species . . . have but one unique and common origin in nature, the entire genus must form but one species" (1764, XI:369).

The original prototype constitutes "the main and common trunk" (*la souche principale et commune*) from which all other congeners issue as "collateral branches" that are formed by the effects of the environment (1766,XIV:335, 349). For Buffon, genera or families are but species writ larger in space and longer in time than one is normally accustomed to; and many of the groups that initially appear as species to us are merely variants isolated by unperceived historical circumstance. Buffon's reinterpretation of the Linnaean hierarchy in "real" terms of spatio-temporal causality thus remains rather fragmentary and diffuse at the species, genus and family levels, although it is clear for him that no true taxa exist above the family or below the species levels.

Buffon, then, conceives of nature's true groups as historically interconnected lineages. But the necessary, if not sufficient, grounds for inferring that the causal criteria of such groups are met remain palpably morphological. Still closely linked to popular notions of family-level fragments, the morphological family could now provide a framework for speculation on the "devolution" (*dégénérescence*) of species and the influence of the environment on living kinds.

Ultimately, this framework would prove an obstacle to a truly historical understanding of nature. But at this stage in the development of systematics, Buffon's method for local historical analysis of morphological families functioned – as the eternal species had – as a strong positive heuristic for inquiry into the scope, limits and means of visible variation in the organic world. The ensuing research would, in turn, serve as a propaedeutic to deeper study of the anatomical, microstructural and paleontological manifestations of underlying biological processes.

Buffon helped push common sense to the limit by presiding over a partial collapse of the phenomenal order. But Buffon himself did not oversee the truly revolutionary changes in our understanding of the order of things that such collapse implied. His reliance on genealogy and factors affecting the process he coined "reproduction" prohibited him from simply patching together phenomenal groups and spanning the breach in everyday understanding that he had opened. But he could neither widen nor deepen enough this breach in the phenomenal order to allow a historically unified understanding of life to emerge in its stead. His methodological subordination of anatomy to morphology and his epistemological credo, that explanation be geared to explaining the visible, saw to that.

8.3 PIECING TOGETHER THE FRAGMENTS

Buffon's acceptance of animal genera, or families, as irreducible natural units within which speciation may occur did not lead him to propose them as a basis for a general, systematic classification. That task of safeguarding the rationality of the system without sacrificing the specificity of life would be the aim of Lamarck's *Philosophie zoologique* (1809) – licensed by a revivifying transference of the natural method from botany into zoology.

According to Adanson, it was Buffon who first encouraged the project of a natural method: "Nobody, as far as I know, had said before M. Buffon that it was from the consideration of the *ensemble* of the parts of beings that one must deduce (*déduire*) the families, or what is the same thing, the natural method" (1763:clv-clvj). Yet, Buffon explicitly rejected any method of inferring a well-connected *series* of families, although he did recommend that all groups, whether strictly phenomenal or also causally based, be distinguished by the ensemble of their external features. Buffon's concern with historical "proof" of the intermittent and separate genealogical composition of morphological families effectively denied ontological status to a family *rank*: there was no guarantee that all of those families commonly accepted on the basis of the "ensemble" of their parts, that is, on the total habitus, would also prove to be historically well-founded descent groups. Because no systematic arrangement of families in a ranked series would be forthcoming, no systematic derivation of commonly accepted morphological genera and species could be expected.

This leads Adanson to dismiss Buffon's reservations about the futility of a true taxonomy and to conclude that a system based on the method of overall morphological resemblance: "differs totally from that pretended scale and filiation of successive beings considered as degradations of one and the same genus" (1763:cccxxiv). Moreover, despite Adanson's vehement denial of the value of Linnaeus' own method for constructing a family series, the project of establishing a full taxonomy based on "the natural method" must undoubtedly be traced to Linnaeus, with Buffon's critique serving as a philosophical corrective of little practical import – at least in botany.

Some family-level groupings, of course, were already recognized in Europe by the herbalists, and were the first to be given names by the systematists: grasses, lilies, cucurbits, composites, umbellifers, labiates, crucifers, legumes. Other groupings, such as the cacti, passionflowers and tilia, were underrepresented in Europe by isolated genera or none at all; hence, they were initially placed within the more prominent European families until further exploration and analysis revealed them as belonging to rich exotic families. It was the method's task to anticipate all possible families and thereby forego the radical revisions in classification that would otherwise attend novel empirical discoveries.

From the first, it was evident that in order to render the results of the method unequivocal, something more was required than mere common-sense intuition of habitually perceived associations. Linnaeus' solution proved unacceptable. It rested on the dubious metaphysical assumption that the functional basis of life is manifest in the fructification parts only; and when applied with any rigor it failed to preserve all previously intuited families, much less account for new ones. Being well aware of the latter difficulty, Linnaeus eventually forsook all pretense to a "philosophical" or "orthodox" method in forming his series of fragments, relying instead primarily on his feeling for aspectual relationships: "*C. Bauhin* and the *Ancients* had marvellously devined by the Habitus of plants their respective affinities ... often the Systematists have deviated, while the Habitus would have indicated the true way" (1751 sec. 163).

In this respect, Linnaeus's "Natural Method of Fragments" (*Fragmenta methodi naturalis*) differs in no significant way from Adanson's method likewise based on the habitus of plants (*Facies seu habitus Plantae*) (1763:clxx). As Candolle's analysis was to suggest, Adanson's "natural method" for completing European family fragments was essentially Linnaeus':

> Hardly has [the naturalist] cast his eye upon the plants, than he recognizes certain well pronounced groups by the *ensemble* of their structure, wherein the individuals, taken together, have a certain family resemblance (*air de famille*), as, for example, the Graminae, the Umbelliferae, the Cruciferae, etc. He will perceive that it is easier to recognize, at first glance (*dès le premier coup d'oeil*), these natural groupings, than to investigate their characters in detail each time he finds them in a new individual; at length, he will think that Europe is not the only part of the world where one can find such groups. As he advances in study, he will perceive that most of the plants of Europe that seem to him isolated by their structure, are part of families in which the majority of individuals are exotic; he will then conceive that it would be possible to arrange all of the well known plants in such natural groups, that is to say, determined by the *ensemble* of their anatomical resemblances, and that such an order will give to whomsoever comes to know it the most faithful image of all that we know of the structure, and consequently of the history, of plants. It is the manner of arranging the plants after the *ensemble* of their essential organs that carries the name of the Natural Method; it is to this study that all of the most celebrated naturalists have consecrated themselves; it is this that Linnaeus, whose name one so often abuses, declared to be the goal of all natural history.   (Candolle 1819:51–52)

Accordingly, it is not altogether surprising that the overall composition of Adanson's families does not substantially differ from that of the Linnaean fragments.

Adanson, though, contends that the habitus had never consistently "been used in any method, except in our own" (1847:14–15).[13] It is in the critique of Linnaeus' fragments that Adanson's own prejudice comes to the fore. He assesses the fragmenta as he does the other "artificial" systems of his predecessors, namely, in terms of the number of his own families that fail to be dissolved. Thus, Adanson finds that twenty of the sixty or so Linnaean fragments do correspond to his own families; however, the rest do not and are therefore to be considered "unnatural." Adanson further justifies his rejection of the fragmenta by citing Linnaeus' own opinion that natural orders (i.e. families) should be ultimately assessed in terms of their entire fructification structure, rather than in terms of the whole habitus.

Admittedly, Linnaeus had argued that the naturalness of the fragmenta were ultimately to be construed according to the principles of the fructification. But such considerations were actually neither necessary nor sufficient factors in the construction of fragmenta. As a matter of fact, there is a general convergence between the fragmenta and Adanson's families, even with regard to those groupings considered ill-formed from a modern point of view. For example, Linnaeus' Tricocca contains only a few more extraneous elements than Adanson's Tithymalia, but both groupings possess an overabundance of virtually the same genera of the modern family Euphorbiaceae.[14]

Adanson also rejects the Linnaean fragment Multisiliquae because it includes the genera *Nigella* and *Garidella* which he excludes from his own family Ranunculi; nonetheless, *all* the Linnaean genera of this fragment are contained in the modern family Ranunculaceae. Although Linnaeus' Succulentae would later be decomposed by A.-L. Jussieu into six distinct natural families, Adanson's Portulacae would fare no better: both the Linnaean fragment and Adansonian family consist of a chain linking a number of then quite exotic genera by very partial overlappings in habitus. Such examples as these are rather typical of the substantive disagreements between Adanson and Linnaeus.[15] In this connection it is painfully amusing to note that Linnaeus was equally disdainful of Adanson's "most unnatural" method, which could only yield "a mixture of everything" (cf. Fries 1911:127).

Although nowadays it is generally acknowledged that Linnaeus' fragments did not substantially differ from Adanson's families, there is still a common refrain among working taxonomists and historians of biology that Adanson's insistence on taking into careful account *all* parts of the plant was of some theoretical moment.[16] To this, Candolle long ago gave a definitive reply:[17]

> This idea is indeed attractive at first sight because of its apparent precision, but it cannot bear a close examination. In fact it presupposes that we know not only all the organs of all plants but also all the points of view from which they can be considered; now it is obvious that this presupposition was false when Adanson made it, and that it will remain so for a very long time, perhaps forever .... This should not cause us to forget that the families he has indicated, as much by way of groping (*tâtonnement*) as by his own method, are in general acknowledged by nature and worth the attention of observers. (1819:67)

Putting aside Candolle's own belief in the primacy of certain functional characters, even if one could enumerate all the parts of the organism, Adanson's theoretical program would still fall through in principle.

Adanson believed that he had succeeded where Linnaeus had confessedly failed in producing a philosophical method that could eventually lead to apodictic results. Only, instead of a rational determination *a priori*, this was to be an empirical determination *a posteriori*: that is to say, from many and studious observations and comparisons one could reasonably hope to a nearly certain estimation of a true scale of being at the family level. This hope is grounded in two "blind posits." The first, as noted by Candolle, involves an uncritical acceptance of the assumption that the parts actually observed and enumerated comprehend all, and only, those items that could possibly enter into the determination of a natural series. The second "blind posit" is an unjustified, and unjustifiable, commitment to the belief that induction by simple enumeration is truth-giving.[18] Ever since Hume (1758/1955), it has been realized that blind induction, which refuses to take cognizance of unavoidable preferences for viewing things in some ways rather than others, just cannot work. No matter how assiduously exercised, it only aggravates our original mistakes and renders nearly certain our never being able to come up with any novel truths.

Adanson regarded the characters that he attributed to families as fallible and corrigible in the manner of the "trial and error method" in mathematics; however, he never doubted that the families themselves were, in fact, invariably placed within the "scale of nature" and that this scale could be precisely calibrated. The scale supposedly consisted of a fixed progression of families that increased in complexity from the simplest plant, to the lowliest invertebrate and, ultimately, to man himself.

The progression is not a simple linear sequence. All that is necessary is that each family be marked by a constant community of characters – although no character need be present in each and every species or genus of the family – and that adjacent families have the most characters in common. The more advanced families, however, have more characters (Adanson 1763:clxx), and there are a greater number of differences between families as one goes up the scale (clxiv). To illustrate, take three families progressively arranged by characters (capital letters): ABCD, CDEFG, FGHIJA. Each family has a unique character-structure; adjacent families have the most characters in common; and no single character need be invariably placed in the scale (e.g. character A appears in the first and third families, but not in the second). In addition, for any given genus or species, for example, DEFGB, there is an unequivocal place for it in one family (in this case CDEFG), even though the genus or species may lack one or more of the defining community of features of its family and possess one or more of the features common to another family.

The gaps, or *distances*, between families are forever "numerically constant" (1763:clxiv). By supposing such a sequence of forms, the intuitive patterns observed could be definitively arranged with respect to future discoveries: additional fragments might be inserted between existing ones (and their defining features slightly altered), but the contours of the scale as a whole would remain the same. Once the general outline of the scale were discerned, its missing pieces could be computed with the same assurance "as the most sublime geometry" (cc).

But on what basis should such a computation turn? Apparently, numerical calculations were to be projected in accordance with some conception of an "equilibrium" of parts (clviij). Although this *ensemble* of "properties" ostensibly incorporates "the habits (*moeurs*), inclinations and faculties" of the organism, it is clear that only the elements of the plane surface enter into the final tabulation: *la figure, la situation, la proportion, le nombre de leurs parties* (clxiv). In other words, each family would be defined by a *correlation* of characters expressed in terms of a mathematical formula. Families, then, would be ordered in a graduated scale of numerical equilibrations, like partial fractions of some integral whole – the integral whole presumably being man himself.

The alleged inviolable integrity of each family's visible plan rests on an unexplicated notion of "organization." On the face of it, there is nothing more to the notion of an "equilibrium" of parts than a relatively constant, or repeatedly observed, correlation of readily perceptible characters. Under the assumption that nature is organized as a "great chain of being", and that many links in the chain were still missing, there would be nothing to block the supposition that the discovery of new species and genera might whittle away at the integrity of each family's tight community of characters and eventually obliterate family boundaries altogether.

Why, then, should one accept as conclusive Adanson's position that species and genera of a family must be defined with respect to their family plan (*selon le génie ou les moeurs propre à chaque famille*) (clxviij)? Why couldn't the position of each species or genus of plant in the natural order be more accurately described by referring to the "chain of being" as a whole, rather than to this or that family? And why should one simply submit to Adanson's declaration that the scale of nature "is really divided into parts relative to us, and that suffices (*et cela suffit*)?" Why mightn't it be that we just don't presently see well or enough?

Why, indeed? Such is Lamarck's attitude in his early botanical treatise, *Flore françoise* (1778). Written under Buffon's tutelage, the work is skeptical of the reality of all generalizations beyond the species, except at the most general level of the "great chain of being." But at this stage, the implications of Buffon's work on animal "genera" would only have alarmed Lamarck the botanist: the intermittent reality of genera or families in the scale of nature threatened to eat away the whole visible fabric of the natural order.

Were genealogical histories to be the criteria for connection in the visible natural order, as with Buffon, then at best one could hope for a spotty demonstration of animal genera and families. Worse, nobody clearly knew how to apply such a demonstration to plants. Should morphological criteria be used exclusively, as with Adanson, then the apparently distinctive characters of families and genera might well fade away with new information. Although one might hope to deal in a numerically rational way with the sheer quantity of this information, as Lamarck would, this would not account for those diverse and special qualities that denote various forms of *life*.

But what of functional anatomy? Like history, it has two things going against it. First, especially in the case of animals, it fails to provide the essential clues to visible connection in the zoological realm. Second, it proves much harder to study in plants. Yet these two difficulties are, as Candolle (1819:57–60) intimates, very much related. The demands fostered by the Age of Exploration on the building of a natural order were more pressing in the case of plants than in that of animals; however, "plant anatomy is more difficult" and "the natural relations between plants, although no less real than those of animals, are less striking to the common eye (*regards vulgaires*). "Because botany rather than zoology thus set the stage for natural history, the focus was on morphology instead of anatomy, with the emphasis on visible over functional connection. This reinforced the general framework of a phenomenal scale of nature. That, in turn, further encouraged use of *prima facie* sensory evidence in support of the dogma that there are no "leaps or interruptions in the series of beings." When the time came for natural history to put the zoological realm in order, even the more evident and compelling aspects of animal anatomy would muster only secondary consideration. For by then, the quest for morphological continuity had become doctrine in natural history.[19]

Although Cuvier credits Buffon with rejecting the disastrous "example of botanists" by calling anatomy to the attention of naturalists (Cuvier 1805,III:xix), Buffon never seems to have wavered from his early conviction that the study of anatomy [and function] was "a foreign object to natural history . . . or at least not its principal object" (Buffon 1749,I:39; cf. Linnaeus 1751 sec. 43). Only for the study of man might anatomy have a primary role to play, while "the internal economy of an oyster, for example, must not be a part of what we have to treat" in natural history (1753,IV:5).

To be sure, Buffon states:

> external differences are nothing in comparison to internal differences; the latter are, so to speak, the causes of the former . . . . [The interior] is the underlying design of nature, the constituent form, the true figure; the exterior is only the surface or drapery; for . . . a very different exterior often covers an interior that is perfectly the same; and conversely, the least internal difference produces very great external differences, and even changes the natural habits, faculties and attributes of the animal.
>
> (1765,XIII:37)

Indeed, comparative anatomy could be useful and sometimes even *necessary* for a correct appreciation of natural affinities. It would show, for example, that, despite the external similarities that mark popular groupings of animals, whales are not fish nor are bats birds.

But internal evidence would not be *sufficient* in itself to completely sunder apparent morphological connections between, say, bats and birds or whales and fish. Still inextricably bound to a phenomenal perspective, anatomy might aspire to partnership with morphology, but not more. It would help to establish principled links in the "chain of being": links that would underscore continuity and visual overlap to preserve the phenomenal order. Thus, Buffon would *expect* that visually intermediate forms, such as the ostrich, would doubtlessly prove to have "other conformities of interior organization with the quadrupeds" and so give the lie to the prejudice of both "popular opinions" and those "naturalists who . . . impatiently suffer any derangement of their methods" (1770,I:396–397).[20]

Although Buffon does not allow functional anatomy to become the arbiter of natural history, he does make it an adjunct – not only of morphology, but of genealogical history as well. Anatomy furnishes morphology with a viable structure and links historical processes to the perfection and degeneration of organic functioning and adaptation. In short, it provides *life* with *organization*.

The breach that Buffon had opened in the phenomenal order would allow functional anatomy the foothold from which it would eventually destroy that order. But there would be a significant series of interim developments. These were meant to renovate and reform the whole visible "chain of being" by giving it an interconnected organic organization. In botany first, where no breach had yet occurred, the effort would be made to simultaneously underscore the distinctiveness of families and their continuity in a chain. This is what the introduction to A.-L. Jussieu's *Genera plantarum* (1789) aimed to accomplish. Once set in place, this framework could then be applied by Lamarck to the whole of the living world, including the animal kingdom in its entirety.

8.4 ORGANIZATION

When Jussieu talks of family "organization," like Adanson he means primarily the whole "structure" of the plant's external parts. But underlying this "equilibrium" of parts (Adanson 1763:clviij) there seems to be a machine-like physiological harmony that makes the family's plan an "action" of parts (Jussieu 1789:ii–iii,xxxiv–xxxv), which is more than a mere correlation of characters. Consider those classes that Jussieu considers superordinate to the families: *Dicotylédones, Monocotylédones, Acotylédones* (a residual category of cryptogams). Ray had recognized a similar division, but he subordinated it to the primary partition of plants into tree and herb life-forms. Linnaeus, too, had proposed such a division, but inasmuch as cotyledons (*placentatio*) were assimilated to the "vegetative" (i.e. habitual) aspect of the plant, they could not serve as the basis for a true division (1751 sec. 163). Jussieu, however, extends the Linnaean scheme in a novel way to accommodate this division; but to do so he is obliged to forsake the quest for a certain computation of the natural order according to its visible characters.

Throughout Linnaeus' work, there is a clear notion that the number and nature of botanical and zoological ranks should be the same. But whereas life-forms may be acceptable candidates for the highest rank in zoology (i.e. the class), they must be rejected in botany. Nevertheless, Linnaeus implicitly sets up a parallel between animal life-forms and cotyledon classes: both sets are quite limited in number and easily diagnosed, and both appear to accommodate all natural fragments and most well-established genera without doing them violence. Animal life-forms, though, could be justified by the fact that their diagnostic characters are drawn from the essential organs of nutrition, and by the physiological integrity of their anatomical plan. Cotyledon classes – that is, classes based on the number of seed "lobes" – seemingly could not. Jussieu removes the ostensible asymmetry by arguing that cotyledon structure is really at the origin of fructification structure and at the heart of the plant's life functions – "a visible structure directing us towards a buried depth" (Foucault 1966/1970:229).

The cotyledon is not one of the most striking visual characters of plants, which indicates that the basis for natural classification is no longer ready visibility. But it is not yet invisible; rather, taxonomy arises from the point where apparent morphologies and hidden functions conjoin to determine the phenomenal order. Because the generation of beings is "the supreme goal of Nature and its primary function," it follows that "the seed, or more exactly the embryo that is hidden within . . . is the principal and most general part of the plant" (Jussieu 1789:xlii–xliv). Moreover, whereas as the cotyledon represents "first life," and insofar as most everyone admits Aristotle's observation that the heart is the first life of the animal, there is a direct physiological parallel between plant and animal classes: the heart of mammals and birds have two auricles, that of fish and reptiles has but one and that of insects and worms has none.

The old Linnaean project of representing life's essence by a single diagnostic may have thus reasserted itself at the level of the class; but the fact that Jussieu refused to consider such a reduction at the level of the family meant that visually apparent families could now be considered biologically complex variations on, and irreducible emanations from, life's simple and essential theme. The essence of life was isolated and visibly reduced at the level of class so that it could be left to widen out at the family level. Henceforth, each family would be marked by a correlation of perceptible characters representing a biologically functioning whole.

Far from being a mere "*a-prioristic* archaism" (Stafleu 1964:xxi), the attempt at the class level to subordinate visible character to underlying physiology, in order to establish an exact parallel between the animal and plant series, had profound and immediate consequences for work in taxonomy. The essential unity and generality of life's varied plans could be duly acknowledged with the class, in order that consideration of the families in all their integral and related detail might proceed without fear of doing violence to the general continuity of the *scala naturae* or the specificity of family structures.

Families, then, would be ultimately grounded in internal, functional processes. But if this were so, what justification could there be for belief in a definitive mathematical progression of *external* parts – be it a deductive sequence, as Linnaeus vainly hoped for, or an inductive progression, as Adanson thought possible? Once conceded that the locus of organization is internal, the very idea of a *mathematical* progression would lose its force. Internal structure could not be scrutinized in accordance with the analytic variables (number, magnitude, geometrical configuration, topological disposition) whose values were to be assigned by a very restricted enumeration of perfectly delimited static elements. For these variables were created solely for the purpose of encoding patterns of surface forms – a flat measure of nature's visible remains rather than its underlying vitality.

Although Jussieu continued to adhere to the *scala naturae*, the nature of this

"Great Chain of Being" altered fundamentally. The progression of plant families would now run parallel, and not end to end, with the progression of animal families. It would no longer be traceable in principle by a tabulation of patterned sequences of similarities and dissimilarities in visible characters. It could be followed instead only by an analysis of the functionally-based relations (*rapports*) between and within correlated character-complexes. The correlation of characters would be subordinated to functional priorities. Each character would thus be weighted in accordance with its unequal contribution to the maintenance of life (cf. Cain 1959a).

No longer separable from one another, characters were not truly functional organs whose operation could only be understood with reference to the entire organism. Reproductive characters might be the most important functionally, but they are not the only characters to be considered inasmuch as reproduction alone does not sustain life. Because characters are functionally based, they need not be severally constant throughout the family. Only the *relations* between, say, the flower and fruit need be relatively constant. In other words, should the elements of one part vary, then the elements of the other part could be expected to vary in conformity with a stable functional response that is flexible rather than absolute (Jussieu 1789:xviii–xix,lvii).[21]

For Jussieu, as for Adanson, there was no necessary conflict between the increasingly evident phenomenal interconnections at the family level and the positing of an essentially discrete series of organizations.[22] Indeed, Jussieu's "natural method" can be taken as an attempt to come to grips with the increasingly blurred array of manifest phenomenal interrelationships among families. This implies a justification of the family series in terms of more or less discrete underlying physiological systems. Even the fact that Jussieu proposed exactly one hundred families – knowing the number to be a choice of convenience – does not mean that he regarded the family itself as arbitrary. For, suppose that each family plan were formed by an ensemble of functional systems; then nature's different vital plans might interlock by sharing parts of their respective ensembles. The motley array of morphological interconnections seen to span families would thus reduce to an ordered series of functional systems, with no family plan – no link in the chain of beings – being completely isolated from the others. Such reasoning would thus seem to constitute an elegant resolution of the *scala naturae*. The ideal taxonomy would structure phenomenal classes so as to best delineate the scope and limits of possible inductions as to shared vital properties. This is what Jussieu's "natural order" seems to strive after.

The implicit purpose of Jussieu's taxonomy appears to be twofold. First, it seeks to fully resolve the visible manifold, saving and further clarifying the commonly agreed upon facts of morphological affinity. In this respect, Jussieu clearly follows the systematic tradition of Cesalpino and Linnaeus whose intention was to supply a principled basis for extending our grasp of what we see to phenomenal reality at large. Second, it endeavors to provide an ordered framework for exact inferences as to the general distribution of vital properties, including biological functions and medicinal virtues. But Jussieu never makes explicit the idea of a full inductive resolution of the morphological *scala* into hierarchically ranked physiological organizations. If the visible relief of botanical forms appears to come to life, it nevertheless remains comatose. This seemingly inchoate resolution perhaps owes to the fact that the underlying physiological organization of plants is less accessible than that of animals.

The explicit idea of a functional resolution of the scale of nature belongs to the German physiologist and comparative anatomist, Johann Blumenbach (1779; cf. Daudin 1926a:218–9). According to Blumenbach, the "manifold affinities" of the animal *scala* sort out into taxa delimited by "the whole *habitus* of the animal" (1779:56–57). But all taxonomically significant morphological correlations are here conceived as direct expressions of underlying physiological organization. The family morphotype is a harmoniously interconnected set of organs arranged on a physiological ground plan. Its species are genetically interconnected manifestations of the type's ground organs, which represent adaptations of the morphotype to external conditions. Ground plans progressively increase across the scale as one approaches man both in terms of the specificity and structural complexity of the functional division of labor. Nevertheless, Blumenbach, unlike Jussieu, believes that nature's thoroughly different types of organizations preclude a continuously graduated "chain of being."

In principle, then, there is a functional resolution of the visible manifold. As a result, inductions concerning inner properties, outward forms and the relations between them should be completely and exactly guided by the taxonomic structure itself: for example, given a functional property that is observed in two organisms, then all organisms belonging to the lowest morphological taxon containing the two should be expected to have the property. A "natural system," built according to a "natural method," would thus constitute an inductive compendium of the living world:

> The Linnaean *Systema naturae*, and similar inventories of modern flora and fauna, are very useful, but hardly incite a young man to make himself in some measure familiar with nature and the knowledge of its creatures . . . . I agree completely with the sublime conception of a compendium, which Bacon of Verulam, one of the wisest men, delimited . . . being the essential summation (*kernige Inbegriff*) of the most important truths of a science.
>
> (1779:iii–iv)

Such a compendium would allow investigation of the most universal phenomena of life as well as the special classes of phenomena that exist at the species, genus, family (or order) and class levels.

8.5 END OF SERIES

At first, in the *Flore françoise*, Lamarck (1778) had followed Buffon in rejecting generalizations above the species level. He also kept with tradition in relegating the study of *structure intérieure* and *fonctions* to physics and chemistry.[23] But by the time of his first contribution to Pancoucke's *Encylopédie méthodique* (1783), Lamarck is clearly inclined to accept the *Méthode* that A.-L. Jussieu had first outlined a decade before. In his *Mémoire* for the Académie des Sciences, Lamarck proposes "un pendant parfait" between six plant classes and the six Linnaean animal life-form classes: *Polypétalées, Monopétalées, Composées, Incomplétes, Unilobés* (monocots), *Cryptogames* (1785:451–453). He also argues that a complete and ascending series of plants, paralleling that of animals, may one day be expected at the family level. But it is only after having turned his attention to zoology that Lamarck would realize a much deeper synthesis than Blumenbach had of Jussieu's static structural-functionalism and Buffon's limited transformationism.

It was during the revolutionary shake-up at the *Jardin du Roi*, and its conversion to the Museum d'Histoire Naturelle (*Jardin des Plantes*), that Lamarck found himself reshuffled into the position of "Professor of Zoology, Insects, Worms and Microscopic Animals." Under Cuvier's influence, Lamarck's study of invertebrates enabled him to cast off the last vestige of single character diagnostics at the class level: "each special organ, even the most essential . . . [becomes] less particular, less isolate," so that life functions are distributed almost evenly over the entire body (Lamarck 1809:213). Under Buffon's influence, an examination of the complexity of mammalian adaptations with respect to varying environmental conditions helped guide Lamarck to the conclusion that the organizations of all extant and extinct species could be linked to a reduced set of functional "masses," that is, classes, orders and families. Although these masses are essentially stable, they form a "progression," which unfolds in the "composition of its organization" over time: from the more generally accommodating and simply structured invertebrates, to the specially adapted and complexly organized vertebrates, and ultimately to man himself "who is the most composed and most perfect" (1809:5).

Initially Lamarck's *scala* "was a flight of minute steps (species), ultimately it became an escalator, moving all the time, not in an endless chain but picking up newly created matter at the bottom" (Stafleu 1971b): "By this I do not want to say that existing animals form a series that is very simple and equally nuanced everywhere; but I say that they form a branching series, irregularly graduated and that has no discontinuity in its parts (Lamarck 1809:59)." But the contours of this escalator were still strongly conditioned by customary ways of viewing things: "Lamarckian evolution . . . appeals to the mind of men far more strongly than Darwinian evolution. Anyone of us, were he to have created the organic world, would certainly have created it according to Lamarck" (Poulton 1908). For, Lamarck views nature exclusively as "if one would compare its different objects with one another and with what is known in regard to man (*à l'égard de l'homme*)" (Lamarck 1809:5).

In his attempt to systematically comprehend the ever increasing morphological diversity of organic forms, Lamarck has effectively pushed understanding to the limits at which it is still directly accessible to common sense. To be sure, the progressive "chain of being" that Lamarck presents in its most sophisticated version is not a direct product *of* basic common-sense dispositions, that is, of the schema of folkbiological taxonomy, in particular, or of an exclusively phenomenal perspective, in general. But neither is this *série* incompatible with basic common-sense dispositions.

As the most mature version of the old "chain of being," it constitutes the furthest development of a cognitive *susceptibility* to elaborate such basic common-sense dispositions within a changing historical context. Although the relation between cognitive susceptibility and basic common-sense disposition will come under scrutiny in the next chapter, observe simply, at this point, that what generally holds for naturally selected bodily dispositions and susceptibilities also seems to hold for human genetically conditioned cognitive dispositions and susceptibilities:

> susceptibilities are side-effects of dispositions . . . . [Both] need appropriate environmental conditions for their ontogenetic [historical] development. Dispositions find the appropriate conditions in the environment in which they were phylogenetically developed [in the phenomenal situation for which they were naturally selected]. Susceptibilities may well reveal themselves only as a result of a change of environmental [contextual] conditions.
> (Sperber 1985a:80–81)

The elaboration of the *scale*, then, is designed to retain continued epistemic access for common sense to a world that has become increasingly problematic.

This natural scale, which forms the fabric of the living world, is woven from two basic threads. First, there is the notion of a vast tableau spanning the visual expanse of organic forms the world over. This tableau primarily owes its origin to reflection on the problem of new plant forms. It is essentially two-dimensional, rendering only the surface of things accessible to the mind. Second, there is the idea of a progression (*marche ascendante*) in the complexity of organic forms. This progression largely derives from meditation on the problem of new animal forms and how they might be understood in relation to man and his more familiar vertebrate cousins. It is three-dimensional: one cannot deny the added dimension that an irreducible behavioral and anatomical articulation gives to each and every kind of animal, anymore than one could deny the integrity of man himself. The first notion lends itself to a belief in a continuous – even homogeneous – visual patterning, which the discovery of new plant forms would tend to confirm. The second idea rather inclines one to believe in a discrete sequence marked by well-defined intervals, which the striking behavior of each new found animal would be apt to highlight.

Never, though, were these two strains completely separated. Even when botany was the preferred subject, the irreducible nature of living kinds that common-sense views of animal life underscored still affirmed itself in the refusal of natural historians to deny the specificity of plant kinds. More a quilted patchwork than a smooth carpet, the tableau of plants would admittedly consist of many partial overlappings in habitus that might seem at first canvass to slur boundaries; but the precise character of the fructification would ensure discreteness. The mathematization of the fructification afforded a formal means of freeing the mind from a welter of sensuous images without loss of generality. True, the mathematical analysis of continuity was still in its infancy and primarily attuned to a very abstract vision of inanimate objects. But eventually it would no doubt prove to be wholly in accord with the organic realm, given the assumption that nature's God and human reason were in fact compatible, if not identical.

As long as consideration was restricted to species and genera, this rationalistic strategy seemed fitting. But no discrete indicators for the family were ready at hand when that rank became the predominant focus of botanical systematics. Linnaeus simply abandoned the attempt. What of Adanson's commitment to an inductive proof that each family could be defined by a unique mathematical correlation of visible characters? This was, as Lamarck implied in his early botanical work (and Candolle later), so much blind faith. Only by giving the correlation of visible characters an added dimension of underlying organization could one justify the biological integrity of families without forsaking belief in a complete tableau of visual overlappings – for the anatomical integrity of families did not preclude their morphological convergence.

This added dimension A.-L. Jussieu borrowed from animal physiology. But he was unable fully to develop it below the class level. He simply presumed that morphological structure provided necessary grounds for inferences as to biological organization. After all, global morphological correlations were fairly apparent at the family level, while knowledge of internal anatomy was very partial, as Lamarck later confirmed: "our knowledge of the organization of plants is much less advanced than that which we have of the organization of a great number of known animals" (1809:112).

Granted, then, that anatomy is simply the vertical infrastructure of a horizontal morphological superstructure. It would, therefore, be best to ground inferences about "laws of affinity" (Jussieu 1789:xxxv) governing overall structure in the latter, simply because it is better known. But in elaborating the principle of the organizational unity of living kinds, Jussieu provided a ready means by which zoology could directly profit from previous work in systematics that had mostly benefited botany. At least this is how Lamarck saw matters: "Thus, for animals, the principal relations will always be determined from the interior *organization*; and, for plants, one will always look for the relations that can exist between different living bodies in the parts of the *fructification*" (1809:44).[24]

Once again, common sense seemed reconciled with the problems that had given rise to science in the biological domain. But this apparent victory for intellectual accommodation turned out to be pyrrhic. Too much had been given over to the realm of nonphenomenal causes to keep natural history hostage to visible affairs. Once taxonomy was grounded in an understanding of underlying biological processes, the study of those processes would soon emerge as the principal object of a new science. This new science of "biology," which Lamarck first coined and helped to inaugurate, would be for others to develop in novel ways little constrained by the phenomenal predilections of common sense.

The scientific development of basic common-sense classificatory dispositions occurred first at the level of the species and then at the genus and family levels in order to augment the *quantity* of phenomenal information that the mind had to process. But the *quality* of information, including ever greater knowledge of overlapping phenomenal relationships, posed an additional problem. On the one hand, neat sortings into well-delimited morphological groupings became more difficult. On the other hand, overlapping phenomenal relationships provided *prima facie* evidence that living kinds were biologically interlinked and that inferences might be made concerning the general distribution of vital properties between them.

Once taxonomy was grounded in an understanding of underlying organic processes, it would be zoology's turn to profit from a marked increase in the quality of information (Farber 1982a, 1982b), including biological (physiological, embryological) and historical (paleontological) information still largely unavailable to botany. No longer could data concerning phenomenal relationships so completely dominate other sorts of hitherto fragmented information. With the new emphasis on functional anatomy and structural morphology, the idea of a regular progression of morphological forms would tend to be less compelling:[25]

> Vicq d'Azyr, Cuvier, and others were finding so much information about organisms that it became easier to see discrete, rather than continuous groups . . . . Although many new plants were being discovered, there was not the same accumulation as in zoology of large amounts of information building up around taxa. On the contrary, the level of knowledge was shallow and diffuse.   (Stevens 1984a:181–182)

Botany's preoccupation with morphology would continue through the early nineteenth century – and beyond.[26] But it could not altogether escape zoology's repercussions: "the most zealous partisans of natural orders recognize today that there are leaps or interruptions in the series of beings" (Candolle 1819:60). Accordingly, it was concluded first in zoology (Cuvier 1812b) and then in botany (Candolle 1833) that there were only a few separate plans of organization in the living world. Such plans, or *embranchements*, could by no means be considered phenomenal plans, because they would accord no theoretical privilege to relations among or between phenomenally compatible genera (folkgeneric-speciemes), families (covert fragmenta) or classes (life-forms). Perhaps for the first time in the history of thought, appearance would no longer constrain the nature of being.

The next chapter further explores the development and demise of the "chain of being" within the framework of the Analogy of Nature – the idea, thought to underlie the world's causal unity, that all of nature's kinds are compounded of the same properties, namely, those found to constitute the readily perceptible "mid-level" phenomena of everyday experience. In natural history, man came to represent the ideal mid-level standard, in relation to which all other things – living and nonliving – were to be arranged according to visibly apparent species, genus, family and class. This cognitive susceptibility to construe man as the fulcrum of the phenomenal order historically provided the scope for further elaboration of humankind's basic common-sense understanding of the organic realm. But an ultimate preoccupation with human biology eventually doomed the whole program by pointing to the arbitrary limits that any dogmatic attachment to the principal Linnaean ranks (i.e. those most compatible with folktaxonomy) would impose on understanding the inner organization of living bodies, that is, on understanding the various conditions for *life*. That is when the epistemological precedence of basic common-sense classificatory dispositions, together with the cognitive susceptibility to elaborate them in a phenomenal "chain of being," finally reached the end of the line.

9

SCIENCE, SYMBOLISM AND
COMMON SENSE

*Although the works of the Creator are in themselves all equally
perfect, the animal is, according to our manner of perceiving, the
most complete work of Nature, and man is its* chef-d'oeuvre.

Georges Buffon, *Histoire naturelle générale
et particulière*, II, 1749

9.1 SAVAGE SAVVY

One important way in which science has managed to transcend the bounds of
common sense is through the deliberate employment of analogy. Unfortunately
the uses of analogy in the development of natural history are often misappre-
hended. This misapprehension owes in large part to a tendency to conflate
symbolic analogy, which is culturally idiosyncratic, with common sense, which
is not, and to confound the formative analogies of scientific theories with
symbolic analogy.

For all the apparent divergence between historians and philosophers of
science, there is a convergence on matters of primitive symbolism and common
sense. Most accounts assume that common sense is bound to symbolism, then
surmise that science must purge this motley savage savvy. Regretfully, anthropologists of all colors have done little to dispel this. Although today many shy
from the conclusion that knowledge must be scientific to be worthy, few
forsake the assumption that inextricably binds local knowledge to socially
peculiar forms of ceremony and symbolism.

To conflate common sense (propositional understanding) with symbolism
(nonpropositional representation), or to confuse the psychological relation of
priority between them, seems but another vestige of a lingering ethnocentric and
positivist world view: in the beginning – goes the story – humankind lived in a
sort of pre- or proto-rational dawn. Here, the symbolic analogies associated
with mythico-religious thought were psychologically primary, historically and
ontogenetically primitive. The intuitive, imagistic and logically undirected (or
semantically "multivalent") thought of savages (common folk, and children)
produced magical adumbrations as to the state of the world. This paleolithic

metaphysics only gradually yielded to a neolithic common sense born of civilized endeavor.

In point of anthropological fact, however, ordinary common-sense kinds aren't at first symbolically built by analogy, and the sort of common-sense relations universally apprehended are invariably consistent. Locke's quip, that it was left to Aristotle to make certain of God's two-legged animals rational, is a quibble – for the Creator had already seen to the matter. Basic rationality, in other words, isn't a historical or cultural construct, but a cognitive universal. Symbolic speculations, though, are culturally idiosyncratic attempts to go beyond the immediate and manifest limits of common sense; that is, symbolic thought is post-rational, or at least posterior to common sense, which is rational.

Whether because of universalist or relativist positions, claims for the existence of highly articulated, transcultural, and domain-specific cognitive principles are often denied by anthropologists, or deprived of substance. Sometimes "formal equivalences" are fabricated and generalized to other conceptual domains: for example, artifacts (Brown *et al.* 1976), diseases (Frake 1961; Brunel & Morisette 1969),[1] kinship (Kay 1971), the classification of ice by the Slave Indians of northern Canada (Basso 1972), and so forth. On other occasions the integrated formal and substantive structure of folkbiological classification is relaxed in favor of "networks" (Friedberg 1970), ambiguous affiliations (Bulmer 1974) and the like in order to accommodate extraneous cultural materials ranging from the purely economic to plant use in magic spells among the Illongots of the Philippines (Rosaldo 1972).

But the set of basic cognitive dispositions responsible for the ranked structure of folkbiological classification appears unique in its universality across human minds and societies. In the development of scientific taxonomy within Western culture, these common-sense dispositions appear to cede to cognitions less constrained in their scope of application and more subject to cultural influences. But such secondary cognitions as those responsible for the elaboration of the eternal-species concept and the scale of nature derive much of their substance and value from the more primary dispositions. Indeed, without continuing recourse to basic dispositions there would be no sustained elaboration and judgment of the more speculative advances in natural history: there would be no grounds for deciding that natural history amounts to more than myth.

In the view of thought as culture-bound to a "world-view" it seems plausible that: "the organic system provides an analogy of the social system which, other things being equal, is used in the same way and understood in the same way all over the world" (Douglas 1973:11–12). Insofar as "social environments" are particular, however, all things are never quite equal. Because comparing across cultures is "like trying to compare the worth of primitive currencies where no common standard of value applies ... one way to solve the problem is to limit predictions of a hypothesis to any given social environment" (15).

In other words, the task of the anthropologist is to show, for instance, how social and biological classifications are mutually determinant within a given culture. What is supposed common to every culture is that social and biological classifications are everywhere linked. Yet we have seen that it is possible to cognitively isolate folkbiological taxonomy from all other domains of categorization, even if people sometimes borrow and manipulate properly taxonomic categories for (culturally parochial) uses in other domains. In fact, without the kind of fixed conception of reality that folkbiological classification manifests, any cultural elaboration would be inconceivable.

Direct attempts at a psychologically adequate evaluation of the whole socio-symbolic "world-view" of a society (or even a part of it) can lead to diametrically opposed speculations about the character of cultural representations across societies. A "world-view" account may be used to underscore "formal universals" of the sort proposed by the structuralist current of (originally French) anthropology. It can also lend support to relativistic interpretations of the kind proffered by the (largely American) hermeneutical school that has people doing more or less "their own thing."

The universalist account accepts the notion of a general "intelligence" or "mental structure" that covers all cognitive domains. According to Lévi-Strauss (1962/1966:139), for instance, zoological and botanical folktaxonomies "do not constitute separate domains"; rather, they "but form an integral part of an all-embracing dynamic taxonomy" that encompasses artifactual, biological and social classifications. Thus, totemic myth supposedly "confirms" that:[2]

> the "system of women" is, as it were, a middle term between the system of (natural) living creatures and the system of (manufactured objects) and secondly that each system is apprehended as a transformation within a single group ... the logical rigor of oppositions can be unequally manifested without thereby implying any difference of kind ... only the semantic level adopted to signify the system changes. (128)

The rationale for linking up the social system with the domain of artifacts and living-kind taxonomy in a single "classification" stems from the fact that the level of terminal contrast in the botanical domain, as exemplified in Conklin's work on Hanunóo botany, presents a confusion of biological forms that can only be rendered intelligible by linking it to concerns that lie outside the exclusive domain of plants or animals. Thus, the "species" of the level of terminal contrast code "by a series of dichotomies" a global conception of the world that relates the eminently practical to the purely abstract, the particular to the general: "The societies which we call primitive do not have any conception of a sharp division between the various levels of classification. They represent them as stages or moments in a continuous transition" (1966:138). This implies that there are no absolute ethnobiological ranks. The whole analysis, though, rests on the captious notion of terminal contrast, which erringly confounds folkspecifics and varietals with basic-level taxa. Specifics and varietals, although culturally important, are by and large incidental to the logical, psychological and biological character of basic-level folktaxonomy (see section 3.2 above).

As for the binary "code," the contention that it is both symbolic and semantic renders the very idea of a code unintelligible. To be a semantic code is to be a function that assigns, correlates and fixes linguistic expressions to designata. Yet, Lévi-Strauss (1964/1969b:341) concedes: "it is pointless to try to discover in myths certain semantic levels that are thought of to be more important than others." In fact, symbolic elaborations of common sense are to be accepted on faith. Literally they are not meaningful, but vague. Their goal is to incite evocation rather than to determine the facts (see Sperber 1975b). But to be effective they require a factual basis, namely, common sense.

If anything, Lévi-Strauss shows the extraordinary richness of the common-sense world upon which symbolism draws. Perhaps more than any other student of nonliterate societies, he has articulated the wealth of worldly knowledge implicit in the "empirical categories" of cultural symbolism; still, in regard to such categories, to "combine them in the form of propositions" is illusional (Lévi-Strauss 1964/1969b:1). Indeed, from an epistemological point of view, Lévi-Strauss's work represents an elegant demonstration to the contrary, namely, that symbolic cognitions differ both from those of common sense and science in their lack of definite propositional (semantic) content and (truth) value.

They are, as Kant (1790/1951, sec. 59) would have it, quasi-schematized "symbolic cognitions" for which "no intuition commensurate with them can be given." Accordingly, symbolic cognitions can only be considered "semi-propositional" representations (Sperber 1985b), that is, representations that carry no truth value. What happens, roughly, is that one seeks some empirically intuitable situation that can serve as a model by reference to which the idea can be made more or less comprehensible (e.g. God putting nature in order on the model of a father disciplining his family). But the fact that the model is underdetermined with respect to its structure leaves many features in the dark. At some point the relation between the real model and the imaginary situation breaks down. Because no cogent isomorphism exists between the model and the modelled, the question of literal truth or falsity cannot arise, "not even vicariously" (Margalit 1979:145).

Now, from a relativist standpoint there are no transcultural truth-values, only truth-values *in a language*.[3] Even within a given culture, whether or not a given utterance is true or false may depend on one's point of view at the moment. What appears logically fickle to us could prove logically coherent to the native. Magic, for instance, may simply be the most intellectually convenient way of importing known causes into hitherto causally opaque situations. From this viewpoint, magic and science are equally propositional. They respectively differ only in their practical, "common-sense" value relative to the whole culture.

Moreover, before some rigidly minded Greeks arbitrarily decided their world was the one and only right one, there were presumably no absolute hierarchies, no underlying natures, no natural distinctions between the artifactual and the living, no facts of the matter to separate the natural and the supernatural:

Archaic man lacks "physical unity", his "body" consists of a multitude of parts, limbs, surfaces, connections; and he lacks "mental" unity, his "mind" is composed of a variety of events . . . . The archaic cosmology . . . contains things, events, their parts; it does not contain any appearances . . . . "Broken in water" belongs to the oar as does "straight to the hand"; it is "equally real" . . . [there is no] concept of an imperceptible essence underlying a multitude of deceptive phenomena.

(Feyerabend 1975:244–45, 263–64)

Yet, presumably because preliterate man attempts to connect anything he knows to most everything, "primitive societies have more detailed classifications of animals and plants than contemporary scientific zoology and botany" (298–299).

From this perspective, the unified "world-view" of a given society owes, not to any overall logic of the mind, as structuralists are apt to think, but to an eminently practical way of thinking – what Geertz (1983:88) deems "common sense as a cultural system":

There is little doubt that the consensus in the field now supports the Lévi-Strauss point of view . . . "primitives" are interested in all kinds of things of use neither to their schemes or to their stomachs. But . . . they are not classifying all those plants, distinguishing all those snakes, or sorting out all those bats out of some overwhelming cognitive passion rising out of innate structures at the bottom of the mind either. In an environment populated with conifers, or snakes, or leaf-eating bats, it is practical to know a good deal about conifers, snakes, or leaf-eating bats, whether or not what one knows is in any strict sense materially useful.

People, it seems, tend to classify trees because wood is materially beneficial, and poison ivy because it is noxious. But they may be just as disposed to categorize useless herbage because it aids us in knowing the habits of various kinds of insects that are, in turn, directly beneficial or harmful, or simply suggestive of other sorts of knowledge.

This view of things plainly confounds basic common-sense dispositions with savoir-faire. The latter kind of pragmatic judgment is culturally relative in ways that Geertz has so revealingly described. What is not relative, however, is humankind's evolutionary disposition to distinguish – as Hamlet suggests any normal human would – say, a hawk from a handsaw, an artifact from a living kind. Inter alia, humankind is universally disposed to believe, or know, to be true that the world of everyday experience is composed of artifacts that exist by reason of the functions humans give them, and of natural biological kinds that exist in virtue of their physically given causal natures. These are among the universally perceived facts.

To the contrary, animism, that is, the transfer of notions of underlying causality from recognized (folk)biological to recognized nonbiological kinds, may well be a convenient and widespread metaphysical fiction to which many folk are religiously devoted. But it can never be held as manifest fact. Even preverbal children make a categorical distinction between animate and inanimate objects (Gelman *et al.* 1983). Young speakers in other societies do not *literally* make regular attributions of animate properties to inanimate things (Keil 1979:131 ff.), nor do children or adults in so-called "primitive" cultures unceremoniously use religious animism in the conduct of their day-to-day lives (Mead 1932). Even when taken in the context of a particular language and culture, assertions pertaining to animism have no definite propositional content. They are believed on authority or as a matter of faith. Such symbolic speculation is not to be confused with common-sense knowledge of matters of fact. Neither is the latter a mature or more civilized refinement of the former.[4]

9.2 COGNITIVE "PATHOGENESIS"

Now if totemism, myth, religion and other speculative activities of the mind do not constitute well-defined cognitive domains, how can the ethnoscientist undertake a cognitive study of these unquestionably pervasive and striking phenomena? More to the point of this inquiry, how are we to make sense of the cognitive processes involved in the use of theory-forming analogies in science?

One promising approach is Dan Sperber's (1985a) proposal to treat culture by means of an "epidemiology of representations". For Sperber, culture consists of mental representations, that is, psychological things produced by individual minds, which become "cultural" to the extent that they are distributed among a given population. Some thoughts, like personal day-dreams, even if recounted hardly carry beyond the individuals who have them. Representations of other things, such as fashion and rumors, spread fairly rapidly but may be rapidly transformed as they spread. Indeed, they may disappear without ever attaining a relatively widespread and constant degree of "steady state" distribution within the culture.[5]

Still other sorts of cognitive "viruses" diffuse "contagiously" through any given community with little alteration over space or time because of their ability to fix onto a psychologically universal basis. From this perspective, consider Lévi-Strauss's (1963:2) insight concerning the persistent use of animal and plant species in totemism and other forms of cultural symbolism. They are "better to think" because all human minds are constitutionally disposed to apprehend them in pretty much the same way with minimum triggering experience from the environment. As they are so easily fixed in the mind, they conveniently serve to anchor more fluid symbolic thoughts. Basic conceptions associated with factual, everyday common-sense domains such as focal color perception, the taxonomic apprehension of living kinds, knowledge of what constitutes an intentional agent, and so forth, are prime candidates for these most "catching" – hence "cultural" – of representations. Such representations might be the product of distinct mental faculties – basic cognitive dispositions naturally selected for survival over the course of millions of years of hominid evolution.

Along with these basic dispositions, evolutionary by-products may have emerged, somewhat as the susceptibility to catch colds emerged as a by-product of the evolution of the respiratory system. Such second-order "cognitive susceptibilities" might include various scientific aptitudes and diverse forms of symbolic activity. They might initially develop in the mind within less constraining parameters than basic representations, and be transmitted through a population with greater elasticity. These second-order representations would lend themselves to a new type of cognitive elaboration precisely because rational constraints on internal consistency and factual compatibility with other beliefs may be relaxed.

Consider the following: People apparently have a basic cognitive disposition to compare animals to themselves. For children in our own society, experimental evidence clearly suggests "a central role for knowledge of humans and human activities in organizing the child's knowledge of animal properties" (Carey 1985a:114). Taxonomically, this basic human disposition is reflected in the unmistakable cross-cultural tendency to underdifferentiate invertebrates, that is, to consider them as phenomenally "residual" or left-over from the primary concern with the "man-like" creatures of blood and bone, especially mammals. Yet it seems that humans everywhere ordinarily make a fundamental ontological distinction between being human and being anything else, even an animal.

One characteristic of both science and mythico-religious symbolism is the endeavour to unify phenomenally diverse sorts of experience, including the integration of fundamental ontological domains that manifest *prima facie* differences (see section 3.5 above). Animistic magic and mythical anthropomorphizations, especially with respect to animals, would "naturally" seem to constitute a core element of the symbolic repertory of many, if not most or all, traditional societies – although actual practice and interpretation vary greatly. Using man as a model, the unknowns of other domains can be variously associated and managed. But the analogy can work both ways so that even the unknown in man might be vicariously handled by external agencies.

The same cognitive susceptibility to use man as the privileged term of analogy is apparent in the development of the science of natural history. The *scala naturae*, or "great chain of being," had man as the perfect standard against which the physiology and anatomy of other creatures could be assessed. The life of the lowest elements of the scale, namely, insects, might thus have been improperly appreciated as but rudimentary vestiges of God's original plan for the creation of life; but at least some of their functioning could thus be better understood if considered an inchoate version of human biology. Conversely, an appreciation of these "lower" systems as incipiently human led to a finer appreciation of the functioning of human systems.

Although, as we shall see, the demarcation between the basic first-order representations of folkbiology and the second-order representations of modern biology is not always clear-cut, the general conceptual distinction remains valid. In this sense at least, Lévi-Strauss aptly notes that the different sorts of knowledge contained in folk, or "neolithic", biology and modern biology "are certainly not a function of different stages of the development of the human mind but rather of two strategic levels at which nature is accessible to scientific enquiry: one roughly adapted to that of perception and the imagination: the other at a remove from it" (1962/1966:15).

Humans thus appear to use their "susceptibilities" to "meta-representation," that is, the capacity to form representations of representations, so as to retain half-understood ideas. By embedding half-baked notions in ideas we can have about them, they can be extended into full knowledge or otherwise further conceptually articulated. The child comes to terms with the world in similar ways each time she hears a new word.[6] In the case of science, as in that of a child's acquisition of ordinary knowledge, this disposition to form second-order representations – to play with the idea of an idea – allows the construction of conceptual stages towards a full understanding. In the case of symbolism, this ability "also creates, however, the possibility for conceptual mysteries, which no amount of processing could ever clarify, to invade human minds" (Sperber 1985a:84).

Unlike second-order scientific speculations, then, second-order symbolic cognitions never become fully assimilated to basic knowledge. They retain an element of mystery not just for outsiders but also, though differently, for the believers themselves. In cognitive terms, this means that religious beliefs are always held meta-representationally. In sociological terms, they are displayed, taught, discussed and re-interpreted as doctrines, dogmas or sacred texts. The fact that religious beliefs do not lend themselves to any kind of clear and final comprehension allows their learning, their teaching and their exegeses to go on forever.

Even mythico-religious beliefs, however, are not unconnected to common-sense knowledge. They are generally inconsistent with common-sense knowledge, but not at random: rather, they dramatically contradict basic common-sense assumptions. For instance, they include beliefs about invisible creatures, beliefs about creatures who can transform themselves at will or who can perceive events that are distant in time or space (see Sperber 1975a, 1975b). This flatly contradicts factual, common-sense assumptions about physical, biological and psychological phenomena. Such dramatic contradictions contribute to making mythico-religious beliefs particularly attention-arresting and memorable. As a result, these beliefs are more likely to be retained and transmitted in a human group than random departures from common sense, and thus to become part of the group's culture.

In brief, mythico-religious beliefs, too, are rooted in basic beliefs, albeit in a "dialectical" way. Thus, within a given religious text or tradition, one might "predict that the likelihood of a transformation from one thing into another should decrease as the distance ... between the [common-sense ontological] categories of these two things increases" (Kelly and Keil 1985). For instance, the metamorphosis of humans into animals and animals into plants may be more common than that of humans or animals into artifacts. To the extent such violations of category distinctions shake basic notions of ontology they are attention-arresting, hence memorable. But only to the degree that the resultant impossible worlds remain bridged to the everyday world can information about them be stored and evoked in plausible grades.

Symbolism thus seeks to draw people ever deeper into unfathomable mysteries by pointedly outraging everyday experience. But these outrages are readily picked up – that is, learned and memorized – by most, if not all, members of the culture. In other words, they are not indiscriminate (if they were – as with free association – they would not likely become part of the cultural repertory). Rather, by contradicting common sense at the most salient junctures of customary empirical knowledge, symbolic analogies provide people with rich conduit metaphors for sharing and linking together diverse phenomena that would otherwise be lost to an uncompromisingly rational mental processor. Science, however, attempts to augment, rather than bypass, the rational processing of empirical reality. Ultimately, symbolic and scientific treatments of second-order speculations about the empirical world tend to be diametrically opposed.

This is not to deny that consideration of mythico-religious symbolism and its supporting social establishments has no role to play in an "epidemiology" of scientific representations. On the contrary, the transmission of those concepts involved in the emergence of a science is invariably conditioned by the surrounding cultural ecology, including the mores and institutions that foster, impede or detour the dissemination of relevant information. Understanding the full epidemiological history and environment of any science would require such consideration. But here we are concerned primarily with the evolving role of common sense in the "pathogenesis" of science – with its successive incarnations in different minds, second-order transformations over time and final mutation into modern biology. The novel thesis is that we can isolate and trace the cognitive pathogens in the growth of natural history, even in its speculative moments.

9.3 SPECULATING

The formative analogies of science are superficially akin to those of myth and religion in that both sorts carry "open texture" or "surplus meaning." That is to say, they convey associations and implications which, for the active life of the analogy, are not completely specifiable. Yet, there is a profound difference. The truly formative analogies of science constitute reference-fixing research programs for the informed practitioner. They suggest strategies for future research intended to reveal significant, and hitherto unforseen, similarities between domains whose initial resemblance is assumedly but the tip of the iceberg. If such research-fixing programs were applied to mythico-religious symbolism, the end result would be "dead" metaphors, platitudes of little evocative or spiritual value.[7]

In symbolic metaphor the goal, rather, is a continuously open-ended reconstrual of the phenomenal world. The reconstrued world could not possibly be *experienced* as true. It is just too outlandish. One can only *suppose* it true, because invariably at some juncture an impossible encounter between phenomena renders this pittoresque world logically and empirically inscrutable. Such a symbolically outlandish world – that of myth and magic – is created in order to incite (an endless) search for commonplace connections (phenomenal relations) in uncommon situations.

Likening, say, essential features of plants and animals, or living kinds and mechanical devices, appears to violate categorical constraints on common sense. Apparently, humans are not psychologically disposed to naturally assume that in *all* essential respects plants are like animals (including people), or that all living kinds are of a nature with just those inorganic entities that can be mechanically construed (cf. Keil 1979). Trespassing on these basic ontological divisions of the everyday world creates phenomenally impossible states of affairs (e.g. that animals should have roots and plants a heart, or that crystals should grow and a person simply be put together). But the invocation of such phenomenal impossibilities in science is not an open invitation to phenomenal reconstrual of an imaginary world that is forever empirically impossible. Rather, it is a directive to make hitherto independent and only partially understood properties of these categorically distinct subjects mutually, and precisely, intelligible.

This is not done by a simple transference of rationality from one term of the analogy to the other; it is not fundamentally an appeal to locate *identical* physical properties in the referents of the terms of the analogy, but to construe certain physical properties of the referents as *analogous*. This means, roughly, positing abstract nonphenomenal attributes that phenomenal properties are thought to share: "Only if we recognize that the analogy . . . is not to be construed in terms of identity or difference of first order attributes, can we appreciate how the use of models in theoretical explanation can generate *genuinely new* conceptual frameworks and justify the claim to have escaped from the myth of the given" (Sellars 1965:183–84).

So, for instance, plants are not thought to have a heart as such; but to possess an organ that functions vitally to maintain the life of a plant much as the heart sustains animals. In postulating the underlying unity of phenomenally disparate natural domains, the scientific quest for a deeper association runs the risk of failure. Should it fail, the analogy must be rejected, or new terms interjected whose connections may be logically and empirically scrutinized.

In natural history, the quest for nonphenomenal connections was, predictably, more bound up with theories of function and generation than with classification as such. The phenomenal patterns encoded in taxonomy were, after all, more or less apparent, either immediately, or after, attention was called to them. But the choice of phenomenal boundaries by which to categorically distinguish morphological groupings, and the highlighting of characteristic perceptible traits by which to systematically relate them, had to be theoretically grounded. Because the intuitive justification for the existence of types amidst token variation lay with the presumption of underlying natures, it is hardly surprising that a theoretical elaboration of the taxonomy of the living world would focus on its largely hidden, organic nature.

Indeed, as a theoretical discipline, natural history may be properly viewed as a *ménage à trois*, wedding theories of morphological affinity with those of organic function and propagation. This is evidently so for those landmark naturalists examined in the course of this study. Tournefort, of course, is the exception; but one who nonetheless appears to prove the rule. For him, the middle term – organic function – is clearly secondary and largely unattended. On the one hand, he proposes an austere picture of a rational taxonomy. On the other hand, he suggests a rarefied "chemical" account of the generation of molecular and crystalline forms. But the lack of articulation between the two marks a break with Aristotelian organicism and leaves the way open for a teleo-mechanical reintegration of the living world that would be in tune with the revolutionary developments in natural philosophy. Still, the break was possible only because previous naturalists had already succeeded in isolating and describing taxonomic characters without regard to all of their functional interrelations.

The fact that early science was unavoidably preoccupied with connecting diverse aspects of the locally manifest phenomenal world, rather than with probing the great functional undercurrents of the universe at large, is one factor in the persistent confusion of philosophers and historians of science as to the difference between early scientific meditation and mysticism. In particular, there is often a failure to distinguish the sustained scientific quest for second-order connections from a freewheeling pursuit of symbolic associations.[8]

Under the pretext that both science and symbolism initially speculate about the possible relations between counter-intuitive phenomena, the "myth of the given" is thought to govern the entire "prehistory" of science prior to the seventeenth century. Prescientific man thus supposedly succumbs to his "animist" desires by promiscuously analogizing about the connections underlying diverse appearances. In truth, however, the quest by ancient and Renaissance naturalists for a natural explanation of classification was anything but sporadic. The major difference on this score between natural history before and after the event of mechanism is that it initially sought to comprehend the set of *specific natures* that make up the living world, while later it endeavored to analyze the various manifestations of *the nature* of living species.

The "myth of the given," or that of "common experience," is an axiom in the intellectual current that stems from the French epistemologist Gaston Bachelard (1980). According to this school of thought, knowledge of the living world barely changed throughout the "prehistory" of natural history, that is, from Aristotle to the Renaissance. On the one hand, "prehistoric" natural historians were admittedly aware of the obvious visual diversity and integrity of living kinds. On the other hand, from Aristotle (see Joly 1968) to Aldrovandi (1668), they supposedly thought that superficial resemblances belied a secret network of invisible forces that linked each living kind to every other, as well as to all other objects in the universe.

As the Nobel biologist François Jacob tells it:

> Each animal, each plant was viewed as a sort of Protean body extending not only to other beings, but to the stones, the stars and even to human activities . . . . The plant becomes an upturned animal, head downwards, Cesalpinus places the heart, abode of the soul, "where we believe there is most reason for placing the vital principle . . . in the lower part of the plant, where the stem joins the root." . . . Amid this tangle of forms, there is no place for the species, as this is to be understood in the seventeenth and eighteenth centuries – namely a persistence of visible structure through succeeding generations. (1970/1973:20–23)

For the philosopher Michel Foucault, the doctrine of superficial resemblance was the prime mover in the creation of new ideas in Western culture through the sixteenth century: "The universe was folded in upon itself: the earth echoing the sky, faces seeing themselves reflected in stars, and plants holding within their stems the secrets that were of use to man."[9] Resemblance operated by way of signatures. Signatures were the visible marks of invisible forms and internal virtues: e.g. the mandragore root, which resembles female genitalia, would be a likely ingredient in potions for sexual dysfunction; likewise walnuts could be expected to import a "sympathy" into treatments of brain disorders.

Within this doctrine, analogy appears to operate as a potent relation: its terms function as *reversible* poles for the evocative attraction of prodigiously many similitudes. This is presumably why Cesalpino not only did not criticize, contradict or dispose of the old analogy of the plant as an animal living head down, but only inverts it: "he gives it added force, he multiplies it by itself when he makes the discovery that a plant is an upright animal, whose nutritive principles rise from the base up to the summit' (Foucault 1966/1970:21). Through the knowledge of signs, then, one could hope to decipher the hidden meanings that connected apparently diverse kinds of things into the totality of existence. But by giving virtually free reign to the imagination in its search for signs, "the sixteenth century condemned itself to never knowing anything but the same thing, and to knowing that thing only at the unattainable end of an endless journey" (30).

The reason is that symbolic resemblance has no strict meaning; rather, its "semantics" is conditionally stabilized: "only if it refers back to another similitude, which then, in turn, refers to others; each resemblance, therefore, has value only from the accumulation of all the others, and the whole world must be explored if even the slightest of analogies is to be justified and finally take on the appearance of certainty" (30). This appraisal of sixteenth–century hermeneutics bears a strong affinity to Lévi-Strauss' (1964/1969b:342) anthropological analysis of mythical thought in preliterate peoples: "The multiplicity of levels appears then as the price that mythic thought has to pay . . . . no factor of diversity can be allowed to operate for its own purposes in the collective undertaking of signification, but only as a habitual or occasional substitute for the other elements included in the same set."

The Medieval and Renaissance hermeneutics described by Jacob and Foucault do indeed appear to harbor a connection with the sort of "open-ended" folk symbolism analyzed by Lévi-Strauss.[10] But it is doubtful that either hermeneutics or symbolic lore is much related to sixteenth-century developments (or lack of developments) in the science of natural history, in general, and Cesalpino, in particular.[11] True, some ancient naturalists, such as Pliny, did partly attempt to establish natural affinities via a "sympathy" in superficial resemblances; but others, like Aristotle, did not. Too, some Renaissance naturalists, like Brunfels, adhered to the "doctrine of signatures"; however, Cordus avoided it and Cesalpino explicitly rejected it.

Assuredly, the analogies employed by Aristotle and Cesalpino were just as much free creations of the mind as symbolic speculation. Actually, their analogies contained terms that also figured in symbolic metaphors of the time (e.g. the plant as an upturned animal). Yet, what matters for science is not where speculative ideas come from, but how they are subsequently treated. Even Pliny and Brunfels managed to carry through *some* of their speculations in a logically and empirically consequent manner, while Aristotle and Cesalpino were consistently firm and careful on this score.[12]

9.4 PLANTS AS ANIMALS

Take the analogy between plant and animal. In *de Anima* (II,4) Aristotle compares the roots of plants to the heads of animals. There he counters the contention of Empedocles that roots grow down because of the earth in them, that is, solely according to the "mechanical" principle of like attracting like. For Aristotle, the roots grow first because the first function of living beings is to eat in order to live, grow to maturity and thus reproduce. They grow downwards because that is where the food is (cf. *PA* 686b35). Roots thus develop before the stem, just as the head of an animal develops in advance of the rest of the body: "The formation of the upper part precedes the lower; in effect, the seed produces a root before the stem" (*GA* 741b35–37).

The analogy, however, goes both ways. Because reproduction is the final end (and first cause) of a being: "It is true that most animals' function is virtually nothing but seed and fruit, like plants" (*GA* 717a21). Clearly Aristotle's use of the analogy between plant and animal is not based on superficial resemblance. Rather, it is grounded in a consistent (if ultimately mistaken) appreciation of functions underlying the organization of life as a whole, but not the structure of stones or stars.

In the *Historia plantarum*, Theophrastus elaborates on the use of Aristotelian analogy. First, it must be cautious:

we should not expect to find in plants a complete correspondence with animals in regard to those things which concern reproduction any more than in other respects; and so we should reckon as "parts" even those things to which the plant gives birth, for instance their fruits, although we do not reckon the unborn young of animals .... And in general ... we must not assume that in all respects there is a complete correspondence between plants and animals. (I,i,3)

Second, comparisons are to be accepted only under particular aspects that can be verified case by case:

if in some cases analogy ought to be considered (for instance, an analogy presented by animals) ... we must of course make the closest resemblances and the most perfectly developed examples our standard: and finally, the ways in which the parts of plants are affected must be compared to the corresponding effects in the case of animals, so far as one can in any given case find an analogy for comparison. (I,i,5)

From this standpoint, it is entirely possible that a plant might resemble an upturned animal in one respect and an upright animal in another. But this does not support the claim of Jacob and Foucault that the terms of the analogy are simply reversible.

According to Cesalpino, for example, one may not just assume that the empirical elements attaching to plants are transferable to animals or vice versa. In *De plantis*, Cesalpino singles out Aristotle and Theophrastus as representative of the high scientific standards he wishes to follow. The first chapter leaves no doubt whatever that Cesalpino rejects symbolic analogies based on superficial resemblance and adopts a cautious analogy between plant and animals as a theory-formative device.

The analogy is less than sweeping, inasmuch as "plants have a structure that is markedly less complex than that of animals" and "in most cases the differences between them are extreme." Thus, the attraction by the heart of the nutritious blood from the veins is emphasized as a feature that *distinguishes* animals from plants. Although animal veins resemble plant roots as conduits of nutriment, animals have need of a more elaborate mode of nutrition that requires enrichment by the heart and redistribution by the arteries.

In the first chapter of *De plantis*, the analogy between plant and animal is thus judged to be "negative" with respect to the system of distribution of nutriments.[13] Similarly, the second chapter begins with the assertion that "whereas in animals we perceive that nutriment is conveyed through the veins to the heart as to the laboratory of internal heat ... in plants we are unable to detect either manifest veins or other conduits, or to feel any sense of warmth" (1583:3). Chapter three commences with the idea that as it is with nutrition, so it is with generation: "germination (*germinatio*) appears to be peculiar to plants," although "possibly in the formation of hair, teeth and horns in certain animals we see something analogous (*similis*) to germination" (1583:5).

On the analogy's positive side, plants appear to have just as much need of a "principle of life" – that is, of a governing program of nutrition and growth – as animals. If such a principle is localized in the heart of animals, might there not be an analogous locus of life, or *cor*, which directs the intake of nourishment for growth in plants? After a considered weighting of the metaphysical and physiological factors involved, Cesalpino (1583:1–3) responds affirmatively.

The argument for a plant "heart" is, at first glance, infelicitous. The *cor plantarum*, or collet, is thought to be the point where the root joins the shoot. Because it appears to be the point of departure for the plant's growth (*germinis principium*), upwards as well as downwards, it is the likeliest seat for life's vital agency. In this, Aristotle's inspiration is unmistakable:

> when the embryo is formed, it acts like the seeds of plants. For seeds also contain a first principle within themselves, and when this, which at first only exists potentially, has been differentiated, it sends out a shoot and a root whereby it takes nourishment; for it requires growth.
>
> (GA 739b35 f.)

Subsequent discoveries showed that growth is not, in fact, directed from this point, but lies with the parts themselves. This led Candolle (1827:147) to declare that the collet is merely a point of demarcation between two parts and hence, as Sachs was to remark, "really no part at all" (1875/1890:47).

Does this indicate that Cesalpino was merely on a wild goose chase after superficial resemblances, or simply an unrepentant Aristotelian? Hardly. Cesalpino's placement of the *cor* was meant as a theoretical solution to an empirical problem: how and why the separation between the root and shoot occurs in the embryo. The evident fact that the problem treats is obvious even to tribal folk (cf. Friedberg 1972:391). Moreover, as Bremekamp notes, the problem of the (hypocotyledonary) transition between root and shoot "remains to this day an unsolved riddle, and we should credit Cesalpino at least for having recognized that this separation presents a problem" (1953a:582).

Cesalpino's conception of the *cor* was inextricably tied to his elaboration of the Aristotelian contrast between the soft and hard composition of animals. Cesalpino supposed the soft inner medullary substance to contain the vital principle, which Linnaeus translated into the source of ovules. The distinction allowed Linnaeus (1764) to justify revision of his views on the eternity of the species and genera in favor of an eternal series of families, or *Ordines Naturales*, without compromising his basic metaphysical principles: genera are the "hybrids" produced in the natural course of time by covering the female medullary substance of any given family with male cortex from the various other families (see section 8.1 above). On the anatomical level, Malpighi and Grew agreed with Cesalpino's implication that the vital elements of the reproductive organs are outgrowths of the plant's inner substance, being composed of the same "tissues." This original notion of likeness-of-tissue had to be theoretically developed, for it was by no means phenomenally manifest.

As it turned out, Cesalpino misplaced the growth principle in plants. But his use of the general Aristotelian analogy between animal and plant structure, and of the specific analogy between the controlling center of animal and plant life, was intimately related to the subsequent development of "classical" natural history in the seventeenth and eighteenth centuries. Harvey, for one, simply reversed the emphasis of the comparison. He took the separation of root from shoot as a sign of the first principle in plants and as a finding that could shed light on animal epigenesis: "In an egg, the first principle, analogous to [that responsible for sending out root and shoot in] plants, I agree with Fabricius in calling the speck or cicatricula, and I have said that this is the principal part, as being that in which all other parts exist potentially and from whence they later arise, each in its due order" (1653/1981:274). The specific analogy thus continued to operate in the later course of science as a vehicle of reciprocal illumination between its terms.[14]

More generally, Malpighi (1675) thought that by following Cesalpino one might discover in the simpler forms of plant life the key to the structure and functioning of higher animal forms; whereas Grew (1682) believed that plant anatomy could be patterned on animal anatomy inasmuch as they are "contrivances of the same wisdom." In this respect, Cesalpino's use of the analogy between plants and animals differed in no significant way from that of the Greeks, on one side, and the classical natural historians, on the other:

> Aristotle, Theophrastus, and their successors had been deeply impressed by the analogy traceable between animals and plants. This, like most analogies, was a two-edged weapon, and its uncritical use in some ways did harm to botany . . . . In opening up new fields of research, however, the comparison was a fruitful one, especially since it led Marcello Malpighi in Italy, and Nehemiah Grew in England, to embark in the latter half of the seventeenth century upon the study of the internal structure of plants.
>
> (Arber 1953:331–332)

The "two-edged weapon" of analogy is just as apparent in the likening of seeds to eggs. Cesalpino followed Aristotle in denying sexuality in most plants; and he thought that "a seed is as it were an egg, in which there is a vital principle" (1583:I,v) akin to Aristotle's "nature" (*physis et psyche*). But Cesalpino went further: located in the seed of plants, as in the eggs of animals, is that hidden *species-nature* of the kind of plant that constitutes the individual. For a given plant or animal only comes to be in virtue of the specific kind of plant or animal it reveals itself to be. Far, then, from denying the fixity of species and the permanence of its visible morphotype, Cesalpino was for all intents and purposes the originator of the taxonomic concept of the eternal species.

Unlike Harvey, Cesalpino did not believe that all plants propagated by seeds, and it is doubtful whether he believed that all animals reproduced by eggs. But in this Cesalpino was actually being more cautious in his use of the analogy between seeds and eggs than Harvey. Harvey had no knowledge of the Graafian follicles, much less the mammalian *ovum*: "Instead he transferred by analogy the properties of the egg of oviparous animals to the mammalian *conceptus*, i.e. the developing embryo in its earliest stages, and saw in their common ovoid shape the symbolic expression of their productivity" (Pagel 1967:273). His subsequent attribution of egg-likeness to plants was not based on any added botanical knowledge, but upon his singular view of generation.[15] Although Harvey's adage *ex ovo omnia* was later adopted by Ray and Linnaeus in an effort to justify a more consequent use of characters in the elaboration of a taxonomic system, it was expressly *Cesalpino's* system that served as their point of departure.

Consider, now, the Cartesian analogy between living kinds and inorganic systems that supposedly signals the break between science and hermeneutics. The original mechanist paradigm involved the confluence of two notions: (i) that of a technical contrivance, and (ii) that of a natural system composed of motive forces that depend exclusively on the interaction of material elements.[16] Although for Cesalpino, as for the Greeks generally, both notions figured in scientific discourse, they did so more or less independently of one another.[17] Analogy with simple contrivances proved to be episodic, incidental and didactic, rather than sustained, reference-fixing and exploratory. For example, Empedocles (*On Nature* frs. 99,100) likens the ear to a bell and illustrates the way the ebb and flow of blood in the nose governs respiration by the manner in which blocking and then unblocking the small opening in a submerged clepsydra controls water intake. In the same vein, Aristotle (*De motu animalium* 707b9–10) related flexing of the forearm to launching of a catapult (cf. Canguilhem 1968:306).

By contrast, Harvey seemed to have been aware of the emerging mechanist program. But far from championing its strict application, he roundly condemned it: "In the generation of animals there is a mystery greater and more divine than the bare assemblage, alteration and composition of the whole out of the parts, for the whole is constituted and to be seen before its parts, the mixed body before its elements" (1653/1981:208). The vital spirit of the blood, for example, could not conceivably be reduced to the arrangement of the blood's material components, and the fertilizing agent of the semen was empowered with superelemental *pneuma*. As for Harvey's presentation of the heart as pump or fire-engine, this occurs "more as an aside than as an idea of principal importance" (Pagel 1967:80; cf. Roger 1971:120). Here, as in Harvey's comparison of the venous valves to lock-gates, mechanical reference seems to act as a purely pedagogical device of no apparent meta-theoretical significance.[18]

Mechanism and atomism undoubtedly came to occupy an important place in late seventeenth- and early eighteenth-century speculations on the constitution of living beings. But the mechanist analogy was by no means the only significant and productive one going. Comparisons between plant and animal still dominated learned discussion: "There is a great analogy between the nourishment and growth of the seeds of plants in the earth, and . . . the seed or egg of a viviparous animal . . . striking as it were root into the womb" (Ray 1674/1928:76; cf. Harvey 1653/1981:314).

Yet, as ever, the productive use of the animal/plant analogy was circumspect:

> Plant nutrition differs from animal in that animals digest food taken
> through the mouth in the stomach, break it up and weaken the union of
> its parts so that they separate more or less spontaneously from one another
> . . . . Plants, however, do not prepare nutritive sap for they have no
> apparatus of parts to carry out this function, but what sap they find in the
> earth is extracted and assimilated by the roots.   (Ray 1686)

Again, there is little, if any difference in Cesalpino's (or Aristotle's) use of the
analogy and that of the classical natural historians. Thus, as late as the mid-
eighteenth century, Alston (1754:5), after citing the definitions of "plant" given
by Tournefort, Jung, Ray and Linnaeus, surmised accordingly: "A vegetable
may therefore be described, to be an organized body, which draws the manner
of its nourishment and growth by pores or vessels placed on the external surface;
and consequently it may be called *an inverted animal*."

Like the classical natural philosophers, these classical natural historians
believed that unifying forces underlay both organic and inorganic existence.
Only, they rejected a materialistic aetiology as too poor and fragmentary to
account for even the simplest and most obvious aspects of life:[19]

> mechanik philosophers being in no way able to give an account [of the
> formation and organization of animal bodies] from the necessary motion of
> matter, unguided by the mind for ends, prudently break off their system
> there, when they should come to animals, and so leave it altogether
> untoucht. We acknowledge indeed that there is a posthumous piece extant,
> imputed to Cartes, and entitled, *De la formation du Foetus*, wherein there is
> some pretence made to salve all this by fortuitious mechanism. But as the
> theory is built and wholly upon a false supposition, sufficiently confuted
> by Harvey in his book of *Generation*, that the seed doth materially enter
> into the composition of the egg: so it is all along precarious and exception-
> able; nor doth it extend at all to the differences that are in several animals,
> or offer the least reason why an animal of one species might not be formed
> out of the seed of another.   (Ray 1691:28)

Nor did this rejection of a thorough-going materialism bespeak a lapse into
mystical hermeneutics: although "any ingenious and imaginative person could
have found as many signatures" as they wished, still this would tell us nothing of
the natural affinities between kinds (Ray 1660:149–50).

Mechanist analogy did eventually come to constitute a new and powerful
research paradigm. But it would neither replace the old analogy relating plant to
animal nor, at least in natural history, would it ever be strictly Cartesian. Like
the older analogy, it inspired a sustained program of theoretical and empirical
inquiry into the unseen connections linking perceptually diverse kinds. Moreover, neither continued acceptance of the old analogy, nor persistent rejection of
a strictly reductionist interpretation of the new one, were intellectually bound
to traditional symbolism. Together these analogies provided the metaphysical

grounding for the theory-formative proposition that guided classical post-Renaissance natural history: that life is a rational architecture whose special organic nature might be mechanically decolorized, deciphered and decocted, but never wholly dissolved.

9.5 THE ANALOGY OF NATURE

From Aristotle to Linnaeus, the justification for natural history comes from the analogy that more or less like causes structure all the various kinds of living things more or less alike. But the analogy governing the causal and structural unity of the organic world is also nested in a larger metaphysical scheme encompassing the natural philosophy of the inorganic realm, which implies the unity of causal forces operating upon inert as well as living bodies. The primary focus in the overarching analogy, however, is the living body, with natural history acting as the "donor field" and the natural philosophy of inorganic substances as the "recipient field."

Transfer confers a teleological dimension, characteristic of the donor, on the recipient's concepts for exploring the motion of celestial bodies and the sublunary behavior of brute substances. There is an unmistakable tendency to hylozoism in this transfer, although it is less explicit in Aristotle than in his successors: "In nature over all there *is* a balance, not only in the sense of equilibrium but of a good and expedient order" (Balme 1972:98). Each body moves and develops towards its own completed and coherent pattern within limits set by the variously acting and interdependent movements of the cosmos at large. Reciprocally, certain properties of the recipient are transferred to the donor: for example, suppression of "corruptible" features relating to extinction and accident in the organic realm, and introduction into the living world of the visible constancy and "perfection" characteristic of supralunary phenomena.

Thus, for Cesalpino (1571) and Harvey (1653/1981), the eternal cycle of a self-perpetuating species-form emulates fixed circuits of heavenly bodies. It thereby seeks and ultimately attains oneness with a perfectly contemplative and undivided God. With Ray (1691) and Linnaeus ([Wilcke] 1760), a more active Divine Artisan uses vital forces, as He does mechanical ones, to govern the "economy of nature" and "police" the material harmony that obtains between the numerical proportions and geographical distributions of the seeds of species. These seeds supposedly originated in the initial act of Creation – "seeds" not only of plants and animals but, as Tournefort conjectures, of mineral crystals as well (cf. Metzger 1918). Either "every kind hath its seed . . . perfectly formed" since the world began (Ray 1691:81–83), or species-specific seeds are the "mixed" products of God-given "principles" that originated with the complete scale of generic (or familial) natures (Linnaeus 1764).

The advent of heliocentric astronomy and mechanical philosophy led to a reversal of the relations between donor and recipient in the scientific program of natural philosophy from the mid-seventeenth to mid-eighteenth centuries. Henceforth, principles of Cartesian mechanism organize the transfer of clock-movement concepts to the study of organic development. This entails the destruction of the neo-Aristotelian scale of original natures.

In the neo-Aristotelian cosmos, no species originates within the course of nature, and the generation of individuals is primarily referred not to the temporal history in which they appear, but to the foundation of the world. Following the creation of man on the sixth day, God's work has been, in Thomist terms, one of administration rather than constitution: simply maintaining the original process for putting new wine into old bottles, decaying matter into sempiternal forms. In the new mechanical philosophy, however, "the giving of the constitution to the cosmos consisted, not of giving it a whole scale of natures, but only of giving a few, universal laws of motion to a universal matter of a single, common nature, solid extension" (Hodge 1987:230). For the most part, though, this view of the world failed to convince natural historians of the period, and for much the same reason that a strictly materialistic aetiology had proved unacceptable to Aristotle: mere matter in motion could not, by any reasonable stretch of the imagination, account for the most interesting aspects of living beings, including the generation of organisms and organs and the specific relations between them.

On Descartes' own account, any adequate mechanical philosophy would have to explain the genesis of all that we commonly see, including the structure of the world and the origins of living things. Even if we know, by revelation, that life is a divine gift, still we should try to discover how Adam might have come into being if God had not been there to help:

> To know the true nature of this Visible World, it is not enough to find those causes whereby one may render understandable that which appears far from us in the Sky; but one must also be able to deduce from them what we see near us, and which sensibly touches us more . . . . so one will know much better the nature of Adam and that of the trees of Paradise, by examining how children form themselves little by little in their mothers' wombs, and how plants arise from their seeds, rather than by considering only how they were when God created them: we will better understand the Nature of all things in the World, if we can imagine a few very intelligible and simple principles, which make us clearly see that the Stars and the Earth, and finally the whole of this Visible World could have thus been produced from a few seeds (although we know it wasn't produced in this fashion). (1681,III,xlii–xliv)

Failure of the Cartesian program on this score did not entail a wholesale abandonment of mechanism by natural historians. It led only to a rejection of the strong version of Cartesian metaphysics whose logical form takes the character of an "all" statement: "All things are clockwork." An attenuated form of Cartesianism was still possible and was, in fact, adopted by Ray, Tournefort, Linnaeus and many others. The logical form of this weaker version has the character of an "all-some" statement: "In everything there is some clockwork."

The atomism and "hidden" mechanism of English (rather than Continental) natural philosophy – particularly the sort elaborated by Boyle, Newton and Locke – would further prod naturalists towards a materialist view of the unity of nature. But the impetus to carry through a "critical" epistemological synthesis came from natural history, which was in crisis. Not only did the pre-existence theory of species-germs block any attempt to causally unify the two cosmogonies – the theory of the earth and the theory of generation – but it also failed to provide a causal basis for the existence of genera, families and classes of organisms. The first sustained attempt to solve this whole array of problems belongs to Buffon.

The epistemology guiding Buffon's scientific program can only be properly understood within the context of the broad metaphysical doctrine of the "Analogy of Nature" (Newton 1714:357) and the methodological procedures that this "Rule of Analogy" (Locke 1689/1848 IV,xvi,12) entails. The analogy combines two older ideas: the theological "chain of being" through which Nature seeks Divine Perfection, and the unity of causal pattern in the macrocosm and the microcosm (see section 6.4 above). Now, however, the chain involves a gradual transmutation of one natural kind into another. There are no original natural kinds; rather, all kinds are constituted by different arrangements of insensible primordial entities ("atoms" or "molecules"). The only causal forces permitted in Nature are those that operate in the realm of "middle proportionals" apparent to the naked eye. This does not mean that forces are themselves necessarily manifest, only that they must operate in exactly the same manner on phenomenal and nonphenomenal (astronomical and molecular) bodies.

For Newton, the "chain of being" involves Nature in a continuous process of reconstitution. Unlike Leibniz's conception, the chain is not simply the unfolding of a foreordained principle of plenitude wherein Nature seeks the greatest possible variety and is allowed no gaps between kinds. A key element of this continuous reconstitution is the "Power of Attraction" that provides the cosmic order with dynamic forces that act at distances and provide accelerations on matter. But like matter itself, the "attractive powers" are organized and reorganized in a great chain. As Newton indicates in Query 31 of the Opticks: "Bodies act upon another by the Attractions of Gravity, Magneticism, and Electricity; and these instances shew the Tenor and Course of Nature, and make it not improbable but that there may be more attractive Powers than these" (1730:376).[20]

Locke similarly extols the methodological virtues of the Analogy of Nature for revealing the essential qualities and forces underlying sensible and intangible things alike. Contrary to Newton, however, Locke asserts that analogy leads only to "probable conjectures" that neither warrant claims for universal laws nor for clear ideas of insensibles. Nevertheless, in things that we cannot discover for sure, that is, for which we have no direct sense-experience "Analogy, in these matters, is the only help we have, and it is from that alone that we draw all our grounds of probability" (1689/1848 IV,xvi,12).[21]

For Locke, as for Newton, the principle of analogy is itself supposedly culled from sense experience. With Locke, however, the epistemological justification for both the application of the principle and its results is less certain the more one moves from sensibles to insensibles and from observations to general claims about nature. Thus, the entire Newtonian edifice rests on shaky grounds, with its superstructure of universal laws of attraction and absolute notions of space and time being least probable. In fact, this superstructure consists of nothing more than "abstract ideas" invented for the convenience they afford us in thinking, and not because they truly (or even likely) describe the natural world.

What applies to so-called laws of nature applies to history as well: we can no more observe past and future than we can observe other planets, atoms or the origins of the cosmos itself. As for natural kinds, including plant and animal species, these, too, are but general ideas: if analogy reveals to us anything at all, it is that there are no clear breaks between phenomenal kinds. What holds for species holds in an even stronger way for genera. At least species do mark resemblances among groups of real individuals – albeit too categorically. By contrast, genera are but further ideas about resemblances; hence, they have virtually no concrete basis in reality.

Locke's sympathetic but critical rendition of his countryman's natural philosophy did much to undermine the epistemological foundations of Newton's cosmos. Coming from a different quarter, Leibniz's attack would appear to many on the Continent to push the already teetering edifice over the brink. For how could it be, argues Leibniz, that absolutes exist independently of, or prior to, the concrete manifold of objects and events that instantiates them? If such were the case, why couldn't the actual world be other than it is? God's decision to create our world, then, would imply the constant intervention of arbitrary decision. But surely God wouldn't do things merely out of wish: if His will were not governed by objective metaphysical necessity, He would have no *reason* to act at all.

We thus could not give any reason to justify this particular world, which is the real one. Yet if we admit, as we must, that reality is found only in the actual relations of concrete bodies, then we may see the general notions of the cosmos, such as space and time, in a different light. Such features do not refer to external frames that hold together the world. Neither are they mere ideas. Rather, they denote a relational, immanent reality formed by the connections between things and events (Leibniz 1957).

Buffon, it seems, began to take the objections of Locke and Leibniz seriously while preparing a translation of Newton's *Fluxions* in the late 1730s (cf. Sloan 1979:116). In following Leibniz, Buffon did not break with English natural-philosophy's metaphysical commitment to the Analogy of Nature.[22] Instead, he used Leibnizian insights to provide it with a firmer epistemological foundation and to give it even wider empirical scope by adding to it a deeper, historical dimension. This also implied converting probabilistic reasoning, which Locke had used to ground skepticism, into a reliable calculus for ascertaining physical truth. By supplementing, and ultimately equating, gravity with heat, and by identifying the species with a historically continuous lineage, he was able to "immanentize" various taxonomic groups along with Newtonian forces. This reading of Buffon both clears up the apparent contradiction in Buffon's early notion of the species, and clarifies the seemingly late change of heart in his view of the possibility of real knowledge.

Buffon does, indeed, conjointly assert that "in nature only individuals really exist" (1749,I:38), and "it is not the individual that is the greatest marvel" but "that species of enduring unity that appears eternal" (1749,II:3).[23] Yet these are not consecutive affirmations expressing a quick change of mind. They are simultaneous conceptions perfectly in accord with one another: "the species being nothing other than a constant succession of similar individuals that reproduce themselves" (1753,IV:386).

Species do not exist as classes: "it is neither the number nor the collection of similar individuals that makes the species." Nor do individuals, taken alone and in spatio-temporal isolation, have any causal grounding in the real world: "an individual is a being apart, isolated, detached, and which has nothing in common with other beings" (1753,IV:384). Only a continuous causal succession of finite beings that gives immanence to time can be considered a *constituent* of reality. Species, then, are constant because time is continuous (and vice versa), individuals being only fleeting moments of Nature's manifold.[24] One *knows* that species are constant (and time continuous) by reason of:[25]

> the true method for guiding one's mind in the sciences ... having recourse
> to observations, assembling them, making new ones, and in enough quan-
> tity to assure the truth of the principal facts, and employing the mathema-
> tical method only for estimating the probabilities of the consequences that
> one can draw from these facts. (1749,I:61–62)

Granted, we may be virtually certain that species exist as "general effects" of Nature; but can we possibly know what are the underlying physical causes of their existence? At first blush the answer appears to be no: "because our senses are themselves the effects of unknown causes, they can only give us ideas of effects, and never of causes; we are thus reduced to calling a 'cause' a 'general effect', and to renouncing any knowledge beyond that" (1749,I:57). Although we may "never penetrate the intimate structure of things," and "never succeed in explaining the mechanism that Nature uses" (1749,II:33–34), still we may aspire to a knowledge of such things that is "right for us" (*juste par rapport à nous*) and a "likely" (*vrai-semblable*) indication of reality itself.[26]

This is because understanding that is not directly attainable by repeated sense experience can still be approached "by analogies" (1749,I:62). While there will always be "a prodigious distance between physical certitude and the kind of certitude deduced from analogies" (in Lyon and Sloan 1981:58), the force of analogy will increase, along with the well-foundedness of its consequences, to the extent that "it will be related to other effects of nature": "it is thus permissible to make hypotheses and to choose that which appears to us to have the greatest analogy with the other phenomena of nature" (1749,II:32).

Accordingly, those analogies with the greatest force will be those that appeal to universal mechanical principles. Following the Newtonian conception of the Analogy of Nature, Buffon holds that such principles need not be strictly Cartesian. Moreover, as with Newton, the Analogy of Nature allows for the possibility – indeed, likelihood – of a hierarchy of "powers of attraction" of which gravity, magnetism and chemical affinity are but the best known:

> The defect of the philosophy ... of Descartes is of wanting to use only a small number of general effects as causes, excluding all the rest. It seems to me that a philosophy without defect would be one that uses only general effects as causes, but at the same time one that seeks to increase their number ... without advancing anything contrary to mechanical principles.
>
> (1749,II:52–53)

As with Newton, commitment to the Analogy of Nature is a commitment to explain the composition of specially occurring complex bodies by means of ubiquitous simples. For Buffon, in particular, this suggests an account of the reproducing germ of an organic species in terms of elemental, inorganic bodies acting under various Newtonian forces.

Buffon, like Aristotle, believes the problem of generation to be inextricably bound to that of growth: "the same power" must govern both: "because it suffices that in an organized body, which develops, there is a part similar to the whole, so that one day this part can itself become an organized body wholly similar to the one it now forms a part of" (1749,II:46–47). How is it possible for a part to augment itself so that it may become a whole, similar in basic composition to the original part? Buffon takes the most apparently simple case of generation and growth in plants and lower animals and initially compares it to crystal formation in simple inorganic compounds (1749,II:19–24).

He goes on to argue, however, that natural growth seems to occur "from within": not by the mere addition of molecules to surfaces as with crystals, but by an "intussusception that penetrates the mass." This leads to the idea of an interior mold (*moule intérieur*): "I know of a quality in nature that one calls *gravity*, which penetrates the interior of bodies; I take the idea of the interior mold relative to that quality" (1749,II:37). Each species has its mold: "a general prototype ... on which each individual is modeled ... the first animal, the first horse, for example, was the exterior model and the interior mold on which all horses – past, present and future – were formed" (1753,IV:215–216).

Although "we shall never have a clear idea of its qualities," "the supposition of these molds is based on good analogies" (32–33). In fact, the mold – spontaneously formed anew when male semen combines with the product of the "female testicles" – is nothing more than a particular, species-specific, cohesion of "organic molecules" (*molécules organiques*). The specificity of the mold is assured by its material configuration, that is, by the selective disposition of "living matter" (*matière vivante*) according to the particular constellation of Newtonian microforces that penetrate and conjoin the organic mass. The perpetuity of the mold is guaranteed by the mechanical principle that like forces act in like manner when in like circumstances.

An epistemological problem arose from the fact that neither Linnaean species nor Newtonian attraction and time followed laws of *succession*. Taxonomic species presented themselves as atemporal classes, and no temporal boundary conditions were placed on the operation of the laws of gravity and other like penetrating forces. The mind thus had no access to a successive order of events; and belief in succession was, for Buffon, the *sine qua non* for seeking what he called "physical certitude" through a probability calculus applied to a series of repeated observations.

The mind can only truly apprehend what sensation reveals, namely, the two-dimensional effects of the causal process; however, causality itself operates in a three-dimensional manifold:

> Let man direct his mind to some object; if he sees right, he takes a straight line, covers the least space and uses the least possible time to attain his goal .... By contrast any step Nature takes goes in every direction; in going forward, she widens out to the side and rises above; she simultaneously covers and fills the three dimensions; and whereas man only attains one point, she arrives at the solid, encompassing its volume and penetrating all the parts of its mass .... If man were to dispose of this penetrating force ... if only he were to have a sense relative to it, he would see deep down into matter. (1766,XIV:22–24)

Analogy, though, does permit us to know *that* such three-dimensional forces exist and *that* added to those powers of attraction required to move the heavens and form crystals is heat, which molds life:

> Man, who wanted to know ... recognized all of Nature's outsides, and not being able to penetrate into the interior with his senses, he guessed at it by comparison and judged by analogy; he found a general force existing in matter ... then turning his sights on living beings, he saw that heat was another force necessary for their production ... that the formation and development of organized beings occurs with the aid of all these forces combined; that extension, the growth of living or vegetative bodies exactly follows the laws of the force of attraction ... and increasing simultaneously in three dimensions; that the mold, once formed by these same laws of affinity, produces others wholly similar to itself. (25–26)

In the year following publication of these thoughts, Buffon embarked on a series of experiments concerning the cooling of globes (cf. Roger 1988:xxii–iii), the results of which would lead him to a unified theory of the world. The findings, which appeared in the second supplement to the *Histoire Naturelle*

(1775,II), encouraged him shortly afterwards to abandon the earlier view of thought as incapable of penetrating nature's mechanism. For Buffon, the conception of heat that he takes over from the Dutch chemist, Hermann Boerhaave, not only changes the temporal course of the cosmos, but also allows the mind to pursue the history of physical effects. As a result, causal change can be ascertained from one effect to another and intellectually followed as a temporal progression. In the final analysis, then:

> the human mind has no limits, it extends to the degree that the Universe does; thus man can and must attempt everything, to know everything he only needs time. In multiplying his observations he could even see and foresee all the phenomena, all the events of Nature with as much truth and certainty as if he had immediately deduced them from causes. And what more excusable and even noble enthusiasm is there than to believe man capable of recognizing all the powers, and discovering by his works all the secrets of Nature! (1776,III:33–34)

Toward the end of his career, Buffon thought he had finally solved the riddle of nature that he had signaled from the beginning: How comes it that every readily perceptible thing "that can be, is"? (1749,I:11) In particular, he could offer an account in purely physical terms for the existence of the all too visible forms of life: not as a timeless, orderly, two-dimensional taxonomic juxta-position of lifeless morphological groups; but as an eventful, temporal scission-ing of the one great "family" of Nature (1766,XIV:29) into *living* species that link up, down and around in a great three-dimensional and multi-directional "chain of being." In this view of life, both chance and necessity are immanent. Consider:

Early in his *Histoire Naturelle* Buffon owned that nature eternally reproduces the various readily apprehended species (1749,II). Later, domestic animal varieties would appear as unique productions contingent on man's intervention (1755,V). Then, local accidents of geography and climate would condition the degeneration of species (1766,XIV). Finally, the living world would acquire a definite age: "one hundred and thirty two thousand years for the absolute duration of this *belle nature*" (1778,V:167). Different species could thus appear at different times depending on the global thermal situation, migrate as the globe cooled, change as they adapted to local conditions, and eventually disappear, never to reappear on the planet. In this late phase of Buffon, the emergent history of species seems irreversible, contingent as it is on the age of the planet and local environmental conditions.

Still, the broad outlines of that history are recurrent. It is most probable that the conditions for life will be met in other solar systems. Very likely, a comet will collide with a regularly orbiting body to unleash Newtonian-Boerhaavian microforces. These will produce organic molecules, which, in turn, will cohere into species molds.[27] Once this happens, the principal family "stocks" (*souches principales*) will necessarily develop and devolve in these other solar systems owing to the universal laws of heat and gravity that govern planetary cooling.

But necessity is not restricted to the formation of higher groups, nor is chance limited to the degeneration of species. Although happenstance may determine the particular timing and sequence in the devolution of species, the general direction of physical degeneration (e.g. of large to small forms) owes to ubiquitous material conditions. Conversely, chance may enter into the formation of at least some *souches principales* that are lateral offshoots in the "chain of being." Unlike Lamarck's chain, Buffon's is not progressively formed in a strict developmental sequence (e.g. widely separated links may appear simultaneously). Real space-time, however, does crucially affect the chain's formation.

The chain's continuity reveals the fundamental unity of nature's plan; but its special and unequal punctuation owes to the emergence of this plan through a changing spatio-temporal manifold. In this manifold there appear to be some glaring irregularities, which are responsible for such "disruptions" and "deformations" of nature as the armadillo, pangolin and porcupine. Unlike the ostrich and the bat, say, these creatures do not show regular continuity with other beings. Instead, they represent lateral branchings that variously link up with a variety of other forms in diverse ways: "armadillos, instead of hair, are covered like turtles, crayfish and other crustaceans by a solid layer; pangolins are armed with scales like those of fish; porcupines have a sort of sharp feather ... similar to birds' feathers" (1763,10:200–202). Neither are these "isolated species" devolved from more regular types (1766,XIV:373). Rather, they appear to be *sui generis* forms indigenous to South America. Possibly, the formation of their "organic molecules" into a regular species "mold" was disrupted in the passage of molecules south across the Andes (1778,V:176–177).

By this time, Buffon has not only rejected pre-existence of the full scale of species, but also a steady-state Newtonian world. Seaparate branches of the historical lineage may come into being at different *époques* of the earth's cooling; and species-molds may actually evolve, or at least devolve, over the course of time as their respective environments change. In fact, the entire solar system seems to change and degenerate owing to the successive action (and inaction) of heat. But in the end, heat is nothing other than a conjunctural, temporal aspect of gravity. Thus, it appears that macrocosmogony – the theory of the earth – is at last reconciled with microcosmogony – the theory of generation – both referring to one and the same gravitational and thermal history of the solar system.

For the first time in natural history, chance informs both general and specific elements in the "chain of being." To the degree that continuity is linear, the mind may predict what must occur in the "chain of being"; but to the extent that such continuity is lateral and irreversible, the mind can only aspire to what nature herself displays, namely, contingent truth. With Buffon, then, the novel possibility arises that the history of species is irreversible and that nature employs both chance and necessity to form the scale of nature.

9.6 MAN DETHRONED

With one foot grounded in Aristotle's codified folkscience and the other already moving beyond Descartes and towards Darwin, Buffon contemplated the world from precisely that juncture where common sense leaves off and counter-intuition begins. He was, however, still too committed to the known to explore the unknown for its own sake. He kept his science bound to everyday intuition and visible affairs.

On the one hand, concern with underlying biological processes and unforeseen historical influences could not sustain a comprehensive account of the phenomenal order that humankind ordinarily represents in folktaxonomy. On the other hand, preoccupation with that order would forestall a complete causal resolution of the domain of natural history. For it entailed accepting the separate *sui generis* natures of those morphological species, genera and families whose historical links could not be shown. That meant swelling the basic ontology of the world *ad hoc* with original and special configurations of supposedly universal forces that would act in intermittently special ways.

From the beginning, Buffon's great effort at a mechanical synthesis of natural philosophy and natural history came under a twofold attack. On the first place, the penetrating forces of the *moule* remained quantitatively inscrutable and otherwise different from the forces of gravity. Unlike gravity, the character of penetrating forces could not be directly assessed in terms of its constituents, nor would such forces appear to act uniformly on matter. Whereas gravitational force could be computed by a law relating to the inverse square of the distance between *any* masses, penetrating forces were effectively teleological forces that selectively influence some kinds of matter but not others. Alston's reaction, for example, is rather typical in this respect:

> I have called them [*moules intérieurs*] feigned forms, because I am entirely ignorant to what kinds of things they belong, since they are to be named neither spiritual, nor material, that analogy also of such modes with gravity, seems to be very far fetched. For let *gravity* be a quality in nature, or an exceedingly active power, and intimately pervading the smallest particles of bodies ... if it be a quality, it is inherent in every particle of matter, and its force is everywhere uniform. But the supposed modes are neither inherent in all matter, nor is any single organic part, nor in the great organical bodies themselves, nor is their influence uniform; and if they are modes of substance, they subsist without substance, or may subsist. (1754:29–30)

In the second place, Buffon's synthesis failed to fully resolve the visible manifold; that is, it did not succeed in generating a unified taxonomic order that would systematically save the generally agreed-upon facts of morphological affinity (see section 8.2 above). True, for Buffon there could be no inference as to historical linkage without a previous notion of overall resemblance in habitus;

but evident morphological affinity alone would not warrant claims of genealogical connection. Mating routines, considerations of climate and other aspects of behavior and environment could weigh for or against an inference from morphological to historical relation.

Also, the fact that original molds could have widely differing extensions – corresponding to taxonomic families, genera or species – implied that there were no taxonomic properties of any sort, be they anatomical or morphological, structural or functional. In other words, no grounds remained for making general inductions about biological (including medicinal) virtues beyond the confines of a single group of ancestrally related lineages. Because such a group would seem never to extend beyond the level of the (morphological) family, a complete, exact and graduated knowledge of biological resemblance and difference for the "natural order" as a whole would not appear possible.

Other attempts at a "Newtonian" synthesis tried to preserve both the inferential framework of the taxonomic system and a hierarchy of morphological affinities. In Germany, for example, Blumenbach's *Bildungstrieb* functioned as an analogue to the principle of universal gravitation much as did Buffon's *force pénétrante*, namely, as the principle of order characteristic of organized bodies (cf. Lenoir 1981). Among the pre-Darwinians, however, it was Lamarck who most thoroughly sought to reconcile these various demands on natural history with Buffon's insights into the historical emergence of natural kinds. He endeavored to effect his own "Newtonian" synthesis of the general principles of natural philosophy and natural history (cf. Conry 1981); to resolve the entire visible manifold into morphological *séries*; to furnish the inductive framework for systematic inferences about biological *organisation* and *rapports* over a fully ranked hierarchy of living kinds; and to genealogically merge *all* species.

Like Buffon, Lamarck holds that nature's constitution is immanent in time. There is no absolute framework of space or time prior to, independent of, or alongside the concrete bodies whose relations actually determine the course of events and the extent of things. Creative movement in the world is not only governed by attraction through the void, but also by heated reaction through the fluid ether:

> At least in our globe, nature has two powerful and general means that she constantly employs for the production of those phenomena we observe; these means are 1) universal attraction . . . 2) the repelling action of subtle fluids . . . [that] incessantly vary in each place, in each time, and that modify the state of relationship between the molecules of bodies.
>
> (1815,I:169–170)

The effects of heated fluids are particularly important for understanding the composition of living bodies in two ways. First, such reactions, although representative of universal forces, are disproportional to actions, and not proportional as Newton would have them. Second, these disproportional effects manifest themselves in the relations between the external bodies and events of the physical surroundings and the internal secretions of living bodies that environments induce.

One disproportionate effect is life itself. In the plants and lower animals, living species are pure effects and vehicles of the environment's constellation of living forces; however, in the higher animals, species are both cause and effect of nature's constitution:

> In the most perfect animals, life's stimulating cause [*cause excitatrice de la vie*] develops in them and suffices, up to a point, to animate them; however it still needs the help of . . . surrounding environments. But in the other animals and all the plants . . . only the surrounding milieu can provide it to them. (1809:367)

In both cases, the environment causes living bodies to excrete adaptations in subtle ways. The morphologically habitual taxa represent the visual summing up of general features of an organism's adaptive behavior. Such general adaptive behavior consists of precisely those heated actions by the organism (*moeurs* and *habitudes*) and on the organism (*toutes les circumstances influentes*) that determine its characteristic morphological and biological organization, that is, the structure manifest in its species, genus, family and class.

By shifting the focus of discussion from mechanics to fluid dynamics, Lamarck thus sought to overcome the two principal defects in Buffon's implementation of the Analogy of Nature. The "disproportions" that characterize living, as opposed to inert, kinds could be accounted for within a suitably modified Newtonian framework, and in a way that unified all those kinds. For the aim of a natural history built on the Analogy of Nature was to find a causal principle of classification: to define the mode of composition of complex beings on the basis of more elementary physical forces and materials; to determine a hierarchy of structural levels that groups such individuals and species into genera, families and classes; and to fit together all these groups in a visible tableau in which all living beings, known or unknown, would have their appropriate place. This is precisely what Lamarck thought he had accomplished in the *Philosophie zoologique*.

Of course, the shift from mechanics to fluid dynamics was not the only factor in Lamarck's more apparently successful implementation of the Analogy of Nature. Intimately linked to the dynamic forces responsible for the structure and development of the living world was his notion of organization or organic structure. This notion, already implicit in A.-L. Jussieu (see section 8.4 above), enabled Lamarck to subordinate visible characters one to another, to link them to internal functions, and to explain the relation between all readily apparent structures by invisible forces. But whereas Jussieu's characterization of the relations between plant architectures merely signaled the importance of underlying functions, Lamarck's system tried to show how the visible structural arrangements of living beings *result* from their obeying functional plants.

As with Aristotle, Lamarck holds readily apparent morphologies to be the products of the way interdependent functions adjust to environments. The center of life, from which the principal masses emerge, consists of a few general functions: respiration, digestion, locomotion, circulation, sensation. The organs and appendages that develop out of these functions gain in flexibility, variability and distinctiveness as the environments governing their operation change. Genera, species and individuals represent ever more peripheral variations on life's essential themes and their differences are mostly a matter of environmental contingency. The fundamental modifications of life – that is, the "masses" of families and classes – represent basically different patterns of interdependence and pre-eminence among vital functions. In the last analysis, these patterns are not determined by the environment, but by their progressive relationship to man.

Man is the perfect organic plan, with the greatest control, elaboration and degree of freedom of essential functions. Speciation within a principal mass occurs so that its representative populations might achieve greater functional control, elaboration and degree of freedom relative to their specific environments. But the progressive transmutation of life from invertebrate to higher vertebrate masses involves an inherent striving for greater functional perfection in absolute terms.

Buffon, it is true, likewise held up man as the standard of morphological and functional perfection. Unlike Lamarck, however, he owned that the anatomical study of man, which was meant to reconcile morphological and functional knowledge, had little relevance for the study of the "chain of being." Morphologically speaking, man appears midway along the quadruped section of the "chain of being" as a lateral offshoot around the level of the orangutang (the elephant being at the uppermost level). Yet man differs qualitatively from all the animals, including apes, by temperament, gestation and so forth: "that is, by the totality of real habits that constitute what is called *nature* in a particular being" (Buffon 1766,XIV:-30,42).

The reason Buffon rejected the lessons of anatomy for natural history was that comparative anatomy and functional analysis failed to capture all, and only, the structural characteristics of readily apparent groupings of organisms (see section 8.3 above). Either, therefore, one would have to abandon the series of phenomenal groupings or accept, as Cuvier would, that the true classes of organisms were those whose functions operate "by means of organs so various that their structures offer no points in common" (1799,I:34–35). For Buffon, however, the implementation of the Analogy of Nature for a unified theory of the world was predicated on a causal resolution of "mid-level proportions," that is, phenomenal groups. Consequently, he was ill disposed to allow the collapse of the visible order under functional scrutiny.

Yet, Buffon's own causal explanation of the visible order not only failed to account for the relations between the great masses of classes and families in the phenomenal "chain of being"; it only intermittently connected the species within them. Where Cuvier came to view this lack of interest in relating species within and between the larger phenomenal masses as a triumph of Buffon's insight and objectivity, Lamarck considered it a partially failed attempt to fully implement the Analogy of Nature. But Lamarck's own causal unification of the living world according to elementary physical principles, which would progressively yield the complex functional organization of man, could only be achieved at the price of a fundamental epistemological inconsistency.

According to Lamarck, it is the common nondimensional view of things that underscores a false belief in the fixity of taxonomic groups: "this apparent *stability* of things in nature will always be taken for reality by the layman (*le vulgaire*) because one generally judges everything in relation to oneself" (1809:71). But it is precisely this phenomenal standpoint that he adopts when arguing that biological complexity must be inferred from morphological complexity in relation to man: "In effect, what is more interesting in the observation of nature than the study of animals; than the consideration of the relations of their organization with that of man" (1809:1). As in other versions of the *scala* (e.g. Bonnet 1782), a rough and ready cognitive susceptibility to measure up other animals to oneself is raised to a metaphysical principle and a methodological procedure: man is the standard for which nature strives and in relation to which the complexity of organic organization must be judged. As a result, the emergence of new species and the emergence of masses through speciation appear as products of both contingent and transcendental causes.

On the one hand, species are not supposed to change when circumstances remain constant: "the individuals of a species must perpetuate themselves without varying, so long as the circumstances that influence their manner of being do not essentially vary" (1809:57). New *kinds* of species come into being when individuals are "exposed to very different situations" (1809:62). Changing conditions, though, do not alter the nature of the scale of masses:

> this scale (*échelle*) . . . has recognizable degrees only in the principal masses
> of the general series, and not in the species, nor even in the genera: the
> reason for this particularity is that the extreme diversity of circumstances
> in which the different races find themselves bears no relation to the
> composition of the organization between them. (85)

On the other hand, the essential cause of speciation is not situationally induced variation within the family, but the impetus to change into a more perfect being. Even if conditions were stable, there would be a gradual transmutation of species along the scale of families:

> If the cause that unceasingly tends to compose the [scale of] organization
> were the only one to affect the form and origins of animals, the increasing
> composition of organization would be a progression, everywhere regular
> . . . . It is evident that if nature had given existence only to aquatic animals
> – and all these animals had always lived in the same climate, the same kind
> of water, the same depth, etc., etc. – then undoubtedly one would have
> found in the organization of these animals a regular and even nuanced

gradation . . . . Note, finally, wherever extreme changes in circumstances have not occurred, one finds this perfectly nuanced *gradation* in diverse portions of the general series, to which we have given the name *families*. This truth becomes all the more striking in the study of what is called *species*; because the more we observe, the more our specific distinctions become difficult, complex and minute. (1809:132–136)

Thus, not only is biological organization subordinate to the phenomenal perspective of the family scale, but so is the entire history of the living world. Life emerges *so as to* fit the scale, but *by way of* purely contingent relations of cause and effect.

Lamarck does not seem to realize that he simultaneously invokes two contrary modes of coming into being, transcendental genesis and contingent causality. Only with respect to man do the contingent causes of genesis appear to be absent, although Lamarck envisions a "hypothetical" world where man-like creatures could have arisen from ape-like creatures under environmental pressure. But even the emergence of this "hypothetical" man would be driven by transcendental causes – effectively the same causes that make the various masses of living beings more or less like ourselves.

In the *Règne animal*, Cuvier finally unhinges inquiry into living organization from anthropocentric visibility, at least in principle:[28]

> I have had neither the pretention, nor the desire to class beings in such a way . . . as to mark their relative superiority . . . that endeavor, according to me, has harmed, to a degree that one would hardly imagine, the progress of natural history. (1829:xxj)

On this account, the putative transcendental structure of the "great chain of being" is not part of the nomological scheme of things, but sheer mental prejudice. Once a causal resolution of the "chain of being" were abandoned, even the intermittent connections between species of a family or genus would prove illusory. Recall that for Buffon a family resemblance constituted only a necessary – and not (as with Lamarck) always sufficient – indication of causal connectedness between the family's species. But even here, privileging of morphological similarity over other sorts of structural and anatomical resemblance must be ascribed to traditional bias. Indeed, from Cuvier's standpoint, it seems Buffon's only mistake was to believe that the Analogy of Nature could be implemented at all.

Unfettered by this skewed vision, the comparative anatomy of animals with man shows a lack of isomorphism between the deep functional analogies of internal organizations and the superficial resemblances of apparent morphologies. Man is a biological island, not the end of a structural series. He belongs to the archipelago of one of the great branches (*embranchements*) of the animal kingdom. Other species belong to other island groups, the contours of which may be only partially visible or not all. One thing is clear: there is no progressive or graduated scale of differences in biological organization that directly corresponds to any presumed phenomenal series.

There is little, if anything in Cuvier, that can justifiably be put down to scholastic or biblical conservatism.[29] Cuvier's dogma of the absolute hierarchy of functions, like Lamarck's own, owed precisely to the unquestioned belief of the age in the positivistic notion of assured truth, or probabilities approaching certainty. Nor did Cuvier abandon mechanism *for* scholastic teleology. Rather, he used the reconstruction of fossil patterns to mount an *attack* on the fundamentalist notion of biblical creation (cf. Cuvier 1812a). The comparative anatomy of living species served as a basis by which to assign fossils to extinct species in accordance with the fundamentally mechanistic principle of a "correlation of parts." According to this principle, animals are perfect engines of a sort wherein the whole lies embodied in the functional implications of any of its pieces. His rejection of evolution does not follow from any commitment to tradition, but from his very strict adherence to "observed fact": given the poor and fragmentary nature of the fossil data, functionally complete reconstructions of organisms were geologically spotty and seemingly very different. Nature thus appeared to be characterized by abrupt and discontinuous changes in faunal and sedimentary patterns.

To Cuvier's mind, rejection of the phenomenal basis for implementing the Analogy of Nature did, however, entail abandonment of the Newtonian program in natural history. Unable to derive life from available mechanical principles, he was compelled to view living kinds as preadjusted machines "conceived as the testimonies of a community of nature and not as the effects of genetic derivation" (Daudin 1926b,II:246) – much as Ray and Linnaeus were forced to accommodate organic arrangements to Cartesianism by populating nature with an original set of special preset clocks.

Darwin would follow Cuvier in repudiating those theories overly accessible to common sense and excessively concerned by a complete reconciliation with mechanism. But he would not reject the Analogy of Nature outright. All living kinds, whether apparent or not, would still have to sequentially arise from the same underlying causal principles, namely, those also responsible for the genesis of man. Lamarck was correct, therefore, to assume that present forms are the outgrowths of past forms; only he was wrong to suggest that current forms could, within the limits imposed by contingent circumstance, be *foreseen* given only knowledge of prior forms.

To accomplish his account of the origins of species, Darwin would use the phenomenal order as a mere heuristic – a ladder to be scaled and then discarded once the true order of things were to come into focus. He would thus preserve the psychological advantage of common-sense intelligibility by rejecting claims for its epistemic value and appropriating its methodological value: by taking the readily observable aspects of morpho-geographic variations at the old family and species levels as indications of more or less comprehensive (precise and prolonged) organizational (adaptive and constitutional) divergence over time. These indications would serve as eminently practical, though by no means infallible, guides for inferences about genealogical connection and evolutionary diversification.

In this way, Darwin could use the turn given the Analogy of Nature by Buffon and Lamarck to advantage: the spatially observed short-run – the domain of "mid-level" proportionals – would presumably consist of general effects by which we may infer the long-run causes of nature's emergent constitution. In other words, the evident synchronic relations between familiar morphologies would constrain speculations about possible diachronic biological connections. As for the mechanics of biological genesis, Darwin would follow Kant in denying the necessity of knowing how, or even whether, life is mechanically constituted.

In a nutshell, Darwin's program goes like this: "give me the first species, and I'll get the rest." This scientific program is certainly less ambitious than Descartes': "give me extension and movement, and I'll build the world." But to argue that this program does not necessarily signal a resolution of the problem of the essence or origin of life, constitutes "no valid objection" in Darwin's eyes. Just as Newton's posit of the "occult faculty" of universal attraction enhanced, rather than undermined, a causal account of the universe, so the acceptance of an unanalyzed conception of the origins of life need not hinder our understanding of the genesis of species, including man:

> Who can explain what is the essence of attraction of gravity? No one now objects to following out the results consequent on this unknown element of attraction . . . . There is grandeur in this view of life, with its several powers, having been originally breathed by the Creator into a few forms or into one; and that, whilst this planet has gone cycling on according to the fixed law of gravity, from so simple a beginning endless forms most beautiful and most wonderful have been, and are being evolved.
>
> (1872/1883:421,429)

In declining to see morphology as a sure guide to biology, and in postponing the need for a thoroughly mechanical account of genesis, Darwin managed to restrict the pretentions of the Analogy of Nature and thus turn it to even fuller advantage. Without denying the future possibility of its completion (as Kant seemed to), he focused it on bringing to maturity the embedded analogy of a unified organic realm of plants and animals:

> Analogy would lead me one step farther, namely, to the belief that all animals and plants are descended from some one prototype. But analogy may be a deceitful guide [again its two-edged character]. Nevertheless all living things have much in common, in their chemical composition, their cellular structure, their laws of growth, and their liability to injurious influences.
>
> (1883:424-425)

Here the analogy between plant and animal is further developed in a theory-formative way, as an expectation for research in microbiology that would confirm a unified evolutionary framework. To this day, the research program inspired by this reading of the analogy continues at an ever accelerating pace. Old puzzles are solved as particular analogies derived from the general analogy are killed off. But new puzzles arise that are increasingly specialized.

9.7 DISPOSITIONS TO SUSCEPTIBILITIES

Our study began with a critical look at some of the widely held inductivist views on the origins of taxonomy. It proceeded to offer a rather different account of the growth of biological thought, in general, and systematics, in particular. Natural history, it appears, advanced not by a continuous and gradual refinement of primitive sensory associations, but by a pointed development of highly specialized cognitive programs for thinking about the everyday world.

This last chapter has looked at those "freer" advances of scientific speculation that bear no direct relationship with common sense. Psychologically, they do not fall directly within the scope of universal common-sense classificatory dispositions. Historically, they cannot be considered the only possible or plausible answers to the problem of overcoming the natural limits of those dispositions. These speculative advances, however, do not appear to represent the sort of "epistemological rupture" with common sense that anti-inductivist historians and philosophers of science suppose.

In effect, the anti-inductivism of the Bachelardian outlook in France shares with Anglo-American empiricism both the assumption that common sense is hopelessly mixed with symbolism and the conclusion that science truly grows to the extent that it purges thought of this confusion. Science, in other words, denies the "naive realism" of folk knowledge (Russell 1940:14–15) by contra-dicting its "immediate and specious" world of phantasmagoria (Bachelard 1980:17). There is also considerable agreement between Bachelardians (cf. Canguilhem 1968) and logical positivists (cf. Reichenbach 1951) on the role of analogy in science. Although it is admitted that analogies between familiar terms, or between familiar and unfamiliar terms, may provisionally serve a heuristic function as a source of psychological stimulation or as a pedagogical convenience, they are at best viewed as dispensable aids to theory construction and potential obstacles to a full grasp of developed theories. Any metaphysical commitment to analogy thus supposedly marks a reversion to the primitive mode of thought.[30]

Anti-inductivists simply do not accept inductivist claims as to the epistemic continuity between symbolism, common sense and science: scientific know-ledge is not achieved by sifting through and refining customary thought, but by discarding the whole mess outright. On Bachelard's account, the distinction between anthropological common sense and science is straightforward: com-mon sense is phenomenal, science nonphenomenal. The one consists wholly of sense-perceptible "givens," the other of abstract "systems of relations" that have been completely disengaged from the "prehistory" of "sensible intuitions" (Bachelard 1965:84). The one is culturally idiosyncratic, including anything from witchcraft to the geocentric theory. The other has a "history" consisting of terms whose meaning and reference can be traced across successive theories, at least in broad outline.[31]

There is also a major difference of anthropological grounding between the aforementioned inductivist and anti-inductivist currents. The inductivist approach is close to the "intellectualist" anthropology – stimulated by Comte and Condorcet – of Tylor (1871) and Frazer (1922). For Tylor and Frazer, primitive thought always contains an element of rationality; however, the rational line in such thought is subject to deviations incurred by the functional requirements of everyday life. These convenient, but short-sighted, attempts to immediately grasp one's relation to the surrounding environment inevitably lead to rash induction, confusion of sign with object, and a tendency to mistake wishful ideas for real causes. Nevertheless, primitive magic and religion must be "rational in intent"; otherwise, suspension of the law of non-contradiction would yield all propositions as consequences of any premise, and this surely no normal human being could live with (cf. Quine 1960:59–60).

By contrast, the "psycho-social" anthropologies of Durkheim (1912) and Lévy-Bruhl (1923/1966) – their differences aside – reject the idea that primitive mentalities are rationally defective. Rather, primitive thought reflects a wholly different mode of conceptual processing, which is neither propositional nor intended to be. Ostensible contradictions in primitive reasoning arise not because savages neglect to verify the validity of their inferences, but because the principle of non-contradiction has no role to play.

Humanity's romantic, prerational dawn had held logic in abeyance. Perception, will and desire were conceptually one. But the modern mind has succeeded in detaching the rationale for everyday life from wishful fantasy. By repression (refoulement) of a "natural" inclination to totalizing mysticism, the abstract has been laboriously disengaged from the concrete and reality extracted from desire. This decantation of affective associations has given logic free reign to put things in their proper order.

Thus, for Tylor and Frazer, science represents the gradual sobering of primitive thought by inductive refinement; whereas for Durkheim and Lévy-Bruhl, primitive thought differs from science in kind rather than in degree – with an "epistemological rupture" radically marking the gap between savage and savant. On both views, folk thought serves as a mere backdrop to the growth of reason. But its earliest and most common cultural posits – initially rash expedients for handling the flux of experience – seem to linger on as vestiges of functional deities outworn: in myth and religion, in the doctrine of signatures and the "great chain of being."

In point of fact, however, common sense is hardly a culturally peculiar construct and is considerably more prosaic than the doctrines and gods of schools and seminaries. Folkbiological thought, for instance, can no more be held directly liable for the speculative excesses committed in the name of the "great chain of being" than for the postulation of the "great chain of being itself." There is even a measure of *prima facie* conflict between folkbiological taxonomy, which posits the existence of basic discontinuities in the living world, and the thesis of overall continuity that underlies the natural scale. That thesis is admittedly skewed to a phenomenal and anthropocentric bias. But there is nothing in folkbiological schema that requires a visual continuity of living forms spanning the whole world. For such a world is not a customary matter of common sense.

Changing environmental and historical circumstance increasingly mitigated the spontaneous, natural exercise of basic common-sense dispositions in discretely partitioning a local flora and fauna. Correspondingly, folkbiological categories, together with presumptions of underlying natures, were submitted to subtle but significant alterations. They were made to fit into more elaborated cognitive schema, such as a *scala naturae* whose underlying organization was gradated in terms of "heat." But such cognitive reformations were susceptible to elaboration only as historically conditioned, second-order representations of the first-order concepts generated by basic dispositions.[32]

There is a clear principled difference between first-order concepts that are the products of basic common-sense dispositions and the nonsymbolic second-order representations that develop in accordance with cognitive susceptibilities: because the rational constraints on internal coherence and consistency with other beliefs may be temporarily waved or relaxed, second-order representations are amenable to further cognitive elaboration. But the substantive nature of the difference, as it pertains to the closure of second-order concepts, is not uniform. For example, the family concept, upon which the scale of being ultimately came to rest, seems to be "implicitly" generated by the universal cognitive schema of folkbiological classification; and the eternal-species concept, upon which the scale was originally founded, appears to be an even more immediate, and less derivative, elaboration of a basic folk concept. By contrast, the graded notion of the scale itself draws little upon everyday knowledge for direct support.

As for the historical effects of cognitive susceptibilities, here too there is no uniformity. The scale itself had a readily apparent morphological bent, with man as the most salient standard at one end and bugs and nonflowering plants as obvious phenomenal "residuals" at the other. This aspect seems more intuitively accessible, and was in fact historically more consistently developed, than was the putative causal aspect of the scale's underlying organization.[33]

The analogy with man was not the only intuitively compelling and historically elaborated analogy involved in forming the scale of nature. Common sense also seems to have supported a belief that whatever goes for plants goes for animals as well: that speculative advances made in understanding plant structures would likely be applicable to animal structures, and vice versa. More was owed to basic common-sense disposition than to the ontological presupposition that plants and animals comprise naturally distinct subcategories of a distinct and natural category of things, namely, living kinds. There was also the universal parallel between folkbotanical and folkzoological ranking. This strict parallel historically broke down, most notably in the case of life-forms. Nevertheless, a strong cognitive inclination to uphold the parallel may have played a crucial role in natural history's subsequent amenability to a series of plant classes more or less equal to animal classes in number and breadth (see section 8.5 above). On an even broader meta-theoretical plane, an apparent human susceptibility to conceive of physical and chemical substances as essential kinds on a par with biological species seems to have stimulated the coordination and mutual advancement of natural philosophy and natural history (see section 3.5 above).

In sum, to get from the familiar to a factual understanding of the unfamiliar does not appear to require so much a radical break with common sense as a sustained development of privileged cognitive tendencies that permit the elaboration of certain scientific ideas. In contrast to basic common-sense dispositions, these tendencies are apparently not so rigidly structured, nor so spontaneously formed, nor perhaps even so tied to specific cognitive domains. But humankind may nevertheless be universally susceptible to comprehend and elaborate them to various degrees, because of their relatively favored relationships with basic dispositions.

The goal of symbolism, unlike that of science, is not to extend factual knowledge, resolve phenomenal paradoxes or increasingly restrict the scope of interesting conceptual puzzles. Instead, symbolism goes the way of eternal truth, and is sustained in that path by faith in the authority of those charged with the task of continually reinterpreting the truth and fitting it to new circumstances. To the contrary, science assiduously searches out falsity in order to eliminate unknowns.

The tree of knowledge, it appears, has a solid trunk of basic common-sense dispositions that branches out in two largely independent developments of cognitive susceptibilities: on the one hand, towards the relatively unfettered growth of symbolism and, on the other, in the direction of well-pruned scientific graftings. This is not to deny that symbolism and science can feed off one another. Only, they do so in fairly distinct ways. Symbolism may imprudently use anything to advantage as a source of evocation, whereas science must carefully pick and choose the elements about which it can speculate.

From Aristotle to Darwin, the speculative program for the elaboration of natural history involved a conscientious exploration of relationships between the elements of three embedded formative analogies: (i) man as the perfect animal, (ii) the plant as an upturned animal, and (iii) the organism as microcosm. Aristotle's own works (at least the existing ones) concentrated on converting (i) into a comparative zoology that could serve as the basis for an integrated theory of animal taxonomy. It is clear, however, that (ii) and (iii) were never far from his mind, nor from the thoughts of those who followed him.

When Harvey acknowledged Aristotle as the "general" he followed and "Nature's most diligent searcher," it is to Aristotle's patient use of analogy and observation that he referred (1653/1981:20). For him, this was the way to the deep sort of empirical inquiry that could even reveal the falsity of the Ancient Master's own conclusions, thereby assuring that scientific progress had been achieved (443). This is evident, for example, in Harvey's comparison of the female genital system of the deer to corresponding human parts. Having found no menstrual blood coagulated by the *semen maculinium* in deer, he generalized these findings to man on the basis of the obvious similarities between mammalian parts. Because all other animals are but "poor cousins" of man, as Aristotle suggested, they too must reproduce like man and the deer. Aristotle's inspiration is also apparent in the unified theory of generation in animals and plants summarized in Harvey's adage, *ex ovo omnia*, and implemented in Linnaeus' *Systema naturae*.

Completion of the program of natural history, however, depended upon a sustained development of (iii), the analogy of the organism as microcosm. For Aristotle, Cesalpino, Harvey, Ray, Tournefort and Linnaeus this meant lawfully relating the ultimate constituents of the universe to one another: preserving the special natures of species and other foundational forms of the cosmos while showing that they follow the same physical patterns of development in their own particular ways. By contrast, with the reversal of the relation between donor and recipient – when hylozoism ceded to mechanism, and teleology to contingent processes – the goal became physical decomposition of all special and complex phenomenal forms into a few general and elementary constituents.

Only when natural philosophy became the principal supplier, and natural history the beneficiary, of ideas about causal law could a unified theory of life and systematics emerge. Only then could man be truly integrated with the rest of the animal kingdom, and the plants with animals. For only to the degree that man were decomposed into his essential mechanical functions would the less perfect functioning of the other animals be understood, and only to the extent that their functioning were understood would the hidden biology of plants even be conceivable.

In the end, sustained elaboration of the "Newtonian" version of (iii) carried the research programs associated with (i) and (ii) to their sought after conclusion. They ceased to be because they ceased to be problematic. The great enigma still remaining was no longer that of the natures of plants, of animals or even of man, but of the origin and nature of life itself.

10

RUDIMENTS OF THE LINNAEAN HIERARCHY: TOWARDS AN ANTHROPOLOGY OF SCIENCE

Much systematic work of the past is in fact not out-dated – just as Pythagoras's theorem is as valid today as ever, or, less absolutely, as Newton's mechanics is all that we need to cope with those many familiar problems where the scale is such that the answers given by quantum mechanics and relativity theory would not differ, at the order of accuracy required, from the Newtonian answers.

L. A. S. Johnson
Rainbow's end: the quest for an optimal taxonomy,
Proceedings of the Linnaean Society of New South Wales
93, 1968

CONCLUSIONS

The scenario that I have explored and defended so far comes to this: Some fields of science have a phenomenal basis. The basis of such a field may be universal and depend upon a specific cognitive domain. Concern with evaluating this basis constitutes much of the initial phases in the field's development. At later stages, problems of *knowing* the field take precedence over issues pertaining to its cognitive *appreciation*. Epistemology divorces psychology: understanding how the phenomenal basis is constructed becomes a manner of regulating inquiry in the field, but no longer constitutes its object. At least this appears to be the case for natural history. Whether other fields, such as optics or the science of chemical substances, develop in ways similar to natural history remains an open empirical question. Hopefully it is one that anthropologists, psychologists and historians and philosophers of science will take up. For, even if the overall research program recommended here fails, the sort of interdisciplinary co-operation required to answer the question promises new insights into cognitive nature and the scientific enterprise.

To resume the general claim: universal domains of cognition produce special forms of worldly knowledge. This part of human nature I call "common sense." It is responsible for the phenomenal givens that people ordinarily apprehend. As such, common sense does not denote just anything that people may tend to acknowledge in everyday contexts. Rather, its primary reference is to domain-specific cognitions that all human beings are given to know indubitably. But folk also hold less-steadfast beliefs that are related to common sense in seemingly privileged ways. These may be responsible for certain themes that reoccur in myths as well as for particular speculative programs in science. Elaboration of these "peripheral" forms of human belief and knowledge, although culturally relative, is liable to be less idiosyncratic than elaboration of other forms that are not significantly regulated by the common-sense "core."

The significance of folk ways of thinking about the living world to the development of systematics is not limited to the elaboration of those *cognitive susceptibilities* that helped to shape the *scala naturae*, namely, concern with a visible order of things and a focus on man as the standard of comparison. A more direct influence of folkbiology on science, and one whose effects have lasted to the present day, pertains to a *basic common-sense disposition* to apprehend and order discontinuity in the living world. The very notion of an absolutely ranked taxonomy sprouts from conceptual schema that are at the root of the layman's belief in a natural hierarchy of groups within groups. Unfortunately, lack of a truly anthropological perspective has led to a serious misapprehension of the cognitive foundations of the science of life. As a result, the origins of taxonomy, in general, and of the Linnaean ranks, in particular, have been lamentably obscured.

It is this circumstance that mars, for instance, Daudin's otherwise subtle and telling analysis of the sources of taxonomic reasoning in the eighteenth and nineteenth centuries. In his opinion, Linnaeus enlists four essential ranks (class, order, genus and species) and one incidental rank (variety) out of a professional "concern for clarity and regularity" expressed in deference to the traditional scholastic sequence: *genus summum, intermedium, proximum, species* and *individuum* (Daudin 1926a:31n.,71; cf. Larson 1971). But such a motivation as this would hardly be compelling in itself, as it would not suffice to explain why Linnaeus considered these ranks to be of a true and fundamental nature. Nor can their existence be explained by referring solely to the logic of his sexual system, as Leikola (1987:48) suggests. It would not elucidate Linnaeus' endeavor to (meta)physically justify them by means of an otherwise rather odd theory of "hybridization" just when he effectively gave up the attempt to define them in purely rational terms of a mathematical combination of fructification characters.

A more plausible conceptual origin for the five Linnaean ranks is common sense. Thus genus and species represent a "binary fission," as it were, of the folk generic-specieme that can be attributed to the requirements of memory storage and hierarchical reasoning imposed on new information by common sense. The causes that initially favored the genus over other ranks, and that prompted its emergence, are not in the least insinuated by scholastic logic.

Folkspecifics more or less correspond to varieties, and covert family-level fragments to Linnaean orders. As for classes, they appear to be modeled on life-forms. This is patently so in the case of zoological classes:

> I will quote an example from zoology in which I have divided all animals into six classes, namely, into quadrupeds, birds, amphibia, fish, insects and worms. If a duck should come before me for examination and I pronounce that it is a bird, that is the same thing as though I had said it was an animal with two feet and the same number of wings, and furnished with feathers and down. If an ignorant person requires a further description of the thing before us, I should add that it is of the Goose order [family]; from which single word he should know that it is a broad-footed aquatic swimming animal.
>
> (Linnaeus 1737b sec. 212)

For reasons previously discussed, Linnaeus is forced to renounce plant life-forms. Nonetheless, he does tentatively propose higher natural-class groupings based on the number of cotyledons (1751 sec. 163): Acotyledons (e.g. mosses), Monocotyledons (e.g. cereals, palms), Dicotyledons (e.g. legumes, umbellifers) and Polycotyledons (e.g. pines, cypresses). These seem to accord somewhat with life-forms, at least in regard to their inclusive scope, limited number and respect for accepted boundaries of family fragments, genera and species. This made it all the easier for A.-L. de Jussieu to re-establish the customary parallel between the plant and animal hierarchies on a new footing that would be causal-physiological rather than behavioral-ecological. Lamarck and Cuvier would, in their somewhat different ways, reassess the nature of classes, families, genera and species accordingly.

Class. Although the seeming well-boundedness of life-form classes is for Lamarck (1809:26), "but an illusion ... resulting from our ways of knowing animals," still they "appear to be actually formed by nature herself, and, surely, one will have a hard time believing that mammals, birds, etc., are not well-isolated classes, formed by nature." Lamarck, like Buffon and Linneaus before him, recognizes the intuitive appeal of animal life-forms as representing broad organizational plans adapted to certain wide-ranging ways of life in the air, on land, in water.

Too visibly abstract to be apprehended in purely morphological terms, they can ordinarily only be grasped within an environmental context, as general structures for *behaving.* For folk, such behavioral plans actually constitute integral parts of the local ecology as it appears in relation to us. For Lamarck, however, the life-form plan is more indicative of the functional organization of organisms in themselves rather than of their ways of behaving in a certain context. Classes, in other words, come to represent general parameters for maintaining life. These undoubtedly vary with the circumstances of their application, and are even "created" by those circumstances in some sense, but they no longer constitute "part of" this or that context. The environment is thus converted into a (semi) independent causal agent, and the life-form transformed into its primary field of operation. In brief, the class now represents the environment's admissible range of possible effects on living nature.

Like all his predecessors since Aristotle, Lamarck was bound to an anthropocentric perspective using man as the standard of reference in relation to which the other visible "masses" of living beings take form. Cuvier, though, refuses to accept common-sense's overriding concern with the readily perceptible patterns of organization. He dismisses the notion of "invertebrate" as a phenomenal residue of no biological consequence: the boneless, bloodless "bugs" that are left over from the common-man's concern with the vertebrates (i.e. the "man-like" creatures of blood and bone).

All the vertebrate classes are thus united under one anatomical *embranchement* roughly corresponding to the modern phylum of Chordates; and the invertebrates are reconstituted as three distinct *embranchements,* as different from one another as each from the category of Vertebrates in its entirety. Cosmically, the insect is thus raised to the level of man, and man is reduced to an object on a par with the lowliest bug. The subjective goal of natural history – to explain the world as it *appears to be* – is replaced by the objective ideal of biology – to explain the nature of living things as they are *in themselves.* The phenomenal order of things was thus overturned, and then reversed in Darwin's account of our humble animal origins.

Family. In the absence of positive proof for common descent, the family (or the new Lamarckian rank of order for lesser-known animals and plants) comes to indicate the most general facies recognizable at a glance. In the case of animals, the family encompasses only species that seem to occupy a similar niche in their particular community.[1] In Lamarck's theory, however, the series of families constitutes an *eternal* progression of basic functional plans within whose confines speciation could occur.

The nature of every such family plan, like that of each life-form class, is *sui generis* and essentially fixed in advance of its actual materialization. As such, it represents a necessary cosmic moment in the general theory of ascent, rather than a contingently formed descent group. There could be no possibility for "evolution" outside the predetermined sequence of families: "the distribution of living bodies must form a *series*, at least in the arrangement of its *masses* [i.e. classes, orders, and, basically, families], and not a reticulate branching" (1809:105).

Also sundered by Cuvier is this last and most accomplished version of the *scala naturae*, that is, the putative progressive order of connections between visibly manifest families. There is tacit acknowledgement that the family's advantage lay in its capacity to furnish the most visibly abstract means whereby common sense could gain access to the non-phenomenal world of biology. But this newly discovered world of "invisible" non-phenomenal causes and processes need no longer be constrained by criteria of manifest perceptibility. Henceforth, the family would have no inherent claim to the status of most-favored rank. This would be so regardless of whatever practical advantages it might continue to have as a touchstone for the accommodation of our empirical intuitions to the theoretical requirements of scientific taxonomy:

> It is in the unity of "families" that [Lamarck and Cuvier's] classification (*distribution*) of the animal realm finds its surest model and guarantee. Only, because animals offer more numerous and more important internal difference of organization than most plants, here recourse to dissection was an indispensable and decisive factor in the scientific appreciation of "relationships" (*rapports*); and it is from the anatomical work Cuvier rendered obligatory, that a correct determination of most of the classes would arise – and even of some of the principal affinities that unite them – independently of any detailed comparison of genera.   (Daudin 1926b,II:241)

But the fact that the family continued to be heuristically, rather than theoretically, privileged provides an important clue to the lasting relevance of scientific groupings that are accessible to common sense. The conscientious development of phenomenal intuitions at the family-level led botany to the first clear-cut conception of a group formed independently of environmental context. True, a genus could be manipulated in thought as a group abstracted from context. But its claim to reality was initially bound to its original identification with a typical (nondimensional) species. Once the family was admitted into natural history, zoology would change its nature. Henceforth the family would represent the most generally visible manifestation of biological organization and the most direct source of speculation as to the material *laws* that might link species together in this larger apparent unity. Even within evolutionary theory, what Candolle (1819:51) had called "family resemblance" (*air de famille*) plays at least this practical role:

> Here [in the Galapagos Islands] almost every product of the land and of the water bears the unmistakable stamp of the American continent. There are twenty-six land birds; of these twenty-one or perhaps twenty-three are ranked as distinct species, and would commonly be assumed to have been here created; yet the close affinity of most of these birds to American species is manifest in every character, in their habits, gestures, and tones of voice. So it is with the other animals, and with a large proportion of the plants . . . . Facts such as these, admit of no sort of explanation on the ordinary view of creation.   (Darwin 1872/1883:353–354)

As for life-form classes, their organizational plan provides a means of access to an understanding of the basic scaffolding of phyletic lines. When simultaneously scrutinized under aspects of their ecology, functional anatomy and structural morphology they provide important insights into convergence (adaptation of characters in separate groups to similar ecological status), analogy (functional similarity not directly related to community of ancestry) and homology (phylogenetic resemblance under a variety of form and function). Although neither Aristotle, Lamarck nor Cuvier clearly anticipated these distinctions, they did develop the bases for the comparative analysis of internal and structural unities by first comparing life-forms.[2]

Genus. To what extent can the genus and species (much less the family or class) be dissociated from their intuitive base? Here Lamarck's viewpoint is more nuanced, and more nearly correct, than Cuvier's view of the fixity of genera and species. For Lamarck, genera are in truth but "small families" (*petites familles*) of species. As a matter of convenience, taxa at the genus level comprise the smallest nontechnical sorts to which the species criterion of cross-fertility need not strictly apply. In principle, though, the genus level supposedly contains taxa delimited by a more distinctive mode of life and a more refined adaptation to circumstance than taxa at the family level.

Within the context of evolutionary theory today, judging whether the genus is ontologically sound revolves around at least two considerations: (1) whether each genus comprises an identifiable phyletic line, that is, a genealogical nexus with its own peculiar constellation of naturally selective causes (Hull 1975; cf. Ghiselin 1966), and (2) whether each genus within the family has more or less the same adaptive range regardless of the number of its species:

> each genus represents roughly the same kind of entity: a distinct mode of life, a distinct evolutionary shift from the basic stock of the family ... each generic name signifies a particular niche. Secondly, a measure of predictability results. Given a slender, long-legged Malaysian bufonid having membranous webbing, one can predict its habitat, some of its habits, the approximate size and number of ova, and the form of its larvae with reasonable confidence. Thirdly, the value of the genus as a synthetic category indicating species interrelationships is maximized [e.g. hybridization].   (Inger 1958:380)

Yet, especially in botany: "a review of interrelationships of different sorts of species and the evolutionary tree shows that the genus cannot now be regarded as a naturally discrete group either in relation to its ancestors and descendants, or at any one time" (Cain 1956:108). Thus, the question of whether genera – or taxa of any other higher rank – are of a real and fundamental nature rests moot.

Still, whether or not phenomenally compatible higher-order taxa prove to be ontologically sound, they undoubtedly provide cognitive, if not epistemic, access to nature; for when set in a rigid taxonomic framework they constitute a means of both storing information and generating it. The synoptic advantage of a ranked classification for information storage and retrieval is considerable. To take a rather typical example from Jaume Saint-Hilaire's *Exposition des familles naturelles* (1805), which represents a synthesis of the work of Linnaeus, Adanson, A.-L. Jussieu and Lamarck: the chapter dealing with the Leguminosae occupies some fifty pages; of these, approximately one page is devoted to a general description of the family and one page to exceptions, possible links with other families, and a discussion of previous literature; each of 100 or so genera is than analyzed in nearly half a page; and each of the 250 or so species is characterized in a few lines – that is, only about a page and a half of description is necessary for all 250 species. Most modern monographs show this summarizing effect of taxonomic structuring (Wharburton 1967). Ever since Cesalpino, this synoptic character of taxonomy has been a motivating force in systematics.[3]

But more than intellectual satisfaction of relief is involved. Taxonomy provides a blueprint for a detailed study of biological processes directly related to evolution: ecologic, zoogeographic, phyletic, genetic, etc. (cf. Bock 1973). It does this not only by summarizing information already given, but also by supplying a framework for finding new information through the systematic extension of observed relationships: properties generally observed in two species are tentatively assumed to be present throughout the smallest-ranked taxon to which those species both belong. Although, in this respect, the higher Linnaean ranks favored by common sense cannot be considered ontologically or epistemically privilged over other ranks of modern taxonomy (e.g. phylum, tribe, order), they continue to enjoy a measure of practical advantage. Because they are psychologically convenient, they have historically provided, and continue to provide, a ready cognitive access to (a first approximation of) scientific taxonomy.

Species. What, then, of species? If, as Lamarck seems to claim, there is virtually unlimited variation between the various groups of organisms, how can such groups be absolutely ranked into species? Nevertheless, for Lamarck, as for Darwin, it was the relative stability of the local species that made variation so striking and such a compelling source of speculation about evolution, once widened temporal and spatial dimensions were at last figured in. Species undoubtedly fluctuate and even disappear across the vast expanses of geological time and geographical space; however, considered locally and nondimensionally, they remain relatively stable and constant communities "which generation perpetuates in the same state, as long as their environmental circumstances do not change sufficiently to make them vary their habits, character and form" (1809:74–75).

Lamarck's initial views on species-change derived from an attempt to save his overriding metaphysical conception of life as a progressive emanation from Cuvier's attack. Cuvier claimed that since certain fossil shells had no contemporary representatives they must have been extinguished by catastrophe. He apparently reached his conclusion, however, without consulting the greatest conchologist of the day, Lamarck. In showing that at least some living species of mussels and other marine mollusks have fossil analogues, Lamarck (1802–1806) reasoned that wholesale extinction of prior forms could not have occurred. Rather, the differences observed between living and fossil species must owe to a gradual change in the nature of the species itself, which is induced by force of circumstance. Unlike Darwin, evidence for hybridization and cross-breeding scarcely plays a role in Lamarck's initial conception of speciation (cf. Burckhardt 1977). Only later would it carry weight: "hybrids, very common with plants, and the couplings often noted between individuals of quite different animal *species*, have shown that the limits between these supposedly constant species were not as solid as one had imagined" (Lamarck 1809:64).

Although Lamarck spent years accumulating evidence for the gradation of species, his interest in *delimiting* species never waned. For Lamarck, knowledge of (nondimensional) species constituted a fundamental precondition for any further inquiry into the system of nature. Throughout his career he continued to describe hundreds of contemporary species, and to infer the existence of numerous fossil species on the basis of morphological analogies with well-delimited living species. In fact, in what appears to be his final word on the subject, Lamarck (1817) considers species to be real units of nature, that is, "products of nature" rather than "products of art." Again he states that species are constant as long as their circumstances are constant. But inasmuch as there is invariably some change in circumstance over time "One cannot conclude in favor of the supposed stability of species" (1817:448–449).

Darwin, unlike Lamarck, considers extinction a primary factor in shaping the course of evolution. Extinction of connecting groups also helps to account for the visible gaps between contemporaneous species. But these gaps are more apparent than real. How, then, can the differences between species be considered to be of a fundamental nature when they appear to owe their origin, at least in part, only to an accident of observation – the extinction of groups of varieties that have disappeared from view?

> In short, we shall have to treat species in the same manner as those
> naturalists treat genera, who admit that genera are merely artificial combi-
> nations made for convenience. This may not be a cheering prospect; but
> we shall at least be freed from the vain search for the undiscovered and
> undiscoverable essence of the term species.   (Darwin 1872/1883:426)

Although the essence of species can be dealt with in this way, this does not imply that what we commonly take to be species – namely, interbreeding morpho-geographic *communities* of organisms – are artificial combinations. With Darwin, as with Lamarck (1809:74–75), species really exist as naturally bounded *sympatric* groups. For there need be no antagonism between the fact that species evolve and the fact that they so obviously cohere as groups of coexisting individuals in a local flora and fauna: "the more distinct two populations are in space and time, the more difficult it becomes to test their species status in relation to each other, but the more irrelevant biologically this also becomes" (Mayr 1969:27). Evolution, in other words, is not a continuous movement of populations through an environmental sieve, but a passage punctuated with local adaptations to specific ecologic and geographic regulations.

Darwin's initial formulation of the theory of natural selection turns on a solution to the problem of how nature is capable of producing *commonly acknowledged species* from races. For Darwin, only those races count as species that are "ancient and perfectly adapted" (*Notebook* E72, mid-December, 1838). As a consequence of slow and gradual adaptions and constitutional divergence under selection pressures, relatively permanent and deeply hereditary changes are wrought over time. These profound historical developments in the race manifest themselves in the sympatric species readily apparent to every naturalist.

Indeed, the argument for natural selection would fail, in Darwin's eyes, if it weren't a solution to the problem of the origin of those entities that were already being counted by naturalists as species:

> and this was a problem that in its very formulation presupposed that the term species had as much of its customary meaning as was consistent with the problem being given that solution. For the argument was Darwin's response to a problem situation that depended on the very norms constitutive of the public enterprise that science was accepted as being by both Darwin and his audience. (Hodge 1987:246)

Wallace (1889:1) is even more explicit on this score when, in his opening account of *Darwinism*, he explains what the term species meant for Darwin in 1859 and what was meant by discovering the origin of species. As Hodge suggests, we have here the basis for Darwin's realism concerning species as taxa.

To be sure, the species criteria that races must fulfil in order to count as real species were not simply those of the folk naturalist, namely, being a relatively well-delimited morpho-geographic community: the criteria of genealogical connection, nonhybridization and interbreeding also had to be met. But these criteria, which natural historians had developed in response to emerging theoretical demands on basic folkbiological notions, were themselves generally inferred from apparent constancies in morphology and ecology. In this sense, all conceptions of species taxa from Cesalpino to Darwin were implicitly required to meet conditions of compatible common-sense realism.

Where Darwin and Lamarck differ from their predecessors, then, is not in denying the existence of species taxa, but in refusing to acknowledge that the ranking of races into species is unequivocal. The "best" of species do pretty much fit the bill. But the criteria can be met only approximatively, never absolutely, even in principle. This means there can be no *essential* difference between species and variety. Nor, therefore, can the species category, or rank, be ontologically true. Context-sensitive truth conditions for the delimitation of species taxa, however, may be given by a correct definition of the species concept. The best candidate around, and the one most compatible with the folkbiological conception, is the modern definition of the biological-species concept proposed by Ernst Mayr: "A species is a reproductive community of populations (reproductively isolated from others) that occupies a specific niche in nature" (1982:273). If anything, evolutionary theory strengthens the non-dimensional concept of the species as a natural unit of reproduction and genetic exchange among sympatric populations.

Mayr's definition was elaborated after a long and careful reflection on the nature of the Avifauna of Highland New Guinea and on local native understanding of the fauna. More than fifty years ago, Mayr found that basic folk

groupings generally correspond with the naturalist's delimitation of phenomenally salient sympatric species. For more than forty years, this discovery was
virtually ignored by biologists and ethnobiologists alike. Assuredly, paleontolo-
gists (cf. Burma 1949) and botanists (cf. Raven 1976) generally have considerably more difficulty in ascertaining whether a given population constitutes a
biological species. However, this state of affairs does not, in itself, necessarily
undermine the adequacy of the biological-species concept. It is just that in these
cases the biological species concept is not much help in actually delimiting
species taxa. Other criteria must be used to *infer* that a given population actually
constitutes a species taxon and fits the definition of the species concept. These
often include extrapolations from the rough and ready means of morphological
or ecological comparison available to most folk.[4]

In fact, the development of all theoretical conceptions of the species owes
significantly to prolonged reflection on the old common-sense problem of the
relationship between the typical, nondimensional form and its presumed
underlying nature (which must allow for individual token variation in a given
niche):

> The history of natural history was dominated by the question of *species*
> .... This constancy is not exclusive of variations, of differences, as it
> imposed an investigation of the conditions of the permanence of unity in
> diversity, an investigation which led to referring the facts of morphology
> to genealogy, and forms to their mode of reproduction, whence questions
> of breeding and interbreeding, of hybridization and intersterility.
>
> (Canguilhem 1981:129)

Inquiry into the species problem had been temporarily suspended after Cesalpino and Harvey. Once the species had been defined as the eternal reproduction
of like from like, and the permanence of visible structures thus assured by
filiation, the basis of taxonomy seemed secure. Underlying the nature of each
and every species was a miniature replica of its typical form ready to leap fully
armed onto the stage of history, like Athena from the head of Zeus when the
right moment presented itself: "every kind hath its seed ... perfectly formed"
since Creation (Ray 1691:81–83). Thus, by linking up visual forms in a universal
taxonomy, one would *ipso facto* connect their corresponding underlying natures,
or essences; and the science of Nature would seemingly be rendered complete.
But the theory of preformed germs was only a postponement of the problem of
underlying nature; for the theory of underlying natures would not only have to
account for the existence of species, but also for the special emergence of higher
forms, especially genera.

Linnaeus, whose investigations of generation were geared to an account of the
visible order by "principle" rather than process, nevertheless recognized that the
obviously visible kind need not be a replica of its underlying structure. Indeed,
principled "mixes" of the underlying parts of very different visible kinds could
form novel and stable types (Linnaeus 1764). Here at last was an excuse to

experiment with fertilization and breeding so as to reveal something new and unforeseen about underlying structure. If Koelreuter (1761–1766/1893) was aghast at Linnaeus' easy "demonstration" of intergeneric hybrids, at least he had an appropriate foil against which to work (cf. Roberts 1929).

In this respect, the lesson of Harvey's discourse "On Conception" should not be forgotten. Theories that lend themselves to refutations after rigorous examination are the stepping-stones of scientific development: "I only ask as my just deserts the liberty I freely allow to all other men, to put forward as true those things which in this whole dark business seem probable until such time as their falsity may be openly proved before all men (1653/1981:443; cf. Popper 1963)."

Buffon's theory of generation also cannot be deemed to be a complete break with preformation theory: "Buffon did not succeed, despite his efforts, to free himself from a mechanist and spatial representation of organization . . . for the germ to deveop into the whole animal, it already has to be that animal, with all its parts materially and actually formed" (Roger 1971:546). But it was novel enough to stimulate original research on the actual physical structure of the germ, that is, on the mechanical *processes* governing what Buffon called "reproduction."

For Buffon, the underlying nature of a kind consisted in a lawful combination of elementary corpuscular units (*molécules organiques*) into a microscopic mold for the visible kind. The problem, then, was to specify the terms of the law, or laws, and the steps of the combinatory sequence in a manner parallel to, and ultimately of a sort with, the specification of those Newtonian forces at work in the combination of atomic elements into crystal formations. The impetus that this approach gave to the immediate and further development of Haller's (1751) embryological speculations and to Spallanzani's (1776) microscopic investigations of conception is undeniable; although Buffon's theory again served mainly as a proper foil (cf. Gasking 1967).

Not until German embryologists provided the intellectual and technical means to explore the nature of the germ in the seed itself, however, could the problem of speciation be directly linked with that of generational processes. Although Darwin himself took little account of the cellular organization of organisms, the contingent phylogeny of Darwinian evolution was, in a real sense, pre-adapted to the emerging theory of cells and contingency in ontogenetic processes. Just as the cell functions as the fundamental unit for regulating the material exchanges responsible for an individual's development, so the species operates as the basic unit in the day-to-day regulation of gene flow, and as such plays a central historical role in evolution.

There is, however, a much closer relation between cell and species than analogy between different logical types. For embedded in the genetic material of the cell is the natural history of the species, and at the origin of the species is a mutation in the cell's genetic program:

If the species are stable, it is because the program is scrupulously recopied sign by sign, from one generation to another. It they vary it is because from time to time the program changes. On the one hand, it is necessary to analyze the structure of the program, its logic and execution; on the other, to examine the history of programs, their drift and the laws governing their changes throughout generations in terms of ecological systems.

(Jacob 1970/1973:8)

The ecologic formation of communities of more or less distinct sympatric groups evolving over time is a snapshot by the ordinary mind's eye. Here is a picture that seems to be largely true to life, at least for most vertebrates and flowering plants that constitute the setting for humankind's wonted existence. That we spontaneously eye such things more or less as they really are is not so very surprising, seeing that our everyday life depends on it; and our own evolution surely must have geared our minds to making such dependence viable.

The ability to recognize nondimensional species may also be a cognitive trait of nonhuman species, yet only humans likely sort species in accordance with presumptions of underlying nature and then recursively apply this procedure for sorting them into higher groups. Without technical aids, hierarchical sorting procedures appear to be severely limited by constraints of memory. But through technological innovation and exploration in the course of history, a greater quantity of information as to number and kinds of organisms, and greater quality of information as to their relationships, were accumulated and processed by introducing additional ranks into a worldwide taxonomy.[5]

The congruence of folkbiological species concepts across cultures, together with the practical concordance of historically elaborated species concepts, suggests a course of both realism and rationality in the development of science from its common-sense origins. If the progress of science is measured, at least in part, in terms of success in solving technical puzzles, then the ongoing inquiry into the "species problem" surely counts as one of the basic sets of scientific puzzles by which to measure success. Of course, common sense itself has no more to contribute directly to a biological unriddling of "the species problem" than it does to a causal resolution of the higher ranks; but it does provide the problem with a transtheoretical grounding.

This is one more assurance that science, in its quest for new horizons, need never go from our mundane world empty or blind. In our intellectual alienation from usual surroundings we, as scientists, may well deny that our familiar setting is the only subject, or even a proper subject, for ontological inquiry; however, it should be kept in mind that without the perseverance of some customary knowledge, a more learned pursuit of what there is would gad into myth. Far from acting merely as an "epistemological obstacle" to science, or being conceptually incompatible with it, common sense has played, and continues to play, a substantial part in tying scientific discourses to one another and to the world.[6] It binds us within the Book of Nature.

By nature, human minds everywhere are endowed with common sense. They possess universal cognitive dispositions that determine a core of spontaneously formulated representations about the world. The world is basically represented in the same way in every culture. Core concepts and beliefs about the world are easily acquired and tend to be adequate for ordinary dealings with the social and natural environment; yet they are restricted to certain cognitive domains and are rather fixed.

Take human beings' spontaneous apprehension of living kinds: simply point out to anyone – anytime, anywhere – animals or plants of apparently different species. Ordinarily, a person will presume them to be essentially different in kind from one another, but collectively of a sort with all animals or plants (as distinct from all the other sorts of things in the world). Folk just "automatically" incline to segregate all, and only, living kinds according to ready presumptions about their distinct underlying natures, and to rigidly join them in an absolute hierarchy. In no other cognitive domain is such a natural taxonomy manifest.

Cultures develop and diversify beyond the common-sense core with practical and speculative systems of representations that are not spontaneously elaborated, like natural history and totemism. These other, harder to master representations tend to be less limited in their domain of application and less fixed in their structure. They involve different cognitive abilities, in particular the typically human ability of retaining only partly understood information in order to work on it and understand it better. Such processing of half-understood information is characteristic of deliberate efforts to elaborate counter-intuitive ideas, and is found in both science and mythico-religious symbolism.

A major difference between spontaneous and nonspontaneous, or sophisticated, conceptualization is that only in the former case are the individual's newly acquired thoughts directly about the objects of the new knowledge: for example, about physical properties or animals. With sophisticated conceptualization, the individual's newly acquired thoughts are initially about the knowledge itself: for example, about notions and ideas in physics or in biology. Only if, and when, these notions and ideas become fully assimilated does the knowledge cease to be non- or even counter-intuitive and become direct knowledge of, say, physical or biological facts.

The passage from representation of knowledge to assimilation of knowledge is often difficult, as in the sciences. Sometimes it is not even possible, so that some forms of knowledge, such as mythico-religious symbolism, remain forever half-baked (meta-representational) notions about ideas. Unlike the propositions of science, which are in principle semantically precise and empirically testable, the quasi-propositions of symbolism are always open to contradictory interpretations of meaning and experience.

Symbolism, then, could never be either a psychologically basic or historically evident stage in the rational extension of factual knowledge, that is, in the scientific elaboration of common sense. Basic and evident are the fundamental, plausibly innately grounded, common-sense dispositions to think about the everyday world in certain cross-culturally recognizable ways. Such are the necessary, if not sufficient, conditions for any symbolic or scientific elaboration of that world.

What makes counter-intuitive ideas understandable at all is that they remain rooted in common-sense intuitions, however remotely. The history of science, for instance, suggests that the breakthroughs that characterize modern theories followed a conscientious probe of the scope and limits of common-sense "givens" in the corresponding naive theories. Evolutionary theory is a case in point. True, evolutionary biology today has gone far against the grain of intuition: not only in denying the common-sense view of the species rank as ontologically true, but also in rejecting the ordinary conception of species taxa as classes of organisms and substituting the notion of the species as a "logical individual." Yet even those axiomatizations of evolutionary theory, that treat the members of a species community as "parts" of an individual spatio-temporal whole, implicitly appeal to a notion of "nondimensional" species that closely approximates the lay conception.

In practice, the field biologist who is initially unfamiliar with a terrain can usually rely on local folk to provide a fairly accurate first approximation of the scientific distribution of the local flora and fauna (at least for vertebrates and flowering plants). To be sure, genetics and molecular biology have little recourse to folk intuitions, but in these fields as well generalizations depend on the acceptance of taxonomic inferences that do make use of notions like species.

This metaphorical talk about a core of spontaneously learned knowledge, and a periphery of further knowledge that requires deliberate elaboration and teaching, not only suggests that the one is more stable and central than the other; it also indicates that they are functionally related: the very existence of the periphery is made possible by the core. Theoretical knowledge elaborates or challenges common-sense knowledge, but never develops in society or the individual without reference to the basic common-sense core.

Admittedly, references to *the* common-sense core of cognition and *the* phenomenal foundation of science seem unduly monolithic (assuming that our ordinary basis for factual knowledge of the world is constituted by various domains with different cognitive make-ups). Indeed, where physics is concerned the psychological and historical evidence for universally consistent interpretations of, say, the causes of motion is none too clear.[7] Moreover, the link between modern conceptions of time and space and corresponding lay conceptions seems tenuous at best. Yet, the psychological and historical relevance of common-sense notions for the emergence of fundamental disciplines like optics and mechanics may be greater than is often supposed. Thus, even preverbal children spontaneously project the spatial trajectories of three-dimensional rigid objects in ways that are crucial to *any* physical determination of the causes of moving bodies. Also, some ostensible obstacles to the advance of natural philosophy that are often attributed to common sense, such as the flat-earth idea, may actually have little to do with common sense.[8]

There may be grounds, then, for supposing that at least some parts of the natural sciences have special common-sense foundations.[9] Of course, one hallmark of scientific progress is the integration of previously separated object domains. But to understand this achievement at all requires an appreciation of the proper scope and limits of the common-sense conceptions that ordinarily define those domains.

The study of the knowledge-structures of various common-sense domains is still in its infancy. For historians and anthropologists of science, the implication that science cannot ignore common sense is ripe with possibilities for further intellectual discovery. But it would probably displease some philosophers and teachers of science. Not only does it suggest that an activity that aspires to cosmic objectivity is riddled through with narrow and naive thoughts that have barely changed since humans emerged from their caves; it also seems to underscore deep-seated prejudices like thinking of species in terms of essences – a thought perhaps congenial to creationists, but abhorrent to evolutionists.

Were science purely a cosmic matter – of interest only to some all-knowing martian deity – then, indeed, the contribution of human nature would seem an insignificant factor in the scientific universe and an impediment to omniscience. Arguably, however, one of the central questions in the philosophy of science is: "How comes it that human beings are capable of thinking scientifically"? If so, then it would be odd to view a fundamental contribution to that capability only as an impediment to realizing it.

Once the proper limits and scope of common sense, science and symbolism are understood, philosophers and scientists can use this knowledge to mark advances in the further quest for insight into reality. Aristotle, no less than Linnaeus, clearly noted where rational and symbolic speculation diverge. Although they may have failed to correctly demarcate the rational bounds of common sense, still their projection and interpretation of common-sense types into organic science provided the framework for thinking about systematic variation between living things. Darwin, refusing to consider variation merely as deviation from type, more clearly saw the limitations of common sense for science. Epistemic claims about the integrity of species that were based on extensions of common sense he handily rejected; but the heuristic value of folk types (species, families, classes) proved crucial to his very formulation of the problem of the origin of species.

The learning of science plainly need not recapitulate the historic process of discovery. But understanding at least some central notions of a science seems to presuppose understanding the corresponding "naive" notions and relating the two appropriately. This pertains to the function of quality and teaching in sophisticated learning: the role of instruction is not merely to present, however clearly, scientific concepts; it is also to help the student gain an "intuitive" grasp of what they mean, by relating them to common-sense experience and knowledge.

In truth, common sense has little to reveal about the dispute between creationism and evolutionary theory. Setting the proper boundary of common sense, however, reveals the fundamental point that both creationism and evolutionary theory elaborate the ordinary meaning attached to species in extraordinary and different ways: the one symbolically, the other scientifically. That is a point the anthropology of science bears on.

The anthropology of science is a paradoxical subject with particular responsibilities. From a purely ethnographic viewpoint, which considers human cultures and social institutions on a case by case basis, science appears as a local phenomenon. Unlike kinship, say, or music, which are universally distributed across cultures, science is more or less restricted to one culture; although today that culture communicates with an ever increasing number of hitherto closed societies. Absent throughout much of human history, science is less widespread even when it exists than, say, totemism or circumcision rites. In this respect it is more akin to sand painting among the Indian tribes of the American southwest, of particular importance only for the practicing culture. Especially for the last twenty years or so, historians and philosophers of science have increasingly adopted such a strictly ethnographic standpoint. This is unfortunate; for ethnographic views of science by no means exhaust its anthropological interest.

Alone among human endeavors, science is forced to answer timeless standards of reality in a cumulative way. No seriously informed person can sincerely dispute that, at least in certain respects, humans are more successful now in probing reality than they were before. If we take common-sense cognition of reality as a base line from which to judge progress, then to grant such an absolute advance is necessarily to deny that it is socially determined. Social factors do invariably affect the pace of scientific progress; in the end, however, only the reality that exists independently of human concerns can truly determine whether science has, in fact, furthered understanding of that reality.

To the anthropologist, then, as for humankind, science proves to be a very special social institution, the only one that endeavors to fix a *univocal* relation between mind and nature. Its ethnographic analysis requires a correspondingly special intellectual outlook, one capable of following that endeavor across time and place. For cognitive anthropology, the central problem of the history and philosophy of science is a search for an answer to the general question, "How comes it that human beings are capable of thinking scientifically?" It is a deep question about human nature – about what may be the one definitely sustained aspect of its improvement.[10]

This way of looking at science is of an altogether different order from the sociological notion of science as a particular cultural phenomenon, or the positivist conception of scientific thinking as consisting in the logical structure of theories, in modes of experimentation and in the rules whereby theory and experiment are brought into correspondence. Given the outlook of this book, problems pertaining to chronology or the historiography of scientific discovery as such are also secondary. Instead, the anthropology of science addresses the nature of scientific thinking generally. It places the central problem of scientific thinking squarely within the larger puzzle of the nature of human thought: "How is it that we acquire such rich systems of ordinary and scientific knowledge after all?" Although our actual experiences with the objects of our thoughts are so fragmentary and individual, how are we nonetheless able to classify and use forms of ordinary and scientific knowledge that are so systematic and extensive?

The problem of ordinary knowledge obviously comes first. But is this priority just a matter of circumstance? Seeing things this way would take us back full circle: to the view of those believers in the intellectual supremacy of science who incline to think of common sense as a mere stepping-stone or as a barrier to science, and unworthy of any claim to "knowledge." But the sticking point in that view is the belief that all pretheoretical understanding of the world is transitory because it springs from human concerns bearing on values relative to time and place. On this view, any ontology of common-sense "givens" would be unsound because they are constantly shifting. The only relatively firm ontology would be science's cosmic one.

At least some basic common-sense dispositions, though, pertain to concerns that transcend all cultural boundaries and are oblivious to human fortune: namely, cognitive concerns with how the world appears to us *as human beings*, as opposed to how it might seem to God or some omniscient extraterrestrial. In those cases where such dispositions apply, science could admit the ontological status of phenomenal kinds as those restricted to "human ecology." Such kinds lawfully relate the human mind to "its" physical surroundings, that is, to those aspects of the environment we are all disposed to notice as natural and manifest.

Historically, of course, the boundary between ordinary and cosmic ontology was initially confused. But as common sense came to play a less direct role in the growth of science, it more clearly relinquished any epistemological claim to scientific verity. Still, its transcultural character continued to give it a privileged position in the development of scientific thinking, and it retained much validity in everyday matters.

Consider that the first significant breakthroughs in science often appear to involve the discovery of critical distinctions that must be drawn between those very kinds to which common sense affords the most direct cognitive access. To give a rather homely example: when bats were definitively dropped from the birds and whales from the fish, so that both could be joined to the mammals, a very profound, even revolutionary, event in systematics thus occurred, based primarily on new knowledge of internal anatomy. But notice how much did not change: neither the abstract hierarchical schema furnished by folktaxonomy, nor – in a crucial sense – even the kinds involved. Bats, whales, mammals, fish and birds did not simply vanish from common sense to spring up full blown again in the new science; rather, there was a redistribution of affiliations between antecedently perceived kinds. What had altered was the construal of the underlying natures of those kinds, with a consequent redistribution of kinds and a reappraisal of properties pertinent to reference. The form of the boxes had not appreciably altered, nor the general manner of stacking them, but only their presumed contents and particular arrangement.

For many in the scientific community, common sense ostensibly offers little more than black bloxes, or worse, Trojan horses containing unduly tenacious and misleading notions as to the uniformity and unity of the contents; trees, for instance, no longer constitute a botanically valid taxon, but most people hang on to the concept of TREE as if their lives depended on it. Yet, when common sense is viewed on its own terms – not as a noxious underling of science, but as an independent and generally faithful ally – then its real worth becomes manifest. Nor is there any compelling reason why it should not be considered in its own right, inasmuch as it is science, and not common sense, which constitutes a rather specialized activity of thought, and one that is hardly required for an apprehension of humankind's immensely rich and varied everyday world.

Quite simply, common sense lights a world for all to see – a world that is, in its fundamental contours, much the same for scientist, layman and bushman. Science may excavate and extend that world in wholly novel ways, but science cannot just confute it and render it useless. Assuredly, the open universe of science consumes the closed world of sense that is humankind's vantage ground. A truly impersonal cosmic science that neglected to ruminate over this peculiar sensibility would suffer at most a trifling irregularity. But when we ask not "What is there in the universe at large?" but "What sort of world do we ordinarily live in?" we dare not rush the course. Indeed science, being only human after all, begs an answer to the second query to broach the first. It has to know what common sense has to offer.

And common sense, in turn, can learn from science. Customary thinking operates adequately with fairly constant factors of mind and nature, but is unaware of them. Lacking self-knowledge as to the range of validity of its beliefs, common sense requires science to define the limits within which its beliefs are valid. Within the confines science thus sets, we learn the extent to which our ordinary vision of the world holds good.

From one angle, then, ordinary thinking initially takes the role of a central historical subject in the growth of scientific thought. It is a role that develops through successive transformations of basic common-sense dispositions into scientific modes of thinking, whose object arises as much from human nature as from the nature of reality. To follow this role is to study an object of thought that is both accessible to common sense and susceptible to further scientific elaboration. From another angle, common sense remains a pre-eminently anthropological subject: cross-cultural in scope and deeply expressive of human nature. The anthropology of science advances from a double perspective; it finds the bounds within which plain thinking stands up and shows us where visibility no longer holds the promise of truth.

Appendix

MILESTONES OF NATURAL HISTORY

I. *Antiquity*

ARISTOTLE (384–322 B.C.) Greek philosopher and naturalist, Plato's student, crowned by Linnaeus "Prince of Philosophers." He introduced the study of systematics by attempting to unify and explain the diverse components of folkbiological taxonomy. Of numerous works on plants and animals, only those are known to us that treat the history, the parts and the movement of animals (*De historia animalium, De partibus animalium, De generatione animalium* and *De incessu animalium*). These describe in detail the characteristics of more than 500 animal species.

THEOPHRASTUS (372–287 B.C.) Greek philosopher and naturalist, succeeded Aristotle as head of the Lyceum, honored by Linnaeus as "The Father of Botany." He was the first to declare that botany should not be occupied firstly with medicinal or practical virtues, but "must consider the distinctive characters and general nature of plants from the standpoint of their morphology, their behavior in the face of external conditions, their mode of generation and their whole manner of living" (*De historia plantarum*).

DIOSCORIDES (*ca.* 40 A.D.–90) Greek physician. His work on medical matters (*De materia medica*) concerns 500 to 600 plant species. His study was to become the standard western pharmacopoeia for 1600 years and the most important ancient source of modern botanical terminology.

PLINY The Elder (23 A.D.–79) Roman naturalist and soldier. His Natural History (*Historiarum mundi*) in 37 books forms an encyclopedia of the theoretical and practical knowledge current in antiquity.

II. *Middle Ages*

HERBARIUM OF PSEUDO-APULEIUS (4th–15th century) the most popular herbal of late antiquity and that most cited by medieval Latin sources. The original Greek text (by an anonymous author who appropriated the name Apuleius) has not come down to us. The work, describing and illustrating over 100 plants, was hand copied and disseminated throughout Europe.

The quality of description and illustration varies greatly from copy to copy and even within any one version; and often it is impossible to know when a given author is referring to the local flora. This herbal was frequently consulted with another, the *Ex herbis feminis* of Pseudo-Dioscorides, which dates back to the fifth or sixth century.

ALBERT THE GREAT (*c.* 1193–1280) German theologian and naturalist, revered as *doctor universalis* for his widespread knowledge. He was probably the greatest naturalist of the Middle Ages. An important part of his writing includes novel empirical observations relating to leaf anatomy and to the propagation of plants and animals. In keeping with Aristotle, he sought to distance his science from superstitions of the time; but his biological work (*De vegetabilibus* and *De animalibus*) is largely a testimonial to Aristotle's authority.

THOMAS AQUINAS (1225–1274) Italian theologian, student of Albert, known as "the angelic doctor" and canonized for his successful reconciliation of Aristotelian philosophy with Roman Catholic doctrine (*Summa theologiae*). He declared "that which engenders, engenders a being of the same species" and suggested that species propagate eternally. This idea, already at a remove from the nonfixity of the Aristotelian species, marks an important advance towards Cesalpino's conception of the eternal biological species.

III. *Renaissance*

BRUNFELS, Otto (1488–1534) German physician and naturalist. He authored "The living images of plants" (*Herbarum vivae eicones*), which did much to dissociate botany from medieval folklore and scholastic herbalism. The work offers a collection of ancient and contemporary commentaries on plants, the census of plant properties providing its main scientific value. The detailed, precise and realistic engravings by the illustrator, Hans Weiditz, are chiefly responsible for the book's success in encouraging herbalists to adopt a naturalistic outlook.

BOCK, Hieronymus (Tragus) (1498–1554) German physician and naturalist. He sought to establish a system of plant classification based on physical characteristics rather than alphabetical order. His masterwork (*Kreütter Buch*) allows ready identification of many of Germany's local plants.

FUCHS, Leonhard (1501–1566) German physician and naturalist. His botanical study (*Historia stirpium*) represents a landmark in the development of natural history owing to its organized presentation, the precision of its designs and the glossary of short definitions for botanical terms.

CORDUS, Valerius (1515–1544) German physician and naturalist. Despite some misconstrual of the nature of the floral organs and plant development, he originated the technique of exact and systematic morphological description for plants. His herbal of local and ancient plants (*Historia stirpium*) was posthumously edited and published by Gesner.

GESNER, Conrad (1516–1565) German physician and philologist. His encyclopedic knowledge of plants and animals (*Historia plantarum* and *Historia animalium*) opened Aristotelian categories and reasoning to new discoveries. From his letters (*Epistolarum medicinalium*), he appears to have initiated the systematic use of herbaria – collections of dried plants first established by Luca Ghini (1490–1556) – as a means for comprehending exotic flora. He also first pointed out the analytic importance of the fruit and seed for future classifications.

CESALPINO, Andreas (1519–1603) Italian physician and philosopher, student of Luca Ghini, esteemed by Linnaeus as "The First True Systematist." Following Aristotle and Theophrastus, his prudent use of analogy between plant and animal structure led to physiological insights into generation and circulation (*De medicamentorium facultatibus*) surpassed only by Harvey's. His classification of plants according to fruit and flower laid the foundation for all succeeding attempts to construct a "natural system" that would wed intuitions of morphological affinity to rational principles (*De plantis*). Here the eternal species acquires its strict biological sense, thus sanctioning the comparison and placement of local forms in a timeless and universal scheme.

BAUHIN, Caspar (1560–1624) German physician and anatomist, student of Fabricius d'Aquapendente (1537–1619). His "Plant chart" (*Pinax theatri botanici*) catalogued all known plants of the time by providing them a universal nomenclature. Despite evident awareness of morphological associations, his index heralds the end of herbalism rather than the start of a quest for a natural system. His compilation includes some 6,000 plant species – about an order of magnitude more than usually recognized by ancient, medieval, renaissance or local folk.

IV. The Era of Systems

GALILEO, Galilei (1564–1642) Italian physician and natural philosopher. An originator of the experimental method in physical science, he proclaimed (*Il Saggiatore*) geometry the ideal mode of scientific reasoning, being that instrument of understanding most apt to model nature and thereby enable deduction and discovery of new empirical facts.

HARVEY, William (1578–1657) English physician and physiologist, disciple of Fabricius d'Aquapendente. He discovered the true nature of the circulation of blood (*De motu locali animalium*). Later experiments on the generation of animals and careful reasoning by analogy to plants led him to conclude that all living beings reproduce in like manner by eggs or seeds (*Exercitationes de generatione animalium*).

JUNG, Joachim (1587–1657) German mathematical and natural philosopher. He was an early champion of atomistic thinking in chemistry. In "Guide to the examination of plants" (*Isagoge phytoscopica*), he established the analytic morphology that would subsequently play a significant role in the inquiries of Ray and Linnaeus: the plant is decomposed into a limited number of fundamental organs, that are defined by their arithmetical, geometrical and topological relations with other parts and with the plant as a whole.

DESCARTES, René (1596–1650) French philosopher, physician and mathematician. His theory of animal-machines offered the first non-Aristotelian conception of unified science by assimilating the organic realm to just those mechanistic and deductive principles thought to govern the inorganic realm (*Les principes de la philosophie*).

MORISON, Robert (1620–1683) English physician and naturalist. He further developed Cesalpino's system (*Plantarum historiae universalis*) and was the first to analyze in monograph a botanical family of morphologically related species (*Plantarum umbelliferarum*).

RAY, John (1627–1705) English naturalist. He applied Jung's analytic morphology to Cesalpino's classificatory system, thus greatly contributing to the development of taxonomy (*Historia plantarum*). Influenced by Locke towards the end of his career, he came to question the empirical veracity of systems based on the priority of the fructification or on any other criteria motivated by essentially rationalist principles (*De variis plantarum*).

LOCKE, John (1632–1704) English philosopher. He rejected pure reason in favor of experience as the source of meaningful ideas, denying the existence of commonly perceived species and doubting the possibility of any true and certain knowledge of the organic or inorganic world (*An essay concerning human understanding*).

NEWTON, Isaac (1642–1727) English mathematician, physician and philosopher. He endowed the world with a mechanistic system of causal laws together with a mathematical method for calculating their empirical effects. But he considered experience, rather than reason as such, to constitute the source of this apparently certain knowledge (*Philosophiae naturalis principia mathematica* and *Opticks*).

LEIBNIZ, Gottfried Wilhelm von (1646–1716) German mathematician and natural philosopher. Independently of Newton, he also discovered in the infinitesimal calculus a sure mathematical basis for the causal analysis of physical relationships. But he rejected the absolute spatiotemporal framework of the newtonian cosmos, arguing that space and time are immanently composed of actual bodies and their movements. Like Descartes, he advocated the primacy of reason over experience (*Discourse on metaphysics* and *Correspondance Leibniz-Clarke*).

TOURNEFORT, Joseph Pitton de (1656–1708) French physician and botanist. He inaugurated the rank of genus as a fixed level of reality immediately superior to that of the species. Shifting the natural system's focus from the more than 6,000 species then known to approximately 600 genera, he effectively reduced the information base by an order of magnitude to regain intuitively manageable proportions. He drew his criteria for a natural classification of plants from the flower and fruit, but conceded that any ordering above the genus-level was likely to be artificial (*Elémens de botanique*).

LINNAEUS, Caroli (1707–1778) Swedish physician, naturalist and explorer. He first codified the rational principles of natural history by naming species of plants and animals according to their genus, arranging genera according to their family and ordering families by their class. His work represented both a culmination of the natural system based on a rational and regular progression of genera, and the initiation of a natural method founded on the empirical understanding of the organization of families and the relations between them (*Systema naturae, Philosophia botanica* and *Genera plantarum*).

v. *A century of method*

BUFFON, Georges-Louis, comte de (1707–1788) French naturalist and philosopher. He instituted the principles of empirical method in natural history in opposition to the rationalist agenda of Linnaeus and other systematists. He rejected the notion of absolute rank, whether based on a system of privileged organs or on intuitions of overall affinity, and held that only groups of genealogically related organisms are natural. The idea of the species as a permanent historical filiation of individuals allowed for action by the environment in forcing separations in the lineage: a species might thus devolve, or "degenerate," from its original stock to form a genus or family of geographically isolated segments. With Newton, Buffon insisted that the only truly natural kinds are those functioning in relations of cause and effect. But he also agreed with Leibniz that the world as a whole – including space and time – exists solely in terms of the causal relationships that actually constitute it (*Histoire naturelle générale et particulière*).

KANT, Immanuel (1724–1804) German philosopher. Unlike Newton and Locke, but like Descartes and Leibniz, he supposed that a science of the universal and necessary derives from *a priori* knowledge of the objects of experience (*A critique of pure reason*). He underscored the importance of teleology as a complement to mechanism, which permits the introduction of systematic unity into the investigation of biological organization (*Critique of judgement*). Allowing that the teleological principle might not be truly constitutive of nature, he nevertheless thought it required by the mind for regulating any empirical research on the organic realm. Following Buffon, he maintained that the only real taxa are those whose members are historically affiliated.

ADANSON, Michel (1727–1806) French naturalist and explorer. He was the first to use the empirical method to complete a classification of the plant world by "family resemblances" (*Familles des plantes*): the diagnosis for each family consists of a set of distinctly perceived morphological characters; and each organism of the family manifests most, but not necessarily all, of the family's characters. The actual extensions of his families hardly differ from those of Linnaeus or Bernard de

Jussieu (1699–1777). But his rejection of *a priori* principles, and his refusal to privilege this or that part of the plant, first made explicit the idea that experience must be the ultimate authority for any classification.

LAMARCK, Jean Baptiste de Monet, chevalier de (1744–1829) French naturalist and philosopher. He initially followed Buffon in affirming that any complete classification must be artificial, although he thought his own system more practical by doing least harm to intuitions of morphological affinity (*Flore française*). Later, he developed Buffon's notion concerning the influence of the environment on the devolution of species into a theory of the temporal emergence of all species from a common origin. But the principal stages and ultimate causes of this evolutionary "ascent" are necessary and transcendent rather than contingent: from the simplest form of life towards the more perfect being of man, the nature and character of the emerging families, orders and classes is ordained prior to any actual transformation of species (*Philosophie zoologique*).

JUSSIEU, Antoine-Laurent de (1748–1836) French botanist. He adopted and developed the system of his uncle, Bernard de Jussieu, by attempting to arrange the families into higher orders and classes according to the characters of the plant embryo (cotyledon). These higher-ranked groups – particularly the monocots and dicots previously noted, but not analyzed, by the likes of Ray and Linnaeus – provided the overarching framework for the modern classification of angiosperms. His families became the standard referents for modern family taxonomies (*Genera plantarum*). By privileging family over genus, and institutionalizing the family as the primary rank of systematics, he effected the further reduction of the growing information base by yet another order of magnitude – from the more than 100,000 species and several thousand genera then estimated to 100 readily discernable families.

BLUMENBACH, Johann Frederich (1752–1840) German physiologist and anatomist. He was the first to demonstrate the value of comparative anatomy for the study of human biology. He interpreted each zoological taxon as a physiological plan that maintains its component parts in constant equilibrium, with higher-order groups representing more general plans of bodily organization. By assigning vital functional processes to essential morphological structures, he thus gave biological content to the organic "laws of affinity" that Jussieu supposed each higher-order taxon must exemplify (*Handbuch der Naturgeschichte*).

CUVIER, Georges (1769–1832) French naturalist and anatomist. He made the art of comparative anatomy and paleontology into a science, advancing the principle that all essential structural modifications of the organism are functionally driven and that certain organs have no overriding influence on its overall economy of life: given a few broken bones or other vestiges of some hitherto unknown species, one might thus hope to give proof of its existence and way of life (*Leçons d'anatomie comparée*). He repudiated the great chain of being and so ended natural history's preoccupation with phenomenal forms (*Le règne animal*). But he also dismissed Buffon and Lamarck's ideas on species transformation, thus apparently safeguarding an absolute and unequivocal framework for generating inferences about the underlying biological nature of the taxonomic order.

DARWIN, Charles (1809–1882) English naturalist and explorer. He formulated the theory of organic evolution: all forms of life are contingently produced by natural selection from a few primeval forms or one. This implies that no evolutionary taxon (including *Homo sapiens*) comprises an eternal or constant class of organisms; rather, all such taxa are temporally and spatially shifting segments of life's ever-transforming genealogical nexus. Neither does any taxonomic rank (including the species category) represent a steadfast piece of the structure of the world: ranks merely indicate relative degrees of natural (i.e. phyletic and perhaps other adaptational) affinities. No taxon or rank – no matter how intuitively compelling or historically revered – has absolute ontological value. What folkbiology knows to be true, and natural history did presume, evolutionary biology cannot abide (*On the origin of species by means of natural selection*).

NOTES

1 *Common sense: its scope and limits*

1. For Moore, common-sense beliefs are not, as Ayer (1976:35) implies, simply widespread popular beliefs that may turn out to be erroneous, like the belief that the earth is flat. Nor is their characteristic feature merely that of being ordinarily, frequently or generally true. They have nothing especially to do with popular opinions, which may be unreasonable, unreliable and epistemologically worthless. Rather common-sense beliefs are universal propositions that "we all commonly" hold and "so far as we know, men . . . have always believed" (Moore 1953:2–3), like belief in the existence of material objects and belief in the fact that people (normally) have thumbs. Belief in God, future life or the objects of science equally go beyond plain thinking about the "things which we all commonly assume to be true about the Universe, and which we are sure that we know to be true about it." On Moore's view, not only do we all hold the beliefs of common sense, but we believe in them. This philosophical axiom of plain thinking is itself a part of common sense, namely, the belief that we know the beliefs of common sense. Skeptics and metaphysicians who reject the validity of common sense must thus deny knowledge of common sense (see Somerville 1986 for an illuminating discussion).

2. Before Moore, the defense of common sense did not carefully disentangle sound judgment from what is universally attributable to the plain man. This is the case with Berkeley's (1734) attempt to vindicate "the genuine uncorrupted judgment of all mankind."

3. The most ardent and articulate proponents of "the dictates of common sense" were Thomas Reid and his student, Dugald Stewart. In contrast to Berkeley, the Scots held that common-sense perception and understanding is actively constituted by innate elements of the mind, and is not merely the passive recording and representation of experience (see Reid 1967,I:120–30, 195ff.). As Madden notes, this nativistic perspective corresponds "to a certain extent with Kant's transcendental aesthetic and categories of the understanding" (1986:255). Peirce parts company with Reid and Kant in disavowing that the native mental capacities responsible for our immediate and primary conception of the world also provide science its epistemic base. The eighteenth-century misconception of the scope and limits of common sense may be partially atoned for by the fact that natural philosophy and natural history were still very much geared to accounts of perceptually manifest phenomena.

4. Use of the term "natural history" to denote the study of wild living nature first emerged in the

early eighteenth century, while "taxonomy" was only coined a century later to describe the hierarchical arrangement of organic groups. But the argument is that underlying conceptions are likely as old and pervasive as *Homo sapiens*.

5. As in modern systematics, category names in folkbiology (generic-specieme, life-form) may ambiguously refer to the rank itself, and the level of reality it denotes, or to any or all of the taxa that fall within that rank (as when we say "'tree' is a life-form"). Unless the context specifically requires disambiguation, I make no effort to distinguish the two senses.

2 Folktaxonomy

1. The thirteenth-century pharmacopy, *Zhenge Bencao*, lists over 1,600 useful plants (Shenwei 1957; cf. Métailié 1981), but over 500 of these are simply added from previous sources with hardly a line of description.

2. In this vein, Needham (1986:2) concedes that "there is no parallel in the Chinese tradition" to the work of Theophrastus, Europe's first true botanist. He cites the *ERH YA*, an ancient Chinese proto-encyclopedia (akin to a *dictionnaire raisonné*) more or less contemporary with Theophrastus. But Needham goes on to suggest that it evinces a concern for detailed morphological analysis similar to that of Theophrastus: "otherwise the technical terms would not have existed" (126–127). One piece of evidence for this claim is that the author of the *ERH YA* acknowledges plant life-forms much as Theophrastus does. But plant life-forms are universally acknowledged by the common folk of any human group. As for the "technical vocabulary" of the *ERH YA*, it shows no more sophistication than the already fairly elaborate knowledge of plant morphology and anatomy that virtually any culture would seem to possess (cf. Friedberg 1972).

3. One discursive tool that does appear to be common to different civilizations is descriptive analogy: the comparison of plants to one another in terms of part of their morphological aspect or some anatomically based virtue. This is evident, for instance, in the sixteenth-century herbals of Europe (e.g. Fuchs 1542), China (e.g. Li Shizen 1590–1596) and Mesoamerica (e.g. the Badianus Codex of 1552, see Emmart 1940). But whereas European herbals of the era were already beginning to develop a regular schema of morphological description and grouping (see section 6.1 below), those of China (Haudricourt and Métailié 1985) and Mesoamerica (Emmart 1940) show little more than an idiosyncratic and irregular use of descriptive analogy.

4. According to Li (1974), the beginnings of classification were inextricably bound to the practice of cultivation. Studies of contemporary neolithic societies, though, indicate this is not so. Morton (1981:1) claims Theophrastus' fourfold division of the plant kingdom into tree, shrub, undershrub and herb "was essentially a tribal classification, reflecting the most primitive, originally functional, division of the tribe into two, later four, and then more numerous moieties." He cites the anthropological work of Durkheim and Mauss (1903/1963) in support. But their claim contains no empirical evidence whatsoever. Moreover, such life-form divisions occur in societies that are not, and likely never were, organized into moieties. Mayr (1982:134) contends that "the first creatures to be named are, of course, those of immediate concern to man." Again, ethnobiology provides scant evidence for this speculative proposition.

5. Tournefort (1694:7–8) well understood that ancient knowledge was more thorough than surviving texts and distorted derivatives might indicate:

> The ancients did not have the aid of engraving for leaving behind the figures of the plants they used. It was not their custom to make exact descriptions. It seems they counted more on tradition than their writings; and from this viewpoint they believed it sufficient to propose the plants most known to them in their time as models for facilitating knowledge of those that were not. Thus they contented themselves with such overall comparisons without describing either [the familiar model or novel plant] exactly. But things have since changed. That which was so familiar to them is a mystery today, and in the absence of knowledge as to these first models, we find only doubt and obscurity in their books.

Tournefort also recognized that ancient knowledge was grounded in local understanding and was not meant to cope with novelty on a world-wide scale:

All of these [ancient] names were founded only upon particular viewpoints: one could not foresee that one day they would have to serve for generic names, that is, names that would be appropriate for all the species of genera that one would establish in the course of time. Hence, we cannot complain that the ancients did not reduce this science to its veritable principles. It was only the experience of many centuries which could show the rules that one would have to follow in imposing names.

But he did not realize that such local understanding was substantially independent of cultural functions and not so spotty with respect to the local flora and fauna as herbals might suggest.

6. Throughout, notations of the sort (date 1/date 2) indicate that page numbers and bibliographical details will be given only for date 2. Date 1 refers to an earlier English or foreign-language edition, the title and publisher of which is mentioned in the later edition.

7. As Hays (1983:594), in his critique of Healey (1978–79), and Brown (1984b), in his response to Randall and Hunn (1984), rightly appreciate.

8. If one accepts the intuitive notion of overall similarity (the only coherent pre-theoretical notion of overall similarity around), then it is false that overall similarity necessarily supports a wide range of inductions. That is, there is no "logically natural" classification in the sense of Gilmour. Take our intuitive classification of artifacts. If Rosch et al. (1976) is correct, there is a basic level which is both general-purpose and indicative of overall similarity; but it would not make much sense to say that such groupings support inductions – that, e.g., we *induce* tables to be quadrupedal from the fact that we usually observe them to have four legs.

9. Accordingly, advocates of the inductivist position in numerical taxonomy have abandoned the "phenomenalism" of Locke and Gilmour in favor of operationally "neutral" attributes and standards of similarity. In other words, a "natural classification" will come about when taxonomy no longer "resorts to either intuition or to complex judgments based on overall appearance of organisms" (Sokal and Camin 1965:180); for, "it seems unlikely that any method of correcting for the distortion can be developed while human beings are directly involved at any stage in the classificatory procedure" (Cullen 1968:179). But even if intuitively-laden notions of observational attribute and observational similarity could be dispensed with, any non-phenomenal substitution would be theory-dependent for criteria of identity, hence, unavoidably "a priori."

10. For rather obvious reasons zoologists and ethnozoologists tend to highlight basic groupings in terms of behavioral and specific features, whereas botanists and ethnobotanists are apt to stress morphological and generic characters.

11. As Darwin (1872/1883:356) notes:

We often take, I think, an erroneous view of the probability of closely-allied species invading each other's territory when put into free communication. Undoubtedly, if one species has any advantage over another, it will in a very brief time wholly or in part supplant it; but if both are equally well fitted for their own places, both will probably hold their separate places for almost any length of time. Being familiar with the fact that many species, naturalised through man's agency, have spread with astounding rapidity over wide areas, we are apt to infer that most species would thus spread; but ... the species which become naturalised in new countries are not generally closely allied to the aboriginal inhabitants, but are very distinct forms, belonging in a large proportion of cases, as shown by Alph. de Candolle, to distinct genera. In the Galapagos Archipelago, many even of the birds, though so well adapted for flying from island to island, differ on different islands; thus there are three closely-allied species of mocking-thrush, each confined to its own island.

12. In cases of species recognition for asexual organisms, Mayr (1969:31) acknowledges that the only "objective" criteria consist "in the fact that each of the morphological entities, separated by a

gap from similar entities, seems to occupy an ecological niche of its own." Moreover, it seems the isolating mechanisms that prevent the interbreeding of sympatric populations are invariably associated with niche specialization. Because such specialization also characterizes uniparentally reproducing organisms, there seems to be *prima facie* justification for the claim that the fundamental "taxonomic species" (Blackwelder 1967) is a "morphological-geographical species" (Davis and Heywood 1963), or "ecological species" (MacArthur 1972) – at least in the first instance, before evolutionary considerations of space and time are weighed in. Perhaps because botanists are more readily confronted with asexual organisms they tend to prefer an "ecological" to a "reproductive" species. Yet, the two notions are inextricably bound to one another. Even uniparentally reproducing organisms come to occupy their position in the economy of nature partly in virtue of their own genealogical heritage and partly in virtue of the place afforded them by other species that *are* characterized by reproductive isolation.

13. Carey (1985a) finds that ten-year-olds seem least disposed to project properties to other animals if the only animals already known to possess those properties are bees (the only invertebrates tested on this particular task). Moreover, the children are apparently aware that bugs and worms lack certain properties that all the other animals possess, such as having bones and having a heart. Adults respond similarly. Such ordinary recognition that the vertebrates, taken as a whole, are inherently different from the invertebrates may have provided some intuitive grounding for the historical elaboration of a super-class (and ultimately a phylum) of vertebrates (chordates).

14. It is true that Tulp (1685) had compared the skeleton of man to that of the ape, and even earlier Belon (1555:40–41) had noted how much a point by point comparison of human and bird anatomy "makes apparent the great affinity between them." But zoology was still restricted as a science to the study of brute beasts: *zoologica physica est scientia brutorum quatenus corpora naturalia sunt* (Sperling 1669:1). Man does not even figure in Gesner's *Historiae Animalium* (1551–1588), although it was the first noteworthy global classification of the vertebrates since ancient times that made use of Aristotle's higher categories.

15. If, e.g. "wood" or "timber" is essential to the emergence of the life-form, "tree," how can Brown maintain his earlier claim that "size," rather than "woodiness," is criterial for "tree"? Moreover, should it be the case that the term for a life-form is polysemous with a variety of its substance's functions (including perhaps a sense of the substance which has no apparent function at all), as Bulmer implies, then "referential expansion" merely indicates that substance terms *per se* are lexically prior to terms for the sources of substances.

16. Elsewhere, Brown (1977:318) argues that "societal complexity and size of folk-botanical life-form lexicons are ... positively associated." The association is such that, e.g. the modern Huichol of Mexico, who have no (named) life-forms, should be found "lacking the complex political integration, social stratification and technological sophistication of peoples who speak languages having three or more life-form terms." But no further evidence indicates that Huichol culture shows less "societal complexity" than, say, the Bunaq of Timor or the Brou of Cambodia; and certainly Israeli society cannot be said to be less complex than, say, Rangi or Karam society.

17. Hunn argues that the opposition may be expressed by a disjunction of features: e.g. "bird" = "warm-blooded animal that flies and/or has feathers"; or "tree" = "plant which is large and/or woody." But disjunctions are not logically required for classification; rather, they appear to mark *identification* procedures. Thus, "bird" may be logically classed in accordance with the conjunctive diagnostic, "winged biped" though disjunctively instantiated at the perceptual level by "feathered and/or flies." Similarly, "tree" may be diagnosed in such cases as "perennial branching plant with branchless self-supporting stem," or something of the sort. The point is that disjunctive features, if allowed, would unduly complicate logico-semantic inference, but could be readily accommodated by the schema of perceptual identification. There is no evidence that life-forms can only be expressed as the disjunction of two concepts (and the notion that a life-form, or any unitary concept, is itself disjunctive, doesn't even seem to make sense). Indeed, it has yet to be shown that *any* ostensibly disjunctive category cannot be reduced to a conjunctive concept.

18. The array of basic-level taxa does not form a contrastive semantic field. It is only necessary that, for any given generic-specieme, all other generic-speciemes lack *some* (though not necessarily the same) feature of the generic-specieme in question. This implies a conjunction of features which necessarily attaches to any given generic-specieme, and to that generic-specieme only. But the conjunction of features attaching to any particular generic-specieme is not related by division to other generic-speciemes. The features that oppose any two generic-speciemes are not complementary characters on a single (set of) character-dimension(s) common to two or more generic-speciemes.

19. A similar circumstance seems to have presented itself to Candolle (Lamarck and Candolle 1815,IV:404) who, in the process of classifying the plants of France according to their natural families, felt obliged to make the cactus a monogeneric family. Nevertheless, he surmised: "one day cacti will probably be divided into many very distinct genera on the basis of habitus." To be sure, here Candolle is elaborating a *theoretical* point about how to handle such "untypical" cases within a general taxonomic framework; but I suspect his insight that there *are* such cases represents an insight of common sense. There is some evidence for, but no direct evidence against, supposing that the Aguaruna consider the cactus peculiar enough – not only in habitus but also in its role in the local economy of nature – to merit life-form status.

20. Of course, one could try to save the formalism in a completely *ad hoc* manner, viz., by isolating out a generic-specieme "level of contrast." But since such a manoeuver is not in the least warranted by the nature of the formalism itself it is hardly more than fudging. This simple mode of extensional definition for Linnaean taxa was first proposed by Woodger (1937) and later adopted by Gregg (1954), to whom Kay appeals for support (see also Hunn 1977:42). Gregg's conception of taxa as sets, like Woodger's, is rooted in the formalist tradition of logical positivism. Later, Gregg (1967) sought to resolve the "paradox" of monotypy: in such cases the superordinate taxon would be left "open," that is, assigned an indeterminate extension containing at least one more organism (as yet unknown) than the subordinate taxon. But there is no factual or conceptual justification for the "solution" other than the *ad hoc* one that such a move would thus allow the formalism to avoid the embarrassment of failing to meet minimal conditions of observational adequacy. Indeed, Gregg goes on to argue that his formalism is not, after all, meant to reflect either the actual processes whereby biological taxa are constructed or understood.

21. An extreme extrapolation from Bulmer's study is Wilson's (1982:552) argument: "it is an anthropological fact that labeling an ostrich a 'bird' will strike natives as more a distortion of meaning than any bomber dubbing." Under certain circumstances an airplane may presumably be labeled a "bird" (or the native equivalent) *even after it has been discovered to be an artifact*. But even if Bulmer had demonstrated the importance of social function in folkbiological ranking (and he hasn't) nothing indicates the Karam would ever think of cassowaries as anything but *animals* – never as artifacts.

22. Bulmer (1974:23) implies, however, that isolates do not have to be phenomenally aberrant; although the cassowary is, the pig and dog are not: "in at least some contexts, [unaffiliated generic-speciemes such as] pigs, dogs and cassowaries are taxa of equivalent [life-form] order to flying vertebrates or game mammals." But the hedge "at least in some contexts" renders the actual status of the pig and dog somewhat obscure. The pig, it seems, is a primary object of the hunt, and the dog is a primary instrument. It is possible that Karam appreciation of the local ecology is so influenced by hunting activity that the dog and pig actually do come to play very distinct roles in the local environment. If this were so, then, as in the case of intensely cultivated plants, cultural activity would have actually *created* a phenomenal environment in which morphological affinity would no longer suffice to determine taxonomic association. Yet, the implication that dogs and pigs are occasionally subsumed under larger groupings seems to indicate this is not so, and that in the neutral, context-independent, case pigs and dogs are basically no different than other speciemes in regard to taxonomic position.

23. Brown, however, questioned the significance of these results. He argued that, in fact, "many unlabeled groupings are in reality not covert at all, i.e., that their taxa are cross-indexed under some nonbiological labeled categories" (1974:327). Such groupings only appear to be covert

because they are actually nontaxonomic. For example, Friedberg (1970) had shown in a study of Bunaq (Timor) classification that certain plant groupings that apparently cut across life-forms such as "tree", "herb" and "vine", pertain more to cosmology than to strictly taxonomic concerns. Since they cut across the named taxonomic groupings, one would not expect them to be consistently named under any one such life-form. If they were, then the named grouping would be essentially incomplete (since the intermediate grouping was recognized to cut across life-forms). Conversely, if the complete intermediate-level grouping were named, then the fact that the grouping ignores life-form boundaries would contradict the (transitive) logic of taxonomic relations.

One such set of Bunaq groupings comprises plants related by their magical and medicinal qualities. These implicitly recognized *kaluk* groupings apparently traverse the major life-forms:

> Nevertheless the systematics of the composition of *kaluks* is not apparent and does not seem to be directly linked to plant classification. In effect, one finds [groupings of *kaluk*] plants to be variable in number and to belong to wholly different [named taxonomic] groupings. (Friedberg 1970:1115)

In other words, *kaluk* groupings may well reflect nontaxonomic (nonmorphological, non-ecological) affinities between plants. So, provided the informant is clear about what kind of information he or she is supposed to give the ethnobiologist, the informant may indeed name these ostensibly "covert" categories. If, for example, the informant shifts from morpho-ecological affinities between plants to more special criteria of usefulness or cosmology – criteria not necessarily restricted to living kinds – then the informant may be compelled to furnish names for groupings which are related by such criteria. Accordingly, for the Brou of Cambodia:

> In addition to these large [life-form] categories that can be qualified as descriptive (it is in effect the aspect of the plant, its habitus and its mode of growth that permits one to classify [a plant] among the trees, herbs or vines, or to designate it as a mushroom), there exist certain others which cover a lesser number of species, but which are important insofar as it is most often a question of useful plants. (Matras & Martin 1972:7)

In his rejoinder to Brown, Berlin (1974) allows for the possibility of groupings organized on the basis of nontaxonomic criteria, but which nonetheless includes taxonomic groupings. Yet such nontaxonomic groupings, whether named or not, do *not* constitute intermediate fragments of the sort elicited from the Tzeltal. Such fragments are not organized on the basis of nontaxonomic concerns of usefulness or cosmology; rather, they reflect affinities of habitus only: "the covert taxa discovered in Tzeltal are formed exclusively on the recognition of gross, visually recognized, morphological similarities and do not represent classes formed on functional considerations" (Berlin 1974:329; cf. 1976:395).

24. That plant life-forms are internally arrayed according to size is indicated by Brown's (1977) data; and the process whereby the label of the typical representative of a part or whole of the life-form space eventually attaches to other generic-speciemes in its "sphere of influence" is intimated by Bright and Bright (1965:253) for the botanical domain.

25. Work in "semantic memory" has produced some suggestive findings concerning the internal structure of zoological life-form spaces. In a study of the semantic field underlying the ordinary English term "animal" (as a polysemous form of "mammal"), Henley (1969) revealed that subordinate terms (generic-speciemes) were simultaneously arrayed along two dimensions, size and ferocity. Rumelhart and Abrahamson (1973) further showed these dimensions to be largely redundant with an appreciation of how close mammals are to humans. Indeed, Miller (1975:9) implies in regard to the Delaware (and this may well be so for other folk as well) that the wild/ tame contrast that anthropologists so often report to be a crucial distinction for folkzoology may actually represent a phenomenal discrimination within life-forms, rather than a strictly utilitarian discimination that overrides and obviates life-forms: "Tameness has more to do with frequent proximity to humans than with domestication. Wildness has to do with remoteness or unfamiliarity to humans."

This would seem to accord with findings involving modern American folk that the internal cognitive structure of a life-form space provides grounds for phenomenal inferences. Accordingly, Rumelhart and Abrahamson (1973) demonstrated one way in which such structure may serve as a basis for judgments of overall similarity. For instance, it is possible to predict that analogies (a) and (b) will have largely overlapping solutions:

(a) GORILLA : DEER :: BEAR : ?

(b) BEAVER : SHEEP :: DOG : ?

Thus, in both cases, subjects will prefer "cow" to "pig", "pig" to "tiger", "donkey" to "camel", "camel" to "elephant", etc. Moreover, when the subject is told that the target is an unfamiliar animal, he or she will be more inclined to impute attributes of cows to the target than attributes of pigs, etc. Rips and his associates were able to extend these analyses to the English term "bird" and to predict the solutions to analogies when two of the terms were from one life-form space and two of the terms from another (e.g. DUCK : EAGLE :: HORSE : ?, MOUSE : BEAR :: BLUEJAY : ?) (Rips *et al.* 1973). Rips (1975) also performed experiments indicating the effects of the internal structure of these life-form spaces on inductions (e.g. the closer an animal is judged to the center, the more likely that subjects will suppose other animals to possess its as yet unknown properties).

26. Although a prior intimation of family-level groupings may have encouraged the domestication of related plants, it is hardly likely that domestication would have preceded family-level perceptions, as Li (1974:719) claims. In fact, there is no evidence that family-level groupings commonly recognized by folk are initially restricted to cultivated plants (or domesticated animals, see Boster *et al.* 1986). Neither is it likely that the supposed symbolic virtues of such plants as the rose first animated the perception of a wider network of family resemblances, as Walters (1961) suggests. Thus, it appears that "there is no flower symbolism to speak of in [subsaharan West] Africa" (Goody 1986), yet mid-level groupings abound. Symbolic or domestic value, however, may have put a premium on *naming* and firmly bounding certain family-related groupings.

3 *The semantics of living kinds*

1. This is not to deny that Hanunóo eloquence on general botanical matters, like specialized Zafimaniry concern with wood, relies on complex modes of transmission governing social "wisdom." Neither is it to suggest that such complex notions as "wisdom" – which comprise the traditional bread and butter of anthropologists – can be studied exclusively with the technique typically employed by cognitive psychologists. It does suggest, however, that basic psychological analysis is pertinent to understanding the cognitive foundations of even these more traditional concerns of anthropology.

2. In another study, Gelman and Markman (1987) found that, 4-year-olds expected the "kind" of thing something is – as indicated by its being called "bird," "fish," "squirrel," etc. – to override misleading appearances in predicting the extension of its "inherent" properties (e.g. what it eats, how it breathes, whether it has eggs or seeds inside, the nature of its eyelids and feet; but *not*, e.g., how much it weighs, how fast it moves, whether it is visible at night, etc.). Thus, when two stimuli (representing a bat and a bird) were assigned mutually exclusive properties ("this bat gives its baby milk," "this bird gives its baby mashed up food"), the children tended to infer of a third stimulus (a bird resembling the bat) that it shared the property of its labeled category ("bird") regardless of the perceptual miscues. Moreover, "at least for animal categories," even 3-year-olds "sometimes drew as many or more inferences to [unnamed] pictures that were from the same [unmentioned] category as the target but differed in appearance than to pictures that were perceptually similar to the target but from a different category" (1987:1540).

3. Warrington and Shallice experimented with four patients affected by herpes simplex encephalitis. They performed very poorly on visual and verbal identification tasks for "animals" (e.g. deer, wasp, ostrich), "plants" (e.g. palm) and "food" (e.g. grapefruit, cabbage, egg), but as well as normal controls for "inanimate" objects, that is, artifacts:

We would suggest that identification of an inanimate object crucially depends on determination of its functional significance, but that this is irrelevant for identification of living things. We would therefore speculate that a semantic system based on functional specifications might have evolved for the identification of inanimate objects. (1984:849)

Now, foods are not living kinds *per se*. Indeed, appreciation of foods clearly depends on functional distinctions, as with artifacts (see sections 3.2 and 3.5 below). But like living kinds and unlike artifacts, foods also have nonfunctional, perceptible defining characteristics. One might thus expect that *both* category-specific impairments for living kinds and for artifacts would affect appreciation of foods. Indeed, Nielson (1946) mentions an impairment with "inanimate" objects, including foods, but not living things.

Sartori and Job (1988) report on a patient whose appreciation of taxonomic structure remains intact but who has difficulty processing basic kinds: "he adds fins to fishes, wings to birds and horns to certain animals, but he has great problems in distinguishing e.g. the horn of a rhinoceros from the antlers of a deer" or in discriminating real from unreal creatures (task 15). Also, "accuracy for vegetables was poor although somewhat better than for animals" (task 18). The "somewhat better," however, may owe to the fact that vegetables, unlike animal and plant kinds as such, also generally involve functional attributes whose appreciation is not impaired. Still, the impairment does seem restricted to only living things without regard to typicality; that is, the patient's performance on typical versus atypical items was "not significant . . . which is the opposite direction of what would be predicted" if living-kind categories were prototypically based (task 6).

4. Until recently, most empirical studies of concept learning regarded the formation of phenomenal concepts, that is, concepts with clearly perceptible correlates, in terms of rather simple conjunctions of sensory invariants. Typically, the experimenter presented subjects a small set of blocks, or other like objects, artificially constituted so as to exhibit some arbitrary array of distinctly different perceptual stimuli: e.g. focal colors, large versus small sizes, simple circular, triangular and rectangular shapes. The subject's task, then, was to learn the "true" concepts the experimenter had in mind by sorting objects into groups "defined" as boolean functions, that is, as severally necessary and jointly sufficient conjunctions of such clearly perceived attributes: e.g. ALL LARGE BLACK SQUARES versus ALL SMALL RED CIRCLES. Any attention the subject gave to such task-irrelevant properties as texture, weight, contiguity with other compresent objects, episodic or semantic associations to things and events in memory, etc., was interpreted as "childish," "simple," "primitive," "savage," "complexive," "concrete," "iconic," "graphic," "pre-logical," "unadult," or "unscientific" (cf. Inhelder & Piaget 1964; Vygotsky 1965; Bruner et al. 1966).

A more "natural" approach to the study of concept formation was then offered by Rosch and her associates. Initially, Rosch's studies were designed to confirm the findings of anthropologists Berlin and Kay (1969) who claim to have found a universal sequence of color terms. Rosch (then under the name Heider) suggested that cognitive-perceptual universals in the categorization of color are just those areas of the color space judged to be most exemplary of basic names found in many languages. Her results indicate that human color categories are structured around a universal set of "focal" colors (Heider 1971;1972). A related cross-cultural investigation of form indicated use of such standard "good forms" of Gestalt psychologists as circles and squares to process form categories much as there is use of focal colors in relation to color categories (Rosch 1973).

Seeking to extend these insights to artifacts and living kinds, Rosch conjectured that "it is possible that children initially define a category by means of its concrete clear cases rather than in terms of abstract criterial attributes," whereas adults would continue to use prototypes "as the basis for processing" (1973:142). She found that both children and adults had faster reaction times when they responded "true" to true statements of the form "An *x* is a *y*" when *x* was a central member (e.g. doll, robin) of *y* (toy, bird) than when *x* was a peripheral member (skates, chicken). Subjects also rated sentences such as, "The tree has about twenty birds perched on it," more acceptable when a typical subordinate (robin) was substituted for the superordinate subject (bird) of the sentence, than when a peripheral subordinate (chicken) was (1975).

5. As Ellen (1986:90) rightly notes, this generally accepted view of taxonomy tends to accompany the claim "that a large number of semantic fields are at all times similarly organized." Nevertheless, he acknowledges that "taxonomy is universally available in the classificatory repertoires of all people." Only, different cultures use the "taxonomic mode" differently and in different domains. Moreover, in no domain can people be said to "operate with an all-purpose classification which is recognized as being in any way separate from, or different to, classifications organized in some other way" (88). Given this view of taxonomy, then, there is little warrant for optimism about "our attempts to tease out convincing domain-specific universals" (94).

The conclusion, however, is spurious because the acknowledged premise is quite simply false. The basic problem does not lie with the fact that psychologists and anthropologists tend to overextend the validity of taxonomy by applying it to myriad sorts of data in Procrustean fashion. Rather, it is the notion of a universal "taxonomic mode" of thought as traditionally defined in the cognitive literature that is entirely specious.

6. Such distinctions are clearly secondary for children as well (Dougherty 1979). Thus, experiments by Waxman (1985) indicate that preschool American children do not seem to appreciate categorical distinctions at these subordinate levels. For example, children labelled TERRIERS and COLLIES identically (as "dogs") with no semantic contrast. Most children tended to contrast subordinate classes only when explicitly prodded, and they did so by using adjectival phrases honoring the head noun of the basic-level class (e.g. "big dogs", "small dogs").

7. An item may be called by a given artifactual term though it bears little (perceptual) resemblance to the prototype and exceeds the normal (perceptual) boundaries associated with the extension of that term; e.g. a varnished mahogany stump located in a living room may be a perfectly respectable table because it could well function as one. Conversely, a given object may bear a close perceptual resemblance to a prototype, yet fail to literally qualify as an instance of the artifactual term under which the prototype falls: e.g. featherweight ceremonial shields and souvenir boats may be intended only to *represent* defining functions, not to serve them. Thus, while artistic artifacts are still artifacts they may not fall under the terms whose items they are intended to represent. There are degrees, though: e.g. a "perfect" prototype of a given object can have functional as well as representational value.

8. Such artifactual terms as "turkey dinner" and "toy tree" are lexically characterized by perceptual as well as functional features. Note also that to count as being an artifact by reason of function served, an item need not itself by physically fabricated according to a plan. In some circumstances it need only be *displayed* consequent to a plan. This holds for natural objects served as food or displayed as art (cf. Wieand 1980).

9. Consider in this light the following supposition as to the ways people's movements are allegedly relevant to a discrimination of "natural objects." How do "pursue, look up, squint, blink" distinguish "bird", as Rosch *et al.* (1976) imply? Presumably, subject-initiated motor attributes are related to the space of human function and use and this space orients our apprehension of living kinds (Rosch 1978:29):

> What attributes will be perceived given the ability to perceive them is undoubtedly determined by the many factors having to do with the functional needs of the knower interacting with the physical and social environment .... Thus, our segmentation of a bird's body such that there is an attribute called "wings" may be influenced not only by perceptual factors such as gestalt laws of form that would lead us to consider wings as a separate part but also by the fact that at present we already have a cultural and linguistic category called "birds."

What little ethnolinguistic evidence there is, though, indicates that the discrimination of animal kinds, as well as their parts, occurs long before any folktaxon such as "bird" emerges (see Berlin 1972; Brown & Chase 1981). Discriminations of living-kind parts *are* linked to the movement of organisms and the relational context of sympatric species, that is, species coexisting at the same locality. But this has little, if anything, to do with the *observer's* movements oriented by the context of human function and use. Quite plausibly humans, like pigeons and frogs, have innate species-pattern recognition schema that can be affected by the observer's situational environment. But there isn't the slightest evidence as to the influence of social context.

10. To give an example: According to Markman and Hutchinson (1984), when children were asked to choose an object similar to a target ("See this [bluejay, birthday cake]? Find another one."), they tended to choose a "thematic" associate (nest, birthday present) rather than a "taxonomic" associate (duck, chocolate cake). In contrast, when the instructions included an unknown *word* for the target ("See this fep? Find another fep."), children preferred a taxonomic associate. The conclusion is that "linguistic input may serve more generally to shape the conceptual structure of the child in the direction of greater taxonomic organization" (25). Yet, there was no control over differences in results for artifactual and living-kind terms. But if, as Wierzbicka (1984) suggests, thematic relations are intrinsically more salient to artifactual than to living kinds, then Markman and Hutchinson's analysis is not fine-grained enough to support their conclusion as it stands.

11. In Putnam's (1975) opinion, however, if we were to find out that the catlike creatures we habitually denote by "cat" are actually cleverly assembled Martian robots, then we should likely agree that we never "really" referred to animals after all. Such counterintuitive situations are notoriously hard to judge. There are no facts of the matter to decide whether we would actually deny that cats are animals, consider them to be like genetically engineered living kinds, or construct a new ontological category that includes, say, LIVING THINGS and ARTIFACTS. An even more radical restructuring of our ontological conceptions is conceivable given the importance of ANIMAL for our general understanding of the world and the central position that cats occupy in our understanding of animals: what, for instance, would become of our scientific ontology upon discovery that such a central cosmological player as the moon is actually made of green cheese? In such a situation, could we ever even hope to understand what's going on? In this respect, Donnellan (1971:47–48) appears to acknowledge the analytic inviolability of the category ANIMAL because it is prior to synthetic judgment: "We decide that something is a cat by seeing what it looks like, how it behaves, etc. Having decided in this way that we are looking at a cat, and if we do not know that cats are mammals, we might investigate to see if this is a *mammal*. But we cannot, it seems, in the same way investigate to see if it is an *animal*. For what has the *gestalt* of a cat thereby has the *gestalt* of an animal."

12. Unfortunately, Hampton's study of non-transitivity in artifact categorization attempts to generalize the findings to living kinds. To this end, he cites Randall's (1976) study of non-transitivity in folkbotany; however, many of Randall's examples evince the same confusion as semantic memory studies that confound, e.g., fruits and berries with living kinds *per se*, and those of Randall's findings that do pertain to living kinds seem to confuse identification strategies (e.g. some willows may not "look like" trees) with classificatory judgments (but they still *are* trees).

13. According to Linnaeus (1751 sec. 259): "No man with any sense would ever say that . . . the Maltese Dog, the Spaniel, the Short-haired Dog, the Mastiff, the Turkish Dog, the Barbet are [not] the same kind." But the "classical" view advocated by Linnaeus must not be confused with linguistic essentialism. For Linnaeus, essences were not, as Smith and Medin suppose, "what we have called defining features," that is, nominal essences; rather, they were possibly unknown real essences.

14. True, one might say that, e.g., a car lost "its" windshield wipers or never had "its" wipers installed. But wipers do not form part of the *definition* of car. Rather, most makes of automobile have wipers by design and not as part of their nature. It is not *necessary* that the plan for making automobiles include windshield wipers or that the design for tables include four legs. Designs and plans are intended to make proper use *possible* – to make it likely that, as a matter of fact, an artifact can serve its prescribed function (cf. Miller 1978). Automobiles with blow-dry windshields and legless tables that hang from the ceiling may be perfectly respectable cars and tables for which it would not make much sense to say that they virtually have "their" wipers or legs or possess them by nature.

15. Propensities seem to come in two varieties. There are those that pertain to behavioral

dispositions (e.g. for a dog to bark), and those which pertain to developmental capacities (e.g. for a lion to be large). The former are related to Lockean dispositions of an entity to display a multiplicity of distinct (though interrelated) modes of comportment at the same or different times without, however, requiring dispositions to have particular molecular and geometrical loci. The latter are closely akin to Aristotelian potentials without, however, implying privation (i.e. that the developed being is ontologically distinct from the undeveloped being). Realization of a developmental capacity for, e.g., mature tigers to be large, causally requires that, e.g., tiger cubs are small. So, the smallness of a tiger cub is just as conditionally necessary to being a tiger (to tiger-ness) as the largeness of mature tigers, and both derive their necessity from the nature and propensities of a tiger that cause it to develop in the ways it should.

16. Speaking of the nature of a kind is ambiguous. Whether people consider the kind itself, together with *its* nature, as a distinct being rather than (as with Aristotle) simply the nature of the kind of (lawful tendency in the) organism that organism is, remains moot. Both alternatives are compatible with daily experience at the commonsense macroscopic level.

17. For certain artifacts (Ford cars versus Chryslers, Erte versus Parish prints) *origin* is salient and one might be tempted to argue that these artifacts have all or most of the properties held to be unique to living kinds. But this isn't so. Insofar as origin figures into notions of underlying nature, it implies transtemporal continuity of (some) constitutive matter, but not continuity in structure. Although the progeny materially "derives" its structure from its progenitors, the identity of progenitor and progeny are distinct. Persistence of one does not entail persistence of the other. As for Fords made at Ford plants, or groceries bought at grocery stores, necessity of origin concerns only place of origin and existence of a causal line from that place to the present whereabouts of the artifact, with no necessary transference of matter along the line. True, for ironwork wrought from iron there is a notion of "being-made-out-of" requiring material transference. But unlike the case for living kinds, it also requires persistence of the thing (iron) that does the becoming.

   Also, for ordinary living kinds (and not bacteria identifiable only with respect to their growth cultures, or the painted roses of Wonderland) willful intrusion of circumstance cannot affect a nature in isolation. But mere reappraisal of circumstance may well alter an artifact's functional "essence," even to the extent that well-intentioned, skilled craftsmen out to create one thing actually produce another. For instance, if a broken table is too flimsy to use, but folk in the current situation are in dire need of firewood or a bedboard and thus unlikely to seek repair, there may be a tendency to deny the object in question is still literally a "table" and to assert it is something else. In short, the role of circumstance is such that artifactual terms, unlike living-kind terms, cannot stand for physical sorts. They cannot have physical natures, because the same material item may, in one circumstance, be one kind of artifact and, in another (possibly concurrent) circumstance, be a different kind.

18. This seems to be a common folk procedure for labeling unfamiliar plants and animals (cf. Witkowski & Brown 1983). Usually, they are labeled with binomials of the sort "foreign x", where x is the base name of the indigenous generic-specieme that the foreign species most closely resembles. Once an unfamiliar species is labeled and identified by perceptual analogy with the facies of the closest generic-specieme, however, it may itself assume the status of a generic-specieme over time. That is, increased familiarity with the once unfamiliar plant or animal may eventually lead to the structuring of a distinct facies which clearly places it on a par with other generic-speciemes. When this happens, the "new" generic-specieme acquires a distinct uni-nomial label and drops the base name of the generic-specieme to which it was originally attached.

19. To put the matter in somewhat modified Fodorian terms: assuming there are a number of highly specialized sensory input systems, or perceptual "modules," and assuming a number of basic, domain-specific concept-forming faculties, we might conjecture that basic faculties have a privileged access to the mental representations that input systems compute (Fodor 1983).

20. It is not altogether clear what Putnam (or Kripke) include under "natural kind." Its domain seems to go beyond living kinds and chemical substances, to dispositions (fragile, malleable),

diseases, artifacts and even colors. But other causalists are more discretionary. Thus, Goosens (1977) excludes dispositions and colors, and Schwartz (1978), artifacts.

21. Of course if there is no prior phenomenal concern to stand in the way, the layman may extend his ontological commitment by proxy to nonphenomenal terms ("cancer virus", "electricity", etc.) and be willing to defer any scientifically motivated decisions about the meaning (or meaninglessness) and reference (or null extension) of such terms.

22. New Guinea Highlanders today readily distinguish the family-level grouping of marsupial mice from the family-level grouping of placental mice, but they also hold to the belief that the placental dog is of a kind with the indigenous marsupial *Satanellus* (cf. Dwyer 1976a). Should other species of the placental dog family Canidae be introduced into the local area, however, it is likely that these New Guinea folk would themselves effect a dissociation as they did with mice. In a related sense, although Americans tend to assimilate the Old World hedgehog (an insectivore) with the New World porcupine (a rodent), science would probably be able to convince most folk that these animals of different mammalian orders are no more of a kind than are any other pair of basically distinct mammals. In the case of the European versus American robin, though, the outcome is not so predictable. These two species of birds are both thrushes, but biologically no more of a kind than are the species of hawk or sparrow. Yet, unlike the European sparrow, the European robin is by and large absent from America. This absence might more readily dispose American folk to the scientific opinion that "robin" ambiguously denotes a disjoint extension rather than (as in the case of "sparrow") a single extension of biologically disparate sorts.

23. This is not to deny that culturally parochial considerations may affect the interactions between science and common sense. It is only to deny that an underlying nature would primarily be sought for just those functional properties assigned the members of a kind. An underlying nature can be held physically responsible for whatever ancillary functional features a kind may have; however, it cannot be presumed to underlie all and only such features as long as the kind *is* considered a natural kind (rather than an artifact-related kind of biological origin like game animal, berry, flower, etc.). Thus, the alliaceous plants (onions, scallions, garlic, chives) are ordinarily thought to form an (intermediate) kind not because of some functional nature, such as "being edible" or "being spicy", but because of their readily perceptible properties (including characteristic odor and taste, and also bulbous form, distinctive sheathing, basal leaves, umbellate inflorescence, etc.). So, e.g., if a poisonous form of onion were found, it would be no less literally an "onion" than a poisonous mushroom is a "mushroom"; although cloves may be functionally of a kind with garlic, phenomenally they are not, etc. Nevertheless, although function is not, in the first instance, responsible for people grouping the onion with its morphological allies, functional considerations may influence the layman's refusal to consider alliaceous plants of a kind with lilies, despite the fact that they belong to the same botanical order. But surely one reason why folk would more readily admit an association of, say, tulips to lilies than onions is because tulips just *are* morphologically closer to lilies than onions.

24. Actually, when these children were told that the property belonged to a central (dog) and peripheral (bee) animal, they were just as likely as adults to project the property to "all of the new animals and the flower" (158). Perhaps instead of the specialized or invented properties, like omenta or golgi, that Carey and others use in order to test young children for inductive generalizations from animals to flowers (and vice versa), it would be more telling to test inductions for properties that children can readily embed in their earliest causal knowledge of living kinds: for instance, properties relating to growing, having babies, etc. This could shed light on the obvious fact that kindergartners readily accept such causal stories as: frogs beget tadpoles that grow into frogs (although tadpoles hardly look like frogs), and trees beget saplings that grow into trees (although saplings may resemble grasses more than trees).

25. Nevertheless, since Keil's (1979) groundbreaking study of the semantic structure of "the ordinary language tree" of basic ontological categories, there has been considerable debate about the possible semantic relations between ontological categories (cf. Gerard and Mandler 1983, Carey 1985a). This debate ranges over some of the same philosophical ground that separates

Sommers (1959, 1963) and Pap (1960), with the former arguing for a strict hierarchy of relations between ontological basic categories and the latter for a less constraining set of relations that allows for only partially connected hierarchies between such categories. The evidence – tentative as it is – does seem to confirm the special status of ontological categories as conceptual cores for distinguishing and representing basically different sorts of things; but it does not appear to support a strict hierarchy of the kind that Keil and Sommers propose.

Keil argues that fundamental ontological categories are canonically arrayed. As a result, predicates in natural language cannot apply to ontological types on different branches of the tree without producing category errors: either (a) any two terms share exactly the same predicates and thus belong to the same ontological category, or (b) one term shares a proper subset of the other's predicates, in which case the former belongs to a category superordinate to the latter, or (c) the terms share no predicates at all and so belong to disjoint categories. But the psychological evidence for connections between the higher nodes – which roughly correspond to the classic Aristotelian categories of substance, quality, relation and so forth – is much too sketchy to warrant the conclusion that there is a rigid ontological pyramid topped by the category of things that can be "thought about." It could always be argued, for instance, that one "thinks about" substances differently than one "thinks about" relations.

More significantly for the present argument, the placement of nodes within the category THINGS WITH MASS is none too clear to me. For example, Keil argues that an unlabelled node in the tree includes the subordinate nodes ARTIFACT and LIVING THING, but not chemical and physical substances. He calls this class of objects "substantial": "meaning that each of their parts is not just a smaller instance of the whole." So, slicing a tiger or airplane in half wouldn't get you two of a kind, but cutting a rock in two would. Keil is surely wrong: cloth, paper and a host of other artifacts of the sort are just as "nonsubstantial" as rocks; and so are living kinds like thyme and coral. Moreover, chemical gases, liquids and solids seem to share properties of natural substance that exclude artifacts, while chemical solids and artifacts share internal properties of cohesiveness that excludes natural liquids and gases. Similarly, humans and animals (beasts) share properties of animacy that plants do not, while animals and plants share internal properties of taxonomic organization according to species that humans do not.

26. There is one way science could assign ontological status to phenomenal kinds, namely, as kinds restricted to "human ecology." These are kinds whose lawfulness consists in the relation of the human mind to "its" physical surroundings, that is, to those aspects of the environment that naturally manifest themselves to us. Most philosophers of science, though, would be unwilling to admit kinds of such a limited scope as genuine ontological posits. From the standpoint of omniscience, as in much philosophy of science, phenomenal kinds are at best faint echoes of reality – starting points on a road that must either end in nomological truth or a false lead. Those cognitive psychologists who accept the causal theory's claim that folk tacitly steer towards omniscience might do well to reflect on the cognitive payoff. What conceptual advantage would assimilation of everyday understanding to scientific knowledge actually afford our species? In our general dealings with the world, science has only a peripheral role to play, while common sense is constantly engaged. To presume humans aspire to omniscience (if not to all particulars, at least to nomic structures) *even when* day-to-day life most requires being down to earth seems a most extravagant faith.

27. Hilary Putnam has recently called to my attention his stated position (in his contribution to the Hahn and Schilpp volume on *The Philosophy of W. V. Quine*) that "ordinary language and scientific language are different but *interdependent*" (Putnam 1986:409). To this statement, I have no objection. But his analyses of ordinary empirical concepts focus almost exclusively on "natural-kind terms" whose correct "meanings" are supposedly provided by specific scientific theories: "we do not and should not treat scientists' criteria as governing a word which has different application-conditions from the 'ordinary' word . . . in the sense of having *unrelated* (or only weakly related) application-conditions" (1986:408). Quine, too, allows that "a theoretical kind need not be a modification of an intuitive kind" and that different systems of intuitive and theoretical kinds may be retained "for use in different contexts" (1969:128–129). Nevertheless, broader and broadening minds would seek to hone their ordinary language concepts according

to scientific standards; for, "science, after all, differs from common sense only in degree of methodological sophistication" (1969:129).

In fact, the application-conditions of ordinary language empirical terms seem to be variously and complexly related to the application-conditions of corresponding scientific terms. In other words, the differences between scientific and common-sense ascriptions of meaning to empirical terms are not merely those of degree (whether of "relatedness" or "methodological sophistication"), but of kind: science obeys cosmic dictates while common sense serves human interests. There is an intricate overlap of obvious significance to the history and philosophy of science; but one which is, after all, of only marginal significance for ordinary language and everyday thought.

4 Essence and environment

1. Actually, Roger Bacon (1930) thought Aristotle a great, if flawed, philosopher. The Stagirite's suggestions about optics led Roger Bacon (as well as Grosseteste) to attempt a mathematical analysis of nature; however, Bacon's natural history, unlike Aristotle's, admitted magical forces. Perhaps Simpson means to echo the opinion of Francis, rather than Roger, Bacon. Much of Francis Bacon's criticism of scholastic "Aristotelianism" proved useful and insightful; however, he seems to have had little real understanding of Aristotle himself. In particular, he appears to have been ignorant of the empirical foundations of Aristotle's biological works, and of the role of Aristotle's method in establishing modern physiology. It is not surprising, therefore, that he ignored the pioneering anatomical research of Harvey who followed the Peripatetic method, although Harvey was his medical attendant. Francis Bacon's unrestricted disdain for the "mischevious authority" of Aristotle and the "superstition" of final causes led Harvey to deride him as one who "writes philosophy like a Lord Chancellor"; for, on Harvey's own account, it was the notion of final cause which guided the research leading to the discovery of the circulation of the blood and to the realization that all living kinds reproduce in like manner (1627/1959; 1653/1981).

As for his own *Sylva Sylvarum, or naturall historie*, Francis Bacon writes:

> The knowledge of man (hitherto) hath been determined by the View, or Sight; So that whatsoever is Invisible, either in respect of finesse of the body it selfe; Or the smallnesse of Parts; Or the Subtiltie of the Motion, is little inquired. And yet these be the Things that Governe Nature principally; And without which, you cannot make any true Analysis and Indication of the Proceedings of nature. The Spirits or Pneumatics, that are in all Tangible Bodies, are scarce knowne .... Spirits are nothing else but a Naturall Body, rarified to a Proportion, and included in the Tangible Parts of Bodies, as in an Integument .... And from them, and their Motions, principally proceed Arefaction, Colliquation, Concoction, Maturation, Putrefaction, Vivication, and most of the Effects of Nature.
>
> (1639:26)

Here Bacon plays down the role of sight that Aristotle had so stressed, as elsewhere he denigrates Aristotle's "notional" theories of form and matter that were meant to account for perceived regularities. Clearly, however, Bacon's natural history is just as "notional," with its animate "spirits" being akin to "explosives" in their power to move bodies: overactive spirits result in alcoholism; putrefaction sets in when spirits try to leave the body; and men see better with one eye closed because the visual spirits are thus able to unite. When Bacon strays from sight he often errs. In fact, his science is much weaker than his philosophy; but his philosophy is not nearly so antagonistic to Aristotle's as it is made out to be.

2. Daudin (1926a5–6) intimates a somewhat better understanding of the matter:

> Natural science is taken up with common thoughts about generic and specific notions. These are criticized and reformed, to be completed and specified in enormous proportions, but not created out of nothing. Natural science gives itself the role of determining, between the concrete objects of these notions, an ensemble of relations that represents

once and for all, definitively, their "affinities." And despite the immense difficulty of such a task, despite the impossibility of supporting each of these operations by rigorous proofs, in effect it succeeds – from the mid-eighteenth to the first third of the nineteenth centuries – in more or less completely establishing such a system of relations, at least in its fundamental lines.

Two caveats are in order, however. First, it is not a matter of gradually refining vague intuitions of the general and the particular which, according to Daudin, correspond to the original "generic and specific notions" of "common thought" (*la pensée commune*). Initially, for Aristotle, it is a question of analyzing the already well-formed ranks of lay taxonomy so as to systematically unify their constituent taxa. Second, only later, with Europe's Age of Discovery, does the problem of "enormous proportions" arise with the consequent attempt to reform the traditional taxonomic ranks so as to extend their scope beyond the limits of the local flora and fauna to the living world at large.

3. According to Lovejoy (1909), the sense current in Greek philosophy and literature before Aristotle closely parallels "the commonest and most familiar colloquial sense of our word 'nature'," namely, "to be of such and such a sort by birth" in virtue of "qualitative character," "make-up," "essential nature." Concerning the Hippocratic Corpus, Bourgey (1953:34) notes that "*physis* rarely designates Nature in general, rather it indicates the particular constitution of a being." For example, in what is likely a late fifth-century BC treatise, *On Regime I*, he notes that *physis* designates a "state of physical composition" or "state of mixture." To know the nature of man, therefore, is to know "from what things he is originally composed" as embodied in the soul (*psyche*) and seed (*sperma*). Therein lie principles (*archai*) and causes (*aitia*) of development.

4. All titles to Aristotle's works are abbreviated in conformity with the Liddell-Scott-Jones lexicon.

5. Although Aristotle never embraces a doctrine of "survival of the fittest," his biology may be compatible with some versions of it (cf. Balme 1980), though *not* with Empedocles's. For what survive in Empedocles's scheme are not so much whole organisms which gradually succeed in acquiring adaptive parts, but disconnected parts which manage to unite by chance into functioning complexes (*On Nature* frs. 57–61). In the prefatory note to the sixth edition of *The Origin of Species*, however, Darwin confounds Aristotle's critical rendition of Empedocles's views with Aristotle's own beliefs. Aristotle emphatically denies what Darwin refers to as "the principle of natural selection shadowed forth," namely, that adaptations occur piecemeal, rather than holistically, and accidentally, rather than to an end.

6. Aristotle uses the terms *schema*, *idea* and *morphe* as non-technical synonyms of *eidos*; in *PA* 640b24–28, for example, he uses all four terms to denote the shape of a bed. According to Bourgey (1953:34n.), it is this "popular" conception of *eidos* that is present in the Hippocratic Corpus (cf. Taylor 1911).

7. Aristotle's appreciation of basic-level intuitions is in some ways actually more nuanced than that of Rosch and her associates; for Aristotle makes a categorical distinction between apprehension of basic-level *artefacta* and basic-level "natural kinds," while Rosch and company do not. It is not merely that "there is much greater finality and beauty in the productions of nature than in those of art" (*PA* 639b21). Finality is altogether different for artifacts and living kinds: in the former, finality is directed by the transcendent purpose of the artisan (*Metaph.* 1041a25–30); in the latter, finality is merely directive and immanent in the material nature of the organism. In the former, the efficient agent of genesis is the *skill* of the artisan; in the latter, it is the motion imparted to female residue by male semen. More significantly for the modern psychologist and epistemologist is Aristotle's denial of "underlying natures" to artifacts (*Ph.* II,1). Although the artisan employs the potentialities of his materials, those materials have no inherently special potentiality that leads to the artifact (cf. Kosman 1987). Artifacts are the way they are by virtue of the functions they serve (*Metaph.* 1032b1, 1043a16–18; *de An.* I.1; *Ph.* II,9)); but living kinds are as they are "by nature" (*physei*), that is, in virtue of an essential and underlying physical constitution (*physis*) that is shaped and developed by an intrinsic "soul" (*PA* 640b24 ff.).

8. Locke (1689/1848 II,xxvii,1–6) argues, *per impossibile*, that these general criteria of identity arise from the particular fragmentary experiences of everyday life. Frege more plausibly views these criteria as prior to, and necessary for, knowledge of objects (cf. Dummett 1973: 75–76). In line with Kant, Pap (1960) considers our ordinary ontological categories to be "synthetic *a priori* insights" (e.g. ANIMAL and HUMAN are subordinate to LIVING KIND). Such categories correspond to what Carnap would call "phenomenological base-principles."

9. There are also essential accidents that are not proper to any species, but are appropriate to the genus: e.g. having a male or female sex is appropriate to being an animal, but not to being a horse or cow (*Metaph.* 1058b22 ff.). A somewhat different case is that of "biped" which appears to be an essential trait of man when he is considered under the genus of footed vivipares (i.e. mammals), but is actually an essential accident because it is not a trait that is unique to man among the animals (birds have it) (*APo.* 75a18; *PA* 643a3).

10. Demonstration must reveal essential accidents (*APo.* 75a39). Knowledge of these form an indispensable part of the natural philosopher's understanding of those consequences of the soul that make an animal what it is (*PA* 641a21).

11. There are, in addition to the essential diagnostics (differentiae) and the proper essential accidents, nonessential accidents such as the color and health of organisms of a kind. But even these accidents are necessitated in virtue of biological ends. That an eye has this or that color owes to the fact that this particular part of the body is (essentially) required to serve some biological function, and there (incidentally) just happens to be this or that clump of matter available as a vessel for efficiently fulfilling that function. The matter that forms the eye of an animal must have *some* color (because all matter is colored); but the color that eye does have is not essential for sight. An explanation of these accidents does not form part of the subject matter of biological science because science concerns only what is best always or for the most part.

12. In *Metaphysics* Z.7 Aristotle states: "Everything that comes to be is (a) "*by something* and (b) *from something*, and it comes to be (c) *something.*" The first item is the efficient agent, the second is matter and the third is the form of the thing that comes to be. In *Historia Animalium* I.6, Aristotle sketches the relevance of this passage to the study of animals. First, "it is necessary to take separately each kind of animal and examine its nature (*physis*) separately." This, as Aristotle makes clear in *de Partibus Animalium* I.4, is the task of common sense. Then, one must go into greater detail, in order to grasp the attributes that distinguish and unite kinds, "according to those differences that pertain to form, to excess to analogy, to opposition." This is the study of material cause; for it is apparent from *de Generatione Animalium* I.1 that "the matter for animals is their parts." It is the subject of *Historia Animalium*. Afterwards, one must attempt to discover the *aitia* of these differences and similarities, that is, those essential parts that define the kind, and point to its essential nature (*PA* 645b ff.). This is the study of formal cause and is the object of *de Partibus Animalium*. So, "one must first take the *phainomena* of each *genos* of animal, and only then go on to speak of their *aitia*, then their *genesis*" (*PA* 640a14). Thus, study of the actual, efficient process of genesis for different kinds of animals completes our essential knowledge of animal nature. This is the topic of *de Generatione Animalium*. Such, then, is "the natural order of investigation once knowledge of each [kind of] animal is acquired. By this method the object and the premises of demonstration will most clearly appear" (*HA* 491a7 ff.).

13. According to A. C. Lloyd (1962:87): "in order to ... be able to distinguish an appropriate differentia from a unique characteristic which belongs to the genus ... it is necessary to observe more than the static facts, namely the [causal] connection between them." Lloyd argues that the causal process itself is also to be observed in nature; however, this "observation" is by no means intuitively obvious. The description of such a process is invariably conjectural and the mechanism thus described partially inscrutable to visible verification.

14. But given the instantiation requirement it could not turn out that no tigers actually exist, as Plato might have allowed.

15. Cf. Vlastos (1969:301): "'participation' here designates the one-way relation of ontological dependence between temporal things and eternal Forms." That is, no exemplar, *x*, could actually exist in space and time and be characterized by *P* unless *P*-ness existed; however, the existence of *P*-ness does not guarantee that it will actually be instantiated.

16. The generative factors, or *aitia*, responsible for coming-into-being have been historically referred to as the four "causes." Recent commentators, such as Vlastos (1969) and Moravcsik (1975), have inclined to view the term "cause" as a misnomer and to consider the doctrine of *aitia* into Plato and Aristotle as a program for understanding in general. On these accounts an *aitia* is a "reason" for something, be it logical consequence in a mathematical proof, the justification of one's actions or an explanation of a fact of nature. Nonetheless, there is ample evidence in Aristotle's physical and biological works that *aitia* applied to natural kinds is a doctrine of physical consequence with respect to underlying nature. As such it seeks to explicate the common-sense notion of natural causality and to systematically extend that notion to unfamiliar objects and events for which no self-evident common-sense intuitions exist.

17. By "irreducible" Gotthelf means that Aristotle believed the male influence in the process of genesis could not be reduced to the sum of contingent material processes. Given the poor state of (bio)chemistry at the time, this teleological effect was a plausible *empirical* supposition pending evidence to the contrary: "If some sum of actualizations of element potentials *were* by itself sufficient for the production of some outcome, that outcome would *not* be subject to teleological explanation for Aristotle" (1987:231).

18. Indeed, because each individual is invariably distinct from every other in all that it happens to be at any moment and in any circumstance, there can be no science of individuals as such. The individual is ineffably unique and cannot be defined in terms of regularities which must be common (cf. *Metaph.* Z 15). But this does not mean that a species definition is anything but a definition of each and every member of the species taken individually rather than all at once. The individual can only be known *sub specie universalitatis*, that is, as an instantiation of some principles of nature that are more or less general in scope: "it is a *preliminary condition* of actual knowledge regarding the single thing that the truth of a universally quantified proposition be recognized" (Leszl 1972:307). In other words, the individual can only be known to satisfy a certain general description; it cannot be known *qua* individual in and of itself. But knowledge of universal principles constitutes mere potential knowledge until actually known to be instantiated in this or that individual, that is, until one knows something *about* particulars. Such universal knowledge coincides with knowledge of the essence of the individual that instantiates the universal; it is, e.g., the structure that the individual man shares with other individuals of the species that is constitutive of his being human (cf. *Metaph.* 1031b20–1).

19. Despite the fact that the proper consequences of a kind may be unique to that kind, they are, in a sense, incidental to nature's overall plan. Thus, the proper consequence that the angles of a triangle sum to two right angles is only an "essential accident" of being a triangle. This is because it does not help to define (the differences) between the essential natures of all *other* geometrical figures. By contrast the essential attribute "three-sided plane figure" would distinguish triangle from quadrangle, etc. (*Metaph.* 1025a30); however, as A. C. Lloyd (1962) notes, in modern ordinary class algebra "there is no criterion for distinguishing an essential or definitory differentia of a species from any unique characteristic."

Similarly, to characterize a Man as "capable of learning grammar" or "capable of learning science" fails to capture the reality of Man as a *species* (*Top.* I,5; VI,3). Because a species is a substantial unity of genus and differentia, the differentia must be as appropriate to the genus as to the species itself. If the attribute is merely unique and necessary to the species, though, there is no assurance that it is also pertinent to the genus; that is, each of the other species of the genus must have as an essential difference a complementary, or co-ordinate, feature taken from a feature-dimension which spans the whole genus.

20. Although in *PA* 639b21, Aristotle uses the coming-into-being of artifacts to illustrate hypothetical necessity, the hypothetical necessity which attaches to living kinds is fundamentally different. In the case of living kinds, the hypothesis that the end will in fact come about reflects the best possible outcome, all things being equal. However, the hypothesis that a statue or a house will come into being is a mere possibility that depends on the whims of human will, desire and convention.

21. In the case of eternal kinds, the best will always come about inasmuch as eternals are intrinsicaly divine and beautiful, whereas natural kinds only *tend* towards the divine and beautiful (*Ph.* 199b34).

5 Materials of logical division

1. An appreciation of the difference between rank and level of inclusion and contrast may help to explain the seemingly contradictory status of man in Aristotle. In *Top.* 1013a14 and *Metaph.* 1016a27 man is referred to as an *atomon eidos* and is listed along with such *eide* of viviparous quadrupeds as the horse and the dog in *HA* 490b18. Yet, in *HA* 505b25 man is listed among the *megista gene*. The difficulty is resolved if one considers man to be a monospecific (or, equivalently, a monogeneric) life-form. Considered as a life-form, Man is in direct contrast to the other *megista gene*. Considered as a basic kind (the only representative of the life-form Man) man is in *indirect* contrast with the basic kinds of other life-forms. In *Metaph.* I, Aristotle allows that two species (e.g. justice and injustice) are in (indirect) contrast even if they belong to different genera (vice and virtue) so long as those genera are themselves in (direct) contrast. Accordingly, man and horse are species in indirect contrast, because their respective genera, Man and Viviparous Quadruped, are in direct contrast.
2. Bourgey (1953:39 n.4) notes a single instance of the logical use of *genos* and *eidos* in the Hippocratic Corpus. The passage from *On Nutrition I*, which may be contemporary with Aristotle, is roughly as follows: "there exists an *eidos* of food, as there exist several; there exists a food which corresponds to a *genos*, [and] one distinguishes the [kinds of] *eidos* of food by their liquid and solid character."
3. Leblond (1945:9,59n.3) argues that the use of *genos* and *eidos* in Aristotle's Logic derives from his Biology. Thus the fact that living organisms naturally tend to form groups embedded within groups presumably leads to the idea of a logical "subalternation" of concepts by genus and species. To the contrary, Balme (1962:98) holds that the logical distinction was introduced into the biological works, though never strictly followed. Both arguments are misleading, though Balme's less so. The technical distinction in Aristotle's Logic has a different logical character than biological ranking. Logically, a genus is a substantial unity. Biologically, a genus is a fixed level of reality containing any number of substantial unities. The technical genus and the biological genus thus belong to different logical types. Aristotle also applied the technical distinction in his Biology; however, he apparently did not intend it to apply to kinds, or taxa, as such, but to organ-systems and function-parts.
4. According to Louis (1975:154–55): "Aristotle ... gave to *eidos* the precise sense of species." As for *genos*: "the most frequent sense is ... more or less that which we give to the word 'genus' in the terminology proper to biology," although "the notion ... can apply to all groups other than species." Yet, in Louis' own translation of the passage in *GA* (746a30–746b10) where Aristotle discusses the relation between reproduction and basic kinds, the word "species" (*espèce*) translates *eidos, genos* and even *phylon*. Moreover, Aristotle actually applies the term *eidos* to higher-order groupings (e.g. the *eide anonyma*), and not only when they are considered in the formal mode. The term *atomon eidos*, however, *is* used to refer to a basic kind whenever it refers to something other than an individual. As for *genos*, this term could in no way correspond to the modern biological notion of "genus," simply because the modern concept of a privileged rank immediately superordinate to the species did not acquire a sense before the latter part of the seventeenth century.
5. To some extent, however, the choice may be conventional and arbitrary. Thus, although Pliny (*Hist. Mundi* X,i,1) like Aristotle, notes the resemblance of the ostrich to the quadrupeds, he nevertheless places it with the birds, whereas Aristotle (*PA* 697b13–26) gives it an independent status (see section 2.4 above).
6. Joly (1960:207) cites Palm's (1933:5–40) study of the relevant passages in *On Regime II* as evidence of the existence of a "zoological system" before Aristotle's "successive and divergent" effort at classification (Joly 1968:253). But there is no evidence of any *principled* system of classification in that work. True, many of the basic kinds and life-forms found in Aristotle are

also found in the Hippocratic treatise. There are also groupings of intermediate generality, such as the leguminous plants which are assembled and distinguished on the basis of their visible aspect. Yet, nothing in the treatise goes much beyond what was probably commonsensically known to the average layman of the time. There is no attempt at reduction of habitual structure to essential parts, or even a systematic attempt at comparing and contrasting morphologies. When principles are introduced to explain the distinctions between animals, the principles are usually nonfunctional and the distinctions often irrelevant to the interrelations among animals; for example, game animals are essentially distinguished from domestic animals by their freer movements, which enable them to throw off moisture and thus be dryer (secs. 47, 49). For Aristotle, though, the distinction between domestic and game animals is not pertinent to classification (*PA* 643b4–5, *HA* 488a29).

Joly notes other ostensible similarities between Aristotle's biological work and *On Regime*. Both are said to rely heavily on *a priori* reasoning and ordinary, run of the mill experience. But the approach to knowledge in *On Regime* seems to run directly counter to Aristotle (*GA* 760b31–3; cf. *Metaph.* 980a21–27); for the Hippocratic text reads: "men confide in their eyes rather than in reason, although the eyes are bad judges, *even in their own domain*; for my part, it is through reliance on reason that I expose this doctrine" (I,4).

7. Nonetheless, Aristotle was still constrained by an all too human phenomenal bias:

> [Aristotle] has been accused, for instance, of ignoring the gnats and mosquitoes, which must have been as prominent [in Greece] as they are now. But he gives their external structures, reproduction from larvae, feeding and habitat – and there is not much more that he could know, having no optical apparatus.   (Balme 1970:282)

8. In the *Gorgias* Plato asks whether or not man is an animal and answers affirmatively. In the *Politicus* he takes the young Socrates to task for dividing the animals into human and nonhuman, and in the *Republic* (596a3) he refers to "men and the other animals." There is also evidence in the Hippocratic tradition which places man among the animals (cf. *On Regime I*, para. 25), as there is in pre-Socratic philosophy: for example, in the attempt of Xenophanes (fr. 15) to reduce anthropomorphism to absurdity.

9. In a later edition of *Systema naturae* (1767,I:17), Linnaeus argues that: "Nature is never more complete than in its smallest beings"; (cf. Linnaeus [Gedner] 1752 sec. 14): "in each insect we shall observe a particular ability that we will not find with other bodies." But Linnaeus's primary division of the invertebrates into *Insecta* and *Vermes* shows a closer attachment to the popular viewpoint and less discrimination than Aristotle's fourfold distinction of bloodless animals into cephalopods, crustacea, testacea and insects. This is not to deny that *within* the two popular classes of invertebrates Linnaeus continually improved upon his subgroupings: incorporating the findings of "amateurs" (i.e., anatomists and morphologists), modifying diagnostics, allowing exceptions in order not to violate intuitions of overall affinity (cf. Winsor 1976). On the whole, these subgroupings show superior discrimination.

10. Buffon (1753,IV) attacks Réaumur and all those who would dare raise the study of insects to the level of man: God is not, and reason thus should not, be preoccupied with ordering a "mob (*foule*) of little creatures" nor with the manner in which their tiny parts are articulated and designed. Buffon and Daubenton also fail to understand Aristotle's position on the invertebrates as a classificatory construct (*Hist. nat.* 1753,IV:149). They thought that Aristotle's rejection of dichotomy implied that the division into blooded and bloodless groups was to be taken as unreal. This is clear from their critique of Ray's (1693) alleged "misuse" of the distinction in his effort to establish a classification of animals. But Aristotle only argues that blood-less, as non-matter, cannot be a differentia of animal. "Bloodless," then, really refers to animals whose matter is analogous to blood (*HA* 532b7; *PA* 655a28 f., 678a31–34; *GA* 726b36; cf. Pliny, *Hist. Mundi* XI,ii). As Lamarck (1809) stresses, Aristotle's bloodless group corresponds to the invertebrates. The fact that Aristotle chose to emphasize blood, rather than bone, owes to the blood's putative connection with life-giving "heat."

11. Granger (1976:241; cf. Mayr 1982:149–54) duly notes Aristotle's disallowance of dichotomy as

an empty formalism (when negative differences are used) or as a Procrustean and arbitrary procedure; but no consideration is given to Aristotle's allowance for *real* division.

12. This appears to be so both horizontally:

> A genus is always divided by differences that are coordinated in terms of a division; for instance, animal is divided by the pedestrian, the winged, the aquatic, and the biped. These must be contrasting terms.　　　　　　　　　　　　　　　　　　　(*Top.* VI,6)

and vertically:

> The division can thus only be this: "of that which possesses feet," there is "that which has a split hoof," and "that which does not," because these are differences of feet: the character "split hoof" is a manner of being a foot. And this process continues until one arrives at undifferentiated species; at that moment one will obtain as many species of "footedness" as last differences, and the [different kinds of] species of animals possessing feet will be equal in number to the difference [of footedness]. If this is so, the last difference will be the substance of a thing and its definition.　　　　　　　(*Met.* 1038a)

Note, however, that the horizontal and vertical examples given here are incompatible with one another: "pedestrian" and "biped" are horizontally contrasting terms, although "biped" is also vertically "a manner of having feet." Moreover, the vertical difference "that which does not have a split hoof" is not a valid difference. Real division can only apply to positive contrasting terms, or *eide*, that share the matter common to their *genos* (*Metaph.* 1055b3ff.); however, a negative term, which is simply non-possibility, shares neither matter nor being with anything at all.

13. According to Balme (1962:91): "If *eide anonyma* means [species] having no [name], it cannot refer to [lion, cerf, etc.]. It must refer to groups that contain these types and are themselves contained within [the viviparous quadrupeds]. What, for example, is the name of the group that contains the lion? We have one ('Cat'), but Aristotle has not. All that he has at this level are *ta lophoura* ['long-haired tails,' i.e. the equids], and the rest are nameless. *Eide anonyma* therefore denotes . . . groups intermediate between the main [*megista gene*] and the [basic] types visible in nature." For the most part, these "intermediate general groupings" to which Balme refers correspond to biological families or orders that are only occasionally named (e.g. *ta selachi*, the cartilaginous fish including rays and sharks): "[Aristotle] designates such groups – comparable to modern families or orders – whenever they naturally impose themselves on him" (Daudin 1926a:17–18; cf. Bourgey 1955:135–37) (see section 2.5 above).

14. Empedocles (*On Nature* fr. 82) also discusses morphological analogies, though not in such a way as to reveal their systematic import.

15. The presence of analogies throughout the animal kingdom, together with the fact that (lack of) perfection in regard to one function does not necessitate (lack of) perfection in regard to another, effectively rules out a monotone *scala naturae*. According to Lloyd (1961), however, such a scale is precisely what Aristotle aims at in his mature work, *de Generatione Animalium*. The sequence proposed in *GA* 733a is: (a) those animals that are hot and wet and bring forth their young in a perfect (man), or near perfect state (the other vivipara); (b) those that are hot and dry and have a perfect egg (scaly reptiles and birds); (c) those that are cold and wet and externally viviparous, but internally oviparous (vipers and cartilaginous fish); (d) those that are cold and dry and produce an imperfect egg (scaly fish, crustacea, cephalopods); (e) those that are simply cold and produce not an egg, but "larva" (insects); (f) and those that are almost lifeless and reproduce spontaneously (testaceans). This sequence is fundamentally no different from that based on the order of complexity of reproductive parts in *HA* 539a10: (a) viviparous and oviparous land animals, (b) birds, (c) (ovo)viviparous and oviparous fish, (d) crustaceans, cephalopods and insects, (e) testaceans. In fact, Balme (1987a) shows convincing internal evidence for *Historia Animalium* being composed *after* the other biological treatises, including *de Generatione Animalium*.

16. Even analogical differences appear to be ultimately quantitative in the sense of proportional. Thus, Aristotle seems to say that the differences between terrestrial and aquatic animals is reflected in a quantitative change in their parts that results from the accommodation of those parts to material nutriment in the course of their genesis and development (*HA* 590a2; cf. *PA* 653b3 and 655a33 where bone and cartilage are spoken of as being analogous and differing by the more and less).

17. Consider the *fundamentum* "organs of locomotion." One of the divisions of this *fundamentum* is the organ that corresponds to "foot" in some animals, "wing" in others, "fin" in still others (*IA* 713a9). Among certain of the invertebrates these organs are "called tentacles" (*HA* 524b). As for "organs of sensation," all animals have similar or analogous parts for smell, hearing, sight and taste, except for those testaceans in which taste is greatly reduced, and hearing and sight "neither sure nor evident" (*HA* IV,8). Concerning the "organs of reproduction," all vertebrate females have a uterus, although the arrangement of uterine parts differs for each major grouping (*GA* 718a35–b5). The invertebrates, too, have uterine parts (*GA* 720b2). This is clearly evident in all of the cephalopods (*GA* 720b20); while in female insects there is an analogous part "which corresponds to the uterus" (*GA* 721a21). For other insects "too small to observe" (*GA* 721a25), and for the testaceans, about which "there is no certainty" (*GA* 720b), there may be no uterine parts because these animals may reproduce not by coupling, but spontaneously or by budding. Like considerations apply to male testes; for instance, fishes and snakes lack testes, but analogously possess two spermatic channels (*GA* 716b15).

18. Although in his progressive development of the complex cortex-medulla theory, Linnaeus does attempt to interpret the *systema naturae* as the product of biological processes (Stevens and Cullen 1988).

19. To underscore the contention that Aristotle is more concerned with eternal and essential nature of a demonstrable rather than phenomenal kind, Pellegrin (1982) cites Aristotle's supposed use of *a priori* reasoning in biological generalization and *ad hoc* interpretation in the face of apparently conflicting experience. Take Aristotle's claim that all sanguineous animals have four feet. Yet, birds have wings (*PA* 639b11) and men have hands (*PA* 687a7) as forelimbs instead of feet. Nonetheless, argues Aristotle, they still have four appendages for support. What, then, of snakes? Well, "the curves they make are alternately concave and convex," so they do have four points of *support*. In effect, this is just another way of saying they have four feet (*IA* 707b22). Or, consider the argument that nature limits secretions so that an animal which secretes in one way secretes proportionately less in other ways: an animal which developed horns does not have developed teeth (*GA* 728b14), and a furry animal, like the bear, does not have abundant reproductive parts *PA* 658b1). Nevertheless the hare has both much fur and much sperm (*GA* 774a30). The discrepancy is ostensibly resolved once it is realized that the hare has such a superabundance of residue that its secretions are excessive.

Pellegrin, like Joly (1968) before him, points to such cases as these as evidence that Aristotle uses observation merely to illustrate arguments which accorded with preconceived doctrines. This is not to deny that experience plays an indirect role by providing tentative correlations which Aristotle would then arrange into fixed arguments; nor is to ignore Aristotle's insightful use of observation to criticize *rival* theories: e.g. "certain physiologers have tried to say such a part forms after such another, but they did not have a perfect experience of the facts" (*GA* 742a16). Such a "perfect experience of the facts," however, means only enough experience as it takes to readily confirm the right arguments, namely, Aristotle's own demonstrations about functional connections between parts.

While it is possible to agree with the opinion that Aristotle does not use observations and experiments in the way modern scientists do, this in no way indicates that Aristotle believes *a priori* arguments to be wholly acceptable. First, experience of various kinds is required to ensure that the phrasing of the argument would be correct: e.g. that "having four feet" and "having four points of support" were equivalent. Second, the experience must be "conclusive" (*GA* 741a34) so that the arguments are easily verified and irrefutable. To this, one could counter that the generalizations of modern science are neither verifiable nor immunizable by experience against refutation. But Aristotle's generalizations differ from those of modern science in that they are restricted to what was commonsensically known to *already* exist; hence, Aristotelian generalizations are in principle verifiable because the relevant experience is in principle exhaustive. Third, and most important, any argument showing the connection between parts of animals must take into consideration the fact that all parts are material, and that their connection exists partly in response to material necessity. Such necessity, however, does *not* operate on parts as such, but on the whole organism-in-its-environment. Aristotle does not ask, "what makes parts go together?" but "how and why do the everyday kinds of animals we know compare and differ as to their parts?" It is for this reason that the only underlying biological natures are those which specifically underlie all, and only, readily visible kinds. This is what Aristotle's definition and classification of animals aims to show.

20. The analogy of plant roots to animal heads does not amount to a *literal* first-order claim of identity in biological function (see sections 4.2 and 5.2 above). Rather, it is a second-order comparison whose interpretation is initially open to theoretical speculation and which is ultimately meant to orient empirical research into possible nonphenomenal connections (see sections 9.3 and 9.4 below).

21. Kirk, however, views the tendency to anthropomorphization as more pronounced in Socrates than in Aristotle. By contrast, Joly sees Aristotle's teleology as a "regression" from the biology of the Hippocratics. Morton considers Aristotle's teleology to be seeking "biological justification for social inequality." Thus, whereas Theophrastus "surveys in detail the effects of climate and soil on plant growth, in a way that is modern in approach, and that implies a rational concept of adaptation" (1981:41), Aristotle's teleology "is essentially anti-scientific, since it implies that development takes place outside natural processes (whether it is called god or divine mind (*nous*) or nature), and thus stands in the way of an analysis of development and adaptation in terms of real existing processes" (1981:55n.65).

Now, Kirk erringly judges animism to be compatible with common sense despite the fact that it violates the logical boundary conditions on ordinary ontological types. Contrary to Joly, such symbolic speculation (e.g. belief that the structure of the macrocosm informs that of the microcosm via inscrutable affinities and action at a distance) is still rampant in many treatises from the Hippocratic Corpus, though not in Aristotle. As for the Platonic Socrates, he merely tells us in the *Phaedo* what teleological causes (*aitia*) should explain, but says he has not found them. Finally, Morton's contention that Aristotle's teleology is merely the fanciful projection of social theory into biology is supported by no evidence at all. Aristotle's concern with the effects of environment is crucial to his biology; the typical morphology of the species, for instance, is integrally bound to the existence of material conditions that are compatible with, and conducive to, the development of such a morphology. If those conditions do not obtain, the species pattern will fail to develop as it otherwise should. In this respect, as in most others pertaining to the effects of the environment, Theophrastus quite clearly follows his teacher.

22. In this respect, the ideas of Lévi-Strauss (1962/1966), Mary Douglas (1966) and other like-minded anthropologists are assumed to "have immediate and obvious relevance to the classicist":

> the apprehension of the social and religious order and of the natural order is a seamless whole. But the explanation of much that looks at first sight unintelligible can be found by reading the texts of the whole system of beliefs. (Lloyd 1983:8)

The opinions of Douglas and Lévi-Strauss in this matter, however, are less than compelling (see section 9.1 below).

23. Indeed, Bonnet (1782:173), after Buffon, also distinguished between ostensible social characteristics of animals, but there is little evidence that such folklore truly affected their science.

24. The taxonomic position of these animals continued to be a matter of vigorous debate until the nineteenth century, when, e.g., Cuvier finally placed the seal and other aquatic carnivores with the terrestrial carnivores.

25. Cain's (1958) celebrated discussion of the empirical implausibility of a logical division of "unanalysed entities" (i.e. entities not known in advance to be in a determinate logical

relationship to one another) may readily apply to entities that are not presumed to be known in advance of their empirical discovery. This assumes, contrary to Linnaeus, that the logical connections between such unknown entities cannot be predicted on the basis of a rationalist principle of sufficient reason. But when the entities that figure into a logical division are presumed to be already known, as with Aristotle, no rationalist principle of sufficient reason is required to suppose that one might go on to discover a determinate set of quantitative relations between them by trial and error.

6 Origins of the species concept

1. Yet, early on at least, the situation seems to have been somewhat less disastrous than generally is supposed. According to Singer (1927:142), the earliest naturalistic plant drawings may be found in the twelfth-century Oxford Pseudo-Apuleius manuscript, Bodley 130. There is also a rendition of the *Herbarius* that replaces some of the entries with representations of plants actually grown in Central Europe (Landgraf 1928). More significantly, it appears that the original author of *Ex herbis* was every bit as circumspect as the great sixteenth-century herbalists in selecting and modifying Dioscorides's descriptions of southeast Mediterranean plants to conform to what was likely the author's own southwest European flora (Riddle 1981). But the originality and accuracy of *Ex herbis* should not be exaggerated. There is no evident conceptual advance over Dioscorides's textual descriptions or Krateuas's illustrations and there is decidedly less information overall. The texts and drawings frequently do not allow ready identification of species by a novice; and the contention (Riddle 1981:46–47) that such entries were "probably" designed for the initiated as generic summaries of related species is anachronistic. The author of *Ex herbis* does not represent overarching morphological relationships in a manner that is uniformly applied to the entries. In any event, by the late Middle Ages the state of the art had largely deteriorated.

2. Turkey was often taken by Europeans as a proximate source of exotica.

3. This is one reason why generic-speciemes cannot be invariably associated with single lexemes. However, this does not mean that binomials are often associated with speciemes that fall under recognized supraspecific groupings corresponding to incipient biological genera. As Dwyer notes, the agreement of binomially labeled folk groupings with morpho-geographical species is, on the whole, "exceedingly poor"; this seems to indicate that "binomial species are of more recent origin in Rofaifo thought than are species designated by mononomials" (1976a:434). To the extent that binomial groupings *are* recognized as speciemes [i.e. as generic-speciemes rather than folkspecifics] they may be expected eventually to acquire a mononomial title. But even if the vestigial binomial label stays (cf. Strathern 1969), the conceptual status of the grouping will have changed. This allows that an appreciation of overarching morphological affinity between the old and new specieme may persist on much the same footing as other, usually "covert" (unlabeled), associations; *ʾisim*, for example, may be taken overtly to refer to indigenous maize, but occasionally it may be taken as a gloss for something like "grains" as well. Still, there is no indication whatever that folk have another morphological rank in the offing – a conceptually pinned down perceptual layer of being over and above that of the generic-specieme – that more or less corresponds to the modern genus. In general, lexical status is only a very rough indication of conceptual status.

4. Fieldwork related to this issue involved the questioning of native Itzá speakers and recent Cakchikuel immigrants to San José, Peten (January 1988).

5. Despite the somewhat overenthusiastic judgment implied in Sprengel's (1817–18) attribution of paternity, the motto has stuck.

6. The outstanding names of the period are centered around two schools: Ghini's in northern Italy (Bologna and Pisa), which is associated with Aldrovandi, Turner, Mattioli, Cordus, Gesner and Cesalpino; and Rondelet's in Montpellier, which also sustained contact with the previous group through the likes of Clusius, Lobelius and Daleschamps.

7. To each plant type, Fuchs allots a chapter divided into the following sections: (1) *nomina* provides Greek, Latin and German synonyms; (2) *genera* occurs only with polytypic forms and

gives the main variants; (3) *forma* offers a brief description of all (or more often some) of the main parts of plants, that is, root, stem or trunk, flower, leaf, fruit, seed and branch; (4) *locus* depicts the local habitat; (5) *tempus* describes the schedule and pattern of maturation and flowering; (6) *temperamentum* characterizes the subjective "temperature" as determined by the taste and texture of the plant parts; (7) and *vires* portrays the virtues of the plant as rendered by Dioscorides, Galen, Pliny, etc.

8. When deciding between classical authorities or advancing his own views, Bock often appeals to how plants are *in nostra Germania*.

9. Much of the credit given Brunfels as the father of German herbalism may actually be due to his illustrator, Hans Weiditz. It seems that Weiditz insisted on figuring even such *herbae nudae* as the pasque-flower, forlorn by the ancients and thus only regretfully included by Brunfels (Arber 1953:323; cf. Sprague 1928:113).

10. It is notable that Bock, like other German herbalists, relies on nonvisual as well as visual cues. In this, as in other respects, the herbalists' means of comparison are more akin to those of ordinary folk than to those of the classical systematists and methodists.

11. The same year saw the appointment of Europe's first professor of field botany (*ostensor simplicium*) at the University of Padua.

12. Gesner himself first described the tulip (*Tulipa turcaram*). Of Persian origin, the plant was introduced to Europe in the late 1550s by the emperor's ambassador to Constantinople (cf. Wellisch 1975).

13. Gesner did, in fact, compile a collection of some 1,500 reasonably accurate plant illustrations with "dissections" (Gesner 1972), many of which were based on dried specimens sent from correspondents all over Europe (cf. Gesner 1584). But none were published in his lifetime and only about a third were in print two centuries after his death (cf. Milt 1936).

14. J. Bauhin trained under Fuchs at Tübingen, worked with Lobelius under Rondelet at Montpellier, studied with Aldrovandi, and traveled with Gesner through the Rhaetian Alps and Val Tellina.

15. The single difference concerns Bauhin's chapter, Cucumis Asininus, whose sole species is included under Tournefort's genus *Cucumis*. But Linnaeus would again accord it a status distinct from the cucumbers, i.e. as *Momordica elaterium* L. (*elaterium* was the name given it by Pliny).

16. Neither Melo nor Melopepo appear as section headings in Pliny. Nevertheless, in bk. XIX, sec. 23, which deals with some of the general properties of cucumbers and melons, Pliny remarks that a "new form" (*nova forma*) has been found in Campania whose fruits are called *melopeponas*.

17. The one exception to the rule is in bk. XX, section Cucurbita. Pliny discusses only a wild variety, while Bauhin's type refers to one of the two domestic varieties Pliny discusses elsewhere (bk. XIX, sec. 24).

18. Tribe, Cucurbitae. Subtribe: A. Benincasinae – *Lagenaria siceraria* (*bohc, cu*), *Citrullus vulgaris* (*santiya*); B. Cucurbita – *Cucurbita ficifolia* (*mayil*), C. *pepo* (*c'ol*), C. *moschata* (*c'um*).

   Tribe, Melothrieae. Subtribe, Cucurminae: *Cucumis melo* (*melones*).

19. A notable exception to such morphological heterogeneity in the section is the group Gramen Paniceum, with five numbered forms corresponding to three species of a single Linnaean genus (*Panicum*); another is the subgroup Gramen nemorosum hirsutum, with six numbered forms corresponding to four Linnaean species of the genus *Juncus*.

20. There are suggestions in Gesner's letters that he was thinking of some of the crucial issues concerning the delimitation of species and genera in ways similar to Cesalpino; however, these ideas were never systematically developed and their direct influence on the subsequent course of natural history appears to have been marginal.

21. This passage and others that I quote from the dedicatory epistle to *De plantis* appear in Greene's chapter on Cesalpino as if they were Greene's own words (Green 1983,II:815–17). Consequently, the editor's notes 23 and 25 (p. 1029) about the reasons for some of "Greene's" statements are inappropriate, although the editor's comments in this chapter as elsewhere are generally insightful.

22. The difficulty that agitated the schoolmen concerning the dual nature of forms and universals is

this: forms exist in nature (*in rerum natura*) only as a many of actual individuals and as a potential universal; but in the mind, form appears to exist as a one, that is, as an actual and unitary universal. Now, if universals-in-the-mind are individual thoughts they cannot be truly universal, for they are embodied in individual thinkers. Communication of ideas and consensus become contradictions in terms, truth and knowledge only illusions. The resolution of this paradox seems not to have especially preoccupied Aristotle (cf. Skulsky 1968).

Cesalpino opts for the Thomist solution (cf. Aquinas' *Tractatus de unitate intellectus contra averroistas*). Men's minds are the same "in species" but not in number. The mind is immaterial. Yet, it can only come to be through embodiment, just as an individual idea is separate from those sensations that initially occasion and confirm awareness of the idea. Once the body dies, though, the mind can survive, just as ideas can operate independently of their original "triggering" experiences. The mind, with its ideas, produces a "likeness" (*similitudo*) of external reality. This picture *represents* reality under its eternal aspect, and not as seen through fleeting sensory images (*phantasmatibus*) of transient experiences. People do not actually share representations, but they have representations of the same things. What people do share is the potential to grasp the world as it truly and always is. This potential is an *a priori* power of the "active intellect" (*intellectus agens*) to sort out sensory experience according to the natural order, that is, by defining natural kinds. It is through this God-loving power to contemplate the eternal order that the mind becomes "part of" that order (1571 II,viii).

23. Contemporary Aristotelian scholars are often at odds over what exactly the import of *nous* is. Lescher (1973), for example, relies on passages from the *Analytica Posteriora* in claiming that *nous* is nothing more than that *state* of induction wherein we grasp first principles. This, according to Plochmann (1963:200), is the sense implicitly adopted by Harvey and intended by Aristotle:

> Harvey does not stress intuition [*nous*], in fact hardly mentions it, but this is because it forms a kind of instantaneous step between the forming of universals and their employment in deduction, and is of interest not so much logically as psychologically. Aristotle himself has little to say about it.

But as Wear (1983) notes, Harvey's "sensationalism" alters the grounds of Aristotelian epistemology and changes the way in which induction is to be understood.

At the other end, Granger (1976:25–7), for one, bases his interpretation of *nous* as "rational intuition" especially on passages from *De Anima*. Here it appears to be an extra process over and above induction. This is one standard reading of Cesalpino's own view of the "active intellect" or "Sovereign Good":

> universals, once formed by abstraction, remain intelligibles not yet thought . . . abstraction alone does not suffice for intellection . . . it does not realize the apprehension of essence, which is the object of the intellect. It is the presence of the intellect that makes us know the ideas latent in sensations and images: just as the presence of luminous bodies brings out colors that escape us in the dark. It acts as a clear measure in itself. Although perhaps unknown to us it is nevertheless innate, not having come from the outside. But because every judgement is made by the application of a known measure to what is measured, once the latter is measured and known it can be taken as a measure and applied to the rest. In this way knowledge of certain terms play the role of *a priori* knowledge and principles. These allow us to know others that [in their turn] permit us to know still others, until the mountain of discoveries piles up . . . the more we know, the easier it is for us to learn the rest   (1571,II,viii).

Dorolle (1929:27), however, denies that Cesalpino is making a phenomenological distinction between the intelligent thought as act and the object that the thought realizes: "The intellect measures values because it is a first value, but it has its origin in its objects." Knowledge, then, is not the function of some innate cognitive schema, but "the complete consciousness that an object comes to have of itself." But whatever the ultimate source of rational measure, it is rational measure alone that provides the "number and nature" of the principles that make classificatory science possible.

24. The point may apply to hypothesis formation as well. The universally quantified proposition that is the implicit content of the major premiss in any syllogistic demonstration is a hypothetical of the following sort: "for all x, whenever x is A (e.g. a man), then x is B (e.g. a rational being)." Such knowledge of the universal is, strictly speaking, only potential or implicit knowledge about reality. As it stands, it has no particular content, not "this's" or "that's" in the real world to which it actually applies. Only when the universal connection expressed in the proposition is instantiated by instances, can knowledge of the universal proposition be deemed actual knowledge.

25. Sloan (1987) suggests that Harvey's attempt to ground *knowledge* of species in perceptual intuition and in reiterated experiences with particulars would be creatively revised by Buffon into an argument for grounding the *existence* of species in a genealogical succession of individuals (see section 9.5 below).

26. Ever since Epicurus, it was acknowledged that for invisible material elements to be considered basic atoms they must have reality separate from compound bodies (but not vice versa). Gassendi (1964,I:268) went on to reason in the *Physicae* that just as there is a visible minimum in the phenomenal macrocosm, so there must be a minimum in things nonphenomenal. Likewise Newton believed that because the readily perceptible world is clearly a world of material objects acting and reacting to one another, so must the intangible realm of astronomical dimensions consist of material bodies acting and reacting to one another as well as to those in the readily perceptible world. Also, the insensible realm of microscopic dimensions must harbor bodies that react to one another and affect the larger compound bodies of the sensible world. But Harvey argues that insensible posits that are supposed to be separate from, or antecedent to, the bodies they compose cannot be ascertained for their effects; hence their existence cannot be established. Thus, for Harvey, astronomy remains mere conjecture drawn from appearances that are not subject to verification by the senses; for example, one must see behind the moon to really appreciate an eclipse (cf. Pagel 1967:30). Indeed, Harvey's methodological rigor on this score actually led to factual error. Inability to observe material contact between the semen and ovum caused him to deny the possibility of such contact. Although he might conjecture about unseen matters of conception, he readily admits his speculation to be a "fable" and his understanding of the actual means of fertilization to be "at a standstill" (1653/1981:447–8).

27. As Sloan (1987:106–107) aptly notes, here the senses of *genus* and *speciem* follow Aristotle's similar uses of *genos* and *eidei* (*De generatione et corruptione* 338a12–15, *de An.* 415a25–b8). But no stock is taken of the proviso attached to the same passage in Aristotle's biological work where mention of eternal specificity is made only in regard to the *genos* of men, of animals, of plants (see section 4.3 above).

7 *The nature of the genus*

1. Gesner may have preceded Cesalpino in recommending the experimental test of seeing whether a plant came true to seed in order to determine which characteristics are really specific and which are accidents. It is doubtful, though, that Ray was aware of this when he proposed the test as an empirical criterion for the species (1686:40–43). It is possible that Gesner influenced Cesalpino through correspondence with Ghini, Cesalpino's teacher; or it may be that Ghini himself conceived the test. It is also worth noting that just as Gesner appreciated Ghini's technique of drying plants, so, too, Cesalpino (1583, dedicatory epistle) expressed a debt to Ghini's concept of the botanical garden.

2. Note, however, that Ray (1686:51–53) effects the same primary division by the presence or absence of buds during winter, rather than by the hardness of the medullary substance.

3. Tournefort (1694:17) acknowledges that Gesner originally suggested the importance of the seed, fruit and flower for judging the relations between plants in two letters written towards the end

of his life; but it was undoubtedly Cesalpino who first systematically applied such ideas. Yet there is no indication that either Gesner (Meyer 1854–1857,IV:334) or Cesalpino (Greene 1983,II:808) had a clear notion of a unique and uniform generic rank.

4. Cesalpino deals with seedless plants in bk. XVI, following his treatment of the herbaceous seed plants (the existence of seedless woody plants was not recognized at the time). On the whole, his seedless groupings reflect sound morphological judgment: first come ferns and their allies (*affines*), next lichens (lumped with heptatics), then mosses (with club-mosses and tree-mosses), algae and, finally, fungi. He also includes some seed plants that are not readily perceived to germinate.

5. In *Historiarum mundi* (bk. XX) Pliny divides the edible "grains" (*fruges*) into cereals (*frumenta*) and legumes (*legumina*). But more often, higher-level groupings are only implicitly formed by listing kinds in sequence, as in the case of the cucurbits. In like manner, Dioscorides implicitly takes stock of the labiates simply by sequencing examples in his *Materia medica* (bk. III, chaps. 31–47): lavender, origanum, thyme, pennyroyal, dittany, *Marrubium, Ballota, Salvia, Mentha, Satureja* and *Marjoram*; another sequence (chaps. 60–71) deals with the umbellifers: *Echinophora, Bupleurum, Angelica, Tordylium, Sison*, anise, caraway, dill, cumin, *Amni* and coriander. Theophrastus is occasionally more explicit in labeling, for example, the common "naked seed" Mediterranean umbellifers *anethon, koriannon, kuminon, marathon* (fennel) and the like as *narthakados* (*narthaks* = ferula) (cf. *Historia plantarum* I,xi,2).

6. Division would proceed through each level by positive and opposed characters that logically exhaust the conceptual possibilities available at each level. Each level would be composed as a complete series of equal fractions of the integral whole. Each progressively lower level would be composed of an integral series of smaller equal fractions. But the smaller the fraction, that is, the lower the rank of the taxon, the more intricate and complex the conformation of variables that constitute the fraction. Thus, all fractions would have a constant numerator (i.e. one or unity), but the equal fractions of each lower level would have a common denominator proportional in complexity to the mathematical conformation of fructification characters defining the taxa of that rank: the lower the level, the more complex the conformation.

7. From the catalog of works in Jung's library compiled by Christoph Meinel (1984b) of the Universität Hamburg, it appears that Jung was conversant with nearly all the published works of Galileo and Cesalpino. Concerning Cesalpino, in particular, Dr Meinel informs me that while Jung attacked much of "scholastic" Aristotelianism he was generally sympathetic to, and even inspired by, Cesalpino and Zabarella. Cesalpino is most evident in Jung's botanical thinking, but also in the composition of the *Praelectiones physicae*: "In fact the authors most frequently quoted by Jungius were Zabarella (24% of all quotations), Aristotle (16%, more than half of which comes from Meteor.), and Cesalpino (5% [most extensively from *De metallicis*, Nürenberg 1602]), followed by Galen (2%)" (personal communication).

8. Ever since Cassirer (1906:134–41) claimed that Galileo's notions of scientific method and explanation had much in common with Zabarella's, a debate has ensued as to whether indeed modern scientific theorizing was initially a further development of the Aristotelian exegetical schools of Northern Italy (Randall 1940) or, rather, a complete breakaway from them (Skulsky 1968). Certainly both Galileo and Zabarella relied on deductive reasoning as a guide to necessary physical truth – a view that other "enlightened" Aristotelians, such as Harvey and Jung, rejected, as did such "modern" exponents of inductivism as Bacon and Newton. But Gilbert (1963) convincingly argues that Galileo's method is more directly inspired by Euclid's account of geometrical analysis, which Galileo converts into a model for inquiry in natural science. At best, contends Jardine (1976), Zabarella's use of syllogism and *regressus* appears to serve as a stimulating *foil* in the Galilean dialogues, whereby the reader is enticed into agreement with the superior merits of Galileo's "geometrical" method.

9. For Theophrastus (*Historia Plantarum* I,iii,2) mallow, when it grows tall it departs from its essential nature (*physis*) (see section 2.3 above). Jung, however, does not think that the philosophical difference between intrinsic "nature" and mere "appearance" applies to such cases, most likely because he realizes the irrelevance of botanical life-forms to a natural order that is based wholly on morphology, and is independent of the (local) economy of nature. But

the systematic relevance of life-forms, though again questioned by Magnol (1689) and Rivinus (1690), was not finally decided until Linnaeus.

10. According to C. Raven, "the discovery of Morison's copy of Cesalpino heavily annotated in his own hand gives the lie to his explicit repudiation of indebtedness" (1942:186). Tournefort was already well aware of Morison's apparent plagiarism:

> One would not have praised this author enough, except that he has praised himself a little too much; far from being content with the glory of having executed a part of the most beautiful project ever made in botany, he dares compare his discoveries to those of Christopher Columbus .... One might have taken him at his word, were it not for his having transcribed entire pages from Cesalpino and Columna .... Ray, without making as much noise, succeeded infinitely better than Morison. (1694:18)

Apart from his revival of Cesalpino's method, Morison is perhaps best remembered for the *Plantarum umbelliferarum distributio nova* (1672), much of which is incorporated in sec. IX of his *Plantarum historiae universalis Oxiensis* (1680–1699). The umbellifers had been called by name since the chapter *De umbelliferis herbis* in Dodoens's *Stirpium historiae* (1583), but Morison's treatise amounts to the first real monograph of a botanical family. Unfortunately, the quality of the fourteen other sections of Morison's *Historia* often falls far short of sec. IX, except where modified by Bobart (in the poshumously edited 1699 volume) to conform more closely with Ray.

11. Although not utilized as a basis for classification, there is implicit recognition of the distinction between monocots and dicots among the ancients as well as among tribal folk. Theophrastus, for instance, is well aware of the distinction between, e.g., monocotyledonous legumes and dicotyledonous cereals, and the Tenejapa Tzeltal lexically generalize the distinction between monocots and dicots (Berlin *et al.* 1974:63).

12. This is hardly proof that Ray, as opposed to Linnaeus, held species to be inconstant and variable, as Singer (1959:194) suggests.

13. Only individuals truly exist. Nature itself is indeterminate, as the existence of borderline cases proves. We choose to ignore such cases only out of a linguistic habit for "presumptive ideas of several species" (Locke 1689/1848 III,vi,29) – ideas which "receive their birth and signification from ignorant and illiterate people, who sorted and denominated things by those sensible qualities they found in them" (III,vi,25). As it is for common sense, so it is for more self-conscious systems that merely extend "this gibberish, which, in the weakness of human understanding, serves so well to palliate man's ignorance" (III,x,14). If discovery and exploration have shown anything at all, it is that so-called "natural kinds" are strictly relative to human interests and purposes. What is constant and singular for one linguistic community is variable and plural for another. Only the scientific community's concerted search for a common vocabulary, requiring "much time, pains, and skill, strict inquiry and long examination," can reasonably hope to produce those complex associations of simple perceptions that most probably reflect species "conformable to those of nature." Such is the task of natural history (III,xi,24), which may yield proper philosophical sorts wholly different from anything that common sense might initially lead us to suspect.

14. Although "a plant is an organized body that has essentially (*essentiellement*) a root" (Tournefort 1694:21), the similarities (or differences) in plant roots are not "essential similarities" (*resemblances essentielles*) (24). They do not mark "the true character of plants (*le véritable caractère des plantes*)" (29) because they do not *systematically* yield "the character of each genus." Such an "essential mark" (*marque essentielle*) (16) simultaneously indicates the "close relationships" between plants of a genus (*leurs rapports prochains*) and provides "the common character that essentially distinguishes [each genus] from all the other plants" (13).

15. Evidence from ethnobotany seems to confirm the cross-cultural aspect of this decomposition. Friedberg (1972), for instance, indicates the importance of the names that the Bunaq of Timor give to these parts (cf. Greene 1983,I:137 for the ancient Greeks). Similarly, for the Tzeltal Maya, Berlin *et al.* note:

> We have arranged plant part names recognized in Tenejapa Tzeltal into groups of expressions referring to stem, bark, leaves, roots, flowers, fruits, and so on . . . . Their recognition of the relevant aspects of plant morphology compares favorably with that of trained Western systematic botanists, given the restriction that they worked unaided by microscopes. (1974:69,79)

16. Sloan wrongly claims that for Tournefort "the characters of the flower and fruit are always necessary and sufficient for defining the genera of plants in those cases where these characters are manifest" (1972:48).

17. For cryptogams, Tournefort offers to mark genera provisionally by the character of the facies. Although systematists anticipated analogies between the fructification of flowering plants and the reproductive apparatus of the nonflowering plants, no lasting advance in the systematic treatment of cryptogams occurred before the detailed study of bryophytes by the German physician Hedwig. From Ray's "Musci" to A.-L. Jussieu's "Acotylédones," cryptogams occupied the phenomenally "residual" place in the plant world that the invertebrates did in the animal world.

18. The first Stockholm edition of the *Philosophia botanica* puts the figure at 5,736, but this expresses an error both in the addition of parts and in the multiplication of the sum total of parts by the four variables. The correct figure appears in the fourth edition (1787).

19. Linnaeus begins the first philosophical outline of his biological thinking, *Fundamenta botanica* (1736), by citing Francis Bacon to the effect that nature must be approached directly through the senses. In this at least, Bacon and Aristotle would agree, as Linnaeus was undoubtedly aware. Like Bacon, Linnaeus was also preoccupied with the usefulness of knowledge and was well aware of the economic benefit that Swedish agriculture and commerce might obtain from a practical system (see Leikola 1987:47).

20. Cesalpino had already assimilated the individual nature to the species essence, without, however, denying an essential metaphysical role to the individual, namely, as the material vehicle whereby and wherein the essence of the species is realized. Linnaeus, however, appears to relegate the role of material actualization of essence to the species itself, and to correspondingly move the existential locus of essence up one rank to the genus: what is peculiarly "essential" to the species is its material role in regulating the distribution of fructifications in the economy of nature.

21. Nehemiah Grew (1682:171) was apparently the first to publish the opinion that the stamen and pollen in flowers correspond to the male organ and semen in animals. Ray definitely adopts this view in his catalogue of European plants (1694). In the same year, Camerarius published his paper, *De sexu plantarum espistola*, which contains an acknowledgement of the views of Grew and Ray, and the first experimental demonstration of the fact that pollen falling on the stigma acts as the male fertilizing agent. Here also are noted different arrangements of stamens and pistils in different kinds of plants. Linnaeus became acquainted with the facts of plant sexuality through the work of Sebastien Vaillant (1717/1728), Tournefort's student and successor as botanist at the Jardin du Roi in Paris. Tournefort himself denied the sexual role of the stamens, probably in deference to the views of Marcello Malpighi, whose work on plant anatomy Tournefort esteemed above all others.

22. Entries of the form, Linnaeus [name of student], refer to works of the *Amoentitas academicae*. These dissertations were likely written by Linnaeus, or at least under his supervision, and each defended by a student whose name figures in the brackets. All references to the *AA* are to the Salvius edition (1749–69), unless indicated otherwise.

23. The Neoplatonic idea of plenitude, or fullness in the world, as an emanation from the Absolute was first definitively formulated by Spinoza. Apart from a profound disagreement on the operation of final causes in nature (with Linnaeus arguing for and Spinoza against), there is much in the metaphysical position outlined in Spinoza's *Ethica* that seems to accord with Linnaeus' own views: e.g. "all things in Nature proceed from an eternal necessity and with supreme perfection" (I,xxxvi [appendix]), "there is no vacuum in Nature" (I,xv [scholium]), etc.

Hagberg (1939/1953:188–189) surmises that Linnaeus may have been exposed to Spinoza's thought while visiting Herman Boerhaave in Holland. In fact Boerhaave, who helped to make Linnaeus's early writings known throughout Europe, may have influenced Linnaeus by rejecting plant life-forms and stressing the importance of all the parts of the fructification as well as its sexual aspect (it was, after all, on Boerhaave's initiative that Vaillant's *Sermo de Structura Florum* was published). But Boerhaave's radical empiricism, upon which he built the first wholly materialist doctrine of human physiology, was very much at odds with Spinoza's rationalist metaphysics.

24. Cesalpino (1583, dedicatory epistle), Ray (1686, preface), Tournefort (1694:2,40) and the other systematists also emphasized the principle of plenitude of forms (*plenum formarum*), or fullness in the world (*natura non facit saltus*), in terms of juxtaposed geographical regions rather than as a great linear "chain of being."

25. At any given time, the natural character will express the essential character; for the essence and natural aspect of a plant owe to its reproductive system (Linnaeus, 1751 secs. 88,167,189). The distinction between underlying essential nature and the natural characters that necessarily follow from the essence has its roots in the Aristotelian distinction between *essentia* and *propria* (see section 4.2 above); however, Linnaeus's understanding of the matter perhaps comes closer to the modern distinction between primary nomic structure (akin to Locke's "real atomic essence") and secondary nomic properties (usually physico-chemical dispositions). For example, when one uncovers the essential nature of gold (i.e. its atomic number) one thereby finds out *what it is* for gold to have the physico-chemical dispositions it necessarily does have (e.g. malleability, solubility in *aqua regia*, etc.). Similarly, if and when one discovers the essential analytic nature of a given plant genus (which is also presumably mathematical in character), then, *ipso facto*, one will have explained what it is for that genus to have the natural reproductive character it does have, and in what ways that natural character is similar to, yet different from, all other natural characters.

26. Although Buffon (1749,I:36–37) roundly condemns Linnaeus for grossly reducing the unknown to the known by assimilating all possible species to a substantially diminished number of generic (usually European) prototypes, it is clear that Linnaeus' intent is not the same as that of common folk, herbalist or lay explorer to which Buffon alludes. Neither is the Linnaean program restricted to an attempt to extend the familiar to the unfamiliar by using the familiar as standard to which the unfamiliar may be associated through analogy or by degrees of more and less, as with Aristotle (*HA* 491a21) and Theophrastus (*Historia plantarum* I,ii,3–4).

27. Like the other classifiers of the time, Linnaeus pays scant attention to anatomical or physiological justification of the choice of taxonomic characters. Microscopists, physiologists and anatomists rank with horticulturalists and medical herbalists as mere "amateurs" (*botanophili*) of botanical science. Only on the subject of floristics do the studies of the amateur appear to hold special interest for the professional. In this respect, Linnaeus would have been heartened in his belief in the (limited value) of microscopy by the work of Malpighi (1675) and Grew (1682). In testing their new found techniques on fruits and flowers (as on other organs), Malpighi and Grew were able to show that apparently anomalous fructifications may, on deeper examination, reveal themselves to be not so atypical after all.

28. The most common form of preformationism circulating at the time was the ovist doctrine of the pre-existence of germs. On this view, the species-typical germs of all present and future organisms have existed since the time of Creation. Encapsulated in the egg or seed of the first female representative of each species, were all of the indefinitely small germs of the indefinitely many future individuals of the species. These germs await only the moment of fertilization by the active, or "vital," fertilizing force of the male semen. Such is the doctrine of Malebranche (1674/1928 bk. 1 chap. 2) adopted by Ray (1691:80–3). A rival pre-existence doctrine that was championed by Leibniz located the germ in the "animalcules," or spermatazoa, which Leeuwenhoek and Hartsoeker found swimming in the male semen. Other, weaker and less clearly formulated, versions of preformationism also existed, such as that suggested by Malpighi and accepted by Tournefort. In this version there is some doubt as to whether there is an infinite embedding of original germs; but there is no doubt that a reasonably well-formed miniature of the adult exists at the moment of conception. Even Buffon's "epigenetic" theory of the internal

molding of organisms constitutes a *de facto* case of pre-existence theory: the species-specific *moule intérieur*, which "instantaneously" molds a well-formed embryo at the moment of conception, is itself practically eternal (cf. Roger 1971:546; and see sections 9.5 and 9.6 below).

29. In the *Species plantarum* (1753/1957–59; cf. Linnaeus [Haartman] 1751), Linnaeus admits in several places that he is unable to determine whether a given kind of plant is actually a species or a variety (e.g. *Rosa indica, Thalictrum lucidum*). With respect to the six species of *Plantago* he suggests that their apparently minimal morphological differences could owe either to the effects of environment (*an loca*) or to crossing (*an copula*). The species of the genus *Scorpius* also seem to differ little from one another. In this case, however, it is clear that these minimal differences are *constantly* reproduced, so the species must have been produced by "mixing." Here, as with *Geranium* and *Calendula*, he argues that the congeneric species must have been derived from a single prototype. In *Disquisitio de sexu plantarum* (1760/1790) it is plain that the "mixing" that produces different species from a single prototype occurs only by crossing the prototype with species of *other* genera (Ramsbottom 1938; cf. Larson 1971).

30. The idea of intergeneric hybrids first arose with respect to *Peloria* (Linnaeus [Rudberg] 1744), a mutant form of the common *Linaria*. Linnaeus was compelled to explain the very different floral structure of *Peloria*, which did not appear to result from the crossing of *Linaria* with a morphologically related species. Because *de novo* mutation, like spontaneous generation, was alien to Linnaeus' beliefs, the only plausible explanation for the intermittent appearance of pelorias among linarias seemed to be cross-generic breeding. In fact, such intergeneric hybrids, Koelreuter (1761–66/1893) was presently to note, seldom occur and rarely, if ever, give rise to new species.

31. The significance of the passage is tied to Linnaeus' belief that all species of plants and animals are perfectly adapted to one another. Thus, while insects live upon plants, birds live upon insects, and insects, in turn, maintain the right ecological proportions between plants. Nature has as many "ministers" as are severally and jointly needed to fulfil all of nature's tasks and functions: "to maintain proportion between plants; to consume that which is error, superfluous, dead or rotten; finally to serve as food for other beings, especially for birds" (1758:340). In this respect, Linnaeus' view of the "economy of nature" (Limoges 1972:20) is closely akin to Ray's "natural theology" (Gillespie 1987).

32. Linnaeus adopted the rule of binomial nomenclature for plants in *Species plantarum* (1753/1957–59) and for animals in the tenth edition of *Systema naturae* (1758), which no longer contains the maxim about the initial number of immutable species. Linnaeus also recognized the possibility of animal species arising through hybridization. He had nothing to say, though, about those "principles" that might be responsible, nor could he give examples of animal species with a probable hybrid origin. But the "horrendous thought" that mankind might not constitute a primordial or unequivocal species seems to have occurred to Linnaeus at least as a theoretical possibility (Leikola 1987:54; cf. Broberg 1983).

33. Nor is Tournefort any less committed to atomism and mechanism than is Ray, contrary to what Sloan (1972) suggests. Gassendi's theory of "molécules," for instance, is very much in evidence in Tournefort's medical thesis of 1695 (cf. Bianchi 1957) and in subsequent lessons given at the Jardin du Roi in Paris (Tournefort 1708). Sloan makes much of the fact that Boyle (and, by implication, Locke and Ray) rejects the Aristotelian distinction between essence and accident in favor of the distinction between primary and secondary qualities. Whereas both essence and accident are thought to objectively inhere *in* a thing, and both are presumably knowable through their direct phenomenal manifestations, for Boyle (1667) only purely subjective secondary qualities are knowable – that is, the colors, tastes, textures, sizes and shapes of objects conveyed to us by the senses. The primary qualities that determine the "real" form of the object refer to the insensible motion, mass and geometrical arrangement of the minute corpuscular constituents of the object. Because primary qualities are insensible, they are unknowable.

Yet, there are other versions of the primary-secondary distinction that do not involve the claim that we can never know the real order of things. In *Il Saggiatore*, for example, Galileo enumerates the primary qualities of matter: these are either geometrical (shape, size, position, contiguity), arithmetical (number) or kinematic (motion or rest). The senses provide us also with secondary qualities of color, taste, texture and so forth; but it is reason alone that allows us to know that there are primary qualities, and to know what, where and when they are. Galileo advances this distinction to justify his opposition to Aristotle's ban on the use of mathematics in natural science. Clearly, the "essential" characters of Tournefort (and even Linnaeus) are more in conformity with Galileo and Descartes than with Aristotle. For knowledge of nature must be consonant with quantitatively expressible, clear and distinct ideas that reason ties to what is readily observable.

8 The method of families and classes

1. One reason Adanson gives for the need to rely on genera rather than species is that species are not stable in time: new species, it seems, may arise by mutation or hybridization. Although later experiments showing the lack of constancy in would-be specific characters caused Adanson to change his mind in favor of the fixity of species, his earlier pronouncement is taken by some to involve "the penetrating recognition that, if organisms change during descent, then natural classification expresses a genetic, or more accurately, a phylogenetic relationships [sic] between them" (Morton 1981:310; cf. Guyénot 1941). But Adanson never drew the conclusion that the transmutation of species might actually give rise to new genera, much less families. No matter how variable (muable & chanjantes) individuals or species may be, the number of families as well as the gaps (vuides ou distances) between them are constant (se conservent constamment) (1763:clxiv). If, as Adanson declares, the natural method "brings together all plants in natural and invariable families, based on all possible relations" (clviij), then past or future variation among species could make no appreciable difference.

2. Thus, the more unfamiliar, or less homogeneous families, would be built around genera that were admittedly artificially well-bounded, but nonetheless substantially natural. Serving as the centerpiece of a family-to-be, such a family prototype would be progressively expanded by associations of habitus, but especially of the fructification, to other species and genera. Eventually, each end of the chain thus formed would link up with one of the more well-established families. Take Jussieu's admittedly vague and largely exotic group, Terebintaceae, whose core is today's cashew family (Anacardiaceae). Starting with the pistachio genus at the center, for instance, one could ultimately form a series, whose outlying genera on one side hook up to the legumes and, on the other side, to the buckthorns (Rhamnaceae). Similarly, the series Rosaceae, with the rose genus as its pivot, would seem to approach the umbellifers and crucifers along one dimension of its floral structure and the lilies and pinks along another. This strategy is meant to hold for zoology as well: "provided that one knows 2 or 3 [kinds of] being from each [family], that is, one from each extreme and one from the middle that provides the liaison, one can be assured of knowing natural history well enough for relating all [kinds of] beings to their natural families" (Adanson 1847:17).

3. Over the course of time Linnaeus increased the number of genera included under his fragmenta, from roughly the same number (746 genera in 1738) as Tournefort's (698 in 1694) to nearly twice as many (1,344 in 1764).

4. A.-P. Candolle, who succeeded Jussieu as the foremost botanical authority of his day, alone named 6,000 new species of plants, or roughly the same number that had been named from the dawn of recorded history to the end of the herbalist period.

5. Linnaeus first mentions in the Critica botanica (1737b) the importance of naming the ordines "which were called by Tournefort sections." But the first rendition of the Fragmenta methodi naturalis in the Classes plantarum (1738) simply lists the sixty-five entries by number. In the revised list of the Philosophia botanica, each of the sixty-seven fragments is designated by a name that is usually derived from a featured aspect of a typical genus. The list, which is accompanied by over a hundred unattached genera, is reduced to fifty-eight named fragments in 1764.

6. This is especially so when the conflict reaches the family core. Because habitual family structure is marked by fewer overall features than habitual generic structure, and inasmuch as these core features form the basis for family construction, there is less leeway for selectively ignoring or emphasizing them.

7. Cuvier (1829:51–52n) suggests that in 1795 he effected the first scientific reappraisal and rejection of the popular invertebrate groupings since Aristotle. Lamarck (1809), however, states that he originally carried through a reform in the spring of 1794. In any event, given Cuvier's prior adherence to the cause of anatomical research, it is likely that in this matter Lamarck was influenced at the time by Cuvier. But neither Cuvier nor Lamarck acknowledge Adanson's reform of 1772 (see Adanson 1847) in which the invertebrates appear to be at least as internally differentiated as the vertebrates. Thus, whereas Linnaeus (1758) argues for just two invertebrate classes that combine for less than 100 genera, Adanson proposes eight invertebrate classes totaling nearly 2,000 genera, or appreciably more than the sum of genera for all of his vertebrate classes combined. Nevertheless, Adanson does not draw out the implications of his reform in the manner of Lamarck and Cuvier. His classification remains geared to a finer appreciation of overall morphological affinity, and is not based on anatomical structure or function.

8. The few attempts at a unitary system of zoology, such as the German naturalist Klein's (1734; 1750) classifiction of animals by feet and ears, never really attained credence as a stepping-stone to a natural system:

> What would one think of the author who, in order to do an elementary book of zoology, classifies the animals after the number of their feet; placing the snakes and worms in the apods; the mollusks and polyps in the beings which have but one foot; man, bats and birds in the class of bipeds; the oviparous and viviparous quadrupeds in a fourth [class], etc.? One would say, without doubt, that this manner of considering the animals might well be of some convenience for finding the names, or of some utility in the study of animal movements; but that this is not science itself, and one must guard against following such an order.   (Candolle 1819:57)

9. By abstracting from successive perceptions, man:

> will come in little time to form a particular idea of the animals that inhabit the earth, of those that reside in the water, and of those that rise in the air; and consequently, he will easily make for himself that division [of animals] into *Quadrupeds, Birds, Fish*. It is the same in the realm of plants; he will distinguish trees from plants [i.e. from herbs and grasses] very well, by their height, by their substance, or by their figure. Here is what simple inspection must necessarily give him, and which with the slightest attention he will not fail to recognize. It is also this that we must regard as real, and which we must respect as a division given [to us] by nature itself.   (Buffon 1749,I:32)

Similarly, according to Linnaeus: "A natural instinct teaches us to know first those objects closest to us, and at length the smallest ones: for example, Man, Quadrupeds, Birds, Fish, Insects, Mites, or firstly the *large* Plants, lastly the *smallest* mosses" (1751 sec. 153).

10. Even those sympathetic to Buffon saw the tendentiousness of the criticism. Daubenton argued correctly that Linnaeus never meant to simply reduce congeneric species one to the other: "Certainly the cat is not a lion, and that is not what Linnaeus wanted to say" (*Séances des écoles normales*, I:293). The anonymous reviewer of the *Bibliothèque raisonnée* (Oct.–Dec. 1750) also surmised that Buffon's lack of familiarity with the many more known species of plants led him to underestimate the practical value of genera in botany; and although one might debate their value as natural units, it is clear that since "the Ancients knew neither number nor measure," they could hardly have treated genera as rational units in the manner of Linnaeus. Moreover, the reviewer notes that while genera formed by multiple affinities "are always superior to others that set apart and bracket together entities by means of a single characteristic," it is not at all evident that Linneaus actually chose the latter.

11. Buffon's influence on Kant's opinion of the genus was decisive. But Kant did not agree that mathematical concepts were pure abstractions or that species were really constituents of nature. For him, only logic could represent the relations between pure ideas, whereas mathematics constituted the concept of time and the means to categorize experience (Kant 1787/1958).

In line with Leibniz, Buffon held that time is composed, and reality constituted, of the succession of events. But Buffon goes further in postulating that every regular series of concrete entities that takes form in time is a constitutive unit of nature (e.g. the species). By contrast, Kant does not accept the concept of such a concrete series as being truly "constitutive" of nature, even if it proves "necessary by nature of the evidence itself." Such a concept is only "regulative" of the perceived relations of experience. As with the idea of teleology, any regulative idea operates as a mental convenience. This does not preclude that such an idea is real; but reason can never be sure it is. Only ideas arising from pure mathematics, or from other "transcendental" notions that represent the unification of *possible* experience (as a totality), can constitute our understanding of nature (Kant 1790/1951).

12. As with Aristotle, Buffon did not consider the species type as an idea in the mind of God prior to, or apart from, material existence. Unlike Aristotle, he did not view the realization of the typical traits of the (prototypical) species as a localized tendency of nature (see section 4.3 above). He held each typical constellation of features to be the lawful product of underlying Newtonian-Boerhaavian microforces common to all members of the species (see section 9.5 below). Left to its own resources, each such special configuration of underlying forces would invariably mold the available organic materials in its own characteristic way: "The *empreinte* of each species is a type whose principal features are carved in forever ineffaceable and permanent characters" (1765,XII:ix). The typical species' features that usually do appear, as the mold fills itself out are actually those that should appear, all things being equal. But as things are not always equal – there being external interference in the operation of underlying forces – nature yields "accessory touches." As a result, "no individual perfectly resembles another, no species exists without a great number of varieties." Also, while the laws governing the formation of species are omnipresent and eternal, species themselves turn out to be neither constant nor everlasting. A given species arises only under certain thermal conditions (that may be different for different species) and vanishes when the planet's inevitable cooling is sufficiently advanced (1778,V:167–169).

13. Adanson does acknowledge that Tournefort's teacher Magnol, a correspondent and admirer of Locke, had recognized the value of the habitus without, however, putting it to consistent use (1763:xxij; cf. Magnol 1689, preface).

14. Adanson cites his mentor, Bernard de Jussieu, as the first to have actually exhibited a partial natural order of families in the layout of the royal garden at Trianon in 1759. Bernard, however, openly took the Linnaean fragments as the basis for his own demonstration beds. Thus, comparing Bernard's Cucurbitaceae with the Linnaean fragment of the same name, on the one hand, and with Adanson's family Bryoniae, on the other, gives an indication of just how convergent were the practices of three otherwise differently tempered natural historians:

Bernard's group omits a genus and adds one to the Linnaean group. Omitted is *Passiflora*, which Linnaeus, together with his student Hallman, acknowledge to be a rather difficult case (Linnaeus [Hallman] 1745). This genus, which is primarily one of the New World, resembles the cucurbits in having a simple perianth and climbing habit. On this basis, A.-L. Jussieu would attach it to the curcubits as an "affiliate" (*Genera Cucurbitaceis affinia*). Indeed, as late as the middle of the nineteenth century, the separate status of the Passifloraceae was still a questionable matter: "Whatever opinion one adopts in this respect, it nevertheless remains very difficult to determine with exactitude the place of the Passiflorae in the series of natural orders" (Richard 1852,II:226).

Added is the genus *Zanonia*, a plant of the East Indies, which is not a cucurbitoid (as are all the other genera in the Linnaean fragment), and which is today the type genus of a distinct subfamily of cucurbits. This genus Linnaeus placed among the list of plants whose affiliations were considered vague or unknown. Adanson's own family is the same as Bernard's, except for the addition of the genus *Ceratosanthes*, which was also later included in A.-L. Jussieu's family, Cucurbitaceae.

15. According to Stafleu (1963:179): "we must recognize in Adanson a remarkable insight never attained by Linnaeus: the conviction that it is necessary for a botanist to look further afield and

to know the vegetation of the tropics." Patently, however, Linnaeus attained such insight. In fact, on Stafleu's own showing, Adanson's families are, on the whole, no more (nor less) natural from a modern viewpoint than are those of Linnaeus (cf. Croizat 1945). How could this possibly be unless Linnaeus understood the importance of exotic plants? Taking as a sample the modern families Malvaceae, Apocynaceae, Solanaceae, Labitae, Ranunculaceae, Euphorbiaceae, Caryophyllaceae and Primulaceae, Stafleu (1963:215–218) notes that Linnaeus and Adanson correctly placed 83% of the then known genera of these six families in their corresponding fragments and families. A slightly lower percentage of correct placement is given for Bernard (80%) and by A.-L. Jussieu (81%).

16. According to the neo-Adansonian movement in modern systematics, the natural method has always consisted of a comparative analysis of *all* the parts of the organism (Gilmour 1940, Cain 1959b, Sneath & Sokal 1973). It is also a principle that has been accepted by a number of historical commentators (cf. Guyénot 1941, Singer 1959, Stafleu 1963, Morton 1981). Thus, to avoid "*a priorism*" the doctrine allows neither intuition nor abstract theory to determine which characters are available in advance for analysis. This, however, is absurd. By excluding "intuition," not to mention more consciously elaborated inferential frameworks, one thereby excludes from possible consideration not only enzymes, nucleotides and chromosomes, but gills, feet, antennae, wings, roots, leaves, stems, flowers, branches, etc. (cf. Mayr 1965; Hull 1968). All such characters depend upon the human-being's intuitive ability to discriminate certain salient sensory-motor configurations in his environment. Indeed, it is precisely intuition which, for Adanson, was to effectively provide "all" of the characters for analysis. He knew little of, and cared even less for, the internal or microstructural characters so important to all modern systematists (including the neo-Adansonians) (cf. Adanson 1763:clvi,clxviii). Adanson was exclusively a phenomenalist who sought to establish the visible order of things.

17. Candolle goes on to argue, however, that even if we knew all the organs and examined them from every possible point of view, Adanson's principle of equal relative importance for all parts of the plant would still be untenable; for, "it is evident that certain organs that are very important in terms of their use have a greater influence than others over the ensemble of the [plant's] organization" (1819:67). It is this argument that leads Cain (1959a:205) to dismiss Candolle's criticism of Adanson as simply Candolle's refusal to shed the prejudice of "weighting according to *a priori* principles." But one may reject Candolle's belief in the *a priori* subordination of characters to selected functions without this affecting Candolle's other argument, namely, that the unbiased analysis of *all* parts of the organism is impossible in practice and deficient as a principle.

18. Roughly, the principle of blind induction runs as follows: when a large number of A's have been observed, and all have been found to be B's, we may go on to assume that very nearly all A's are B's. But suppose that $a_1, a_2, \ldots a_n$ are members of A that have been observed and have been found to belong to a certain class B. Suppose further that a_{n+1} is the next A to be observed. Now, if it is a B, then substitute for B the class consisting of B *without* a_{n+1} so that the induction breaks down. Should it be argued that nature disallows such "contrived" classes as, say, "all animals save cows," it must be admitted that *our* disallowance of such a class rests on a *prior* inference as to nature's predilections for forming certain classes rather than others. Such an inference cannot be arrived at by enumerative generalization from observed instances on pain of infinite regress. The patterns we see confirmed in our observations are patterns that the mind's eye has itself imposed, whether or not we are consciously or reflectively aware of this fact.

19. Candolle and Cuvier would both signal the irony: The idea behind natural history was to make sense of the diversity of living forms, by showing them as patternings of life. Botanists initially made rapid progress toward a natural order by ignoring plant anatomy. The greater the pressure imposed by the welter of new plant forms to comprehend a natural order, the greater the reliance on external characters. But the greater the reliance on external characters, the farther astray this led natural historians from a true appreciation of the underlying structures and connections of existence. Such an appreciation, one might have eventually hoped to extract from the anatomical study of animals. But the transference of natural history's botanical program into zoology seemed to rule out the interest of such study.

20. In his earlier collaborative effort with Buffon (1753,IV:142–167), Daubenton argued that the considerations of anatomy invoked by Ray and Linnaeus in their respective classifications of cetaceans were inconsequential. Although Ray (1693) realized that cetaceans have mammalian hearts, he nevertheless classified them with the fish in concession to the prejudice of the common man (*au préjugé du vulgaire*); and while Linnaeus (1735) first classed them as an order (Plagiuri) of fish, he subsequently classed them as an order of mammals (Cete) simply because he wished to preserve symmetry and the appearance of consistency as he changed one set of class diagnostics in favor of a more convenient set. Later arguing from anatomical considerations, Daubenton (1782:xiv–xv; also Vicq-d'Azyr 1792) came to reject Buffon's (also Bonnet 1782) bias in favor of the intermediate status of such groupings as an equally unacceptable concession to the *a priori* dogma of continuity. But Daubenton, like many commentators since, never fully grasped the fundamental similarity of these apparently conflicting approaches to classification: rival metaphysical principles operated only in the service of seemingly more effective attempts to meet the deeply felt (and often religiously sustained) need to preserve a phenomenal order of things. If possible, an attempt would be carried through in conformity with the expanding inquiry into nonphenomenal structures and processes, but if necessary, in spite of it.

21. Later, the principle of *corrélation des formes* and that of *balancement des organes* would be integrated in a strictly anatomical doctrine of *subordination des organes* (see Desmoulins 1822).

22. True, the arrangement of families in a *scala naturae* is marked by overlapping polythetic groupings having a certain "family resemblance." In other words, each family is associated with a cluster of morphological characters that is sufficient to isolate the taxon as a whole from all others, but no character in the cluster is necessarily associated with all, or only, members of that family. Most members of the family, however, will manifest most of the characters in the cluster most of the time (cf. Beckner 1959:22; Sneath and Sokal 1973:20). Nevertheless, although a taxon be morphologically polythetic, it may be monothetic in other respects. For instance, it may be associated with a unique set of well-delimited physiological systems, or a specific structural or functional anatomy whose constituent features are severally necessary and jointly sufficient for defining the membership of the taxon. Thus, the phenomenal continuity of the family *scala* and the typological notion of each family as a fundamental organizational plan need not be incompatible (cf. Stevens 1984a:171; Sober 1980).

23. Although Tournefort's original title at the *Jardin du Roi* was "professor and demonstrator of the interior and exterior of plants," the "interior" of plants meant only pharmaceutical botany: plants would first be classified by external characters without regard to internal structure, and only afterwards would the groupings thus formed be examined for their medicinal virtues. Bernard de Jussieu's initial appointment was as "sub-demonstrator of the exterior of plants."

24. There is no warrant for Sloan's (1972) claim that A.-L. Jussieu's acceptance of the principle of subordination of characters was incompatible with the analysis of "all" characters advocated by Lamarck and Candolle. Consider the following:

> Among the plants, the natural method is extremely difficult to establish, because of the obscurity that reigns in the characters of the interior organization of . . . the plants that diverse families offer. Nevertheless, ever since the learned observations of M. Antoine-Laurent de Jussieu, one has taken a great step in botany towards the natural method.
>
> (Lamarck 1809:24)

> Sensing the vagueness of simple methods of intuitive groping (*tâtonnement*), the exaggeration of the principle of uniform and general comparison of organs, [Bernard and A.-L. de Jussieu] were the first to note with care that all the organs, all the points of view from which they can be considered, do not have equal importance, nor permanence; some of them, so to speak, dominate the others; so that by first establishing the classification upon the predominant organs . . . one is led to imitate as much as possible the order of nature in that of classification.
>
> (Candolle 1819:69–70)

25. Consider the claims that Cuvier's work on functional anatomy had little real effect on systematics in Cuvier's time and that functional anatomy today constitutes more a hindrance than a help (Simpson 1961:72; cf. Cain 1959a). The importance of Cuvier's anatomical line of reasoning to the systematic work of his time can hardly be overestimated. Even Lamarck and Geoffroy Saint-Hilaire drew a great deal on Cuvier's studies. For Lamarck, considerations of functional anatomy revealed both the continuity and progression in living forms; while for St Hilaire understanding function was not sufficient, but it was necessary, to understanding structural correlations. Granted, functional anatomy cannot distinguish well between organs subject to evolutionary processes of convergence and those which remain structurally stable indicators of a true lineage (e.g. the jaws and teeth of present-day bats and carnivores are convergent analogues, not evolutionary homologues). Nevertheless, an appreciation of functional anatomy remains of crucial concern to systematics. Even vestigial organs, which are so important to evolutionary considerations because they represent those features least subject to selection pressures, can properly be appreciated only after their outworn functions have been understood. Furthermore, the structural similarities between, say, a man's hand, a porpoise's paddle, a horse's leg and a bat's wing can arguably be linked to functional considerations of movement and displacement, even though these homologous organs reflect widely different habits of life. In brief, structural homology is not wholly independent of functional anatomy.

26. Although still morphological, the "laws of affinity" that determine the relationships of the plant realm would take on the formative character of those mechanical principles evident in zoological thinking since the 1730s. But whereas zoology at first inclined to a processual analogy with magnetism, gravity, electricity and chemical affinity, botany would more readily tend to a structural analogy with the organization of crystal symmetries. At least this seems to be the case with Augustin-Pyramus de Candolle, the early nineteenth-century's foremost plant taxonomist and theoretical botanist (Candolle 1827,II:236–44; cf. Stevens 1984b). True, Lamarck and Buffon also employed analogies between crystallography and zoology; but abstract notions of structural symmetry did not dominate their thinking about the organization of animals.

Nevertheless, given the dynamic interchange between Parisian botany and zoology, it is not surprising that the organizational principle of a "more or less abstract [morphological] symmetry" also played an important role in the animal systematics of the day (cf. Farber 1976). The principle had a crucial part, for instance, in Geoffroy Saint-Hilaire's (1818) elaboration of morphological *analogie* as the foundation of his *philosophie anatomique*. This nonfunctional conception of *analogie* – which Darwin (1883:382), via Owen, later interpreted as structural "homology" – would prove indispensable to the theory of evolution (cf. Russell 1917:108). Henri de Blainville also continued to rely heavily on morphology – especially external morphology – in his construction of an animal series that would reconcile Lamarck, Cuvier and St Hilaire (cf. Appel 1980); and, as Corsi (1983) suggests, it is the circulation and reworking of great ideas by the population of lesser (or less remembered) thinkers, such as Blainville, Virey and others, that is in a large part responsible for their eventual adoption.

9 *Science, symbolism and common sense*

1. The seventeenth and eighteenth centuries witnessed the rise of the *Indiculus universalis*, which represented an attempt among learned men of the age to compartmentalize man-made and inorganic objects often along taxonomic lines. The taxonomic classification of diseases, in particular, owes much of its impetus to Linnaeus:

> [Linnaeus] felt obliged, as a professor of medicine, to compel all different diseases to take their places in a framework of classes, orders, genera, and species; here he could follow his friend Boissier de Sauvages of Montpellier, who had already drafted such a classification. Later on, the Finnish physician Johan Haartman, a student of Linnaeus ... completed a still more detailed nosology in the same spirit. (Leikola 1987:47).

Of course, any strictly taxonomic nosology would fail to capture the relations between disease "morphology" (i.e. symptoms) and "underlying nature" (i.e. pathology). Jaundice and diarrhoea, for instance, are symptomatic of diverse pathologies, while the pathologies of dementia and syphilis are associated with diverse symptoms. In fact, concern with taxonomic nosologies seems by and large restricted to doctors and naturalists of the seventeenth and eighteenth centuries, and to twentieth-century ethnolinguistics and ethnomedicine. Most folk have no need or use for it.

2. What exactly this "logic of oppositions" is intended to express is actually logically unfathomable. Mathematical analogies are given ranging from lattice-theory (Lévi-Strauss 1949/1969a), to group-theory (1962/1966) to category-theory (1971). But the supposed social manifestations of "lattices" lack all formal power (see Chomsky 1968) and the "groups" invariably contain principles in contradiction to mathematical axioms (see Regnier 1968). Myth, argues Lévi-Strauss, is perhaps analyzable in terms of category theory, which was developed as a foundation theory for mathematics. The implication seems to be that the formal foundations of mathematics and myth are structurally of a sort: mathematics alone of the activities of thought is like myth in representing, as it were, the free play of the mind reflecting upon itself. But the "category-theory" he actually cites concerns purely descriptive models of social networks and contains little, if anything, of significance to mathematical foundation-theory.

3. Particularistic interpretations of cultural norms, values, behaviors, institutions and social history are not only worthwhile, but indispensable to an understanding of actual human performance and all that goes with it: from "what makes Johnny run?" to the causes of conflict. But relativism as a professional doctrine of ethnologists runs the gamut from the strident to the ludicrous. Jorion (1986), for example, calls upon anthropology to "begin again from zero" so that peoples studied may be able to break through the official jargon to "speak for themselves," as it were. On this view, formalist arguments for cross-cultural universals are not only dubious, they are downright suspicious (perhaps vestiges of imperialism, or at least eurocentrism). On a less ideological plane, Pollock (1986) provides a telling example of the theoretical and substantive value of unbridled relativism in her article, "Food classification in three pacific societies." In the introduction we are told that "the concept of food in Fiji, Hawaii, and Tahiti contrasts markedly with that in parts of the western world." This is only to be expected in view of the fact that even the nature of the grammatical construction "my taro" in Fijian is different from that of, say, "my apple" in English. How surprising, then, to find in the conclusion that: "whatever the proto-historic and pre-European links of the food system between the three societies, it is clear from the post-contact records and ethnographic reports that *food was highly valued in many Pacific societies*" (my italics). An astounding conclusion that requires the author to cite further sources in support of the idea that food may be important to people other than ourselves.

4. Young children may, however, ascribe peculiarly human psychological properties to other animals until they learn otherwise (Carey 1985a). Also, children may make empirical mistakes about what is or is not alive, especially in regard to distant (e.g. the sun) or ill perceived (e.g. coral) objects (Klinberg 1957). But the idea that there is a genuinely prelogical or precausal thought, whether for preliterate folk (Lévy-Bruhl 1923/1966; Durkheim and Mauss 1903/1963) or children (Piaget 1928), is frankly unintelligible given the behavior of any normal human that manages to walk and talk. Nor is possession of logical and causal cognitive competence in the least cast into doubt by the fact that preliterate folk "while expert in the practical skills and details necessary to operate their institutions, are usually unable to view and describe their operation as a whole, or to formulate general principles of their operation as a whole or . . . to distinguish between logical and narrative order" (Hallpike 1976:266). Take the case of language as a social institution. Perhaps the day will come when science can explicitly formulate the laws of language structure and use that humans spontaneously employ so effortlessly yet are scarcely able to articulate. But this does not imply what Hallpike's reasoning would suggest – that until that day humanity remains "prelinguistic."

5. Other sorts of representations, like those associated with notions of honor or equality, may have a long-lasting and wide distribution in a given society, but not in other societies. Such representations, although culturally idiosyncratic, may proliferate among a population because

of their ability to affix themselves to a large range of institutionalized hosts in the cultural ecology. Alfred Gell has suggested that social equality, for example, may be rooted in psychologically more primary representations of physical or numerical equality; but the root sense within political and social discourse has been simplified to an intrinsically dimensionless notion of "sameness" that can be attached to virtually any cultural dimension – like a bacterium that readily adapts to practically any habitat.

As such, "equality" can be imbued with as much or as little "meaning" as the Maoist cliché, "let a thousand flowers bloom." It thus becomes a convenient ideological accompaniment to other ideological constructs such as "democracy" and "communism." As an ideological construct it may serve as prop (or blind) to such institutional parameters in the cultural ecology as social mobility and political participation, and it may transform as those parameters change. While the psychologist may find little definite cognitive structure to study in such a notion, the anthropologist has a full-time (and rather traditional) job of analyzing this sort of "pathogen."

6. Adults, too: Take the empty word "dax" and try it out on someone. Tell the person anything you like about "dax," such as its "being cute." The learner, perhaps after failing to find it in the dictionary, may assume it's a child or a pet. If no irony seems intended, it is likely at least to be thought of as a physical object. If you later say, "so I put it on my kid's shelf," perhaps the hearer will call to mind a stuffed animal or some other artifact. Because the possibilities of association and understanding are initially far underdetermined by context, the information already evoked will be stored and manipulated meta-representationally. Then, when new contexts and occasions of use arise, the learner can further attempt to hone down meaning.

7. The term "metaphor" is loosely used here as a synonym for analogy. Actually, metaphors and all other figures of speech differ from pronouncements containing symbolic and scientific analogies in that they lay no claim to truth.

8. Admittedly, in the early stages of any speculative advance there may be little to distinguish scientific from symbolic uses of analogy. Thus, it may well be that western creation myths initially incited Newton to conceptualize matter in terms of force while the oriental symbolism of yin and yang may have inspired Bohr's view of subject and object as complementary determinants of physical reality (cf. Holton 1973); and divination doubtlessly played a part in provoking thought about the underlying nature of living kinds. But as speculation matures, the methodological differences between scientist and mystic quickly render the epistemological distinction obvious.

To be sure, symbolic analogies may also find their way into scientific discourse as sacred dogmas and so impede scientific progress. To some extent, belief in a scale of physical perfection may have been ethnically driven by religious expectation and hence, for a time, rendered morally unassailable. Still, the socially contrived aspect of the "epistemological block" can usually be divorced from any cognitive impediment generated by the analogy as such. With respect to science, Providence has no cognitive import unless it proves logically consistent and empirically consequent (and scientists generally come to an accord on such matters once they agree on terms).

9. In line with Foucault, Lloyd sees the atavistic symbolism of traditional lore reasserting itself following the decline of Greece: "In the Middle Ages and Renaissance a similar predilection for the marvellous or anecdotal only gradually yielded once again to attempts at more systematic zoological taxonomies" (1983:57).

10. Actually, Jacob conceives of mythico-religious tales as "moral" stories "repeated in the same form, with the same words, from generation to generation" (1981:29–31; cf. Smith 1984). To the contrary, Lévi-Strauss views myth as neither fixed nor necessarily moral; it carries no particular message of social value because its elements are constantly in flux from telling to telling. Here at least, Lévi-Strauss's notion of mythical thought relates to hermeneutics. In any event, Jacob does not claim that the hermeneutical tradition was particularly marked by "moral" tales, nor does his conception of "myth" have much to do with the subject of mythology as usually construed by anthropologists. Still, his rendition of the "signatures" of Renaissance hermeneutics, like Foucault's, closely follows Lévi-Strauss's analysis of the "semantics" of folk myths. In this connection, it merits note that Lévi-Strauss, Foucault and

Jacob wrote on these related subjects while contemporaries on the faculty of the Collège de France.

11. Also, "such a hotchpotch" of superficial similarities does not have the relevance to the classificatory aspect of "folk biology in contemporary, small-scale, non-literate societies" that Ellen (1979:29) suggests.

12. Clearly unwarranted is the assertion that only in the age of Ray, Tournefort and Linnaeus did it become *conceivable* for natural history to arrange living kinds among themselves by "restricting analysis to phenomena alone" (Jacob 1970/1973:30), that is, "undertaking a meticulous examination of things themselves for the first time, and then ... transcribing what it has gathered in smooth, neutralized, and faithful words" (Foucault 1966/1970:131). The apparent source of this miraculous view of intellectual change is the dubious Bachelardian assumption that prescientific thought was (and is) culturally idiosyncratic and capricious, while the proto-scientific thought of the seventeenth and eighteenth centuries broke with the "specious" knowledge of similitudes: "against natural training, against the diverse and colored fact ... by purifying natural substances and ... arranging scrambled phenomena" (Bachelard 1980:23). In point of anthropological fact, however, the "arrangement" of "scrambled phenomena" proves to be a cognitive mainstay of all prescientific folk. As for "the diverse and colored fact," it already appears somewhat bleached in Brunfels and positively monotone in Cesalpino.

13. The deliberate isolation of an element of "negative analogy" is, as Hesse (1966) stresses, a hallmark of theory building in science. The recognition of a negative analogy allows one to make a distinction between a familiar system and that system used as a model in connection with a theory formed by stripping away the negative analogy. Although Hesse's analysis of the relative importance of negative analogy to scientific-theory construction pertains to the use of analogy in semiformal or mathematical models, the point can also be made more generally to cover genuine theoretical advances in hitherto obscure empirical domains. This is also the case with Cesalpino's (1593) revolutionary theory of the circulation of the blood flow in animals. For clarity and insight, it was unsurpassed by any of Cesalpino's predecessors; and for the better part of a century, only Harvey's theory of "closed" circulation can be deemed a marked improvement (cf. Pagel 1967:169–81).

14. It was Wolff's (1774) microscopic investigations at the growing point of the plant stem that provided him with the key to an understanding of the early stages in the formation of the chick embryo. These findings underscored his claim that plants and animals are similarly composed, at least in the initial stage. He conjectured that embryological development proceeds under the influence of an admittedly unknown essential nature (*vis essentialis*): beginning with the primary "cellular" substance (*Zellsubstantz*), an organism progressively emerges that is presumably structured in accordance with its essential nature.

15. According to Harvey:

> The conception in viviparous animals is analogous to the seed and fruit of plants, just as is the egg in viviparous creatures and the worm in spontaneous productions, or some bubble containing moisture with vital heat. In all these the same thing is inherent whereby we may truly call them seeds, that is, that thing out of which and by which as the pre-existent material, artificer and organ, every living creature is first made and born.
>
> (1653/1981:282)

Harvey's lack of detailed empirical knowledge of mammalian reproductive anatomy caused him to misplace the locus of conception, to deny the necessity of physical contact between semen and egg, and to underplay the role of the uterus. Like the mammalian *conceptus*, the seed of plants seemed to be a virtually autonomous and detachable entity – a vital primordium. This accorded well with his metaphysical view of an eternal species-form prior to, and apart from, the vagaries of environmental or parental influence.

16. Broadly speaking, early mechanism had it that through the mere disposition of the material bases in which the motive forces of a device inhere, action is generated and power channeled for the performance of particular tasks suitable to the device's specific constitution.

17. Concerning the notion of an atomistic or corpuscular system, whereas followers of Leucippus, Democratus and Epicurus used analogies to bring living things under the aegis of such a material organization, Aristotle, like Cesalpino after him, rejected such attempts to simply reduce the organic to the inorganic.

18. In general terms, pedagogical analogies are heuristic aids that use the organizing principles of a familiar base-domain to guide inferences in an initially less familiar target-domain. Other examples are Aristotle's likening of ontogenesis to intention, Harvey's comparison of the heart to a pump or Bohr's modeling of atoms as miniature solar systems. Such heuristics deliberately simplify, and even falsify, the empirical situation to facilitate exposition and application. By contrast, formative analogies imply a measure of metaphysical commitment that heuristics lack. Examples are Aristotle's likening of plant to animal life, Candolle's comparison of generation and crystallization and the "functional" interpretation of human conceptualization capabilities in terms apposite to the information processing capacities of a computer.

    To some extent, of course, the boundary between these two sorts of analogy is fuzzy, dependent as it is on how deeply the (ontological) attachment to the analogy goes (cf. Kuhn 1977). Moreover, those formative analogies of yesterday that were intimately associated with the development of powerful theories now known to be false may become the pedagogical analogies of tomorrow. But at any given moment in the development of a scientific theory it is usually possible to distinguish the "exegetical" from the "constitutive" metaphor by the fact that the former, but not the latter, is replaceable by nonmetaphorical teaching techniques (Boyd 1979).

19. Few, if any, natural historians subscribed to the orthodox view of such natural philosophers as Huygens:

    > Des Cartes recognized better than his predecessors that in Physics one can not understand more than may be related to Principles that do not extend beyond the scope of our mind, such as those that depend on bodies considered without qualities, & on their movements.
    > (1690, preface)

    Thus, Garden typifies the natural historian's lament: "We see how wretchedly Descartes came off when he began to apply the laws of motion to the forming of an animal" (1691:476–477; cf. Lyon and Sloan 1981:16).

20. As McGuire shows, in Newton's case the metaphysics of analogy is meant to justify "transduction," that is, the methodological procedure of applying axioms and hypotheses concerning the sensible realm to the world of intangible entities. Indeed, the postulate that there are such intangible entities at all is itself grounded in the analogy:

    > knowledge of essential qualities of sensible bodies is more securely transferred to the imperceptible in terms of the postulation of a chain which exists between the two orders ... primordial entities differ only in size, but not in kind, from sensible bodies. Moreover, they have in common only the essential qualities of the latter which we know from experience .... Though we cannot observe the primordial particles we can give content, by thinking through and by means of the underlying analogy, to a claim to know the nature of matter in general.
    > (McGuire 1970:40)

21. It is upon analogy, then, that the more plausible speculations of natural philosophy and natural history depend:

    > Observing, I say, such gradual and gentle descents downwards in those parts of the creation that are beneath man, the rule of analogy may make it probable, that it is so also in things above us ... ascending upwards towards the infinite perfection of the Creator, by gentle steps and differences, that are at every one at no great distance from the next to it. This sort of probability, which is the best conduct of rational experiments, and the rise of hypotheses, has also its use and influence; and a wary reasoning from analogy, leads us often into the discovery of truths and useful productions, which would otherwise lie concealed.
    > (Locke 1689/1848 IV,xvi,12)

22. For those natural historians adopting Leibniz's general view of things, the complete dissolution of the phenomenal world, progressively and by degrees, into ubiquitous mechanical principles could no longer be taken as a plausible program. The scale of natures would reappear in a Leibnizian world with a vengeance. Natural kinds would be multiplied indefinitely across the phenomenal spectrum, each representing an immanent reality, containing the preformed germs of all past, present and future *individuals* destined to actualize the kind's existence in the course of time (see Bonnet 1782).

23. According to Lovejoy (1936/1964:228–229), Buffon followed Locke in rejecting "the concept of species" but "soon abandoned this position" (see also Canguilhem 1968:342; Roger 1971:583; Jacob 1970/73:146; Mayr 1982:334). But nowhere does Buffon deny the existence of species. It is the following passage that seems to have confounded the commentators:

> In general the more one increases the number of divisions of natural productions, the more one approaches the truth, because in nature only individuals really exist;

"and," the passage continues, it is:

> that orders and classes exist only in our imagination (& *que les genres, les ordres & les classes n'existent que dans notre imagination*). (1749,I:38)

But species, which exist "in succession, in renewal and in duration" (1749,II:3), cannot be considered merely general ideas. (Note that the ideas expressed in the first two volumes of Buffon's *Histoire naturelle* were formulated before 1746 and published together in 1748).

A further source of confusion is Adanson's (1763:clxiij–clxiv) misquote of the passage from the first volume of *Histoire Naturelle* to the effect that what exist are "only individuals and genera" (*que des individus et les genres*). This leads Stafleu (1963:183) to express "surprise" at the privileged position that Buffon would then seem to inconsistently accord genera.

24. Buffon declares:

> An individual is nothing in the universe, a hundred or a thousand individuals are still nothing. Species are the only beings in nature; perpetual beings, as ancient and permanent as nature herself . . . each may be considered as a whole that may be counted as one in the works of creation and that, consequently, is but one unit in nature . . . a day, a century, an age, all the portions of time do not come to a part of its duration; time itself is only relative to individuals, to beings whose existence is fleeting; but species being constant, their permanence constitutes duration, and their difference constitutes number.
>
> (1765,XIII:i)

Sloan (1979:114–5) notes that Buffon's idea of time being coextensive with species does not come directly from Leibniz, but from von Wolff's elaboration of Leibniz. According to Leibniz, time is immanent in the relations between concrete bodies; whereas for von Wolf (1736), it is the *successive ordering* of concrete bodies in a *continuous series* that constitutes time. On Buffon's account, species are precisely, and preeminently, such series.

25. If species are indefinitely extended in time, while our experience is limited, how can we know they *really* exist? As Sloan (1987) points out, Buffon's answer appears to rely on arguments similar to those first formulated by Jakob Bernoulli (1713) in his work on the probabilistic foundations of human knowledge. For Bernoulli, as for Leibniz, reality consists in the ordering of concrete events. But contrary to Leibniz, knowing to what extent the order we observe corresponds to the real metaphysical order demands more than intuition. It requires a probability calculus. Such a calculus must be designed to quantitatively justify induction from an observed series to a true series by degrees of "moral certitude."

In Buffon's "moral arithmetic" (in Lyon and Sloan 1981:51–73), first developed around 1730, the mere addition of confirming observations geometrically increases probability: "certitude doubles with each new experiment." Although we can never be more than "morally" certain of our finite experiences with a series, we can be "physically" certain about the extension of that series to the degree that repeated experiences confirm the pattern we perceive. Applied to species, this manner of reasoning assumedly afford human beings the greatest possible certitude with respect to Nature. Not only does the species provide an inexhaustible number of confirmations for a repeating series, but the recurrent succession of physical individuals of which we may be morally quite certain constitutes the very stuff of which time and nature are actually composed. Just as a finite number series constitutes the only true series of natural numbers, so the recurrent order of physical individuals constitutes the only persistent sort of causal line, or lawful kind of "general effect," in nature. In matters of truth, abstract mathematical notions, such as the infinite number series or geometrical infinity (1749,II:27), are as specious – as "gratuitous" – as the notional genera and species of Linnaean taxonomy (1749,I:37–40).

26. Farber (1973:67) writes that: "Buffon worked within the Lockean tradition that rejected real essences." Yet, neither Locke nor Buffon ever denied the existence of real essences. All Locke claimed was that real essences are unknowable, and that we cannot presume the real essences of individuals to be the same in kind, because there is never any guarantee that our nominal phenomenal kinds coincide with real nomic kinds. Buffon, however, always believed that we could locate real nomic kinds (e.g. species) in Nature, and he eventually came to believe that true knowledge of the intimate, mechanical structure underlying their generation was possible.

27. It is this *moule intérieure* that makes heat, attraction, space and time immanent in the living world. Each mold is a particular configuration of molecules that became organic because they were heat-sensitized. Organic molecules therefore differ from brute matter only with regard to their heat-retaining (because originally heat-sensitized) capacities. Insofar as the particular historical circumstances that obtained in our solar system with respect to its thermal character have changed, there is virtually no possibility that new organic molecules and molds will arise on earth. They will on other planets.

28. Not even Cuvier himself, though, was free from talk about "higher" and "lower" animals. Darwin was dead set against the distinction; but it nevertheless appears in terms similar to those used by *scala* theoreticians in accounts of evolution well into the present century (e.g. Wells *et al.* 1934).

29. Stafleu (1971b; cf. Szyfman 1982) opposes Lamarck's dynamic and "revolutionary" "romanticism" and "empiricism" to Cuvier's static and "conservative" "neoplatonism" and "essentialism":

> It is clear that Lamarck is essentially a scientific positivist . . . observed facts are the only basis for science. Scientific concepts should be free from metaphysics . . . . [Cuvier], however, was thoroughly eighteenth century and still imbued with many *a priori* assumptions.

But Lamarck, no less than Cuvier, was "imbued with many *a priori* assumptions," including belief in the anthropocentric *scala naturae* as a cosmic "final cause." Moreover, Lamarck's every assumption about the effects of the environment on organic change are biased to his own peculiar brand of Newtonian physicalism. Of course, such "metaphysical" frameworks as these may have skewed observations, but they also told one where to look for "facts" and thus provided a necessary foothold in the flux of data; for, there just is no such thing as a simple "observed fact" independent of all (*a priori*) conceptual frameworks.

30. This stance is somewhat independent of the very real issues concerning the problematic role of models in science, generally, and physics, in particular. In that regard, the influence of Duhem on the Bachelardian school and of Mach on logical positivism is clearly legitimate. But when wrongheaded anthropological and psychological claims are invoked to resolve epistemological issues in scientific-theory construction the arguments become spurious. So, for instance, given the Greek commitment to common-sense realism, the whole Aristotelian ontology of essence, form and matter is misconstrued as the lingering vestige of a primitive disposition to the "analogical fallacy" called "substantialization of abstracta" (Reichenbach 1951; cf. Joly 1968).

31. As Gaukroger notes, however, the distinction Bachelard draws exhibits a fundamental inconsistency: if common sense is only given *in a culture*, and not in an absolute way, then "both the objects of science and common sense are not strictly 'given', but must be 'constructed' in some way" (1976:236). Moreover, although Bachelard implies that concepts judged by present standards to be "scientific" *always* have a role to play in future scientific discourse, in fact there is no guarantee that the natural kinds denoted by predicates in current scientific theories will persevere as law-abiding referents in future theories. Any given scientific discourse is therefore no more secure against fundamental alteration than is common-sense discourse. This leads Gaukroger to argue for some positive measure of historical interaction between common sense and science.

Gaukroger thus correctly suggests that common sense is not invariably an obstacle to science. But this is not because they are merely relative to one another and to the culture they emerge in. Rather, common sense serves as a psychologically absolute standard against which the progress of science can be measured. Bachelard is basically right to claim that common sense is phenomenally "given" while science is not. Only, he is wrong to assume (as Gaukroger also does) that these givens are culturally parochial.

32. Consider, by comparison, the relationship between Riemannian geometry (the geometry of modern astronomy) and Euclidean geometry (the terrestrial geometry of the ancients and quite possibly the natural geometry of all folk). Riemannian geometry has both logical incompatibilities with Euclidean geometry as well as intuitive affinities (e.g. one understands a straight line in the former by thinking of a great arc in the latter). Indeed, it may be that Riemannian geometry is not even *conceivable* independently of Euclidean geometry, yet is logically distinct from it. Provided use of Euclidean geometry is restricted to its natural domain of application in earth measurement it remains plausibly not only the most natural geometry we can think of but also manifestly true – not in a cosmic sense, but phenomenally. Moreover, when exploring the microscopic and astronomical dimensions of the nonphenomenal universe we dare not leave all our terrestrial baggage behind, lest we be left flailing aimlessly about in the lurch. The point is that science goes beyond ordinary knowledge by a selective and nonarbitrary development of basic common-sense dispositions.

33. From Aristotle to Buffon, heat constituted a locus of speculations as to the causes underlying the coming into being of living kinds; however, the properties of this internal "fire" were never obvious: "Now although to our sense of feeling heat may not be manifest, its presence for that reason is not to be denied; for whatever is not warm to the touch we habitually feel as cold" (Cesalpino 1583:4). The characteristic warmth associated with the pulse of vertebrates was extended to invertebrates and plants by variously invoking a diverse range of "hot" phenomena: from brimstone to passion, from starlight to the sirocco.

10 *Rudiments of the Linnaean hierarchy: towards an anthropology of science*

1. In time, increase in information as to morphological and anatomical relationships at higher levels led to a conception of Order wherein the relationships between families seemed as compelling as relationships within families on any of the current interpretations of what taxonomy was supposed to represent in nature. In botany, it seems, the idea of orders superordinate to families stems directly from an acknowledgement of the importance of interfamily relationships within the flowering plants, especially those relationships established by the techniques of comparative morphology first developed by Auguste-Pyrame de Candolle and Robert Brown. But through the first half of the nineteenth century there was still no comprehensive system of orders (Sachs 1875/1890:145; cf. Richard 1852).

2. Even plant life-forms have long continued to serve as convenient, and not entirely "unnatural," frameworks for organizing an understanding of a *local flora* for professional naturalists who otherwise reject life-forms as general botanical taxa. Thus, we find Linnaeus reporting exotic genera in terms of their life-form status; for example, in the *Critica Botanica* (1737b sec. 238) three new American genera are introduced: *Hernandia* (*arbor Americana*), a tree, *Plumeria* (*arbuscula Americana*), a bush, and *Milleria* (*planta Americana*), a herb. Similarly, Bartlett (1935;

cf. Bartlett 1926), in his report on the flora of the Batak lands of North Sumatra, employs the sorts of life-forms used by the Batak themselves in organizing the local flora: (a) tree and shrubs, (b) herbs, (c) ferns, and (d) mosses. Many an ethnobotanist and field naturalist does likewise.

3. This space-saving agency of the hierarchical system, however, cannot be applied in unrestricted fashion to evolutionary taxa, especially when there is reversal or parallel evolution.

4. Ultimately, however, the adequacy of the species concept in an axiomatized account of evolutionary theory will depend on whether it can be lawfully instantiated, that is, on there being evolutionary *principles* of competitive exclusion and reproductive isolation that yield all and only species. Maybe there are just no *general* conditions on the relations between geographical boundaries and genetic isolating mechanisms that allow for a regular determination of species status. But even if delimitation of species proves to be a purely local and contingent affair there is little warrant for Dwyer's contention that the ecological species usually apprehended by tribal folk constitutes the only "objective species" and that reproductive criteria merely reflect "attempts to rationalize the 'reality' of the species in terms of the ideology of evolution" (1976a:433). The morpho-ecological criteria that folk apply do tend to yield relatively stable local groupings because human minds are predisposed to pick out stimuli that evolution rather consistently reproduces (at least in the short term).

Still, given the general concordance between ecological and reproductive criteria, it is not surprising to find that basic-level folk taxa may, in the case of species relatively unfamiliar to the modern biologist, initially prove a more correct guide to taxonomic status than does scientific classification; following an ethnobiological analysis of the Karam (New Guinea) frog speciemes *kosoj* and *wyt*, for instance, biologists came to agree that there were indeed two species (*Hyla angiana* and *H. disrupta*), rather than the one (*H. becki*) previously thought (Bulmer and Tyler 1968:376). But basic folk kinds do not invariably circumscribe genetically self-regulating populations, which are hardly "ideological" constructs. Thus, herpetologists have shown that morphologically dissimilar and geographically separated local populations can actually belong to the same species (e.g. *Holbrookia maculata*) and, conversely, that geographically coexisting and morphologically similar populations may constitute distinct species (e.g. *Rana chiricahuensis* and *R. urticularia*) (cf. Cole 1984). Even though folk may be, or may become, aware of reproductive distinctions that do not fully accord with morpho-geographic distinctions, they may well persist in believing that only morpho-geographic kinds are basic (cf. Dwyer 1976b).

5. The legacy of taxonomic ranking, like that of the species, is not entirely without problems. The psychological and historical impulse to render phyletic branching as a taxonomic hierarchy has given short shrift to a careful analysis of the branching process itself. Perhaps because of these constraints on representation, only now are taxonomists really beginning to grapple with the difficult issues of hybridization and lateral gene transfer in evolutionary branching and diversification.

6. Of course, the fact that a given conceptual framework is well tried does not warrant the claim that it is, *ispo facto*, true and natural: "Do not work with stable concepts . . . . Do not be seduced into thinking that you have at last found the correct description of the 'facts' when all that has happened is that some new categories have been adopted to some older forms of thought, which are so familiar that we take their outlines to be outlines of the world itself" (Feyerabend 1975). The fact of the relative constancy of taxonomy across changes in theoretical interpretation is not necessarily proof of the reality of taxonomy, as Dobzhansky (1937:305) seems to suggest. On the contrary, it may indicate an epistemologically lax proclivity to put new wine in old clouded bottles (Stevens 1984a). If the relatively steadfast historical thread is considered not a direct line on truth, but a filiation of real puzzles to be explained – a means of weaving successive theories to one another and to the world that appears to us – then the undeniable progress of science in understanding nature makes rational sense, even if nature ultimately dissolves the stitching.

7. Although, where there is evidence of consistency in the performance and interpretation of certain tasks, lay notions of the causes of motion may be simply wrong from a sophisticated standpoint (cf. Clement 1982; McCloskey 1983).

8. As with natural history, appreciations of the relation between natural philosophy and common sense have been skewed by a failure to distinguish the respective bounds of ordinary factual

thinking, mythico–religious symbolism and scientific speculation. Thus, for Popper (1958–1959), some early theories, or "myths," are more closely related to common sense than others: Thales's explanation of earthquakes, in terms of the movement of the earth upon the water it supposedly rides, is "at least inspired by observational analogy." But Popper goes on to argue that common sense itself can actually be a hindrance to the progress of science because it leads otherwise powerful and independently motivated speculation back to artificially constraining observational analogies. Take the case of Anaximander: his speculation on the free suspension of the earth was assumedly a properly scientific theory in that it was both a direct criticism of a previous theory (Thales's) and a direct antecedent of modern scientific findings; however, he was misled by "common-sense theory" to suppose the earth was flat like a column-drum.

Granted, such observational analogies as "the earth is flat like a column-drum" or "the earth rides on water like a ship" are compatible with common sense; for, sheer intuition about what is self-evidently true cannot, by itself, falsify the putative claims to truth expressed by such analogies. Yet, assertions to the effect that such analogies convey truth (or even likelihood) are not claims *of* common sense, as Popper insinuates, nor are they in any way implied by common sense. For if common sense can provide no intuitions to falsify such claims, neither can it provide the intuitions to verify them. Such analogies lie beyond the natural, innately determined, phenomenal bounds of common sense. Moreover, neither the free-suspension theory nor the theory that the earth is a sphere are *incompatible* with common sense. Indeed, in *de Caelo* Aristotle points to the readily apparent character of the horizon in defense of the earth's sphericity, while the idea of free-suspension in Anaximander is supported by the visibly fixed distance of the stars.

In his debate with Popper over the contribution of the pre-Socratics to natural philosophy, Kirk (1960) suggests that: e.g. (1) Thales's idea of a water-supported earth was "borrowed" from the myths of the riverine civilizations; (2) these myths, in turn, were "natural ideas" that were "firmly based . . . upon observation and experience" (327); and (3) such myths derived from common-sense notions that were themselves "inductive" in the sense of being "based on an indefinite number of particulars," although the inductions could be "intuitive" and "subconscious" (321). But Kirk also mistakes the relation between science, symbolism and common sense; (3) particulars can only confirm, but logically they cannot produce, any general intuition; (2) myths symbolically reconstrue common experiences, but not in any firm or consistent way; and (1) to the extent that Anaximander was able to criticize (the propositional content of) Thales's theory, there could be nothing mythical about it. The putative sequence observation → common sense → myth → science is not logically consequent.

9. It would be misleading to talk of a special human common-sense disposition as if it were merely a matter of norms and deviation, as with the pseudo-scientific notion "I.Q." The selection of mutations responsible for the development of any such cerebral disposition would be no more a fluke or mystery than that responsible for the development of any regularly identifiable bodily organ. In this sense, it would be no more misleading to talk of *a* human cognitive disposition than of, say, *a* human retina.

10. A good argument, however, might be made for basic improvements in technology being largely independent of advances in science.

REFERENCES

Adanson, M. (1763) *Familles des plantes*, 2 vols. Paris: Vincent.

   (1847) *Cours d'histoire naturelle. Fait en 1772 par Michel Adanson*. Paris: Fortin, Masson and Cie.

Aldrovandi, U. (1668) *Dendrologiae naturalis scilicet arborum historiae libri duo*. Bononiae: Ferronii.

Alston, C. (1754) *A dissertation on botany*. London: Benj. Dodd.

Anglin, J. (1977) *Word, object, and conceptual development*. New York: W. W. Norton and Co. Inc.

Appel, T. (1980) Henri de Blainville and the animal series: a nineteenth-century chain of being. *Journal of the History of Biology*, 13:291–319.

Aquinas, T. (1955) *Somme théologique [Summa theologiae]*, 6 vols., trans. A.-M. Rouget. Paris: Desclée.

   (1946) *Tractatus de unitate intellectus contra Averroistas*. Rome: Gregorian University.

Arber, A. (1950) *The natural philosophy of plant form*, Darien, Conn.: Hafner.

   (1953) From medieval herbalism to the birth of modern botany. In: *Science, medicine and history*, ed. E. Underwood. Oxford.

Aristotle (The abbreviations are those of the Liddell-Scott-Jones Lexicon).

APo	*Analytica Posteriora*
APr.	*Analytica Priora*
Cat.	*Categoriae*
de An.	*de Anima*
GA	*de Generatione Animalium*
HA	*Historia Animalium*
IA	*de Incessu Animalium*
Int.	*de Interpretatione*
Metaph.	*Metaphysica*
PA	*de Partibus Animalium*
Ph.	*Physica*
Pol.	*Politica*
Top.	*Topica*

Armstrong, S.; Gleitman, L.; & Gleitman, H. (1983) What some concepts might not be. *Cognition*, 13:263–308.

Ayer, A. (1976) *The central questions of philosophy*, Harmondsworth: Penguin.

Bachelard, G. (1965) *L'activité rationaliste de la physique contemporaine*, Paris: Presses Universitaires de France (originally published in 1951).

(1980) *La formation de l'esprit scientifique*, 11th ed. Paris: Vrin (originally published in 1938).

Bacon, F. (1639) *Sylva sylvarum, or naturall historie*, 5th ed. London: Rawley.

Bacon, R. (1930) *Opera hactenus medita Rogeri Baconi*, vol. 10: *Questiones supra libros prime philosophie Aristotelis*, ed. R. Steele. Oxford: Clarendon Press.

Balme, D. (1962) GENOS and EIDOS in Aristotle's biology. *Classical Quarterly*, 12:81–98.

(1970) Aristotle and the beginnings of zoology. *Journal of the Society for the Bibliography of Natural History*, 5:272–85.

(1972) Notes to Aristotle's *De partibus animalium and de generatione animalium I*. Oxford: Oxford University Press.

(1980) Aristotle's biology was not essentialist. *Archiv für Geschichte der Philosophie*, 62:1–12.

(1987a) The place of biology in Aristotle's philosophy. In: *Philosophical issues in Aristotle's biology*, ed. A. Gotthelf and J. Lennox. Cambridge: Cambridge University Press.

(1987b) Aristotle's use of division and differentiae. In: *Philosophical issues in Aristotle's biology*, ed. A. Gotthelf and J. Lennox. Cambridge: Cambridge University Press.

(1987c) Teleology and necessity. In: *Philosophical issues in Aristotle's biology*, ed. A. Gotthelf and J. Lennox. Cambridge: Cambridge University Press.

Bartlett, H. (1926) Sumatran plants in Asahan and Karoland, with notes on their vernacular names. *Michigan Academy of Sciences, Arts and Letters*, 6:1–66.

(1935) The Batak lands of North Sumatra. *Natural and Applied Science Bulletin*, 4:211–323 (University of the Philippines).

(1940) History of the generic concept in botany. *Bulletin of the Torrey Botanical Club*, 47:319–62.

Basso, K. (1972) Ice travel among the Fort Normal Slave: folk taxonomies and cultural rules. *Language in Society*, 1:31–49.

Bauhin, C. (1623) *Pinax theatri botanici*. Basel: Regis.

Beckner, M. (1959) *The biological way of thought*. New York: Columbia University Press.

Belon, P. (1555) *L'histoire de la nature des oyseaux*, Paris: Cavellat.

Benson, L. (1962) *Plant taxonomy*. New York: Ronald.

Berkeley, G. (1734) *A treatise concerning the principles of human knowledge ... to which are added three dialogues between Hylas and Philonous ... first printed in the year 1713*, London: Tonson.

Berlin, B. (1972) Speculations on the growth of ethnobotanical nomenclature. *Language and Society*, 1:63–98.

(1973) The relation of folk systematics to biological classifications and nomenclature. *Annual Review of Systematics and Ecology*, 4:259–71.

(1974) Further notes on covert categories. *American Anthropologist*, 76:327–331.

(1976) The concept of rank in ethnobiological classification: Some evidence from Aguaruna folk botany. *American Ethnologist*, 3:381–399.

(1978) Ethnobiological classification. In: *Cognition and categorization*, ed. E. Rosch and B. Lloyd, Hillsdale, N.J.: Lawrence Erlbaum Assocs., Ltd.

(1982a) Predicting discontinuities in ethnobiological classification. Paper presented at the Department of Anthropology Faculty Seminar, 22 November 1982, University of California, Berkeley.

(1982b) Natural and not-so-natural higher order categories in ethnobotanical classification. Paper read before the Anthropology Section of the New York Academy of Sciences, 26 April 1982, New York.

Berlin, B., Boster, J., and O'Neill, J. (1981) The perceptual basis of ethnobiological classification: evidence from Aguaruna folk ornithology. *Journal of Ethnobiology*, 1:95–108.

Berlin, B., Breedlove, D., and Raven, P. (1966) Folk taxonomies and biological classification. *Science*, 154:273–75.

(1968) Covert categories and folk taxonomies. *American Anthropologist*, 70:290–99.

(1973) General principles of classification and nomenclature in folk biology. *American Anthropologist*, 75:214–42.

(1974) *Principles of Tzeltal plant classification*. New York: Academic Press.

Berlin, B. and Kay, P. (1969) *Basic color terms: their universality and growth.* Berkeley: University of California Press.

Bernoulli, J. (1713) *Ars conjectandi.* Basel: Thurnisiorum.

Bianchi, H. (1957) Tournefort et la médecine. In: *Tournefort,* ed. R. Heims. Paris: Muséum National d'Histoire Naturelle.

Blackwelder, R. (1967) *Taxonomy.* New York: John Wiley and Sons, Inc.

Bloch, M. (1988) The concept of "wisdom" in Madagascar and elsewhere. Working Paper presented to the King's College Research Centre Conference on "The Representation of Complex Cultural Categories," Cambridge University, 22–24 March 1988.

Blumenbach, J. (1779) *Handbuch der Naturgeschichte.* Göttingen: Dietrich.

Bock, W. (1973) Philosophical foundations of classical evolutionary taxonomy. *Systematic Zoology,* 22:375–92.

Bock, H. (1539) *Kreütter Buch.* Strasbourg: W. Rihelius

[Hieronymi Tragi] (1552) *De stirpium.* Strasbourg: W. Rihelius.

Bonnet, C. (1782) *Contemplation de la nature,* 2nd ed. Hamburg: Virchaux.

Boster, J. (1980) How the exceptions prove the rule: an analysis of informant disagreement in Aguaruna manioc identification. Ph.D. dissertation, University of California, Berkeley.

(1987) Agreement among biological classification systems is not dependent on cultural transmission. *American Anthropologist,* 89:914–20.

Boster, J., Berlin, B., and O'Neill, J. (1986) The correspondence of Jivaroan to scientific ornithology. *American Anthropologist,* 88:569–83.

Bourgey, L. (1953) *Observation et expérience chez les médecins de la collection hippocratique.* Paris: Vrin.

(1955) *Observation et expérience chez Aristote.* Paris: Vrin.

Boyd, R. (1979) Metaphor and theory change: what's "metaphor" a metaphor for? In: *Metaphor and thought,* ed. A. Ortony. Cambridge: Cambridge University Press.

Boyle, R. (1667) *The origine of formes and qualities,* 2nd ed. Oxford: Davis.

Bremekamp, C. (1953a) A re-examination of Cesalpino's classification. *Acta Botanica Neerlandica,* 1:580–93.

(1953b) Linné's views on the hierarchy of taxonomic groups. *Acta Botanica Neerlandica,* 2:242–53.

Bretschneider, E. (1893) *Botanicon sinicum.* Notes on Chinese botany, from native and western sources. *Journal of the China Branch of the Royal Asiatic Society,* 25:1–468.

Bretzl, H. (1903) *Botanische Forschungen des Alexanderzuges.* Leipzig: Teubner.

Bright, J. and Bright, W. (1965) Semantic structure in Northwestern California and the Sapir-Whorf hypothesis. In: *Formal semantic analysis,* ed. E. Hammel. American Anthropologist Special Publications, vol. 67.

Broberg, G. (1983) Linnaeus's classification of man. In: *Linnaeus: the man and his work,* ed. T. Frängsmyr. Berkeley: University of California Press.

Brown, C. (1974) Unique beginners and covert categories in folkbiological taxonomies. *American Anthropologist,* 76:325–27.

(1977) Folk botanical life-forms: their universality and growth. *American Anthropologist,* 79:317–42.

(1979a) Folk zoological life-forms: their universality and growth. *American Anthropologist,* 81:791–817.

(1979b) Growth and development of folk botanical life-forms in the Mayan language family. *American Ethnologist,* 6:366–385.

(1982) Growth and development of folk-botanical life-forms in Polynesian languages. *The Journal of the Polynesian Society,* 91:213–243.

(1984a) *Language and living things: uniformities in folk classification and naming.* New Brunswick: Rutgers University Press.

(1984b) Life-forms from the perspective of "Language and living things". *American Ethnologist,* 11:589–93.

Brown, C. and Chase, P. (1981) Animal classification in Juchitan Zapotec. *The Journal of Anthropology,* 1:61–70.

REFERENCES

Brown, C., Kolar, J., Torrey, B., Truong-Quang, T., and Volkman, P. (1976) Some general principles of biological and non-biological classification. *American Ethnologist*, 3:73–85.

Brunel, G. and Morissette, L. (1969) Guérison et ethno-étiologie populaire. *Anthropologica*, 21:43–72.

Bruner, J., Olver, R. and Greenfield, P. (1966) *Studies in cognitive growth*. New York: John Wiley and Sons, Inc.

Brunfels, O. (1530–1536) *Herbarum vivae eicones*. Strasbourg: Schottu.

Buck, R. & Hull, D. (1966) The logical structure of the Linnaean hierarchy. *Systematic Zoology*, 15:97–110.

Buffon, G.-L. (1749–1767) *Histoire naturelle générale et particulière*, 15 vols. Paris: Imprimerie Royale.

Vol. 1: Premier discours. De la manière d'étudier et de traiter l'histoire naturelle [1749].

Vol. 2: Histoire des animaux [1749].

Vol. 4: L'asne [1753].

Vol. 5: De la chèvre [1755].

Vol. 9: Animaux communs aux deux continents [1761].

Vol. 10: Les tatous [1763].

Vol. 11: Le mouflon [1764].

Vol. 13: De la nature. Seconde vue [1765].

Vol. 14: Nomenclature des singes & De la dégénération des animaux [1766].

(1770) *Histoire naturelle des oiseaux*, 9 vols. Paris: Imprimerie Royale.

(1774–1789) *Histoire naturelle générale et particulière. Supplément*, 7 vol. Paris: Imprimerie Royale.

Vol. 2: Théorie de la terre. Partie hypothétique [1775].

Vol. 3: Des mulets [1776].

Vol. 5: Epoques de la nature [1778].

Bulmer, R. (1967) Why is the cassowary not a bird? *Man*, 2:5–25.

(1970) Which came first, the chicken or the egg-head? In: *Echanges et communications: mélanges offerts à Claude Lévi-Strauss*, ed. J. Pouillon and P. Maranda. The Hague: Mouton.

(1974) Folk biology in the New Guinea Highlands. *Social Science Information*, 13:9–28.

(1979) Kalam classification of birds. In: *Classifications in their social contexts*, ed. R. Ellen and D. Reason, pp. 57–79. New York: Academic Press.

Bulmer, R. and Tyler, M. (1968) Karam classification of frogs. *Journal of the Polynesian Society*, 77:333–85.

Burckhardt, R. (1977) *The spirit of system: Lamarck and evolutionary biology*. Cambridge, Mass.: Harvard University Press.

Burma, B. (1949) The species concept: a semantic review. *Evolution*, 3:369–73.

Cain, A. (1956) The genus in evolutionary taxonomy. *Systematic Zoology*, 5:97–109.

(1958) Logic and memory in Linnaeus's system of taxonomy. *Proceedings of the Linnaean Society of London*, 169:144–63.

(1959a) Deductive and inductive methods in post-Linnaean taxonomy. *Proceedings of the Linnaean Society of London*, 170:185–217.

(1959b) The post-Linnaean development of taxonomy. *Proceedings of the Linnaean Society of London*, 170:234–44.

Camerarius, R. (1694) De sexu plantarum epistola. *Academicae Caesareo Leopold*, vol. 8. Tübingen.

Candolle, A.-P. (1813) *Théorie élémentaire de la botanique*. Paris Déterville.

(1819) *Théorie élémentaire de la botanique*, 2nd ed. Paris: Déterville.

(1827) *Organographie végétale*. Paris: Déterville.

(1833) Note sur la division du règne végétal en quatre embranchements. *Bibliotèque Universelle de Genève. Sciences et Arts*, 18:259–68.

Canguilhem, G. (1968) *Etudes d'histoire et de philosophie des sciences*. Paris: Vrin.

(1981) *Idéologie et rationalité dans l'histoire des sciences de la vie*, 2nd ed. Paris: Vrin.

Carey, S. (1978) The child's concept of "animal". Paper presented to the Psychonomic Society, San Antonio.

(1985a) *Conceptual change in childhood*. Cambridge, Mass.: MIT Press.

(1985b) Constraints on semantic development. In: *Neonate cognition: beyond the blooming buzzing confusion*, ed. J. Mehler and R. Fox. Hillsdale, N.J.: Lawrence Erlbaum Assocs., Ltd.

Carnap, R. (1928) *Der logische Aufbau der Welt*. Berlin: Weltkreis-Verlag.

Cassirer, E. (1906) *Das Erkenntnisproblem in der Philosophie und Wissenschaft de neueren Zeit*. Berlin: Bruno Cassirer.

Cesalpino, A. (1571) *Questionum peripateticorum libri quinque*. Venice: Juntas.

(1583) *De plantis libri XVI*, Florence: Marescot.

(1593) *De medicamentorium facultatibus libri II*, Venice: Juntas.

Chomsky, N. (1968) *Language and mind*. New York: Harcourt Brace Jovanovich, Inc.

(1988) *Language and problems of knowledge: the Managua lectures*, MIT Press.

Clement, J. (1982) Students' preconceptions in introductory mechanics. *American Journal of Physics*, 50:66–71.

Cole, C. (1984) Taxonomy: what's in a name? *Natural History*, 93:30–4.

Colloquium (1986) "Les inuit du Nouveau-Quebec: appropriation du milieu naturel et savoirs autochtones". Centre National de la Recherche Scientifique, Paris, 28–30 May 1986.

Conklin, H. (1954) The relation of Hanunóo culture to the plant world. Ph.D. dissertation, Yale University.

(1962) Lexicographical treatment of folk taxonomies. In: *Problems in lexicography*, ed. F. Householder and S. Saporta. Report of the Conference on Lexicography, 11–12 November 1960, Indiana University Press.

Conry, Y. (1981) Une lecture newtonienne de Lamarck est-elle possible? In: *Lamarck et son temps. Lamarck et notre temps*. International Colloquium C.E.R.I.C. Paris: Vrin.

Cordus, V. (1561) *Valerii Cordi Simesusij Annotationes in Pedacij Dioscoridis Anazerabei de medica materia libros V [Historia stirpium]*, ed. C. Gesner. Strasbourg: J. Rihelius.

Corsi, P. (1983) *Oltre il mito: Lamarck e le scienze naturali de suo tempo*, Bologna: Il Mulino.

Croizat, L. (1945) History and nomenclature of the higher units of classification. *Bulletin of the Torrey Botanical Club*, 72:52–75.

Cronquist, A. (1968) *The evolution and classification of flowering plants*. New York: Houghton Mifflin Co.

Cullen, J. (1968) Botanical problems of numerical taxonomy. In: *Modern methods in plant taxonomy*, ed. V. Heywood. New York: Academic Press.

Cuvier, G. (1799) *Leçons d'anatomie comparée*, t. 1: *Organes du mouvement*. Paris: Badouin.

(1805) *Leçons d'anatomie comparée*, t. 3: *Organes de la digestion*. Paris: Genets.

(1812a) *Recherches sur les ossements fossiles*, 4 vols. Paris: Déterville.

(1812b) Sur un nouveau rapprochement à établir entre les classes qui composent le règne animal. Museum d'Histoire Naturelle de Paris, *Annales*, 19:73–84.

(1828) *Rapport historique sur le progrès des sciences naturelles*. Paris: Verdière & Lagrange.

(1829) *Le règne animal*, 2nd ed., vol. 1. Paris: Déterville.

D'Andrade, R. (1970) Structure and syntax in the semantic analysis of kinship terminologies. In: *Cognition: a multiple view*, ed. P. Garvin. New York: Macmillan.

Darwin, C. (1883) *On the origins of species by means of natural selection*, 6th ed. New York: Appleton (originally published in 1872).

(1960–1967) Darwin's notebooks on transmutation of species, ed. G. de Beer, M. Rowlands and B. Skarmovsky. *Bulletin of the British Museum (Natural History)*, 2:27–200; 3:129–76 (Notebooks B,C,D,E).

Daubenton, L.-J.-M. (1753) Exposition des distributions méthodiques des animaux quadrupèdes. In: Buffon's *Histoire naturelle générale et particulière*, vol. 4, pp. 142–68. Paris: Imprimerie Royale.

(1782) Introduction à l'histoire naturelle. In: *Encylopédie méthodique: histoire naturelle des animaux*, pp. i–xv. Paris: Panckoucke.

Daudin, H. (1926a) *De Linné à Jussieu: méthodes de la classification et idée de série en botanique et zoologie (1740–1790)*. Paris: Alcan.

(1926b) *Cuvier et Lamarck: les classes zoologiques et l'idée de série animale (1790–1830)*, 2 vols. Paris: Alcan.

Davis, P. and Heywood, V. (1963) *Principles of angiosperm taxonomy*. New York: Van Nostrand Reinhold Co., Inc.

Descartes, R. (1681) *Les principes de la philosophie*, 4th ed. Paris: Theodore Gerard.

(1907) *Discours de la méthode*. Paris: Cerf. (Originally published in 1637).

Desmoulins, A. (1822) Anatomie. In: *Dictionnaire classique d'histoire naturelle*, vol. 1. Paris: Baudouin Frères.

Devitt, M. and Sterenly, D. (1987) *Language and reality*. Cambridge, Mass.: MIT Press.

Diamond, J. (1966) Zoological classification of a primitive people. *Science*, 15:1102–4.

(1972) *The avifauna of the Eastern Highland of New Guinea*. Cambridge, Mass.: Nuttall Ornithological Club.

Dioscorides (1959) *The Greek herbal of Dioscorides, illustrated by a Byzantine A.D. 712, Englished by John Goodyer A.D. 1655*, ed. R. Gunther. New York: Hafner Press.

Diver, C. (1940) The problem of closely related species living in the same area. In: *The new systematics*, ed. T. Huxley. Oxford: Clarendon Press.

Dobzhansky, T. (1937) *Genetics and the origin of species*. New York: Columbia University.

Dodoens, R. (1583) *Stirpium historiae*. Antwerp: Plantini.

Donnellan, K. (1971) Necessity and criteria. In: *Readings in the philosophy of language*, eds. J. Rosenberg and C. Travis. Englewood-Cliffs, N.J.: Prentice-Hall.

Dorolle, M. (1929) Introduction to: *Césalpin, questions péripatéticiennes*. Paris: Alcan.

Dougherty, J. (1979) Learning names for plants and plants for names. *Anthropological Linguistics*, 21:298–315.

(1983) *West Futuna-Aniwa: an introduction to a Polynesian outlier language*. University of California Publications in Linguistics, vol. 102.

Douglas, M. (1966) *Purity and danger*, London: Routledge and Kegan Paul.

(1973) Introduction to *Rules and Meanings*, ed. M. Douglas. Harmondsworth: Penguin.

Dughi, R. (1957) Tournefort dans l'histoire de la botanique. In: *Tournefort*, ed. R. Heim. Paris: Museum National d'Histoire Naturelle.

Dummett, M. (1973) *Frege: philosophy of language*, London: Duckworth and Co.

Dupré, J. (1981) Natural kinds and biological taxa. *The Philosophical Review*, 90:66–90.

(1986) Sex, gender, and essence. *Midwest Studies in Philosophy*, 11:441–457.

Durkheim, E. (1912) *Les formes élémentaires de la vie religieuse*. Paris: Alcan.

Durkheim, E. and Mauss, M. (1963) *Primitive classification*, trans. R. Needham. Chicago: Chicago University, (originally published in French in 1903).

Dwyer, P. (1976a) An analysis of Rofaifo mammal taxonomy. *American Ethnologist*, 3:425–45.

(1976b) Beetles, butterflies and bats: species transformation in New Guinea folk classification. *Oceania*, 14:188–205.

Ellen, R. (1979) Introduction to *Classifications in their social contexts*, ed. R. Ellen and D. Reason. New York: Academic Press.

(1986) Ethnobiology, cognition and the structure of prehension: some general theoretical notes. *Journal of Ethnobiology*, 6:83–98.

Emmart, E. (1940) *The Badianus manuscript: an Aztec herbal*. Baltimore. (Originally composed in 1552).

Empedocles (1964) Fragments. In: *Les penseurs grecs avant Socrate*, trad. J. Voilquin. Paris: Garnier-Flammarion.

Evans-Pritchard, E. (1963) Notes on some animals in Zandeland. *Man*, 63:139–42.

Farber, P. (1973) Buffon and Daubenton: divergent traditions within the "Histoire naturelle". *Isis*, 66:63–74.

(1976) The type concept in zoology during the first half of the nineteenth century. *Journal of the History of Biology*, 11:93–119.

(1977) The development of taxidermy and the history of ornithology. *Isis*, 68:550–66.

(1982a) The transformation of natural history in the nineteenth century. *Journal of the History of Biology*, 15:145–52.

(1982b) *The emergence of ornithology as a scientific discipline, 1760–1850*. Dordrecht: Reidel.

Feyerabend, P. (1975) *Against method: outline of an anarchistic theory of knowledge*. London: New Left Review.

Fodor, J. A. (1983) *Modularity of mind*, Cambridge, Mass.: MIT Press.

Fodor, J. D. (1977) *Semantics: theories of meaning in generative grammar*. New York: Thomas Y. Crowell, Co.

Foucault, M. (1970) *The order of things*, London: Tavistock Publications Ltd. (originally published in French in 1966).

Fox, R. (1953) The Pinatubo Negritos: their useful plants and material culture. *The Philippine Journal of Science*, 81.

Frake, C. (1961) The diagnosis of disease among the Subanun of Mindanao. *American Anthropologist*, 63:113–32.

Frazer, J. (1922) *The golden bough*, 3rd ed. London: Macmillan.

Friedberg, C. (1970) Analyse de quelques groupements de végétaux comme introduction à l'étude de la classification botanique bunaq. In: *Echanges et communications: mélanges offerts à Claude Lévi-Strauss*, vol. 2, ed. J. Pouillon and P. Maranda. The Hague: Mouton.

(1972) Elements de botanique bunaq. In: *Langues et techniques: nature et société*, vol. 2: *Approche ethnologique et naturaliste*, ed. J. Barrau. Paris: Klincksieck.

(1984) *Les Bunaq de Timor et les Plantes*, t. 4, *MUK GUBUL NOR "La Chevelure de la Terre"*. Thèse d'Etat, Université de Paris V.

Fries, T. (1911) *Bref och Skrifvelser af och Carl von Linné*, afd. 1 del. 5. Stockholm.

Fuchs, L. (1542) *De historia stirpium*. Basel: Insengrin.

(1542) *Neu Kreüterbuch*. Basel: Insengrin.

Furth, M. (1987) Aristotle's biological universe: an overview. In: *Philosophical issues in Aristotle's biology*, ed. A. Gotthelf and J. Lennox. Cambridge: Cambridge University Press.

Galileo, G. (1623) *Il Saggiatore*. Rome: Mascardi.

Garden, G. (1691) A discourse concerning the modern theory of generation. *Philosophical Transactions of the Royal Society of London*, 17:476–77 (published in 1693).

Gasking, E. (1967) *Investigations into generation (1651–1828)*. London: Hutchinson.

Gassendi, P. (1964) *Opera omnia*, Band 1: *Syntagma philosophicum*. Stuttgart-Bad Cannstatt.

Gaukroger, S. (1976) Bachelard and the problem of epistemological analysis. *Studies in History and Philosophy of Science*, 7:189–246.

(1978) *Explanatory structures: concepts of explanation in early physics and philosophy*, Atlantic Highlands, N.J.: Humanities Press, International, Inc.

Geertz, C. (1983) *Local knowledge: further essays in interpretive anthropology*. New York: Basic Books, Inc.

Gelman, R. (1980) What young children know about numbers. *The Educational Psychologist*, 15:54–68.

Gelman, R.; Spelke, E.; and Meck, E. (1983) What preschoolers know about animate and inanimate objects. In: *The acquisition of symbolic skills*, ed. D. Rogers and J. Sloboda. New York: Plenum Publishing Corp.

Gelman, S. (1988) The development of induction within natural kind and artifact categories. *Cognitive Psychology*, 20:65–95.

Gelman, S. and Markman, E. (1987) Young children's inductions from natural kinds: the role of categories and appearances. *Child Development*, 58:1532–1541.

Geoghegan, W. (1976) Polytypy in folk biological taxonomies. *American Ethnologist*, 3:469–480.

Gerard, A. and Mandler, J. (1983) Sentence anomaly and ontological knowledge. *Journal of Verbal Learning and Verbal Behavior*, 22:105–120.

Gesner, C. (1551–1558) *Historiae animalium libri V*. Zürich: Froschover.

Bk. 1–2: *Icones animalium quadrupedum viviparorum et oviparorum* [1553].

Bk. 5: *De piscium et aquatilium animatium natura* [1558].

Gesner, C. (1584) *Epistolarum medicinalium*. Wittenberg: Gronenberg.

(1972) *Conradi Gesneri historia plantarum*, Zurich: U. Graf.

Ghiselin, M. (1966) On psychologism in the logic of taxonomic controversies. *Systematic Zoology*, 15:207–215.

(1981) Categories, life, and thinking. *The Behavioral and Brain Sciences*, 4:269–313.

Gilbert, N. (1963) Galileo and the School of Padua. *Journal for the History of Philosophy*, 1:223–31.

Gillespie, N. (1987) Natural history, natural theology, and social order: John Ray and the "Newtonian ideology." *Journal of the History of biology*. 20:1–49.

Gilmore, M. (1932) Importance of ethnobotanical investigation. *American Anthropologist*, 34:320–27.

Gilmour, J. (1937) A taxonomic problem. *Nature*, 137:1040–1042.

  (1940) Taxonomy and philosophy. In: *The new systematics*, ed. J. Huxley. Oxford: Clarendon Press.

Gilmour, J. and Walters, S. (1964) Philosophy and classification. In: *Vistas in botany*, vol. 4: *Recent researches in plant taxonomy*, ed. W. Turrill. Oxford: Pergamon Press Ltd.

Goody, J. (1986) La culture des fleurs. Paper presented to the monthly seminar of the Centre d'Ethnologie Française, Musée National des Arts et Traditions Populaires, 15 April 1986, Paris.

Goosens, W. (1977) Underlying trait terms. In: *Naming, necessity, and natural kinds*, ed. S. Schwartz. Ithaca, New York: Cornell University Press.

Gotthelf, A. (1976) Aristotle's conception of final causality. *Review of Metaphysics*, 30:226–54.

  (1987) Aristotle's conception of final causality. Postscript 1986. In: *Philosophical issues in Aristotle's biology*, ed. A. Gotthelf and J. Lennox. Cambridge: Cambridge University Press.

Granger, G. (1976) *La théorie aristotelicienne de la science*. Paris: Aubier.

Greenberg, J. (1966) *Language universals with special reference to feature hierarchies*. The Hague: Mouton.

Greene, E. (1983) *Landmarks of botanical history*, 2 vol. Stanford: Stanford University Press.

Gregg, J. (1954) *The language of taxonomy*. New York: Columbia University Press.

  (1967) Finite Linnaean structures. *Bulletin of Mathematical Biophysics*, 29:191–206.

Grew, N. (1682) *Anatomy of plants*. London: The Royal Society.

Guyénot, E. (1941) *Les sciences de la vie aux XVIIe et XVIIIe siècles*. Paris: Albin Michel.

Hagberg, K. (1953) *Carl Linnaeus*, trans. A. Blair. New York: E. P. Dutton (originally published in Swedish in 1939).

Hage, P. and Miller, W. (1976) "Eagle" = "bird": a note on the structure and evolution of Shoshoni ethnoornithological nomenclature. *American Ethnologist*, 3:481–87.

Haller, A. (1751) *Réflexions sur le système de la génération de M. de Buffon*. Geneva: Barrillot et Fils.

Hallpike, C. (1976) Is there a primitive mentality? *Man*, 11:253–70.

Hampton, J. (1982) A demonstration of intransitivity in natural categories. *Cognition*, 12:151–64.

Hart, J.; Berndt, R.; and Caramazza, A. (1985) Category-specific naming deficit following cerebral infarction. *Nature*, 316:439.

Harvey, W. (1959) *De motu locali animalium* (English version), trans. G. Whitteridge. Cambridge, Cambridge University Press (originally published in Latin in 1627).

  (1981) *Disputations touching the generation of animals* [*De generatione animalium*], trans. G. Whitteridge. Oxford: Basil Blackwell (originally published in Latin in 1653).

Haudricourt, A. and Métailié, G. (1985) Description et illustration des plantes en Chine et en Europe au XVIe siècle. *Bulletin de la Société d'Ethnozoologie et d'Ethnobotanique*, 16:16–25.

Hays, T. (1976) An empirical method for the identification of covert categories in ethnobiology. *American Ethnologist*, 3:489–507.

  (1979) Plant classification and nomenclature in Ndumba, New Guinea Highlands. *Ethnology*, 18:253–270.

  (1983) Ndumba folk biology and general principles of ethnobotanical classification and nomenclature. *American Anthropologist*, 85:592–611.

Healey, C. (1978–79) Taxonomic rigidity in folk biological classification: some examples from the Maring of New Guinea. *Ethnomedizin*, 5:361–84.

Heider, E. (1971) "Focal" color areas and the development of color names. *Developmental Psychology*, 4:447–55.

  (1972) Universals in color naming. *Journal of Experimental Psychology*, 93:10–20.

Henley, N. (1969) A psychological study of the semantics of animal terms. *Journal of Verbal Learning and Verbal Behavior*, 8:176–84.

Hesse, M. (1966) *Models and analogies in science*. Notre Dame: University of Notre Dame.

Hirschfeld, L. (1988) On acquiring social categories: cognitive development and anthropological wisdom. *Man*, 23:611–38.

Hodge, M. (1987) Darwin, species and the theory of natural selection. In: *Histoire du concept d'espèce dans les sciences de la vie*, International Colloquium organized by the Fondation Singer-Polignac, May 1985, Paris: Fondation Singer-Polignac.

Hofsten, N. (1959) Linnés naturppfattnig. *Svenska Linné-Sällskapets Arsskrift*. Arg. 41, 1958. Uppsala: Almqvist and Wiksell.

Holton, G. (1973) *Thematic origins of scientific thought: Kepler to Einstein*. Cambridge, Mass.: Harvard University Press.

Horton, R. (1967) African traditional thought and Western science. *Africa*, 37:50–71, 159–187.

Hough, W. (1897) The Hopi in relation to their plant environment. *American Anthropologist*, 10:33–44.

Hull, D. (1965) The effect of essentialism on taxonomy – two thousand years of stasis. Part 1. *The British Journal for the Philosophy of Science*, 15:314–26.

(1968) The operational imperative; sense and nonsense in operationalism. *Systematic Zoology*, 17:438–457.

(1975) Central subjects and historical narratives. *History and Theory*, 14:253–274.

(1978) A matter of individuality. *Philosophy of Science*, 45:335–60.

(1985) Linné as an Aristotelian. In: *Contemporary perspectives on Linnaeus*, ed. J. Weistock. Lanham, Mass.: University Press of America.

(1987) Genealogical actors in ecological plays. *Biology and Philosophy*, 1:44–60.

Hume, D. (1955) *An inquiry concerning human understanding*. New York: Bobbs-Merrill (originally published in 1758).

Hunn, E. (1975a) Cognitive processes in folk ornithology: the identification of gulls. Language-Behavior Research Laboratory, Working Paper No. 42, University of California, Berkeley.

(1975b) A measure of the degree of correspondence of folk to scientific biological classification. *American Ethnologist*, 2:309–27.

(1976) Toward a perceptual model of folk biological classification. *American Ethnologist*, 3:508–24.

(1977) *Tzeltal folk zoology*. New York: Academic Press.

(1982) The utilitarian factor in folk biological classification. *American Anthropologist*, 84:830–47.

(1987) Science and common sense: a reply to Atran. *American Anthropologist*, 89: 146–149.

Huygens, C. (1690) *Discours de la cause de la pesanteur*, Leiden: Pierre Vander Aa.

Inger, R. (1958) Comment on the definition of genera. *Evolution*, 12: 370–84.

Inglis, W. (1966) The observational basis of homology. *Systematic Zoology*, 15:219–28.

Inhelder, B. and Piaget, J. (1964) *The early growth of logic in the child*. London: Routledge and Kegan Paul.

Jacob, F. (1973) *The logic of life*, trans. B. Spillman. New York: Pantheon Books, (originally published in French in 1970).

(1981) *Le jeu des possibles*. Paris: Fayard.

Jacobs, M. (1980) Revolutions in plant description. In: *Liber gratulatorius in honorem H.C.D. De Wit*, ed. J. Arends, G. Boelema, C. de Groot and A. Leeuwenberg. Wageningen: H. Veenman & Zonen.

Jaeger, W. (1948) *Aristotle: fundamentals of the history of his development*, 2nd ed., trans. R. Robinson. Oxford: Oxford University Press. (originally published in German in 1923).

Jardine, N. (1969) A logical basis for biological classification. *Systematic Zoology*, 18:37–52.

(1976) Galileo's road to truth and the demonstrative regress. *Studies in History and Philosophy of Science*, 7:277–318.

Jaume Saint-Hilaire J. (1805) *Exposition des familles naturelles*, 2 vols. Paris: Treuttel and Würtz.

Jeyifous, S. (1985) Atimodemo: semantic conceptual development among the Yoruba. Ph.D. dissertation, Cornell University.

Johnson, L. (1968) Rainbow's end: the quest for an optimal taxonomy. *Proceedings of the Linnaean Society of New South Wales*, 93:1–45.

Joly, R. (1960) *Recherches sur le traité pseudo-hippocratique du régime*. Paris: Belles Lettres.

(1968) La biologie d'Aristote. *Revue philosophique*, 158:219–53.

Jorion, P. (1986) Reprendre à zero. *L'Homme*, 97–98:299–308.

Joseph, H. (1916) *Introduction to logic*. Oxford: Clarendon Press.

Jung, J. (1662/1747) *Opuscula botanico-physica*, ed. M. Fogel and J. Vagetius. Coburg: Ottonis. (The *Isagoge phytoscopica* was originally compiled in 1678–1679 and *De plantis doxoscopiae* in 1662).

(1982) *Praelectiones physicae. Historisch-kritische Edition*, Herausgegeben von Christoph Meinel. Göttingen: Vandenhoeck and Ruprecht.

Jussieu, A.-L. (1774) Exposition d'un nouvel ordre de plantes adopté dans les démonstrations du Jardin Royal. *Mémoires de l'Académie des Sciences*, 1774:175–197.

(1789) *Genera plantarum*. Paris: Herissant.

Kant, I. (1951) *Critique of judgement*, trans. J. Bernard. New York: Hafner Press (originally published in German in 1790).

(1958) *A critique of pure reason*, trans. N. Kemp. New York: Random House Inc. (originally published in German in 1787).

Kästner, H. (1896) Pseudo-Dioscorides *De herbis femininis. Hermes*, 31:578–636.

Kay, P. (1971) On taxonomy and semantic contrast. *Language*, 47:866–87.

(1975) A model-theoretic approach to folk taxonomy. *Social Science Information*, 14:151–66.

Kay, P. and McDaniel, C. (1978) The linguistic significance of the meaning of basic color terms. *Language*, 54:610–46.

Keil, F. (1979) *Semantic and conceptual development: an ontological perspective*, Cambridge, Mass.: Harvard University Press.

(1983) On the emergence of semantic and conceptual distinctions. *Journal of Experimental Psychology*, 112:357–385.

(1986) The acquisition of natural kind and artifact terms. In: *Conceptual change*, ed. A. Marrar and W. Demopoulos. Norwood N.J.: Ablex Publishing Corp.

(1988) Intuitive belief systems and informal reasoning in cognitive development. Working Paper, Department of Psychology, Cornell University.

Keller, J. and Lehman, F. (1988) Complex concepts. Working Paper presented to King's College Research Centre Conference on "The representation of complex cultural categories," Cambridge University, 22–24 March 1988.

Kelly, M. and Keil, F. (1985) The more things change . . . : metamorphoses and conceptual structure. *Cognitive Science*, 9:403–416.

Kempton, W. (1978) Category grading and taxonomic relations: a mug is a sort of cup. *American Ethnologist*, 5:44–65.

Kesby, J. (1979) The rangi classification of animals and plants. In: *Classifications in their social contexts*, ed. R. Ellen and D. Reason. New York: Academic Press.

Kirk, G. (1960) Popper on science and the Presocratics. *Mind*, 69:318–39.

(1961) Sense and common-sense in the development of Greek philosophy. *Journal of Hellenic Studies*. 81:105–17.

Klein, J. (1734) *Naturalis dispositio echinodermatum*. Dantzig: Schreiber.

Klein, J. (1750) *Historiae avium*. Lübeck: Schmidt.

Klinberg, G. (1957) The distinction between living and not living among 7–10-year-old children, with some remarks concerning the so-called animism controversy. *The Journal of Genetic Psychology*, 90:227–38.

Koelreuter, J. (1893) Vorlaeufige Nachricht von Einigen das Geschlecht der Pflanzen betreffenden Beobachtungen. *Ostwald's Klassiker der Exacten Wissenschaften*, no. 41. Leipzig: Engelmann (monographs originally published between 1761 and 1776).

Konorski, J. (1967) *Integrative activity of the brain: an interdisciplinary approach*. Chicago: University of Chicago Press.

Kosman, L. (1987) Animals and other beings in Aristotle. In: *Philosophical issues in Aristotle's biology*, eds. A. Gotthelf and J. Lennox. Cambridge: Cambridge University Press.

Kripke, S. (1972) Naming and necessity. In: *Semantics of natural language*, ed. D. Davidson and G. Harman. Dordrecht: Reidel.

Kucharski, P. (1964) Anaxagore et les idées biologiques de son siècle. *Revue philosophique*, 154:137–66.

Kuhn, T. (1962) *The structure of scientific revolutions*. Chicago: University of Chicago Press.

(1977) Second thoughts on paradigms. In: *The structure of scientific theories*, ed. F. Suppe. Urbana: University of Illinois Press.

Labov, W. (1973) The boundaries of words and their meanings. In: *New ways of analyzing varia-*

tions in English, ed. C. Bailey and R. Shuy. Washington, D.C.: Georgetown University Press.

Lamarck, J.-B. (1778) *Flore françoise*. Paris: Imprimerie Royale.

(1783) *Encyclopédie méthodique: botanique*, vol. 1. Paris: Panckoucke.

(1785) *Mémoire sur les classes les plus convenables à établir parmi les végétaux. Mémoire de l'Académie des Sciences*, année 1785.

(1802–1806) *Mémoires sur les fossiles des environs de Paris*. Museum d'Histoire Naturelle de Paris, *Annales*, tomes 1–8.

(1809) *Philosophie zoologique*, Paris: Dentu.

(1815) *Histoire des animaux sans vertèbres*, t. 1. Paris: Déterville.

(1817) Espèce. In: *Nouveau dictionnaire d'histoire naturelle*, t. 10. Paris: Déterville.

Lamarck, J.-B. and Candolle, A.-P. (1815) *Flore française*, 6 vols. Paris: Desray.

Landgraf, E. (1928) Ein frühmittelaltericher Botanicus. *Kyklos*, 1:3–36.

Larson, J. (1971) *Reason and experience: the representation of nature in the work of Carl von Linné*. Berkeley: University of California Press.

Laughlin, R. (1975) The great Tzotzil dictionary of San Lorenzo Zincatán. *Smithsonian Contributions to Anthropology*, 19.

Leach, E. (1964) Anthropological aspects of language: animal categories and verbal abuse. In: *New directions in the study of language*, ed. E. Lennenberg. Cambridge, Mass.: MIT Press.

Leblond, J. (1939) *Logique et méthode chez Aristote*. Paris: Vrin.

(1945) *Aristote: philosophe de la vie*. Paris: Aubier.

Lehman, H. (1971) Classification and explanation in biology. *Taxon*, 20:257–68.

Leibniz, G. von (1902) *Discourse on metaphysics*, trans. G. Montgomery. La Salle, Ill.: Open Court.

(1957) *Correspondance Leibniz-Clarke*, ed. A. Robinet. Paris: Presses Universitaires de France.

Leikola, A. (1987) The development of the species concept in the thinking of Linnaeus. In: *Histoire du concept d'espèce dans les sciences de la vie*, International Colloquium organized by the Fondation Singer-Polignac, May 1985, Paris: Fondation Singer-Polignac.

Lennox, J. (1980) Aristotle on genera, species, and "the more and the less." *Journal of the History of Biology*, 13:321–46.

(1985) Are Aristotelian species eternal? In: *Aristotle on nature and living things* (Festschrift for David Balme), ed. A. Gotthelf. Pittsburgh: Pittsburgh University Press.

(1987) Divide and explain: the *Posterior analytics* in practice. In: *Philosophical issues in Aristotle's biology*, ed. A. Gotthelf and J. Lennox. Cambridge: Cambridge University Press.

Lenoir, T. (1981) Teleology without regrets. The transformation of physiology in Germany, 1790–1847. *Studies in History and Philosophy of Science*, 12:293–354.

Lescher, J. (1973) The meaning of NOUS in the *Posterior analytics*. *Phronesis*, 18:44–68.

Leszl, W. (1972) Knowledge of the universal and knowledge of the particular in Aristotle. *Review of Metaphysics*, 26:279–313.

Lévy-Bruhl, L. (1966) *Primitive mentality*, Boston: Beacon, (originally published in French in 1923).

Lévi-Strauss (1963) The bear and the barber. *The Journal of the Royal Anthropological Institute*, 93:1–11.

(1966) *The savage mind*, Chicago: University of Chicago Press, (originally published in French in 1962).

(1969a) *The elementary structures of kinship*, trans. J. Bell and J. von Sturmer. Boston: Beacon, (originally published in French in 1949).

(1969b) *The raw and the cooked*. New York: Harper & Row Publications Inc. (originally published in French in 1964).

(1971) *L'homme nu*. Paris: Plon.

Li, H.-L. (1974) Plant taxonomy and the origin of cultivated plants. *Taxon*, 23:715–24.

Li Shizhen, (1975–1978) *Bencao gangmu*, 4 vol. Beijing: Renmin weisheng chubanshe (originally published from 1590–1596).

Limoges, C. (1972) Introduction to Linnaeus' *L'equilibre de la nature*, trans. B. Jasmin. Paris: Vrin.

Linnaeus, C. (1735) *Systema naturae*. Leiden: Haak.

(1736) *Fundamenta botanica*. Amsterdam: Schouten.

(1737a) *Genera plantarum*. Leiden: Wishoff.

(1737b) *Critica botanica*. Leiden: Wishoff.

(1738) *Classes plantarum*. Leiden: Wishoff.

(1744) *Systema naturae*, 4th ed. Paris: David.

(1749–69) *Amoenitates academicae*, 7 vols. Stockholm: Salvius.

Vol. 1: D. Rudberg [1744] *Peloria*.

　J. Hallman [1745] *Passiflora*.

　O. Söderberg [1748] *Curiositate naturali*.

Vol. 2: I. Biberg [1749] *Oeconomia naturae*.

Vol. 3: J. Haartman [1751] *Plantae hybridae*.

　C. Gedner [1752] *Cui bono?*.

Vol. 6: C. Ramström [1759] *Generatio ambigena*.

　H. Wilcke [1760] *Politia naturae*.

　J. Graberg [1762] *Fundamentum fructificationis*.

(1751) *Philosophia botanica*, Stockholm: G. Kiesewetter.

(1756) *Systema naturae*, 9th ed., Leiden: Haak.

(1758) *Systema naturae*, 10th ed., vol. 1. Stockholm: Salvius.

(1764) *Genera plantarum*, 6th ed., Stockholm: Salvius.

(1767) *Systema naturae*, 12th ed., 2 vol. Vienna: Trattner.

(1787) *Philosophia botanica*, 4th ed., Geneva: Pietre & Dellamolière.

(1790) *Disquisitio de sexu plantarum*. In: *Amoenitates academicae*, vol. 10, pp. 100–31. Erlangen: Schreber, (originally presented as the prize essay of the Imperial Academy of St Petersburg in 1760).

(1792) *Praelectiones in ordines naturales plantarum*. Hamburg: Hoffmann.

(1957–1959). *Species plantarum*, 2 vols. London: Ray Society (originally published in 1753).

(1972) *Discours sur l'accroissement de la terre habitable [Oratio de Telluris habitabilis incremento]*. In: *L'équilibre de la nature*, trans. B. Jasmin, pp. 29–55. Paris: Vrin. (Originally published in Latin in 1744, subsequently in the *Amoentitates academicae*, vol. 2).

Lloyd, A. (1962) Genus, species and ordered series in Aristotle. *Phronesis*, 7:67–90.

Lloyd, G. (1961) The development of Aristotle's theory of classification of animals. *Phronesis*, 6:59–80.

(1968) *Aristotle: the growth and structure of his thought*. Cambridge: Cambridge University Press.

(1979) *Magic, reason and experience: studies in the origins and development of Greek science*. Cambridge: Cambridge University Press.

(1980) *Aristotle: the growth and structure of his thought*. Cambridge: Cambridge University Press.

(1983) *Science, folklore and ideology: studies in the life sciences in ancient Greece*. Cambridge: Cambridge University Press.

Locke, J. (1848) *An essay concerning human understanding*. London: Tegg (originally published in 1689).

Loftus, E. (1977) How to catch a zebra in semantic memory. In: *Perceiving, acting and knowing*, ed. R. Shaw and J. Bransford. Hillsdale, N.J.: Lawrence Erlbaum Assocs., Inc.

Louis, P. (1961) Notes to Aristotle's *De la génération des animaux*. Paris: Belles Lettres.

(1975) *La découverte de la vie. Aristote*. Paris: Hermann.

Lovejoy, A. (1909) The meaning of PHYSIS in the Greek physiologers. *The Philosophical Review*, 18:369–83.

(1964) *The great chain of being*. Cambridge, Mass.: Harvard University Press (originally published in 1936).

Lyon, J. and Sloan, P. (1981) *From natural history to the history of nature: readings from Buffon and his critics*. Notre Dame: Notre Dame University.

MacArthur, R. (1972) *Geographical ecology: patterns in the distribution of species*. New York: Harper and Row Publications Inc.

Macnamara, J. (1982) *Names for things: a study of human learning*. Cambridge, Mass.: MIT Press.

Madden, E. (1986) Was Reid a natural realist? *Philosophy and Phenomenological Research*, 47:255–276.

Magnol, P. (1689) *Podromus historiae generalis plantarum*. Montpellier: Pech.

Magnus, Albert (1955) *Opera omnia*, vol. 12: *De natura et origine animae, de principiis motus processivi, quaestiones super de animalibus*, Monasterri Westfalorum.

Malebranche, N. (1928) *De la recherche de la verité*, ed. D. Roustan and P. Schrecker. Paris: Boivin (originally published in 1674).

Malpighi, M. (1675) *Anatome plantarum*, London: (John) Martin Publishing Ltd.

Mann, T. (1940) *Magic mountain*. New York: Vintage.

Margalit, A. (1979) Open texture. In: *Meaning and use*, ed. A. Margalit. Dordrecht: Reidel.

Markman, E. and Hutchinson, J. (1984) Children's sensitivity to constraints on word meaning: taxonomic versus thematic relations. *Cognitive Psychology*, 16:1–27.

Matras, J. and Martin, M. (1972) Contribution à l'ethnobotanique des Brous. *Journal d'agriculture tropicale et de botanique appliquée*, 19:1–49, 93–139.

Mayr, E. (1941) *List of New Guinea birds*. New York: American Museum of Natural History.

(1965) Numerical phenetics and taxonomic theory. *Systematic Zoology*, 14:73–97.

(1969) *Principles of systematic zoology*. New York: McGraw-Hill Bk. Co.

(1982) *The growth of biological thought*. Cambridge, Mass.: Harvard University Press.

McCarthy, A. and Warrington, E. (1988) Evidence for modality specific meaning systems in the brain. *Nature*, 88:428–29.

McCloskey, M. (1983) Naive theories of motion. In: *Mental models*, ed. D. Gentner and A. Stevens. Hillsdale, N.J.: Lawrence Erlbaum Assocs., Inc.

McCloskey, M. and Glucksberg, S. (1978) Natural categories: well defined or fuzzy set? *Memory and Cognition*, 6:462–72.

McGuire, J. (1967) Transmutation and immutability: Newton's doctrine of physical qualities. *Ambix*, 14:69–95.

(1970) Atoms and the "Analogy of Nature": Newton's third rule of philosophizing. *Studies in History and Philosophy of Science*, 1:3–59.

Mead, M. (1932) An investigation of the thought of primitive children with special reference to animism. *Journal of the Royal Anthropological Institute*, 62:173–90.

Meinel, C. (1984a) *In physicis futurum saeculum respicio: Joachim Jungius und die Naturwissenschaftliche Revolution des 17 Jahrhunderts*. Göttingen: Vandenhoeck and Ruprecht.

(1984b) *Der handschriftliche Nachlass von Joachim Jungius in der Staats-und Universitätsbibliothek Hamburg. Katalog*. Stuttgart: Ernst Hauswedell.

(1985) Révolution scientifique et expérience en chimie: méthodologie et réforme chez Joachim Jungius vers 1630. Paper presented to International Colloquium, "Hélène Metzger", Centre International de Synthèse, Paris, 21–23 May, 1985.

Mervis, C. and Rosch, E. (1981) Categorization of natural objects. *Annual Review of Psychology*, 32:89–115.

Métailié, G. (1981) Bibliographie indicative concernant la botanique et l'ethnobotanique de la Chine (ancienne et contemporaine). *Journal d'agriculture traditionelle et de botanique appliquée*, 28:353–378.

Metzger, H. (1918) *La genèse de la science des cristaux*. Paris: Alcan.

Meyer, E. (1854–1857) *Geschichte der Botanik*, 4 vols. Köningsberg: Bornträger.

Mill, J. (1889) *A system of logic*. London: People's Edition.

Miller, G. (1978) Practical and lexical knowledge. In: *Cognition and categorization*, ed. E. Rosch and B. Lloyd. Hillsdale, N.J.: Lawrence Erlbaum Assocs., Ltd.

Miller, G. and Johnson-Laird, P. (1976) *Language and perception*. Cambridge, Mass.: Harvard University Press.

Miller, J. (1975) Delaware alternative classification. *Anthropological Linguistics*, 17:434–44.

Milt, B. (1936) Conrad Gessner's "Historia plantarum" (Fragmenta relicta). *Vierteljahrsschrift der naturforschenden Gessellschaft in Zürich*, 81:285–91.

Moore, G. (1953) *Some main problems of philosophy*. London: Allen and Unwin (Publishers) Ltd.

(1962) *The commonplace book of G. E. Moore 1919–1953*, ed. C. Lewy. London: Allen and Unwin (Publishers) Ltd.

Moravcsik, J. (1975) AITIA as a generative factor in Aristotle's philosophy. *Dialogue*, 14:622–38.

Morison, R. (1669) *Praeludia botanica*. London.

(1672) *Plantarum umbelliferarum distributio nova.* Oxford: Sheldoniano.

(1680–1699) *Plantarum historiae universalis Oxiensis,* vol. 2–3. Oxford: Sheldoniano.

Morris, B. (1976) Whither the savage mind? Notes on the natural taxonomies of a hunting and gathering people. *Man,* 11:542–57.

Morton, A. (1981) *History of botanical science.* New York: Academic Press.

Needham, J. (1986) *Science and civilisation in China,* vol. 6(1): *Botany,* Cambridge: Cambridge University Press.

Needham, R. (1975) Polythetic classification. *Man,* 10:349–369.

Newton, I. (1714) *Philosophiae naturalis principia mathematica.* Amsterdam: Societatis.

(1730) *Opticks or a treatise of the reflections, refractions, inflections and colours of light,* 4th ed. London: W. and J. Innys.

Nielsen, J. (1946) *Agnosia, apraxia, aphasia, Their value in cerebral localization.* New York: Hoeber.

Owen, R. (1866) *The anatomy of vertebrates,* vol. 1: *Fishes and reptiles.* London: Longman, Green and Co.

Pagel, W. (1967) *William Harvey's biological ideas.* Basel: Karger.

Paillet, J. (1973) Eskimo language animal and plant taxonomies in Baker Lake. Unpublished manuscript.

Palm, A. (1933) *Studien zur hippokratischen Schrift PERI DIATES.* Tübingen.

Pap, A. (1960) Types and meaninglessness. *Mind,* 69:41–54.

Paso y Trancoso, F. (1886) La botanica entre los Nahuas. *Anales del Museo Nacional de Mexico,* 3.

Peirce, C. (1935) *Collected papers of Charles Sanders Peirce,* 6 vol., ed. C. Hartshorne and P. Weiss. Cambridge, Mass.: Harvard University Press.

Pellegrin, P. (1982) *La classification des animaux chez Aristote.* Paris: Belles Lettres.

(1987) Logical difference and biological difference: the unity of Aristotle's thought. In: *Philosophical issues in Aristotle's biology,* ed. A. Gotthelf and J. Lennox. Cambridge: Cambridge University Press.

Piaget, J. (1928) *Judgement and reasoning in the child.* London: Routledge and Kegan Paul Ltd.

Plato (1899–1907) *Platonis opera,* 5 vols., ed. J. Burnet. Oxford: Oxford University Press.

Pliny [Pline] (1829) *Histoire naturelle de Pline* [*Historiarum Mundi*], 20 vols. Paris: Panckoucke.

Plochmann, G. (1963) William Harvey and his methods. *Studies in the Renaissance,* 10:192–210.

Pollock, N. (1986) Food classification in three Pacific societies: Fiji, Hawaii, and Tahiti. *Ethnology,* 25:107–117.

Popper, K. (1950) *The open society and its enemies.* Princeton N.J.: Princeton University Press.

(1958–59) Back to the Pre-Socratics. *Proceedings of the Aristotelian Society,* 59:1–24.

(1963) *Conjectures and refutations.* New York: Harper and Row Publications Inc.

Poulton, E. (1908) *Essays on evolution.* Oxford: Clarendon Press.

Putnam, H. (1975) The meaning of "meaning". In: *Language, mind and knowledge,* ed. K. Gunderson. Minneapolis: University of Minnesota Press.

(1986) Meaning holism. In: *The philosophy of W. V. Quine,* ed. L. Hahn and P. Schilpp. La Salle, Ill.: Open Court.

Quine, W. (1960) *Word and object.* Cambridge, Mass.: Harvard University Press.

(1966) Three grades of modal involvement. In: *The ways of paradox.* New York: Random House.

(1969) Natural kinds. In: *Ontological relativity and other essays.* New York: Columbia University Press.

Ramsbottom, J. (1938) Linnaeus and the species concept. *Proceedings of the Linnaean Society of London,* 150:192–219.

Randall, J. (1940) The development of scientific method in the school of Padua. *Journal of the History of Ideas,* 1:177–206.

Randall, R. (1976) How tall is a taxonomic tree? Some evidence for dwarfism. *American Ethnologist,* 3:541–57.

Randall, R. and Hunn, E. (1984) Do life forms evolve or do uses for life? Some doubts about Brown's universals hypothesis. *American Ethnologist,* 11:329–49.

Raven, C. (1942) *John Ray naturalist, his life and works.* Cambridge: Cambridge University Press.

Raven, P. (1976) Systematics and plant population biology. *Systematic Botany*, 1:284–316.

Raven, P., Berlin, B. and Breedlove, D. (1971) The origins of taxonomy. *Science*, 174:1210–13.

Ray, J. (1660) *Catalogus plantarum circa Cantabrigiam nascentium.* Cambridge: Field.

 (1682) *Methodus plantarum nova.* London: Faithorne and Kersey.

 (1686) *Historia plantarum.* London: Smith and Walford.

 (1691) *The wisdom of God manifested in the works of creation.* London: Smith and Walford.

 (1693) *Synopsis methodica animalium quadrupedum & serpentini.* London: Smith and Walford.

 (1694) *Stirpium Europeanarum extra Britannias nascentium sylloge.* London: Smith and Walford.

 (1696a) *Synopsis methodica stirpium Britanicarum.* London: Smith and Walford.

 (1696b) *De variis plantarum methodus dissertatio brevis.* London: Smith and Walford.

 (1703) *Methodus plantarum emendata et aucta.* London: Smith and Walford.

 (1848) *The correspondence of John Ray*, ed. E. Lankester. London: Ray Society.

 (1928) A discourse on the specific differences of plants. In: *Further correspondences of John Ray*, ed. R. Gunther. London: Ray Society (communication originally presented before the Royal Society, 1 December 1674).

Réaumur, R.-A. (1734–42) *Mémoires pour servir à l'histoire générale des insectes*, 6 vol. Paris: Imprimerie Royale.

Regan C. (1926) Organic evolution. Presidential Address, Section D. British Association for the Advancement of Science, 1925.

Regnier, A. (1968) De la théorie des groupes à la pensée sauvage. *L'homme et la société*, 7:201–13.

Reichenbach, H. (1951) *The rise of scientific philosophy.* Berkeley: University of California Press.

Reid, T. (1967) *Reid's philosophical works*, with notes and supplementary dissertation by Sir William Hamilton. Hildesheim: Georg Olms.

Rey, G. (1983) Concepts and stereotypes. *Cognition*, 15:237–62.

Richard, A. (1852) *Nouveaux éléments de botanique et de physiologie végétale*, 2 vols. Paris: Béchet Jeune.

Richards, D. and Siegler, R. (1986) Children's understanding of the attributes of life. *Journal of Experimental Psychology*, 42:1–22.

Riddle, J. (1981) Pseudo-Dioscorides' *Ex herbis femininis* and early medieval medical botany. *Journal of the History of Biology*, 14:43–81.

Rips, L. (1975) Inductive judgments about natural categories. *Journal of Verbal Learning and Verbal Behavior*, 14:665–81.

Rips, L.; Shoben, E.; and Smith, E. (1973) Semantic distance and the verification of semantic relations. *Journal of Verbal Learning and Verbal Behavior*, 12:1–20.

Rivinus, A. [Bachmann] (1690) *Introductio generalis in rem herbarium.* Leipzig: Günther.

Roberts, H. (1929) *Plant hybridisation before Mendel.* Princeton, N.J.: Princeton University Press.

Roger, J. (1971) *Les sciences de la vie dans la pensée française au XVIIIe siècle.* Paris: Colin.

 (1988) Introduction à: *Buffon- Epoques de la nature. Edition critique.* Paris: Muséum national d'Histoire naturelle.

Rogers, D. (1963) Studies of the *Manihot esculenta* Crantz and related species. *Bulletin of the Torrey Botanical Club*, 90:43–54.

Rondelet, G. (1554) *De piscibus marinis libri XVIII.* Lyon: Bonhomme.

Rosaldo, M. (1972) Metaphors and folk classification. *Southwestern Journal of Anthropology*, 68:83–99.

Rosch, E. (1973) On the internal structure of perceptual and semantic categories. In: *Cognitive development and the acquisition of language*, ed. T. Moore. New York: Academic Press.

 (1975) Universals and cultural specifics in categorization. In: *Cross-cultural perspectives on learning*, ed. R. Brislin, S. Bochner and W. Lonner. New York: Halstead.

 (1978) Principles of categorization. In: *Cognition and categorization*, ed. E. Rosch and B. Lloyd. Hillsdale, N.J.: Lawrence Erlbaum Assocs., Ltd.

Rosch, E. and Mervis, C. (1975) Family resemblances: studies in the internal structure of natural categories. *Cognitive Psychology*, 8:382–439.

Rosch, E.; Mervis, C.; Gray, W.; Johnson, D. and Boyes-Braem, P. (1976) Basic objects in natural categories. *Cognitive Psychology*, 8:382–439.

Ross, W. (1949) *Aristotle*, 5th ed. London: Methuen.

Rosskopf, M.; Steffe, L.; and Taback, S. (1971) *Piagetian cognitive development research in mathematical education*. Washington, D.C.: National Council of Teachers of Mathematics.

Roué, M. (1986) Taxonomie et savoir INUIT concernant le caribou. Paper presented at the Colloquium "Les Inuit de Nouveau-Quebec: Appropriation du milieu naturel et savoirs autochtones". Centre National de la Recherche Scientifique, Paris, 28–30 May 1986.

Royaumont Center for a Science of Man (1980) *Language and learning: the debate between Jean Piaget and Noam Chomsky*, ed. M. Piatelli-Palmarini. Cambridge, Mass.: Harvard University Press.

Rumelhart, D. and Abrahamson, A. (1973) A model for analogical reasoning. *Cognitive psychology*, 5:1–28.

Russell, B. (1940) *An inquiry into meaning and truth*. London: Unwin and Allen.

  (1945) *A history of Western philosophy*. New York: Simon and Schuster, Inc.

Russell, E. (1917) *Form and function: a contribution to the history of animal morphology*. New York: E. P. Dutton.

Ryle, G. (1938–39) Categories. *Proceedings of the Aristotelian Society* 38:189–206.

Sachs, J. (1890) *History of botany (1530–1860)*, trans. H. Garnsey. Oxford: Clarendon Press (originally published in German in 1875).

Saint-Hilaire, G. (1818) *Philosophie anatomique*. Paris: J. B. Ballière.

Sartori, G. and Job, R. (1988) The oyster with four legs: a neuro-psychological study on the interaction of visual and semantic information. *Cognitive Neuropsychology*, 5:105–132.

Scheffer, W. (1958) *Seals, sea lions, and walruses*. Stanford: Stanford University Press.

Schwartz, S. (1978) Putnam on artifacts. *Philosophical Review*, 87:566–74.

  (1979) Natural kind terms. *Cognition*, 7:301–15.

Sellars, W. (1965) Scientific realism or irenic instrumentalism. In: *Boston studies in the philosophy of science*, vol. 2, ed. R. Cohen and M. Wartofsky. New York: Humanities Press.

Shenwei, T. (1957) *Chongxiu zhenghe jingshi zhenglei beiyong bencao*. Beijing: Renmin chubanshe. (Facsimile of 1249 A.D. edition).

Simpson, G. (1961) *Principles of animal taxonomy*. New York: Columbia University Press.

Singer, C. (1927) The herbal in antiquity. *Journal of Hellenic Studies* 47:1–52.

  (1959) *A history of biology*. New York: Abelard-Schuman.

Skulsky, H. (1968) Paduan epistemology and the doctrine of the one mind. *Journal of the History of Philosophy*, 6:341–61.

Sloan, P. (1972) John Locke, John Ray, and the problem of the natural system. *Journal of the History of Biology*, 5:1–53.

  (1979) Buffon, German biology, and the historical interpretation of biological species. *The British Journal for the History of Science*, 12:109–153.

  (1987) From logical universals to historical individuals: Buffon's idea of biological species. In: *Histoire du concept d'espèce dans les sciences de la vie*. International Colloquium organized by the Fondation Singer-Polignac, May 1985. Paris: Fondation Singer-Polignac.

Smith, C., Carey, S., and Wiser, M. (1985) On differentiation: a case study of the development of concepts of size, weight, and density. *Cognition*, 21:177–237.

Smith, E. and Medin, D. (1981) *Categories and concepts*. Cambridge, Mass.: Harvard University Press.

Smith, E., Shoben, E. and Rips, L. (1974) Structure and process in semantic memory. *Psychological Review*, 81:214–241.

Smith, J. (1984) Science and Myth. *Natural History*, 93:11–24.

Sneath, P. and Sokal, R. (1973) *Numerical taxonomy*. San Francisco: Freeman.

Sober, E. (1980) Evolution, population and thinking, and essentialism. *Philosophy of Science*, 47:350–383.

Soja, N. (1987) Ontological constraints on 2-year-olds' induction of word meaning. Ph.D. dissertation, MIT.

Sokal, R. and Camin, J. (1965) The two taxonomies: areas of agreement of conflict. *Systematic Zoology*, 14:196–195.

Sokal, R. and Sneath, P. (1963) *Principles of numerical taxonomy*. San Francisco: Freeman.

Somerville, J. (1986) Moore's conception of common sense. *Philosophy and Phenomenological Research*, 47:233–253.

Sommers, F. (1959) The ordinary language tree. *Mind*, 68:160–185.

(1963) Types and ontology. *Philosophical Review*, 72:327–363.

Spallanzani, L. (1776) *Oeuvres de M. L'Abbé Spallanzani*. Paris: Senebier (originally published in Italian in 1765–66).

Spelke, E. (1987) The origins of physical knowledge. Paper presented at the Fyssen Symposium, "Thought without language." Versailles, France, 3–6 April 1987.

Sperber, D. (1975a) Pourquoi les animaux parfaits, les hybrides et les monstres sont-ils bons à penser symboliquement? *L'homme*, 15:5–34.

(1975b) *Rethinking symbolism*. Cambridge: Cambridge University Press.

(1985a) Anthropology and psychology: towards an epidemiology of representations. *Man*, 20:73–89.

(1985b) *On anthropological knowledge*. Cambridge: Cambridge University Press.

Sperling, J. (1669) *Zoologia physica*. Wittenberg: Kirchmajer.

Spinoza, B. (1972) *Opera*, 4 vols., ed. C. Gebhardt. Heidelberg: Winter.

Sprague, T. (1928) The herbal of Otto Brunfels. *Journal of the Linnaean Society of London*, 48:79–124.

(1940) Taxonomic botany, with special reference to the angiosperms. In: *The new systematics*, ed. T. Huxley. Oxford: Clarendon Press.

Sprague, T. and Sprague, M. (1939) The herbal of Valerius Cordus. *Journal of the Linnaean Society of London*, 52: 1–113.

Sprengel, K. (1817–1818) *Geschichte der Botanik*, 2 vols. Altenberg: Brockhaus.

Stafleu, F. (1963) Adanson and the "Familles des plantes". In: *Adanson: the bicentennial of Michel Adanson's "Familles des plantes"*, ed. G. Lawrence. Pittsburgh: Hunt Botanical Library.

(1964) Introduction to reprint of A.-L. Jussieu's *Genera plantarum*. Weinheim: Cramer.

(1971a) *Linnaeus and the Linnaeans*. Utrecht: International Association for Plant Taxonomy.

(1971b) Lamarck: the birth of biology. *Taxon*, 20:397:442.

Starkey, P., Spelke, E. and Gelman, R. (1983) Detection of 1–1 correspondences by human infants. *Science*, 222:79–81.

Stearn, W. (1957) An introduction to the *Species Plantarum* and cognate botanical works of Carl Linnaeus. In: *Species Plantarum*, A Facsimile of the first edition, 1753, vol. 1. London: Ray Society.

(1958) Botanical exploration to the time of Linnaeus. *Proceedings of the Linnaean Society of London*, 169:173–96.

(1959) The background of Linnaeus's contributions to the nomenclature and methods of systematic biology. *Systematic Zoology*, 8:4–22.

Stevens, P. (1984a) Metaphors and typology in the development of botanical systematics 1690–1960, or the art of putting new wine in old bottles. *Taxon*, 33:169–211.

(1984b) Haüy and A.-P. de Candolle: crystallography, botanical systematics, and comparative morphology, 1780–1840. *Journal of the History of Biology*, 17:49–82.

Stevens, P. and Cullen, S. (1988) Linnaeus and the cortex-medulla theory of plant form and his appreciation of natural relationships. Working Paper, Harvard University Herbarium.

Strathern, M. (1969) Why is the Pueraria a sweet potato? *Ethnology*, 8:189–98.

Stross, B. (1973) Acquisition of botanical terminology by Tzeltal children. In: *Meaning in Mayan languages*, ed. M. Edmonson. The Hague: Mouton.

Swammerdam, J. (1685) *Histoire générale des insectes*. Utrecht: Ribbins.

Szyfman, L. (1982) *Lamarck et son époque*. Paris: Masson.

Taylor, A. (1911) The words EIDOS and IDEA in pre-Platonic literature. In: *Varia Socratica*. Oxford: Parker.

Taylor, P. (1978–1979) Preliminary report on the ethnobiology of the Toberlorese of Hamalhera, North Moluccas. *Majalah Ilmu-ilmu Sastra Indonesia*, 8:215–29.

(1984) "Covert Categories" reconsidered: identifying unlabeled classes in Tobelo folk biological classification. *Journal of Ethnobiology*, 4:105–22.

Theophrastus (1968) *Enquiry into plants [Historia plantarum]*, trans. A Hort. London: Heinemann.

Tournefort, J.-P. (1694) *Elémens de botanique*. Paris: Imprimerie Royale.

(1697) *De optima methodo instituenda in re herbaria. Epistola. In quâ respondetur Dissertationi D. Raii de variis plantarum methodus*. Paris: Jardin du Roi.

(1708) *Materia medica, or a description of simple medicines generally used in physick . . . their operating and acting upon human bodies according to the principles of the new physiology, chymistry and mechanism*. London: Bell (lessons given at the Jardin du Roi, Paris, and first published in English).

(1717) *Relation d'un voyage au Levant*, 3 vols. Paris: Imprimerie Royale.

(1719) *Institutiones rei herbariae*, 3rd ed. Paris: Imprimerie Royale.

Trager, G. (1939) "Cottonwood" = "tree": A southwestern linguistic trait. *International Journal of American Linguistics*, 9:117–18.

Tulp, N. (1685) *Observationes medicae*. Amsterdam: Elzeverium.

Turiel, E. and Davidson, P. (1986) Heterogeneity, inconsistency, and asynchrony in the development of cognitive structures. In: *Stage and structure: reopening the cognitive debate*, ed. I. Levin. Hillsdale, N.J.: Lawrence Erlbaum Assocs., Ltd.

Tylor, E. (1871) *Primitive culture*. London: John Murray Publishers Ltd.

Vaillant, S. (1728) *Discours sur la structure des fleurs, leurs différences et l'usage de leurs parties prononcé à l'ouverture de Jardin royal de Paris le Xe jour du mois de juin 1717*. Leiden: Van der Aa.

Valmont-Bomare (1791) *Dictionnaire raisonné universel d'histoire naturelle*, 4th ed., 20 vols. Paris: Bruyset Fréres.

Vicq-d'Azyr, F. (1792) Discours préliminaire. In: *Encyclopédie méthodique: système anatomique des quadrupèdes*. Paris: Panckoucke.

Vines, S. (1913) Robert Morison and John Ray. In: *Makers of British botany*, ed. F. Oliver. Cambridge: Cambridge University Press.

Vlastos, G. (1950) The physical theory of Anaxagoras. *The Philosophical Review*, 59:31–57.

(1969) Reasons and causes in the PHAEDO. *The Philosophical Review*, 77:291–325.

Vygotsky, L. (1965) *Thought and language*. Cambridge, Mass.: MIT Press.

Wallace, A. (1889) *Darwinism. An explanation of theory of natural selection with some of its applications*. London: Macmillan.

Walters, S. (1961) The shaping of angiosperm taxonomy. *The New Phytologist*, 60:70–84.

Warrington, E. and McCarthy, R. (1983) Category-specific access dysphasia. *Brain*, 106: 859–878.

Warrington, E. and Shallice, T. (1984) Category specific impairments. *Brain*, 107:829–854.

Waxman, S. (1985) Hierarchies in classification and language: evidence from preschool children. Ph.D. dissertation, University of Pennsylvania.

Wear, A. (1983) William Harvey and the way of the anatomists. *History of Science*, 21:223–249.

Wellisch, H. (1975) Conrad Gessner: a bio-bibliography. *Journal of the Society for the Bibliography of Natural History*, 7:151–247.

Wells, H., Huxley, J. and Wells, G. (1934) *The science of life*. New York: The Literary Guild.

Wharburton, F. (1967) The purposes of classification. *Systematic Zoology*, 16:241–45.

Wieand, J. (1980) Defining art and artifacts. *Philosophical studies*, 38:385–89.

Wierzbicka, A. (1984) Apples are not a "kind of fruit": the semantics of human categorization. *American Ethnologist*, 11:313–28.

(1985) *Lexicography and conceptual analysis*. Ann Arbor: Karoma.

Wilkins, J. (1668) *Essay towards a real character and artificial language*. London: The Royal Society.

Williams, M. (1985) Species are individuals: theoretical foundations for the claim. *Philosophy of Science*, 52:578–90.

Wilson, M. (1982) Predicate meets property. *Philosophical Review*, 91:549–89.

Winsor, M. (1976) The development of Linnean insect classification. *Taxon*, 25:57–67.

Witkowski, S. and Brown, C. (1983) Marking-reversals and cultural importance. *Language*, 59:569–82.

Witkowski, S., Brown, C. and Chase, P. (1981) Where do trees come from? *Man*, 16:1–14.

Wittgenstein, L. (1958) *Philosophical investigations*, trans. G. Anscombe. New York: Macmillan.

Wolf, J.-C. (1736) *Philosophia prima, sive ontologia.* Frankfurt: In Officina Libraria Rengeriana.

Wolff, C.-F. (1774) *Theoria generationis.* Halle: J.-C. Hendel (originally published in 1759).

Woodger, J. (1937) *The axiomatic method in biology.* Cambridge: Cambridge University Press.

Xenophanes (1964) Fragments. In: *Les penseurs grec avant Socrate,* trad. J. Voilquin. Paris: Garnier-Flammarion.

Zabarella, G. (1608) *Iacobi Zabarellae Patavini opera logica.* Frankfurt: Zetzneri.

Ziff, P. (1960) *Semantic analysis.* Ithaca, New York: Cornell University Press.

INDEX

nature
  analogy 230–8
  balance of 230
  of being 210
  causal of living kinds 60–1
  causal process 290
  essential and cross-cultural presumption 62
  fundamental unity of plan 238
  hidden of vegetative soul 147
  ideal economy 179, 230
  intrinsic 6
  of kind 285
  and necessity 58–64
  reproduction of readily apprehended
    species 237
  scale of 206
  specific 147
  universal 146
nature, underlying 71, 74, 77, 78, 286
  and appearance 178
  causing growth and development 141
  order 86
Ndumba (Highland New Guinea) 44
necessity for mathematic eternals 96
Needham, J. 276
neo-Adansonian movement 25, 309
New Guinea Highlanders 286
Newton, I. 11, 146, 232–3, 235, 272–3
  metaphysics of analogy 315
  perceptible world 300
nomenclature 129–33
  ancient Greek 129
  binomial 131, 305
  common sense naming 137
  English colonists 129
  Latin 134
  local of species 132
nomic
  relations 66
  theory 64–71
non-substance 91
Notebooks 78
nous 299
nutrition, fundamentum in zoology 192

oak 129, 130
observation, causal 53
Occam's razor 159, 164
offspring, species-likeness 96
On the origin of species by means of natural
    selection 274
ontological
  categories 286–7, 290
  definition 93

ontology
  boundary between ordinary and cosmic
    268
  essential nature 85
Optiks 273
orders 318
ordines 306
organ-compex 178
organic variation 12
organs
  analogy 110–11
  function 100, 102, 105, 120
  systems 100–1
  value judgements 117
ousia 88
overall similarity 277
ovist doctrine 304
ovum as uniform primordial pattern 147–8

Pagel, W. 228, 300
  blood circulation 314
palms, Aguaruna 38–9
paradeigma 91
Paradise 179
particulars, knowledge of 145
Paso y Trancoso, F. 20
Peirce, C. 3, 90
Pellegrin, P. 113–14, 295
pheneticist movement 25
phenomenal
  conformation to specific types 94
  interconnections at family level 205
  kind, ontological status 287
  order 196, 203, 211, 245
  reality 64–71, 119
  world, symbolic metaphor 221
phenomenalism 277
Philosophia botanica 273, 303
Philsophiae naturalis principia mathematica 273
Philosophie zoologique 196, 241, 274
philosophy
  mechanical 230, 231
  natural 232
phyletic lines 256
Physica 144
Piaget, J. ix, x, 282, 312
pig 279
Pinatubo Negritos (Philippines) 103
Pinax theatri botanici 135, 137–8
plant
  anatomy 303, 304
  characteristics 191, 302
  growth 226
  part names 302–3